WHEN TO USE WHAT RESEARCH DESIGN

When to Use
What Research Design

W. Paul Vogt
Dianne C. Gardner
Lynne M. Haeffele

THE GUILFORD PRESS
New York   London

© 2012 The Guilford Press
A Division of Guilford Publications, Inc.
72 Spring Street, New York, NY 10012
www.guilford.com

Printed in the United States of America

This book is printed on acid-free paper.

Last digit is print number: 9   8   7   6   5   4   3

Library of Congress Cataloging-in-Publication Data

Vogt, W. Paul.
   When to use what research design / W. Paul Vogt, Dianne C. Gardner, Lynne M. Haeffele.
     p. cm.
   ISBN 978-1-4625-0353-7 (pbk. : alk. paper) — ISBN 978-1-4625-0360-5 (hbk. : alk. paper)
   1. Social sciences—Research—Design.   2. Social sciences—Methodology.   I. Gardner, Dianne C.   II. Haeffele, Lynne M.   III. Title.
   H62.V623 2012
   001.42—dc23
                                      2011045572

Preface

This book discusses how to choose research designs and their associated research methods. Because *choosing* methods is a very large topic, the book deals only indirectly with the question of how to *implement* methods once they are chosen. The scope of the work is vast. Large handbooks are devoted to the topic of each of its chapters. The field of research methods is richly endowed with excellent texts at all levels devoted to *how* to conduct survey research, interviews, grounded theory, experiments, and so on. We are less well supplied with works that help us decide *when* and *whether* to use these methods. "*Which method?*" is the necessary prior question. One cannot look up how to do something until one has decided what that something is.

Our overall topic is research *design.* This term is used in several ways. Most narrowly, a design means a method of data collection, such as an interview, survey, or experiment. More broadly, a research design is a comprehensive plan for conducting an investigation that stretches from the initial research question through the methods of data analysis, interpretation, and reporting. Like many researchers, we sometimes use the term both ways. In this book we discuss research design first (in Part I) as the choice of method(s) for collecting data, such as surveys, interviews, participant observations, and experiments. We then review methods of identifying, selecting, and sampling people, organizations, documents, and cases to be studied (Part II). Finally, we look at the ethical choices that arise at the intersection of the method of data collection and the identification of the participants and cases selected for study (Part III). We think of these three parts—Design, Sampling, and Ethics—as a sort of "design package" that gets you ready as a researcher to collect, analyze, and interpret your data. Analysis and interpretation are discussed in a companion book.

This volume aims to help fill a gap in the text and reference book literature. It emphasizes *how to choose* (not how to execute) designs, methods of sampling, and strategies for addressing ethical dilemmas. The book is inclusive in that it discusses methods drawn from many schools of thought. The field of research methodology is divided by several controversies. Proponents of particular approaches often claim too much for their own methods and accede too little to practitioners of other methods. Choices among methods can become more ideological than methodological. We have tried to avoid this tendency. But controversy *cannot* be avoided. Even the terms one uses to describe the topics of discussion—such as case, theory, design, archive, hypothesis, inductive, object, and subject—can and often do engender heated debate. Writers in a controversy-laden field such as ours must try to define and use terms carefully keeping in mind that readers will often prefer other labels. We hope that the Glossary at the end of the volume may help clarify how we are using terms as well as serve as a useful reference.

Like all researchers, we have preferences and are more experienced with some methods than others. But we have attempted to be ecumenical, and our approach is most often intentionally pluralistic (though not anarchistic). When asked which method is best, our answer is almost always: "It depends." We find value in all approaches, from thick descriptions of individual cases to mathematical models that seemingly transcend any concern whatsoever with empirical cases. Any can be effective for particular research problems, but saying this is not very instructive. It is not particularly helpful to make a general statement that all methods can be useful *somehow* in *some* circumstances. The trick is to develop rational grounds for choosing among specific methods in particular instances. Which methods under what circumstances work better for which types of research problems and research questions? These are the questions we address in this book.

When choosing research methods, technical advice may not be the most important kind. No simple decision tree can help one choose among designs: focus group interviews versus individual interviews, randomized field trials versus quasi-experiments, or participant observation versus a survey. We deal with these types of choices. They are not technical. They are often controversial. We cannot claim that our recommendations represent more than the suggestions of investigators who have regularly pondered issues of research methodology while consulting with many clients and advising numerous doctoral students in several fields over the course of three decades. Mostly what we offer are arguments or reasons, not algorithms and decision trees. The reader will decide whether the arguments are persuasive.

Our most important piece of advice is: Don't take our advice *exclusively*. Our second most important piece of advice is: Don't take anyone else's advice exclusively either. Decisions about a serious piece of research should be informed by as many advisors as you can persuade to help you, either in person or through reviews of the research literature on your topic. Although we explain the reasons behind our advice, we have not spent a lot of time detailing the numerous debates about methods. These are referenced in footnotes and Suggestions for Further Reading (at the end of each chapter), but we have kept them to a minimum in the main body of the text.

All this being said, we haven't been shy about giving advice. While we try to explain the reasons behind each suggestion for selecting one method over another, we also see a value to succinct summaries. These are provided in the Summary Tables at the end of each chapter. The statements in these tables are necessarily declarative (when *this*, use *that*), but the guidelines and lists of recommendations are not *rules* that tell you what to do. We think that looking for rules is less fruitful than weighing the reasons that can lead to various methodological choices. We are most definitive in our recommendations when reacting negatively to the rules of other writers—*X* is *always* the best way to do *Y* (infer cause, understand meaning, evaluate efficiency, describe culture, etc.). We think it is a mistake to claim that *one* good way to do something is the *only* good way.

We have used a footnote citation system instead of using in-text citations. We based this decision on the results of a little "market research" with some potential readers. Three classes of doctoral students in various fields in the social sciences were given two versions of the same paragraph about sampling bias in Internet surveys. One version used citations in parentheses within the text; the other used footnotes. Of 47 students anonymously surveyed, 5 said the format was a matter of indifference; 42 preferred the footnotes. Not one student preferred the in-text citation system. In discussions after the surveys, respondents who preferred footnotes said they found the citations-in-text paragraph "cluttered," and that "the names and dates got in the way of the ideas." While in-text citation is important, and the best choice in some contexts, especially in research reports, we agree with the students that footnotes are more effective for a reference and text book such as this.

For whom is this book written? The market research just discussed makes clear that one audience is graduate students in the social sciences—including applied fields such as education, nursing, and marketing—who are trying to decide what methods to use to carry out a research project. Different parts of the book are likely to be of interest to different kinds of readers. For example, the sections on design and sampling will often be more useful for researchers in the early stages of their research on a topic. This could include both novice researchers and more experienced researchers investigating a new area or contemplating a new method. The companion book, on analysis, will almost certainly be of more interest to readers who have already made their most important design, sampling, and ethical choices. Our goal is to broaden the range of options among which researchers can make choices. Our assumption is that researchers making decisions at any stage can benefit from considering a wide range of alternatives.

As we mentioned earlier, large handbooks are devoted to the topics of each of this book's chapters. Getting to your goal in research is something like hiking to a remote point of interest. To arrive at the trail head you need a roadmap, which is what this book provides. Once you get to the trail head, you take out your detailed topographical trail guide. Continuing the analogy, for specific instructions on implementation you'll have to consult methodology handbooks, prior studies, and other sources cited in the notes and Suggestions for Further Reading. While there is considerable detail in the chapters that follow, at some point there is no recourse but to refer you to more specialized sources.

EPISTEMOLOGICAL STATEMENT

Some traditions in research, especially research using qualitative data, encourage researchers to reveal anything that might uncover their biases. And in medical research, authors are often required to report any conflicts of interest. In books like this one, such self-disclosure is probably a good idea if not overindulged. Our biographical information is available elsewhere. Here, we would like to focus on our approach to knowledge, that is, our epistemological position. Epistemology is the study of the origins of knowledge and the justifications of knowledge claims. Sketching epistemological beliefs may be an especially good idea in works on methodology, since methodology is a kind of applied epistemology. As will be obvious, our emphasis in this book tends to be practical and applied rather than theoretical and philosophical. But we can understand why some readers of a reference book on research methods might nonetheless find the following discussion too theoretical and insufficiently applied. (Others will surely find it insufficiently theoretical and too superficial.) If you are one of those readers, please feel free to skip the rest of this preface.

Epistemology is a complicated and demanding philosophical discipline. As practical researchers in the social sciences, we have found it necessary to simplify. The three of us have not always done so in the same ways, and we sometimes use quite different terms for the same concepts. The following is our attempt to lay out some basic ideas—very compactly.

There are three basic types of epistemological belief: (1) empiricism/sensationalism, in which the sources of and justifications for knowledge claims come from observation through the senses; (2) rationalism/idealism, in which knowledge arises from and is verified by reasoning using internal mental categories; and (3) sociocultural relativism, in which knowledge is shaped by the specific social and cultural circumstances of those making knowledge claims. This third type can be considered a special case of the first two: Are our empirical observations shaped by our social position? Are our rational/mental categories determined by our culture?

One can also think of these three epistemological approaches as implying different learning styles or preferences. They are different entry points into knowing that are likely to be favored by different people. These preferences shape the questions we ask and our predilections about answering them through research methods. In the case of empiricism/sensationalism, direct experience provides the data or evidence for developing and then answering our questions. Without direct observation, research questions simply would not occur to us. Rationalism/idealism manifests as a preference for deductive learning. We begin with a truth or premise, then, through logical deduction, generate new truths or elaborate on that premise; this sometimes, but not invariably, results in a testable hypothesis. The third learning style demands metacognition of us: How do our socially and culturally mediated preferences shape what we know, what and how we investigate, and how we go about turning the results of our investigations into usable knowledge in context? Ultimately, we believe that we learn best when we use multiple learning styles and use them differentially to frame and then answer questions.

We have not found it helpful to get more specific than these typologies, though much contemporary epistemological discussion does so. Among the unhelpful things sometimes done is labeling every new wrinkle: neo-post-positivism, critical-queer-constructivism, or whatever. The obsession with "positivism" also strikes us as increasingly a waste of time. Positivism is a derivative combination of empiricism and rationalism. It joins knowledge derived both from sense data and from logical deduction, albeit in a very restrictive way. The members of the Vienna Circle are all dead. So are most of their followers, and it has been a long time since someone has said something new about their shortcomings. Criticizing logical positivism no longer suffices as a way to establish one's *bona fides*. It is still a socially important ritual among some researchers, but its intellectual importance has faded over the last 50 years.

Another unhelpful distinction that sometimes is included under the rubric of epistemology is the "quant–qual" debate. This is a category mistake. The adjectives *quantitative* and *qualitative* refer to the symbols we use, not to the knowledge claims made by using them. The symbols (words, numbers, or pictures) we use to make knowledge claims do not determine whether these claims are built upon empirical, rational, or relativist foundations.

In sum, if the only helpful general categories of epistemology are empiricism, rationalism, and relativism, which is correct? Our answer is: all of the above, in various combinations in various circumstances. The most helpful combinations vary with the problem being studied. That answer adds up to a kind of pragmatism, because the key criterion is helpfulness or usefulness. Our goal is *usable knowledge*, in the broadest sense of the term. Usable knowledge helps us to think, to understand the world better, to interact with others, to act on the physical environment. Who decides if something is useful? The community of users/knowers decides.

Given this decidedly eclectic theory of knowledge, how do we make claims in this book about when to use which methods or about which methods are better for what? Our ultimate standard is a kind of Deweyan pragmatism or progressivism. One method is better than another if it tends to foster more *growth* in usable knowledge. A method is worse than another if it tends to restrict or narrow the scope of the growth of knowledge. We find that this standard—fostering rather than restricting the growth of knowledge—can be applied to most problems of interest. But it is no straightforward algorithm. Applying it always involves reflection, debate, and judgment.

The standard is difficult to apply, but it is not a matter of relativism. We do believe that knowledge is possible, though it is not very tidy. We reject claims that knowledge, fairness, and lack of bias are impossible. They are difficult, moving targets and are always only approximately achieved. By contrast, relativism in its various forms tends to self-destruct; it contains the seeds of its own incoherence. If "everything is relative," and one cannot make any knowledge claims, what about the claim that everything is relative? To make a claim that one cannot make a claim is literally absurd, because it is self-contradictory.

We would not want to read a book about research design by authors who claim that attempting to learn anything is futile because all knowledge claims are extensions of our social position, gender, ethnicity, personality traits, and so on. All of these things tend to *influence* our perceptions and ideas, of course. That is the kernel of truth in relativism. But they do not wholly *determine* our perceptions and ideas. To claim that they do is the kernel of falsehood in relativism.

In brief, knowledge in the social and behavioral fields is possible. It is possible to make cogent arguments that various approaches to learning have advantages and disadvantages that we can weigh as we make rational judgments about selecting research designs and methods that are likely to be effective at answering our questions. Our goal in this book is practical: to assist researchers in making effective methodological decisions by discussing the advantages and disadvantages of various methods.

Where do these methodological guidelines come from? How do we study methodology in order to give advice? We have found it most useful to study the actual *practices* of researchers and their reflections on how they came to make the decisions they did. This does not lead us to "correct" versions of research and how to do it. Research wouldn't be so fascinating if there were always clear, unambiguous conclusions about methodology. In the same way, the guidelines offered in the following chapters would also be very dull if they were completely uncontroversial. It might be handy if all methodological choices could be reduced to straightforward algorithms and decision trees. But that would distort reality, and it would certainly make research much less interesting and creative than it is.

Acknowledgments

First of all, we want to thank C. Deborah Laughton, Publisher, Methodology and Statistics, at The Guilford Press, who has tended this project from the outset. She suggested the initial idea for the book, helped in its development, encouraged us when we faltered, was patient with the numerous delays, and provided thoughtful advice on the work at several strategic points along the way. The book would not have been started or finished without her counsel.

We are also indebted to colleagues who anonymously reviewed the manuscript. The first reaction when receiving dozens of pages of commentary from reviewers is: Gulp! Upon reading the extensive and closely argued suggestions for improvement, however, we could feel only gratitude. We couldn't always follow their advice, sometimes because their recommendations pointed us in opposite directions, but we carefully considered every one of them. In our introduction to Part III, on research ethics, we say that peer review is the foundation on which scholarship is built and that it is researchers' chief ethical responsibility to their colleagues. We did our best to take our colleagues' reviews as seriously as they took their responsibilities when making them.

Some reviewers remain anonymous; we are no less indebted to their efforts. Those who have allowed us to thank them by name are: Tracey LaPierre, University of Kansas, Department of Gerontology; Karen Staller, University of Michigan, School of Social Work; Susan Kushner Benson, University of Akron, Department of Education; Theresa DiDonato, Loyola University of Maryland, Department of Psychology; Rosemary Hopcraft, University of North Carolina at Charlotte, Department of Sociology; and Kory Floyd, Arizona State University, Hugh Downs School of Human Communication.

We also thank Bridget Delaney, a graduate assistant at Illinois State University, who did her best to keep us from making errors of commission and omission, both in the footnotes and in the reference list. And she did this work efficiently and cheerfully, even when we made our "emergency" requests at inconvenient times. Elaine Vogt, Illinois Wesleyan University, reviewed the entire manuscript and gently pointed out some harsh realities: many passages where our prose was in serious need of improvement and in which our reasoning contained gaps; we benefited greatly from her stylistic and substantive counsel. Rosalie Wieder and Anna Nelson at The Guilford Press did superb editorial work getting the manuscript ready for typesetting. Despite all the help and suggestions for improvement, we know that the volume is imperfect in many ways and we acknowledge, of course, that the remaining errors and infelicities are ours alone.

Brief Contents

General Introduction: Design, Sampling, and Ethics 1

PART I. Research Questions and Designs 9

CHAPTER 1. When to Use Survey Designs 15

CHAPTER 2. When to Use Interview Designs 31

CHAPTER 3. When to Use Experimental Designs 48

CHAPTER 4. When to Use Naturalistic and Participant Observational Designs 67

CHAPTER 5. When to Use Archival Designs: Literature Reviews and Secondary Data Analysis 86

CHAPTER 6. When to Use Combined Research Designs 103

PART II. Sampling, Selection, and Recruitment 115

CHAPTER 7. Sampling for Surveys 121

CHAPTER 8. Identifying and Recruiting People for Interviews 141

CHAPTER 9. Sampling, Recruiting, and Assigning Participants in Experiments 159

CHAPTER 10. Searching and Sampling for Observations 180

CHAPTER 11. Sampling from Archival Sources 198

CHAPTER 12. Sampling and Recruiting for Combined Research Designs 217

PART III. Research Ethics: The Responsible Conduct   227
            of Research

CHAPTER 13. Ethics in Survey Research   241

CHAPTER 14. Ethics in Interview Research   253

CHAPTER 15. Ethics in Experimental Research   266

CHAPTER 16. Ethics in Observational Research   281

CHAPTER 17. Ethical Issues in Archival Research   297

CHAPTER 18. Ethical Considerations in Combined Research Designs   307

            Conclusion: Culmination of Design, Sampling, and Ethics   317
            in Valid Data Coding

            Glossary   335

            References   357

            Index   371

            About the Authors   378

Extended Contents

General Introduction: Design, Sampling, and Ethics   1

Part I. Research Questions and Designs   4
Part II. Sampling, Selection, and Recruitment   5
Part III. Research Ethics: The Responsible Conduct of Research   6
Combining Methods and Concluding Comments   6

PART I. Research Questions and Designs   9

Introduction to Part I   9
What Is the Role of Theory in Research Questions and Designs?   10

CHAPTER 1. When to Use Survey Designs   15

When Are Surveys Likely to Be a Wise Design Choice?   15
  Are the Data Best Obtained Directly from the Individuals
    You Are Studying?   16
  Can Most of Your Data Be Obtained by Brief Answers
    to Structured Questions?   16
  Can You Expect Respondents to Give You Reliable Information?   17
  Do You Have a Clear Idea of How to Use the Answers
    to Your Questions?   18
  Can You Anticipate an Adequate Response Rate?   18
When Should You Use Which Mode of Administering Your Survey?   19
What Design Should You Use to Study Change over Time?   23
  When Should You Use a Panel Design to Study Change over Time?   23
  When Should You Use a Cohort Design to Study Change over Time?   23
  When Should You Use a Cross-Sectional Design to Study Change
    over Time?   24
  When Should You Use Event-History Methods?   25
What Question Formats Can You Use in a Survey Design?   25
Conclusion on Survey Designs: So Many Questions, So Little Time   27
Suggestions for Further Reading   28
Chapter 1 Summary Table   29

CHAPTER 2. When to Use Interview Designs   31

     Comparing Interviews with Surveys   33
         How Surveys and Interviews Differ   33
         What Interviews and Surveys Have in Common   34
     Specific Interview Types, Approaches, and Procedures   36
         The Relation of Interviewers' Research Questions and the Kinds
           of Questions They Ask   37
         More and Less Structured Interview Questions/Interview Schedules   39
         Social Rather Than Individual Interviewing, as in Focused
           Group Interviewing   41
         Different Modes of Conducting Interviews and the Formality
           of the Interview Setting   42
         When Should the Researcher Co-Create the Interview Text
           with the Interviewee?   43
     Conclusion   45
     Suggestions for Further Reading   46
     Chapter 2 Summary Table   47

CHAPTER 3. When to Use Experimental Designs   48

     What's Wrong with Gold-Standard Thinking?   49
     When Is an RCT a Good Option?   50
     When Is an Experimental Design a Good Option for Your Research?   50
         Can Cases, Subjects, or Participants Be Randomly Assigned?   51
         Can Key Variables Be Manipulated?   51
         Are RCTs Effective for Your Research Problem?   52
         Would an Experimental Intervention Distort the Object of Study?   53
         Is the Research Question More Focused on External
           or on Internal Validity?   53
         Is the Research Question More Focused on Causal Processes
           or Outcomes?   54
     When Should You Use the Basic Types of Experimental Design?   56
         When Should You Replicate Previous Experiments?   56
         When Should You Use "Blinding"—and How Much Should You Do?   57
         When Are There Advantages to a Within-Subjects Design?   57
         When Are There Advantages to a Between-Subjects Design?   57
         When There Is More Than One Factor, Should You Use a Crossed
           or a Nested Design?   58
         When Is It Useful to Use Pretests?   59
         When Should You Use a Matched-Pairs Design?   59
         When Should You Control for Pretest Sensitization if Pretests
           Are Used?   59
         When Should You Control Aspects of the Laboratory Environment?   59
         When Should You Plan for a Laboratory Experiment and When
           for a Field Experiment?   60
         When Should You Worry about Treatment Fidelity and Conduct
           Manipulation Checks?   60
         When Should You Categorize Continuous Independent Variables
           in an Experimental Design?   60
         When Do You Add More Factors or Independent Variables
           to Your Design?   61
         When Should You Use Quasi-Experiments?   61
         When Should You Use Natural Experiments?   62
         When Should the Experiment Be Combined with One or More
           Other Designs?   62

General Conclusion on When to Use Experimental Designs   63
Suggestions for Further Reading   64
Chapter 3 Summary Table   65

CHAPTER 4. When to Use Naturalistic and Participant Observational Designs   67

Overview of Observational Designs   68
When Is Observation a Good Design Choice?   69
    *. . . When You Can Best Answer Your Research Question by Studying
Social, Cultural, or Political Processes as They Unfold*   69
    *. . . When You Want to Identify, Develop, or Refine Sensitizing Concepts
or Variables*   70
    *. . . When It Is Important to Cultivate a Rich or Thick Description
within a Particular Context*   71
    *. . . When You Want to Uncover or Explore Causal Mechanisms
or to Recognize Interactive Links between and among Variables*   73
Further Distinguishing between Naturalistic and Participant Observational
Designs   73
    Cell I: Naturalistic/Covert Research   74
    Cell II: Naturalistic/Overt Research   75
    Cell III: Covert/Participant Research   75
    Cell IV: Overt/Participant Research   76
When Should You Use a Naturalistic Observational Design?   76
    *. . . When You Can Take Advantage of Public Events with Little Chance
of Influencing What You Observe*   77
    *. . . When You Are Making Initial Entries into the Field to Explore
Sensitizing Concepts or Variables*   77
    *. . . When It Is Particularly Important Not to Influence the Participants
or the Setting*   78
    *. . . When Participant Observation Is Impossible or It Would Raise
Ethical Concerns*   78
When Should You Use Participant Observational Designs?   79
    . . . When You Want to Witness a Phenomenon from the Inside   79
    *. . . When You Are Particularly Interested in Diverse Perspectives and in
the Social Nature of What You Are Studying*   80
    *. . . When You Want to Study Something over Time as It Unfolds,
Perceptions Emerge, and Meanings Are Ascribed*   80
    *. . . When You Want to Influence the Attributes, Variables, Settings, and
Practices You Are Studying*   81
Conclusion: Characteristics of All Observational Designs   81
    Using a Sensitizing Concept or Framework   82
    Studying Change over Time   82
    Triangulation and Corroboration   83
Suggestions for Further Reading   84
Chapter 4 Summary Table   85

**CHAPTER 5. When to Use Archival Designs: Literature Reviews   86
and Secondary Data Analysis**

What Kinds of Archival Data Are Available for Researchers?   88
When Should You Collect and Use Preexisting Data Rather Than Produce
Your Own?   88
Types of Archival Research   89
    Reviews of the Literature, Research Synthesis, and Meta-Analysis   89

Database Archives   93
  When Should You Use Such Database Archives?   95
  When Should You Not Use Database Archives?   95
Organizational Records   95
Textual Studies of Documents   96
  When Should You Study Phenomena, When Texts,
    and When Contexts?   97
  When to Use Textual Archival Research   98
  When Not to Use Textual Archival Research   98
New Media, Including Internet Sources   99
Conclusion   100
Suggestions for Further Reading   101
Chapter 5 Summary Table   102

CHAPTER 6. When to Use Combined Research Designs   103
Simple versus Multipart Research Questions   104
When to Combine Research Designs   106
Types and Qualities of Combined Designs   106
  When Should You Sequence Your Design Methods?   106
  When Should One Design Method Predominate?   108
  When Should Your Design Methods Interact or Be Used Iteratively?   109
Logistical Considerations in Combined Research Designs   110
  When Should You Consider Engaging More Than One Researcher?   110
  When Should You Triangulate?   111
Conclusion and Summary   112
Suggestions for Further Reading   112
Chapter 6 Summary Table   113

PART II. Sampling, Selection, and Recruitment   115
Introduction to Part II   115

CHAPTER 7. Sampling for Surveys   121
Probability Samples   122
  When Should You Use Simple Random Sampling?   122
  When Can You Make Inferences about Populations from Which You
    Have Not Randomly Sampled?   123
  When Should You Sample with Replacement?   123
  When Should You Use Systematic Sampling?   124
  What Can You Do to Obtain a Sampling Frame?   124
  When Should You Use Stratified Random Sampling?   125
  When Should You Use Cluster Sampling?   126
Nonprobability Samples   126
  When Should You Use Convenience Samples in Surveys?   126
  When Should You Compare Sample Statistics
    to Population Parameters?   127
  When Should You Use Quota Samples?   127
  When Should You Use Judgment (Purposive) Samples in Surveys?   128
  When Should You Use Snowball Sampling
    and Respondent-Driven Sampling?   129
  When Can You Learn from Nonprobability Samples?   130
When Should You Try to Improve Response Rates?   131
  How Big Does Your Response Rate Have to Be?   133

How Big Should Your Sample Be? 133
  When Might Your Sample Be Too Big? 134
  When Do You Need to Increase Your Statistical Power? 134
  When Should You Increase Your Sample Size? 135
  When Should You Trade Size for Representativeness—
    or Vice Versa? 138
Conclusion 138
Suggestions for Further Reading 139
Chapter 7 Summary Table 140

CHAPTER 8. Identifying and Recruiting People for Interviews 141
How Interview Strategies Are Shaped by Research Questions 143
  When Your Research Question Seeks to Gather External
    versus Internal Data 143
  When Your Research Questions Are Descriptive 144
  When Your Research Questions Are Exploratory 144
  When Your Research Questions Seek Explanations 145
  When Your Research Question Involves Theory Testing 145
  When Your Research Questions Aim at Theory Building,
    Including Finding Causal Mechanisms 146
Conclusion on the Influence of Research Questions 146
Making Basic Decisions about Interview Sampling 147
  Whom Should You Interview and Where? 148
  How Many Interviewees Do You Need? 149
  How Many Times and for How Long Should You Interview? 150
  How Will You Contact or Recruit Your Interview Subjects? 150
  When Should You Select, Invite, and Recruit for Focused
    Group Interviews? 153
Conclusions on Selecting People to Interview 155
Suggestions for Further Reading 156
Chapter 8 Summary Table 157

CHAPTER 9. Sampling, Recruiting, and Assigning Participants in Experiments 159
Randomized Controlled Trials 159
  When Identifying the Target Population 160
  When Recruiting a Pool of Volunteers 160
  When Sampling and Assigning Operationalizations of a Variable 161
  When to Use Group Rather Than Individual Randomizing 162
  When to Use Pure Random Assignment or One of the Other Assignment
    Methods 163
  When Deciding Sample Size and Experimental Group Size 164
  When Adding Cases or Participants Is Expensive 166
  When to Use Pretests—and When during the Experiment
    to Administer Them 167
  When Things Go Wrong in Your Experiment 168
  When to Report What You Have Done 168
  When You Sample for Field, Not Laboratory, Experiments 169
Alternatives to RCTs 170
  Natural Experiments 171
  Quasi-Experiments 172
  Single-Case Experiments 174
  Regression Discontinuity Methods 174
Controlling for Covariates 175

Conclusion: Sampling, Recruiting, and Assigning Cases
    in Experiments   177
Suggestions for Further Reading   177
Chapter 9 Summary Table   178

CHAPTER 10. Searching and Sampling for Observations   180

Overview of Searching and Sampling Concerns
    in Observational Research   182
Appropriateness and Relevance of the Sample   183
    When Do You Search and Sample for Relevance?   184
    When Do You Search and Sample for Representativeness?   185
Accessing Observation Sites   186
    Witnessing Authentic Phenomena   187
Decisions Influenced by Resources and Other Practical Considerations   187
Four Basic Sampling Decisions   188
Sampling and the Five Types of Research Questions   190
    Sampling for "Thick Description" in Response to
        "What?" Questions   191
    Sampling to Explore Described Phenomena in Depth   192
    Sampling for Explanatory Studies   192
    Sampling to Test an Emerging Theory   193
    Sampling to Establish a Theory   194
Conclusion   195
Suggestions for Further Reading   196
Chapter 10 Summary Table   197

CHAPTER 11. Sampling from Archival Sources   198

When Do You Search and When Do You Sample?   199
    When Do You Stop Collecting Data: When Do You Have Enough?   200
Sampling Research Literature to Build Upon and Synthesize It   200
    When Do You Use Electronic Databases to Do Your Searching?   201
    When Is It OK to Be Selective Rather Than Comprehensive?   203
Database Archives   205
Organizational Records   207
Textual Studies of Documents   210
    When Do You Use Computer-Assisted Methods for Searching
        and Sampling Texts?   211
New Media, Including Various Internet Sources   212
Conclusion   214
Suggestions for Further Reading   215
Chapter 11 Summary Table   216

CHAPTER 12. Sampling and Recruiting for Combined Research Designs   217

When Should You Use Probability Samples in Your Combined
    Design Study?   219
When Should You Use Purposive Samples in Your Combined
    Design Study?   220
When Should You Use Both Probability and Purposive Samples
    in Your Study?   221
Conclusions   223
Suggestions for Further Reading   224
Chapter 12 Summary Table   225

PART III. Research Ethics: The Responsible Conduct   227
of Research

Introduction to Part III   227
Responsibilities toward the Persons Being Studied   229
Responsibilities toward Other Researchers   233
   Collegiality   234
   Honesty   235
   Fairness   236
Responsibilities toward the Broader Society/Community   236
   Moral Suasion   236
   Legal Penalties   237

CHAPTER 13. Ethics in Survey Research   241

Consent: Informed Participants Willingly Joining the Research Project   242
   Design   242
   Sampling   243
   Data Collection   244
   Analysis and Reporting   244
Harm: Preventing Injury to Respondents   244
   Design   244
   Sampling   245
   Data Collection   245
   Analysis and Reporting   245
Privacy: Ensuring Respondents' Anonymity and/or Confidentiality   247
   Design   247
   Sampling   248
   Data Collection   248
   Analysis and Reporting   249
Conclusion   250
Suggestions for Further Reading   251
Chapter 13 Summary Table   252

CHAPTER 14. Ethics in Interview Research   253

Consent: Informed Participants Willingly Agreeing to Be Interviewed   254
   Design   254
   Sampling and Recruiting   255
   Data Collection   256
   Analysis and Reporting   257
Harm: Preventing Injury to Interviewees during the Interview   257
   Design   257
   Sampling and Recruiting   257
   Data Collection   258
   Analysis and Reporting   259
Privacy: Ensuring Interviewees' Confidentiality   259
   Design   259
   Sampling and Recruiting   260
   Data Collection   261
   Analysis and Reporting   262
Conclusion   263
Suggestions for Further Reading   263
Chapter 14 Summary Table   264

CHAPTER 15. Ethics in Experimental Research   266

    Consent: Informed Participants Willingly Joining the Research Project   268
        Design   268
        Sampling and Assigning   271
        Data Collection   272
        Analysis and Reporting   272
    Harm: Preventing Injury to Experimental Participants   272
        Design   272
        Sampling, Recruiting, and Assigning   273
        Data Collection   275
        Analysis and Reporting   275
    Privacy: Ensuring Participants' Anonymity and/or Confidentiality   277
        Design   277
        Sampling and Recruiting   277
        Data Collection   277
        Analysis and Reporting   277
    Conclusion   278
    Suggestions for Further Reading   278
    Chapter 15 Summary Table   279

CHAPTER 16. Ethics in Observational Research   281

    Seeking and Acquiring Informed Consent to Observe   282
        Design   282
        Sampling   285
        Data Collection   287
        Analysis and Reporting   287
    Avoiding and Minimizing Harm to Participants While Conducting
        the Study   288
        Design   288
        Sampling   289
        Data Collection   289
        Analysis and Reporting   290
    Ensuring Participant Privacy   291
        Design   291
        Sampling   291
        Data Collection   291
        Analysis and Reporting   292
    Conclusion   293
    Suggestions for Further Reading   294
    Chapter 16 Summary Table   295

CHAPTER 17. Ethical Issues in Archival Research   297

    Ethical Practice in Reviews of the Research Literature   298
    Ethical Practices in Employing Database Archives   299
    Ethical Obligations When Using Institutional Records   300
    Ethical Issues Using Documents, Including Public Documents   301
    Ethical Issues When Using Blogs and Other Sources Published Online   303
    When Might the Honest, Correct Reporting of Archival Research Cause
        Harm?   303
    Conclusion   304
    Suggestions for Further Reading   305
    Chapter 17 Summary Table   306

CHAPTER 18. Ethical Considerations in Combined Research Designs   307

    Consent   307
     Design   307
     Sampling   309
     Data Collection   309
     Analysis and Reporting   309
    Harm   310
     Design   310
     Sampling   310
     Data Collection   311
     Analysis and Reporting   311
    Privacy   311
     Sampling   312
     Data Collection   312
     Analysis and Reporting   313
    Conclusion   314
    Suggestions for Further Reading   314
    Chapter 18 Summary Table   315

Conclusion: Culmination of Design, Sampling, and Ethics   317
in Valid Data Coding

    When to Use Qualities or Quantities, Names or Numbers,
      Categories or Continua?   319
    What Methods to Use to Code Concepts with Reliability and Validity   321
    What Methods to Use to Improve Reliability   321
    What Methods to Use to Enhance Validity   323
    What to Use to Code Concepts Validly   325
    Coding Decisions Shape Analytic Options   330
    Suggestions for Further Reading   334

Glossary   335

References   357

Index   371

About the Authors   378

General Introduction
Design, Sampling, and Ethics

Our aim in this book is to assist researchers in choosing research methods by helping them select designs to gather data and select samples from which to collect data. We also discuss the ethical concerns that arise from the interaction of design and sampling choices. (A companion volume addresses how to select data analysis techniques.) Coding and measurement form the transition between design, broadly conceived, and analysis. That is why we conclude this volume with a design-relevant discussion of coding and measurement and begin the companion volume by considering coding and measurement from the standpoint of analysis.

We have written this book mainly for readers who have a research question, problem, or topic to investigate. If you don't have your research goals already in mind, you will want to define those goals before you make important decisions about how to do your research. Although it is not uncommon to hear students say, before they have a research question, "I want to do interview research" or "I'd like to conduct an experiment," we think that choices among research designs and sampling methods are better made after you have decided on your research topic and question(s), not before. Once you have defined your research questions and goals, then you can better face the many choices among designs, sampling methods, and ethical procedures. Our hope is that we can help make your design, sampling, and ethical choices more deliberate and defensible.

Many researchers pursue multiple goals using multiple research methods to attain them. Of course, all research goals and all potentially useful methods cannot be pursued at the same time. Researchers must choose among goals and methods or, at minimum, rank the order in which they will be tackled. Another way to put this is that choosing among methods always entails "opportunity costs." Taking advantage of an

1

opportunity by making one choice may preclude making another. For example, one opportunity cost of selecting a specific research method is that other methods cannot easily be used simultaneously. This tradeoff problem[1] is central to making informed choices about research methods, because choices made early in your design may limit how you can analyze and interpret your data later.

The three parts of this book take up methodological choices in a logical order: from design to sampling to ethics. These three together constitute the initial "design package" that prepares you for data collection and analysis. We deal with the initial design package in this volume. Analysis choices are reviewed in a companion volume.[2] This book is meant to help researchers establish a defensible research design, which in turn can lead logically to a justifiable and replicable method of data collection, and to adopting responsible ethical safeguards necessary given your design and sampling choices. Our companion book focuses on choosing strategies for coding, measuring, and analyzing your data. This is a logical order in which to address the choices researchers need to make. We depict this logical order as a series of stages in Figure 1. Of course, in practice, researchers encounter many feedback loops in their work, in which later choices encourage reconsideration of earlier decisions.

In theory, it would be possible to enter the stream of choices illustrated in Figure 1 at any point. And, it is almost always true that thinking about later choices (e.g., coding and analysis) is likely to affect the thinking about and lead to revisions in prior choices (e.g., sampling). Clearly, no simple linear algorithm describes the empirical reality of researchers' thoughts and decisions. One of the themes brought up by reviewers of sample chapters for this book was that certain topics—such as research ethics, concepts and constructs, units of analysis, validity, and reliability—should be discussed earlier in the sequence. We almost always agreed with their points. Each choice in the series of decisions that constitute a research plan would be improved if the other decisions had already been made. But there is a problem. Everything cannot come earlier. Everything cannot be first. Something must come later. To put it another way, writing a book requires authors to impose a structure. The five steps we have used—design, sampling, ethics, coding, and analysis—are our attempt to structure the complexity of the process of selecting the methods used to investigate research questions.

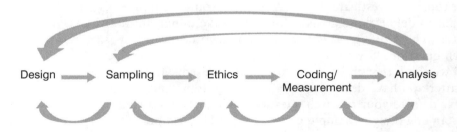

FIGURE 1. Natural sequence of methods choices with feedback loops.

---

[1] Vogt (2002); Brady and Collier (2004).

[2] Tentatively titled *When to Use What Analysis Methods*.

Design is the master category. By "designs," we refer here to the basic methods of collecting evidence: surveys, interviews, experiments, observations (participant and naturalistic), archival research (data and textual archives), and combinations of these methods. Design is fundamental because everything ultimately flows from the design choice, and because this choice is the one most closely tied to the investigator's research questions and theories.

Subsequent parts of the book are organized under the rubric of design types. Thus, when we discuss sampling, it is sampling for each of the designs (surveys, interviews, experiments, etc.), and when we discuss ethics, the same is true. However, we have tried to structure the book so that readers can move among the parts, chapters, and sections in several different ways. The book may be read from the first page to the last—*and* it may be dipped into at will. Table 1 shows the organization of the book's three parts (design, sampling, and ethics) and its six design themes (surveys, interviews, experiments, observations, archival studies, and combined methods). For example, a reader might wish to consult only the interview chapters (Design Theme 2, Chapters 2, 8, and 14) or to read only chapters dealing with research ethics (Part III, Chapters 13–18) or to peruse only the chapter on research ethics in interviews (Chapter 14).

Having this flexibility to navigate by part or by design theme or by chapter is important because the order we have used, while logical enough for researchers beginning a new project, many times does not capture the empirical reality of what researchers actually do. For example, all three of the authors of this book have worked on projects in which the measurement decisions were essentially made before the research team began its work. For example, when studying family income in an investigation comparing states over time, our only reasonable option was to use measures and data from the Current Population Survey. A second example was a statewide study of the academic achievement of thousands of students. Here, the only viable measure was standardized state achievement test scores. Nonetheless, the research question was determinative in each case. It was the research question that required a design that collected income data from all states. And it was a different research question that necessitated a design that examined data collected from thousands of students. Different research questions might have led to different designs—for example, interviews with wage earners in the first case or observations of classroom interactions, in the second.

TABLE 1. Organization of the Volume, by Parts and by Design Themes

	Part I: Design	Part II: Sampling	Part III: Ethics
Design Theme 1: Surveys	Chapter 1	Chapter 7	Chapter 13
Design Theme 2: Interviews	Chapter 2	Chapter 8	Chapter 14
Design Theme 3: Experiments	Chapter 3	Chapter 9	Chapter 15
Design Theme 4: Observations	Chapter 4	Chapter 10	Chapter 16
Design Theme 5: Archives	Chapter 5	Chapter 11	Chapter 17
Design Theme 6: Combined	Chapter 6	Chapter 12	Chapter 18

Perhaps the greatest departure of this book from the current norm in discussing research methods is that we do not initially organize our thinking about research choices using the distinction between quantitative and qualitative research. For many researchers, the "quant-qual" decision is the first and most important choice. We agree that deciding how to code one's data—quantitatively, qualitatively, graphically, or all three—is an important decision, but we think it is more effectively made later in the process: after the research question has been decided upon, after the design has been chosen, and often after the cases have been selected. Since all designs can be (and have been) used to generate either quantitative or qualitative data, design types are not mutually exclusive in the kind of data they can generate. Therefore, designs cannot properly be categorized according to whether they are quantitative or qualitative. All designs can be either quantitative or qualitative, or both. On the other hand, when we address analysis choices in our companion book, the quant–qual distinction moves from the periphery to the center of attention.

The following overview of the volume's Parts I, II, and III helps to clarify the scope and structure of the book.

PART I. RESEARCH QUESTIONS AND DESIGNS

Part I raises the crucial questions: Given my research problem, how shall I conduct the study to collect evidence? What evidence do I need in order to address my research questions? Where and how can I most effectively obtain it? The design choices, which are plans for collecting evidence, are divided into five main groups. A sixth category is that of combining two or more of these five in the same research project.

- Surveys
- Interviews
- Experiments
- Observational Research: Naturalistic and Participant Observations
- Archival Research: Data and Textual Archives
- Combining Designs

This categorization focuses on methods of collecting evidence, not on other criteria used to classify research methods. For example, one such criterion is so-called correlational research designs. Correlations are analysis tools, not design types. Correlations may be used in all of the above designs—or none. This means that "correlational" is not a useful design criterion. It is neither exhaustive nor mutually exclusive. The same is true, as noted above, of so-called quantitative and qualitative designs. The adjectives *quantitative* and *qualitative* refer to matters of coding measurement, not design. All of the designs listed above can be used to generate either quantitative or qualitative data or both. Both continuous quantitative data and categorical qualitative data can be analyzed with correlational techniques.

Another distinction that is often used to classify research is between experimental and nonexperimental research. This is a real distinction and many writers like it. But the residual category, nonexperimental, is so huge that it is not very useful for organizing a book covering the full spectrum of choice of research methods. Saying that research is nonexperimental is not sufficiently specific for most purposes. Imagine how you would react if an author claimed that all research naturally falls into two categories: interview research and non-interview research. Some proponents of interview research might think this reasonable, but most of us would find it bizarre to categorize the majority of published research as "non-interview." The fact that we tend to find the label nonexperimental a reasonable way to describe the majority of published research is an indication of the degree to which, rightly or wrongly, the concept of experimental research is privileged in methodological writing. Even if experimental research truly ought to hold a place of honor, "nonexperimental" is at best a vague and ineffective category.

The advantage of the proposed classification scheme used to organize the design chapters of Part I is that it can be directly linked to the investigator's research questions and to the general disciplinary or theoretical problems that motivated those questions. Categories such as correlational or non-experimental are less helpful for displaying the range of choices researchers face or for tying the choice of methods to what is needed to answer research questions.

PART II. SAMPLING, SELECTION, AND RECRUITMENT

Key questions addressed in Part II include: Whom or what shall we study, how many will we study, and how shall we choose them? Once designs have been decided upon, researchers then need to turn their attention to finding cases to study. We use the term *cases* generically to describe any unit of analysis or object/subject of study. Many researchers, especially perhaps those in psychology and education, prefer *participant* as the generic term. That is a good term for many designs, such as experiments or participant observations in which people are being studied directly. But it seems awkward if used for many other kinds of social research. For example, the geographic regions in a study of residential patterns, the articles in a meta-analysis, the demographic influences on unemployment rates, the political reactions to trends in hate crimes, the data in a database archive, or the movies in a study of the depiction of teenagers in Hollywood films are not well described as "participants" in the research. But all have to be sampled or selected in some way—from the demographic regions to the movies—and there doesn't seem to be a more generic term for what is being sampled than *cases*. Certainly, cases differ greatly from one type of research to another. Cases may be of many kinds: individuals, institutions, events, trends, social groups, political entities, and so on. Part II reviews methods of sampling among a population of cases. The methods range from drawing full-blown probability samples of thousands of cases to the purposive selecting of a single case to investigate.

Each set of sampling choices stems from and is related to the design choices. Methods of selecting cases to study may vary greatly depending on the choice of design. An approach that could be very appropriate for sampling articles from newspaper archives would be of little value for choosing a site for participant observation. The chapter topics are organized as follows.

- Sampling for Surveys
- Selecting and Recruiting for Interviews
- Sampling, Recruiting, and Assigning Participants in Experiments
- Selecting Sites for Naturalistic and Participant Observation
- Finding and Sampling from Archival Sources
- Selecting Cases for Combined Designs

Sampling often occurs at several stages. If one is sampling, one is selecting from a larger group: the population or universe. So, the first choice is which population (or universe) will be sampled. This is true even if one is doing a study involving a single case—such as an individual life history or single particular organization—as long as the case is a case of something. The "something" is the population concerning which the lessons learned from studying the case are relevant. The population may be more or less clearly defined and the process of selecting from it may be more or less systematic, but the general intellectual problem is similar for all types of research. In one way or another, most researchers address the question: What kind of population, composed of what units of analysis, is appropriate for my research question, and how can I learn more about that population? Clearly, to answer a research question, choosing the population is fully as important as applying rules of sampling when selecting the cases to be studied.

PART III. RESEARCH ETHICS:
THE RESPONSIBLE CONDUCT OF RESEARCH

Ethical issues emerge most saliently at the intersection of design and sampling. Once the researcher has considered the basic methods of gathering the data and decided from whom they will be gathered, ethical issues become very concrete. Even though ethical choices are (or should be) based on important general moral principles, it is often not very practical to discuss the ethics of research in general. These important and complex discussions are usually more fruitful in the context of a specific design and sampling plan. It is easiest to consider, for example, the rights of experimental research participants after one knows who those participants will be and what the researcher will be asking of them. That is why the chapters on ethics in research will have the same design-guided structure used in the first two parts of the book. After a general introduction in which some overriding themes are discussed, ethical issues, problems, and choices will be considered in turn for survey research, interviews, experiments, observational research, archival research, and combined designs.

COMBINING METHODS AND CONCLUDING COMMENTS

The last chapter of each of the three parts—design, sampling, and ethics—addresses the question of combined or multiple research methods. Combining different methods in the same research project can take many different forms. Categories of these forms are labeled differently by researchers (and researchers can be quite insistent that the "correct" label be used). *Mixed method* research focuses on approaches that cross the quantitative–qualitative boundary. Answers to surveys coded numerically and answers to interview questions coded verbally are a frequent example. *Multimethod* research may include approaches that mix quantitative and qualitative data, but multimethod research can also refer to research that does not necessarily cross the quant–qual border. A sociologist using verbal documents and qualitatively coded observations to better understand an institution would be conducting an example of multimethod research that is qualitative. A psychologist combining numerical data from field observations and numerical data from laboratory experiments would be an example of conducting multimethod research that is wholly quantitative.

Whatever the specific combinations, the general disposition behind such approaches described in the combined methods chapters (6, 12, and 18) is methodological pluralism. One consequence of this pluralism is that it increases the range of choices, which is already extensive when selecting noncombined methods. And this increase is dramatic. Any increase in the already large set of choices highlights the most important lessons this book tries to convey. First, selecting research methods is a matter of choice. Second, methodological choices are better if they are made with systematic deliberation. Our goal is to provide some tools to assist researchers engaged in such deliberations.

We have written this book both as a reference tool for making decisions about the research method(s) you might want to use and also as a survey of research methods that is a more general overview of the choices available to researchers. We hope that the book may be helpful to researchers at various stages of their careers, from those about to tackle their first project, through master's level and doctoral students, and perhaps even to seasoned investigators thinking about branching out in a new direction.

PART I

Research Questions and Designs

INTRODUCTION TO PART I

The relation of the research question to the research design is among the most intellec-tually challenging parts of the entire research process. And, it is the part of this book where it is hardest to give straightforward, if–then advice. One can almost never simply say: If you want to do this, then use that method. Or, if such advice is given, it may be too simplistic. How does one move from a research problem to a design?

Research questions come in several varieties. Among the questions you could ask about a research question the following are common: Does the question mainly involve description or causal inference? Is the goal in-depth understanding of how and why something occurs or is it generalizing broadly about when and to whom it happens? Is the research question exploratory or confirmatory? Does it focus more on prediction or explanation? These are handy ways of categorizing questions about questions, and they sometimes help one choose research designs.

Where do researchers get research questions? Problems, which the research ques-tions are meant to resolve, typically come from three sources: the external world, a researcher's personal interests, or from a discipline-based theory. Of the three, the lat-ter is by far the most prestigious, especially among discipline-based researchers, but it is probably the least common. Wherever it comes from, the initial formulation of the research question is typically refined by a review of the research literature on the topic. The literature review is important in several ways. Whether it is to provide ideas for turning a general area of research into more specific research questions, or to help avoid researching a largely resolved question, or to steer you away from false method-ological paths, the literature review is essential. It keeps you from trying to reinvent the wheel, and, just as important, from reinventing the flat tire. The research review also directs you to the standard methods for handling the problem your research question is intended to solve.

9

A good research design is justifiable in terms of the research question. At minimum, the researcher should offer an argument that the design adopted is an effective one for the job. This is less often done than one might expect. Frequently, even major projects such as doctoral dissertations offer little more than a few sentences by way of justification of what is arguably the most consequential of all the choices made in planning a research project. More is usually said on the issue of how the research question emerges from "theory."

WHAT IS THE ROLE OF THEORY IN RESEARCH QUESTIONS AND DESIGNS?

When should your research question and design be based on theory? "Always!" would probably be the answer of most methodology text authors. Graphically, the relation of theory, research question, and design is often described as a linear sequence, and sometimes called the "hypothetico-deductive model." This sequence is depicted very simply in Figure I.1.

In this standard theory-testing model, a research question (or hypothesis) is a statement of what ought to pertain if a theory is true. In the standard model, you reflect on a theory, deduce a hypothesis, and then test the hypothesis. Theory-based research is often research that tests the accuracy of a prediction that should pertain if the hypothesis is true. That kind of research is very important and, according to many, the only way science progresses, but it is not the only kind of valuable research. Investigations that *explore* empirical reality more inductively or that aim to *create*, not test, a theory are also legitimate and, indeed, essential to intellectual progress. These will be discussed at several points in the following chapters, but they are not the typical textbook model.

There are advantages to conducting theory-based research, but they are not so overwhelming that one would never want to do anything else. You might have a hunch, and if you think about it systematically, you might build a good research question and then a good design based on that question. In that case, your hunch stands in for theory in Figure I.1. For example, you might believe that a commonly accepted belief (or theory) is really just a prejudice, so you want to design a research project to test that belief. But teachers of methods in social science graduate programs usually discourage this approach. The discouragement is likely to be especially strong in subdisciplines that are rich in theories that direct most of their research work, especially experimental work. In other fields, in which theories are less determinative, students are often encouraged to search in the research literature to find a theory applicable to their topic or question. It is usually not too hard to find a theory that can stand in for your hunch or your interest. Whether this is an improvement has to be decided on a case-by-case basis. As longtime readers of research articles, we have sometimes found that theories seem to have been

Theory ⟶ Research Question ⟶ Research Design

FIGURE I.1. Theory's relation to design.

tacked on to a question that was perfectly interesting in its own right. However, adding the theory in such circumstances at least helps tie the research report, more or less directly, to a broader literature.

What is a theory? This is not an easy question because there is much difference of opinion about what counts as a theory. Theories range from broad sociopolitical beliefs such as Marxism or feminism to highly specific theories that all but define a subdiscipline; *expectation states* theory in social psychology is one example in which the theory has been tested and refined through hundreds of experiments.[1] Given this range in what counts as a theory, any all-purpose definition tends to be vague. We offer the following: A theory is a more-or-less ordered set of propositions about how something works; it is a series of logically linked statements about why something happens or about relations among phenomena.

There is no shortage of theories in the social sciences. Unfortunately, many of them are fairly weak. Most do not predict as much or explain as well as we would like. Basing your work on a mediocre theory is not likely to do you a lot of good. Our view is that, after a thorough review of the literature so that you know what has been done in your area of research, you may decide to construct your own theory. So yes, you should often base your work on a theory, but it does not *necessarily* have to be based on the thinking of any previous researcher.

On the other hand, you take a big risk by doing research on a subject in which others have no interest. If others have an interest, there will be theories. You might think that X does not cause Y. But if no one else does, "Well, duh!" as they say. If you want to show that something is *not* true, you need to show that lots of people think it is true and that important consequences follow from their misunderstanding. If you want to show that something *is* true, then you need to show that this is not already widely known and perhaps that some folks, whose opinions matter, think it is not true. You don't want to sound like a fool or waste your time testing a long-defunct hypothesis, so you need a thorough grounding in the research literature in your area. To be effective, your research question has to address a subject about which a reasonable number of people, especially researchers, have beliefs.

This is why the literature review is so important. It is also quite frequent, when reviewing previous research, to find conflicting theories or models. This provides an opportunity for the researcher to craft a research question aiming to resolve the dispute.[2] Another advantage of a thorough literature review is that it occasionally turns up a lead, suggested by a researcher some time ago, that was not taken seriously and that now seems promising to you. This is less a matter of finding a theory to test and more a case of getting ideas to help you refine your hunches. Such use of initially-ignored work is fairly common, especially in the natural sciences (Gregor Mendel's genetics research is the classic example). In brief, reviewing research literature can be important at any stage of a research project, but it is perhaps most important at the stage where you are formulating research questions and selecting a design.

A theory is a belief, often a testable belief. But many theories are more descriptive and explanatory than predictive and cannot be tested directly. Theories about the

---

[1] For discussions, see Rashotte, Webster, and Whitmeyer (2005); and Kalkhoff and Thye (2006).

[2] See Classen (2007) for an example.

origins of war, patterns of economic inequality, or the relation of democratic forms of government to other variables such as economic development are examples.[3] Whether you base your work on a named theory or not, it is often very important to have a series of ordered propositions that directs your investigation. You need a clearly enunciated question (or hypothesis) that helps you determine what will count as evidence for and against the hypothesis or lead to an answer or answers to your research question, but all this need not be tied to a standard theory or to resolving a dispute between standard theories.

As we mentioned earlier, your research question might lead you to try to create a theory. What research design would you use in that case? This is a very difficult question, because the processes of creating theories are much more uncertain than the processes of testing them. It is often said that qualitative research is better at generating theories and hypotheses, while quantitative research is better at testing them. The history of theory creation is not, we believe, well described by this generalization. Theories do not seem to come more often from either quantitative or qualitative work. Theories are the product of reflection on evidence. That evidence may be quantitative or qualitative, but the process of coming up with a theory is neither quantitative nor qualitative (these are measurement distinctions). Rather, theorizing involves some form of reasoning about intuitions triggered by evidence. The evidence might be generated by the theorist or the theorizing may be based more on evidence obtained by reviewing the literature.

In practice, the full design process is often expanded to include some earlier steps, including the literature review, as seen in Figure I.2.

As an example, as a doctoral student, one of us had a general *area of interest* in high school students' college readiness (or lack thereof). Within that broad area of interest, she *identified a problem*, in that some students seem to have greater support than others from peers and adults as they proceed through high school, and these more strongly supported students seem to be more prepared for and more likely to attend college. She conducted a *literature review* that revealed previous studies in this area of interest, and particularly on the problem of student supports (or lack of supports) for college-going. In the process, she also learned about *social capital theory*, which could potentially be tested as a way of explaining how more highly supported students benefit in terms of college readiness and college-going. Her *research questions* focused on how those in relatively new adult supporting roles emerging in some high schools, called "postsecondary coaches," actually did their jobs, and how much social capital (if any) they were accumulating for their students. As her *research design*, she settled on a comparative case study of two post-secondary coaches in two high schools of relatively similar size and student demographics, but with markedly different outcomes in terms of students attending college, particularly for minority and low-income students.

FIGURE I.2. Expanded design process.

[3] See, respectively, Senese and Vasquez (2003), Moran (2006a, 2006b), and King and Zeng (2007).

In brief, the origins of research questions are many and complex. Once a researcher has a research question, then the work of designing an investigation can begin in earnest. We can address the main question in Part I of this book by asking: *Given my research question, when should I . . .* use a survey? conduct interviews? conduct experiments? do naturalistic or participant observation? investigate secondary or archival sources? combine designs? The abbreviated answers in Table I.1 provide an overview of the chapters of Part I.

TABLE I.1. Given My Research Question, When Should I . . .

. . . Use a survey? **Chapter 1**	• When answering your research question requires broadly representative answers to questions asked of a large group • When good data about your research question can be obtained by asking structured, short-answer questions • When you can expect a high percentage of intended respondents to respond to your questionnaire
. . . Conduct interviews? **Chapter 2**	• When in-depth exploration of participants' meanings is a key part of your research question • When you can gain access to informants willing to talk with you, either individually or in (focus) groups about issues that will help answer your research questions • When you are more interested in generating new hypotheses than testing existing ones
. . . Conduct experiments? **Chapter 3**	• When causal processes are your main concern • When the independent variables are manipulable • When the causal processes you are interested in can be simulated in controlled conditions • When internal validity is more important than external validity
. . . Do naturalistic observation? **Chapter 4**	• When you can observe without being observed and without greatly influencing what you are studying • When you want to explore social processes • When participant observation is impossible or would raise ethical questions • When you are more interested in identifying new variables than in measuring established ones • When you want a rich description of a particular context
. . . Do participant observation? **Chapter 4**	• When simple observation leads to participation as a consequence • When you need to get inside a social or political process • When merely asking questions (interviewing or surveying) is too distant from what you need to know to address your research question • When you want to discover or examine the causal mechanisms linking associated variables • When you want to study variables in particular contexts
. . . Investigate secondary or archival sources? **Chapter 5**	• When available data for answering your research questions are better than what you could reasonably expect to generate yourself • When the documents themselves are the object of investigation, such as union contracts or the research reports in a literature review • When the object of investigation is not available to researchers but it can be approached indirectly through documents or other archival materials • When the subject involves the past and, consequently, other designs are impossible
. . . Combine designs? **Chapter 6**	• When you want to corroborate results with several methods • When you want to use one method to inform another • When you want to continuously look at a question from new angles, looking for unexpected findings and/or potential contradictions • When you want to elaborate, clarify, or build on findings from other methods • When you want to "tell the full story" in an area of inquiry

CHAPTER 1

When to Use Survey Designs

Beginning our discussions of when to use which method by starting with survey designs is reasonable, since surveys are probably the single most commonly used research design in the social and behavioral sciences. Many studies of the research published in various social science fields have documented the predominance of survey methods.[1] It is probably accurate to say that more data in the social sciences have been gathered using surveys than any other design. This is especially true if we count as surveys official reports that people and organizations must file, such as those required by the Securities and Exchange Commission or by the Integrated Post-secondary Education Data System. When the term *survey* is used, this usually refers to a *sample survey*,[2] meaning that information is gathered from only a part of the total population. When an entire population is surveyed, this is typically called a *census* (of a population) rather than a survey (of a sample), although the methods of collecting the data may be the same.

The first question to ask when deciding whether a survey design is good for your study is simple: Can you learn what you want to know by asking people? If not, a survey is a poor design choice. The second design question is when to use the various modes of surveying: should the questions be asked face-to-face, over the telephone, on paper, via e-mail, or on a Website? Also important to survey design is asking whether you intend to study change over time. Last is the issue of which question formats will be effective, given the nature of your research questions. Guidelines for answering these four questions are provided in this chapter.

WHEN ARE SURVEYS LIKELY TO BE A WISE DESIGN CHOICE?

Surveys are popular because they can be efficient, providing researchers with a great deal of evidence at a relatively small monetary cost. More important than the issue of the cost per unit of evidence is the issue of whether the evidence you can gather using a

---

[1] For example, see Hutchinson and Lovell (2004).

[2] Surveying is so closely tied to sampling that it is difficult to discuss the two separately; see Chapter 7, this volume, on sampling for surveys and the Glossary for brief definitions of terms.

survey is appropriate for answering your research questions. To decide whether survey research is a good design choice for you, consider the circumstances in which surveying respondents will be an effective way to address your research questions. The following are among the most important criteria for deciding whether a survey is a good design for your research. Surveys are an effective research design when:

1. The data are best obtained directly from the respondents;
2. Your data can be obtained by brief answers to structured questions;
3. You can expect respondents to give you reliable information;
4. You know how you will use the answers; and
5. You can expect an adequate response rate.

We next examine each of these criteria in more detail.

Are the Data Best Obtained Directly from the Individuals You Are Studying?

Often the only efficient way to obtain information about people is by asking them. This is especially true of "subjective" data, that is, data about the inner states of the subjects being studied, such as their attitudes, beliefs, or values. For example, depression is diagnosed by asking people about their *feelings*—of helplessness and hopelessness, among other symptoms; election predictions are made by asking likely voters about their *intentions*.

You can also use surveys to collect "objective" data when this is most easily obtained directly from respondents. Although data such as respondents' age, income, and years of work experience (because they do not refer to respondents' internal states) could possibly be obtained in some other way, it is usually more efficient simply to ask. On the other hand, when you have access to records, as educational and medical researchers often do, using records can be more accurate and possibly more efficient (you can learn faster with less cost). For example, asking patients how many times they visited their HMOs over the past 2 years relies on their memories, their honesty, and their definitions of "visit." If you can get the information directly from HMO records, this would be quicker and more accurate. When the information you seek can be obtained from records or other secondary sources (see Chapter 5), consider doing so. It is not only inefficient, but also unethical to waste respondents' time asking needless questions. Unimportant questions can also annoy respondents and make them less willing to make the effort to answer your other, more important, questions to the best of their ability.

Can Most of Your Data Be Obtained by Brief Answers to Structured Questions?

Surveys work most effectively when asking structured questions. Structure refers to the degree of control you want to exercise over the kinds of answers you will get. The questions you might ask of persons who have agreed to participate in your research can be almost completely unstructured and purposefully vague, suggesting very little about how they ought to respond. On the other hand, the answers could be highly structured and limited to one-word options that you have predetermined. Although some survey questions may be—and often should be—open-ended, surveys are not the best design if you want to ask the kind of broad and exploratory questions typical of interviews (see Chapter 2).

Can You Expect Respondents to Give You Reliable Information?

Sometimes surveys are an unwise choice because respondents may find it difficult to answer accurately. Perhaps the information you seek is hard to remember or too sensitive for respondents to be willing to reveal to a stranger. It is often assumed that *social desirability bias* reduces the validity of much survey research, meaning that respondents may answer questions to reflect what they think is socially appropriate rather than what they really believe or do. Racial beliefs and attitudes provide a good example. In the second half of the 20th century, the number of people answering national surveys (such as the General Social Survey) in ways indicating they held racist prejudices dropped quite rapidly.[3] Were people really less prejudiced or did they just more often give the socially "correct" answers in the 1990s than in the 1950s? It is impossible to know for certain. It is clear, however, that the *behavior* of respondents to the same survey questions changed dramatically from the 1950s to the 1990s. Perhaps their attitudes about race changed, or perhaps their attitudes about what was politically correct or socially desirable[4] changed, but something definitely changed in those years.

Another example comes from the Centers for Disease Control (CDC). The CDC collects survey data from a large sample of the U.S. population for its ongoing Behavioral Risk Factor Surveillance System (BRFSS), which is conducted using random-digit telephone surveying. State by state, this survey charts changing levels of risk factors, such as being overweight or obese. Obesity has been increasing in recent years. In 1995, no states had an obesity rate of more than 20%; by 2000, 22 states had a rate greater than 20%; by 2005, 46 states did.[5] These figures are based on respondents' *self-reports* of their height and weight during telephone interviews. Can we trust them? Because the suspicion is that people underestimate their weight and overestimate their height, the obesity rate is probably even higher. On the other hand, it could be that obesity levels have not changed. Rather, survey respondents in more recent years could have more accurately reported their heights and weights. A more likely interpretation would be that, although precise rates of obesity cannot be known, the trend toward increasing obesity levels is very clear.

In our own survey and interview research, we have found that people who are willing to participate in research seem eager to try to give honest answers or to make an effort to remember correctly. Several have said they felt it was a kind of civic duty to do so, much like voting. In our experience, respondent memory can be a bigger problem than dishonesty. In any case, if you, as a researcher, doubt that respondents will be honest or will be able to remember what they need to remember in order to answer your questions, then you should choose a different method.

---

[3] Vogt (1997).

[4] Such effects are often referred to, especially in psychology experiments, as "demand characteristics."

[5] CDC (2006).

Do You Have a Clear Idea of How to Use the Answers to Your Questions?

You need a clear understanding of what each question on your survey contributes to solving your research problem. Structured surveys are not the place to just throw in questions to see what answers you get (although one or two carefully chosen follow-up or exploratory questions can be valuable). Your respondents' time is important, so don't waste it. The shorter your survey and the more to the point your questions, the more likely respondents are to pay attention and finish the survey. Most respondents can distinguish between a serious investigation of a topic and idle curiosity, and they often become irritated when they suspect the latter.

Your research question is often operationalized into half a dozen or so subquestions. One way to make sure that each of your survey questions works to answer your research questions is simply to match them up. Go through your list of survey questions and identify to which research question each survey question applies. Then go through the list of research questions and make sure that each is addressed by survey questions. It is remarkable how often you can identify gaps in this way. If there is an item on the survey that does not answer one of your research questions, delete it. If one of your research questions is not probed by enough survey questions, write more.

You should also have a pretty good idea of what methods you will use to analyze the results of your questions. Although it is easier to repair an analysis mistake (e.g., using ANOVA [analysis of variance] when regression would have been better) than a design mistake (you surveyed when you should have interviewed), your overall design should include the basics of an analysis plan. Without such a plan, you might realize, after you collected the data, that you didn't write the questions in the most effective way or that you could have learned more from the answers had you attended to issues of analysis from the beginning. If you plan to bring in a statistical consultant to help you with this, do so *before* spending hundreds of dollars printing and mailing the survey.

Can You Anticipate an Adequate Response Rate?

An otherwise excellent survey design can be ruined by a low response rate. Unless you have some reason to believe that a substantial proportion of those you ask to respond will in fact do so, you should consider another method. What is a "substantial" proportion? There is no fixed minimum, but if your response rate is less than 50%, you can have little confidence in the generalizability of your answers. We have often seen statements such as the following: "Given that the typical response rate for a survey of this type is less than 20%, my response rate of 25% is quite good." No—it isn't. In fact, it's terrible, at least if you want to make any claims about how representative your sample is of the population. Unless your 25% who responded are a random sample of your original random sample—and you would have to be wildly optimistic to assume so—you can no longer generalize from the sample to the population. Of course, you *can*, but it is no longer legitimate to use inferential statistics to generalize to a population. For this reason, if you think a low response rate is quite likely, you might be better off to use your judgment to select (not randomly) a smaller number of respondents and interview them. You could then make up in depth of interview data what your group of interviewees lacks in generalizable breadth.

What is an acceptable response rate, and how can you tell in advance what yours will be? You have no way of knowing for certain, but reviews of the research literature can give you a likely range for studies like yours. Also, you can sometimes be more optimistic about your likely rate if you have "connections" of one sort or another. For instance, if you are surveying members of an organization, are you a member, and will that organization endorse your research? If so, you can feel more confident about your probable response rate.

Much research has been conducted on the issue of response rates, and there are several rules of thumb useful for maximizing them. If your research is sponsored by a university, you may expect response rates higher than they would be if you contact possible respondents as an individual scholar. Guaranteeing respondents that their answers will be anonymous often helps. Confidentiality (the researcher knows, but promises not to tell) is a second-best option. Because so much is known about response rates, if you are planning to conduct survey research, consult one or more of the many books and articles in the field.[6] Such works can suggest ways to improve an adequate response rate, and just as important, ways to avoid spoiling your survey with a rate of response too low to use.

If you have no connections and if your review of the literature suggests that you are likely to get a paltry response rate, an alternative is to sample records rather than persons. To do this, a researcher often uses cluster sampling. First, take a random sample of institutions. Then try to obtain access to a random sample of records from those institutions. One doctoral student, a practicing school administrator, took a random sample of school districts in New York State. In the selected districts, he then drew samples of schools and contacted the administrators of the selected schools. He asked these administrators to provide him with anonymous records of a sample of third-grade students in the schools. He obtained a highly representative sample with an excellent response rate, perhaps because, as an administrator himself, he was deemed by other administrators to be trustworthy.

WHEN SHOULD YOU USE WHICH MODE OF ADMINISTERING YOUR SURVEY?

The three modes of administering a survey are face-to-face, telephone, and self-administered (on paper or electronically). How do you decide whether to have the respondents administer the survey to themselves, as they would for a mail or Internet survey, or whether to talk to respondents directly, either on the telephone or in a face-to-face setting? There is no single best method; all three modes have both advantages and disadvantages. We have summarized many of these in Table 1.1. As you reflect on this table and ponder your own research topic, you will often find that many advantages of a method tend to be offset by its disadvantages. The best you can do is assess the modes in terms of their suitability to your research question, weighing the pluses and minuses to select the method that is most likely to accomplish your purposes—or the method

---

[6]On confidentiality, see Singer (2004) and Chapter 13 of this book. See Curtin, Presser, and Singer (2005) on declining response rates and Salant and Dillman (1994) for a general text, especially for the problem of response rates.

that is least likely to inhibit them. While there is no single best method for all surveys, or even for one research topic, usually one mode is most suitable for a particular project. A good researcher can offer a thoughtful and convincing explanation of why he or she has chosen the survey mode used. Table 1.1 can be useful for thinking about these issues.

A self-administered survey has many advantages, but it is inappropriate for respondents who cannot read well or cannot read at all for some reason, such as lack of education, visual impairment, or mental impairment (#1 on Table 1.1). If respondents do not understand a question (#2), they can ask the telephone or face-to-face researcher for an explanation. So, if you think that many of your respondents will require clarifications, you or a member of your research team need to be there to provide those clarifications. Of course, this is impossible on self-administered surveys. Another disadvantage of self-administered surveys is that the researcher cannot be certain who completed the survey instrument (#3). For example, having worked as administrators, we know that high-level administrators sometimes delegate the responsibility of completing a survey. If a survey you have mailed is returned to you, you can be fairly certain that someone at that address responded to and returned it, but you can be less certain of who did so.

TABLE 1.1. Comparing Three Modes of Administering Survey Questionnaires

Advantages and disadvantages	Mode of administration		
	Face-to-face	Telephone	Self-administered
1. Usable with respondents who cannot read	Yes	Yes	No
2. Researcher can explain the meaning of a question	Yes	Yes	No
3. Researchers' certainty about identity of respondent	High	Medium	Low
4. Interaction with administrator of questionnaire	High	Medium	Low
5. Certainty that all respondents get exactly the same question	Low	Medium	High
6. Cost per respondent	High	Medium	Low
7. Time per question	High	High	Low
8. Possible to administer to groups	Yes	No	Yes
9. Effort required to obtain a large sample size	High	Medium	Low
10. Problems of access to respondents in remote or unsafe areas	Yes	No	No
11. Researchers' efficiency tied to that of the postal, Internet, or telephone system	No	Yes	Yes

Interaction with the survey researcher allows respondents to ask for clarifications, and that's good (#4). But that can also be bad—because it adds an element of uncertainty to the data. Many studies have shown that the gender or race or accent of the survey researcher can influence some respondents' answers in face-to-face and even in telephone surveys. When the survey researcher is accessible to the respondent, she or he can clarify the meaning of a question *and* may bias the answers—simultaneously. Is the danger of bias greater or smaller than the need to clarify? There can be no all-purpose answer, but you should have good reasons for how you have structured your research project. If you want to get rid of interviewer bias by using a self-administered survey, then you need to make special efforts, such as rigorous pilot testing, to ensure that your questions are clear.[7]

With a self-administered questionnaire, you can be certain that the respondents have been asked exactly the same question in the same way (that's the advantage of writing over speaking), and you can be confident that there is little chance of the respondents being influenced by the gender or race of the researcher (#5). But the same question, while presented verbatim, may not *mean* the same thing to different respondents, and you will not be able to determine that on a self-administered survey. You might be able to do so face-to-face or on the telephone.

You are not completely powerless in the face of possible concerns about race-of-surveyor or gender-of-researcher effects. And you can do something about the fact that the same words can have different meanings for different people. A good solution is to conduct survey experiments.[8] If you are worried about gender effects, for instance, then randomly assign respondents to survey interviewers. This enables you to test to see whether the gender of the researcher had an effect and if so, how big it was. In the same way, if you expect that two different wordings of a question could influence the way respondents answer it, word the question one way on half of the surveys and the other way on the other half. Randomly assign the two versions to your respondents. If there is no difference in the responses of the randomly assigned groups to the two different wordings, they can be pooled and analyzed together. On the other hand, if a statistically significant difference exists between the two versions, you can report that as an important finding.

The per-respondent cost of your survey and the speed with which you can collect the data are related (#6 and #7). Face-to-face surveying is by far the most expensive in time and money. Except for travel time and costs, telephone surveying does not save much, although random-digit-dialing, invented in the 1960s, has made national surveys possible with no travel costs. By comparison, self-administered surveys are a huge bargain. The respondents do all the work. The usual cost is seldom more than a dollar or two per completed survey for printing and postage in a mail survey, and it is dramatically less when using the Internet for self-administered surveys.

Because one can survey huge numbers of respondents essentially without cost, Internet surveying, either by e-mail or using Web pages, is increasingly popular. One can even use commercial organizations to tabulate your responses for you, but this requires caution since you lose some control over your data by doing so. In our experience, Internet surveying has worked both quite a bit better *and* quite a bit worse than mail surveys.

---

[7]These issues are discussed in Chapter 1 of our companion book on coding and analysis.

[8]For an excellent overview of survey experiments see Gaines, Kuklinski, and Quirk (2007).

It depends on who is being surveyed; different populations respond differently. Right now, we think the safest and most effective approach is to offer self-administered survey respondents the option of responding by mail or by Internet. And, be sure to add faxing as another option. One small survey with which we were involved obtained a 100% response rate, about one-third each by mail, Web, and fax. Research on these topics is extensive and knowledge is growing rapidly.[9]

Related to the questions of time and cost is the ability to administer your survey to groups (#8). You can visit sessions at a conference or classrooms at a university and distribute and collect batches of surveys. This combination of face-to-face and self-administered surveying is often effective for obtaining a large sample in a relatively short time (#9). For example, organizational climate surveys are sometimes administered by sending them to the organizations and having a contact person distribute, collect, and return them. This is hardly an ideal method, for several reasons, but it does allow researchers to collect thousands of surveys from dozens of organizations in a reasonable amount of time. That advantage is lessened by the fact that you have little control over how the data were collected. Were the instructions to the respondents clear? Were they the same at each organization? Were respondents given enough time to complete the survey? Was it explained to respondents that their answers were anonymous? And did they believe it? And was it true?[10] If you are a lone researcher without substantial funding, such as a doctoral student working on a dissertation, and you want to collect thousands of surveys from dozens of organizations, you may not have much choice. But you always have the option of constructing a better design that is more commensurate with your resources.

Another excellent feature of the telephone survey and the self-administered survey is that it is possible for you to contact respondents who reside in inaccessible areas (#10). The disadvantage is that these modes put you at the mercy of the telephone and/or postal and/or Internet systems. Furthermore, places that are geographically remote, such as villages in less developed countries, often do not have highly reliable phone, postal, or Internet connections. In brief, if you can expect to run into a great many barriers to gaining access to respondents, then perhaps survey research is not the best design choice for answering your research questions.

Deciding on the mode you will use to administer your survey requires making tradeoffs. The methods that are cost-efficient (cheapest) and methods that are most effective for answering your research questions may not be the same. If your ideal method does not coincide with what you can easily afford, what should you do? Take out a loan? Do an inferior study? Try a different design? Don't give up until you spend some time searching for a compromise technique that can salvage your study. If you review textbooks and research on surveying, you will probably be surprised by the many inventive ways other investigators have used to circumvent your problem. Don't even think about undertaking survey research without reviewing some of these texts and research

---

[9]For Internet surveying, see Hembroff, Rusz, Rafferty, McGee, and Erlich (2005); Kaplowitz, Hadlock, and Levine (2004); Alvarez, Sherman, and Van Beselaere (2003); Blumenthal (2005); and Sanders, Clarke, Stewart, and Whitley (2007).

[10]Wells, Petralia, De Vaus, and Kendig (2003) provide a sobering case study of how hard it can be to convince respondents. See Chapter 13 of this book on guarding against exerting unethical pressures when using this approach.

reports.[11] Try to use works written by well-known survey researchers, such as those referenced in the notes to this chapter. Also, your review of the research literature on your topic should focus on the methods sections of the research reports as much as on their substantive findings. The best way to get good ideas about methods is to review and reflect on the ways others have done research on your topic.

WHAT DESIGN SHOULD YOU USE TO STUDY CHANGE OVER TIME?

If your research question includes studying change over time, and your design is survey research, you have several options. Although these options are in part a matter of sampling (the topic of Part II of this volume), they also involve issues of design. The basic point is that if you want to study change over time, you need to measure your variables at more than one time. The three basic approaches to time in survey research are: panel studies, cohort studies, and cross-sectional studies. In a panel study, you survey the same group (called, for no good reason, a *panel*) of respondents two or more times. In cohort studies, you take samples from the same population two or more times. In a cross-sectional study, you survey a "slice" of the population at a single point in time. Most surveys are cross-sectional, in large part because other designs are much more demanding in time and other resources. Strictly speaking, a cross-sectional survey cannot be used to study time as a variable, because by definition, in a cross-sectional design, time is a constant, not a variable. Still, researchers using cross-sectional data to make temporal inferences have some options, as we will see below.

When Should You Use a Panel Design to Study Change over Time?

When you want to record changes in respondents and when you have access to a group of respondents over time, a panel design, sometimes called a true longitudinal study, is a good option. The obvious disadvantage for an individual researcher conducting a longitudinal study that spans a considerable period of time is that he or she will have a lengthy wait before being able to collect the data needed to finish the study. For this reason, longitudinal studies by individual researchers are often limited to periods of fairly short duration. Program evaluation is a common setting for such research. For instance, survey research has often been used to evaluate programs designed to improve intergroup relations. In this kind of research, individuals are surveyed to determine whether their attitudes changed as a result of participating in a program.[12]

When Should You Use a Cohort Design to Study Change over Time?

If you want to study change over time in a large population, a cohort design can be effective. Rather than pursuing the same individuals, which can be very difficult if the interval between surveys is long, one can take samples from the same population. A cohort is a group that has a statistical feature in common. Often age or birth cohorts

---

[11] Good texts include Fowler (2008); Gaines et al. (2007); and Weisberg, Krosnick, and Bowen (1996). Also see the Suggestions for Further Reading at the end of this chapter.
[12] Stephan and Vogt (2004).

are studied. For example, you could sample the birth cohort of 1980 (those born in that year) in the presidential election years 2004, 2008, and 2012. The disadvantage of the cohort approach is that, by sampling two or more times, you increase sampling error.[13] Adjustments can be made for this error, however. And that error is often less than the bias that comes from attrition, which occurs when respondents drop out of, or cannot be found for, subsequent rounds of surveying in a longitudinal (panel) study.

When Should You Use a Cross-Sectional Design to Study Change over Time?

Of the methods considered here, the least appropriate for studying change over time is the cross-sectional design, but it is not completely irrelevant for studying change, and it is, of course, the least costly in time or money. The huge advantage of a cross-sectional study is that you have to collect data only once. But having only one datapoint for time means that time cannot be a variable in your study. It is a constant. It is worth explaining this at some length, because so many researchers have tried to squeeze dynamic conclusions out of static data.

Say it is the year 2010 and you have the results of surveying a large, representative sample of adults' political attitudes. You are particularly interested in two groups: (1) people born in the 1940s, who grew up in the 1950s, and who are now in their 60s; (2) people born in the 1970s, whose formative years were the 1980s and who are now in their 30s. Any differences between the two groups could be attributable to their ages: senior citizens in their 60s versus adults in their 30s. The differences could be attributable to the generation in which they grew up: the 1950s versus the 1980s. Differences could be due to their ages or the era in which they grew up or to some combination of the two.

To add one more wrinkle to an already tricky problem, let's say you also have results of a similar survey done in the year 2000, one that you have replicated in your 2010 survey. Putting the two together would give you a cohort study. What if you compared people in their 50s in 2000 with people who were in their 60s in 2010? These two samples would have grown up at the same time, so you could control for generational effects.[14] If members of this same generation were more conservative in 2010 than 2000, could that be attributable to their having aged? Could it be that their attitudes changed because they started moving out of the labor force and into the ranks of the retired? Perhaps, but it could also be due to the differences arising from the fact that the political climate in 2000 was different from that in 2010. At the time of the 2000 survey the nation was at the end of a long period of prosperity and the 9/11 terrorist attacks had not yet occurred. Maybe people in 2010 had different attitudes than in 2000 not because they were older, but because 2010 was a different time than 2000.

To put it a little more technically, the problem when using cross-sectional data and even cohort data to study differences over time is that it is nearly impossible to separate period effects, age effects, and generational or cohort effects. Age, period, and generation are confounded. It is possible to control for one or two of the three on a fourth

[13]See Chapter 7 of this book and the Glossary for a brief definition.

[14]For example, someone 55 years old in 2000 was born in the same year (1945) as someone who was 65 years old in 2010.

variable, such as attitudes, but it is often not possible to control for the effects of all three on a fourth. If surveying is your research design and your question involves change in respondents over time, you will need to consult more specific and more technical works.[15]

When Should You Use Event-History Methods?

Another approach to studying change over time is *event-history analysis* (EHA). It gives researchers a means of studying change using only a cross-sectional survey. In contrast to the so-called *prospective* approach (repeated surveying planned for the future), event history analysis is *retrospective*. Respondents are asked to remember biographical data concerning *states* and *events*. States refer to such categorical variables as employed/unemployed, or married/single, or alive/dead (in medical research, EHA is usually called *survival* analysis). Events, in this usage, refer to changes from one state to another. The goal of such research is to investigate change and duration. How long does a state last, and what brings about change from one state to another? One might, for example, compare the employment histories of men and women in the same occupation.[16]

One advantage EHA has over panel and cohort designs is that panel and cohort designs in fact use a series of cross-sections. A panel design tells you about respondents in, say, 2000, 2005, and 2010, but not what happened in the intervening years—in 2004 or 2008, for example. EHA fills in those gaps by asking such questions as: When did you get your first full-time job? How long did you remain employed in that position? What did you do when that position ended? Say you got your first full-time job in 2004, were laid off in 2007, and then got your second job in 2009, which you still hold. EHA routinely provides that level of detail. A researcher using a panel design, however, might only know that you were not employed in 2000, but were employed in 2005 and 2010.

WHAT QUESTION FORMATS CAN YOU USE IN A SURVEY DESIGN?

Although question format is closely linked to issues of measurement, it is also an integral part of research design. One of the distinguishing features of survey design, as opposed to most forms of interview design, is that surveys usually employ structured questions, often forced-choice questions in which the respondent selects a predetermined response—yes/no, agree/unsure/disagree, and so forth. Sometimes surveys use unstructured questions in which respondents are asked to answer a question in their own words. These are often called "open-ended" questions. The measurement implications of forced-choice versus open-ended questions are discussed in our companion book on measurement and analysis. Here, we briefly review some of the options available to the researcher, mostly to illustrate the broad range of design possibilities.

---

[15] A good place to start work on this complex topic is Glenn (2003). On the highly difficult issue of how to separate the effects of period, age, and generation, see the works of Kenneth Land and colleagues, who have developed statistical techniques for the purpose. See Yang and Land (2006, 2008).

[16] A good introduction is Allison (1984). See also Belli, Shay, and Stafford (2001); Juster, Ono, and Stafford (2003); and Singer and Willett (2003).

One important way to structure or format survey questions is known as *free listing*. Respondents are asked to think of and list all the kinds of something that they can. This can be done face-to-face or on the telephone, but it often works out well for self-administered surveys too. For example, men and women or people from different ethnic groups or different age groups can be asked to "think of all the kinds of crime you can." The researcher can study at least two types of differences between and among groups of respondents: number and order. How many are listed? Which examples come early on lists and which ones come late? Free listing is an excellent way to understand how different groups perceive a cultural category such as parenting ("think of all the examples you have seen of bad parenting, of parents not treating their kids in a good way"). If members of one group routinely mention physical punishment as bad parenting and it occurs early on their lists and respondents from another group rarely mention it or include it as an afterthought, you have good evidence of difference between the groups—at least as the groups are represented by the samples you have selected.

Another option among question formats is *semantic differential scaling* (SDS). This is an excellent method for studying the meanings of language and/or to investigate quantitatively how respondents evaluate phenomena. It has been widely used to study topics as diverse as product preferences, cultural variety, and political attitudes. The main focus tends to be on similarities and differences across groups, such as age, gender, education, and ethnic groups. Respondents are asked to locate their attitudes or feelings on a group of scales composed of opposing adjectives, such as fair/unfair, passive/active, valuable/worthless, cruel/kind. The scales usually have 7 points between the polar adjectives, and 15 to 20 or more adjective pairs are used for each object being evaluated.

Should you opt to use SDS, you should obtain the adjective pairs in some systematic way, such as reviewing the research literature on the topic or from interviews with members of your target population. One important advantage of SDS is that it is fairly easy to construct and administer. Another is that you can detect more subtle meanings and nuanced differences using SDS than by using one or a small number of approve/disapprove questions. Finally, the method can be applied to just about anything: gun control legislation, artificial sweeteners, church attendance, or classical music. If you decide that your research question is one that SDS can address well, then this pretty much commits you to factor analysis and/or multidimensional scaling as methods of data analysis. You may consider this to be a disadvantage. While it is true that these analysis techniques are conceptually demanding, they are worth the effort if your research question involves examining the relationships among subtle variables and intricate meanings and you want to study a large sample. The availability of easy-to-use software means that you can focus on the meanings and concepts involved in your findings and not have to worry too much about the technical details.

Finally, saving the most widely used format for survey questions for last, we come to the Likert scale, named after its creator. It employs the familiar pattern of a statement followed by a series of options, such as strongly agree, agree, neutral, disagree, and strongly disagree. Likert scales are especially good for assessing degree of agreement with or support for a belief, policy, or practice. In terms of measurement,[17] they are popular because it is easy to sum responses to individual items to make scales. One

---

[17] See Vogt, Vogt, Gardner, and Haeffele companion volume (forthcoming).

need not, as novice researchers increasingly do, confine oneself to Likert-type scales, despite their many advantages. Free listing and semantic differential scaling are important options, and there are others.[18]

CONCLUSION ON SURVEY DESIGNS: SO MANY QUESTIONS, SO LITTLE TIME

Think of all the questions you should address when deciding on your research design. Before doing a survey you should ask yourself: Are the data best obtained by asking people? And by asking them structured questions? Can I trust respondents to give accurate answers? Do I know what I want to do with those answers once I get them? And, finally, can I expect a reasonable response rate? If the answer is a definite "no" to any one of these questions, survey research may not be appropriate for your study. If the answers are "yes," more choices await you.

What mode of surveying should you use: face-to-face, telephone, or self-administered? Then consider your sampling design: Do you use a panel, a cohort, or a cross-sectional approach to sampling? Finally, think about question format: Should you use open-ended or forced-choice questions? Forget, for the moment, that there are many types of open-ended and forced-choice questions. Forget also, for the moment, that there is no reason you cannot combine these methods—for example, by asking both open-ended and forced-choice questions through both face-to-face administration and on the telephone.

Just three stripped-down categories of mode (face-to-face, telephone, and self-administered), sample design (panel, cohort, cross-sectional), and question format (open-ended and forced choice) offer a total of 18 different possible design combinations (three modes times three sample designs times two question formats). So, after you have decided to choose survey research as your design (rather than interviews or observations or experiments), you still have a *minimum* of 18 combinations from which to choose: telephone a cohort and ask forced-choice questions, or meet face to face with a cross-sectional group to ask open-ended questions, and so on.

The numbers of choices proliferate still further as we drill down the choice menu to issues of selecting respondents, deciding among measurement methods, and opting among analysis techniques. That is why it is important to decide *what to use* before getting deeply absorbed in *how to implement* the decisions. Life is short. Learning how to do something just in case you should want to do it someday is not the best use of your time. First decide what to use; only then is it efficient to learn how to use it.

The multiple and interconnected questions addressed in this chapter on survey design are just as numerous and intricate when you consider each of the other main design options. The design option most closely related to surveying, so closely related that it actually overlaps, is interviewing. As we will see in the next chapter, many of the conceptual problems of surveying and interviewing are identical.

The table on pp. 29–30 summarizes when to use survey designs, and their mode, sampling, and format options.

---

[18] For a good survey see Bernard (2000); more technical detail is available in Presser et al. (2004).

SUGGESTIONS FOR FURTHER READING

The research literature on surveying is enormous, and texts based on that research are available at all levels from very introductory to highly advanced and technical. For specific suggestions about particular points see the references cited in the notes to this chapter. Here we highlight more general works. While the following works are all excellent, they do tend to focus more on *how* to conduct survey research; they are less devoted to addressing our main question in the book: *when* to do so.

General Texts

The third edition of Dillman and colleagues' *Internet, Mail, and Mixed-Mode Surveys: The Tailored Design Method* (2009) updates a classic study that is justly credited with having ratcheted up standards in surveying and providing solid guidelines for reducing survey error. Comparing the most recent edition to the first (1978) is an excellent way to see how much has changed in four decades of survey research—and how much has remained the same. Robert Groves and colleagues' *Survey Methodology* (2nd edition, 2009) is, like Dillman's book, a solid text based on recent research. If you had to make only two books suffice as background for your survey research, we can think of no two better choices than the volumes by Groves and Dillman. For a shorter and more introductory overview, Fowler's *Survey Research Methods* (4th edition, 2008) is a good beginning.

More Specialized Works

Presser et al.'s collection, *Methods for Testing and Evaluating Survey Questions* (2004) is a handbook by highly respected survey researchers; it has much information on choosing different survey question formats.

A very interesting and enlightening article on changes in modes of surveying and the problems and promise of new modes, particularly telephone surveying, is Curtin et al. (2005), "Changes in Telephone Survey Nonresponse over the Past Quarter Century."

An excellent test of Internet surveying can be reviewed in Sanders et al. (2007), "Does Mode Matter for Modeling Political Choice?: Evidence from the 2005 British Election Study." The authors found, somewhat surprisingly, that there were few differences in results between different survey modes.

Dealing with change over time using survey research can be very complicated. Paul Allison's *Event History Analysis* (1984) is an old, but conceptually very clear discussion of the basic issues. A more thorough and up-to-date scholarly account is Singer and Willett's *Applied Longitudinal Data Analysis* (2003).

CHAPTER 1 SUMMARY TABLE

USE SURVEY DESIGNS WHEN . . .

- The data are best obtained directly from respondents.
- Data can be obtained by brief answers to structured questions.
- You can expect respondents to give you reliable information.
- You know how you will use the answers.
- You can expect an adequate response rate.

MODES OF SURVEY ADMINISTRATION

Use face-to-face survey administration when . . .

- You need to be sure who is responding to the questions.
- You may need to explain the meaning of the questions.
- Respondents cannot read.
- You have plenty of time and money.
- You don't mind putting in the effort needed to attain the necessary sample size.

Use telephone survey administration when . . .

- You may need to explain the meaning of the questions.
- Respondents cannot read.
- You need to reach remote or unsafe areas.
- You have sufficient time and money.

Use self-administered survey administration when . . .

- Respondents can read.
- You want to be certain that all respondents receive exactly the same questions.
- You have limited time and money.
- You don't need to be certain about the identity of the respondents.
- You don't want to put a lot of effort into obtaining the necessary sample size.

SAMPLE DESIGN

Use a panel survey design when . . .

- You want to record changes in respondents.
- You have access to a group of respondents over time.

Use a cohort survey design when . . .

- You want to study change over time in a large population.
- You can't necessarily survey the same individuals, but can sample from the same population over time.

Use a cross-sectional survey design when . . .

- Time is not an important variable in your study.
- Your research question involves comparing respondents at a specific time.
- You are able to collect data only once.

Use event history design when . . .

- Time is an important variable but you can only collect data once.
- Your respondents' memories of events are likely to be reliable.

QUESTION FORMAT

Use free listing when . . .

- You want to understand how different groups perceive a cultural category.
- You want to study response differences of number and order among respondents.

Use semantic differential scaling when . . .

- You want to study how respondents evaluate phenomena.
- You want to study similarities and differences across groups.
- You want to detect subtle meanings and differences.

Use Likert scaling when . . .

- You want to gauge respondents' perceived agreement with, or the impact of, beliefs, policies, or practices.
- You are looking for large, not subtle, differences across groups.
- You want to sum responses to several items to make a scale.

CHAPTER 2

When to Use Interview Designs

Interviews are surely the oldest form of research. Asking questions of others and paying attention to their answers is probably nearly as ancient as the invention of language. The data for the oldest extant book-length research report, Herodotus's *The Histories*, written some 2,400 years ago, was gathered through interviews. Herodotus collected what we might today call oral histories as well as quite a lot of folklore tales. He had a clear research question, stated in his first paragraph: how did two peoples, the Greeks and the Persians, come into conflict? Their stories, or histories, differed, as Herodotus sometimes wryly noted: "such then is the Persian story," but, of course, "the Greeks have a different story." The point of this account of Herodotus's work is simple: the oldest book in the social sciences was written by an author who used interview research to gather almost all his data. The method hasn't changed much today, whether it is Bob Woodward describing White House policymaking for the Iraq War[1] or Rory Stewart's explorations of life in the Afghanistan countryside immediately after the fall of the Taliban.[2]

Because it is so familiar, such a natural way of gathering information, beginning researchers often assume that interviewing will be easy. A discussion or conversation in which you want to learn what the other person thinks is the basic building block of the interview. Because such discussions are very common, a regular part of ordinary discourse, one can be deluded into believing that interviewing takes no extraordinary preparation or talent. It is well to remember, however, that an equally common part of ordinary discourse is misunderstanding. People often do not understand one another. The ease with which we can get it wrong is at the heart of the reason why research interviews can be exceptionally difficult to conduct effectively.

Not only are the informal interviews of everyday private discourse familiar, so too are the more formal interviews of journalists and public interviews appearing in the entertainment media, such as those conducted by Oprah Winfrey, Barbara Walters,

---

[1] Woodward (2008).

[2] Stewart (2006).

Larry King, Jon Stewart, and Terry Gross. The main difference between research interviews and either ordinary discourse or journalistic interviews is that research interviews are usually much more systematic. Research interviewers often ask several people, perhaps dozens, the same or similar questions, aiming to pursue answers to broader research questions. Notes are taken. Responses may be tape recorded, transcribed, and analyzed at great length. In short, research interviewing is distinguished mainly by methodological rigor. Elaborate methodological superstructures are erected upon the familiar foundation of conversations in which questions are asked and replies made. The price paid for rigor is structure, and structure makes research interviews less natural than conversations. An interview is an organized conversation in which one person asks the questions, and another answers them. The agenda is set by the researcher. There is usually a minimum of give and take. (Of course, minimal give and take can also occur in an ordinary conversation with a loquacious friend.)

It is important to point out that our subject is the *research* interview. There are many other types. Therapeutic interviews are equally interesting and important, and therapists also do research. Clinical interviews, such as taking a medical history, can also be linked to research, but medical interviews are meant to convey information as much as to gather it, as well as to plan a course of action.[3] We also do not discuss job interviews by employers or forensic interviews used by the police investigating a suspect. Given how widespread interviews are in modern life, it is not at all extreme to say that we live in "an interview society."[4] It surely is the case that interviews are as pervasive as they are because of a widespread feeling that they are fascinating, that everyone has something valuable to say, and that they are a good way to learn.

While our discussion is limited to research interviews, this does not mean that our topic is narrow. Research interviews are used in virtually all disciplines, in applied as well as in basic research. And interview designs are routinely combined with other methods of collecting data. When researchers use multiple methods, one of them is usually interviewing. Interviews are used to help write the questions and to interpret the answers in survey research. They are used in experimental designs to screen potential participants for eligibility and to debrief them after the experiment is over. And most forms of participant observation are inconceivable without more-or-less formal interviewing as part of the process. Even archival research is combined with interviewing, for example when, to supplement documentary sources, biographers interview friends and relatives of an individual being studied so as to complete a biographical portrait. One might think, given the ubiquity and importance of interviewing in research, that it would be easier than it is to find firm guidelines for a researcher deciding when to use what kinds of interviewing for which types of research questions. But, "the interview remains an area of richly diverse practice about which few convincing generalizations can be made."[5] Nonetheless, we will attempt some generalizations for researchers pondering when to use interviews, when to use particular types and modes of interviewing, and to some extent, when to combine interviews with other designs (see Chapter 6).

---

[3]Zoppi and Epstein (2001).

[4]Gubrium and Holstein (2001).

[5]Platt (2001, p. 51).

COMPARING INTERVIEWS WITH SURVEYS

Comparing interviews with surveys helps to clarify their common problems and can be instructive for deciding when to choose one design over the other, and perhaps when to combine them. Both designs are built on the same foundation. The basics of the two methods are the same: you ask people what you want to know and record their answers. The basic problems of survey and interview design are also the same: you need to make sure to ask the right questions, to ask them in the right way, and to make special efforts to understand the answers. It is also useful to compare surveys to interviews, because interviewing in surveys has been studied very extensively[6]—more extensively than the kind of extended, in-depth interviewing that is the subject of this chapter. Comparison involves differences as well as similarities, of course. Differences are especially useful for answering the question: when is it likely to be better to use interviews instead of surveys?

How Surveys and Interviews Differ

Surveys and interviews can tap different aspects of social life, and they usually ask different kinds of questions. For example, when you step into a voting booth, you pull a lever or otherwise reply to a short-answer question: "On this list, what's your preference?" You don't have to write an essay explaining why you prefer one candidate over another. Surveys are a very good method for studying voting behavior. On the other hand, when you go to a town meeting, you introduce yourself, tell your story, and explain your position on an issue. Interviews are a form of research much more consonant with the town meeting. Surveys are also most often shaped by a desire to generalize to a broader population, such as predicting the outcome of an election. Of course, interview researchers also generalize. Even when the interviews are part of a study of a single case, a case study is a case *of something*, a broader phenomenon about which one hopes to generalize. While interviewers usually generalize, at least to some degree, the typical survey research project is, by design, aimed at generalization ("How is the population going to vote?"). Interviews are more aimed at understanding ("Why are some people so strongly opposed to this policy?").

Several differences distinguish the sampling and coding practices of survey research and interview research. Survey researchers usually ask questions of more people (a bigger sample) than do interviewers. Interviewers usually select interviewees through purposive or judgment sampling targeting individuals with specific knowledge, experiences, or characteristics. This means that the interviewees in a study often have much in common, while respondents in surveys are usually some sort of cross-section or representative sample of a broader population. Indeed, survey questions are often asked of the entire population of interest, such as all the students at a college or all clients who visited a clinic in the past year. In part, because of the large numbers of people typically surveyed, survey questions are usually shorter. The answers are also constrained to be short. That is why survey questions and methods are usually better at obtaining answers to comparatively direct, low-inference questions, such as "If the election were held tomorrow, for whom would you vote?" or "Do you think that race relations in the United States in the last 10 years have gotten better, or worse, or stayed about the

---

[6]Tanur (1992) is a useful discussion. See also Willis (2005).

same?" Interview questions and methods are more suited to pursuing complicated matters in depth, such as "What characteristics of a candidate for political office would lead you to trust what he or she says?" or "What are your personal relationships with persons of different races, and how do you feel about those relationships?" In other terms, the standardization of survey questions helps improve the *reliability* of answers, while the in-depth probing of interview questions enhances the *validity* of the answers. We delve into these issues more in the Conclusion to this volume.

What Interviews and Surveys Have in Common

Three main traits are shared by surveys and interviews: (1) both methods can be directed to gathering personal/internal information or external/less personal information; (2) both are based on trusting respondents or informants to answer honestly; and (3) both struggle with complicated problems of interpreting meanings.

First, both interviews and surveys can be categorized by what you want to learn from your respondents/informants, particularly whether what you seek is more external or internal to those who answer your questions. Do you seek information they can provide because of their expertise or experience or do you want to learn about them personally—about their attitudes or feelings, for example? Imagine the interview research in which you might ask the same individual one of the two following questions: (1) What is the relation of the marketing and the research departments in your company? (2) How did you feel after your recent cancer diagnosis? In the first instance you are asking mainly for information largely external to the person. The answer to the first question might not be simple, and your informant might have strong opinions about departmental relations, but the answer would likely differ in kind from an answer about feelings following a cancer diagnosis. Feelings are internal or *subjective*[7] phenomena in several senses of the term. Here we use the term *subjective* mainly in a methodological way: to emphasize that the answers you seek can most reliably be obtained from the specific subjects of the research. Departmental relations are more objective in the sense that they are external to the particular subjects of the research. You could ask someone else about departmental relations, find documents pertaining to them, or perhaps observe them yourself. Few such options exist for the study of subjective phenomena. Surveys and interviews have in common the important characteristic that they both can be and are used to plumb either objective or subjective information. Of course, the kinds of questions will differ depending on the design. Even for a complicated issue, an interviewer might need to ask only one or two open-ended questions. For the same issue, a survey researcher would likely have to ask a dozen or more short-answer questions, each trying to get at various aspects of the topic.

Second, both surveys and interviews are built on trust. You need to be reasonably sure that respondents or informants/interviewees[8] will not intentionally deceive you

---

[7] We use the terms *subjective* and *objective* with some hesitancy because discussions of the objective–subjective continuum have often been heated and bitter. Still, those terms seem more appropriate for the distinctions made in this paragraph than others we can think of, although internal and external can often be substituted.

[8] For consistency, we follow the somewhat established practice of calling those who answer survey questions *respondents* and those who reply to interview questions *informants* or *interviewees*.

about what they know, think, believe, or feel. If you are not confident about that, neither the survey nor the interview is likely to be a valid method. You also need to be fairly certain that informants will be *able* to express their thoughts and feelings in ways you can understand.

Finally, and most important, the central common problem for both surveys and interviews is meaning. What do the questions mean? Do they mean the same thing to all respondents or informants? Do they mean the same thing in all settings or contexts? What do the answers mean? How can meaning be inferred from the answers? The relationship of meaning and language, of words and the world, is problematic for both surveys and interviews, but tends to be more so for interviews because, among other reasons, interviews usually involve longer questions and answers containing many more words that can be misunderstood. (On the other hand, the lengthier exchanges can provide more opportunities for clarification). In any case, researchers can be fairly certain that all the survey respondents or interview informants have been asked the same questions in the same way. But it is a big step from there to assume that respondents *understood* the same words in the same way.

For example, one of us co-taught a seminar on research methods for doctoral students in educational administration. All were practicing administrators, some in colleges and universities, some in elementary and secondary schools. The instructors thought that it would be good for the seminar to have a few substantive themes. To decide on the themes, they surveyed prospective students about whether they thought "retention" would make a good theme. Most said yes, but building the course around that theme just didn't seem to work in practice. It was not until the third week of the course that the professors realized—or remembered—that for college administrators, retention meant holding on to students so that they did not transfer to another college or drop out of higher education; for school administrators, retention meant not promoting a student from one grade to the next (and for teachers it meant remembering subject matter). The professors had not expected any problems of meaning because they had given the survey to a largely homogenous group of middle-class educators, of about the same age, living in the same region of the country, and entering the same doctoral program. But differences of meaning still got between the question and the answer. Think of how much more likely differences of meaning are to occur when your respondents/informants differ by age, class, ethnicity, or gender. The professors probably would have had the same problem had they interviewed rather than surveyed the doctoral students about "retention," but they probably would have identified the source of confusion more quickly in interviews. This example illustrates why it is important to pilot a survey questionnaire or an interview protocol; it is the main way to spot such problems of meaning.

Interpreting the meanings of respondents and informants is complicated in both surveys and interviews because meaning is highly dependent on word choice and meaning can vary with context. This phenomenon has been extensively studied in survey work. Features as apparently innocuous as the order in which questions are asked or changes of a single word in a question have been shown to be capable of having important effects.[9] Context can be more important still. Where was the interview conducted? Who asked

---

[9]Schumann and Presser (1981); Tanur (1992). More recent examples are available in Willis (2005).

the questions? Was anyone else present? Most empirical evidence about the importance of question content and the context of the interaction between researchers and respondents has been done for survey research, but it is likely to be even more important in interview research if for no other reason than that the question wording and contexts are more likely to vary in interviews.[10] Because contexts such as these can be very important, survey researchers and interviewers ought to describe them thoroughly. Interviewers and survey researchers could take a page from the work of experimentalists and observational researchers, who often describe their study settings in great detail. Thorough descriptions can help with interpretation of findings as well as facilitate replication of studies.

Thus far we have seen that interviews can be an effective design option for several kinds of research questions. How effective they are depends on characteristics of the populations studied, the types of questions to be asked, the forms of generalization required by your research question, and the formats and settings for eliciting answers to questions. Interviews tend to be effective: when you are seeking knowledge that is best obtained from members of your target population because it is subjective or internal to the people interviewed; when you seek in-depth answers from research participants; when generalizing to a large population is less important than learning in detail about a smaller group; and when the questions you ask require that informants have time to reflect and seek clarification before answering, often because your questions probe difficult or sensitive matters of meaning and belief.

SPECIFIC INTERVIEW TYPES, APPROACHES, AND PROCEDURES

While the guidelines summarized in the preceding paragraph are a good start, a researcher contemplating using interview designs has many decisions to make, including decisions about the types of interviewing to use, about approaches to the research interview, and about procedures for conducting the interviews. There are several ways interviews and interview questions can be categorized.[11] We cannot touch on them all, but we will consider five ways your choices are likely to be especially important for your design and can lead to different approaches to interviewing:

- The kinds of questions you ask
- The amount of structure in the interview questions
- Different modes of conducting interviews—including face-to-face, telephone, and e-mail—and the formality of the interview sites
- Social settings for interviewing, such as focused group interviews
- The degree to which the researcher co-creates the interview text with the interviewee

---

[10] See Weinreb (2006) for interviewing by strangers versus acquaintances and men versus women. For interviewing in a non-native language, see Winchatz (2006).

[11] See Bernard (2000) for a good overview. One classic in the field—Spradley (1979)—lists 30 types of questions. Hermanowicz (2002) discusses 25 strategies for conducting a "great interview."

The Relation of Interviewers' Research Questions and the Kinds of Questions They Ask

It is easy, and wholly correct, to assert that your research questions should always lead to the kinds of interview questions you should ask. But that generalization, while usually true, does not provide enough detailed guidance. For more specific suggestions about when to use what kinds of questions, we need to ask more precise subquestions. First, when should your interview questions be exploratory and descriptive and when explanatory or confirmatory; when should they test, build, or shun theory? Second, when does your research question lead you to seek external information, narratives, or contexts?

When Should Your Interview Questions Be Exploratory and Descriptive and When Should They Be Explanatory or Confirmatory? When Should They Test, Build, or Shun Theory?

These are among the first questions to ask yourself, and the answers can usually be directly inferred from your research question. Many discussions of interviewing assume or assert that confirmatory, theory-testing research questions are not appropriate for interview designs.[12] It is true that the interviews one most often sees in research journals are more likely to be conducted with an exploratory or descriptive research question in mind, but this is a social tendency, not a logical entailment. Interview research is often crucial for testing a theory of causation or for discovering a causal mechanism. For example, one of the most persistent findings in the sociology of health is that people with strong social ties seem to derive many positive health outcomes from those ties. One often-studied social tie is marriage, which appears to have many health benefits, especially for men. In one study using the huge SEER database[13] to study over twenty thousand men who had testicular cancer, it was found that being married was an independent predictor (after controlling for many other variables) of 10-year survival. Married men were less likely to die. For obvious reasons, one cannot use experimental designs to test theories of why this might be true by randomly assigning some people to the married experimental group and others to the unmarried control group. Finding the causal mechanism or intervening variable accounting for the positive effects of marriage could have important consequences for designing social support resources for people with this, or perhaps other, diseases.

The interview research needed to study the causal mechanisms would not be simple. You would probably want to ask general open-ended questions as well as targeted ones aimed at testing any hypotheses you might have. Perhaps one hypothesis is that being married helps cancer patients avoid some of the despair that can follow diagnosis and thus makes them more inclined to follow treatment plans. You would probably want to interview couples, both individually and singly, and you would want to think long and

---

[12] For examples of this point of view, see Denzin and Lincoln (2005) for discussions of qualitative research of which interview research forms a large part and Gubrium and Holstein (2001) for discussions focused solely on interview research.

[13] Abern, Dude, and Coogan (2010); SEER stands for the Surveillance, Epidemiology, and End Results database maintained by the National Cancer Institute.

hard about when and how to do that. You might also want to talk with focus groups of single and married men. You might expand the research to inquire whether this type of cancer is a particular instance of cancer patients with and without partners. This and similar questions could be pursued with interview research—and not very effectively in any other way.

At one end of the interview spectrum is *explanatory/confirmatory* research such as theory testing and identifying causal mechanisms, as in the cancer example just described. At the other end of the interview spectrum is *descriptive/exploratory* research, such as the life story or life narrative approach. The goal of this kind of research is "to learn as much as possible about how one person views his or her own development over time and across the life cycle."[14] This kind of research is considered especially important because of the belief that most people, perhaps all, organize their understanding of themselves in the form of stories or narratives.[15] To what extent these stories are true—or even consistent from one telling to the next—is of less interest than the story, the overall life narrative, at the moment of the telling. Of course, it is rare, even in this very descriptive approach, where all stories are considered worth telling and analyzing, for there to be no focus, no aiming for something. It is seldom the case that researchers pursue just anyone's story. For example, sometimes researchers try to find life histories of people who have been heretofore ignored or unknown.

A third option, situated roughly between theory testing and pure description, is the grounded theory approach. We locate it toward the middle of the interview spectrum— ranging from confirmatory to descriptive research—because while researchers engaged in grounded theory interviewing do not initially test a theory, they do aim to build one that they subject to a sort of provisional testing. Researchers using grounded theory begin with in-depth, largely descriptive research interviews. But their ultimate goal is to *construct* a theory inductively (from the ground up) through a process of reinterviewing people and reanalyzing what they say so as to gradually construct a theoretical understanding of what interviewees have been telling the researcher.

The term *grounded theory* is used both strictly and loosely by researchers. Many use it loosely to mean any systematic analysis of interview transcripts; they borrow more or less closely some of the analytic stages advocated by the method's founders—Anselm Strauss and Barney Glaser.[16] For some time researchers followed the founders closely. But Strauss and Glaser had a falling out, and now there are more or less "positivist" and "constructivist" camps among grounded theory advocates. These are split mainly between those who see the theories as emerging more or less empirically from the data versus those who stress that the theories are constructed by the researcher.[17] The various forms of the grounded theory approach have been widely adopted, as a reading of the interview research literature makes clear. The method's combination of an open-ended exploratory beginning with a systematic method leading to rigorous conclusions has won it many adherents. Being able to go back and forth between data collection

---

[14] Atkinson (2001, p. 124).

[15] Bruner (1990) is one prominent theorist to advocate this point of view.

[16] Glaser and Strauss (1967).

[17] See Charmaz (2008) for one side and Corbin and Strauss (2008) for the other. For an overview and suggestions for making grounded theory more rigorous, see Wasserman, Clair, and Wilson (2009).

and analysis (theorizing) is a feature of the method that has a great deal of appeal.[18] When deciding on the approach to theory they want to take, researchers often find the grounded theory middle ground an attractive option.

When Does Your Research Question Lead You to Seek External Information, Narratives, or Context?

One reason to interview people is that they know things researchers want to know. Interviews can be a very useful method when seeking information. They need not be only about feelings or personal interpretations of meaning. For example, historians often conduct oral history interviews to gather interviewees' recollections of specific eras or events. Political scientists might interview members of Congress or their staffs to better understand the legislative process. The authors of this book have interviewed state and federal education officials to better understand the intent and effects of specific educational policies. By contrast, the life history interviewers just discussed are not seeking expert information; rather they want the interviewee's story, the narrative, which is itself the topic of interest. As we discussed above, interviewers can pursue subjective or objective data—data about the interviewees' internal worlds or the world external to the interviewees. A third option is studying the interviewees' context: interviewers might study a group, such as a clan or a church or a political organization, to understand the relations among its members as well as their relations with a broader community. So there are three options when interviewing: seeking external information to learn about external phenomena, *or* generating narratives which themselves are the data of interest, *or* uncovering networks of information, narratives, and meanings to understand the context in which they operate. Such contexts could be important when you are trying to learn about the culture of a group. The individuals in the group are interesting and important, but your goal could be to learn about the culture of the group, such as how much consensus there is among its members. This is not a direct informational question, but rather a question that has to be answered by piecing together information, narratives, and meanings.

In any case, for many researchers today, the topic of interest has changed from "the interview as an adequate measure of a reality external to it, to the content of the interview as [being] of interest in its own right."[19] Such potentially different areas of focus in interviews have, as we shall see, some close parallels to the options that face researchers when they do archival research (see Chapter 5). When researchers confront archival texts, are they interested in the texts themselves, in the information in the texts, or in the contexts in which the texts are located and were created?

More and Less Structured Interview Questions/Interview Schedules

When do you use different levels of structure in the interview questions? Interviews and interview questions can be unstructured, semistructured, or highly structured. The

---

[18] Grounded theory is discussed at length in our companion volume on when to use what methods of analysis.

[19] Platt (2001).

highly structured interviews and questions tend to approximate survey-type questions, but the questions, though constrained, are usually open-ended. This kind of question is probably most useful when you are seeking factual information.

By contrast, an interview and its questions can be unstructured and informal, as when in the course of participant observation, the researcher chats briefly with an interviewee. In covert participant observation, such a chat would be sort of a stealth interview. Ethnographers traveling among or living with groups of people might have discussions with them. But they might not have a formal sit-down, face-to-face session explicitly treated as an interview. Only at the end of the day would such an interviewer take some time to record as field notes the useful things learned in discussions with informants. Even when the informants know you are visiting them as a researcher, the discussions can be quite informal.[20]

Interview protocols, or lists of questions you plan to ask, will usually parallel the degree of structure. The list might be quite formal, written, and shared with the interviewee. Or it might be just a few nagging thoughts at the back of your mind. Some people dislike the very idea of an interview *protocol*. They consider it a "positivist" thing, and the term *protocol* is a turnoff. Consensus about the best approach is hard to reach on this issue. Our view is that even when you plan to do an informal interview asking only a few broad, open-ended questions, it is often a good idea to have a more thorough list as a backup to use with interviewees who don't respond to your more general questions. One tactic, even when you hope for an open-ended informal interview, is to arrive with three protocols: one with 2 or 3 questions, one with 8 to 10, and one with 20 or so.

Another strategy is to vary the level of the question structures. This is especially useful when you are approaching the interview with very little idea of what to expect. You begin with broad, open-ended questions (what some call *grand tour* questions). On the basis of what you learn, you then construct, on the fly, more targeted questions. Whether to use this approach also depends significantly on your level of skill as an interviewer, especially your comfort level with and ability to improvise.

Even when conducting structured informational interviews, researchers may decide to change the questions in the course of interviewing. Or they may, and probably most often will, change the interview protocol based on what is learned in the early interviews. Changes often come about when interviewees themselves make it clear that you need to add or change questions. When interviewing, we almost always conclude by asking: What else should I have been asking? Are the questions I've been asking getting at the most important things? Sometimes the people you interview will have excellent ideas about what questions you should ask. At other times, it only becomes clear that you need to revise your question list after reviewing some interviewees' responses and you realize that you need to pursue a new line of questioning. In sum, even the most formal interviews benefit from flexibility. And even the most informal, unstructured interviews can benefit from some goals and plans and ideas to keep you on track in the pursuit of your research questions.

---

[20]This was the approach used by Stewart (2006) in the Afghan countryside and Venkatesh (2008) in Chicago housing projects.

Social Rather Than Individual Interviewing, as in Focused Group Interviewing

Focused group interviews, or *focus groups* for short, are not widely used by social researchers,[21] but they seem to have considerable potential. They may be especially appropriate when the topic of your research deals with interaction in groups. Pioneered by Robert K. Merton and others in the 1940s, focus groups began as a research tool, and focus group data were almost always combined with quantitative data about opinions. By the 1960s, focus groups were used almost exclusively to collect qualitative data in marketing research.[22] Perhaps because of their association with marketing research, researchers in the social sciences have not eagerly adopted what seems like a useful technique, at least in some circumstances. Most interview researchers who discuss methods mainly talk about individual interviews. They have paid less attention to group interviewing. Survey researchers sometimes use focus groups as a handy supplement, often for brainstorming about individual survey questions.

Focus groups seem especially good at addressing questions that are targeted or focused—hence the name. Two famous marketing examples, almost iconic in the literature, were minivan features that "soccer moms" would like and candidate traits that could be used to frighten voters. Perhaps the easiest link for social researchers wanting to build on what has been learned in marketing research would be in the field of evaluation research. As one advocate put it, "existing procedures for generating discussions of commercial products could also fit discussions of social services."[23]

One practical issue that is sometimes relevant for deciding when to use focus groups rather than individual interviews can come up when your research problem requires that you talk to more people than you can contact for individual interviews. It is easier to interview more people in groups than individually. While focus groups can be hard to organize, a dozen focus group sessions can comfortably yield responses from 100 or more people. Conducting 100 individual interviews would be dramatically more time-consuming. Another consideration relevant to when to use focus groups is the possibly greater generalizability of focus group results as compared to individual interview results. Perhaps because of the larger numbers typically involved in a focus group study and the greater focus on a narrower range of issues, they seem to produce results that are more generalizable than individual interviews—at least their results have been generalized fairly successfully, certainly more so than most sampling theory would lead one to expect.

The most relevant situation when focus groups seem the ideal method occurs when your topic involves group dynamics or social relations. When social interaction or cultural interaction[24] is part of the subject, focus groups have great "ecological validity," that is, they are research settings that approximate the topic being studied. The parallels with individual and group therapy can be fairly close. If you are studying family

---

[21] They may be used more often than the publication record indicates, but hugely more published interview research reports on individual interviews.

[22] Merton, Fiske, and Kendall (1956, 1990); Morgan (2001); Morgan, Fellows, and Guevara (2008).

[23] Morgan (2001, p. 145).

[24] Munday (2006).

dynamics, either as a researcher or as a therapist, meeting with the family as a group is often the most effective interview situation. If you are studying intergroup relations, bringing the groups together in discussion can be a tool for better understanding and perhaps improving intergroup communication.[25] While group interviews are especially suited for group subjects, they can also be good for stimulating brainstorming. People help one another to come up with ideas. Groups can actually learn in discussions, and the researcher can chart the process of learning.[26]

Different Modes of Conducting Interviews and the Formality of the Interview Setting

Face-to-face interviewing is so frequently thought of as the standard option that sometimes researchers do not consider other modes of conducting interviews. But there are occasions when face-to-face interviewing may not be feasible, or even when feasible it may not always be the best choice. As with surveying, modern modes of communication have greatly expanded a researcher's range of options. A review of Table 1.1 in Chapter 1 on survey designs touches on most of the tradeoffs among the different modes, and those tradeoffs are similar to the ones faced by interview researchers. Obviously, researchers can conduct many more telephone interviews than face-to-face interviews, thus saving themselves and the people they question a great deal of time. And some interviewees may prefer to be contacted by telephone rather than in other ways.[27] E-mailing seems to be more controversial in the methodology literature, perhaps because it is more remote from the interview's foundations in ordinary conversation. But e-mail and other Internet-based forms of communication are expanding rapidly and have their advocates. For example, one group of researchers found it easier to elicit discussions about adolescents' risky behaviors using e-mail communications than in face-to-face discussion.[28]

Of course, the practical advantages of e-mail are enormous, outpacing even the telephone for low cost, ease of covering distances, and simplicity of data collection. For example, e-mail responses to questions do not have to be transcribed—a savings in time and transcription fees that can sometimes outweigh the absence of face-to-face interactions, at least for some types of research questions. Compared to ordinary "snail-mail" letters, e-mail communications differ mostly in terms of speed and quantity. Many researchers resist e-mail and other written forms of communication as less "genuine" than personal, face-to-face interaction. But it is far from clear that oral communication is always better—that it is less prone to misunderstanding or deception—than written communication. Unfortunately, the researcher deciding when to use which modes of interviewing has less research-based guidance than would be helpful.[29] In the absence of research, we researchers exchange thoughts on our experiences. In our experience, seconded by some colleagues, using multiple modes of communication in interview

---

[25] Stephan and Vogt (2004).

[26] Wibeck, Dahlgren, and Oberg (2007). For a striking example of learning in group discussions concerning medical ethics, see Bok (1999).

[27] For an example, see Stephens (2007).

[28] Hessler et al. (2003).

[29] See Couper and Hansen (2001) on computer-assisted interviewing and Menchik and Tian (2008) for a detailed study comparing various modes of communication.

research is quite common. You might e-mail someone to ask if they are available for a telephone interview; then you might inquire on the phone whether they would be willing to meet with you face-to-face, either individually or in a focus group; finally you might engage in e-mail communication to clear up any final questions and perhaps to exchange documents. In light of the impressive range of easily combined and helpful options—including electronic as well as in-person face-to-face technologies like Skype—privileging one form of communication seems archaic.

When Should the Interview Site Be Formal or Informal?

The formality of the site is mainly an issue in face-to-face interviews. Since interviewing is a form of conversation, and conversations happen in most kinds of sites and contexts, so too can face-to-face interviews. They may be conducted in interviewees' homes or in a public place. They may be in a researcher's office. Informal interviews are often combined with eating or having a coffee or other drink. The degree of formality in interview site is likely to vary greatly depending on the needs and characteristics of the people being interviewed and on the nature of the topics being discussed. Again, it is hard to point to conclusive research guidelines. Opinions are frequent, evidence is rare. Researchers have to use their common sense—for example, not asking questions about sensitive issues in a crowded cafeteria. But common sense may not lead to guidelines as clear as you would like. What might seem to you to be a reasonable way to go about conducting the interview could appear completely inappropriate to the person you are interviewing. Perhaps the best advice, when deciding on the setting for the interview, is to give the persons you want to interview as much choice as possible. When you decide about the formality of the site for conducting the interview, one issue that will probably influence your decision is the advantages and disadvantages of consistency. If you want consistency, and through consistency to eliminate site characteristics as a variable, you will probably need to be more formal in your site selection. If the natural variability of informal sites and situations is important for pursuing your research questions, then that will have implications for your analysis.

When Should the Researcher Co-Create the Interview Text with the Interviewee?

As a researcher, you interact with interviewees. Their answers to questions will be influenced by how they view you. And the way you ask the questions will be influenced by how you view them. In short, the interview is an interaction between two or more individuals, neither of whom is a blank slate. Researchers aren't passive question-asking machines, and interviewees aren't databases of answers to be accessed by asking the right questions. All this is obvious, but what should researchers do about it? When should they maintain a certain formality and professional manner and consistency in the questions they ask and the way they ask them? And when should researchers and interviewees jointly embrace their roles as co-creators of the interview experience? We have already discussed some of these issues above. Here we rephrase the question and make it more specific to capture some recent thinking about the research interview: *When should the researcher set aside the researcher role and join together as a partner with the interviewee to create the interview experience?*

One contemporary view is that an interview is a social setting in which knowledge, meaning, beliefs, and so on are jointly produced or constructed. Researchers work with interviewees to construct the interview situation, and ultimately the transcript.[30] Interviews in participant observation, action research, and ethnography are most likely to fit this model. An opposite point of view is that the researcher is initially a ghostwriter at best, perhaps only a stenographer. Subsequently the researcher can become an analyst of the transcripts thus produced. This approach is most likely to make sense when the research questions lead the researcher to pursue a purely informational interview in which the goal is to learn about events and processes largely external to the interviewees.[31]

The answer to the question of when one of these two extremes—or what point along the continuum between them—is most appropriate must initially be shaped by your research question and thereby by the people you interview to answer it. Some interview situations and interviewees almost demand a high level of intimacy and joint effort; in others this would be inappropriate. In some circumstances, in order to elicit responses, you might want to ask questions passively. In others, you might need to be more intrusive. There is the old joke about the physician who when asked about why he decided to specialize in psychiatry answered, "Because surgery wasn't invasive enough." Psychiatry may require an exceptionally high level of probing, but not all interviews do.

Answers to questions about the importance of intimacy and co-creation become more complicated when the research project's interviews are conducted by several interviewers, who are trained more or less thoroughly for their work. One of the authors of this book was undergoing such training in a project studying parolees' experiences with the parole system. During question time, one of the other trainees asked a rambling question (made a statement really, a sign that he might not be a good interviewer) about how much we as interviewers should empathize with our informants and work with them to co-construct a common understanding, perhaps by revealing our own struggles with bureaucratic oppression. The project director sighed and responded: "Sure, sure, the difference between the interviewer and interviewee can get blurred, and the final transcript is a joint product. But let's not get carried away here and forget that we are interviewing parolees because we are interested in *them* and in *their* experiences with the system; and learning whether the system is fair; and learning how to make it better. We're not interested in the thoughts of interviewers who can't hold their egos in check long enough to listen to and try to learn about somebody besides themselves."[32] The trainee who asked the question left; he did not return for the second day's training. Obviously, feelings can run high on this issue.

Another way to look at this set of issues is to ask: When is the interviewer–interviewee interaction a unique experience, an unrepeatable encounter, which cannot be reproduced? Or, when is the interview replicable, at least to some degree? When would two different investigators learn pretty much the same thing were they to interview the same person? There is no question that different interviewers can draw different conclusions

---

[30] Fontana (2001); Bhattacharya (2008).

[31] Woodward (2008) is an example.

[32] The quotation was reconstructed shortly after the training session from notes taken during the question and answer period.

from interviewing the same people.[33] How different? Here's a thought experiment that might help clarify thinking about the issues involved: Imagine that two interviewers, A and B, each interview the same 20 people. They flip coins to decide on interview order, each going first with half of the interviewees. Say they are both sociologists using the same interview protocol to pursue the same research questions. Finally, say that A is a 30-year-old African American woman and B is a 55-year-old European American man. How different, or similar, are the two sets of interviews likely to be? There isn't a lot of research to guide our thinking,[34] which is why we find thought experiments to be useful when pondering perennial questions about the role of the researcher in the interview experience.

Our overall view is that even when we as researchers are most deeply involved with the people we are studying—and this is most likely to occur when we interview in the course of participant observations—our purpose is to learn about others, not ourselves. Of course, when doing research, one learns about oneself, but that is a happy by-product, not the main goal. We are pretty sure from having worked on various interview teams over several decades that there can be reliability or consistency in interviewing. This means that one qualified interviewer can sometimes be substituted for another, that each social situation is not *wholly* unique, and that there will be *some* consistency in what is learned. Of course, no two interviews will ever be identical. Perfect replication is never possible, but this does not justify ignoring consistency as well as paying attention to variability. We are strong advocates of interviews. An interview is a superb way to gather evidence precisely because of its flexibility and adaptability to the needs of researchers and the interviewees, *and* because each interview is not a completely spontaneous, improvised creation, unique unto itself.

CONCLUSION

We have seen that interviews can be a good general design choice depending on features of your research question, the nature of the kinds of populations you need to study, the kinds of questions you need to ask participants, and your descriptive and analytical goals. Depending on your research goals different kinds of questions, alternate modes of interviewing and various ways of relating to interviewees can be helpful. The table on p. 47 summarizes these and related points.

---

[33] Johnson (2001) reviews some famous cases in which findings were challenged based on re-interviews of the same people.

[34] Studies have been more often conducted on coding interview transcripts and field notes (which we address in a forthcoming companion volume); interviewer effects in surveys have also been studied extensively.

SUGGESTIONS FOR FURTHER READING

Interviewing is the oldest documented method of gathering data for social research, but interview designs are less codified than others discussed in this book, such as surveys and experiments. Because interviewing tends to be less rule-bound (than, say, survey sampling or random assignment) the literature describing interview methods contains fewer standard texts, especially at the intermediate and advanced levels. On the other hand, classics in interview research seem to have a longer shelf life; they are more likely to remain relevant decades after they were written.

For example, Spradley's *The Ethnographic Interview* (1979) is widely read, remains influential, and is still in print after more than three decades. Mishler's *Research Interviewing: Context and Narrative* (1986) is also very popular, especially among education researchers. Spradley's book is more often consulted for practical advice, while Mishler's is more influential for his attitude toward interviewing and interviewees. To bring these two classics up to date, a good place to start is Gubrium and Holstein's very thorough collection, *Handbook of Interview Research* (2001).

The insights and methods of grounded theory have become very influential among interview researchers. The founding classic by Glaser and Strauss, *The Discovery of Grounded Theory: Strategies for Qualitative Research* (1967), is still widely read. Grounded theory has been around long enough to have spawned opposing schools, which are related to a clash between its two founders. Very accessible descriptions of the two approaches are Charmaz's *Constructing Grounded Theory: A Practical Guide through Qualitative Analysis* (2006), which outlines the more constructivist approach. Corbin and Strauss's *Basics of Qualitative Research: Techniques and Procedures for Developing Grounded Theory* (3rd edition, 2008), presents the more traditional approach.

The enduring importance of classics in interview research can also be seen in the focus group approach to interviewing. The classic, foundational work by Robert K. Merton et al., *The Focused Interview* (1990), originally published in 1956, is still very much worth reading. Indeed, we think that if you are going to do extensive focus group interviewing, Merton's work remains a must. A good modern text is Krueger and Casey's *Focus Groups: A Practical Guide for Applied Research* (4th edition, 2009).

Specialized methodology articles in interview research are very useful. We use them in our work and have cited several on specific topics in the notes to Chapter 2. But we also have the impression (based partly on our own experience) that interview researchers often find the most useful guidelines for selecting their approaches by reading examples of good interview research rather than reading methods texts. We have mentioned several of these exemplary works in Chapter 2, ranging from Herodotus 2,400 years ago to Bob Woodward in 2008, because sampling the work of other researchers seems an indispensable way to learn the interviewer's craft.

CHAPTER 2 SUMMARY TABLE

WHEN IS THE RESEARCH INTERVIEW LIKELY TO BE A GOOD DESIGN CHOICE?

- When you seek "subjective" knowledge that is most effectively obtained from the interview subjects.
- When questions call for in-depth answers not easily answered in survey formats.
- When in-depth information is more important than the ability to generalize to a larger population.
- When informants need time to think about and elaborate on their answers.

SPECIFIC INTERVIEW TYPES, APPROACHES, AND PROCEDURES

When should interview questions be exploratory and descriptive?	• When you want to learn as much as possible about a phenomenon or person. • When context is important.
When should interview questions be explanatory or confirmatory?	• When testing theories and/or identifying causal mechanisms.
When should you use structured interviews?	• When you seek information.
When should you use focused group interviews?	• When you are asking targeted ("focused") questions. • When your topic involves group dynamics or social relations/interactions.
When should you use different interview modes (e.g., face-to-face, telephone, e-mail)?	• When a particular mode fits your research question and/or personal approach. • When combining modes will give you greater access to information.
When should the interview site be formal or informal?	• When the needs or characteristics of the informants may be influenced by the site.
When should you join together as partner with the informant to create the interview experience?	• When your research question requires a high degree of intimacy and joint effort with informants. • When the interviewer/interviewee interaction is unique and cannot be reproduced.

CHAPTER 3

When to Use Experimental Designs

For many, *experimentation* is synonymous with *scientific*. Yet experiments are a natural way to learn, much older than scientific disciplines. The authors of this book like coffee and drink a lot of it, so at one time or another, each of us has experimented with it. The main variables are types of coffee maker, number of scoops of coffee, amount of water per pot, and brands and roasts of coffee. The basic idea of an experiment is the same whether you are investigating the effects of medical treatments, psychological reactions to different stimuli, or espresso roast versus house blend. You want to control or keep constant all the variables you are not investigating so as to focus on the ones you are interested in. So, if we want to compare espresso roast to the regular house blend, we use the same pot, the same amount of water, the same brand, the same filters, and so on—but we use different roasts.

Early on in our discussion, it is important to clear up a common misconception. Experimentation is not necessarily quantitative; it does not generate only quantitative data. The dependent variable in the coffee experiment is taste, which is about as qualitative and subjective a variable as one can imagine. One can turn a subjective judgment of taste into a number ("On a scale of 1 to 10, I'd give it a . . ."), but this is not necessary. And the variable remains subjective even when quantified. The experimental method is rigorously systematic, but it does not deal only with quantities. For example, one frequent topic in experimental research in medicine is pain relief. Since there is no "painometer" to assess the effects of pain medication, researchers ask patients for their subjective opinions, often quantified on a scale of 1 to 10, to be sure, but subjective nonetheless. In brief, as with the other designs we are examining, experimentation has nothing to do with the quant–qual dichotomy.

Our chief question for this chapter on experimental design is "When is it most useful to employ experimental methods?" That raises a related question: are experiments always the best option? In other terms, are experiments—specifically randomized controlled trials—the gold standard against which other methods of investigation should be measured? Our answer is: no. The premise of this book is that gold-standard *thinking*—the belief that there is a clear criterion that identifies the best method for all purposes—is a huge mistake. Sometimes experiments are the best approach; at other times they are not feasible or, if feasible, not as effective as other methods.

If you were to survey investigators and ask them which was the best research design, the most common answer would probably be randomized control trials (RCTs). The term RCT[1] is sometimes used to mean experiments in nonlaboratory settings, but has recently come to be used more broadly to mean any experimental trial in which subjects are randomly assigned and researchers have control over the delivery of the independent variables. RCTs are not a recent innovation. They date, depending on your historian, to Fisher's agricultural experiments in the 1920s or to drug trials in the 1940s. The use of RCTs in social research, especially program evaluation, has been greatly emphasized in recent years, even to the point of being virtually mandated for some government-sponsored programs. When RCTs are feasible, they are indeed a good tool for detecting program outcomes, but they are not necessarily the best method in all cases.

WHAT'S WRONG WITH GOLD-STANDARD THINKING?

When R. A. Fisher compared crop yields in the 1920s and helped establish the metaphorical "gold standard" in research methods, there was a real gold standard—in monetary policy. But, the monetary system's gold-bullion standard collapsed during the Great Depression. It was too inflexible to deal with financial shocks. Inflexibility is also the main problem with seeing all other research methods in terms of the RCT. Ironically, the complete irrelevance of the gold standard in monetary policy has coincided with the prominence of gold-standard thinking in research methodology.

Today, instead of a gold standard in monetary systems, most currencies are in open market competition with one another. Users decide what a currency is worth, mostly by comparing it to other currencies. That is a better model for the international monetary system, and a better model for assessing research designs. In other words, "deregulation" would improve our thinking about the comparative advantages of research designs. To be clear, this is not a criticism of RCTs or any other method. It is, rather, a challenge to *gold-standard thinking* about methods. Researchers and policy makers would be equally ill advised to suddenly elevate multilevel modeling or semistructured interviews or participant observation or any other good method to the single standard against which all others had to be compared.[2]

Gold-standard thinking violates the premise upon which this book is built. We start with the assumption that all research questions can be approached in multiple ways, each of which has advantages and limitations. Of course, that assumption could be wrong, but if it is correct, one's choice of design should be driven by the research question, the context in which one is trying to answer it, and the objectives of the research. It is not helpful to try to make research questions conform to preexisting criteria that assign ranks to designs and methods apart from considerations of topics, contexts, and units

---

[1]RCT can stand for randomized control(led) trial, randomized clinical trial, and randomized controlled clinical trial. A variant is randomized *field* trials in which experiments are conducted in natural settings rather than laboratories.

[2]We first developed some of these ideas in a discussion of comparative case study research in program evaluation; see Vogt et al. (2011).

of analysis. The inflexibility of gold-standard thinking has two main facets. First is the assumption that evidence gathered using RCTs will always be superior, regardless of the topic or setting, to evidence gathered in any other way. Second is the belief that research problems for which RCTs are impossible cannot be studied scientifically. Both of these assumptions are fundamentally wrong. Evidence-based conclusions about real-world problems require a broadening, not a narrowing, of the range of research models.

WHEN IS AN RCT A GOOD OPTION?

Although it can be very difficult to implement, the basic RCT design is very simple, and that simplicity leads to clear, direct, and powerful forms of analysis. This simplicity, clarity, and power are the source of much of the RCT's appeal. The basic question typically asked in an RCT is no more complicated than our coffee experiments: Does the expensive espresso roast taste significantly better than the regular coffee blend? The core of the method includes four steps. First, you assign participants or cases randomly to control and experimental groups—two identical coffee pots. Second, you provide a treatment or intervention—the independent variable—to the members of the experimental group (use espresso roast in one pot). Third, you provide no treatment or a standard treatment to members of the control group (regular blend in the second pot). Fourth, you compare the outcomes on a dependent variable for the control and experimental groups (taste the difference). Note that credibility is greatly enhanced if the experimenters do not know which is the experimental and which is the control group. That is why blind tasting is used for judging wines and why it would be important in our coffee-tasting experiment too. In an experiment with human participants, ideally everyone would be "blinded": the participants should not know whether they are in the control or experimental group, nor should the researchers, nor should the data analysts—until the findings are revealed.

This four-step procedure is a very powerful design for identifying effective treatments or interventions. The key source of its remarkable strength is experimenter control of the independent variable and the comparison of groups to which people or other cases are randomly assigned.[3] The purpose of random assignment (and blinding) is to make the groups equivalent or, more precisely, to make differences between them due solely to random variation. As always, our purpose in this book is less to describe how to carry out a method and more to decide whether it is the right one to use for your research question.

WHEN IS AN EXPERIMENTAL DESIGN A GOOD OPTION
FOR YOUR RESEARCH?

When deciding whether to use the experimental option for your research, answering the following questions will be important:

---

[3]When implementing an experiment, "real-world" complications often intrude on the ideal model of the RCT. For a discussion of when this is likely and suggestions for how to respond, see Baker and Kramer (2008).

- Can cases, subjects, or participants be randomly assigned?
- Can the variables be manipulated?
- Are RCTs effective for your research?
- Would an experimental intervention distort the object of the investigation?
- Is the research question more focused on internal or external validity?
- Is the research more concerned with causal processes or outcomes?

Each question is discussed in more detail in the following sections.

Can Cases, Subjects, or Participants Be Randomly Assigned?

When research participants can be randomly assigned to control and experimental groups, one of the necessary conditions for experimental research has been met. If cases, subjects, or participants can be randomly assigned, give serious consideration to using an experimental approach in your research. But, in some circumstances, random assignment is impossible. And, even when it is possible, many people do not like it. Resistance on the part of potential participants may undermine the validity of the randomization process. In the provision of education, health, or other social service benefits, people are often unwilling to participate if they are not guaranteed access to the new drug or program or procedure. Governments do not have, or do not often wish to exercise, the power to compel potential participants to be randomized, and researchers have even less ability to do this. Ironically perhaps, governments may have the authority to compel *all* schools or social service providers to change, but compelling some of them to join the randomization pool for an experiment is much rarer. When random assignment is not possible, or would raise insurmountable practical and ethical difficulties, one of the conditions for experimental research is not met. When that happens, consider other designs. Examine methodological alternatives. Don't spend too much time regretting the fact that one research option is unavailable. That kind of gold-standard thinking will not help you very much.

Can Key Variables Be Manipulated?

When variables can be manipulated by the investigator, another of the necessary conditions for experimental research has been met. When the research question's variables are manipulable and random assignment of participants is possible, then the case for taking an experimental approach is *very* strong. But, many variables of great interest in social research cannot be managed by investigators. Sex/gender, race/ethnicity, income levels, crime rates, and neighborhood characteristics are impossible for researchers to manipulate. While some simulations have been successful, direct manipulation is difficult or impossible. Of course, nonmanipulable variables can frequently be studied either as outcomes or covariates using well-established statistical techniques. Gold-standard thinking would call these techniques poor alternatives, at best. Perhaps they are. But many important human problems cannot feasibly be addressed by experimental methods. For these problems—such as child abuse, revolution, inequality, war, economic crises, and so on—it is irrelevant at best to compare the methods used to study them to RCTs. It is far too hypothetical to assert that *were we* able to study a problem with RCTs, this *would be* better than studying the problem using other methods. Surely it is more useful to think about how to choose among feasible methods.

On the other hand, one shouldn't give up on experiments too quickly. Many variables that cannot be manipulated can be simulated fairly directly. For example, in political science, where experimental research has traditionally been quite rare, experiments have increased significantly in recent years, and that research has been quite influential.[4] Much of this research has been based on laboratory simulations of political processes. In economics, approaches to the psychology of economic decision making have been well approximated in simulation games. One such study used simulation games to address the question of whether the foundations of economic theory were equally applicable across cultures; the authors found dramatic variation in what most economic theorists have postulated to be human universals.[5]

Are RCTs Effective for Your Research Problem?

This is a different type of question than the first two. Random assignment and manipulable variables are necessary conditions for RCTs. Effectiveness is a comparative question. RCTs are more effective for interventions (independent variables) and outcomes (dependent variables) that are relatively uncomplicated and easily defined and measured. One widely discussed example is the effect of class size on student learning. This has been studied experimentally—most famously in the 1980s and '90s in Tennessee.[6] For complex, long-term social programs, methods other than RCTs can sometimes yield a higher caliber of data for fewer resources and less effort. For example, we find a comparative international study using archival data on class size and student performance to be equally persuasive and to have greater generalizability than the aging data from the Tennessee experiment.[7] It is erroneous to believe that no matter the research question, or the context in which it is studied, RCTs will inevitably produce the highest grade of evidence. Experimental methods are often inadequate to evaluate long-term multifaceted programs because uncontrollable covariates can intervene. The basic problem is known as the history effect: variables not under the researcher's control emerge over the life of the study to confound interpretation. The standard RCT can be too inflexibly structured to capture and control for such covariates.

RCTs are designed to collect evidence on outcomes after the experiment has run its course. For some questions, this may not be the most effective approach. When studying the effects of fertilizer on wheat crop yields, Fisher had to wait until the end of the experiment, until harvest time, to measure outcomes. In long-term program evaluation it is neither necessary nor effective to refrain from analysis until the conclusion of the trial. Researchers can use many methods—from grounded theory interviews to Bayesian statistical analysis—to gather data and learn from them as the program unfolds.[8]

---

[4] Druckman et al. (2006).

[5] Henrich et al. (2005).

[6] Finn and Achilles (1999).

[7] Pong and Pallas (2001).

[8] Chatterji (2007); Palmer (2002).

Other important questions seem ideally suited to the kinds of variables and time frames that experiments handle well. For example, social psychologists have long studied the roots of conformity. Our understanding of variables that would be difficult to observe as they naturally occur in social life has been importantly enhanced by experimental studies, because the variables are relatively easy to create in small-group laboratories. For example, one study asks: how is it that people come to support norms and to pressure others to support norms that they do not or would not support absent social pressure?[9] The authors' answers are persuasive and would have been difficult or impossible to study other than in a laboratory environment. Another long-standing social theory with roots going back to Kant and extending to modern social theorists of democracy, such as Rawls and Habermas, is the importance of discussion and deliberation in decision making. Do people arrive at different kinds of decisions when they discuss their reasoning with others? A significant contribution to our understanding of this important question in social theory was possible because it was quite susceptible to laboratory test—by randomly assigning people to make decisions individually or in deliberative groups.[10]

Would an Experimental Intervention Distort the Object of Study?

One might think of this as a type of Heisenberg effect[11]—in brief, it is hard to study something without changing it. For example, many federal education grants require partnerships between universities and schools. For obvious reasons, it would be very difficult to randomly assign meaningful partnerships; therefore, a requirement to use the experimental method would create an artificial situation that would be different from what one would otherwise observe. Other types of reform, such as whole-school reform, require enthusiastic volunteers; teachers and administrators have to vote to join the experimental condition. This obviously makes randomization impossible and introduces self-selection bias. But reasonable causal inferences are possible using techniques such as difference-in-difference regression.[12]

Is the Research Question More Focused on External or on Internal Validity?

Internal validity refers to the extent to which a study's results can be correctly attributed to the treatment or independent variable. A study is internally valid when one can rightly draw accurate conclusions about the causal effects of the treatment on the outcome in the sample studied. An internally valid study may not be externally valid. *External validity* is the extent to which the results of an internally valid experiment can be generalized beyond the sample of people who participated in the study. Such generalizability is importantly related to the representativeness of the sample (a topic discussed in more detail in Chapter 9). Here we briefly note that there are many ways

---

[9]Willer, Kuwubara, and Macy (2009).

[10]Schneiderhan and Khan (2008); the answer is yes, there is a "deliberative difference."

[11]Named for particle physicist Werner Karl Heisenberg, who noted that the act of observing particles changed their behavior.

[12]Bifulco (2002). This is discussed in more detail in the regression chapters of our volume on analysis.

in which the external validity of an experiment can be limited. For example, in drug trials of the cost-effectiveness of COX inhibitors, it was found that observational data from actual clinical practice was far superior to data from RCTs.[13] The clarity of the implementation of the variables in the RCT was not matched in clinical practice. As that study showed, external validity is an empirical question, not something to be settled by stipulation. Another area of limited external validity occurs in programs funded by grants that have eligibility and selection criteria that preclude random assignment. To be eligible, a community or an institution such as a hospital or a university might have to provide matching funds. Thus, only communities with sufficient resources or institutions with enthusiastic managements might qualify. It would be hard to generalize from such groups of enthusiastic volunteers to a more general population of communities or institutions. Such limitations on external validity are not confined to evaluation of social programs.[14]

Is the Research Question More Focused on Causal Processes or Outcomes?

When your focus is on outcomes, experimental approaches are a very attractive alternative—presuming that the conditions necessary for experimentation have been met (random assignment and manipulable variables). Experiments may be less useful for identifying causal processes. The outcome question might be: Do smaller classes (independent variable) increase student learning (dependent variable)? The process question (intervening variable) might be: *How* do they do so? Clearly, an interest in causal processes does not mean that causal effects are unimportant. If there is no effect or outcome, the only process there is to study is a fruitless one. Even that can have some value if, for example, you can specify *why* an intervention that has been successful in other cases was not effective in this one. Such studies of processes often focus on *fidelity of implementation*, which is important in all experimental studies. Examinations of the fidelity of implementation and other questions about processes are often conducted using interviews, observations, or document analysis—and frequently with some combination of the three. In general, the tendency to separate process from outcome is a mistake, but studying both is often more than one researcher or one team can accomplish simultaneously in a single study.[15] Processes may also be studied with follow-up experiments. As with many other questions, researchers disagree about the best approach to studying causal processes versus causal outcomes.

It is clear that experiments have many advantages and disadvantages. Were we all not so accustomed, through years of repetition, to believing claims about the invariant superiority of RCTs, it is unlikely that we would so automatically accept those claims today. While RCTs are truly superb when it comes to the internal validity of causal generalizations about variables that can manipulated, they are often substantially less persuasive when it comes to external validity, especially in studies in which cases or participants cannot be randomly assigned and variables cannot be manipulated. We

---

[13] van Staa et al. (2009).

[14] The classic study on the external validity of experiments is by Bracht and Glass (1968). For an argument that experiments can be designed so that the results are more generalizable, see Highhouse (2009).

[15] Plewis and Mason (2005).

have summarized the main advantages and disadvantages of experimental designs in Table 3.1. As the structure of the table suggests, pluses and minuses tend to be balanced. While, in general, for every advantage there is an equal and opposite disadvantage, for any *particular* research project, the positives and negatives are *not* likely to be equally balanced. For your project, the balance is very likely to tilt in one direction or another.

The general point conveyed in Table 3.1 is that for some types of research questions the experimental approach is ideal. When random assignment of cases to control and experimental groups is possible, investigators can reduce, further than with *any* other method, the confounding effects of variables in which they are not interested. When the experiments are conducted in a laboratory setting, this reduces still further the chances of confounding variables. In short, experiments are especially good at ensuring *internal* validity, that is, drawing correct conclusions about your sample, especially regarding causal effects.

Of course, there are also important limitations of experimental designs. As discussed above, many topics of great importance cannot be examined experimentally. For example, if you are interested in the issue of which intervening variables account for the association between social background characteristics and longevity (life or death is pretty high on the importance scale), it is clear that most relevant variables are not manipulable and that most effects are too long-term to be investigated in experimental settings. Since experimental approaches are not feasible, other designs, if feasible, will necessarily be more effective, despite any limitations they might have.

The external validity of experiments may be limited by the very thing that gives experiments their strength—the purity of the laboratory environment. The laboratory enables researchers to isolate potential causal effects. But real-world variables are not isolated in this way. The ability to isolate them is a source of internal validity *and* a

TABLE 3.1. Advantages and Disadvantages of Experiments

Features of experiments	Advantages	Disadvantages
Random assignment	Within the bounds of probability it controls for all confounding variables.	Many important subjects of research are not susceptible to random assignment.
Manipulable variables	The presence, duration, and intensity of independent variables are determined by researchers.	Many important causal variables are impossible or difficult to manipulate.
Effectiveness	Better at investigating short-term, relatively uncomplicated variables.	Long-term effects may be obscured by the history-effect threat to validity.
Artificiality of treatments	Keeps contaminating influences to a minimum.	Can be too distinct from real-world complexities (too short-term and too mild).
Validity	Best for internal validity of conclusions.	Often less strong for external validity or generalizability.
Causation	Often the strongest design for identifying causal outcomes.	Often less effective at discovering causal processes.

concern for external validity. Experiments are also hard to generalize from because of another of their features: researchers are prohibited by ethical and legal rules from harming research participants. (We discuss these issues in depth in Part III of this volume.) Real life is not so kind. Harsh realities, such as the effects of unemployment on mental health or of residential segregation on crime rates, cannot be studied experimentally. Participants cannot be randomly assigned and variables cannot be manipulated. But these variables can be studied using observations, surveys, interviews, and archival data. Finally, another reason that experiments are often weak on external validity, or the ability to generalize from a sample to a population (see Part II of this volume), is that most experimental samples are not representative.

In sum, in many circumstances, experimental methods are far superior to other designs. If you decide that your research is best served by an experimental approach, then you have a host of additional choices to make. Mostly these choices involve selecting among the various types of experimental designs.

WHEN SHOULD YOU USE THE BASIC TYPES OF EXPERIMENTAL DESIGN?

Many ingenious experimental designs have been devised to increase internal validity. Most of the problems you are likely to encounter when conducting experiments have been encountered before, and many techniques have been developed to avoid those problems or reduce their impact. As with other methods, such as survey research, you will face numerous second-level choices—after you have made the first choice to conduct an experiment. The most practical way to seriously examine your options and obtain the best results from your experimental investigations is to review some of the standard texts in the field. Here you can learn what experienced researchers have done to address typical problems and avoid unexpected ones.[16] This section briefly introduces some experimental research design choices and when to use them. The section is structured using a series of "when" questions. In each case, there is no invariably right answer. Rather, each question asks what is best for your project, given your research question and the context in which you are attempting to answer it.

When Should You Replicate Previous Experiments?

The quick answer is *often*, because there are many advantages to doing so. First, replication links your research with that of others. Science progresses by replication. Second, replication is one of the best ways to improve the external validity of experiments. One caution is that replication can be much harder than it looks, even in fields where replication is considerable.[17]

---

[16] Good resources include Shadish, Cook, and Campbell (2002) and Myers, Well, and Lorch (2010). Helpful texts can be found at all levels of readers' expertise: Ryan (2007) is advanced; Abdi, Edelman, Valentin, and Dowling (2009) is intermediate; and Gonzalez (2009) is elementary.

[17] For a study of possible difficulties in replicating experimental instructions, see Rashotte et al. (2005).

O   X   O

FIGURE 3.1. Simple within-subjects experimental design.

When Should You Use "Blinding"—and How Much Should You Do?

The basic answer is *whenever possible* and the more the better, since each level of blinding eliminates a possible source of bias. In single-blind experiments, participants do not know which treatment they are receiving. In double-blind experiments, the researchers do not know either. In triple-blind experiments, the data analysts are likewise ignorant. The basic idea is to eliminate wishful thinking on the part of the experimenters, the research participants, or the data analysts.[18]

When Are There Advantages to a Within-Subjects Design?

A within-subjects design is a before-and-after study, also called a repeated-measures design. You measure, treat, and measure again. It is easiest to begin this and relate questions using the notation developed in the 1960s by Campbell and Stanley and used subsequently in many descriptions of experimental designs.[19] They use X's and O's for describing designs: O stands for observation and X stands for treatment ("X-perimental" treatment). The simplest within-group experiment without a control group in this notation is depicted in Figure 3.1. The advantage of this design is its simplicity. It is a simple pretest, posttest design using one experimental group. In this case, the first O is the first pretest or first "observation." The X is the experimental treatment, which is then followed by a posttest or second observation. This design might be adequate for many purposes, but adding a control group to make the experiment a between-groups study would likely be a great improvement.

When Are There Advantages to a Between-Subjects Design?

Between-subjects experiments make comparisons between groups of participants—those in the control and experimental groups. To describe this design, we can use the same notation. Now we make random assignments of participants (symbolized by R) to control and experimental groups. The experimental group is subject to the treatment while the other is not. This design is depicted in the Figure 3.2. Group 1 (with the X) is the experimental group; Group 2 is the control group. The experimental group is treated exactly as in Figure 3.1, but in this design, the members of this group are randomly assigned. The second group, also randomly assigned, receives no experimental treatment (no X in the figure). By comparing the final observation between the two groups, the researchers can be much more confident about the effects of X than they could be without the comparison/control group.

---

[18] For a study of 200 clinical trials indicating that blinding may be claimed more often than practiced, see Haarh and Hrogjartsson (2006).

[19] Campbell and Stanley (1963); Cook and Campbell (1979); Shadish et al. (2002).

Group 1 R   O   X   O
Group 2 R   O   O

FIGURE 3.2. Basic between-groups experimental design.

When There Is More Than One Factor, Should You Use a Crossed or a Nested Design?

In a crossed design, each participant receives each level of treatment; the scores compared are before-and-after scores and comparisons are within-subject. In a nested design, each participant receives only one level of treatment; the scores compared are between groups of participants.

In the following example, two factors are being studied for their effects on solving math problems. The research question is: is the speed of solving math problems affected by problem difficulty and work context? Speed of solving math problems is the dependent variable. The two factors (independent variables) are: Level of Difficulty (D) and Work Context (C). There are *two levels of problem difficulty*: easy (D1) and hard (D2), and there are *four work contexts*: solitary work (C1), working with others present (C2), working in silence (C3), and working with music playing (C4).

Both the crossed and the nested experimental designs utilize the two levels of difficulty and four work contexts, but the participants are treated quite differently. In the crossed design, you utilize only one group, and the speed of problem solving in the group is measured eight times (two difficulty levels × four work contexts). In the nested design, you utilize eight groups of participants and each group is measured once, on only one of the possible combinations of difficulty and work context. A comparison of the two designs is shown in Figure 3.3.

Which is better: one group measured eight times or eight groups measured once? There is no single right answer, but two things are obvious: you need fewer participants with the crossed, within-group approach, but you need to worry about all the things that repeated testing can cause: pretest sensitization, fatigue, practice effects, and so on. In the nested, between-groups approach, you don't need to worry about practice effects and so on, but you need many more participants. Also, as a general rule, nested designs

Crossed Design

	Treatment							
Group 1	D1C1	D1C2	D1C3	D1C4	D2C1	D2C2	D2C3	D2C4

Nested Design

	Group							
	1	2	3	4	5	6	7	8
Treatment	D1C1	D1C2	D1C3	D1C4	D2C1	D2C2	D2C3	D2C4

FIGURE 3.3. A version of crossed and nested designs (D = difficulty; C=context).

are much more complicated to analyze. A *split-plot* design combines nested and crossed designs in one study.

When Is It Useful to Use Pretests?

It is always a good idea and is by definition necessary in within-subjects (single group) designs. But it can be very helpful to control for pretest scores even when participants have been randomly assigned to different groups. You can use regression or ANCOVA to adjust results for pre-experimental differences. In quasi-experiments (see below), conducting pretests to gather data may not be possible but a similar goal is achieved by collecting baseline data. (Analysis issues about such adjustments are controversial and will be discussed in our companion book on analysis.)

When Should You Use a Matched-Pairs Design?

When you think participants have characteristics that may affect their reaction to a treatment, you can elect to use a matched-pairs design. This design matches participants on those characteristics, usually after some type of pretest or initial observation. After the pairs are determined, one member of each pair is assigned at random to the experimental group; the other is assigned to the control group. (Without random assignment, matching is less effective.) Groups receiving similar treatments are called *blocks*, and there are several ways in which blocking can be accomplished. In general, blocking in experiments is parallel to stratifying in surveys.

For example, if professors wanted to test the effectiveness of two different text books for an undergraduate statistics course, they might match the students on quantitative aptitude scores before assigning them to classes using one or another of the texts.

When Should You Control for Pretest Sensitization if Pretests Are Used?

When it seems probable or possible that the first observation (before the experimental intervention) could influence the second (after the intervention), as in a scenario where a pretest would influence scores on a posttest, you could use the "Solomon four-group design." The Solomon design is summarized in Figure 3.4. Groups 1 and 2 are the same as in Figure 3.2, but Groups 3 and 4 omit the first observation or pretest. Adding Groups 3 and 4 to the design controls for any effects the first observation has on the second.

When Should You Control Aspects of the Laboratory Environment?

The laboratory environment should always be controlled to eliminate extraneous variables that may confound results. There is a tendency to think that random assignment takes care of everything, but the laboratory environment is a clear exception. Designing the context in which your experiment will be conducted requires experience and judgment. In many laboratory studies, experimental sessions extend over days or weeks. Maintaining consistency from one session to the next requires much effort and rigorous attention to detail.

1. R	O	X	O
2. R	O		O
3. R		X	O
4. R			O

FIGURE 3.4. Solomon four-group design.

When Should You Plan for a Laboratory Experiment and When for a Field Experiment?

Laboratory settings are appropriate when controlling for extraneous variables is important, and when the consistency of the laboratory environment can be maintained for the duration of your study.

However, most social science researchers are interested in how well a treatment works in the real world, not just in the artificial environment of a laboratory. One of the big advantages of a field experiment is that real practicing professionals, not researchers, administer the experimental treatment. Studies conducted in natural settings have the advantage of not requiring researchers to generalize from the artificially pure world of the laboratory to the messy real world. But the messy field environment in the real world can cause big problems for researchers. So much is typically going on in the real world that it is hard for researchers to be sure about what they are studying due to the introduction of many unaccounted-for variables. When the authenticity of the field environment is more important than controlling for extra variables, a field experiment is a logical choice.

When Should You Worry about Treatment Fidelity and Conduct Manipulation Checks?

These two are related in that they have to do with determining how the independent variables were delivered. They should be considered when conducting all types of experiments, but tend to be more problematic in field experiments when researchers rely on practitioners to administer the treatments. Was the intended treatment actually delivered? Was it delivered according to the specifications in the design? Qualitative observations of the practitioners administering the treatment are often helpful when studying treatment fidelity.

Manipulation checks investigate whether the intervention is strong enough or consistent enough to have the intended effect. These checks are important in both laboratory and field research. Again, they can be more important in field experiments, where investigators often have only limited control over the way the treatment is implemented. It is important both to conduct a manipulation check in a pilot study and to check for treatment fidelity several times during the actual course of the experiment.

When Should You Categorize Continuous Independent Variables in an Experimental Design?

The classic experimental design already uses categorical independent variables: cases or participants are either in the treatment group or not—yes/no, 1/0. But many variables are inherently continuous, such as minutes of practice or scores on a test. Typically, such variables are categorized into high and low (dividing at the median) or small, medium, and large. There are many reasons to do this, mostly having to do with ease of analysis, but there are also many reasons to be cautious when contemplating such "data mutilation."[20] In general, categorizing a continuous variable is most reasonable when the continuum contains natural break points or thresholds.

When Do You Add More Factors or Independent Variables to Your Design?

Each independent variable adds a level of complication to your analysis, but often, each will increase external validity. When interaction effects are a key part of your research questions, you will of course need to include the potential interacting variables. When studying the *joint* effects of two or more independent variables on a dependent variable you are conducting a factorial design. When doing a factorial design, you will also need to decide whether your factors should be crossed or nested (see p. 58).

When Should You Use Quasi-Experiments?

Quasi-experiments are often an attractive alternative to true experiments, especially in real-world, rather than laboratory-world, contexts. Quasi means "resembling to some degree." You use quasi-experiments when you are unable to assign *individuals* to control and experimental groups, but you can select *groups* at random to receive different treatments—or you can assign treatments at random to groups of recruits or volunteers.

Quasi-experiments are very common in studies of social, medical, and educational interventions; the units of analysis are agencies, clinics, and schools, not individual clients, patients, or students. When these aggregate units of analysis can be chosen at random, the investigation can resemble a true experiment to some degree.[21] Group randomization makes statistical analyses more complicated, and there is a considerable body of research about the effects of this kind of randomization.[22] Despite the complications, most methodologists would probably advise that when it comes to a choice between a quasi-experiment, a natural experiment, and archival research, the quasi-experiment is better—all else being equal. But all else is seldom equal. It can be difficult to decide, for example, whether your research goals are better served by conducting a quasi-experiment with control over an intervention at, say, 6 sites with 240 cases or gathering data from records with no controlled intervention at, say, 30 sites with 1,200 cases. There is no right answer. You have to make your decision and justify it given your research question and the comparative advantages of a controlled intervention versus a larger sample.

---

[20]Cohen (1983) is a classic discussion; see also Preacher, MacCallum, Rucker, and Nicewander (2005).

[21]On quasi-experiments in general, see Mark (2008).

[22]See Murray and Blitstein (2003); Hedges (2007).

When Should You Use Natural Experiments?

A favorite alternative to the RCT in the social sciences is the "natural experiment." The term is often used loosely to apply to the study of any naturally occurring differences among groups. It is also used to describe independent variables that arise as a result of social or political action, such as policies or legislation. Making a distinction between an archival study of existing variables and a natural experiment can be difficult; the difference is mostly a matter of degree—or semantics.[23] In what most people would term a natural experiment, the data are generated in a more-or-less natural process or by an event that can approximate an experimental intervention. You use natural experiments when you can "find" experimental conditions and collect the data generated by natural or social forces. For example, if the topic is the effects of different residential patterns, researchers cannot manipulate these in order to collect data. But a natural disaster, such as a hurricane, can provide an exogenous source of variation in residential patterns. The consequent residential changes can be studied as though they had been experimentally generated.[24]

Some advocates of the natural experiment believe the natural intervention needs to be clear enough that simple methods of analysis, such as t-tests of mean differences, can be used. Indeed, this is how some methodologists would define a natural experiment. But that confuses the design used to collect the data with the methods used to analyze them. There is no reason beyond tradition to prefer rudimentary methods of analysis in either true or in natural experiments.[25] Difference-in-difference regression[26] and interrupted time series designs[27] are effective alternatives.

When Should the Experiment Be Combined with One or More Other Designs?

It is more common to combine experiments with other methods than many researchers believe. For example, adding observational methods to an RCT protocol can raise the overall quality of the study. RCTs are structured to focus on overall mean effects. In program evaluation, these can be less interesting than differential effects, which help identify which program elements work better with subgroups of the population. Discovering these effects often requires observational methods.[28] One might think initially of bringing in additional methods to supplement experimental work, but sometimes experiments can be used to assist in other designs.

The survey experiment is the best developed of these supplementary methods. An experiment can be incorporated into a survey by, for example, randomly selecting survey respondents to reply to different forms of questions. By studying the results, survey researchers can learn how to improve the quality of survey questions and understand patterns of responses to them. For example, researchers examining the question "does

---

[23]Rutter (2007); Dunning (2008).

[24]Kirk (2009).

[25]Palmer (2002).

[26]Card and Krueger (2000).

[27]Mandell (2008).

[28]Plewis and Mason (2005).

race matter in neighborhood preferences?" showed control and experimental groups of survey respondents different videos depicting neighborhoods that were identical except for having "residents" (actors) of different races. While race was not the only factor shaping neighborhood preferences, it was a very important one.[29] One special advantage of combining surveys and experiments, such as the one in the previous example, is that they have complementary strengths. Surveys are often good at generalizing (exernal validity) because they are built upon random samples of populations, something quite rare in experiments. And experiments are excellent at identifying causal relationships (internal validity), something quite elusive in surveys. Combining them, the strengths of the two designs can be united and their weaknesses mitigated.[30]

GENERAL CONCLUSION ON WHEN TO USE EXPERIMENTAL DESIGNS

The experiment is actually a large cluster of related designs, rather than one design. Of course, all experimental designs have some features in common: they are especially suitable when your research question is causal, when you can manipulate the causal variables of interest, and when you can randomly assign cases to experimental (or treatment) and control (or comparison) groups. Random assignment and control over the independent variables make causal inferences drawn from experimental studies particularly powerful: experiments are very strong when it comes to internal validity of causal inferences. Because experiments tend to focus on a small number of variables and a small number of cases per study, they are less strong on external validity or generalizability. One common strategy researchers use to improve external validity is to conduct a series of related experimental studies, changing a variable or a population subgroup in each study. In this way the scope of the inferences that can be drawn may be broadened. Even when the inferences are of limited or unknown scope, they nonetheless are unusually certain. One can never *prove* anything in empirical disciplines, but levels of certainty can be high—usually higher with inferences based on experimental evidence than on evidence gathered with other designs.

One reviewer of an early draft of this chapter complained that we constantly point out that experiments can have weaknesses as compared to other methods and that we make this kind of unfavorable comparison much more when we discuss experiments than when we discuss other designs. This is correct, and there is a good reason for it. None of the other major designs that we discuss here—surveys, interviews, observations, and archival research—has long been held by so many people to be ineluctably superior to all others. Only about experiments has there grown up an unconvincing claim of inevitable superiority that has become a textbook platitude. By challenging some of the improbable claims that have been made on its behalf, perhaps we can contribute to putting the experiment in its proper place. That place is one of honor. The experiment is a powerful and logically elegant solution to *some of* the researcher's more difficult and important problems. As such, it is a crucial option for researchers to con-

---

[29] Krysan, Couper, Farley, and Forman (2009).

[30] An excellent overview of survey experiments is Gaines et al. (2007). For a discussion of combining RCTs with regression discontinuity designs, see Mandell (2008).

sider when choosing a design. The table on pages 65–66 summarizes the experimental design considerations discussed in this chapter.

SUGGESTIONS FOR FURTHER READING

Ronald Fisher's pioneering work *The Design of Experiments* (1935) is the classic original account, though many of the basic ideas were adumbrated in the 17th-century writings of Francis Bacon. Fisher's work is not as widely read as it once was, and it's not in print any longer, but many libraries have it. Ironically, the book by Fisher's great rival, Karl Pearson, *The Grammar of Science* (3rd edition, 1911), is still in print. But unlike the classics of interview research, these older volumes by Fisher, Pearson, and Bacon are not often read by practicing scientists unless they also have an historical bent.

Among the best-selling works today on experimental design a real standout is Shadish, Cook, and Campbell's *Experimental and Quasi-Experimental Designs for Generalized Causal Inference* (2002). Its popularity is due to a lively writing style and its ability to deal with advanced concepts in a largely nontechnical way. It is also popular because it updates two earlier highly influential works: Campbell and Stanley's *Experimental and Quasi-Experimental Designs for Research* (1963) and Cook and Campbell's *Quasi-Experimentation: Design and Analysis Issues for Field Settings* (1979). The first of these introduced the key and highly influential concept of "threats to validity." Each subsequent work expanded on its predecessor's list of threats.

Helpful texts can be found at all levels of readers' expertise. Gonzalez's *Data Analysis for Experimental Design* (2009) is short and elementary; like much methodology writing on experimental design in social research, it mainly uses examples from psychology. Abdi and colleagues' *Experimental Design and Analysis for Psychology* (2009) is an intermediate-level text, again based in psychology. A very advanced and quite comprehensive text is Ryan's *Modern Experimental Design* (2007). It draws heavily on engineering examples, but is more broadly useful because of its extensive, though concise, review of types of experimental design. Perhaps the best compromise among these levels of difficulty and fields of coverage is Myers, Well, and Lorch's *Research Design and Statistical Analysis* (3rd edition, 2010), which also includes some comparisons with other designs.

Finally, we cannot fail to mention a brief article (published in 2003), something of an Internet phenomenon, one that seems to be attaining underground classic status, called "Parachute Use to Prevent Death and Major Trauma Related to Gravitational Challenge: Systematic Review of Randomized Controlled Trials." The authors, Gordon Smith and Jill Pell, argue that because there are no RCTs (only observational studies) on the question, they are unable to draw any evidence-based conclusions about the effects of using a parachute during a free fall. They suggest that radical advocates of evidence-based medicine would do a great service were they to organize and volunteer to participate in such trials of parachute use.

CHAPTER 3 SUMMARY TABLE

WHEN IS AN EXPERIMENTAL DESIGN A GOOD OPTION FOR YOUR RESEARCH?

- When cases or subjects can be randomly assigned.
- When variables can be manipulated.
- When random control trials are cost-effective.
- When an experimental intervention will not distort the object of your investigation.
- When research questions are more focused on internal validity than external validity.
- When your research is more concerned with causality than with outcomes.

WHEN SHOULD YOU USE THE BASIC TYPES OF EXPERIMENTAL DESIGN?

When should you replicate previous experiments?	• Often, because it links your research with others' work and improves external validity.
When should you use "blinding"?	• Whenever possible to eliminate sources of bias.
When are there advantages to within-subjects design?	• When the number of potential subjects is limited and a simple design is sufficient for your research question.
When are there advantages to between-subjects design?	• When enough subjects are available and when you want to be confident about treatment effects.
When should you use a crossed or nested design?	• Use a crossed design when number of subjects is limited and you can control effects of repeated testing. • Use a nested design when enough subjects are available and you have sufficient analysis resources.
When is it useful to use pretests?	• It is always a good idea to do so, especially with within-subjects designs.
When should you randomly assign after first matching on a pretest?	• When characteristics of subjects may affect their reaction to a treatment.
When should you control for pretest sensitization?	• When it seems probable that the first observation (pretest) may influence the posttest results.
When should you control aspects of the laboratory environment?	• The laboratory environment should always be controlled to avoid introducing additional variables.
When should you use a laboratory experiment and when should you use a field experiment?	• Laboratory experiments should be used when controlling for extraneous variables is important. • Field experiments should be used when your main interest is how well a treatment works in the real world.

When should you worry about treatment fidelity?	• Fidelity should be considered in all experiments, but especially in field experiments where practitioners administer the treatment.
When should you categorize continuous variables in an experimental design?	• Seldom; only when the continuum has natural breaking points or thresholds.
When do you add more factors or independent variables to your design?	• When you want to increase external validity. • When interaction effects are key to your research question.
When should you do quasi-experiments?	• When you are unable to assign *individuals* to control and experimental groups, but you can assign *groups*.
When should you use natural experiments?	• When you can find experimental conditions generated by natural or social forces and collect the data.
When should an experiment be combined with other designs?	• When you need to supplement the experiment to fully answer your research questions. • When an experiment can assist with other designs, such as survey development.

CHAPTER 4

When to Use Naturalistic and Participant Observational Designs

Naturalistic and participant observational research designs take us back to research questions when we seek to decide "when to use what." Often the hunches and propositions that are the origins of research questions come from life experience and observation. If research questions result from reflection on evidence, then what is a better source of evidence than naturally occurring phenomena, especially where usable knowledge is the goal? *Observational research*, as we use the term here, means studying events, situations, settings, practices, and other social phenomena as they occur. Rather than intervene in the natural course of events by using an interview, survey, or experiment, researchers observe social phenomena "on the fly," as they actually happen. They gather evidence rather than generate it. As with any research endeavor, tradeoffs are made. In the case of observational research, what researchers may lose in terms of the control that comes with intervention, they may gain in the possibility of investigating a world less artificial than one shaped by researchers. They may see something familiar with fresh eyes and new insights, and perhaps shed assumptions that may be getting in the way of developing usable knowledge.

In this chapter, we first consider when to use observational designs overall. We then distinguish between naturalistic and participant observational design options for various types of research questions. In a sense, observation is the root of virtually all research. Research is an enterprise that attempts to explain variation—variation that is observable in one way or another, and so, strictly speaking, all research designs employ observation. Surveys and interviews capture and observe perceptions in response to structured protocols that elicit those perceptions. Experiments make tightly controlled observations through the lens of carefully selected and manipulated variables. We have addressed those types of observations in preceding chapters.

OVERVIEW OF OBSERVATIONAL DESIGNS

You might consider using an observational research design when you want to get close to the action and glean diverse aspects of lived experience from interaction with others. In other words, your research question can demand that you be right in the thick of things. Some research questions simply cannot be answered without investigating real-life experiences. Observational research is for those occasions when "seeing is believing." It is the difference between seeing the coral reef in a *National Geographic* documentary and making the dive yourself, or between observing human interaction in the social psychology lab and observing it on the street.

The two main types of observational research are *naturalistic* and *participant*. In naturalistic observation, researchers seek to keep their influence on the observed phenomena to a minimum; they want to be as unobtrusive as possible. However, there are not actually very many opportunities to observe people without having any interaction with them at all, and ethical concerns for privacy often require that you make your presence known. Once you do so, even the slightest amount of interaction could influence those you are observing, taking you out of the realm of purely naturalistic observation. Thus, participant observation is much more common in social science research. The amount of participation you engage in while observing may vary from very slight to full immersion, and will be guided by your research question and study design.

Settings for observations may also vary, and are discussed in detail in Chapter 10, where we address sampling strategies and case selection. Here, we will just mention that, depending on the nature of the observational study, settings can range from remote villages to corporate headquarters to Internet chat rooms.

Whether you observe in real or virtual spaces, it makes sense to turn to observational designs when your research questions ask about *variation, context, detail*, and *depth*. We use the term *variation* to mean those phenomena or concepts that represent something new, or that differ from each other in observable ways. They pique our interest, generate our research questions, and serve to structure those questions. Often, a variation we observe triggers a host of why and how questions that can only be answered by observing the phenomenon as it happens. These initial why and how questions lead to questions about *context*. What are the specifics of a particular observational setting? How do environmental, cultural, and other contextual factors interact with and influence the phenomenon of study? *Detail* and *depth* are related issues. While some may say "the devil's in the details," an observational researcher may say that the muse of understanding also resides in those details. Detailed observations may help to illuminate a rich web of interconnections, exceptions, and paradoxes that we associate with in-depth understanding. Observational research incorporates these four considerations as its particular set of constituent parts. At the heart of the matter, you can use observational designs when studying human social interactions in real settings to help you explore what matters to people and how they interpret their own experiences.[1]

Figure 4.1 depicts the observational research process when you seek to answer questions about *variation, context, detail*, and *depth*. The observation process and the four considerations help us think through when to select observational designs to answer research questions.

---

[1]Rennie and Fergus (2006).

Observe → Gather Data in "Real Setting" → Code/Measure → Analyze
  Considerations:

- **Variation** (sensitizing concepts, variables, attributes of interest, causal connections)
- **Context** (settings, practices)
- **Detail** ("thickness" of description)
- **Depth** (exploring something new versus studying established variables)

FIGURE 4.1. Observational design processes and key considerations.

Research questions, regardless of your design choice, may be categorized based on their intent. In this volume, we often refer to research that is (1) descriptive, (2) exploratory, (3) explanatory, (4) testing a theory, or (5) developing a theory. Observational designs can be useful for answering any of these types of research questions. In Chapter 10, we use these categories to determine when to apply particular methods of sampling and site selection. In this chapter, we assume that you may be using any of the five. When you employ one of these research categories, we recommend that you take the four chief considerations (variation, context, detail, and depth) into account.

When we observe processes, we can quickly find ourselves swamped if we fail to decide what we want to witness: variation, context, detail, and/or depth. We tend to see more by deciding what it is that we are initially looking for, even while we know that we will need to conduct multiple observations and that these observations may modify our design as we proceed. Studying social processes entails investigating phenomena over time, and that in turn requires that the observations be trustworthy and buttressed by multiple observations—either within combined designs and/or using additional researchers observing the same phenomena. Triangulating with other evidentiary sources also adds to the trustworthiness of observational evidence.

WHEN IS OBSERVATION A GOOD DESIGN CHOICE?

Observation is an effective research design choice when your research question leads you to:

1. Study social, cultural, psychological, or political processes as they unfold
2. Identify, develop, or refine sensitizing concepts or variables
3. Cultivate a rich or thick description within a particular context
4. Uncover or explore causal mechanisms or recognize interactive links between and among variables

The following sections discuss each of these situations in some detail.

. . . When You Can Best Answer Your Research Question by Studying Social, Cultural, or Political Processes as They Unfold

Observation is the design of choice when it is necessary and feasible to witness social, political, or cultural phenomena and mine your observations for insights about research variables of interest. Social, cultural, and political processes are, by their nature, inter-active and dynamic, durable and largely stable over time, both conceptual and practi-cal, and often characterized by stages or phases so that patterns can be discerned and described.[2]

Observation of social, political, or cultural processes has two features that make it a logical choice. First, *social processes are complex* and often require actual physical presence in the field, creating a tension between what you think your guiding concepts or variables are and what you might learn through observation. Observational designs are tools to help us describe what actually happens in the social, cultural, psychologi-cal, and/or political spheres that reshape our understanding and help us capture prac-tical and significant variation. Second, *social processes are by nature interactive and dynamic*. As situations occur, observational designs allow you to engage with others and make decisions as you go. It is essential to document these in-the-field design deci-sions to help others understand your choices and improve their own designs.[3]

When your research question concerns culture, observational research is almost always at least one component of the design. Definitions of culture abound, but they share a few key features that include shared values, beliefs, attributes, practices, and norms of behavior among study populations. Culture is a slippery concept. While it can be studied at some level using surveys and interviews, it is hard to dispense with observation. Observing culture as it is enacted and experienced in natural social con-texts tends to suggest ideas for further study, in order to establish it as a phenomenon or—more likely—a cluster of phenomena.

. . . When You Want to Identify, Develop, or Refine Sensitizing Concepts or Variables

When you want to understand, describe, or thoroughly characterize ongoing social pro-cesses or refine your ideas and those of others in all their complexity, relevancy, and vibrancy, then observational designs are a good choice. You might choose an observa-tional design when you are focusing on clarifying a *sensitizing concept* or framework. A sensitizing concept is an idea that guides observation; it makes us more alert (sensitive) to seeing certain phenomena; it tends to evolve over the course of a research project as more observations are made.[4] Observational research is also a good choice when you are developing a set of research variables rather than investigating established ones. Obser-vation's open, real-life quality makes it ideal for the early phases of research. Thus, observational design may be a good choice for descriptive, exploratory, explanatory, or theory-developing studies.

Observational designs may also be useful when you want to develop and refine research variables that prior scholarship has identified. The research literature may define previously studied variables, which you now seek to understand in relation to each other, perhaps seeking causal mechanisms that can be converted into usable knowledge. As another example, you may have a hunch or emerging idea about a phenomenon.

---

[2]Bowen (2010).

[3]Owens (1982).

[4]Like many concepts in qualitative research, this one has its origins in grounded theory. See Corbin and Strauss (2008).

In this case, you would not be exploring relationships among pre-identified variables; instead, you would be using a sensitizing concept or framework that leads you to seek and define variables for future study.[5] In such cases, observation helps to "establish the phenomenon" with sufficient "regularity to require and allow explanation."[6]

Over the course of its development, social science scholarship has identified and clarified variables in the quest to understand and explain social phenomena. When you conduct a literature review, you are garnering emerging ideas for study, but you may find wild variation in the ways a term, concept, or construct is defined, used, coded, or analyzed by scholars. Or, you may find that scholars write about something that they never even attempt to define. The end result can be an entire literature of cross-talk where you are not sure what a study is about or how usable knowledge could come from it. For example, the authors of this book are members of a team that studies assessment and evaluation practices. The related phenomena "assessment" and "evaluation" are fabulous illustrations of scholarly gaps. These terms are defined in multiple and contradictory ways, the research literature uses mixed and confusing definitions, and occasionally researchers skip the definitions altogether! Observational research that focuses on how these terms are used, who uses them, and in what contexts they are used could do much to help clarify practice in this area of research.

Observational research opens the possibility of seeing something new, describing variation that has not been noticed before. Without observation, causal mechanisms are difficult to establish regardless of the research methods used, including experiments and statistical analyses of all kinds.[7] For example, a field experiment might determine that two variables (X and Y) are causally related, that is, that an increase in X leads to a predictable increase in Y. But observation of X and Y in action is often needed to identify the actual causal mechanism: to understand *how* X leads to Y.

Prior scholarship reveals sensitizing concepts or frameworks that help you to focus on the parameters of your research question. Descriptive studies based on observation can stand on their own merit and also support an array of research enterprises that follow. To be effective, researchers must notice and then confront tacit assumptions about phenomena, compare descriptive categories, synthesize or distinguish among related concepts and variables, and evaluate emerging categories, definitions, and characterizations of phenomena. Observational designs support all these research endeavors.

. . . When It Is Important to Cultivate a Rich or Thick Description within a Particular Context

The notion of rich or "thick" description of social phenomena is foundational in observational research.[8] The idea of thick description originated in philosophy but quickly became a key concept in anthropology after Geertz described it, and it is now common in social science research across disciplines. In simplest terms, thick description means portraying a phenomenon, such as a behavior, in context, because without the context,

---

[5]This situation is the particular domain of observational designs. Standard texts on naturalistic inquiry and participant observation frequently discuss it. One good source is Hobbs and Wright (2006).

[6]Merton (1987).

[7]Cronbach (1975).

[8]Geertz (1973).

it cannot be fully understood. Our goal is to witness human actions in context so that we can analyze, interpret, and ascribe meaning to them. Context is the setting for the observed phenomenon, and consists of various circumstances and facts that both inform your observations and affect the situation you are observing. We can see that context is an interrelated set of varying conditions that include setting, time (including historical time), practices, and other attributes in the observational milieu. Context offers special opportunities to witness meaningful variation that can translate into practical application. From your "insider" position as observer, your analysis and interpretation of both the phenomenon of interest and its surrounding context become meaningful to "outsiders" who may want to understand or to use what you have learned. Inside knowledge of a particular field may even be essential when studying complex phenomena.[9] It is difficult to imagine studying cultures, political movements, or other complex social phenomena without taking great pains to capture them in situ—as they happen and as participants find (and indeed cultivate) meaning in them.

Without thick description, variation that matters is often missed. School improvement research provides one example. Researchers studying Chicago public school reforms used triangulated methods that included observation, and found that subtle differences among low-wealth neighborhoods could help explain variation in the success or failure of school reforms.[10] Observation of public school council meetings contributed to this understanding, coupled with socioeconomic data, crime statistics, and other measures from longitudinal databases. While the quantitative data were critical to developing a preliminary understanding of these micro-community influences, observational research uncovered new contextual variables that made a significant contribution to answering research questions about effective urban school reform. Variation among schools and the communities in which they were located yielded rich research themes that could be translated into action plans for making urban schools better places. These important contextual variations only came to be understood because the researchers were immersed in Chicago's schools and neighborhoods as they gathered, coded, and analyzed both verbal and quantitative data. Taken together, these words and numbers could be used to construct thick descriptions of contexts for educational practices—in given times and places, developed under a given set of policy mandates, with particular mixes of individuals.

We may turn to observation when we seek to understand something in a fundamental way, to describe or characterize it for the first time, to explore what something means to those engaged in it, or to illuminate something familiar with fresh insight. No social phenomena are fixed forever and none are utterly uninfluenced by context. Usable knowledge will take contextual influences into account. If action plans result from research implications and recommendations, then understanding and accounting for contextual variation can determine whether the plan "makes or breaks."

In sum, you should consider observational designs when you believe that contextual variation will help you to better understand phenomena. Without understanding contextual variation, researchers would discover little that could be converted into usable knowledge.

---

[9] Iacono, Brown, and Holtham (2009).

[10] Bryk, Sebring, Kerbow, Rollow, and Easton (1998); Bryk, Sebring, Allensworth, Luppescu, and Easton (2010).

. . . When You Want to Uncover or Explore Causal Mechanisms or to Recognize Interactive Links between and among Variables

Understanding causal and other types of associations between and among variables is a primary purpose of doing research, especially when you intend to influence real-world practices and policies through the development and refinement of usable knowledge. Observation can distinguish between causal relationships and other kinds of interactions among variables. Say, for example, an observer noticed that something happened often in the morning but never in the afternoon, or often in fall but rarely in winter. Research questions about timing and other variables of interest would emerge naturally. Or suppose you notice certain non-work-related behaviors among workers in offices with exterior windows, which you see rarely or never among workers in interior office spaces. Observation could help you discern if the windows are causing the behaviors (maybe because of access to outside distractions), or whether other variables are at play. Observational researchers are often the first to notice the regularities that researchers then use other designs to measure and test.

Statistical analyses alone have limited utility in establishing causation. Statistical regularities can suggest that variables are related, but may provide only circumstantial evidence about cause and effect. Observation often identifies the mediating variables that explain the regularities. Also, observational research may lead to identifying variables and their potential relationships that subsequent experimentation can test. In a classic example from the early days of public health, Goldberger's observations in orphanages and prisons allowed him to rule out contemporary myths about the causes of the devastating disease pellagra, and assert a connection between pellagra and diet. Although we now know that pellagra is caused by a niacin deficiency, at the time, medicine generally did not recognize nutritional causes for disease.[11] Goldberger's initial observations led to experimental designs much later in the research process. Recently, Gawande studied cystic fibrosis clinics, all of which used the same treatment regimen, but with dramatically different success rates. Only by detailed observational research was he able to discover the causal mechanisms underlying the excellence of some clinics.[12] In education, a coherent instructional program was statistically linked to student achievement, but the analysis demonstrating this link was developed only after observing other manifestations of instructional coherence in Chicago elementary schools.[13] In all three cases, the human presence, perception, and perspectives of observers were necessary to recognize sources of variation, identify variables, and discern associations among those variables.

FURTHER DISTINGUISHING BETWEEN NATURALISTIC AND PARTICIPANT OBSERVATIONAL DESIGNS

In practice, naturalistic and participant observational designs are not separated by a bright line, but rather represent a continuum reflecting the researcher's level of participation.

---

[11] Bollet (1992).

[12] Gawande (2004).

[13] Newman, Smith, Allensworth, and Bryk (2001).

	Covert	Overt
	Not identified as researcher	**Identified as researcher**
Naturalistic or passive observation	I. Observing in public places: streets, crowds, cafeterias	II. "Job shadowing" or "ride alongs" in police cars
Participant or active observation	III. Undercover studies of institutions or practices	IV. Action and evaluation research, participating in social life

FIGURE 4.2. Observational research: Covert/overt and passive/active.

At one end, the researchers are passive observers. This is *naturalistic* observation. At the other end of the continuum, researchers actively participate with those in the field who are being studied. This is *participant* observation. There are many potential gradations along this continuum, depending on the degree of active involvement by the researcher. Another dimension of observational research, which also tends to be something of a continuum, is the distinction between when researchers identify themselves as such versus when researchers conceal the fact that they are doing research. These differences are referred to in Figure 4.2, and they lead to a two-by-two categorization with four possible combinations. Each cell in Figure 4.2 (labeled I–IV) represents an observational design option. Each option is illustrated with examples of types of research.

Cell I: Naturalistic/Covert Research

Naturalistic/covert research is what one might think of as the "pure" type of naturalistic observation. The researcher witnesses events, often in the public sphere, without self-identifying as a researcher, noting what is observed and making as little impact on others as possible. Naturalistic/covert observation might bring to mind those natural scientists who study animal behavior in the wild, using high-powered field glasses and night-vision cameras. In social science research, the naturalistic observer may talk to participants in the field or otherwise minimally engage them, but will not self-identify as a researcher for fear of influencing the phenomenon of interest. This kind of investigation is rare in published research in the social sciences, but it is probably more common than the publication record suggests, at least as an informal prelude or supplement to other research methods. It is rarer in social research than in natural science research, mainly because the perceptions of the study population are so often needed to answer research questions, and these perceptions are difficult to determine through external observation alone. When it is important to your research question that your data collection be "unobtrusive and non-reactive,"[14] naturalistic/covert observation is an obvious choice. Sometimes it is the only practical choice—in the study of crowd behavior, for example.

We can expand the concept of naturalistic observation to include clinical observations of young children. Research focused on infants and very young children is often called naturalistic observation, regardless of setting. Early in her career, one of us

---

[14]The terms are from the classic work by Webb, Campbell, Schwartz, and Sechrest (1966/2000).

studied early childhood language acquisition, taking samples of children's utterances in a clinical setting. These utterances were audio-recorded for transcription and analysis. While adults would clearly notice the audio recorder and other signs that they were in the midst of a research study, the children were relatively uninfluenced by the presence of the researcher (and the bulky cassette recorder); it therefore seems appropriate to call this a form of naturalistic observation. In a classic example of naturalistic observation, Swiss psychologist Jean Piaget's studies of his own children still enjoy a major influence on child development scholarship.[15] Some might not call Piaget's work "naturalistic" because of his extensive interactions with his children while observing them. As in many areas of research, agreement on labels is less than total.

Cell II: Naturalistic/Overt Research

In naturalistic/overt research, your role as researcher is explicit, but you do your best to remain in the background while you observe. A common example is job shadowing, where you learn about an occupation by tagging along. This began as a way for students to learn about possible occupations, but has evolved into a fairly well-developed research technique, especially in organizational research.[16] A similar technique is the so-called "ride-along" used in the study of police officers in their patrol cars. Observers in naturalistic/covert research are expected to maintain their neutrality and not participate in what they are studying. Such lack of involvement can be hard to maintain in practice and trying to maintain it can undermine the rapport between the observer and the research participants.[17] When there is no way to do your research without the knowledge and consent of those you wish to observe, but you want to keep your influence on the people and their contexts to a minimum, the naturalistic/overt approach can be an effective choice.

Cell III: Covert/Participant Research

Participant observation is more common in social science research than naturalistic observation, whether covert or overt. In participant observation, the researcher is a witness but also more: the researcher is engaged to one degree or another in the action and discourse. Participant observers can participate either covertly or overtly. Covert/participant observation has a long history. A famous example is Goffman's study of institutionalization in asylums, in which he observed for a year pretending to be an assistant athletic director.[18] A somewhat infamous example is Humphreys's observations of homosexual behavior in public toilets; he served as a "watch queen" who warned men about police or other intruders.[19] While covert/participant observation is still a standard part of the toolkit of investigative reporters, it has become much less common in social science research in recent years, in part because of institutional review

---

[15] Piaget (1955).

[16] McDonald (2005).

[17] Spano (2006).

[18] Goffman (1961).

[19] Humphreys (1970).

board (IRB) regulations and perhaps because of greater ethical sensitivity on the part of researchers.[20] When you believe that your credibility as a participant would be compromised if you revealed that you were a researcher, or if it might raise safety concerns, covert/participant observation is a possible choice—assuming that you can resolve the ethical problems it almost always entails. We discuss these ethical considerations further in Chapter 16.

Cell IV: Overt/Participant Research

Overt/participant research has become the norm for most scholars doing social science observational research today. In many cases, perhaps most, participation is unavoidable: the observers must participate or they will not be able to gather plentiful, high-quality evidence. (Even the famous nature scientist Jane Goodall, when she studied chimpanzees in Africa, had to "join" the ape troops in order to make her detailed observations of their behavior.) In a study of partisan conflict, researchers argued for participation in the public demonstrations they observed because participation provided the only way to understand intergroup conflict in all its richness. Also, had they not participated, the people they studied would not have trusted them enough to provide them with extensive data.[21] The fact that they revealed themselves as researchers seems not to have impeded their data collection—at any rate, not as much as trying to be neutral in a highly charged situation would have done. Another excellent example is Duneier's study of street vendors in Greenwich Village.[22] He usually introduced himself as a researcher, but over his extended observations, he became part of the life he studied by helping with the vendors' work. Over the course of the study, his level of participation increased. Duneier had few, if any, qualms about this. Other equally prestigious participant observers have been less comfortable with the blurring of the boundary between their roles as researcher and participant.[23] When you need to conduct an observational study in order to address your research questions, it will often have to be participant observation, and it is increasingly common for this kind of research to be conducted overtly, with researchers identifying themselves as such. The growth in overt/participant observation may be fostered in part by an increasing familiarity with the researcher's role in modern society.

WHEN SHOULD YOU USE
A NATURALISTIC OBSERVATIONAL DESIGN?

Naturalistic observation is an effective design choice when you have one or more of these special conditions:

---

[20] One exception is Calvey's (2008) study of nightclub bouncers.

[21] Drury and Stott (2001) argue that intergroup conflicts that play out as demonstrations and other crowd situations require a participant observer and advance the idea that subjectivity is a special advantage in this kind of research.

[22] Duneier (1999).

[23] Bosk (2008).

- You can take advantage of events unfolding in the public sphere.
- You are making initial entries into the field to explore sensitizing concepts or variables.
- It is particularly important not to influence the participants or the setting.
- Participant observation is impossible, dangerous, or would raise ethical concerns.

. . . When You Can Take Advantage of Public Events with Little Chance of Influencing What You Observe

When you can take advantage of social phenomena in the public sphere, you might consider naturalistic observation. With public events, it is possible for researchers to witness social actions as they would unfold with or without their presence. Few studies rely solely on naturalistic observation because few research questions can be satisfactorily answered with it. For example, in Adeline Gordon Levine's 1982 sociological study of the Love Canal community,[24] her reliance on naturalistic observation of public meetings and events led to criticism that she was overly speculative about participants' motives.

Internet social media create public spaces that are increasingly important as potential sites for naturalistic observation. Sometimes the candor of online revelations is surprising, but they are nonetheless there for the plucking by the savvy researcher who can use them to answer a question or to make novel observations that lead to new questions. This area is ripe for enterprising researchers who can use it to extend their studies into new public spheres.

If you are interested in a particular research area, you can go into social networking websites and discussion boards and simply lurk; you can learn a great deal that way without posting a word yourself. However, if you post, then you are participating. One decision will be whether to participate overtly as a researcher. In our example (see Chapters 5 and 11) of the Web forum devoted to helping family members cope with a person with borderline personality disorder, can there be any doubt that you could follow several discussion threads and learn a great deal about what it means to be the spouse or child or sibling of someone diagnosed with this disorder? You can imagine the detail and "thick description" that could result from long-term observation of virtual spaces such as these. There are millions of websites. They provide enormous amounts of publicly available evidence about critical social, cultural, psychological, and political questions.

. . . When You Are Making Initial Entries into the Field to Explore Sensitizing Concepts or Variables

To develop and hone your research questions, it makes sense to enter the field and make observations before you have invested too much in a particular idea or design. The process begins with watching and witnessing. In fact, assuming the role of naturalistic researcher in almost any social setting can be useful for honing your observational skills. Seeing the familiar with a new consciousness is one of the best reasons for choosing an

---

[24]Levine (1982).

observation design, but it takes practice. If your literature review has led you to an array of potential study variables, naturalistic observation may initially help you to narrow them down to those that are most salient to your research questions and that can be feasibly observed and documented during the projected course of your study.

. . . When It Is Particularly Important Not to Influence the Participants or the Setting

Whether you are in the public sphere to describe something that is broadly observable or you are just casting about in public spaces for a fresh research question or insight, you will likely not reveal yourself as a researcher or wish to influence the social processes that you are observing. You are a covert operator and passive witness, even if you talk to people on the scene.

Of course, a primary reason for not wanting to influence participants is so that you can observe what really happens when you aren't there—in other words, observing the natural course of events in the study setting. Your research may require that participants not feel inhibited by your presence, nor encouraged to "perform" for you. In reality, this is not easy to achieve, because adding any new person into a situation will inevitably have some ripple effects. Not identifying yourself as a researcher will increase the likelihood of observing more natural interactions, but does raise some ethical concerns, which we address in Part III of this volume.

One way that observers can view naturally occurring events is through the use of video recordings. This technique has been used in many organizational settings, often to observe and study particular behaviors such as teaching or presentation styles. In these cases, the participants consent to the recording process, but are assumed to be acting as they would if the camera were not present. (Whether or not this is a valid assumption is always something of an unknown.) A related source of potential observational data is surveillance videos. These are often placed in public places for safety reasons, such as in subway stations, at ATM machines, and in the parking lots of convenience stores. Depending on the phenomenon of interest, observation and analysis of these types of video artifacts would certainly qualify as naturalistic observation, at least in the sense that the researcher is not influencing the observed behaviors. On the other hand, participant knowledge of the camera's presence may differ and could certainly influence what is being observed. (With the recent proliferation of "reality television" shows, we see many examples of people being videotaped with their full knowledge and consent, yet behaving in ways we can hardly believe they would want to make public!)

. . . When Participant Observation Is Impossible or It Would Raise Ethical Concerns

The research enterprise invariably generates a set of tradeoffs between benefits versus costs and risks. Naturalistic and participant observation designs have a symbiotic relationship in this way: naturalistic observation will not get you as into the action as will participant observation research, but it is an option that helps you avoid the potential disadvantages of participant observation. Taken with other design options, naturalistic observation may be an effective choice when you cannot participate either overtly or covertly because of access or ethical considerations. Particularly in studies where the participants do not know they are being observed, costs and benefits must be carefully weighed.[25] Participant observation is impossible when the presence of a researcher cannot or will not be tolerated and access is denied. Where participant research is not possible, naturalistic observation may be one among several design options.

Ethically, covert operations are invariably troublesome and should only be attempted when the benefits outweigh the potential risks to the participants, and the researcher is committed to doing everything possible to minimize those risks. Chapter 16 deals in greater detail with the special ethical dilemmas of observational research.

WHEN SHOULD YOU USE PARTICIPANT OBSERVATIONAL DESIGNS?

Participant observation is an effective design choice when you have these special considerations:

- You want to see what a phenomenon looks like from the inside.
- You are particularly interested in diverse perspectives about what you are studying.
- You want to study something over time as it unfolds, perceptions emerge, and meanings are ascribed.
- You want to influence what you are studying.

. . . When You Want to Witness a Phenomenon from the Inside

We addressed the basic answer to this question earlier in this chapter, but it is useful to emphasize that observational research focuses on perspectives, meanings, and lived experiences. It is often difficult to understand something by passively witnessing it, as when choosing naturalistic observation. In participant observation, you can think of yourself as a participant with a special vantage point. While there are several famous examples of covert participant observation, most participant observation is conducted with the full knowledge of the people being studied. Participant observational research allows you to engage other participants in conversations and share experiences with them. For example, in a 7-month study of how academic achievement in urban schools is mediated by school practices, Hatt spent 4 hours weekly overtly observing and assisting teachers in a General Educational Development (GED) classroom to understand the lived experiences of the 18- to 24-year-olds attending to get "back on track."[26] Only after a 3-month period did Hatt begin to interview the students. The study continued for another 4 months during which she interviewed each of 18 students twice and gathered documents from the site. But it was her months of participant observation that laid the foundation for the work that followed, buttressing her confidence that she had something to report

---

[25]Increasingly, institutional review boards provide oversight and weigh potential harm against possible benefits of research.

[26]See Hatt (2007) for an example of participant observer research that included the intent to build relationships with the student population in the study to develop trust and elicit a well-developed and nuanced picture of the ways schooling had shaped perceptions of who is and is not "smart."

about "book smarts" and the lives of the young adults she got to know. Of course, the more time you spend in the field with the other participants, the more comfortable they will feel with you. The human dimension, where relationships form, provides unique opportunities to understand something from others' perspectives.

Participant observation is also a response to a serious limitation of naturalistic observation if we seek insider perspectives. Human behaviors may contradict what people say they value, believe, or intend. In order to understand social, political, or cultural processes, we often want to explore these contradictions, noting them with sympathy for the human condition. Data gathered by participant observation can serve as a check against the limitations of both naturalistic observation and self-reports. It can also serve as a means of verifying findings from other data sources such as interviews.

. . . When You Are Particularly Interested in Diverse Perspectives and in the Social Nature of What You Are Studying

When we establish research protocols for surveys, interviews, experiments and other designs, we are likely basing these on our own tacit assumptions or familiar themes in the scholarship on the subject. Unexamined assumptions can prevent us from learning from variation in the messiness of real life and from the complexity of human interactions and relationships. Participating with others with different viewpoints is a strong antidote to the blinding effects of our own assumptions. Proximity allows us to be sensitive perceivers of human characteristics, tensions, emotions, body language, and a host of other unnamed nuances that may come to the researcher as a "felt sense"[27] about something. There is no reason to assume that such perceptions are tainted and not useful to researchers. These twinges and perceptions may form the basis of something quite formidable upon further reflection and investigation. This is the power of the interacting human perceiver in the research enterprise.

. . . When You Want to Study Something over Time as It Unfolds, Perceptions Emerge, and Meanings Are Ascribed

Naturalistic observation designs are frequently time-limited. Although technically a sampling issue, time spent in the field as a participant observer is priceless when it comes to perceptions, meanings, and lived experiences, not only because these are dynamic, but also because they are complex. Participant observers must be patient and allow the stories to unfold, and then subject each narrative line to reflection to uncover layers of meaning and look at a phenomenon in depth, often through multiple lenses.

Let us return to our Chicago school research example. The researchers, committed to the neighborhoods in the vicinity of the University of Chicago, spent years gathering data using combined methods that included observation. The result is a body of work that gives educators powerful narratives of neighborhoods changing and schools changing with them. Not all research can have this scope, but the example is illustrative of the value of taking the time to follow the story, building understanding of one circumstance or context that will have applications elsewhere. From this long-term research, new

---

[27]Gendlin's (1981) book *Focusing* offers a description of what a "felt sense" or gut level feeling is. In observational research, the researcher is a tool of the enterprise, making self-awareness critical.

models have emerged for improving student achievement in urban settings that might work in other urban areas such as Cleveland or Newark or Los Angeles.

... When You Want to Influence the Attributes, Variables, Settings, and Practices You Are Studying

As researchers, our first reaction is probably never to knowingly influence the study population in the field. But there are exceptions. Even though rare in basic research disciplines, those exceptions are important and make significant use of observational research. In many fields of practice, emerging research trends differ in important ways from traditional definitions of the research enterprise. We address two of them here: (1) action research, and (2) evaluation as a form of research. These two exceptions share a key feature that distinguishes them from traditional research: a short feedback cycle between developing an answer to the research question and using findings to influence practice. Lewin described action research, a term he coined, as "comparative research on the conditions and effects of various forms of social action and research leading to social action . . . composed of a circle of planning, action, and fact-finding about the result of each action."[28] The same description could apply to many contemporary examples of program evaluation research.

As ideas about what constitutes research expand to include practitioner-as-researcher models, it makes sense to think about research designs where findings are quickly put to use. Traditional research or scholarship relies on an extended feedback cycle and formal documentation of findings, refinement processes that include peer review, and dissemination through such venues as publications and presentations. Even when answers to the research questions are disseminated, the audience is usually the research community, not practitioners who might put the knowledge to use.

In the case of program evaluation, the researcher is often a participant observer in the field of clinical practice, intending to influence the setting and the people in it in order to clarify key variables and to change practices based on findings. Action and evaluation research change the audience and emphasis. One audience for evaluation research is the agencies that fund social projects; they understandably want to know whether the projects are effective. In fact, funding agencies were the original audience for the work of evaluation researchers. Increasingly, the audience has been extended to include those delivering services: the practitioner communities in health care, education, criminal justice, and other fields in which research is applied. Evaluation emphasis has shifted from compliance auditing to improving practice by building knowledge, and developing organizational learning through improved strategies and practices. In these cases, the researcher may be fully engaged as a participant.

CONCLUSION: CHARACTERISTICS OF ALL OBSERVATIONAL DESIGNS

Naturalistic and participant observational designs share some features that can help us decide when to use them and whether naturalistic or participant observation will best serve to answer research questions. We discuss here three of these features: using a

---

[28]Lewin (1946).

sensitizing concept or framework, studying change over time, and using triangulation and corroboration.

Using a Sensitizing Concept or Framework

As we discussed earlier, sensitizing concepts get to the heart of using observation designs. You turn to observation when you want to learn by directly experiencing a social phenomenon but you first need to describe or otherwise characterize it. It is unlikely that you have *no* clues about what you are studying or it would be difficult even to begin, hence the idea of a sensitizing concept or framework. You probably have your own ideas, which, together with those of other scholars and practitioners, have made you sensitive to something that you have now embodied in a research question; these ideas are the sensitizing concepts. A great deal is written about the preliminary ideas that guide research, especially in the literature on qualitative research and grounded theory.[29] When making design choices based on your research questions, consider what made you craft the questions as you did. You can decide whether the questions include or imply variables that are well developed, sensitizing concepts that are less well developed, or some combination of the two. These should be clearly identified in your study. The sensitizing concepts will tend to evolve.

Studying Change over Time

If your research question includes studying change over time, and your design includes naturalistic and/or participant observation, you will most often enter the field more than once. For example, many participant observation studies seek to understand organizational cultures. The researcher would need access to the organization over time to observe a range of occasions, from day-to-day work to special cultural events. Researchers need to adjust depending on the research questions and what they learn while observing. Without repeated visits, you will see only a small slice of the organization's life and work. It is difficult, for example, to understand organizational "climate," if you only experience the "weather" on a particular day.

Research studying change over time often does so by developing sensitizing concepts; teasing out variables and their complex relationships; providing thick, contextual description; and cultivating the diverse perspectives of study populations. This will invariably require multiple observations and often necessitate combined research designs. In fact, it is sometimes fear of how much time and effort observational designs can take that drives researchers to undertake survey or interview research instead. While you will surely need to set some limitations on your field time, studying phenomena that develop in situ will take you back to the field again and again. This raises sampling issues, because with observation research sampling is not just about populations and cases—it is also about when and where to go and how long to stay. One may study only one case but make thousands of observations in so doing. We discuss these sampling issues in more detail in Chapter 10.

---

[29] "Grounded theory" is an influential line of scholarship in qualitative research design that looks to designs like observational research as a means of generating theory inductively. See seminal works by Glaser and Strauss (1967) and Strauss (1987).

Triangulation and Corroboration

It is a good idea in observational research to use triangulation and corroboration whenever you can. While naturalistic and participant observational research designs are essential forms of social science research, it would be rare for social science research focused on creating usable knowledge to rely on observation alone. The unstructured or semistructured interview is a natural addition to participant observation research, as is document analysis. Indeed, most other approaches can be used to corroborate observation research. In our Chicago school research example, we described how both quantitative and observational analyses were merged to develop a more complete picture of effective school practices.

You can also employ multiple researchers in the field together seeking evidence in response to shared research questions. The benefits are obvious, especially in a design intended to capture detail and depth through observation. The more detail the research team can bring to the table, the greater the likelihood of developing key themes and patterns, understanding interactions and developing variables, and understanding contextual variations. The researchers can serve as checks on one another for bias and other perennial research concerns. Researchers can follow up with participants and elicit their feedback at almost any stage of the research process to test their evidence, codes, analysis, findings, and implications or conclusions. One form of such corroboration is the member check, where researchers present participants with an orchestrated opportunity to correct any misperceptions, mischaracterizations, or omissions. Member checks increase the trustworthiness of the observations and the themes and patterns generated from them as well as enhancing sensitivity to ethical concerns.

Many of the challenges in the observational research tradition develop because fewer design and analysis decisions can be made initially. Observational designs are more improvisational and require gathering data with all its real-life complexity, as compared to data that are generated according to protocols developed in advance of data gathering. Research questions serve as guides as you enter the field as a naturalistic or participant observer, open to the idea that you will need to refine your initial decisions in light of what you find and to choose wisely between and among the alternatives that present themselves. As we decide when to use what, conceptual and practical tools from the naturalistic and participant observation research tradition are likely to be part of the answer when the usable knowledge we seek is complex. Because there are no algorithms in observational research, there is no better way to prepare than to review and ponder examples of successful projects (see the footnotes and Suggestions for Further Reading for some guidance).

We use naturalistic and participant observations on their own and also when we want to buttress our confidence in the surveys, interviews, and other designs used to answer our questions. For many complex phenomena, naturalistic and participant observation research give us an indispensible set of useful design options to complement other research approaches so that we can develop and refine usable knowledge for understanding and practice. The table on page 85 summarizes considerations for using observational designs.

SUGGESTIONS FOR FURTHER READING

Naturalistic and participant observational designs, like interviews, are commonly used, and there are many supplemental resources available, historic and current, practical and arcane. We ignore some of the controversies you will find if you dig into readings about observational research, including epistemological arguments, wildly variant philosophies of science, and the meaning and appropriate applications of research. For an overview of philosophical influences, we recommend two philosophical equivalents of road maps for the philosophies affecting your research: (1) *The Dictionary of Qualitative Inquiry* (Schwandt, 2007); and (2) *From Archetype to Zeigeist: Powerful Ideas for Powerful Thinking* (Kohl, 1993). Additionally, there are discipline-specific approaches in health care, social work, industrial psychology, and other fields. A search at any university library will reveal these resources.

Reading the Classics

We recommend Guba and Lincoln's classic, *Naturalistic Inquiry* (1985). It is still in print and is nicely supplemented by Norman Denzin's essay "The Logic of Naturalistic Inquiry" (1971). Note that these and other authors eschew causal and explanatory research and its application. They are more interested in ascribing meaning from their observations. To balance this perspective, we recommend Cronbach's 1975 classic, "Beyond the Two Disciplines of Scientific Psychology," which calls for more observation in psychological research and offers observational designs for those who want to explain what they observe. A classic text that takes up these knotty but perennial issues is *The Structure of Science: Problems in the Logic of Scientific Explanation* (Nagel, 1961). For participant observational designs, we recommend Clifford's "On Ethnographic Authority" (1983). These designs originate in cultural ethnography, and anthropology is a dominant influence. A seminal work on ethnography and participant observation within this tradition is Van Maanen's *Tales of the Field* (1988).

Reading Beyond

Observational design discussions are often embedded in resources that ostensibly treat other topics, but you are likely to find useful insights by investigating these related resources. Most often, these resources are written from a qualitative perspective. Observational designs are so common in cultural ethnography, for example, that it is difficult to divorce them from that tradition. Reading in this area is recommended for studies that rely on observation as a major data source, so that you can justify your design choices on philosophical grounds. First among this group of resources is the *Sage Handbook of Qualitative Research*, now in its fourth edition (Denzin & Lincoln, 2011). The handbook addresses multiple topics and includes advice for observational designs, interviews, observations in the case study context, and other research approaches and issues common to field work. These resources are dense, but reading them selectively provides nuanced views of how these designs might be used and findings applied. Past editions may be helpful as well. Each edition is new and different. The fourth edition's many essays include: "The Observation of Participation and the Emergence of Public Ethnography" and "Participatory Action Research: Communicative Action and the Public Sphere."

CHAPTER 4 SUMMARY TABLE

USE OBSERVATIONAL DESIGNS WHEN . . .

- You can witness social processes as they unfold.
- You want to explore something that is not well understood.
- You need to create a rich portrait in context through "thick description."
- You hope to uncover causal mechanisms or to recognize other links between and among variables.

DISTINGUISHING NATURALISTIC AND PARTICIPANT OBSERVATIONAL DESIGN

Use naturalistic observational designs when . . .

- You can take advantage of events unfolding in the public sphere.
- You are making initial entries into the field to figure things out.
- You don't want to influence the other participants.
- Participant observation is impossible or would raise ethical concerns.

Use participant observational designs when . . .

- You want to study something from the inside.
- You seek diverse perspectives and use the social nature of what you are studying to find them.
- You want to study something over time as it unfolds.
- In rare circumstances, you want to influence what you are studying.

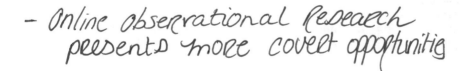

- Online observational research presents more covert opportunities

—

CHAPTER 5

When to Use Archival Designs
Literature Reviews and Secondary Data Analyses

We refer to the large number of data sources to be discussed in this chapter by the general term *archival*. Much of what we discuss in this chapter is called *secondary data analysis* by other researchers; we use "archival" only because it is a somewhat more general term. Archival data exist prior to any actions by current researchers, although they may have been assembled by previous scholars. These preexisting data are gathered by current researchers. Archival research data may be collected from numerical records, verbal documents, or visual artifacts such as those on websites. The key distinction in terms of research design activities has to do with whether current researchers *gather* data from available sources or whether they *produce* it through some sort of action such as interviews, surveys, observations, or experiments. In other terms, the difference is between *collecting* secondary data versus *generating* primary data. Archival researchers collect data they have not generated.

The distinction between collecting data generated by others and generating one's own data is not often used as a way to categorize research designs, nor is calling all methods of gathering secondary data "archival." But we think the distinction between the two is an important one that captures real differences in the researcher's craft. All schemes for dividing up research designs (such as experimental and nonexperimental or quantitative and qualitative) are somewhat arbitrary. We are making no ontological claims about our six-part division (survey, interview, experiment, observation, archive, and combined). Rather, in a book like this, what matters is whether the system of categories is useful for readers who are trying to find suggestions and make choices. We hope ours is, but that is for readers to judge.

There are many kinds of research that are archival, broadly speaking. Historical research is the most closely tied to what most people mean by "archives." Reviews of the research literature (including meta-analyses) are another type of fundamentally archival method based on secondary sources. Because literature reviews are fundamental to good research, even when you plan to generate your own data, any study you conduct will have an archival aspect if you review previous research. Archival research is often combined with other designs. For example, researchers who study organizations by interviewing and observation often also consult archives of organizational records. Probably the most common type of archival research in the social sciences in the United States involves employing huge public-use databases generated by the Bureau of the Census, the National Center for Educational Statistics, the Centers for Disease Control (CDC), survey organizations such as the General Social Survey, and so on. The largest single depository for social science data in a digital format, and one of the easiest sources to which to gain access, is the Inter-university Consortium for Political and Social Research (ICPSR). The number and quality of options for archival researchers are really quite overwhelming.

Archives are not without flaw, of course. In the first place, there is no such thing as a completely neutral collection. Interpretation is built into any collection. What was thought to be valuable and kept, or useless and discarded, or embarrassing and destroyed? Even huge public databases entail the interpretations of their compilers. But the best archives use explicit and public criteria for inclusion, criteria that specify procedures used to handle missing data or records. Perhaps the most striking advantages of archival collections are that they can be huge and, because they are often created by groups of researchers over decades of work, they can be of exceptional quality. They routinely exceed by several orders of magnitude what solo researchers can accomplish on their own. Still, it is essential that you learn all that you can about how the data in an archive you use were collected and by whom.

On a related note, we don't mean to make using archival data sound too easy. Archival data are rarely as simple to use as a novice might think. Often, the data have not been collected with the needs of researchers in mind. Therefore, much searching and sorting must be done before the archival materials are usable. Even when archives are designed for investigators to consult—as with U.S. Census archives or other national and international statistical databases—the data have *not* been collected with your specific research question in mind. Researchers need to spend substantial time (a few weeks is probably the norm) cleaning, recoding, sorting, and otherwise getting the data ready for use. Still, for many research questions, the benefits can outweigh the costs.

It is not surprising, perhaps, that in fields such as sociology, political science, and economics, generating one's own data is rather uncommon. For example, 130 research articles were published in volumes 72, 73, and 74 (2007, 2008, and 2009) of the *American Sociological Review*. Over three-quarters of these (101 of 130) used data the researchers collected from archives rather than generated themselves. The most common sources were survey archives, census data, and other publically available data, usually as generated by government agencies. When authors generated their own data, the most common methods were interviews and observations, often combined at the interview site.[1]

In brief, social scientists and researchers in related applied disciplines, such as education and business, rely very heavily on archival sources for data. But authors of methodology texts seldom discuss this common fact at any length. Instead, methodology texts more often expound on the virtues of experiments. As our quick review of the leading sociology journal (as well as reviews in other fields) makes clear, we authors

---

[1] These counts are approximate since some articles used data gathered from more than one source.

of methodology texts often do not "preach what we practice."[2] We mostly talk about experiments but we mostly use archives. Even in psychology, where the archival research is less predominant, archival sources play an important role, and not only in reviews of the research literature and meta-analyses.[3]

WHAT KINDS OF ARCHIVAL DATA ARE AVAILABLE FOR RESEARCHERS?

Archival data are found in many places. Some examples include:

- Published textual materials such as books, scholarly journals, magazines, and newspapers.
- Governmental and other public official records including data archives such as the census, the Current Population Survey (CPS), the American Community Survey (ACS), vital statistics from sources including the CDC, and educational data from sources such as the National Center for Educational Statistics (NCES).
- Depositories of data intended for the future use of researchers, such as those maintained by the Library of Congress, presidential libraries, universities, the previously mentioned ICPSR, and so on.
- Records such as school, hospital, police, and organizational files and documents.
- Internet sources such as Web pages and blogs.

WHEN SHOULD YOU COLLECT AND USE PREEXISTING DATA RATHER THAN PRODUCE YOUR OWN?

The obvious answer is when you can better answer your research question by doing so. In order to answer your research question, do you need to generate your own data, or can you answer your question more effectively by using records or publicly available data archives? The answer depends on whether archival materials exist; detective work to find archival data must often precede data collection. If there is no way you could possibly generate data as useful for your research question as that which is available in archives, you *select* among data generated by others.[4] While this in itself can be considered a kind of data generation, it is certainly very different from running experiments,

---

[2]The phrase comes from Bennett, Barth, and Rutherford (2003). Several other studies of what has been published in journals lead to similar conclusions. For example, on experiments in political science, see Druckman et al. (2006). On the same question for journals in education, see Vogt (2007, p. 116). Reviewing publications based on quantitative data in the major journals in economics, political science, and sociology, Herrera and Kapur (2007) conclude that a large majority of these studies are based on datasets collected not by the researchers but by institutions such as government agencies (census, education ministries, etc.) and international organizations (UN, OECD, etc.).

[3]See Trzeniewski (2010); also Gosling and Johnson (2010).

[4]We discuss searching and sampling archives in depth in Chapter 11.

conducting interviews, or surveying respondents. Another consideration is the cost–benefit ratio: taking advantage of archival sources can be very attractive to researchers whose resources are limited, since many archival materials are freely available.

TYPES OF ARCHIVAL RESEARCH

We review the options for types of archival research, and when you might want to engage in one of them, in five general categories:

- Reviews of the research literature, research synthesis, and meta-analysis
- Database archives
- Organizational records
- Textual studies of documents
- New media, including various Internet sources such as Web pages and blogs

Reviews of the Literature, Research Synthesis, and Meta-Analysis[5]

We begin where you will almost inevitably begin your research, with a review of the research literature on your research question. It is a good place to start our review of archival research because of its ubiquity (every researcher has to do literature reviews) and because much of what is true about reviewing the research literature is true of other forms of archival research as well.

It is routine and wholly correct to say that one should incorporate into any research project a systematic review of previous research on the subject.[6] Such reviews are often iterative, with each iteration being more focused than the previous ones. You might begin with an exploratory review of a general subject area to help you refine your research questions and to identify your variables and the methods you could use to study them. Reviews of the literature often also point to databases and other archival sources you could use. Then you might move to a more focused review that concentrates on studies that investigated the particular variables you have decided to study. Finally, it is not at all uncommon to revisit the research literature on your question toward the end of your project. You do this to help with the interpretation of your findings and to integrate them into the broader discussions of the topic in your field.

How extensive and intensive should your literature review be? A review may be a relatively simple introduction to how your research question has been dealt with in the past; this is particularly appropriate when the research reports on your topic are not very numerous or difficult to summarize. On the other hand, your review may be so extensive and detailed that you decide to conduct a review instead of doing primary, data-generating research on your topic. There are several terms to describe different

---

[5]There are many good works describing how to conduct literature reviews and meta-analyses. A brief one is Chapter 17 of Vogt (2007). Good general accounts are Cooper (2010) and Lipsey and Wilson (2001). Of course, our focus is less on "how to" and more on "when to."

[6]Some proponents of grounded theory argue that reviews of previous work get in the way of researchers' attempts to build a theory inductively, from the ground up.

approaches and levels of thoroughness in reviewing the research literature on a topic. Most common, especially in early drafts of dissertations, are what we have elsewhere called *boring lists*, and, among more seasoned researchers, *biased impressionistic summaries*. When should you do one of these? Well, never! But all textbook chiding aside, these are remarkably persistent.[7]

However, it does not follow that every research topic will always require rigorous, time-consuming reviews—but most will. When the research on your topic is limited and the scope of your research is very modest, an *introductory review*, which is a short overview of a sample of the research on your subject, may be appropriate. A *systematic review* is a more methodical and intensive review that plays an important role in elaborating your research question and in shaping the course of your data collection and analysis. A *research synthesis* is an even more rigorous and detailed review; it is often so extensive that you may decide that it can stand on its own; it forms the entirety of your research report. A *meta-analysis* is a type of research synthesis in that it reviews the literature extensively—often attempting to review the total population of studies on the topic. What distinguishes a meta-analysis is that it *quantitatively* summarizes and analyzes its results. Which of these is right for your topic? The answer depends on the nature of the literature on your topic. That answer leads to something of a paradox, but an unavoidable one: to decide what kind of literature review to do, you first have to review the literature.[8]

When to Do an Introductory Review

It is often hard to justify this level of review, even though it is widely practiced. One consequence of the emergence of meta-analysis and other forms of systematic review is that it has generally raised the standards for all reviewing of the literature. Most people would agree, at least in principle, that the research reports in a literature review should be dealt with in as rigorous, reliable, and unbiased a manner as any study of research evidence. If that is the case, an introductory review is appropriate only for a small preliminary study or when your topic is covered in only a small number of studies.

When to Do a Systematic Review

This will probably be the choice for most researchers in most cases. You want to do primary research—experiments, interviews, a survey—and you do not want to replace that original work with a secondary analysis of research reports and of data collected by others. However, if you want to do a good job with your primary research, you should not be casual, biased, or haphazard. Doing primary research is not a license to work in ignorance of what other researchers have done. To make a serious contribution to knowledge, researchers need a thorough command of the research literature on their topics, acquired through a systematic review.

---

[7]See Boote and Beile (2005) for a discussion of the sorry state of reviews of the research literature in dissertations in education.

[8]This is an example of the classic (dating back to Plato) paradox of inquiry. For a blog post on the subject, see *vogtsresearchmethods.blogspot.com*.

When to Do a Research Synthesis or a Meta-Analysis

The main difference between the research synthesis and the meta-analysis is that the latter is necessarily quantitative. Note that you should not try to duck doing a thorough synthesis because your data are qualitative and inappropriate for meta-analysis. Good examples of qualitative syntheses of the research on a topic are readily available in virtually all fields in the social and behavioral sciences.[9]

One circumstance in which a synthesis may be especially appropriate occurs when the research literature is extensive, but there is confusion about what it says or perhaps the research reports actually contradict one another. Conflicting reports can often be due to differences in the studies, differences that the synthesizer is uniquely positioned to discover. Maybe older studies conclude one thing, newer studies another. Maybe laboratory experiments come to different conclusions than field experiments. Perhaps differences occur among subpopulations or sites or contexts: results might vary according to the age of the individuals being studied, research sites (public or private), or the context in which institutions are located (rural, suburban, urban). One of the big outcomes of syntheses, whether of quantitative or qualitative data, is discovering and explaining differences like these. A synthesis can have more external validity than the studies it summarizes, because it synthesizes data pertaining to different methods, groups, and contexts.

Examples from medical research have frequently shown that syntheses can help reduce previous uncertainty about a treatment or intervention. This is perhaps most frequent when the studies being synthesized have mainly been conducted using small groups (as is common in experiments). Only when the data are pooled does the sample become large enough to have enough statistical power to detect an effect or to clarify apparently contradictory results.

When __Not__ to Do a Research Synthesis or a Meta-Analysis

First, of course, there may be a limited number of studies worth synthesizing on your topic. However, consider that this may indicate that researchers in your field do not consider your topic very important. Second, you could have been "scooped." When someone has just conducted a good synthesis or meta-analysis on your topic, there may be little point in conducting another. However, it is pretty rare, even in archival research, to be so totally scooped that there is no point in continuing. Usually, the way you would conceive the synthesis will have some differences with previous work. You will want to consider some variables that others haven't or to operationalize variables in a different way.

The most likely reason that a meta-analysis would be inappropriate to synthesize research on your topic is that the data aren't amenable to the main techniques of meta-analysis. Despite some recent advances in the field, meta-analysis works best when the outcomes data from the studies are fairly simple. Meta-analysis has been most successful summarizing the results of experiments with one dependent variable, one independent variable, and few if any covariates or control variables. That is because the common tools for meta-analysis (standardized mean differences, correlations, and odds ratios)

---

[9]For an exemplary study of how the effects of media violence have been studied, see Gunter (2008).

work best with relatively simple bivariate data. With more complex models it is harder to find appropriate tools for synthesis. Complex statistical models with dozens of variables analyzed with one version or another of regression analysis are especially difficult to summarize across studies because the size of any outcome will depend importantly on the specific variables in the model. Even standardized regression coefficients cannot be properly compared across studies that include different variables in the models.[10] However, what we might call a *mini-meta-analysis* is often a good option. Even if most of the studies are not amenable to quantitative meta-analytic summary, it makes sense to meta-analyze those that can be quantitatively pooled. Then combine the results of the mini-meta-analysis with less quantitative studies before synthesizing the research on your topic.

When to Include Other Sources of Knowledge about Research

There is no need to limit yourself to documents. The idea is to review the *research*, not only the *literature* or documents. As you are learning about a field, it usually doesn't take very long to figure out who the active and respected researchers are. Contact them, especially if you have specific questions about something they have written or you want to ask whether they are planning further investigations that they might be willing to tell you about. Most researchers don't get so much "fan mail" that they will ignore an honest request.

Another source for reviewing the research, not the documents, is scholarly and professional meetings. Unless your topic is very unusual, it is likely to be discussed, at least obliquely, in several sessions of the major scholarly meetings in your field. By attending these sessions you will often hear and perhaps meet the less well-known but highly active members of your research community.

It is often advisable to treat sources such as e-mail correspondence and observations at scholarly meetings as forms of *data* to be researched, not merely as personal contacts supplementing the document analysis. The full gamut of interview and observational methods can be used to make this part of your review of the research systematic too.[11]

When to Challenge, Not Build Upon, Previous Research

It is important to remember that literature reviews, of whatever kind, have many purposes. They are generally described in a fairly uncontroversial way as a means of building upon prior work and contributing your little brick to a growing edifice of knowledge. In the famous words attributed to Newton (and many others),[12] "if I have seen farther, it is by standing on the shoulders of giants." But research reviews have sometimes played a more dramatic and controversial role in the evolution of research on a topic. For example, your thesis might be that previous work in the field is seriously lacking. You review it, not to build on it directly, but to discredit it. Your review is aimed at demonstrating its weaknesses—or at least showing that it contains important "gaps." You may, as someone once put it, "stand on the shoulders of giants—in order to step on their faces."

---

[10] Some progress is being made in this area; see Aloe and Becker (2011).

[11] Onwuegbuzie, Leach, and Collins (2011) in Williams and Vogt (2011) review some options.

[12] Anyone writing a review of the literature should ponder Merton's (1985) erudite and humorous history of this oft-repeated phrase.

A similar approach to reviews of research is taken by scholars conducting theoretical research, scholars who plan to *create* theories, not test them. Where do theories come from? When we use theories to shape our research questions, we probably don't often think of them as arising from research; but they do. They do not fall from the sky into the minds of theorists; they are usually the product of systematic research, typically research reviewing existing research. The theorist's premise is that sometimes we can get new knowledge merely by thinking hard about what we already know. Theoretical physicists are best known for this. They have sometimes discovered relationships among natural phenomena years before laboratory physicists were able to gather evidence about them. Einstein was the famous example; he never collected his own data for any of his published works. But he was an assiduous reader and eager discusser of the research of others. How did that reading and discussing lead to path-breaking theories? The process is more than a little mysterious, but it involves a lot of reflection followed by leaps of insight followed by more reflection. How does one prepare oneself to increase the likelihood of having an insight; on what does one reflect? The answer is, by studying previous research. Ultimately the value of theoretical research depends on whether one's insights are of use to others in the field. Even if you happen not to have a flash of insight that leads to a path-breaking theory, your systematic review of the research literature gives you something useful to show for your efforts.

DATABASE ARCHIVES

The number and scope of public and quasi-public statistical archives are really quite staggering. These data are often collected by governments. When governments survey citizens and institutions, responding is often mandatory—whether the data are crime statistics, higher education enrollments, stocks and commodities trading, or vital (births and deaths) statistics.[13] That means that the response rates are unusually high. International organizations such as the United Nations or the Organization for Economic Cooperation and Development also collect extensive data, usually from governments. It is difficult for governments to carry out their functions without such data, and it would also be hard for citizens to hold governments accountable without it. The expansion of and continued demand for such data is relentless. How good are these data? Collecting data in ways that are perfectly objective may be an ideal, but, like most ideals, it can never be fully realized. On the other hand, the people who work in statistical agencies have a vested interest in being accurate. In fact, even crooks need to keep good records if they are to effectively plan their campaigns to rob us more.

None of this means that such data are without flaws. And the fact that several of the best-known national and international databases have serious weaknesses is a legitimate cause for concern.[14] Hence, researchers, delighted as they may be at the availability of such wonderful datasets, need to be critical in their use of them. Even when a given database is the state-of-the-art source for a particular question, responsible researchers will be informed consumers, not merely downloaders, of the data they use. It has

---

[13] For the state of official statistics in the United States see Torrieri (2007) and in the United Kingdom see Holt (2007). For a good example of the use of UN data to investigate a research question, see Patel, Roberts, Guy, Lee-Jones, and Conteh (2009).

[14] Herrera and Kapur (2007) provide an important review.

been the case that serious scholars working for public agencies have labored to improve databases,[15] but the extraordinarily demanding nature of that work makes it the exception rather than the rule for all but the most important public databases. What should you do? If you use a large database archive, be sure to read all the technical literature accompanying it and make sure your literature review focuses on the notes and appendices of the work of other researchers using it.

Finally, one shouldn't assume that computerized data archives contain only quantitative data. Photography and oral history archives are two examples of qualitative data sources that the archival researcher may wish to use. For ethnographic data, the granddaddy of all databases is the Human Relations Area Files (HRAF), founded and housed at Yale since 1949.[16] One of the best archives of qualitative data (mostly interview data) is the marvelous archive called Qualidata. This is maintained by the Economic and Social Data Service in the United Kingdom. Its resources are usually freely available to qualified researchers.[17] Social science researchers (except for historians) are much less likely to use archival qualitative data than quantitative databases, but there is more of it than most social and behavioral scientists realize. While there is sometimes reluctance among qualitatively oriented researchers to use oral history and interview archives, often on ethical grounds, researchers studying qualitative data are increasingly influenced by the general trend toward using ever larger and more systematic archival data sources.[18]

Note that it is possible to make *predictions* to test a theory using archival sources. The researcher predicts what will be found in the archival data. Because this is not a prediction about a future event, it is sometimes called a "retrodiction." And this sort of prediction is widely practiced in economics, political science, and sociology. For example, to test Durkheim's theory of egoistic suicide, data were obtained from the CDC about U.S. suicide rates in the early weeks of the Gulf War of 1991. As the theory predicted, suicide statistics dipped during the war and returned to their baseline levels after it ended.[19] *Causal inference* is also possible using documentary evidence. One potential cause of the rising incidence of autism was a mercury-based preservative called thimerosal, which was once commonly added to vaccines. The additive was rarely used in the United States after 2001; it had earlier been removed from vaccines in Canada, Sweden, and Denmark in the 1990s. But there has been no decline in the incidence of autism since this presumptive cause was removed. The causal inference is strong and clear: if thimerosal caused autism, its removal should have led to a drop in the occurrence of autism. It didn't; ergo, it wasn't the cause.[20]

---

[15] Clifford Adelman's work with the National Longitudinal Study is one example (see Lin and Vogt, 1996).

[16] The website is *www.yale.edu/hraf/collections*.

[17] The website is: *www.esds.ac.uk/qualidata*.

[18] See Parry and Mauthner (2004) for claims that using such archives may not be ethically appropriate. For a contrary view, see Fielding (2004).

[19] McKenna and Vogt (1995). In some respects this was a prediction in a stricter sense of the term, because the data were just becoming available as the paper was being written.

[20] See *www.who.int./vaccine_safety* and *www.cdc.gov/vaccinesafety* for summaries.

When Should You Use Such Database Archives?

As always, the first recommendation is to follow the exigencies of your research question. It is almost always a good idea to make inquiries about whether appropriate archival sources exist. If you are a solo researcher and your research question requires a large nationally representative sample, there may be few alternatives. Like most methodologists, we routinely recommend letting your research question be your guide, "the dictatorship of the problem,"[21] in other terms. But we know that this is sometimes naïve. Researchers do not always draw their decision trees starting with the problem, topic, or question. It is actually quite common in the social sciences to shape one's research question so as to take advantage of an especially good dataset. This kind of opportunism, taking advantage of an opportunity, is hardly "wrong," even though it is rarely considered the ideal.

When Should You *Not* Use Database Archives?

Obviously, of course, you shouldn't use them when there aren't any data archives that contain sufficient data for your topic. Or, if data exist, they might be too old to address your research question. The age of data doesn't always stop researchers from making contemporary claims. Even when the most recent case available in the dataset is 10 years old, it is not uncommon to read a phrase in a research report such as "the data clearly indicate that the problem *is* . . ." with unabashed avoidance of the past tense. Old data should be put into historical context. If you don't want to do that and your approach requires very up-to-date and recent data, you'll probably have to collect it yourself. To get recent data, you may have to give up sample size and representativeness. For some research questions, this could be an effective trade—for others, not so much.

ORGANIZATIONAL RECORDS

Although the use of survey archives and government documents predominates in sociology, economics, and political science, there are several other good sources of archival data and therefore ways to do archival research. In pursuit of a research question, perhaps initially just searching for background information, you may find that a great deal of data is already available on your subject in organizational or institutional records. Sometimes these require special permission to gain access, but often the records you need can be obtained from public sources. For example, Leahey studied the determinants of academic salaries—particularly two variables that had gone largely unstudied in previous research.[22] Earlier research examined the influence of faculty members' years of experience, research productivity, and the types of university they worked in, as well as their gender and ethnicity. To this list Leahey added research specialization and research visibility. Neither had been studied before for the two disciplines she examined in depth: sociology and linguistics. Her study is instructive, because nearly all of her data came from publically available documents and records. She took a 20% prob-

---

[21] Vogt (2008).

[22] Leahey (2007).

ability sample of faculty at research universities. The sampling frame was lists provided by professional organizations and department websites. Evidence about research productivity was gathered from electronic databases: *Sociological Abstracts* for sociology faculty and *Linguistics and Language Behavior Abstracts* for linguistics faculty. The keyword descriptors listed for each publication indexed in these resources were used to construct the measure of specialization. The measure of visibility was constructed using citation indices. Finally, because salary data for faculty in public universities are public information, Leahey was able to gather this from public records. Thus, the author did not directly use a database generated by others, but her sources were organizational records, publicly available.

When collecting data from organizational records that are not openly available, it becomes especially important to be very specific about your data collection methods.[23] Unlike when you use publicly available databases, which other researchers can access at will, organizational records will rarely be available to other researchers. Sharing one's data and the methods used to collect them is one of a professional researcher's highest responsibilities. As the old adage goes, "In God we trust; all others must show their data." It is quite common for researchers to agree that it is a good idea to describe their methods and the rationale for them, but it is less often believed that the data themselves should be easily accessible to other researchers. Jeremy Freese[24] makes the strongest case we know of for doing so.[25] It is not exactly a new idea. For example, several important economics journals make data availability a condition of publication. And *Demography*, a sociological journal, has a similar requirement. Freese argues that publishing one's data makes social research a *social* activity and not something at the discretion of the individual researchers. And, it requires little effort to make one's data accessible to others, since several online data archives have been created for the purpose. Of course, we are not arguing for making organizational records available. That would likely violate confidentiality and the trust organizations placed in the researchers. But the databases constructed from those records could be routinely made available.[26] To be trustworthy, the data and the criteria used to collect and analyze them have to be accessible to other researchers. As Freese points out, the less your data are available, the less persuasive your findings will be to readers skeptical of your conclusions.

TEXTUAL STUDIES OF DOCUMENTS

The world is awash in documents, and this is hardly a recent phenomenon: books, newspapers, magazines, diaries, contracts, and treaties are a few examples. Although much archival data is quantitative and comes in computerized forms such as spreadsheets, when the media are more traditional and the reading is more conventional, the documents are usually referred to as texts and the research as textual analysis. After your

---

[23] See Moss (2009).

[24] Freese (2007).

[25] Not all would agree; see Denzin (2009).

[26] An exemplary case of this is the work of Bowen, Chingos, and McPherson (2009). They pooled institutional records from 68 universities to construct two new databases; these are available online along with technical appendices that describe how they used them to reach their conclusions.

research question has led you to a particular type of document, then you need to choose your orientation to the documents. This is also mainly determined by your research question.

When Should You Study Phenomena, When Texts, and When Contexts?

Three broad subjects can be studied through textual analysis:

1. The *phenomena* that the texts refer to, as when texts describing a political movement are analyzed to learn about the movement;

2. The *texts* themselves, as when memoirs are read as examples of a literary genre; and

3. The *context*, as when the main issue the researcher is interested in is how context might influence a text, such as how a law (the text) might be influenced by social prejudice.

Actually, these three objects of study overlap, but their differences illustrate important distinctions in research strategy. Contexts may influence texts; texts may describe non-textual phenomena; and contexts can influence phenomena, as depicted in Figure 5.1.

Do you study texts because you are interested in what they are about, or because you are interested in the texts themselves, or because you are interested in how contexts shape texts? For example, do you study political documents because you are interested in politics, because you are interested in the rhetorical devices used in political documents, or because you are interested in how political forces shape the ideas expressed in the documents? All three are legitimate kinds of questions, but it is advisable to pick a strategy or an emphasis to add clarity to a research project. Meta-analysis is a good example. It works mainly with documents, but it is highly focused on the phenomena being studied in those documents. In the distinction among contexts, texts, and phenomena, meta-analysis is mostly concentrated on the phenomena, in this case, the research findings.

Of course, one could also conduct a review of the literature because one is interested in the character of analysis that is used in the documents or because one is interested in the history of the discipline as represented by those documents. For example, in recent years, one theme in the writing about the development of the social sciences, especially sociology, has been the importance of the "ethnographic turn." According to many accounts, sociology has been transformed in recent decades by a greater emphasis

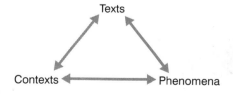

FIGURE 5.1. Subjects for textual analysis.

on qualitative research, particularly ethnographic methods of data collection and analysis.[27] To investigate this ethnographic turn, one group of authors did a review of publications in major sociology journals.[28] Their goal was not that of a meta-analysis, in which one wants to sum up the substantive findings on a specifically defined topic. Rather, the authors wanted to examine the recent history of their discipline. Their conclusions were quite interesting. First, phenomena: despite the lack of agreement about what "ethnography" actually is, there is considerable consensus in the major journals that many more ethnographic studies are being conducted now than in the past. Second, texts: some of the change from past years has involved the embrace of the *term* ethnography, which is now often used broadly to mean nearly any method of qualitative data collection and analysis. Third, contexts: ethnographic methods have expanded in U.S. sociology journals more by adding new journals than by being incorporated into older journals.

When to Use Textual Archival Research

It is actually virtually impossible to avoid textual archival research altogether. Even the most quantitatively oriented social science research typically contains as many words as numbers, so when you summarize this for your review of the literature, you will need to do some kind of textual summary as well as a quantitative summary. And, when your main research design is aimed at *generating* verbal data, these data often take on an archival character. It is quite common for researchers first to *generate* the data that they *subsequently* treat more or less archivally. For example, it is routine in interview research to make audio recordings and then transcribe the tapes. At some point these transcribed texts become fixed. They become "objective" in the sense that, while they remain open to interpretation, altering them would be dishonest. Similar processes are often at work in regard to observational researchers' field notes. Many researchers believe that the notes are better than, and take priority over, memory. It is also increasingly common for the coding and analysis of the interview transcripts and field notes to be done by members of the research team other than those who collected the raw data.[29]

When *Not* to Use Textual Archival Research

Again, of course, when textual archives are insufficient for treating your topic, you need to consider other approaches. Or, your topic may be so recent that the sometimes slow process of assembling textual archives lags far behind what you need to discuss a pressing current issue. If you are interviewing or observing lived experiences or your research question requires that you interact with persons, texts are not going to be your primary source. Still, eventually your data will probably become textual—as interview transcripts or field notes, for example. Thus, data you generated at the design and sampling stages of your research will probably become textual at the coding and analysis stages. You will be coding and analyzing your own "archives."

---

[27]See Gans (1999).

[28]Culyba, Heimer, and Petty (2004).

[29]For examples, see Kurasaki (2000), Weston et al. (2001), and Sigaud (2008).

NEW MEDIA, INCLUDING INTERNET SOURCES

Internet sources provide researchers with a vast new arena of archival research. An excellent example is the Web log or *blog*. Blogs are online essays or diaries. They have proliferated at an astonishing rate since they first emerged in the 1990s. While they resemble documents that social researchers have long used in their work, they are distinct in several ways. Historians and biographers have long used diaries, journals, and other private papers in their research. One huge difference between those resources and blogs is that blogs are public as well as being personal papers. They seem to straddle the border between public and private. Sociologists and psychologists have also sometimes used diaries in their research. But these have usually been solicited from participants by researchers, not something that research subjects generated on their own. Another difference is that the conventional diaries used in the past have been rare and precious. But we have a glut of blogs. Rather than painstaking searches or anxious solicitation of diaries, researchers now have to resort to sorting and winnowing using technologies as new as the materials being hunted. The problem is finding, among hundreds of thousands of possibilities, a set of blogs on the topic in which you are interested. As we will see in the chapter on sampling archival sources, high-tech solutions, such as Web crawlers, are often necessary.[30]

Websites are another obvious source. There are literally billions of them. Just about any social movement or group will have websites devoted to it. Consequently, scholars who conduct research on political action groups, social movements, game enthusiasts, and so on will find websites a potentially useful source.

A form of website conducive to analysis is the Web forum or discussion board. Such sites are topical and attract users or members eager to share their stories, feelings, information, and advice with each other. For example, one such forum deals with borderline personality disorder, and is specifically designed for people who regularly deal with sufferers of this disorder.[31] Separate message boards on this site are set up for new members, family members, friends, spouses and significant others, those divorcing or separating, and those rebuilding their lives after separating from the individual with the disorder. Users post profiles with basic demographic data, and the site includes a world map showing where users currently online are located. Users start discussion topics or "threads," and other users reply. The site provides quantitative data regarding the forum traffic: which sections get the most postings, which members post most often, top topics by number of replies, top topics by number of views, average time online per day, and other statistics.

A researcher might be interested in the personality disorder itself (the phenomenon). In that case, textual data from specific informational postings might be useful to study. The researcher might instead be interested in the type of discourse in which the users engage (the text). In that scenario, the data regarding forum traffic might be of great interest and the researcher may want to follow specific discussion threads in depth. Or, the researcher might be interested in the forum environment and how it influences communication (the context). In that case, forum postings could be compared with other forms of communication regarding the personality disorder phenomenon.

---

[30]Hookway (2008) provides a good introduction.

[31]*www.bpdcentral.com/index.php.*

A final example is online economic activity. Many economic transactions take place online. Studying these requires online data that the researcher samples and analyzes, but does not generate. The fact that these transactions occur rapidly, and that the buyers and sellers can view one another's actions in real time, has changed the nature of markets, which can be studied with online data archives. Studying them can require elaborate statistical and graphical techniques, but the data are readily available.[32]

As the online world grows, so does the scope of potential research topics dealing with it. Access to this world is rarely available other than by going online yourself. Researchers in the social and behavioral sciences are probably most likely to use online sources to do archival research on populations that would be otherwise difficult or impossible to contact, such as newly emerging social and political groups or movements. Among the main attractions of new media archival research is the fact that the data are available not only to researchers but to everyone. This kind of transparency and openness has implications for democratizing knowledge production and consumption, which as Deweyians, we can only applaud.

CONCLUSION

This chapter has reviewed archival designs using five broad categories: summarizing the research literature, using database archives, investigating organizational records, undertaking textual studies of documents, and exploring new media as a source of data. While the design problems and prospects can be quite distinct among these five types, there are also several overriding themes that apply to designs taking any of these approaches. First, in these designs you select secondary data; the study is not "primary" in the sense that the data are initially collected by you. Second, researchers frequently resort to these designs because there is no reasonable alternative; they couldn't possibly collect better (or equally good) data on their own. As compared to what a solo researcher or even a well-funded team could collect in perhaps one year, archives vastly extend the range of data available, including large, nationally representative samples containing thousands and even millions of cases. Third, archival research can have three distinct foci, depending on the use to which the data are put; these may be addressed singly or in various combinations: the data as representation of external phenomena; the social forces and contexts that create and shape the data; and the data as a topic of study in its own right. For example, one might study organizational records because one is interested in organizations, one wishes to learn how social and organizational variables influence data records, or one wishes to undertake an analysis of the nature and evolution of organizational records. Finally, as vast as archival resources are, all archives are limited, incomplete, and biased. The absence of data in archives is not proof (though it is an indicator) of the absence of phenomena in the world. The table on page 102 summarizes these and related points concerning when to use archival designs.

---

[32] For example, Hyde, Jank, and Shmueli (2006) studied *eBay.com* auctions this way.

SUGGESTIONS FOR FURTHER READING

While some archival research requires travel to collections of data or documents, much of it can be done without ever leaving the library and often, given Internet resources, without ever leaving your desk at home. That does not mean gathering data produced by others is somehow inferior to generating your own or that it is an easier kind of research, as a review of the following suggested readings makes clear.

Reviewing the research literature on your subject is a well-established tradition in the social sciences, but systematic reviews and meta-analyses date mostly from the 1970s, specifically to the work of Gene Glass and Robert Rosenthal (foreshadowed in some earlier articles by Karl Pearson). Good books on the methods of meta-analysis and other ways of synthesizing research came quickly. In 1984 Light and Pillemer published what is still a very important discussion, *Summing Up: The Science of Reviewing Research*. It is a font of wisdom that we continue to consult and recommend to our students. A good textbook is Cooper's *Research Synthesis and Meta-Analysis* (4th edition, 2010). A somewhat more advanced textbook, but still accessible to the non-specialist, is Lipsey and Wilson's *Practical Meta-Analysis* (2001).

There are more published guidelines for researchers conducting research reviews than for other types of archival research. Very often researchers seeking advice will have to search in examples of actual research rather than use textbooks and handbooks, which, although it can be more work, can also be more rewarding. In any case, a few good recent works on using database archives to conduct your research are available. Vartarian's *Secondary Data Analysis* (2010), although focused on examples from social work research, is a good general overview, and the edited collection by Trzeniewski, *Secondary Data Analysis: An Introduction for Psychologists* (2010), is also quite helpful.

Textual analysis of documents is as old as documents. Diplomats perusing treaties and lawyers looking for legal precedents are familiar examples. Advances that began with Renaissance scholarship were ratcheted up when Mosteller and Wallace published their analysis of the Federalist Papers, *Influence and Disputed Authorship: The Federalist*, in 1964. Not just any analysis of textual content will count as *content analysis* in the strict sense of the term insisted upon by those who advocate doing content analyses with computer software. Neuendorf's *The Content Analysis Guidebook* (2002) is a good example of work using this approach, the influence of which is very rapidly increasing.

Not surprisingly the fewest traditional resources (textbooks, handbooks, reference works) are available for the most recent type of archival research, that which uses new Internet-based media and documents. A good place to begin is the collection edited by Gosling and Johnson, *Advanced Methods for Conducting Online Behavioral Research* (2010). Published by the American Psychological Association, it naturally focuses on research in that field, but its suggestions are broadly applicable to other disciplines.

CHAPTER 5 SUMMARY TABLE

Reviews of the literature, research synthesis, and meta-analysis

When to do an introductory review	• For a very small or preliminary study. • When your topic is covered by only a small number of studies.
When to do a systematic review	• Necessary for most studies.
When to do a research synthesis or meta-analysis	• When the research literature is extensive but contradictory or confusing. • When you want to pool data across studies with relatively simple outcomes data, creating more statistical power to detect effects.
When to include other research knowledge	• When you have specific questions to ask researchers. • When information from scholarly meetings is relevant to your study.

DATABASE ARCHIVES

When to use database archives	• When your research requires a large, nationally representative sample.

ORGANIZATIONAL RECORDS

When to use organizational records	• When records are available (either publicly or with permission) that match your research subject.

TEXTUAL STUDIES OF DOCUMENTS

When to use textual archival data	• To study phenomena of interest. • To learn about aspects of the texts themselves. • To learn about the environment (context) and its influence. • When you have collected field notes, transcribed interviews, or collected artifacts during a field study.

NEW MEDIA, INCLUDING INTERNET SOURCES

When to use new media	• To research phenomena in populations that would be hard to contact or observe through other means. • When you need current rather than historical data.

CHAPTER 6

When to Use
Combined Research Designs

In the previous five design chapters, we have often emphasized a key point: your research questions guide your decisions about how to design your study.

In Chapter 1, we discussed when to select a survey design for research questions that seek brief answers to structured questions. In Chapter 2, we described how interviewing can provide data for those types of research questions that require in-depth answers from informants. In Chapter 3, we recommended that you choose to use experiments if your research question includes variables that you can manipulate and allows random assignment of participants or cases to control and experimental groups. In Chapter 4, we discussed how participant or naturalistic observation can provide data for research questions that seek to describe and explore phenomena in particular contexts. Finally, in Chapter 5, we explored ways that archives can yield data to answer specific research questions for which archival sources are more complete or more pertinent than data you could collect yourself.

But what if your research questions are more complex or have multiple parts? What if a single study design approach cannot adequately provide the data you need to answer your questions? That is when you must consider *combining research designs*. Combining designs is not simply a matter of using two or three methods to gather data. Some up-front thought must be given to the strengths and weaknesses of various methods in relation to your research questions, as well as to the order and logistics of how you will employ your selected methods, and how the methods will logically complement each other.

In this chapter, we continue the focus on matching designs to your research questions, but now with the added considerations involved in combining designs.

SIMPLE VERSUS MULTIPART RESEARCH QUESTIONS

Many research questions, even if addressing important or controversial topics, may still be stated rather simply, and they can sometimes be addressed using straightforward, single-method research designs. In practice, you may actually need to combine two or more research methods to adequately answer these "simple" questions, even when the questions themselves are essentially direct and uncomplicated. Other research questions require multiple levels of inquiry, whether stated explicitly or by implication. Table 6.1 provides contrasting examples of simple and multipart research questions that address similar topics. Our discussion in this chapter focuses primarily on multipart research questions.

Just to be clear: when we classify these sample research questions as "simple," we do not mean that finding the answers will be *easy*, or that such questions are less valuable than others. By simple, we mean that these questions imply a straightforward research design using a single *dominant* method to gather data that may be analyzed in a straightforward way. While even the simplest designs may encounter complicated problems (such as missing historical data or low survey response rates), the designs themselves are still simple.

In contrast, the research questions that we classify as "multipart" imply several layers of inquiry. For example, the multipart race relations question in Table 6.1 has two parts, explicitly stated: first, determining the trend in interracial marriage rates over the past 20 years, and second, determining factors contributing to that trend. This type of question automatically implies a design that combines at least two methods: archival research on marriage trends and survey and/or interview research to identify potential contributing factors. A third design component is also implied: analyzing the data to determine the actual contribution of each identified factor.

The research question about whether there is a positive-outcomes bias in reviewing research articles can be (and has been) studied with fairly straightforward experiments[1] in which reviewers are randomly assigned to two groups. One group reads an article reporting a statistically significant difference between two treatments. The second group reads an otherwise identical article except that it reports no statistically significant difference between the two treatments. If the experiment addressing the simple question determines that a bias exists, then the researcher can turn to the more complicated question of why this difference in reviewer behavior occurs. Interviews with the experimental participants could be used to investigate the more complicated question: what were the reviewers' reasons for their decisions?

The multipart health care delivery question is more subtle; while it might initially look like a question that suits a survey design, it also asks for information about change over time. Even the survey component itself can be complex. Since surveys take place in the present, survey data could provide the current status of patient attitudes and beliefs. But to build the survey, you might have to interview patients to determine the appropriate attitude and belief questions to include in the survey. To get the historical perspective implied in the question, you would need to mine archival data sources—possibly past surveys, patient satisfaction questionnaires, or other health care system sources. And to

---

[1] Emerson et al. (2010).

TABLE 6.1. Contrasting Simple and Complex Research Questions

Topic	Simple research questions	Multipart research questions
Race relations	What proportion of marriages in the population is interracial? How does this compare with the proportion 10 and 20 years ago?	How has the proportion of interracial marriages in the population changed over the past 20 years and what factors have contributed to this change?
College access and completion	How does the 6-year college graduation rate compare by gender, race, and socioeconomic status?	What effects do student support programs have on student motivation, resources, and capacity to complete college?
Bias in research reports	Are submitted research articles that report positive, statistically significant results more likely to get published?	Why do reviewers rate research articles that report statistically significant differences more highly than articles that do not do so?
Program effectiveness	What percentage of program participants completed all program elements at the satisfactory level?	How do program participants apply their learning in the workplace after program completion?
Business organization dynamics	What financial factors predict the impending turnover of upper management staff in not-for-profit organizations?	Why do upper management staff members leave not-for-profit organizations?
Health care delivery	How have health care costs changed over the past 20 years?	How have patient attitudes and beliefs regarding the quality of their health care changed over the past 20 years?

determine "change," you would need to make sure that most, if not all, of your attitude and belief factor data were comparable across the years.

In fact, with multipart questions, the first step is to "dissect" the question into its component parts and analyze the research implications of each part. As you do this, at least two scenarios could emerge. On the one hand, you might decide to pare down your research question and just study one of the parts. This could simplify your research design and take you back to one of the more straightforward designs we have discussed in previous chapters. On the other hand, you might embrace the complexities of your question and all the design requirements it implies, with the expectation that your findings will be of significant value to researchers and/or practitioners. In other words, don't let a multipart research question scare you; careful parsing of the question into its component parts can lead to a clean and elegant research design, in turn leading to results with practical applications. Many social problems are indeed complex, and might only be usefully addressed with multipart research questions.

The approach that involves conducting utilitarian research with practical significance has been termed *pragmatism*. *Pragmatic* can be taken to mean practical and useful, but not necessarily neat and straightforward. In order to conduct this type of research, you have to be practical about how you seek your answers; that is, you must be willing to use whatever methods are logical and useful, even if that means combining research designs in new ways. Being too dogmatic—for example, exhibiting too much adherence to seeking simple correlations among observed phenomena—can cause researchers to find "significant" but, practically speaking, meaningless connections.[2]

The following section offers guidance about when it may be a good idea to use a combined research design.

WHEN TO COMBINE RESEARCH DESIGNS

There are at least six reasons to use combined research designs.[3] These are shown in Table 6.2, along with examples for each reason. As you look at the "Reason" column in Table 6.2, you can imagine the types of research questions that might go with each, which brings us back to our earlier comments in this chapter: your research questions guide the research design, and may lead you to choose a combined design.

TYPES AND QUALITIES OF COMBINED DESIGNS

If you do choose a combined research design, you have some important decisions to make about how and when to implement different research methods, so as to gather the data you need to answer your research questions. Knowing the strengths and weaknesses of each of your methods is particularly important in combining designs: two weak methods, even if somewhat complementary, may not fully compensate to create a strong combined design.

When Should You Sequence Your Design Methods?

Let's say you have a research question that conforms to Reason #2 from Table 6.2; that is, you want to use one research method to inform another research method. Ideally, after you employ both methods, you will get better (more valid) results. However, as you can see in the example given for Reason #2, there are two ways to go about this: either do the survey first and use it to inform the interview process, or do the interviews first and use them to inform the survey process. How do you know which to do? This is where you must think again about your research questions and the types of data you need to answer them.

If your research is attempting to generalize your results to the overall population, then it makes sense to use your interview process first, to give you good ideas for how to construct the best possible survey. Then you select your random survey sample and conduct your survey to collect your data. After all, as we discussed in Chapter 1, often the main purpose of surveying is to generalize your findings to a broader population, so it makes sense for this to be the last big step of your data collection.

---

[2]The philosophical basis of pragmatism can be found in the works of George Herbert Meade and John Dewey, among many others.

[3]Jennifer Greene and her colleagues provide excellent discussions on how to blend research methods to answer specific types of research questions. The information in this section is adapted from their work, with the addition of a case study for theory building, which we added. See Greene (2007) and Greene, Caracelli, and Graham (1989).

TABLE 6.2. When to Combine Research Designs

Reason	Examples of combined design(s)
1. When you want to corroborate results obtained from other methods	• Conduct comparative analyses of two quantitative datasets, a set of survey responses and a set of ratings by observers, to see if they confirm each other's findings.
2. When you want to use one method to inform another method	• Use interview data from selected informants to guide the construction of a survey for a broader sample of the population. • Conversely, use survey data to construct interview questions that can probe in greater depth areas of inquiry raised in the survey.
3. When you want to continuously look at a question from new angles, and look for unexpected findings and/or potential contradictions	• Reanalyze multiple sources of archival data in several previously untried ways, revealing new patterns formerly undetected or ignored. • Use observational research data to suggest relations among variables to test in a laboratory setting.
4. When you want to elaborate, clarify, or build on findings from other methods	• Use public school performance reports of state test results to identify schools that are outperforming those with similar demographics, then conduct observational research to look for effective practices that may be contributing to the results.
5. When you want to "tell the full story" in an area of inquiry	• Conduct a survey of hospital patients regarding their perceptions of care; follow with interviews of selected patients with differing survey responses; analyze public hospital complaint records; document patient care information and services provided by mail, in person, and on websites; interview hospital personnel regarding perceptions of patient care; observe public examples of patient care scenarios.
6. When you want to develop a theory about a phenomenon of interest	• Conduct a comparative case study of two organizations that exhibit contrasting examples of the phenomenon you are studying. For example, compare the social capital developed and deployed by guidance staff in (1) a high school with a philosophy of brokering resources for students and (2) a high school with a philosophy of serving as a clearinghouse for resources that students must access of their own volition.

Conversely, if your research is attempting to examine in more depth those things that people report on forced-choice survey questions, you are asking a much different question. In this case, your survey would be administered first, telling you what "most people" think about the survey issues. Now your real interest is to test whether there is more to know than just the relatively simple forced-choice answers gathered from the survey. Questions like "why did people answer this way?" and "how did people choose their answers?" are not easily explored with surveys themselves. Subsequent in-depth interviewing of selected survey respondents, possibly using follow-up probing for interesting responses, can provide much more detail and insight into the survey answers. You could select interviewees by how they answered the surveys (providing you have created a means to identify them). For example, you could select them based on the demographic information they provided, or based on their answers to particular survey questions related most directly to your research interest. In this case, your survey answers are informing your interview process.

The same thought process applies if you are considering a research study that combines any of the approaches we have discussed in Chapters 1 through 5. How you state and dissect your research question should logically determine the sequence of your design methods.

For example, one study sought to examine child custody decisions as determined by courts in divorce cases, and their subsequent effects on families.[4] In this design, the researchers included four sequential phases:

1. Phase 1 conducted an archival statistical review of the body of recent custody cases to determine the types of custody issues being handled and their relative frequencies and respective outcomes;

2. Phase 2 selected a subsample of cases and conducted archival case studies to investigate in more depth how cases were handled by the courts;

3. Phase 3 surveyed the population of parents involved in the larger set of recent cases to gain knowledge about their perceptions of positive and negative aspects of their court experiences; and

4. Phase 4 interviewed a subset of parents from Phase 3 to garner in-depth understanding of the issues these parents faced related to the custody decisions.

When Should One Design Method Predominate?

A companion consideration to deciding the order of your research methods is that of deciding which, if any, of the chosen methods will be "dominant." Again, depending on your research questions, your research design may have more than one component, but some parts get more to the heart of your question than others.

Let's consider Reason #4 from Table 6.2, in which we want to elaborate, clarify, or build on findings from other methods. The example we provided is from an actual study we conducted to seek effective practices of K–12 schools that outperformed schools with similar student demographics. We started with an analysis of multiple years of publicly available archived state test data. The purpose of this step was to find schools serving high percentages of low-income students whose aggregate state test scores were consistently higher than those of other schools with similar high-poverty student populations. But our main purpose was not to show simply that such schools exist; we were more interested in knowing *how* these schools were fostering such strong test performance.

Our predominant research design step was a comparative case study of high-performing schools and average-performing schools: conducting interviews and participant observations, collecting and analyzing archival materials, developing individual school case studies, and comparing our findings across cases. In this example, the first step of quantitatively analyzing the archived test data was obviously necessary—we had to identify the schools before we could recruit them for the study and visit them. But

---

[4] May (2007).

our case study research addressed the core of our research interest—finding out how the "outlier" schools attained their sustained high performance.[5]

In many discussions of mixed method research designs, the underlying assumption is that the "mixing" always involves combining quantitative and qualitative methods, as in the high-performing school study described above. Elaborate typologies have been proposed to help determine and classify the predominant methods within mixed method designs.[6] Practically speaking, however, you could certainly combine two or more qualitative approaches, or two or more quantitative approaches in a single study design. For our purposes, we refer to all of these options as "combined designs." The question of predominance of one method or another within that design is considered more in relation to your research questions and how they may best be addressed than in relation to assigning a classification or "type" to your combined design.

When Should Your Design Methods Interact or Be Used Iteratively?

In combined designs, the various methods will inevitably be interactive in some way. As we have already mentioned, they may fall into a linear sequence, with one method following another in predetermined order within your design. Alternatively, your research question could have multiple parts, one addressed with one method and the other with a different method, both of which can be conducted simultaneously. In the latter case, data collected from the two methods would most likely not be combined until the analysis stage of your study.

It would not be unusual for your methods to need to be reiterated several times, when one method informs the other. Let's say, for example, that survey research is your predominant method, and you intend to seek broadly generalizable results. It would obviously benefit you to hone your survey to a high level of quality. You might combine survey and interview methods in a linear, repeating sequence: (1) interview a small sample of potential participants to determine and/or refine survey questions; (2) administer the survey as a pilot; (3) use the survey results to formulate in-depth interview questions for a broader sample of informants; and (4) revise your survey based on the interview results and administer it again to your sample of respondents drawn from the target population.

Very often in combined qualitative designs, findings from one method provide clues for how to conduct other parts of the research, or to extend it further. To return to the school study we referenced earlier in this chapter, the cross-case analysis led to a set of universal effective practices documented in every high-performing school, and missing or incomplete in the average schools. As an extension of this study, some researchers have taken these findings and created a "school audit" or inventory, which other schools can use to determine which, if any, of these validated practices they are currently using. School personnel can use the results to formulate improvement plans, and researchers can then use the school audit data to study how and why these effective practices are present or absent and under what conditions.[7] The potential opportunity for interactivity and/or repetition across methods in order to increase the validity of findings is an important positive attribute of combined research designs.

---

[5] Haeffele, Baker, and Pacha (2007).

[6] See, for example, Johnson and Ogwuegbuzie (2004).

[7] *www.nc4ea.org/index.cfm/e/initiatives.corework_diagnostics.*

Case study research is a classic example of employing combined and iterative methods. By their very nature, case studies utilize multiple methods to gather data from a variety of sources: interviews, observations, archives, questionnaires, and often various forms of quantitative data such as financial or performance data. As we discuss further in our companion volume, in case study research, data analysis begins almost immediately and early findings serve to continuously refine both the research questions and the data collection process. Good sources for case study designs in various areas of social science research have been provided by Stake, Yin, Ragin, and George and Bennett.[8]

LOGISTICAL CONSIDERATIONS IN COMBINED RESEARCH DESIGNS

When Should You Consider Engaging More Than One Researcher?

It is quite possible that when you develop a combined research design, you will not personally have the expertise to conduct all the components within your design. In this case, you become somewhat of a "general contractor," finding experts to take on particular aspects of the study. However, portioning out all the data collection may not be a good option; usually the principal investigator must participate to a high degree in the data collection process in order to later perform the data analysis.

One such study was conducted in Britain to investigate the financial implications of the death of a spouse.[9] The study united two researchers, one with expertise in interview research, and one with expertise in archival database analysis. The interview component was appropriate to the research focus because of both the personal and financial consequences of losing a spouse. The archival component relied on longitudinal data from the British Household Panel Survey, which compiled an extensive database from sequential interviews over 13 years of a nationally representative sample of adults, and provided general financial trends for both couples and widowed respondents. The investigators were able to bring their different areas of expertise to bear on their shared research question.[10]

Another possibility is that the actual on-the-ground work involved may be too much for one person to handle within a given time frame. This is especially common when combining designs, which usually have sequential or simultaneous components, causing a lot of scheduling logistics and juggling of effort. Some types of data collection, such as interviewing and conducting observations, are just naturally time-consuming and labor-intensive. Others, such as self-administered mail surveys, temporarily shift the labor to the respondents to some extent, but also may require intensive follow-up to obtain the desired response rates. In this case, you may need to include administrative support staff time in your plan.

If you do need to engage other researchers or field workers in your research, it is important to understand that every time you do so, you run the risk of adding unforeseen variables to your design. Even within a single component of your project, this can

---

[8] Yin (2009), Stake (1995), Ragin (2008), and George and Bennett (2005).

[9] Corden and Hirst (2008).

[10] While combining the knowledge of multiple researchers in a combined-method project may be desirable and even necessary, current practices in doctoral programs seldom allow for this, which is one reason why combined designs are comparatively rare in dissertation research.

be problematic. For example, face-to-face or telephone interviewers asking questions in slightly different ways can lead to potentially serious reliability problems with interviewees' answers. Therefore, it will be imperative to establish protocols and assure that members of the research team are consistent in their application.

When Should You Triangulate?

Triangulation should be a consideration from the beginning of your design process. Just as combining two weak design elements will not make a strong combined design, a combined design alone does not necessarily create opportunities for triangulation; this must be a more deliberate consideration.

Triangulation—the use of several means to examine the same phenomenon—can occur within or between methods, and for several purposes. Traditionally, triangulation is expected to lead to confirmation of findings from several different methods, thereby conferring more validity upon your results. But, can you actually determine ahead of time that you will indeed get the confirmation you seek? In reality, the answer is no. A more productive way to think about triangulation is that it will broaden your understanding of the phenomenon of interest, whether by confirming a finding or by contradicting it—or by discovering new variables. In other words, the results of triangulation can improve your research.[11]

You can build triangulation into your combined design in several ways: by using data sources, multiple methods, or multiple investigators.[12] Deciding to use any or all of these depends on your research question, your resources, and your capacity to manage multiple aspects of the project. Examples of each approach are shown in Table 6.3.

TABLE 6.3. Triangulation Examples

Multiple data sources	Multiple methods	Multiple investigators
Within a mixed method field study to evaluate an experiential education program, researchers compared two quantitative datasets, one from participant questionnaire ratings and one from observer ratings, to determine the error within the quantitative measurements.[a]	To document and examine sources and symptoms of job anxiety among corporate employees, researchers created a "research package," combining findings from interviews, observations, and surveys to seek convergent findings across all methods.[b]	To examine factors that affect dissemination of health information, report texts and interview transcripts were coded by multiple researchers using a coding scheme based on earlier analyses. Researchers' codings were compared and showed strong coding dependability (interrater reliability).[c]

[a]Kadushin, Hecht, Sasson, and Saxe (2008).
[b]Jick (1979).
[c]Farmer, Robinson, Elliot, and Eyles (2006).

---

[11]See Mathison (1988) for a good discussion of reasons to triangulate.
[12]Denzin (1978).

CONCLUSION AND SUMMARY

As we stated in our general introduction, this section of the book is intended to help you decide *when* to use particular research designs, not to provide the details of *how* to execute them. In recent years, the arena of combined research design has developed a broad literature complete with typologies, frameworks, and numerous examples of well-designed studies. Should you decide on a combined research design, we recommend you consult this literature extensively[13] as well as examine examples of recently published studies that provide details of design. Don't restrict your study of examples to those within your own particular branch of social science research; sometimes other subdisciplines can provide valuable design concepts that can inform your thought processes and improve your combined research design.

The table on page 113 summarizes the combined research design guidance in this chapter.

SUGGESTIONS FOR FURTHER READING

Most literature on combining research designs concentrates on "mixed methods," in which quantitative and qualitative methods are combined. In our usage, "combined designs" use more than one method, but these methods can be qualitative, quantitative, or both. Bearing this in mind, useful references for mixed methods research designs include Creswell and Clark's *Designing and Conducting Mixed Methods Research* (2010) and Greene's *Mixed Methods in Social Inquiry* (2007). Creswell and Clark walk through the process of selecting a mixed method design, provide useful examples, and discuss data collection, analysis, interpretation, and reporting of results. Detailed examples are also included in the book's appendices. Greene provides a good discussion of the "quant–qual" debate, and makes a useful distinction between paradigms and methods. The book provides helpful guidelines for designing a mixed methods study.

Case study research is often where methods must be combined and integrated into a coherent whole. We recommend Yin's *Case Study Research: Design and Methods* (4th edition, 2009). This book provides a good discussion of combining research methods in case study designs in order to answer "how" and "why" questions. Yin also provides a useful explanation of the relationship of research design to theory (e.g., explanatory, descriptive, exploratory, theory testing).

---

[13]We recommend Creswell and Clark (2010), Tashakkori and Teddlie (2003), and Brewer and Hunter (2006) as representing current standards in combined research designs.

CHAPTER 6 SUMMARY TABLE

When should you combine designs?	• When you want to corroborate results obtained from other methods. • When you want to elaborate, clarify, or build on findings from other methods. • When you want to use one method to inform another method. • When you want to "tell the full story" in an area of inquiry. • When you want to continuously look at a question from new angles, and look for unexpected findings and/or potential contradictions. • When you want to develop a theory about a phenomenon of interest.
When should you sequence your design methods?	• When your research question calls for phases, with earlier phases informing later phases. • When the data from one phase determines how you will conduct a later phase.
When should one design method predominate?	• When one part of your research design gets more to the core of your research questions than others.
When should your design methods interact or be used iteratively?	• When one method informs another. • When your design involves repetitive processes, as in case study research.
When should you consider engaging more than one researcher?	• When you don't personally have the expertise to conduct all phases or components of the study. • When the work involved is too much for one person to complete. • When you want triangulation among investigators (see below).
When should you triangulate?	• When you want to broaden your understanding of a phenomenon. • When you want to increase confidence in your results.

PART II

Sampling, Selection, and Recruitment

INTRODUCTION TO PART II

Sampling is important in every research project. All researchers sample in the sense that they *select* from a pool of possible cases, respondents, participants, or informants (the terms differ depending upon the design). If you study a whole population, you are selecting one population from among other populations. The seemingly simple questions "Who (or what) should I study, and how many of them?" raise numerous subsidiary questions, whether your research focuses on thousands of cases or only one. These questions are addressed in the chapters of Part II on sampling, selecting, and recruiting cases.

We use *case* here as a general term, not because it is ideal, but because it is the most generic (i.e., it is less tied to particular designs in the way that *respondent, interviewee, participant*, and *informant* are) and because we cannot think of an alternative.[1] The term isn't ideal because "case study" is also used as a shorthand term for an in-depth study of one case, a *single*-case study. Why do we need a general term? Because there is a general reality being described, one that transcends particular forms of research. Whatever you study you have to select the people, things, events, and so forth that you will study, and the general principles for doing so are parallel across most forms of research. We think it is important to be cognizant of those parallels.

Regardless of the design employed, it is crucial to describe the rationale for why you selected the population and cases you chose and to provide the details of how you did so. This practice is perhaps more frequently followed in surveys and experiments, but it is essential in interview, observational, and archival research as well. In surveys

---

[1] One possibility is "unit of analysis." This seems more infelicitous than *case*, if for no other reason than case is one syllable while unit of analysis is seven.

and experiments, the details can often be easily summarized because there are well-established routines and a commonly understood terminology for selecting respondents and assigning participants. In interview, observational, and archival research, investigators more often start from scratch and less often follow a pattern; frequently they have to adjust as they select and recruit cases depending on what they find in the earlier stages of their investigations. The creativity stemming from a lack of methodological routines makes it even more important to explain what you did and why.

Such explanations are perhaps especially needed in single-case study research. Case studies are not a distinct design; all designs may be used in the study of single cases. Rather, case studies are defined by *sampling*: a case study examines one instance (or sometimes, in a comparative case study, a small number of instances) of a given phenomenon. Selecting the phenomenon of interest is roughly equivalent to selecting the population of interest when investigating larger samples.

Two key criteria for selecting cases are that respondents, informants, interviewees, or participants should be *able* to participate and *willing* to do so. These criteria apply regardless of the design and the method of selecting cases. Survey respondents and interviewees must be able to understand questions and willing to answer them. Experimental participants must be able and willing to undergo the experimental treatment—or to forgo treatment if they are in the control group. People in settings studied by a participant observer must be able to engage in their regular activities in your presence and be willing to try to do so. Even in archival research, access to data often depends on the willingness or ability of those who control the archives to provide access. Case studies of institutions, rather than of individuals, raise similar issues of access and permission from those in charge.

Generalizability or external validity is always an issue when selecting and sampling. There are two steps: first, select the *population* (universe, group, category) to which you want to generalize; second, choose cases from this population. The second step can often be based on established routines, but the first is based on knowledge of the topic being investigated and on wisdom. In other words, whether you study a few cases or thousands, you first need to establish what you are sampling *from* and why you are doing so. If you are to generalize, you need to identify to whom the generalizations might apply. Concerning generalizability (or external validity), it is accurate to say that choosing the population (universe) is fully as important as techniques for sampling from that population. A meticulously drawn sample selected from an inappropriate population will be of little value for answering a research question.

One standard for determining a population of cases is *causal homogeneity*, which means that the causal processes identified have the same form across all cases. Even if you are aiming to make descriptive inferences only, you need to have some sense of *descriptive homogeneity*, that is, an idea of how widely your descriptions might apply. If you are not going to make any inferences whatsoever, at least implicitly, why would anyone care about your study? Research employing one case or a small number of cases is interesting, not (as is sometimes claimed) because it abandons all attempts at generalization, but because the cases are cases *of something*: a typical institution, an unusual group, a surprising event. The criterion is in the adjective: to identify the institution, group, or event, you have to know what is typical, unusual, or expected. These adjectives are generalizations: if something is surprising, that is because you know what is expected; if it is unusual, that is because you know what is usual; if it is typical, that is because you have an understanding of what is general or predominant.

Single-case study research is often considered a particular type of design, but it is more effective to treat it as a particular kind of selecting universes and sampling cases—one that focuses on one case or a small number of cases rather than on variables. Single-case studies are important in many fields. All of the main research designs— experiments, interviews, surveys, participant observation, and archival analysis—can be applied to the study of a single case. Given this ubiquity, it is also clear the case study has little to do with the quant–qual distinction. It may be that collectors of qualitative data are more likely to be engaged in single-case studies than are collectors of quantitative data, but this is a tendency, not a logical entailment. In brief, a single-case study is an investigation of a population or universe using a sample of one. That single case could be a political revolution, a neurology patient, a support group, a natural disaster, or a school.

The discussion of selecting populations and sampling cases in the chapters of Part II follows our established pattern of investigating these according to the ways the main issues of selecting and sampling come up in each of the major designs: surveys, interviews, experiments, observational research, archival research, and combined designs. As an overview, we provide a few introductory remarks about each.

Many sampling methods have been most fully developed in the context of *survey research* (Chapter 7). That is why it is an excellent place to begin our consideration of selecting cases to study. But parallel issues arise in all research designs and many of the same techniques can be used to address them. Two questions are most important in sampling from a population in order to use sample data to make inferences or generalizations about the population: is the sample big enough and is the sample sufficiently representative of the population? Other questions naturally follow: Will those who are selected participate? If they participate, will they persist to the end? In survey research, these questions are mostly covered under the rubric of selection bias, response rate, and nonresponse bias, but versions of them are important in most forms of research.

In *interview research* (Chapter 8), the issues are similar: is the population selected useful for answering the research question? Even if you only wish to understand cultural meanings of the data obtained from interviewees and intend no generalizations, you still need an appropriate population and a sufficient number of interviewees who are typical or representative enough of the population selected for study. The same considerations apply whether you do individual interviews or focus group interviews. The big difference in sampling between the typical interview and the typical survey is that in interviews, participants are usually chosen deliberately, not randomly. Whether the person studied is right for the research project is a matter of judgment rather than of sampling technique.

Sample size is also important in *experimental research* (Chapter 9), especially for purposes of statistical power (which can also sometimes be important in survey research). How many participants do you need to detect effects of the experimental treatment? Once this is determined, the emphasis in experiments tends to be more on recruiting and assigning participants than on representative sampling. Ideally, a pool of experimental participants would be randomly sampled from a population of interest, and then the sampled participants would be randomly assigned to control and experimental groups. This ideal is rarely met except in survey experiments. Even in experimental medical research, it is usually not the case that researchers draw a random sample of all patients with a particular condition. Rather researchers usually study eligible individuals who have a particular condition in particular hospitals or clinics and are available to be recruited to the experiment. Members of this nonrandom group of recruits are randomly assigned to treatment and control groups. The randomness that allows for hypothesis testing comes from random assignment, not from random sampling.

In *observational research* (Chapter 10), it is not uncommon to conduct a detailed study of one case. Sampling one site from among many possible sites is equivalent to selecting a universe from which observations are then sampled. Sampling here refers to what is in fact observed. What does the researcher pay attention to as relevant to the research question? What method is used to decide what to observe? The sampling of observations is influenced by two questions about the role of the observer: Is the observation done openly so that those being studied know it? Is the researcher a participant as well as an observer or merely an observer?

The range of sampling possibilities in research using *secondary/archival sources* (Chapter 11) is huge: diaries from historical figures, published research reports, epidemiological databases, survey archives, transcripts of oral history and other interviews, and so on. Because the range is vast, the selection problem is great. Although archival researchers are constrained by what exists, and do not generate their own data, those constraints can be less of an issue than it might seem. Selection in archival work often involves imagination and detective work. First there is deciding what kind of data would be helpful for answering the question. Then there is discovering whether such data exists, and if it exists how to select among an often overwhelming amount of it. In database archives you hardly ever use all variables and cases, just as in newspaper archives you would never attempt to read all issues, pages, and articles.

When addressing a research question using *combined designs* (Chapter 12), all the case selection and sampling issues pertaining to each individual design constituting the combined design are present. Also important are special problems that can arise from the intersection of different designs and therefore different sampling schemes. Even with a single design, a researcher can combine recruiting, assigning, or sampling methods: one group of cases might be selected using random techniques and a second group on the basis of recommendations of members of the first group (snowball sampling).[2]

Selecting a design shapes the choices one can reasonably make when it comes to selecting a population to study and sampling a case or cases from that population. But

TABLE II.1. General Sampling Questions
• Is the population (or universe) appropriate for the research question?
• Is the sample of cases appropriate for the research question?
• When the cases are individuals, are they able and willing to participate?
• When the cases are organizations or archives, can the researcher gain access?

---

[2]A general summary of sample size recommendations is found in Onwuegbuzie and Collins, 2007, Table 3. For discussions of when to focus on effect sizes and confidence intervals (rather than on hypothesis testing) when calculating sample size, see Parker and Berman (2003) and Kelley and Rausch (2006).

Chapter	Design type	Sampling issues
7	Survey	Is the sample large enough and representative enough of the population to draw inferences?
8	Interview	Are the interviewees typical enough of the group(s) they represent that the researcher can make generalizations?
9	Experimental	Is the sample big enough for statistical power; are the control and experimental groups large enough?
10	Observational research	Can the researcher gain adequate access to the case(s) to make a number of observations sufficient for making generalizations?
11	Archival research	Do archival data exist in sufficient supply to draw valid and reliable conclusions about the research question?
12	Combined designs	Does the use of multiple methods of case selection and their possible interactions cause sampling problems?

TABLE II.2. Main Sampling Issues/Questions by Specific Design Types

the design does not tightly constrain the choices. Numerous methods exist for sampling in surveys, finding interviewees, recruiting experimental participants, selecting sites for observation, and choosing data from archives. It is important that the criteria used to decide among all the possibilities be conscious so that the decisions are systematic, describable, and justifiable. Researchers who cannot explain what they have done seldom inspire confidence. Haphazard decisions rarely lead to valuable research. In Tables II.1 and II.2 we summarize some of the major issues pursued in the next six chapters.

CHAPTER 7

Sampling for Surveys

Whom should you survey and how many respondents do you need? These are the two basic questions of survey sampling. The answers depend on several considerations, most of them stemming directly from your research question. Most important is whether you plan to generalize from your group of respondents (the sample) to a broader group (the population). Most survey researchers hope to make valid generalizations from samples to populations. If you are choosing a sample in order to generalize to a broader group, then the main issue is whether your sample is representative.

As with most research methods, sampling builds on common sense and is a natural way to learn. We all sample all the time. If you use the remote control to flip through the channels to find something to watch, you are sampling programs. If you go to the bakery and take a free taste of the new poppy seed muffin, you are sampling. You don't watch the whole program or eat the whole muffin to see if you like it. A small sample usually suffices. How small a sample can you get by with? It has to be big enough and representative enough, but what's *enough*? Two seconds of a program or a tiny crumb of the muffin might not do. But you usually don't need 20 minutes of the program or three-quarters of the muffin. Can you systematically determine what "enough" is? Sampling theory provides good guidelines. Note that these sampling questions—who and how many—apply, more or less directly, to all research designs, not merely to surveys. The issues may have been discussed more frequently among survey researchers, but they are important to selecting cases for any research design.

Conducting survey research or using any other research design (interviews, experiments, observations, or archival investigations) does not *require* you to take a sample with the aim of generalizing to a population. You might not wish to generalize from a sample; rather you could want to study the entire population, such as all residents of a small town or all the students in a school or all the clients at a clinic. But the selection process is still crucial. If you are studying the whole population, then the main issue is whether this population is a good one for the purposes of answering your research question.

Two broad categories of survey sampling are probability and nonprobability sampling. In *probability sampling*, each respondent has a known probability of being selected for inclusion in the study. Because the sample probabilities are known, techniques of inferential statistics can be used to make generalizations about populations. In *nonprobability sampling*, as the name indicates, the probability of inclusion is not known. When the sample probabilities are not known, using inferential statistics to generalize about populations is technically inappropriate, although quite common.

Do you want to make inferences about a larger group from your sample? Then you must use

PROBABILITY SAMPLES

Of the two main categories of sampling, probability samples are *always* preferable in survey research. The defining characteristic of a probability sample is that the researcher knows the probability that a particular case will be selected from the population. That knowledge is very useful. But probability samples are not always possible. In other kinds of research—interview research, for example—they are not even preferable. In survey research, probability sampling is the standard against which a project is judged. How do you choose among the four main types of probability samples: random, systematic, stratified, and cluster?

When Should You Use Simple Random Sampling?

The answer is short: whenever you can. Random sampling is also known as *simple random sampling* to distinguish it from other forms of random sampling. Simple random sampling uses a random process to select respondents, such as having a computer generate random numbers to use in identifying people on a numbered list. In that way, it gives each member of the population an equal probability of being selected for inclusion in the sample. This equal probability means that the sample is probably representative of the population. The chief reason to conduct a random sample is to eliminate *bias*. A biased sample is one in which some members of the population are systematically over- or underrepresented. Because random sampling ensures that every member of the population has an equal probability of being selected, it removes *bias* from the process of selection.

Random sampling does not remove *error* from the process of selection, however. *Sampling error*, defined as the difference between the sample and the population, is unavoidable. While discrepancies between the sample and the population as a whole are inevitable, random sampling allows you to estimate both the size and the likelihood of sampling error. Estimating the likelihood of sampling error is a key component of *significance testing*. Significance testing assumes random sampling. What is being tested in significance testing is the likelihood that a result would occur *in a random sample* if no such result occurred (null hypothesis) in the population from which the sample was drawn. The estimate of that likelihood is the *p*-value (short for *probability* value).

Because random sampling eliminates bias and allows you to estimate sampling error, it maximizes *external validity*. External validity refers to the degree to which the results drawn from the sample can accurately be generalized beyond the respondents to the population at large. Such generalization is the whole point of taking a sample, and random sampling accomplishes it best. In brief, simple random sampling in surveys eliminates bias, reduces sampling error, and maximizes external validity. You can ask no more from a process of selection.

When Can You Make Inferences about Populations from Which You Have Not Randomly Sampled?

You *can* compute a *p*-value if your sample is not random, but you probably shouldn't. Indeed, many statistical packages assume that your sample is random and compute a *p*-value automatically. However, computing a probability value using a nonprobability sample makes little sense. If you compute a *p*-value from a nonprobability sample, implicitly you are asking a hypothetical question: *if* this were a random sample from population, what *would be* the statistical significance of my findings? It isn't really a random sample, but what would the significance be if it were? Researchers routinely do this, but the results should be treated with skepticism. Of course, if you are a student learning how to conduct significance tests, it's fine to practice on nonprobability samples.

When might it be more or less reasonable to *assume* that your sample will be like a population even though it was not drawn from that population? One case is when you are talking about the future. You can't sample a future population for the obvious reason that it does not yet exist. You might want to *assume* that the future will be like the past. That is a risky assumption, and it is definitely not a statistical assumption. However, if you are willing to make that assumption, you can generalize from a past sample to a future population. We believe that, in most circumstances, using a *p*-value to do so is inappropriate, but many researchers disagree.

A second category of potentially reasonable inference from a nonprobability sample to some other population occurs most often in studies of the natural rather than the social world. Medical generalizations, for example, can often be more stable than social, political, and psychological generalizations. That stability can give you a reason for *assuming* the sample will resemble a population from which it was *not* drawn. While such inferences are not based on statistics and sampling theory, they can be valuable. For example, it is not unreasonable to assume that something learned about kidney disease by studying patients in Wisconsin will be true of kidney disease patients in other states as well. But the reasonableness of that assumption is not based on probability and sampling theory.

When Should You Sample with Replacement?

One answer is: whenever you can. Strictly speaking, statistical inference based on sampling *assumes* that the sampling was done with replacement. Sampling with replacement means that after a case has been selected, it is returned to the population before the next case is selected. If this procedure is not followed, equal probability is undermined. Cases selected later will have a higher probability of being chosen.

Think of drawing a sample of playing cards one at a time from a standard deck of 52 cards. The probability of drawing any particular card is .0192 (1 ÷ 52). If you draw a second card without replacement, without returning the first card to the deck, the probability becomes .0196 (1 ÷ 51). Do it again, and the probability on the next draw will be .0200 (1 ÷ 50). If you draw a small sample from a large population, sampling without replacement causes only minor inaccuracies. Sampling with replacement tends to be awkward and impractical, and it is in fact very rarely done in practice.[1] You should be aware, however, that sampling without replacement technically violates assumptions about probability sampling.

When Should You Use Systematic Sampling

Systematic sampling is widely used when simple random sampling would be inconvenient. In practice, simple random sampling is often inconvenient and frequently not feasible. In systematic sampling, you select every "*n*th" person from a list of the population, such as a membership list. (Systemic sampling is also called list sampling.) For example, if you wanted to survey 600 members of a union, and the membership list contained 60,000 names, you would select every 100th member. Your starting point on the list, the first member you select, should be chosen at random. You could use a computer program to generate a random number as a starting point. Say that number was 228. For your sample, you would start by selecting the 228th name, then the 328th, the 428th, and so on.

Most member lists are alphabetical. Using systematic sampling from an alphabetical list can generally be *assumed* to be indistinguishable from simple random sampling from the same list. Non-alphabetical lists are more likely to contain some unknown bias. In order to test whether your systematic sample might be biased in some way, you can divide your planned sample size in two and take two samples. If you plan to sample 600 from a list, take two samples of 300 instead. Use different intervals and start points for each sample and test your results for statistically significant differences between the two samples. If there are none, then combine your samples for analysis.

Even though random sampling involves more work than systematic sampling, if you have a good list, why not use the better method? Why run the risk of a biased sample if you don't need to do so? When might the risk be worth it? The question is not a statistical one. Rather, it has to do with how industrious you are. How much work are you willing to do in order to reduce the risk of bias? You might decide that simple random sampling was not worth the effort if you were selecting from a telephone book for a city with a population of one million. Simple random sampling might seem just too unwieldy. With a smaller, more manageable list you might make a different choice.

What Can You Do to Obtain a Sampling Frame?

How good is your list of the members of the population? This is an important question in all sampling techniques, but is especially salient in systematic sampling. The list of population members is called a *sampling frame*. It doesn't do you much good to use the very best methods to avoid bias when selecting from a list when the list itself is biased. And no list is perfect. For example, a telephone directory is an incomplete and therefore biased record of a population. Some people are not included because they do not have phones; others only have cell phones; still others have unlisted numbers. Some people are included but are no longer part of the population, such as those who moved after

---

[1]The big exception is resampling methods such as bootstrapping; see our companion book on when to use what methods of analysis.

the directory was printed. Differences between the population and the *sampling frame* are an important source of error. One way to improve your survey research is to use the best possible list of the members of the population. For instance, a membership list from an organization's central office is usually harder to get than the organization's telephone directory, but it is much better as a sampling frame.

When you don't have a sampling frame, it may be possible to create one. Sometimes when you cannot get a list, you can get a map. For example, if you want to interview a representative sample of residents in a town and you cannot find a directory, you can use a map as your sampling frame. Randomly select map coordinates and sample households at those locations. The possibilities for using this type of geographic or area sampling have been greatly enhanced by the development and widespread availability of global positioning system (GPS) technology. One problem with the older approach of using a map was that it was hard to identify sampling units that were small and accurate enough to be useful. GPS technology has solved this problem since the GPS can be used almost anywhere on the planet and can precisely specify very small areas. The researchers then sample from those small areas, often surveying everyone living in each area. When the population is unknown or highly mobile, GPS area sampling will be better than any list. Indeed recent research on the use of the GPS indicates that it yields an equal probability sample, arguably better than one available in any other way.[2]

When Should You Use Stratified Random Sampling?

The answer is, not as often as you might think. To conduct a stratified random sample, you first select groups or "strata" from a population and then use the techniques of simple random sampling within each of those groups. Why would you do that? One good reason is if you want to compare groups that are not equally represented in a population. For instance, if you wanted to compare the opinions of male and female mechanical engineers, a simple random sample probably would probably not yield enough female engineers for statistical analysis. In that case, you could stratify on the basis of gender. To do this you might need two sampling frames, one for male and one for female mechanical engineers. From each list you could randomly select 300 engineers. Each sample would be representative of its population. But the combined sample of 600 would *not* be representative of the total population of engineers; women would be overrepresented. The bias would be reversed if you were studying the opinions of octogenarians. Women generally tend to live longer. Assuming you could get complete lists of men and women in their 80s (a big assumption), if you used the same procedures as with the engineers (300 from each group), you would have enough in each group to make meaningful comparisons, but men would be overrepresented in the combined sample.

Avoid stratification except in cases where you *know* that using simple or systematic random sampling will yield too small a group of respondents in some category. Beginning researchers sometimes think that stratification will make their samples more representative. It won't. Stratification makes samples *less* representative. Often stratifying is just unnecessary work. You don't need to divide the sample into subgroups before you collect the data; you can do that afterwards, in the analysis phase. In brief, either simple random sampling or systematic sampling is better for most purposes than stratified

---

[2]See Bernard (2000) for additional suggestions. On GPS sampling, Landry and Shen (2005) is definitive.

sampling. Random methods have the greatest probability of producing a sample that is representative of the population on all variables, including—and this is a key point—variables you don't know about.

When Should You Use Cluster Sampling?

Cluster sampling—also called multistage or multilevel sampling—is very widely used. Simple and systematic random samples are impossible when sampling frames are unavailable. For example, there is no aggregate list of all of the approximately 15 million college and university students in the United States. If you want a national sample of college and university students, what do you do? Because there are lists of all colleges and universities, you could use these as *clusters*. First take a random sample of colleges and universities. Then contact those institutions to obtain lists of their students. Then take a random sample from each of those lists. Combine those samples to make your national sample. Of course, it would be no small task to do all this, but the principle is clear.

Cluster sampling is very efficient. It is used in many, probably most, national surveys. The main drawback is that each stage of the sampling process increases sampling error (the difference between the population and the sample). First, there will be sampling error in your sample of colleges and universities. Second there will be sampling error in your samples of students. The easiest way to compensate for the extra sampling error is to increase your sample size. The time and effort saved by cluster sampling is so great that you can usually come out ahead even if, in order to keep sampling error in line, you have to increase your sample size substantially.

NONPROBABILITY SAMPLES

Random, stratified random, systematic, and cluster sampling are *probability samples*. They are called this because cases or respondents have a *known probability* of being selected. Much sampling for educational, anthropological, and medical research is not probability sampling. This can be very justifiable when the research design employs interviews, observational research, or experiments. When is it okay to use nonprobability samples in survey research? In general, there are two justifications: when you have no choice and when representativeness is not important in your research. The three most common types of nonprobability samples are convenience samples (also known as opportunity samples), quota samples, and judgment samples (also called purposive samples).

When Should You Use Convenience Samples in Surveys?

The answer to this question is simple: *very* rarely. Convenience samples are hardly ever justifiable, but they are used all the time because it's so easy to do so. If the group you are studying is a good one for answering your research question, and it also happens to be convenient, then the convenience is just your good luck. Such good fortune is rare. Because convenience samples are often included in lists of kinds of samples (including this one), there seems a tendency for some beginning researchers to think of them as a fully legitimate option. They aren't. They should be a last resort; professional researchers should be embarrassed when they use one. Again, we don't mean to suggest that you shouldn't use a convenience sample if you are a student learning how to conduct a survey. What might be an excellent learning exercise can be inappropriate in professional practice.

Inferential statistics are inappropriate with convenience samples. They are often computed, but they have no clear meaning. Inferential statistics *presume, require, necessitate* (we don't know how to emphasize this more strongly) a probability sample drawn from the population about which you wish to generalize. Unless you have used a probability sample, it is wrong to use probability statistics to make inferences about a population. It is done all the time, but it is wrong—again except as a class exercise. Note, however, that this rule is routinely contradicted in practice. You might even be asked to do it in order to publish your results.

Researchers hardly ever want to say what they should say about convenience samples: "I studied this sample because it was easy, not because it was most appropriate for answering my research question." Of course, feasibility always figures into the design of a research project. But feasibility is not merely convenience. If you cannot gain access to the group you want to study, even if it would be the best one for answering your research question, then you must do something else. On the other hand, if two populations or samples really are equally good for answering your research question, by all means choose the one that is more convenient, whether that is because they live closer to your home, are more likely to have access to e-mail, or whatever.

When Should You Compare Sample Statistics to Population Parameters?

One way to check the representativeness of your sample is to compare statistics computed on your sample to statistics computed on your population. Population statistics are called *parameters*. For example, if you did a cluster sample of college and university students, you would want to compare your sample to known population parameters. We know quite a bit about the population of college and university students—what percent attend 2-year colleges, what percent are women, and so on. If you have succeeded in drawing a representative sample, then your sample percentages and the population percentages should coincide fairly closely. Making this kind of comparison is always important in all samples, but it is especially important in convenience samples and other nonprobability samples. In nonprobability samples, there is no other way to assess the representativeness of your sample. The similarity of some sample statistics to some known population parameters is no guarantee that your sample is representative; it merely suggests that it might be.

When Should You Use Quota Samples?

Quota sampling is essentially stratified convenience sampling. If used well, it can increase the credibility of convenience sampling. You decide how many respondents you want in each of several categories. The number for each category is the quota. Then you approach members of the population seeking to fill your quota of women, men, African Americans, and so on. We have seen this kind of sampling several times in shopping malls. One of us (Vogt) recently asked a pollster why he hadn't been asked to respond to a survey (he was disappointed because respondents got a free coupon). The surveyor said, "Sorry, dude, I've already got my quota of old white guys."

Quota sampling has obvious advantages over simple convenience sampling. Using it ensures that you will get representation in each of your categories. It also means that some categories will not be overrepresented. When pollsters are simply turned loose in a shopping mall, they tend to survey people they feel comfortable approaching—usually, people like themselves. Quota sampling helps reduce this tendency. And quota sampling has been used quite effectively by national commercial polling organizations, perhaps most extensively in exit polls on Election Day. Pollsters are given quotas for each time period and each main demographic group. Although the polling organizations have not always been accurate in their predictions of the total vote, and on occasion they have been very inaccurate, the percent of correct predictions of the winner is high, and it is hard to see what other method could be used to collect sample statistics in just a few hours of one day.

When Should You Use Judgment (Purposive) Samples in Surveys?

When you cannot do a probability sample, judgment sampling can help mitigate the disadvantages. Rather than employ a random process to select respondents, you use your judgment. In surveys, judgment sampling is often done to give some legitimacy to a nonprobability sample. By contrast, in interview research, judgment sampling is exactly what is required. In interviews, you need a few good informants—not a large, representative group of respondents.

In judgment sampling, the cases might be selected because they seem typical or perhaps because they are diverse. In cluster sampling, the judgment may have to do with the clusters of respondents to use. Sometimes within the clusters, random sampling is used. But using nonrepresentative clusters, and then sampling from them randomly, does not yield a representative sample. Judgment sampling is very common in experiments and quasi-experiments, but it is widely used in surveys too. One good use of judgment sampling is to obtain a group with whom to pilot test a survey. In that case, you select respondents whom you judge to be sufficiently like those you expect to select in your actual sample; you try out your survey on them.

If you are a lone researcher, for example working on a dissertation, and you do not have extensive funding, judgment sampling may be the only way you have of adding an element of representativeness to your sample. For example, one student Vogt worked with wanted to survey female engineering students. She did not have the resources to do a cluster sample, so she decided to survey all female engineering students in four different universities. She used two criteria to select them: public versus private and large versus small. The survey was then distributed to all women engineering students at a small private, a large private, a small public, and a large public university. The sample was not ideal, but it was much better than simply selecting the four engineering programs nearest to her home.

Judgment sampling can sometimes be the only practical method, even in well-funded national studies. For example, the National Institute of Child Health and Human Development (NICHD) has studied over 1,000 children for its longitudinal "Study of Early

Child Care and Youth Development." The sample was meant to be representative, but methods of random sampling were not used. Rather, on one specific day at 10 hospitals across the United States, all women giving birth "were screened for eligibility and willingness to be contacted again." The screening criteria were mostly designed for the convenience of the researchers: the mother had to speak English, live within 3 hours of the hospital, and in a "neighborhood [that] was not too dangerous to visit." About 5,000 mothers met these criteria. From that group, a stratified random sample (using education level and ethnicity to stratify) was drawn. Finally, about 1,300 mothers "completed a home interview when the infant was 1 month old and became study participants."[3] These women and their children have been followed over several years.

Writers of books on research methods often assert that the only good sample is a probability sample. But the difficulties can be formidable. Even massive, government-funded research studies often cannot achieve perfection. Despite its limitations, the NICHD group has collected what is, without doubt, the best current database for studying problems of child development. Think of how it was constructed. Judgment sampling was used to select the 10 sites. Convenience sampling was used to screen the mothers. Only then was stratified random sampling used to select among those who lived close enough and were English speaking. Hardly a perfect design, it is true, but it would be churlish to criticize.[4]

The frequency with which convenience, quota, and judgment samples are used does not change the general rule: the more representative the sample, the more accurate any generalizations inferred from it; the more it is based on principles of probability, the more representative it is. Random sampling is an ideal. Like most ideals, people cannot always live up to it.

When Should You Use Snowball Sampling and Respondent-Driven Sampling?

Snowball sampling involves asking initial contacts for further contacts. It is used both by survey researchers to find comparatively large pools of respondents and by interview researchers to identify smaller numbers of informants. It is especially helpful for populations that are rare or difficult to access. The key assumption of snowball sampling is that members of your target population know one another. Although it is a nonprobability technique, snowball sampling has been developed into a much more formidable method called respondent-driven sampling (RDS). Pioneered by Heckathorn, RDS is probably the best known and definitely the most technically well developed of the methods for studying hidden and/or rare populations. RDS can be used to derive unbiased, probability-based estimates about the populations studied. This is true even though RDS is based on snowball sampling, which is in no sense a method of probability sampling. Here is an example of the method: visitors to a drug rehabilitation clinic who are willing to participate in a study are interviewed and paid for their time. They are given three coupons that they can give to acquaintances who might be eligible for the

---

[3] National Institute of Child Health and Human Development (2002, p. 136).

[4] For examples of the range of sampling difficulties and the methods researchers used to deal with them, see Lee, Ready, and Johnson (2001); Lynn (2003); and Wells et al. (2003).

study. Interviewees recruited from among the coupon holders are also given coupons to distribute. This technique enables researchers to learn about the network; they use this knowledge to draw inferences about the population. In addition to the attractiveness of a method that uses nonprobability methods to make unbiased estimates, RDS has proven to be comparatively easy and inexpensive to implement. It has even been applied to sampling an Internet-based network.[5]

When Can You Learn from Nonprobability Samples?

Valid generalizations from unrepresentative samples can be made. Good examples come from biomedical research, in which we have learned a great deal about human diseases and how to treat them by studying laboratory animals. The animals studied in medical experiments are clearly not a representative sample of humans. They are not even a representative sample of animals: mice, rats, and so on. (The old joke is that even the mice are white males.) Lab animals are used because they are *sufficiently like* humans in their reactions to provide the basis for a generalization. For example, testing a new drug on laboratory mice can be used as the first step in approving the drug for human use. Before the drug wins approval, however, it has to pass through Stage 2 and Stage 3 trials, which do use human *volunteers* (again not a representative probability sample).

In some circumstances, the identity of your sample may not be of great concern. For example, in a 12-year study of 2,500 men in Minnesota who filled out questionnaires and received medical exams, it was discovered that those who took aspirin daily had a much-reduced risk of developing benign prostatic hyperplasia (BPH). Hazard ratios of the components of the syndrome ranged from .51 to .79 (1.0 indicates no difference), and they were statistically significant.[6] There isn't much reason to suspect that results would have differed had the men been from Georgia or Arizona. The results *might* have differed. Perhaps environmental or climate factors would have influenced the findings. But prostate glands in one state are probably *sufficiently like* those in other states so that we can make a generalization. By contrast, social variables such as attitudes and beliefs are more likely to vary than medical ones. While there are some medical differences among subgroups, and they can be important, similarities tend to be much greater.

Another study involved research on 1,836 elderly Japanese Americans living in the Seattle area. As in the Minnesota study, patients were surveyed about their dietary and other habits as well as given periodic medical examinations. Over a 10-year period, the incidence of Alzheimer's disease was 76% lower among participants who drank fruit and vegetable juices more than three times per week—compared with those who drank them less than once per week.[7] Can we trust these results? They are surely true for Japanese Americans living in the northwest, but how broadly can the findings be generalized? Would they apply to African Americans living in Washington, D.C.? The two studies—Minnesota aspirin takers and Seattle juice drinkers—have much in common. The key independent variables (aspirin and juice) were studied using self-reports of

---

[5] See Farquharson (2005) for traditional snowball methods and Salganik and Heckathorn (2004) for RDS. For RDS applied to Internet sampling, see Wejnert and Heckathorn (2008).

[6] St. Sauver et al. (2006).

[7] Dai, Borenstein, Wu, Jackson, and Larson (2006).

survey respondents. In both cases, the effects were impressive. Both samples were large, but neither was representative. The reported effects were surely true in the samples studied. What does that tell us about the rest of the world?

The outcomes were too important to ignore. It would have been nice had the studies used random samples, but almost no one has the resources to do that. Even in well-funded medical research, nationally representative random samples are rare except for studies conducted by government agencies such as the CDC. Both the aspirin and the juice studies provide important clues. Next steps would be first to see whether the results held in the study of other populations and, second, to try to determine the mechanisms by which aspirin and juice provided their beneficial outcomes, ideally in controlled experiments. The parallels with social, psychological, and educational variables are close. Lessons learned in studies of nonrepresentative, nonprobability samples can only be generalized to a broader population when it can be assumed that the sample and the broader population are *sufficiently alike.* That is a vague criterion and usually a heroic assumption, not something based on the statistics of sampling theory. The assumption is most likely to be reasonable for variables in physics and chemistry, less likely for variables in biology and medicine, and still less likely for social and psychological variables.

WHEN SHOULD YOU TRY TO IMPROVE RESPONSE RATES?

Because *nonresponse bias* is a huge source of problems with most surveys, an effort to improve response rates is time well spent. Nonresponse bias arises from the fact that if a substantial number of those in your planned representative sample do not respond, those who do respond no longer constitute a representative sample.

Even if you are studying a whole population rather than taking a sample, nonresponse is still a problem. If any substantial number of respondents do not respond, you are now surveying a sample, not a population. And it is not a representative sample because nonrespondents cannot be assumed to be similar to respondents. They might be similar, but they probably aren't, and you cannot tell—because they did not respond. The larger your group of nonrespondents, the less representative your sample is. This is why, if you have good reason to suspect that you will get a low response rate on your survey (review the research literature for response rates in studies similar to the one you are planning), you should consider an alternative research method.

Advanced statistical techniques, particularly the multiple imputation methods pioneered by Donald Rubin,[8] enable researchers to estimate and correct for nonresponse bias. But these methods are technically difficult and cannot easily be used with small samples. And they are used for missing answers to questions on a survey, not for missing people (survey respondents). Everyone agrees: the best advice for dealing with missing data is to do everything *in advance* to avoid it. But it can never be totally avoided. A conscientious researcher will have a missing data strategy and describe it for the reader. Unfortunately, many of the easiest and most widely used strategies (such as listwise deletion), which are the default options in popular statistical packages, can do more harm

---

[8] Rubin and Little (2002).

than good. You need to review your options and make a choice.[9] Handling missing data is more of an analysis issue, and we will discuss it in the companion book on analysis. Here we can say that choosing a method is complicated because most of the advanced software programs for imputation are not easy to use. Nothing can match the ease of packaged default procedures such as listwise deletion, but these should be avoided by all serious researchers. Again, there is nothing wrong with experimenting with these easy but flawed procedures as part of a class project to explore statistical techniques, but you would want to use them on your dissertation only with the greatest caution.

While we tend to avoid software recommendations because of the speed with which they can become obsolete, once in a while an exception seems appropriate.[10] One set of data imputation procedures in one particular program is considerably more user-friendly than others. It is called AMELIA (named after Amelia Earhart) and is based on bootstrapping techniques. Available as freeware since the late 1990s, it is both faster and easier to use than the other advanced imputation alternatives.[11] In 2008, it became available as a package in the R freeware program. Its ease of use has made it very popular, and you can't beat the price.

Good imputation procedures for missing data are a godsend, but statistical fixes at the analysis stage are a last resort, and they cannot be used for all types of missing data. It is much better to concentrate on prevention at the design and sampling stages to keep the use of cures to a minimum at the analysis stage. This means you need to take all reasonable steps to ensure a good response rate.

A great deal of research has been conducted on the issue of response rates. Survey research is a big industry and much is at stake. For the most up-to-date research, do a literature review specifically on the issue of survey response rates in your field. Response rates tend to differ sharply by mode of administration, and response rates for specific questions can differ greatly by question format. Random-digit dialing to find participants for telephone interviews has become common in recent decades. To stem the sharp decline (presumably due to cell phones and caller ID) in the response rates using this technology,[12] some researchers have sent letters or postcards in advance of the attempted telephone contact. Letters and postcards can increase response rates and lower the number of calls that need to be made, often enough to more than cover the cost of postage.[13] Mail and e-mail surveys and combinations of e-mails and letters also yield different response rates and have sharply different costs. There are no firm rules, only judgment, for deciding whether the extra cost of mail versus e-mail is worth the increased response rate.[14]

There is little doubt that the response rate for individual questions is in large part determined by the clarity of the questions and format of the response choices.[15] How-

---

[9] A good place to start is McKnight, McKnight, Sidani, and Figueredo (2007).

[10] See Horton and Kleinman (2007) for a thorough review of missing data software.

[11] Honaker, Joseph, King, Scheve, and Singh (1999).

[12] For documentation of the decline, see Curtin et al. (2005). An excellent review of strategies for dealing with the decline is Groves (2006).

[13] Hembroff et al. (2005).

[14] Kaplowitz et al. (2004).

[15] Christian, Dillman, and Smyth (2007).

ever, which wording is clearer and which formats for indicating answers are more likely to elicit responses are not easy questions to answer. Intuitions are often wrong, so turn to empirical data, often from survey experiments, whenever possible. One way to keep up with empirical research is by thumbing through recent issues of journals such as *Public Opinion Quarterly*. In sum, anything you can do to increase the number of potential respondents who actually respond can only improve your study.[16]

How Big Does Your Response Rate Have to Be?

The bigger the better. Select the people in your sample randomly and do all that you can to find them and convince them to participate. Big national surveys—such as the American Community Survey (ACS), which is compulsory—often achieve response rates over 90%. Such national organizations have large staffs, adequate budgets, and prestigious names. It is hard for individual researchers to do as well, but it is not impossible. Researchers who avoid the miserable response rates of the typical survey often use their knowledge of the population to tailor their sampling plan to that population.

Say you achieve a response rate of 70%. How good is that? It is better than the typical survey, but it is a far from comfortable rate. Say you mailed out a survey to 1,000 people, and 700 responded (365 women and 345 men) for an overall rate of 70%. If 60% of the women who responded favored a particular policy and 45% of the men did so, the difference of 15% between men and women would be a large and statistically significant difference by most standards. But, given your response rate, how confident can you be? The total number of women favoring the policy is 219 (365 × 60% = 219). The total number of men is 155 (345 × 45% = 155). The absolute difference between men's and women's responses to this survey question is 64 (219 − 155 = 64). But the number of people who did not respond (300) is nearly *five times* as great. It is not too pessimistic to worry that your statistically significant difference of 64 people would have been swamped if the 300 nonrespondents had responded. You do not know. You cannot know. You ought to worry. If you get a sample statistic so overwhelming that it would stand even if all of your nonrespondents contradicted your conclusion, only then can you be confident that it would still hold up against any nonresponse bias. One way to reduce the worry would be to do something already suggested: compare characteristics of your sample to known characteristics of the population. If your sample statistics are close to these known population parameters, you can be *somewhat* more confident that nonresponse bias has not invalidated your conclusions.

HOW BIG SHOULD YOUR SAMPLE BE?

The bigger the better. The representativeness of the sample is much more important than its sheer size, but size matters too. Among equally representative samples, bigger is *always* better. The bigger the sample, the more accurately it will represent the population and the less likely you are to overlook something. Putting it the other way around, the smaller your sample, the less certain you can be of your findings.

---

[16]Some studies have shown that smaller response rates, as with Internet surveys, have little effect on substantive results. One of the most persuasive of these is Sanders et al. (2007).

When Might Your Sample Be Too Big?

Sometimes textbooks will warn you that samples can be "too" large. This is misleading advice—a false alarm. There is *no* statistical downside to a large sample. What textbook authors sometimes worry about is that with large samples one can find *statistically* significant results that are not *practically* significant. That is true, and it is also true that researchers should not confuse practical significance with statistical significance. But this is no reason to use a small sample or worry about using a big one. Our advice is twofold: (1) don't automatically assume that a statistically significant finding is practically important, *and* (2) use the biggest sample you can afford. The only disadvantage of large samples is that they require more money, time, and work.

When Do You Need to Increase Your Statistical Power?

Statistical power is the ability to use a sample to detect a relationship in a population. Not seeing a relationship in the sample when it actually exists in the population is Type II error.[17] In other words, Type II error is retaining the null hypothesis when it should have been rejected. Type I error is rejecting one that should have been retained. Clearly, power and statistical significance are the two halves of statistical inference. The two are inversely related. All else being equal, if you reduce the chances of one kind of error, you increase the chances of the other kind. But, it is possible to reduce *both* kinds of error. This happy result is achieved by increasing your sample size.

If your research question involves uncovering important but hard-to-detect relationships in a population, you need sufficient power. How do you increase your statistical power? The most direct way to increase power is to increase sample size. Other means of increasing statistical power include increasing the sensitivity of your measurements or decreasing sample variance, but these tend to be less clear than increasing sample size, especially prior to taking the sample and conducting the measurements.

Is the increase in power worth the cost in money and work that comes with increasing sample size? "Worth it" is both a scientific and an economic criterion. It is a waste of time and money to increase sample size to the point that you can detect things that are too small to be of interest. That would be like using one of the Palomar Observatory's telescopes to go bird-watching. You do want to be able to detect important things. What is "important" in your area of research? Again, the most important considerations are not statistical ones, but are matters of judgment and careful research design.

Increasingly, researchers are asked to calculate the statistical power of their samples. The standard formulas for computing statistical power are not especially complicated and should cause you no problem if you have already drawn your sample and have computed various sample statistics.[18] However, it is increasingly common for you to be expected to compute the sample size you need to attain a given level of power *in advance*. The results of such computations are often required in grant applications and dissertation proposals. No problem, right? Wrong: the standard formulas require you to

---

[17]These issues are discussed in greater detail in our companion volume on analysis. Here we touch on them only to discuss questions of sample size.

[18]For the formulas see Kraemer and Thiemann (1987) or Cohen (1992). A very important source for the topics discussed in this chapter is the American Association for Public Opinion Research. See "Response Rates: An Overview" and other documents available at *www.aapor.org*.

plug in data that you do not have, such as the variance of the sample's dependent variable. As Vogt explained elsewhere:

> Of course, you won't have this before you collect the sample, but in order to decide how big your sample should be, you need to have it. This puts you in the impossible situation of having to compute things on the sample you have not yet collected in order to decide how big a sample you should collect![19]

The way around this catch-22 is to *estimate* what you need to plug into the formula. Estimates can be based on a review of the research literature for similar studies, presuming that such are available. Failing that, determining the required values involves creative writing or inspired guesswork.[20] But one thing you can count on: if you want to be more confident in your statistical power, increase your sample size. That conclusion gets us to our next question.

When Should You Increase Your Sample Size?

The basic answer is simple: When you need more confidence in the precision of your results. Again, this is a decision that can be informed by statistics, but much nonstatistical judgment is inevitably involved. Most discussions of sample size concern calculations pertaining to statistical power, but that is not the only consideration. Several recent commentators have argued that it is much more important to focus on a sample size large enough to provide strong evidence for a conclusion, or for narrower confidence intervals around effect sizes.[21] These commentators are on the right track, but it will take a long time to break the mindset that power is the only or the main thing to be concerned about when calculating sample size.

To see what kind of judgment is involved in making sample size decisions, consider a hypothetical example. Say you draw a random sample from a population and compute the mean for the respondents. You get a mean of 600 and a standard deviation of 100. The mean of 600 could be Graduate Record Examination (GRE) scores of university graduate students, or 600 could be the weekly income of hospitality industry workers, or 600 could be the number of deaths per 100,000 patients taking a medication. If you want to generalize to the population and say that 600 is a good estimate of the mean in the population, how confident can you be? How precise is your estimate likely to be? The answer depends mostly on your sample size.

If you have taken a random sample, your precision and confidence can be estimated precisely. First, you need to compute the standard error (*SE*) of the mean. The formula is simple. You divide the standard deviation (*SD*) of the sample by the square root of the size of the sample (*n*), as in the formula in Figure 7.1.

The standard deviation (*SD*) is 100; the mean is 600. What happens to the precision of 600 as an estimate of the population mean as you increase sample size? What if your sample is 10 or 50 or 100 or 1,000? To find out, compute the *SE* at each of those sample

---

[19] Vogt (2007, p. 86).

[20] Berk (2004).

[21] Three examples are Strug, Rohde, and Corey (2007); Parker and Bergman (2003); and Kelley and Rausch (2006).

$$SE = \frac{SD}{\sqrt{n}}$$

FIGURE 7.1. Formula for standard error of the mean.

sizes. That will give you the different margins of error. The range from two SEs below to two SEs above the mean gives you the range at the 95% confidence level. (Actually, it's the 95.4% confidence level.)[22] Table 7.1 shows what happens to the precision of your estimate as the sample size increases from 10 to 1,000. Clearly, the standard error drops and the confidence interval narrows. In brief, the bigger the sample, the more precise the estimate.

How could you summarize your results at the different sample sizes? Using Table 7.1, depending on your sample size, you could say, "The mean of the population is around 600—give or take about 63, or about 28, or about 20, or about 6." How much precision do you need? How narrow does your confidence interval need to be? It would depend on what you were measuring.

A sample size of 10 yields a margin of error around the mean of about 63: 600 plus or minus 63. That would not even be good enough for GRE scores. Why bother if you weren't going to be more accurate than that? A sample of 50 might be okay for GRE scores, and a sample of 100 surely would be. How about for weekly income? Again, you could get by with a sample of 50 in a pinch, but 100 would be more reasonable, and probably good enough for most purposes. But for the survival rate for a medical treatment, saying "600 deaths, but I could be off by 20 either way" strikes us as too crude. We would not want to be off by that much when discussing a life-or-death issue. A sample size of 100 would be inadequate. Even a sample size of 1,000 might not be good enough, though it surely would be for the other two examples. On the other hand, a sample size of 1,000 for the GRE might be overkill and a waste of time and effort. This example illustrates that determining the sample size combines statistical calculations

TABLE 7.1. How Error Declines and Precision Increases as Sample Size Goes Up

Sample size	Sample mean	Standard deviation	Standard error of the mean	Sample mean ±2 SEs (95.4% confidence interval)
10	600	100	31.6	536.8 – 672.2
50	600	100	14.1	571.8 – 628.2
100	600	100	10.0	580.0 – 620.0
1,000	600	100	3.2	593.6 – 606.4

---

[22]If you use three SEs above and below the mean, this gives you the 99.7% confidence level. One does not often encounter 95.4% and 99.7% levels of confidence. Rather, it is typical to use 95% and 99%. To get the 95% level you multiply the SE by 1.96 (not 2); for the 99% level you multiply by 2.58 (not 3). Which number do you prefer to round off, the multiplier or the level?

inferential Stats measure probability that an outcome could have happened by chance - no relation between independent variables

with judgments about the nature of the population studied and the research question, which together help you to specify the level of precision required.

A final caution: even a large probability sample *could* be unrepresentative of a population. All samples contain *sampling error*. Sampling error is the difference between a sample statistic and the true population value. Anything can happen in a random sample, but some things are more likely than others. The beauty of probability samples is that you know the probability that the results drawn from it are unrepresentative. That probability declines as the sample size goes up.

A final reason to use larger samples concerns the validity of descriptive and associational statistics. The most common analytic techniques used for survey data come from the correlation and regression family. These techniques, especially the advanced ones, are all "case hungry." Factor analysis, structural equation modeling, and multilevel modeling all demand hundreds of cases if their conclusions are to be stable. Even for ordinary linear (OLS) regression, a sample of 30 cases or 50 cases is almost always too small, especially when your research involves more than a couple of independent variables. The more variables studied, the larger the number of cases (sample size) required.

So is there anything wrong with the recommendation to increase sample size? No, but it is a costly thing to do. You need to increase the sample size by a lot to get a sizable drop in error. When you double the sample size, the standard error is not cut in half. To halve the standard error, you need to quadruple the sample size. Figure 7.2 uses the same mean of 600 and shows graphically what happens to the standard error as you

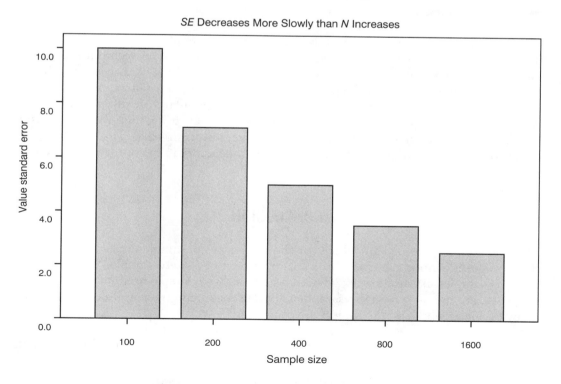

FIGURE 7.2. Sample size and standard errors.

double the sample size. It goes down, but rather slowly, with each doubling of sample size reducing the error only by about 30%.

When Should You Trade Size for Representativeness—or Vice Versa?

Both the size of your sample and its representativeness are crucial. Ideally, you would want a sample that is both large and representative. If you cannot afford both, if you have to choose, which should you emphasize? Again, the answer is clear: representativeness is *always* more important. You are much better off with a sample of 200 that is representative than a sample of 1,000, or even 10,000, that isn't.

A famous example of a huge sample that led to erroneous conclusions was collected by the *Literary Digest* magazine in 1936. Using a sample of over two million of its readers, the magazine predicted that the winner of the 1936 presidential election would be Alf Landon. Never heard of President Landon? That's because Roosevelt was reelected by a comfortable margin. The problem, in brief, was that readers of the magazine were not a representative sample of the population. Modern samples of one thousand have rarely been as far off the mark as the magazine's sample of two million. Today, no one but historians would have ever heard of the *Literary Digest* were it not the poster child for a hugely embarrassing error illustrating the importance of sample representativeness. It isn't too risky to predict that a 21st-century version of this famous mistake is likely to occur. Current telephone polling is done on landlines, but at least one-fifth of the population uses only cell phones (regulations, which are in a state of flux, currently bar "cold calls" to cell phones). Landline users tend to be older, whiter, and Republican—sort of like readers of the *Literary Digest*.

Modern sampling is not perfect, by any means. All samples contain error. A sobering example of sampling error, as well as other differences in survey technique, occurred during the 2004 presidential election campaign. National polling organizations (Harris, Pew, and Gallup) using good samples of about 750 to 800 likely voters, produced quite divergent results. In September 2004, estimates of the popular vote difference between Bush and Kerry varied by as much as 17%. If professionals using high-tech methods to sample the same population at the same time can get results this divergent, think of how likely *you* are to err and how risky it is to put too much faith in the results of one sample survey, even one using the best methods of sampling.

CONCLUSION

This chapter has provided guidelines for choosing types of samples and sample sizes for surveys, but it cannot substitute for a full treatment of *how to* sample. When actually drawing samples, be sure to seek advice on how to do so. Simple random sampling isn't simple to do; nor is systematic sampling. Because sampling is a well-developed field, many excellent works on the subject are available.[23]

Our next chapter investigates sampling in the context of interview research. In both interview and survey research, you need to find people who are willing and able

---

[23] Two widely available works are Jaeger (1984) and Sudman (1976). For coverage of some newer issues, see Groves et al. (2004) and the Suggestions for Further Reading at the end of this chapter.

to answer your questions. So some sampling choices you will make will be similar to those just discussed. But the kinds of questions and the nature of the expected answers in interviews are different from the questions and answers in survey research. Those differences will lead to a distinct set of strategies from which to choose as you locate and recruit interviewees. The table on p. 140 summarizes the survey sampling guidance in this chapter.

SUGGESTIONS FOR FURTHER READING

The theory and the practical applications of survey sampling have been well honed over the course of several decades. In addition to the chapters on sampling in the two works recommended in Chapter 1's Suggestions for Further Reading—Dillman and colleagues' *Internet, Mail, and Mixed-Mode Surveys: The Tailored Design Method* (2009) and Groves and colleagues' *Survey Methodology* (2nd edition, 2009)—there are two undisputed classics in the field. They are still read and still in print, although they are surprisingly pricey. Leslie Kish's *Survey Sampling* (1965) did much to establish the modern foundations of the field as did William Cochran's *Sampling Techniques* (1977). A more up-to-date intermediate text book is Lohr's *Sampling: Design and Analysis* (2nd edition, 2009). Sarndal's *Model Assisted Survey Sampling* (1992) remains quite useful.

Good short introductions to online survey sampling are Sue and Ritter's *Conducting Online Surveys* (2007); this is a general book on the topic with some sections on sampling. More focused on sampling is Schonlau and colleagues' *Conducting Research Surveys via E-Mail and the Web* (2002).

Researchers are more likely to be able to find up-to-date answers to questions about specific sampling issues, such as the effects of survey mode on response rates, in research articles rather than in texts. This is particularly true in the case of newer technologies such as social networking and telephone videoconferencing. We have cited several of these in the footnotes, but current knowledge is, as always, a moving target.

CHAPTER 7 SUMMARY TABLE

USE PROBABILITY SAMPLING WHEN . . .

- You know the probability that a particular case will be selected from the population.
- You want to generalize to the larger population, using inferential statistics.

Use simple random sampling when . . .
- You want to eliminate bias in your sample (always an important factor).
- You want to maximize external validity.

Use systematic sampling when . . .
- Simple random sampling is inconvenient or infeasible.
- You can obtain a good list (sampling frame) of the population.

Use stratified random sampling when . . .
- You want to compare groups that are not equally represented in a population.
- You know that simple or systematic random sampling will yield too small a group in some category.

Use cluster sampling when . . .
- Sampling frames are unavailable, making simple and/or systematic random samples impossible.
- You can increase your sample size to compensate for extra sampling error created in the clustering stages.

USE NONPROBABILITY SAMPLING WHEN . . .

- Representativeness is not important in your research.
- There is no way to get a probability sample.

Use convenience sampling when . . .
- You have no other options.
- You don't want or need to make inferences about populations.

Use quota sampling when . . .
- You want to increase the credibility of convenience sampling.
- You need to ensure that you will get representation in each of your research categories or groups.

Use judgment (purposive) sampling when . . .
- You cannot do a probability sample.
- You need to obtain a group to pilot test a survey (to be administered later to a probability sample).
- You have limited resources, and want to add credibility to a convenience sample.

Use snowball sampling/respondent-driven sampling when . . .
- You are studying a population that is rare or difficult to access.
- You need a method that is relatively easy and inexpensive to implement.

CHAPTER 8

Identifying and Recruiting People for Interviews

Criteria for methods to select cases should vary by design. Much of what we have said in the previous chapter on survey sampling is not relevant or needs to be qualified when considering methods of selecting cases in other designs. For example, interview informants[1] usually have a lot in common. This is true whether the interviews are individual or focused group interviews. By contrast, in surveys the researcher usually wants a representative sample of a diverse population; if all respondents were alike, this would amount to a biased sample. To repeat, techniques and criteria for choosing the people to participate in the research will differ by design. For instance, in survey research, purposive sampling is usually thought of as a second-best, makeshift method, one that is only slightly less lackadaisical than convenience sampling. But in experimental research, purposive sampling is an important supplement that can be especially useful for increasing the generalizability of findings. And in interviewing, purposive or judgment sampling is the method of choice. It might sometimes be supplemented with other methods, but the lead method is nearly always purposive. In purposive sampling, you deliberately select the cases you want to study. In interview research, this means that you first specify your target population; then you identify a pool of potential interviewees; then you invite specific members of that pool to participate.

Fishing expeditions are rightly dismissed as inappropriate in most research methods texts. Just dropping in a line to see what bites or whether you might snag something interesting is not a thoughtful or systematic method, and it is also unlikely to be successful. But *hunting* expeditions are precisely what are needed in interview research. When hunting, you know what you are looking for (you look with a purpose; hence, purposive

---

[1] What shall we call the person interviewed? *Interviewee* is one option and the one we use most often here; *participant* is another; anthropologists sometimes use *informant*. *Respondent* could work well for both surveys and interviews. Feelings can be very strong about this and similar issues of naming. Researchers' feelings about naming would probably make a good topic of research for social psychologists or anthropologists trying to understand identity group and clan formation.

sampling) and have a general idea of where to look, but you are not exactly sure whether and where you will find it. Of course, no matter how deliberative your searching is, you need to be ready to take advantage of opportunities that present themselves. Purposive sampling is often combined with opportunistic sampling. For example, when Rory Stewart walked across Afghanistan (from Herat to Kabul), he had a route planned; but at each stage along his route, he had to find people who were willing to talk with him—and often to put him up for the night. This kind of opportunistic procedure can lead to many delightful surprises. But it can also lead to bias. For example, because of traditional cultural constraints, Stewart was unable to interview women. His rich detailed portrait of a nation recovering from war omits half the population.[2]

Stewart was shown great courtesy over many months in Afghanistan. Successful researchers often tell how they were fortunate to be treated better than anyone has a right to expect and how that made their study possible. A striking example of opportunistic sampling combined with a courteous welcome extended to a stranger can be seen in Kai Erikson's sociological classic describing a disastrous flood in an Appalachian mining community that killed more than 100 and left some 4,000 homeless.[3] Erikson had been hired as a sociological expert in community relations to study the impact of the flood. His employer was a law firm preparing a suit for damages to be filed by the survivors. This consulting job, in which he served his clients well, also led to the opportunity to conduct sociological work that is rightly recognized as making an important contribution to sociological methods. His work was based largely on interviews with 142 survivors of the disaster. Some might think that he "exploited" both this opportunity, and the people he interviewed, but probably not after they read the book.

The distinction between opportunity sampling and convenience sampling may sometimes be unclear. To continue with one of our examples, convenience sampling for Stewart in his study of Afghanistan might have been staying in a hotel in a major city and interviewing Afghans who happened to stay there too. Or, more adventurously, Stewart could have interviewed people who lived in places served by public transportation. Instead, Stewart *walked* across the country and then took advantage of the opportunities that presented themselves. So the distinction between convenience sampling versus opportunity sampling is between doing what's easiest for you versus having a sampling plan based on your research question, while remaining flexible enough to recognize opportunities that occur as you implement your plan.

Apart from the observation that interview case selection is usually purposive and the selection of people you wind up talking with is often based partly on what we might call opportunistic sampling, generalizations about sampling and case selection in interview research are almost always subject to many qualifications. Algorithms are all but absent. This means that we will often illustrate points with examples.

Our discussion is organized in two parts: first, we discuss how interview sampling strategies are shaped by research questions. Second, based on how you interpret your research questions, we discuss more practical decisions you must make about interview sampling, such as who, how many, and where.

---

[2] Stewart (2006).

[3] Erikson (1976).

HOW INTERVIEW STRATEGIES ARE SHAPED BY RESEARCH QUESTIONS

There is hardly a more fundamental point to make than that strategies for finding, choosing, inviting, and recruiting people to interview need to be shaped by the nature of your research questions. Research questions are particularly important for identifying target populations and pools of potential interviewees. Recruiting from the pool is often more improvisational. It is easy to agree about the importance of research questions, at least in general terms. To make the discussion more concrete, we focus below on different kinds of research questions and what they imply for approaches to sampling. To organize our discussion, we discuss the nature of research questions under the following headings, realizing that any such organization is too rigid to describe what skilled researchers often actually do.

Our first topic focuses on when your research question leads you to seek external data compared to when it requires internal data from interviewees. Then we turn to a set of headings that form a continuum based on the extent to which your research question is theory centered. Some questions are clearly—to borrow from advertising slogans—"theory lite," while others contain the "concentrated formula." They range from descriptive research questions in which theory plays a modest role through exploratory and explanatory investigations, where theory becomes more salient, through theory testing and building, where theory is the main focus.

- When your research question seeks to gather external versus internal data
- When your research questions are descriptive
- When your research questions are exploratory
- When your research questions seek explanations
- When your research questions involve theory testing
- When your research questions aim at theory building

When Your Research Question Seeks to Gather External versus Internal Data

We discussed in Chapter 2 the distinction between interview researchers pursuing data that is either external or internal to the interviewee. This is parallel to the distinction between objective (external) or subjective (internal) data. Obviously, the people you identify as possible interviewees will differ greatly depending on the kind of data your research questions lead you to pursue. If you are interested in studying the origins of the "surge" in the U.S. war with Iraq, as Bob Woodward did,[4] you will seek a different sort of interviewee than if you are trying to understand how people cope with chronic illness and pain, as Kathy Charmaz did.[5] In the first case, you will seek individuals who have unique knowledge about external events, which you can often verify with external sources. In the second case, you seek individuals willing to explore with you and explain

---

[4] Woodward (2008).

[5] Charmaz (1991).

to you internal meanings and processes; verification usually involves returning to the same individuals for further clarification.

When Your Research Questions Are Descriptive

Descriptive goals have long predominated in interview research. While there is always some element of description in any research, the emphasis can vary. Even when the researcher's goals are more theoretical, the route to theoretical understanding through interviewing usually passes through thick descriptions and lengthy quotations from what interviewees say. We began our discussion of interview research in Chapter 2 by referring to Herodotus, who authored the first extant book-length interview research report. In his work, description and exploration were just about equally balanced. One research question involved exploring how it happened that the Greeks and Persians came into conflict, a conflict that altered the course of their subsequent histories for many decades. But Herodotus also had a more descriptive research goal: simply to record and describe for posterity what the Greeks and Persians had to say. To put it in modern terms, he described the cultures of the two peoples and how the conflict influenced them. When you pursue descriptive goals, accuracy and fairness are among the highest criteria of success. The fairness of Herodotus's descriptions is perhaps attested to by the controversies surrounding his works. Some found him an apologist for the Greeks while others, especially Greeks, thought of him as a "Persia lover." There was great diversity among the people with whom Herodotus talked. When he explored the origins of the conflict he focused on a different type of informant than when he collected the folklore that showed how people's beliefs were shaped by the devastating wars.

When Your Research Questions Are Exploratory

There are different ways to explore—with a microscope or with a telescope. Do you peer deeply into a subject or scan its horizon? Your research question will determine whether you want to delve deeply or roam widely in your explorations. In the first case, you will most likely want to pursue a small number of very in-depth interviews with particularly informative interviewees. But a larger number of shorter interviews can also work for some research questions. Shorter interviews generally have to be more targeted. It can be tricky to combine exploratory and targeted approaches, almost by definition, since to target an area of research is to narrow the range of exploration. For example, Adams explored the role imagination plays in social life by interviewing cross-national couples about how they decided where to live (his country, hers, or a third).[6] Adams's work was exploratory because social researchers have largely ignored the topic. She addressed a broad question by using a very specific group as they focused on a very specific question. By contrast, Udry's search for interviews was less specific; he searched broadly to explore more specific questions, in this case about the nature of economic institutions and practices in rural Ghana.[7] Although his aim was ultimately to move toward more theoretical work, he needed first to explore his topic through conversations with many people, which led to "opening up new questions [and] being surprised."

---

[6] Adams (2004).

[7] Udry (2003).

When Your Research Questions Seek Explanations

Sometimes your research question is quite exploratory and you can roam widely in your search. More typically, in what we call explanatory research, the searching involves weighing alternative explanations by delving deeply into the evidence from a comparatively few cases. For instance, seeking explanations for success (or failure) is quite common in evaluation research. In one project, we interviewed state higher education officials in states that, as indicated by our archival research, had done especially well in maintaining access to public higher education and curbing the rate of cost increases. We had some ideas (not really fully developed "hypotheses") about the political climate in states that kept cost increases moderate and maintained college access for students from less advantaged backgrounds. We used the interviews with knowledgeable state officials to ask them what their explanations were for the apparent success, at least comparatively speaking, of their states. We also asked them about some of our primitive hypotheses. In general, these interviews helped hone our explanatory tool kit. We retained some of our ideas as plausible, dropped others, and added new ones based on what our interviewees told us.

But none of this means there were no real surprises. When interviewing, researchers should always be ready for unexpected responses. For example, after introducing ourselves to one interviewee by explaining that we wanted to talk with her because of her key role in a state that was, based on our statistical indicators, comparatively successful at maintaining access to higher education, she said: "I'm surprised you came here. This state has a *terrible* record [her emphasis]." This interview was one of our most productive, even though—or precisely because—it contradicted our initial premise.[8]

When Your Research Question Involves Theory Testing

The question of the function of generalizations or theories is one of the most contentious issues in interview research. The reader will probably guess that we do not believe that any particular orientation is the only correct one. Erikson's discussion of the issue, as he describes his orientation in the study of the disastrous Appalachian flood, nicely summarizes the main points:

> Sociologists usually select the scenes they study because those scenes shed light on some more general proposition in which they were interested beforehand . . . My assignment . . . however, was to sift through the store of available sociological knowledge to see what light it might shed on a single human event, and this, clearly, reverses the normal order of social science research.[9]

As Erikson makes clear, either of these approaches—the order usually followed, and the reverse order he took for his study—can be appropriate. We also think it can be useful, in the course of the research, to *alternate* perspectives, sometimes frequently, between the generalization-driven and the case-driven approaches.

When taking a confirmatory or theory-testing approach, you are more likely than with most other types of interview research to sample in ways that approximate experimental

---

[8]Hodel et al. (2006).

[9]Erikson (1976, p. 12).

research or comparative case study research. For example, your theory might be that organizations with a particular type of management culture tend to have labor problems of a specific type. You plan to interview key individuals at each organization to learn about its management culture. If the presence or absence of the labor problems is a matter of public record, you could select two groups of organizations—one group with and another group without the labor problem.[10] Then you could use your interviews to see whether the management culture was what it "ought to" be if your theory was correct. Having decided on contrasting groups of organizations in which to conduct your interviews does not determine the number of organizations you would study. You might study 40 organizations (20 with the labor problem and 20 without) for 2 days each. Or you could study 2 organizations (1 with and 1 without the problem) for 40 days each. Your decision would probably be based on how much time per organization you would need to understand its management culture. And you might not know how much time you would need until after you had conducted interviews at a few organizations. You might expect to need a large number of interviews and a great deal of time in each organization, but find that you rather quickly reach the saturation point. Or you might expect to be in and out in a couple of days, but find that you have hardly scratched the surface of what you need to know in that amount of time. In that case, you would pursue fewer interviews in much greater depth. In theory *testing*, a larger number of cases is commonly studied in less depth. In theory *building*, in-depth interviewing and a smaller number of cases is the norm. Note that these are tendencies, not rules.

When Your Research Questions Aim at Theory Building, including Finding Causal Mechanisms

Theory building usually involves looking deeply into a limited number of cases, often with the goal of finding a causal link or mechanism. You are looking for (exploratory) a likely causal link (explanatory) for an outcome or event. Often this search involves "process tracing," where you reconstruct the steps leading to an outcome.[11] At other times it involves "grounded theory,"[12] in which researchers construct an explanation out of intensive examination of interview data. The kinds of outcomes one theorizes about can vary widely. They can range from single events to broad trends. They can be public or personal. In any case, while successful theory building emerges from flashes of intuition, creative insights, and other mysterious processes, these "eureka moments" are usually constructed atop months of in-depth probing of processes and meticulous examinations of mounds of data.

CONCLUSION ON THE INFLUENCE OF RESEARCH QUESTIONS

The types of research questions you pursue strongly shape your target populations and pools of potential interviewees. The influence of research questions is also important

---

[10]This is known as "selecting on the dependent variable," and it is controversial. The best known argument against is King, Keohane, and Verba (1994). For an opposing position, see Brady and Collier (2004).

[11]George and Bennett (2005).

[12]Corbin and Strauss (2008).

for the number of people you interview and how long you interview them, but it is less determinative. In short, research questions have a stronger effect on whom to interview than on how many of them to interview. When your research question is heavily descriptive and lightly theoretical, you might want interviewees who have good memories, are adept at noticing details, and have sufficient experience with the topic of your research. The kinds of interviewees you choose is probably least determined and most open-ended when you pursue an exploratory research question; if you knew precisely who to interview, you'd probably be investigating an explanatory research question or you might be testing a theory. When your questions are explanatory or involve testing a theory, your choices of people to interview tend to be more circumscribed. But when we move to the highest degree of theory-centeredness—that is, when the research question directs you to try to *build* or create a theory—the constraints implied by the question again become less important, certainly less than they were for theory testing or even explanatory research.

These conclusions are suggestive, but they are far short of the much firmer guidelines that can be offered for selecting respondents in surveys or assigning participants to groups in experiments. The suggestive nature of any recommendations we offer about interview research is in the nature of this design. Researchers uncomfortable with uncertainty and wanting clearer paths to follow when making decisions about case selection would do better pursuing questions that could be answered through survey or experimental designs. There is also a lack of clear rules for deciding the more nuts-and-bolt issues discussed in our next section, such as how many interviewees to invite and try to recruit.

MAKING BASIC DECISIONS ABOUT INTERVIEW SAMPLING

We have organized interview sampling decisions into four categories of questions, and the last contains several subquestions. The answers to the questions usually must be combined to create a complete sampling plan. Interviewees are almost never thought of as a sample from a population; rather, they are cases or examples. They may exemplify a population, usually a subgroup in a population, but they do not represent it in a statistical sense. If you gain unique access to a group or an organization, one that is important for addressing your research questions, you need not worry too much about representativeness, sampling frames, sample size, and random selection.[13] This does not mean that selecting people to interview can be approached casually; just the opposite is true. You need to exercise great care when deciding *whom* to interview, *how many* to interview, *how long* to interview them, and *how to contact* them.

- Whom should you interview and where?
- How many interviewees do you need?
- How many times and for how long should you interview?

---

[13] See Venkatesh (2008) for an example of a researcher who attempted to do survey research and was laughed at, but in the process managed to gain unique access to members of a group whom he observed and interviewed intensively.

- How will you contact or recruit your interviewees?
  - When should you offer incentives?
  - When should you consider variations in case selection by mode of interviewing?
  - When should you use snowball sampling and its modern elaborations?
  - When should you select, invite, and recruit for focused group interviews?

Whom Should You Interview and Where?

Whom do you ask to participate in your interview study? Interviewees have to have beliefs, experiences, or knowledge relevant to your research questions. And they need to be willing to talk with you and able to express themselves. Often, it is not easy to tell whether potential participants in your study are knowledgeable or experienced or able to express themselves well enough until you have started interviewing. You may need some initial screening questions, such as: "How long have you worked as a nurse?" Your criteria for screening based on that kind of question are dependent on your research problem. If you want to study the early occupational socialization of nurses, you don't want veterans. If you are interviewing "Palestinian female citizens of Israel,"[14] your population is quite targeted. You may wind up interviewing all you can find who are willing to talk to you. When Ralph Ezekiel studied the "racist mind" of white supremacists, he interviewed the leadership of national organizations and members of local adolescent gangs in one city.[15] Remarkably, as a member of one of the groups his target population despised (he was Jewish), and because he made no secret of his disagreement with virtually everything he heard, Ezekiel encountered no shortage of individuals—all white males—willing to talk to him.

There is no such thing as a generic interviewee. Each will have background characteristics and experiences that will influence how they view you and your questions, and that will shape the responses they make to your questions. And there is also no such thing as a generic researcher. Interviewees aren't "vessels of answers,"[16] and interviewers are not question vending machines. All bring their backgrounds, needs, and desires to the interview situation. What Goffman called "the presentation of the self" is universal and particularly salient in interviews.[17] This is hardly a new insight, but over the past few decades much more attention has been paid to its importance. Today, a researcher must attend to the question: When should the characteristics of the interviewees, and how they relate to your characteristics, be a focus in your study? There really are no rules, except perhaps: don't stereotype. Any answers will usually lie in the nature of your research questions. If your research question involves focusing on individuals who are members of a particular social category, it is important to remember two points. First, we are all members of *many* social categories (gender, age, ethnicity, occupation, and so on); no individual represents just one category. Second, the membership of *all* social categories is heterogeneous to one degree or another. So again we emphasize that

---

[14] Herzog (2005).

[15] Ezekiel (1995).

[16] Gubrium and Holstein (2001).

[17] Goffman (1959).

while it is important to pay attention to social background, don't stereotype: "avoid presuming very much based on membership in *any* categories and rely instead on the interview itself to reveal the individual."[18]

A related question is: what do you do when you have a personality conflict with one of your interviewees? You might annoy an otherwise good informant—or vice versa. When you find the informant irritating but are still learning from the interview, you should probably continue. But when you rub the informant the wrong way and he or she clams up, you might do better to move on and find someone more willing to talk to you.

The issue of *where* to conduct the interview can also be quite important. First, you need to decide whether you want location to be a variable or a constant in your study. More important, you need also to think about the contexts in which potential interviewees are willing to be interviewed. This was especially important in the example of the Palestinian women living in Israel mentioned in a previous paragraph. Locations for those interviews, and who chose them, were a key component in that study. In the study of the white racists, location was less of an issue, but the author found that it was important to attend meetings and rallies where he could observe his interviewees talking to one another, not only to him.

How Many Interviewees Do You Need?

How many informants should you interview? Why? Even in survey sampling, where statistical guidelines can be a big help, there are no invariably correct answers to this question. A fortiori, in interviewing, determining the number of respondents is largely a matter of judgment—hence judgment or purposive sampling. You can interview a single informant to write a biography or a "life history" as a way to study a broader culture. A handful of life histories is another option. What we confidently said of survey sampling—"the bigger the better"—is unlikely to be true of the number of cases in interview research.[19] As always, there is the inevitable tradeoff between breadth (many interviewees) and depth (fewer). Because one tends to interview similar individuals, one often doesn't need a sample size large enough to generalize to subgroups. As discussed above, the size will vary with the population being studied and the research question.

When have you interviewed a sufficient number of informants? How can you tell? It is much harder to decide in advance in interviews than in surveys. Our informal review of research articles and dissertations indicates that 20 to 40 interviewees is a normal range. For example, the authors conducted "in-depth interviews with 38 Arab Americans"; in another case "32 black women" were interviewed.[20] The number of interviewees will also be influenced significantly by the amount of time you have to devote to the project. Stewart, Erikson, and Ezekiel in the examples discussed above interviewed hundreds. But they collected data for years, often working full-time as they prepared their books. This is probably more time than most researchers envision working on a project.

---

[18] Schwalbe and Wolkomir (2001, p. 206).

[19] Crouch and McKenzie (2006).

[20] Respectively, Read and Oselin (2008) and Moore (2008).

How Many Times and for How Long Should You Interview?

How many times should you interview informants, and for how long each time? The amount of interview time is as important, perhaps more important, than the number of informants. Some of the classic texts in the field presume that you will conduct long interviews and that repeat interviews with the same interviewee will be common.[21] You might interview 20 people five times each in 1-hour sessions for a total of around 100 hours of interviewing. While reasonable, this is not inevitably the best way to "spend" 100 hours of interviewing. In some cases, a 1-hour interview with each respondent is plenty, and you might want to interview 100 of them, for the same total of 100 hours of interview data collection. Your strategy depends on what you want interviewees to explain to you, which in turn depends on your research questions.

Do potential informants have the necessary time to discuss all that you want to ask them about? One often worries about not getting enough time with informants, but many interview researchers have had the opposite problem—finding it hard to get respondents to let you wrap it up. Sometimes, after your initial screening questions, you discover that a particular interviewee is not the kind of person you were looking for, but this doesn't mean that the interviewee will gladly give up the opportunity to talk about him or herself. And there is a frequent tendency for interviewees to want to continue the discussion, sometimes after the formal interview is over—for example, after the tape recorder is turned off. It is sometimes the case that you pick up key insights and information after the formal interview, particularly when "the interviewee may have few opportunities to talk to someone so obviously interested as the interviewer."[22]

Reinterviewing can be done almost forever—assuming the interviewer is tireless and the interviewee is tolerant. You can always go to another level of depth. How deeply do you sample? When do you stop? Of course, the answer will be practical in part. You cannot spend your whole life studying one group or community or individual. But you should have a better justification than "I'm tired and out of time." Several metaphors have been suggested. The "point of diminishing returns" is a good one: when you have begun to learn considerably less from each additional interview, then it is time to stop. Most commonly in interview research, this is called the point of "saturation."[23] These points—diminishing returns and saturation—tend, like beauty, to be in the minds of the beholders. Experience can sometimes suggest a rule of thumb. For example, when conducting focus groups, researchers have often found that after eight or nine groups they do not learn much more. Ultimately, you will have to make a judgment. The rationale for that judgment should be part of your reporting.

How Will You Contact or Recruit Your Interview Subjects?

When you get to the details of actually finding folks to talk with, the entire process—from conceptualizing the ideal interviewees (the target population), to finding people to

---

[21] Spradley (1979); Mishler (1986).

[22] Warren et al. (2003) give numerous examples and discuss the ethical problems that can arise when learning from interviewees after the session covered by the informed consent form is over.

[23] See Wasserman et al. (2009) for a review and some suggestions for making the criterion of saturation more rigorous.

contact (the pool of potential interviewees), to convincing some of them to participate—usually involves several steps. When you have decided on the kinds of persons you want to interview, you still have to get them to the table. Recruiting is usually done by some combination of judgment and quota sampling, but probability sampling is not always absent. For example, in a study of graduate students' perceptions of their relationships with their advisors,[24] 12 programs were selected at random from an official list of the relevant programs. Then the training directors of those programs were contacted to solicit their participation, specifically to ask whether they would provide a list of the relevant graduate students. Nine of the 12 directors agreed to send a list of students whom the researchers could contact. Of 52 students on those lists, 16 agreed to be interviewed. Did the random sampling from a list of programs help make the study's conclusions more generalizable? Perhaps, but given the fairly low response rate from students who had not been selected at random (they accepted an invitation and volunteered to participate), any *statistical* generalizations would be very limited. Random sampling from a list of programs was certainly a reasonable way to select a dozen programs, but it would have been hard to fault the authors of the study had they done quota or purposive sampling. They could have used such criteria as programs that were large or small, at universities that were public or private, or in different regions of the country. For this research project, either random or purposive sampling would seem to work well. Most important is the fact that the authors *explained* how they found and recruited the interviewees. This is fairly rare in interview research. Descriptive narratives of how researchers invited and selected people to interview are not provided as often as they ought to be.[25]

When Should You Offer Incentives?

Opinions differ, but there is little doubt that you should always consider one question: What could motivate interviewees to answer my questions, especially difficult questions? Most research evidence about incentives pertains to participation in either survey research or experiments, where incentives seem to be effective at increasing participation rates—"complete this survey for a chance to win a gift certificate" or "participate in this experiment for extra credit." Opinions among interview researchers differ more over the issue of appropriateness of incentives than their effectiveness. One incentive that is fairly common, often appropriate, and raises few ethical concerns is to offer to share preliminary results of the research with interviewees. Such sharing can be combined with soliciting reactions to those results, which can be used to improve the research's quality. This procedure was followed in the research on graduate students' perceptions just described. It is also quite common to provide courtesy incentives, such as soft drinks and snacks. This practice is especially widespread in focus group research; some researchers have even found it necessary to offer lunch or dinner in order to get 8 to 12 people to show up at the same time and place. Providing lunch or dinner in a room quiet enough to conduct research can get very expensive; and it can be complicated—what do you do about dietary restrictions, for example? Direct cash rewards for participating are used in some kinds of interview research, perhaps most effectively in respondent-driven

---

[24]Schlosser, Knox, Moscovitz, and Hill (2003).

[25]Johnson (2001). By contrast, such narratives are routinely a part of the write-ups of experimental research.

sampling (see below) to recruit members of subpopulations such as intravenous drug users or the homeless to study health issues pertaining to those groups.[26]

When Should You Consider Variations in Case Selection by Mode of Interviewing?

As briefly discussed in Chapter 2, when modes of interviewing change, sampling strategies tend to differ as well. The main modes of interviewing are face-to-face, telephone, and various Internet-based forms of communication such as e-mail. It is increasingly common to combine these, for example, sending an e-mail describing your research project and asking whether the addressee would be willing to be interviewed on the telephone on the subject: "If so, would you please suggest some dates and times it would be convenient for me to call? If you would prefer to communicate by e-mail rather than over the telephone, I would be happy to do that as well." Another frequent combination strategy is asking respondents to a survey whether they would be willing to discuss the topic in greater depth either on the telephone or through one form or another of computer-mediated communication, such as e-mail. When you need to cast a broad net to find interviewees, you can sometimes write en masse to subscribers to an e-mail list or participants in a chat room or bloggers asking them whether they would be willing to be contacted for purposes of your research.[27]

Face-to-face interviewing is still the most frequently discussed mode in research methods texts, but we doubt that it is or will long be the mode actually used most frequently by interview researchers. Still, much of our methodological discourse about interviewing (including rules and procedures for ensuring interviewer privacy and confidentiality) presumes the normality of the face-to-face interview. At minimum, online modes of communication are likely to increasingly supplement face-to-face interactions. And hybrids, such as video-chatting, are becoming routine as the technology gets better and cheaper. The advantages and disadvantages of online modes of communication have the same roots—impersonality and lack of context are the losses that usually trouble researchers the most. Other research designs have been influenced by technological developments in communication, but none so fundamentally as interview research. The Internet makes interviewees easier to find but harder to know, at least in the ways researchers have traditionally thought of getting to know the people they interviewed.

When Should You Use Snowball Sampling and Its Modern Elaborations?

When the people you want to interview are hard to find, either because they are rare or because they are hidden in some way or both, then snowball sampling is likely to be the best method—perhaps the only method—for finding a reasonable number of potential interviewees. Snowball sampling means asking individuals who have agreed to be interviewed whether they would suggest other individuals who might be willing to be interviewed. This is a very widespread procedure, and one that many interview researchers find all but indispensable. Of course, snowball sampling will work only if

---

[26] Salganik and Heckathorn (2004).

[27] Garcia et al. (2009) provide a useful overview. For blogs, see Hookway (2008). On e-mail interviews, see Hessler et al. (2003) and Menchik and Tian (2008).

your interviewees know other members of your target population and are willing to trust you with their names. The popularity of the method is in part due to researchers' need. Often there is no practical alternative. Snowball sampling not only provides the researcher with leads but also with implicit references—"so and so suggested that you might be willing to be interviewed for this study."

Although it is often considered a technique especially appropriate for research collecting qualitative data, and it is most often referred to in that way, snowball sampling's roots are statistical.[28] When Leo Goodman first pioneered snowball sampling, the goal was to learn about individuals' communities or networks, not primarily to find individuals to interview. Building on this purpose of learning about networks, more recent statistically inclined researchers have elaborated on ways that researchers can use the "chain referral" method to identify *probability samples* of individuals to be interviewed. As probability samples, they can allow statistical generalizations from samples to populations. The most fully developed of such methods is respondent-driven sampling (RDS). Using the techniques of RDS, it is possible to use snowball samples to make unbiased estimates of population parameters. While the math behind RDS is formidable, researchers have demonstrated that it is relatively easy to implement and that it is a cost-effective method.[29] In short, when you want to use your findings from a sample of interviewees to make statistical generalizations to a broader population, RDS is a promising alternative—assuming that members of the population about which you want to generalize know one another.

When Should You Select, Invite, and Recruit for Focused Group Interviews?

The big differences when recruiting for focused group interviews (focus groups, for short) are contained in the two words *groups* and *focused*. Opinions vary, but most researchers agree that a good range for the size of a focus group session is between 8 and 12 people. This size means that the interview is a group discussion, but that the group is small enough that each individual has an opportunity to participate in a 60-to-90-minute session. The number of groups is also often recommended to be in the 8 to 12 range. Since each group contains 8 to 12 individuals, the total number of individuals heard from will be between 64 and 144. But the *groups* matter more than the specific number of individuals in them. The group is usually the unit of analysis. This means that for any given investigation, the number of group members should be similar from session to session. A group discussion among three people is very different from a discussion among 20. Groups that differ in size by that much are not really the same kind of interactional unit of analysis. In any case, a focus group is not designed to be a quick and easy way to interview a lot of individuals. When your research question aims at *individual* beliefs, attitudes, and opinions, you are better off interviewing 20 or 30 individuals *as individuals* rather than processing them en masse in groups.

---

[28] Goodman (1961).

[29] See Farquharson (2005) for traditional snowball methods as well as the related approach of "reputational sampling." See Salganik and Heckathorn (2004) for RDS. For RDS applied to internet sampling see Wejnert and Heckathorn (2008). An alternative is the so-called "capture-recapture" method; see Bloor (2005) for a review.

Recruiting groups means finding common times when and places where people are able and willing to meet. As anyone who has ever tried to schedule meetings or social events for a dozen people can attest, finding a date and time when everyone can make it is often surprisingly difficult. The recruiting task is made easier in focus groups because the specific 8 to 12 individuals to meet at a particular day, time, and place can be drawn from a larger pool of 100 or so. What should this pool of 100 or 150 potential focus group interviewees be like? First, they should be fairly homogeneous and therefore willing and able to focus on a particular topic. For example, in one study the topic of interest was teachers' attitudes toward the rights and liberties of high school students.[30] Obviously, non-teachers or university professors or grade school teachers could not be part of the pool of possible participants. The researchers looked for volunteers from among teachers at several high schools in their area. Once they had a sufficient pool, they tried to find common days, times, and places for the focus groups to meet. Following standard practice, when the potential participants differed significantly in background characteristics—for example, between younger and relatively inexperienced teachers versus older veteran teachers—these were put in different groups whenever possible.

As discussed in Chapter 2 on interview research designs, focused group interviews make most sense when your research question involves social dynamics and collective influences on beliefs, attitudes, and emotions. When groups of people are interviewed together and discussion among them is encouraged, it is possible for researchers to gain insight into the processes through which collective identities and opinions are formed. The most relevant situation when focus groups seem the ideal method occurs when your topic involves group dynamics or social relations. In one study of the women's movement in Britain,[31] focus groups were ideally suited to the researcher's goals: she wanted to understand the processes by which feminist identities were formed. This researcher also made use of what is sometimes called a "mini-focus-group" approach: that is, using groups of 4 to 6 individuals. The argument in favor of smaller groups is that they allow more intensive interaction among participants and between participants and the interviewer. The size of the group can vary considerably and any rule of thumb is no more than a suggestion to get you started. One key point when using focus groups is that your research question should be based on the idea that the focus group participants will provide you with something that you could not obtain by interviewing them individually. This usually means that the group process will be one of learning or change for the participants. Researchers often want to study the change or learning processes. One striking example involved discussions of ethics by medical students. After a mostly nondirected discussion on the topic of when it would be reasonable to lie to patients ("for their own good"), most participants changed their opinions from a rather breezy acceptance of dishonesty to conclude that the situations where lying was justified were quite rare.[32] Of course, the learning in group situations is not always marked by such happy outcomes, as social psychologists who study conformity have long demonstrated.[33]

---

[30] Vogt and McKenna (1998).

[31] Munday (2006).

[32] See Wibeck et al. (2007) for the women's movement and Bok (1999) for the lying medical students.

[33] See Willer et al. (2009) for a good overview and a recent extension.

CONCLUSIONS ON SELECTING PEOPLE TO INTERVIEW

Beginning researchers have a tendency to want to interview people like themselves or what they aspire to become. Students interview students, aspiring social workers interview social workers, and so on. This is acceptable. Each of the authors of this book has done it at one time or another. But we don't believe that it is necessarily the most effective research strategy. Our view conflicts with that of several methodologists writing about interviewing, particularly those who stress the importance of social and cultural relativism. There is a belief that men cannot understand women, or Anglos understand Hispanics, or straights understand gays, and therefore are inappropriate as interviewers.[34] We do not always share this belief. It is certainly easy to think of excellent interview work that has crossed gender, national, social class, and ethnic categories.[35] Of course, there are advantages in being an insider interviewer, but being an outsider can be also useful, precisely because you bring a different perspective to the interview. What we reject is the view that *only* someone from a particular social category can understand other members of that category. One of the beauties of in-depth interviewing is that it enables you to learn something new, to understand a different culture or way of thinking. This is a point most forcefully made by ethnographers,[36] but it has more general applicability.

Whatever your plan for finding potential interviewees and selecting among them, you will execute it imperfectly. That is to be expected in all forms of research. When it happens, you are obligated to explain, as limitations to your study, what these imperfections are. Sometimes difficulties with sampling can be revealing and can actually lead to some tentative conclusions about the subject. For example, one of us was on an interview research team studying people who were in so-called "open marriages." The team had a great deal of difficulty finding any. It was much easier to find individuals who *had been* in such marriages than people who were currently in them. Their tentative conclusion was that open marriages are inherently unstable. The couple either abandons the experiment or breaks up. Perhaps their strategy for finding interviewees was flawed. They certainly could not generalize their provisional conclusion to communities other than the ones in which they did their research, but they would not have been surprised to learn that open marriages were unstable elsewhere. In any case, the researchers on this team redirected their attention to related questions on which it was possible to find people to interview.

When you do not have a defined population and a sampling frame, such as a list of the members of the population, it is almost inevitable that you will have to adjust your research questions to align with the sample of people you can find and recruit. This phenomenon is not widely discussed in the research methodology literature. Perhaps it is too embarrassing. But it is almost certainly quite frequent. And it shouldn't be embarrassing; it is in the nature of interview research. The only bad choice that should embarrass researchers in the face of the inevitable need to improvise is hiding extemporized adjustments from the readers of their research reports. One way to address methodological

---

[34]Kong, Mahoney, and Plummer (2001).

[35]LaMont (1992), Henrich et al. (2001), and Winchatz (2006) are three examples.

[36]See Spradley (1979) and Emerson, Fretz, and Shaw (1995).

"full disclosure" would be to consult the decision criteria in this chapter, perhaps using the following concluding table as a checklist.

The table on pages 157–158 summarizes this chapter's interview sampling guidance.

SUGGESTIONS FOR FURTHER READING

Guidelines for identifying a potential pool of interviewees and then sampling and recruiting from that pool are not widely discussed in the research methods literature. Specific research reports often describe who was interviewed and how they were chosen, but there seems to be little general guidance. (For examples, see works cited at the end of Chapter 2 and in the footnotes to that chapter and this one.) Perhaps it's in the nature of interviewing that sampling methods are specific to particular research problems and populations. Techniques which are useful for identifying and interviewing samples of homeless people, state officials, surgical nurses, college students, or business managers are unlikely to be useful from one group to the next—or are they? Because it is not easy to find general guidance, do we necessarily conclude that it is impossible that there could be any? As one reads examples in which authors explain how their interviewees were chosen, one often finds a tendency for the writers to allude to general principles. Often the allusions take the form: "Typically one does X, but that wasn't appropriate or feasible in this case, so I. . . ."

There are several good general texts on interview research, for example, Kvale and Brinkmann's *Interviews: Learning the Craft of Qualitative Interviewing* (2nd edition, 2009) and Kink and Horrocks's *Interviews in Qualitative Research* (2010). But these provide very little guidance on whom to interview. They focus on how to conduct interview research, not on sampling and recruiting. It's a big step to go from saying that "we don't know of any" such texts to claiming that "there aren't any," but we're willing in this case to put a foot hesitantly forward. As always, we'd be happy to be corrected by readers who point out to us sources that we overlooked or how we otherwise got something wrong.

CHAPTER 8 SUMMARY TABLE

HOW INTERVIEW STRATEGIES ARE SHAPED BY RESEARCH QUESTIONS

When your research question seeks to gather external or internal data	• *External:* Seek individuals with specific and/or unique knowledge about external phenomena. • *Internal:* Seek individuals willing to explain/explore internal meanings, feelings, and processes.
When your research questions are descriptive	• Seek accuracy and fairness in reporting what you learn from interviewees.
When your research questions are exploratory	• Determine if you seek depth or breadth. • Be open to unexpected opportunities.
When your research questions seek explanations	• Prepare to delve deeply.
When your research question involves theory testing	• Prepare to sample in ways that are similar to experimental or case study sampling.
When your research questions aim at theory building	• Prepare to look deeply into a limited number of cases.

MAKING BASIC DECISIONS ABOUT INTERVIEW SAMPLING

Whom should you interview and where?	• Pay attention to social background and personal knowledge, but don't stereotype. • Decide if the location is a variable or a constant in your study. • Think about the contexts in which people will be willing to be interviewed.
How many interviewees do you need?	• Prepare to use judgment based on your research question(s). • Take into account the amount of time you have to spend.
How many times/for how long should you interview?	• Prepare to use judgment based on your research question(s). • Be alert for reaching a "saturation point."
How will you contact/recruit your interviewees?	• Usually combine judgment and quota sampling.
When should you offer incentives?	• To motivate interviewees to answer questions. • Provide courtesy incentives (such as refreshments), especially for focus groups. • In respondent-driven sampling (RDS), especially for hard-to-reach groups.

When should you consider variations in case selection by mode of interviewing?	• When you need to cast a broad net (e.g., consider recruiting and interviewing via e-mail). • When combining modes will create more options for access to participants.
When should you use snowball sampling?	• When the people you want to interview are hard to find. • When your interviewees are likely to know other members of your target population. • When your interviewees are likely to trust you with the names of other potential informants. • When you want to make statistical generalizations to a broader population using RDS.
When should you use focused group interviews?	• When your research question involves social dynamics and collective influences on beliefs, attitudes, and/or emotions. • When your topic involves social/group relations or the social processes of change. • When group participation will provide you with something you could not obtain by interviewing people individually.

CHAPTER 9

Sampling, Recruiting, and Assigning Participants in Experiments

Once one has decided to use experimental methods as the basic design, the next questions involve where and how to find participants for the experiment. Although the participants are usually called a "sample," they are seldom a sample in the sense of being drawn at random from a known population with the goal of then generalizing to that population. Rather, experimental participants are usually recruited from pools of volunteers. Then randomness enters the picture, when the volunteers are assigned to control and experimental groups. As discussed in Chapter 3, random assignment is part of the definition of an experimental design. That means that some sections of this chapter on assigning participants to experimental conditions will parallel parts of Chapter 3 on experimental design.

As always, we focus on options and when you would want to choose particular research methods. The choices in experimental research are numerous and often intricate. This reflects the extensive efforts experimental researchers have made to refine designs and methods for assigning cases to experimental conditions. Some of the choices may not be familiar to many readers. When that is the case, we describe them briefly as well as suggesting when it might be most effective to select which options.

When finding participants for experiments, as with any design, the basic questions are: Who? How many? Where? Who do you recruit? How many do you need? Where do you find them? The general steps are first to identify a target population, then to recruit a pool of volunteers, and finally to assign volunteers to experimental and control groups—also called treatment and comparison groups. These steps vary as between randomized controlled trials (RCTs) and various alternatives to RCTs.

RANDOMIZED CONTROLLED TRIALS

As discussed in Chapter 3, the two main characteristics of randomized controlled trials (RCTs) are (1) random assignment of cases to experimental and control groups and

(2) researcher control over the implementation of the independent variable. After you determine that you wish to and are able to use an RCT, many "when" issues need to be resolved. They include identifying a target population, recruiting volunteers, assigning operations of the independent variable, whether to use group or individual randomization, possible improvements on simple randomization, determining sample size, estimating statistical power, controlling for pretest scores, adjusting for missing data and other imperfections in implementation, and whether to conduct laboratory or field experiments. We discuss each of these in turn.

When Identifying the Target Population

Identifying a target population clearly depends on your research question, usually in a straightforward way. When the research question involves an educational or training program (e.g., does the program significantly increase scores on the outcome measure?), let's say for high school students or for senior citizens, your general population is clear. But you still might have many questions about subpopulations. If it is a program to improve pass rates in high school algebra, do you want students from public and private schools, in rural, urban, and suburban settings, and who are representative of different ethnic groups? If your question is about an exercise program for senior citizens designed to lower blood pressure and improve related health outcomes, similar questions pertain. Do you want participants from nursing homes or only those living independently?

Like high school students, senior citizens in nursing homes are clustered in easily accessible groups. And it is quite common to approach recruiting from your target population using groups and institutions such as schools, nursing homes, and community centers. These clusterings mean that your sampling from your population will not be random (see the section below on group randomization). Unlike cluster sampling, where the clusters are first selected randomly, and then samples are drawn randomly from those clusters, in recruiting for experiments the clusters are usually chosen with a combination of quota and purposive sampling. In a big study of a high school algebra program, for example, one might mostly select at the classroom level and choose students from large and small classrooms in large and small high schools, in rural, urban, and suburban communities, and so on. Or more typically, you would make these selections in stages by first running the experiment with recruits from, say, public urban high schools. In subsequent rounds of experimentation, you might recruit from rural high schools, private high schools, and so on.

When Recruiting a Pool of Volunteers

You can sometimes count on civic-mindedness or idle curiosity to find participants in your experiments, but even when you are blessed with eager volunteers, you will still need to do some recruiting, if only to let people know that there is an opportunity to volunteer. Generally, recruiting is more active than merely making an announcement. And to obtain volunteers, incentives are often necessary. Paying people for their time seems reasonable, as does providing a token of appreciation. But the incentive should not be closely related to your outcome variable, because this could influence your results. When using incentives there are some questions you should ask yourself: Does your incentive make your recruits less representative? If the recruits aren't representative, does that matter for the outcomes of the experiment? With monetary incentives, do you end up recruiting mostly poor people? Without monetary incentives, do you recruit only the independently wealthy? Does it matter for your research question? One common incentive is possible access to a new and promising treatment. When that is the case, potential participants may resist randomization. A way around this resistance is to use winning the random assignment lottery to decide who goes first. Those who "lose" are the control group for a time, but later also receive the treatment. This kind of staggered implementation of the treatment is also handy when you do not have resources to treat all participants at one time.

When Sampling and Assigning Operationalizations of a Variable

Sometimes, when your research question does not specify a population very precisely, any handy pool of potential recruits will do. This is often when the ubiquitous college student participants come into the picture. They are used mostly when the focus is on variables and their relations, not on generalizing to specific populations. For example, in a study of the effects of deliberation on decision making, "participants [were] drawn from introductory courses . . . at our university."[1] A total of 122 students were assigned at random to one of two kinds of groups of five students each: deliberation or discussion. A third (control) group engaged in an exercise on the topic (essay writing) that required no social interaction. The three groups of students differed from one another on the outcome measures of how they reached decisions and whether they changed in their decisions from pretest to posttest. These differences supported the theory being tested. To take a second example, an article on how pressure to conform is generated in groups, three studies were described (reporting multiple experiments in the same research article is a frequent practice). In the first study, 76 "undergraduate students (57 women, 19 men) at a large public university participated in the study for extra credit in a sociology class."[2] Students were given an unintelligible text to read and evaluate. They were randomly assigned to read it individually or in groups with "conformist confederates," who pretended they thought the article meant something and exerted pressure on the actual experimental subjects to conform. Students who read the article individually were more likely to recognize that the text was gobbledygook than were students who discussed the text in groups. This confirmed the authors' theory about the roots of conformity.

   As in most experiments, in these two studies—one about the virtues and the other about the dark side of group decision making—the focus was on *internal validity*. In such experiments, the goal is to make valid causal inferences about the relations among variables and the theoretical constructs they represent. This means that it is often important to sample among operationalizations of a variable and to be sure those operationalizations represent the theoretical construct. This sampling is usually purposive; the researchers use their best judgment about how to "sample" among the myriad ways the independent variables can be operationalized. This usually means that the operationalizations used to deliver the independent variable are varied, if not within one experiment, in subsequent iterations of the experiment. Indeed, experimental instructions are

---

[1] Schneiderhan and Khan (2008).
[2] Willer et al. (2009).

among the ways to deliver variations on an independent variable. Paying attention to the way the independent variable is administered can be more important than so-called "ecological validity," or the degree to which the experimental setting is similar to real-world settings. In brief, what matters most in laboratory RCTs is "the degree to which the operationalizations of constructs are true to the constructs."[3] Good operationalizations of constructs lead to justifiable causal inferences about the theory being tested.

Relatively small differences in delivery of the independent variable can have big effects. While the basic idea of an experiment is simple and the inferences can be straightforward and summarized in less than one line of text,[4] implementation can be exceptionally tricky. One good practice is to maintain consistency in administering a treatment, or, if you vary it, to treat these variations as a study variable. We discuss below the pretesting of variables related to the outcome variable, but pretesting experimental instructions is also a good idea. There is no escaping meaning. In experiments, just as in surveys and interviews, the participants' understanding of your explanation of the experiment is a key to a successful study. What do experimental participants understand by your instructions? The instructions, which are part of the operationalization of the independent variable, need to fit the theory.[5]

There are several kinds of potentially confounding variations in the operationalization of variables. Researchers sample among those—when they are aware of them. *Experimenter effects* have been studied fairly thoroughly and can be considered different operationalizations of a theory—do male subjects react differently in pain tolerance experiments when the experimenter is male or female? *Order effects* occur when there is more than one treatment in an experiment; then, the order in which the treatments are administered is another operationalization of the independent variable. *Counterbalancing* is the typical method for dealing with these effects on the delivery of the independent variable—when the order in which participants receive experimental treatments could affect their reactions to those treatments. Counterbalancing involves presenting treatments in random orders to ensure that you do not mistake order effects for treatment effects. Both can be important, but they need to be distinguished. For example, if there were three treatments—X, Y, and Z—there are six possible orders: XYZ, XZY, YXZ, YZX, ZXY, and ZYX. Participants should be assigned not only to control and experimental conditions, but also to different categories of conditions. In this example there would be at least seven groups: at least one control group and six different treatment groups.

When to Use Group Rather Than Individual Randomizing

Randomizing at the group rather than the individual level is done more often than one might suppose and surely more often than most textbooks suggest. That is because finding pools of unassociated individuals can be much more difficult than finding individuals who are clustered in one way or another. Researchers cannot assign customers to real estate offices to measure the customer satisfaction that results from a new

---

[3] Highhouse (2009).

[4] For example, a typical summary might read: H_0 not rejected; $p = .126$; Cohen's $d = 0.14$; 95% CI, −.21, +.18.

[5] One thorough discussion of these issues can be found in Rashotte et al. (2005).

service; the customers choose the offices. Researchers cannot assign patients to different hospitals to assess outcomes using different surgical techniques; health insurance plans have predominant influence in assigning patients to hospitals in many cases. And researchers cannot assign students to schools or classrooms to evaluate the effectiveness of an experimental curriculum; school and classroom assignments are made according to district and state policies. It is much more practicable in such cases to use clusters of cases (such as offices, hospitals, or classes), rather than individuals (such as customers, patients, or students).

Classic experimental designs can be effectively employed when groups rather than individuals are the experimental units. Sometimes groups can be selected at random even if individuals cannot be (see the discussion of quasi-experiments below). The main disadvantage of using groups as the unit of analysis is a drastically reduced sample size. If you have 1,200 students, 600 of whom receive the new curriculum and 600 of whom receive the old, your N would be sufficient for virtually all conceivable purposes of statistical inference and power. But what happens if instead of randomly assigning 1,200 students you randomly assign 60 classrooms, with each classroom containing 20 students? You might have the same 1,200 students, and you might be interested in individual students' learning, but, since the students are clustered in classrooms, your N is now 60. You would have 30 classrooms in the control and 30 classrooms in the experimental group. That may be enough, but it comes close to dipping below one rule of thumb about minimum sample size. Will you have enough statistical power to detect an effect of the new curriculum?[6] Surely moving from an N of 1,200 to an N of 60, though convenient and often the only practicable alternative, is a serious disadvantage in terms of statistical power and assessing statistical significance. A potentially more serious disadvantage of group randomization is that it means you are comparing classroom averages, even though your interest is in individual students. Generalizing from group averages to individuals is known as the *ecological* fallacy, and it should be undertaken only with extreme caution, some would say never. These disadvantages of group randomization can be mitigated somewhat by controlling for group differences, either through matching and propensity-score matching (discussed below) or through regression techniques such as ANCOVA and multilevel modeling (discussed in the companion volume on analysis).

When to Use Pure Random Assignment or One of the Other Assignment Methods

Pure random assignment is elegantly simple and highly effective. It should always be the first choice. It can be supplemented in various ways to improve it, but if random assignment is possible, it should rarely if ever be replaced. Supplements to pure random assignment employ additional means for assigning participants to groups or treatment conditions. These supplements are usually called "designs." They are designed to reduce error variance, which in this case means differences between participants in the control and experimental groups that were not removed by random assignment. While random assignment *eliminates* bias in the *process* of assigning participants, it only *reduces*

---

[6] Three articles in *Educational Evaluation and Policy Analysis* (Vol. 29, No. 1, 2007) have examined these questions in depth.

error variance in the actual assignment. Since there will always be some error variance, the control and experimental groups will never be perfectly equal, but it is possible to reduce these differences. Such reductions are particularly desirable when the number of participants is small, because when you have a small N, randomization is not as effective at reducing error variance. The use of these methods to supplement random assignment also importantly influences the size of the sample and the number you need in each treatment/control group, so we discuss them in the next section.

When Deciding Sample Size and Experimental Group Size

Probably no question is more frequently asked of a statistical consultant than: How many cases or subjects or participants do I need? Unfortunately, there is almost never an answer as simple as the question. All else being equal, bigger is better. But experiments can be costly to implement, and it is often difficult to recruit volunteers. As briefly discussed in Chapter 3, the design you pick influences the number of cases you will need. There are several basic choices: (1) within-subjects versus between-subjects, (2) blocked versus fully randomized, (3) crossed versus nested, and (4) Latin squares.[7] We do not review them in detail, but concentrate on how these choices affect your needed sample size for calculating statistical significance, power, and generalizability. When you pick a design, you also influence the number of cases you will need.

Within- versus Between-Subject Studies

The standard model in RCTs is between-subjects. That means that there are control and experimental groups, and they contain different participants. By contrast, in the within-subjects model, each participant serves as his or her own control. With this design, you have the highest certainty that there are no differences between participants receiving and not receiving treatment. Because they are the same people, there can be no differences, except those caused by the passing of time between the pretest and the posttest. The simplest within-subjects design is a plain before-and-after study. You measure the participants before the experimental treatment and after. Of course, whenever you use a pretest and a posttest of the dependent variable you are collecting data within-subjects, but in the between-subjects approach you are looking at two groups of subjects—those receiving treatment and those in the control group. In the within-subjects design, you collect data only on the treatment group; it is the only group you have.

It is fairly common to have both within-subjects and between-subjects variables in the same study. Such designs are called *mixed* or *split-plot* designs. For instance, you might want to study gender and number of practice sessions—one, two, or three—as the independent variables or factors; outcome on a performance measure would be the dependent variable. Gender would be the between-subjects factor, and number of sessions would be the within-subjects factor. *Repeated-measures designs* are a particular type of within-subjects design. Instead of having three groups with one, two, and three practice sessions respectively, in a repeated-measures design, all subjects would get three sessions and their performance on the outcome variable would be measured after each.

---

[7]Myers et al. (2010) review the numerous alternatives with special attention to their consequences for statistical analysis.

Single-case designs are also repeated-measures, within-subject designs (see the section on p. 174 on single-case designs).

When to Use Random Assignment within Blocks

The "blocks" in this design are roughly equivalent to strata in surveys. A blocking variable is one the researcher wishes to control. The participants are placed into groups determined by scores on the variable, usually a continuous variable, that the researcher wants to control. Participants with similar scores are assigned at random to blocks. Each block is then given a different experimental treatment. So, if you had two treatments and a control, you would need three blocks. When you have only one treatment and a control, the blocks become *matched pairs* (see below). Blocking is important when the sample size is small. The smaller the size the less sure you can be that random assignment will work its magic. With blocking, as with stratifying, the "general idea is to have experimental units that are more homogeneous within blocks than between blocks."[8]

When to Use Crossed versus Nested Designs

The basic outlines of the two methods are described in Chapter 3. Here we discuss the implications for sampling. The most obvious difference between the two is that researchers need many fewer participants with the crossed, within-group approach—at least 50% fewer. And depending on the number of experimental conditions, it could be many fewer than that. But the problems with within-subjects designs are also clear. Lack of a control group is the greatest. And repeated testing can lead to difficulties in implementation and interpretation, such as pretest sensitization, fatigue, practice effects, and so on. In the nested, between-groups approach, these difficulties are mitigated, but the cost can be high: you need many more participants. You may often be forced to decide based on your resources rather than on what you think the best design would be if your resources were unlimited. An awful question confronts us as researchers more often than we would perhaps like to admit: Is what I can afford to do good enough to bother doing?

When to Use Latin Squares and Related Designs

This is an extension of the randomized blocks design. It gets its name from the fact that Latin letters are used to label the blocks.[9] In any case, you use Latin squares to allocate treatments to participants in a within-subjects design—or, looking at it the other way around, it is a way to assign participants to treatments; the two are equivalent. As with counterbalancing, the Latin-squares method is used to negate order-of-treatment effects by rotating the order of treatments. A Latin square has to be square: the number of rows and columns, which represent the treatments and participants, must be equal. The number of participants is a multiple of the number of treatments. In a 3 × 3 square, the number of participants would be 3, 6, 9, 12, or some other multiple of 3. There is not only one set of ordered treatments that can be used with the Latin-squares method.

---

[8]Ryan (2007, p. 57).

[9]The Greco-Latin squares method adds variable orders and a different Greek letter to each Latin cell.

With three treatment groups, there are 12 possible 3 × 3 Latin squares. With four treatment groups, there are 576 4 × 4 possible squares. How do you choose among them? Randomly, of course.

When Adding Cases or Participants Is Expensive

When the experimental treatment is elaborate and requires special expertise and/or equipment (the functional MRI is a current favorite among expensive technologies),[10] then you want to be precise in your sample size estimate, not only for analytic reasons, but also because adding a modest number of cases can be a budget buster. That explains the good market for fairly expensive software packages for estimating sample size. For most purposes in the social and behavioral sciences, researchers can find a free package or one that is included in software to which they already have access. Even when recruiting and administering independent variables to additional participants is not terribly expensive, there is little point in going far beyond what is needed for purposes of the study. Resources might be better spent doing a second study rather than conducting only one study with a bloated number of participants.

In an experiment with a small number (N) of participants, you need to ensure that you have enough power to detect an effect. This involves planning your sample size to make sure it is adequate. There are formulas to help you do this planning. But, in order to use them, you have to insert into the formula values that you will not actually know until after you have completed the study. To determine the optimal sample size (N) in an experiment, you need to know the power and the effect size. Or, to figure out the power, you need to know the N and the effect size. Of course, you don't know the effect size. The whole point of the experiment is to gather data so you can calculate it. So you must estimate it to determine power and/or sample size.[11] After the experiment, of course, you can actually measure power and effect size, but by then it will be too late to increase your sample size should it have been insufficient. Unless you have a strong indication from the research literature of likely effect sizes,[12] this decision will have to be made largely on the basis of educated guesswork.

Statistical power is important. Power determines the likelihood that you can detect an effect. But the current emphasis on statistical power (and the related issue of statistical significance) may deflect attention from equally important concerns. Among them is making certain to have sample sizes large enough to detect effect sizes that are big enough and confidence intervals around effect sizes that are small enough to be important for practice. Findings that are statistically significant may not be sufficiently large and precise to be useful in professional practice. The procedures for making the sample size calculation will differ when the aim is effects that are large enough and margins of error that are small enough to be practically important.[13]

---

[10]See Tingley (2006) for an overview and Duster (2006) for a critique.

[11]A good practical discussion of statistical power and of how to use free software to estimate it can be found in Raudenbush, Martinez, and Spybrook (2007).

[12]See Hedges and Hedberg (2007) for a review.

[13]See Parker and Berman (2003) and Kelley and Rausch (2006) for a discussion. Kelley and Rausch also provide links to software that can be used with the freeware package "R" to make the calculations.

There are no *analytic* disadvantages to overestimating the needed sample size, so, when in doubt, it is much better to overestimate than to underestimate. The disadvantage of overestimating is increased cost—in money, time, and other resources. You have to decide: Are you more willing to risk having a sample size that is too small in order to save time and money? Or are you more willing to spend extra time and money in order to improve the chances that you have sufficient power to detect an effect? This is more an economic decision based on what you value than it is a methodological decision.

When to Use Pretests—and When during the Experiment to Administer Them

Pretests of participants on the outcome variable are almost always a good idea. However, pretest sensitization is often a worry. For example, if your experimental treatment is aimed at reducing prejudice, and you administer a pretest measure of prejudice level, this could be a tip-off to participants of the purpose of the experiment, and that prior knowledge could influence the effectiveness of the experimental treatment.

Pretests can be used to screen potential participants, to match members of the control and experimental groups, and to collect information on covariates (such as age, education, and ethnicity) that you might wish to control for when analyzing outcomes data. It is usually better to pretest before assignment to control and experimental groups. The later the pretest, the less useful it is as a "before" measure. Of course, it is necessary to pretest before assignment if you wish to use pretest scores in order to screen participants for eligibility. Despite the desirability of early pretesting, it is often practically difficult to pretest before random assignment. Late pretests probably do little harm, as long as they come before the experimental intervention.[14] Because pretests are usually targeted at your dependent variable, they are usually better than other "before" measures, such as evidence from records. But consulting records (such as student achievement test scores) can be cheaper and easier than writing and administering your own pretest. You could devote the time saved by using records—rather than writing, scoring, and analyzing pretests—to increase your sample size. Whether that trade-off (pretest vs. sample size) is worth it has to be answered on a case-by-case basis; you would compare the benefits of a larger sample size with the advantages of having more targeted pretest data.

When matching participants on pretest scores, the researcher's intention is usually to strengthen the conclusions drawn from an experiment by making members of the control and experimental groups more similar than might occur with simple random sampling. Matching is used both in experiments and in quasi-experiments, and there are several matching techniques. The simplest and clearest is the matched pairs approach. We use it here to illustrate the general idea. When using matched pairs, the researcher matches participants on a variable that is likely to affect their reaction to the experimental treatment or that is related to the dependent variable. For example, if the experiment was to test the effectiveness of a program designed to increase tolerance for nonconformity, the experimenter could give a pretest of attitudes about unconventional activities. The participants with the two highest scores would be matched; one would be assigned at random to the control and the other to the experimental group. The second-

---

[14]Schochet (2010).

highest-scoring pair would be similarly assigned at random to control and experimental groups, and so on until all participants were paired and assigned. The strength of the technique is that while using random methods of assignment, it also ensures that the match between the control and experimental groups will be very strong on a key variable—probably stronger than it would be had simple random assignment (without matching) been used.

One form of pretest matching that should be avoided is the "extreme groups" approach. This is very common, probably because it makes the researcher's work easier, but there are many reasons it should not be used. The typical extreme-groups method is to divide the participants, measured on a continuous variable, into thirds or quarters and compare the upper third or quarter with the lower. There are no good reasons to do this beyond tradition and sloth—and many reasons to avoid it. Noted researchers have denounced it for decades, using terms like "data mutilation," a "dodge of the lazy," and a way to foster "blissful ignorance." There is no question that the extreme groups approach can lead to serious overestimations of statistical power, effect sizes, and reliability.[15] Its continued use is somewhat perplexing. Perhaps the answer lies in social psychology—as an illustration of how poor practices can be perpetuated by imitation.

When Things Go Wrong in Your Experiment

Things always go wrong, at least a little. Conditions rarely live up to textbook ideals. Even with random assignment, the participants assigned are almost never randomly selected from a population to which the researcher wants to generalize. Then, after random assignment, participants may not show up because they had hoped to be in the experimental group but the lottery didn't go their way. Or they find the treatment boring or stressful and they drop out before it is over. Or they neglect or refuse to answer some questions on the pretest or the posttest, so that there are missing data. These limitations are routine, and they all cause threats to the validity of any causal conclusions experimenters might draw. While there is little that can be done to enable researchers to generalize to a population from which they did not sample, there are statistical techniques to address many other problems, such as missing outcomes due to participants dropping out or failing to comply with experimental protocols.[16]

When to Report What You Have Done

Full description is always good, and most good experimental studies contain considerable narrative detail about how the experiment was conducted, who the participants were, and any difficulties implementing the experimental design. The parts of this narrative addressing assignment to control and experimental groups can usually be covered in a sentence or two, since there are routine labels for most procedures of assignment. Despite the relative ease with which the basics of experimental design can be described, incomplete descriptions are still surprisingly common. For example, in an otherwise good article in a respected journal, we find the following: "A between-participants

---

[15] See Preacher et al. (2005).

[16] Baker and Kramer (2008) provide a good review.

pretest-postest experiment was used . . . Research participants ($N = 271$) were assigned to one of two . . . conditions."[17] What is missing is specification of *how* participants were assigned, but since the study is described as an experiment, we *could* assume that they were assigned at random. Also not specified is who comprised the pool of 271 participants. How old were they? How many were male and female? Were they recruited from a larger population? We could assume that they were young adults, since this is the target population for the research, and we might guess that they were university students, but we don't know this for sure. The moral of the story? Even when the method of assignment can be assumed, and when it can be assumed that random assignment was used to reduce differences between control and experimental groups, and when it is likely that the group of participants was not a sample drawn from a population to which the researcher wants to generalize, it is not good practice to neglect to specify these things. When such details are omitted, readers do not have sufficient information to judge the quality of the study and to decide whether to be confident about the validity of the conclusions.

When You Sample for Field, Not Laboratory, Experiments

Sometimes it is impossible to conduct an experiment in a laboratory or, even if possible, it is preferable to conduct your experiment in the real social, economic, or political world. Laboratory studies are usually simulations. Field experiments, or randomized field trials (RFTs), involve studying people in real-world settings. One loses some control over the variables and assignment mechanisms, but many researchers would consider this well worth it in terms of ecological validity, that is, the extent to which the experimental setting matches real-world settings. Some of the best-known RFTs have been massive government-supported attempts to study social and economic policies, such as, in the United States, "the effects of programs for job training, housing, health insurance, Food Stamps, Medicaid, unemployment insurance, and earnings and wage subsidies."[18] Despite huge investments in these studies, the strength of the inferences about causal conclusions is somewhat disappointing. One well-known author involved in such research concludes that the best way to strengthen these inferences is through multimethod research.[19] Similar ambitious studies have been undertaken in the United Kingdom, such as a study of 16,000 workers covered by the "Employment Retention and Advancement" program; in this and similar field experiments, clients of actual social agencies are randomly assigned (after giving informed consent) to different implementations of the program so as to compare their effectiveness.[20] When participants cannot be randomly assigned, for either logistical or ethical reasons, one runs the risk of "intervention selection bias," which stems from the obvious fact that those selected for an intervention are not likely to be a random sample, and therefore it would be inappropriate to generalize from this biased sample to a more general population.[21] Many

---

[17]Tedesco (2007).

[18]Moffitt (2004).

[19]Moffitt (2005).

[20]Walker, Hoggart, and Hamilton (2008).

[21]Larzelere, Kuhn, and Johnson (2004).

would say that studies plagued with this problem are not actually RFTs, but are instead quasi-experiments.

While the best-known RFTs have been government-sponsored studies of social policy, more modest field experiments are possible and may even be more fruitful. For example, one team was uncertain about the accuracy of conclusions drawn from experiments on market behavior using undergraduate laboratory simulations (this research often goes under the name "behavioral economics"). So they supplemented the laboratory research and tested their laboratory-based conclusions by conducting experiments in the field, in real markets.[22] They recruited numismatists at a coin show to participate in their experiments on market behavior, using silver dollars at a show where such coins were bought and sold. The details, though fascinating, are unimportant for our purposes. The main point is that it is possible to test theories in real-world settings using randomized experiments. It requires quite a lot of ingenuity by researchers to find real-world settings amenable to experiments, but it seems worth the effort in terms of increased ecological validity.

None of the above emphasis on the benefits of conducting studies in real-world settings should be taken to mean that we think field research is always preferable to laboratory research. Any research design has to be ready for obstructionism or resistance from participants. In laboratory experiments, uncooperative participants can be dealt with fairly easily by dropping the recalcitrant participant and replacing him or her with another. In field experiments, this is often not so easily done. A difficulty reported by one of our colleagues can illustrate. In a project studying the effects of training on elementary teachers, one school principal did not like the fact that "his" teachers were becoming more knowledgeable than he, and he especially seemed to resent that they were no longer quite so acquiescent. He did his best to undermine the study. Unlike in the typical laboratory setting in which an unruly participant can be invited to leave, in this case, the program officers and researchers evaluating the program were forced to try to work around this uncooperative real-world participant in the field experiment.

ALTERNATIVES TO RCTS

The main experimental alternatives to RCTs are natural experiments, quasi-experiments, single-subject experiments, and regression discontinuity (RD) designs. RCTs and their alternatives are mainly defined by the degree to which the researchers can manipulate the independent variables and can randomly assign cases to treatment and control conditions. These differences are summarized in Table 9.1. As can be seen, in RCTs and RFTs, experimenters exercise maximum control over experimental conditions. In natural experiments, they have the least mastery over the variables. The other designs represent intermediate states. In these, researchers implement the independent variables but do not use random assignment of individuals to control and experimental groups.

For many writers on research methods, there are only two major classes of research design: experimental and observational. Some would call natural experiments and quasi-experiments observational, because they are not "true" experiments. For such

---

[22] Harrison, List, and Towe (2007).

TABLE 9.1. Researcher Control over Variables and Case Assignment in Different Designs

	RCT and RFT	Quasi-experiments	Single-subject	Regression discontinuity	Natural experiments
Experimenter control, independent variables	Yes	Yes	Yes	Yes	No
Random assignment, cases	Yes	Yes for groups, not individuals	No	No	Sometimes, but not by researcher

writers, the observational category is a catchall and, like most residual categories, this is not very informative. We use the term *observational* research too, but we use it to refer specifically to research in which the investigator does some actual observing of social phenomena as they happen. For nonexperimental research involving preexisting data not generated by the investigator, we use the term *archival* research, but most textbooks refer to this as *observational* as well. Of course, all this reflects little more than a difference of opinion about which terms are more informative. We mention it here mainly to alert readers about what they will find in this and subsequent chapters. Of course, we think our terms are more descriptive and natural, but ultimately, the concepts matter more than the labels attached to them.

Natural Experiments

Natural experiments are widely used and have a history as long as or longer than RCTs. In a natural experiment, the researcher finds a situation in nature or in society that approximates an RCT. The data come from archives or observations and are not created by the researcher's actions. The "sampling" of the natural experiment occurs in the *finding* of natural or social events or settings that approximate experiments. To the extent that the naturally occurring variables operate *as if* they had been manipulated by an experimenter and *as if* cases were assigned at random, the better they are for causal analysis.[23] Sometimes researchers have been able to study variables truly assigned at random, as when the topic was the income of lottery winners or the effects on young men who "lost" the military draft lottery in the 1970s. But, while cases were randomly assigned, these assignment mechanisms were not under the researchers' control.

The classic example of a natural experiment, and probably the first formally recognized as such, dates to the 1850s. It was also a milestone in the history of epidemiology. John Snow believed that cholera was caused by contaminants in the water supply. He was able to subject this belief to a definitive test after 1852 (a time when the germ theory of disease was at best only vaguely understood), when one of the two companies that supplied water to London moved its intake pipe farther upstream; its water was then less contaminated by fecal matter and other London sewage. The second company

---

[23]The "as if" criterion is discussed in Dunning (2008). Other useful sources are Rutter (2007) and Robinson, McNulty, and Krasno (2009).

continued to supply tainted water, thereby providing Snow with a definitive test. Snow had to demonstrate that other differences, besides the condition of the water, could not explain any association between the company from which people obtained their water and the incidence of the disease. It is worth quoting Snow directly, as his logic still perfectly summarizes the kinds of conditions investigators seek in natural experiments:

> Each Company supplies both rich and poor, both large houses and small; there is no difference either in the condition or occupation of the persons receiving the water of the different Companies. . . . It is obvious that *no experiment could have been devised which would more thoroughly test the effect* of water supply on the progress of cholera than this [emphasis added].[24]

The death rate from cholera for those Londoners imbibing sewage-laced water was over eight times as high as that of those drinking the purer water piped in from farther upstream. Most readers of Snow's book—and it remains worthy of perusal today—have been convinced that "no experiment could have been devised" that would have allowed Snow to reach more certain conclusions. Few natural experiments are as good as this one, because few natural or social or commercial settings provide the kind of test that Snow was able to find—or, few researchers have been insightful enough to recognize them.

Quasi-Experiments

The quasi-experiment is an experiment "to some degree," and that degree is researcher manipulation of the independent variable, but without control over the assignment of cases to treatment groups. Most often, when conducting experiments out of the laboratory and in the real world, researchers are not able to conduct randomized field trials because they cannot randomly assign participants to control and experimental groups. Instead, they conduct quasi-experiments in which, to the extent there is randomization, it involves random assignment of treatments to preexisting groups formed by choice or by regulation, such as students in schools. The researchers do not assign cases to groups, but they do retain some control, often considerable control, over the administration of the treatments to the groups.

The quasi-experiment is the most frequently used field design, since researchers rarely have control over assignment to real-world groups, and it is certainly a design that has been very thoroughly discussed in the methodological literature. The best source is Shadish and colleagues' *Experimental and Quasi-Experimental Designs for Generalized Causal Inference*. Published in 2002, this book is a hugely expanded third edition of the famous little monograph published by Campbell and Stanley in 1963, which set the terms of the debate for nearly all subsequent discussion of experimental designs and which introduced the term *quasi-experiment*. Shadish et al. put their main emphasis on field experiments, which mostly means quasi-experiments, and on external validity, which is what the authors mean by the term *generalized causal inference* in the title. We cannot summarize their main arguments here, nor can we review the extensive literature on the subject that has appeared in the decade or so since the book was published.

---

[24] Snow (1855).

Rather, we focus on a few key points about case selection and how to adjust for absent or imperfect randomization.

In RCTs, matching is a supplement to improve upon simple random assignment. It is designed to increase the similarity between control and experimental groups. When you use a quasi-experiment, by definition you do not have random assignment of individuals to control and experimental groups. Therefore, matching becomes dramatically more important. In most quasi-experiments, the matching is similar to the kind of grouping done in comparative case studies. For example, when quasi-experimenters plan to study clinics, schools, or restaurants, they group them by such attributes as size and location before administering treatments. In that way, the cases in the treatment and comparison groups are similar on a few important variables. Note that this matching is done at the organizational, not the individual, level. When the research question concerns effects of treatment on individuals, and when the number of those individuals and data available on them is extensive, it is possible to greatly improve the quality of the matching by using a technique called *propensity score matching* (PSM). Although it is an analytical technique implemented after the experimental treatment, it makes sense to discuss it briefly in this chapter on assigning cases, because it is a method that can be thought of as the virtual assignment of cases.

When conducting a quasi-experiment, we think that researchers should always consider PSM.[25] We explain why by describing a hypothetical but fairly typical example. Say you want to test the effectiveness of a program to improve math achievement of students in the 4th grade. You find 14 schools in a large urban school district that are willing to participate. You explain that you have resources to implement the program at only seven schools in the first year; this is Group 1. The other seven, Group 2, will implement the program in the second year; in the first year they serve as the control group. The schools agree to decide who goes first by a drawing. With this staggered implementation, and with the order determined by drawing lots, you have introduced an element of randomness into your assignment of cases. This is a pretty good design, and you can congratulate yourself on how well you've done. But, without further work, it is unlikely that you would be able to detect an effect of the program, even if the effect size were considerable. At the end of Year 1, any differences between the average math achievement scores of the schools in Group 1 (treatment) and Group 2 (control) are not likely to be statistically significant, if for no other reason than your number of cases, seven in each group, is too small for you to detect a difference. Besides, you are interested in the effects of the program on individual student achievement, not on school averages—and certainly not on averages of school averages! Here is where PSM can come to the rescue.

If each of the schools in your quasi-experiment enrolls about 60 4th-grade students, each of your two groups, experimental and control, contains about 400 individual cases. Now you're talking! If you have, from school records, typical data about the individual students in your two groups (and these can usually be obtained anonymously), you have what you need for PSM. PSM is a form of matched pairs that combines scores on multiple variables into an overall propensity score. That score is then used to match participants in the quasi-experiment. Say you have, for most students, scores on a previous standardized math test, prior math grades, and information on demographic variables

---

[25] A good overview is available in Stuart and Rubin (2008). See also Rudner and Peyton (2006).

such as socioeconomic status. Rather than trying to match students on each of the variables individually, you combine the variables' scores, using regression techniques, into propensity scores on which you match students. In our example, you might select the 200 closest matches from Group 1 (treatment) and Group 2 (control) and compare their math achievement. PSM is a powerful technique, far better, we believe, than any other that could be used for this kind of data collected in a quasi-experiment. The main disadvantages are technical: you need a lot of participants and a lot of covariants. It takes a lot of time to collect the data, to compute the propensity scores, and to use them to match participants. Considerable technical skill is required, and it is not as easy to explain the results to the lay public and school officials as it would be if you used school averages. But, if you are interested in whether your program actually has an effect on individual students, you would be ill advised not to consider the method.

Single-Case Experiments

Single-case experiments are also known as single-subject experiments and as "ABA" designs. These are true experiments in that the treatment is manipulated, but given that there is but one case, of course there is no random assignment of cases to control and treatment groups. Instead, they are within-subjects designs applied to one case at a time. Treatments are applied, stopped, applied again. Repeated measures of the outcome variable are made following each change in the treatment. This approach is most frequently used in therapeutic contexts, when patients or psychological clients have rare ailments. The focus is on individuals, not on treatment and control groups. Participants are studied one at a time. As in most case-oriented research, whether the cases are nations, companies, or individuals, the researcher's emphasis is seldom on variables, but rather begins with the case. Any theoretical understanding of variables tends to be built up inductively. When applying this design, the experimenter works by assigning treatments to cases, not be assigning cases to treatment conditions. The results are usually summarized as a time series and often depicted graphically.[26]

Regression Discontinuity Methods

Regression discontinuity (RD) methods of assigning participants to control and experimental conditions are most often used when considerations of fairness argue against random assignment to treatment groups.[27] Instead, those most in need of the treatment are assigned to it. Needless to say, this *assumes* that the treatment is beneficial. Of course, if that were known with certainty, there would be no need to conduct an experiment. To make the assignment, a cutoff score is used, not random assignment, to place participants into control and experimental groups. Often the assignment criterion is a pretest on the dependent variable. The cutoff score is often the mean of the scores on the assignment criterion. Other scores may be picked for the cutoff point on substantive grounds; on statistical grounds the mean is best, but only on statistical grounds (statistical power is greatest if the mean is used). As with the single-case experiment, results are usually depicted graphically in RD by using a regression line. If the treatment has

---

[26]Kennedy (2005) provides a good introduction.

[27]The best general source is Shadish et al. (2002, Chap. 7).

been effective, there will be a sharp break in the regression line that coincides with the cutoff score. The RD approach has a great deal of potential, because it can employ an assignment mechanism more likely to be perceived as fair, while also providing unbiased estimates of the effects of the independent variable—the only nonrandom method of assignment to do so. RD has not been widely used outside of education, perhaps because of resistance to innovation, especially when innovation requires considerable technical expertise.

CONTROLLING FOR COVARIATES

A covariate is a variable other than the independent variable that is correlated with ("covaries" with) the dependent variable.[28] When attempting to make causal inferences, all researchers, whatever designs they use, hope to control for covariates and thereby to eliminate other possible explanations for a causal connection indicated by an association between an independent and a dependent variable. In experiments, this control is accomplished very effectively by researcher manipulation of the independent variables and, of particular focus in this chapter, researcher assignment of cases to conditions. In an RCT, random assignment tends to take care of covariates "automatically," by equalizing control and experimental groups, at least within the bounds of probability.

When wanting to improve upon or supplement random assignment to control for covariates, the researcher has a range of methods from which to choose: matching or assigning subjects to blocks on the basis of scores on a covariate, using repeated measures or within-subject designs, and, for the greatest reduction in error variance, Latin-squares methods. These improvements and supplements can be complicated to implement and costly in time and effort. In most experiments, it is beneficial to control for covariates. All else being equal, it would always be helpful to use prior information about experimental participants to increase the study's statistical power and thereby to increase the precision of the estimates of the size of experimental effects. Or, looking at it the other way around, you can reduce the sample size needed to attain a particular level of statistical power if you control for prior information. But all else is rarely equal; the researcher has to assess the likely benefits of using supplements to random assignment against the costs of implementing those supplements. The general idea is to minimize the differences between control and experimental groups, specifically differences not attributable to the experimental effects. Random assignment does a good job at this, particularly when the number of cases assigned is large. The smaller the number of cases, the more likely controlling for other variables is needed to improve the quality of the study.

When you do not have the RCT researcher's control over administration of the independent variable and assignment of cases, the need to control for covariates is greatly increased. The further you move from the pure RCT ideal, the greater the need becomes. Thus, the need to control for covariates is greater in quasi-experiments than in RCTs and greater still in natural experiments. Of course, in archival designs, in which you

---

[28]Usage is not perfectly consistent. Sometimes *covariate* is used to mean independent variable. A covariance is a nonstandardized correlation coefficient, *r*. Or looking at it the other way around, *r* is a standardized covariance.

investigate variables that you did not generate and which do not approximate random assignment, controlling for covariates is the whole ball game. Remembering that the covariate is a kind of correlation (unstandardized) helps explain why archival research is often called "correlational"—despite the fact that correlational methods are routinely used in RCTs, too.

Just how important is the use of prior information to control covariates? The bigger the differences between the groups, the more variation there is to control. The difference between groups—that is, the variance in the outcome measure attributable to group differences rather than to experimental conditions—is often measured by the *intraclass correlation* or ICC. The ICC measures the proportion of the total variance associated with the dependent variable due to between-group differences. Ideally, you would want differences between control and experimental groups to be zero before the experiment and large after the experimental treatment.

Only when the ICC is substantial is there much point in controlling covariates. What is substantial? Rules of thumb differ, as always, but an ICC less than .05, or 5%, would usually be too small to bother with. ICCs have been computed often enough for public health outcomes and for educational effects that we can generalize. In "firms, hospitals, group medical practices," the ICCs are "typically much smaller [seldom higher than .10] than those for measures of student achievement within schools [usually between .10 and .30]."[29] This means that controlling for covariates is typically useful when studying these institutions, especially schools. In the absence of prior knowledge, the researcher should expect to benefit from controlling for covariates in schools more than, for example, in hospitals.

How do we get scores on covariates and which covariates do we choose? The most useful covariate is almost always the score on a pretest of the dependent (outcome) variable. Second best is a covariate that is likely highly correlated with the dependent variable, but not with the independent variable (in economics, this is called an "indicator variable"). Group mean pretest scores can be effective, even when the goal is to understand effects of experiments on individuals, but they are never as helpful as individual pretest scores. Demographic and other background variables can be useful too, especially when pretest scores are not available. Pretest scores on some outcomes may be difficult or impossible to obtain (for example on surgical outcomes or on customer satisfaction). In those cases, background variables can be a useful substitute.

All this leads us back to where we almost always begin in causal research—to John Stuart Mill's three conditions for causation. To conclude that variables are causally linked, the researcher must demonstrate three things: first, the presumed cause must precede the effect ("after" cannot cause "before"); second, the hypothesized cause and effect must covary (if they don't occur together, they can't be causally linked); and third, no other explanation accounts as well for the covariance of the postulated cause and effect. The third one is the tough one. All research methods concerned with causality are attempts to improve the degree to which we can claim that no rival explanation better accounts for the one posited in the theory. Experiments, particularly the methods they use to assign cases to control and experimental conditions, are among the most successful (some would say the *only* successful) ways researchers have for eliminating otherwise plausible causal theories.

---

[29] Bloom, Richburg-Hayes, and Black (2007, p. 53).

CONCLUSION:
SAMPLING, RECRUITING, AND ASSIGNING CASES IN EXPERIMENTS

As in every chapter, we conclude this one with a table summarizing what your options are and when we think it is advisable to choose to use which ones. The number of options described in this chapter is quite large. This reflects the extensive efforts experimental researchers have made to improve designs and methods of sampling and assigning cases in experiments. The chapter has also been more complicated than some of the others because many of the options (the "whats") needed explanation. When we discussed options that might not be familiar, such as Latin squares, propensity score matching, or regression discontinuity approaches to assigning cases, we first had to describe these. So we have not been able to say simply: (1) when to use X and (2) why. We have often needed an extra step: (1) here's what X is; (2) here's when to use it, and (3) why.

The table on pages 178–179 summarizes this chapter's guidance on sampling for experiments.

SUGGESTIONS FOR FURTHER READING

Because random assignment and its approximations are part of the design of experiments, many of the sources listed in the Suggestions for Further Reading in Chapter 3 will also be relevant for this one.

It is often most interesting to get ideas about experimental design during your review of the literature by looking at what others have done rather than by using textbook accounts. However, some textbooks describe important experiments others have conducted. Mook's *Classic Experiments in Psychology* (2004) provides a nice overview and gives a very readable description of 60 well-known experiments. Another popular text taking the same approach is Hock's *Forty Studies That Changed Psychology* (6th edition, 2008). As these two books illustrate, most experimental work in the social sciences occurs in psychology and psychology-based disciplines. A very good overview that discusses experiments in other fields—including sociology, economics, and political science—is edited by Webster and Sell: *Laboratory Experiments in the Social Sciences* (2007). This is more of a handbook than a textbook; individual chapters are written by specialists in the various disciplines.

Because random assignment is often difficult to apply for practical and ethical reasons, there is an extensive literature on "work-arounds." Most of the sources are quite advanced. A brief general text that covers a lot of ground in a nontechnical way is Dattalo's *Strategies to Approximate Random Sampling and Assignment* (2010). For more on propensity score matching and related techniques that can be used to make adjustments when random sampling isn't possible, see Gao and Fraser's *Propensity Score Analysis* (2010). And the key book by the one of the creators of several of the techniques we discuss in this chapter is Donald Rubin's *Matched Sampling for Causal Effects* (2006).

CHAPTER 9 SUMMARY TABLE

Situation	Options
SAMPLING AND ASSIGNMENT OPTIONS WHEN USING RCT EXPERIMENTAL DESIGNS	
• After identifying a target population	• Use your knowledge of the population to find cases (usually purposively) to assign randomly.
• To recruit a pool of volunteers	• Use appropriate incentives, but not incentives closely tied to the dependent variable. • Use a lottery to determine which cases get access to a desired treatment, or in a staggered implementation, which get early access.
• Operationalizing a variable	• Use different operationalizations of the independent variable to represent various aspects of the theoretical construct. • Consider possible experimenter and order effects when operationalizing the independent variable.
• When to use group and when to use individual random assignment	• Individual randomization (the preferred method) is often impossible because cases are naturally grouped. • Group randomization is often more feasible than individual, but reduces sample size.
• Design influences on sample size	• Between-subjects designs require more subjects than within-subjects designs. • Use mixed or split-plot designs when your research question requires combining within-subjects and between-subjects variables. • Use blocking when the sample size is small and you want to increase the similarity of the control and experimental groups. • Use the nested, between-groups design (rather than the crossed within-groups approach) if you have sufficient resources. • Use Latin-squares methods of assigning cases when counterbalancing treatment orders is important.
• Choosing an appropriate sample size to ensure statistical power	• When adding cases is expensive, precise estimation of the sample size needed for sufficient power is especially important. • Choosing a sample size always involves estimation; precise calculations of statistical power can only be conducted after the experiment.
• When to use pretests	• Pretesting cases on the dependent variable, ideally before random assignment, can improve assignment and, by controlling for pretest scores, lead to stronger conclusions.

When to use pretests (cont.)	• Matching participants on pretest scores can add to the internal validity of your conclusions.
	• Avoid extreme-groups matching on pretest variables or any other variables.
What to do about imperfect implementations	• Report the imperfections (refusals, dropouts, missing data, etc.) and what you have done to adjust for the problems they cause.
Reporting your sample size and methods of assignment	• Only full details about the size of the sample and the methods of assignment enable your readers to be confident about the validity of your conclusions.
When to use field (not laboratory) experiments	• Field experiments sample from a different universe than laboratory experiments. Lab experiments are tidy but artificial; field experiments are messy but realistic. Consider the nature of your research question when making the inevitable tradeoff.

SAMPLING AND ASSIGNMENT OPTIONS WHEN USING ALTERNATIVES TO RCTS

When to use natural experiments	• When you can find naturally occurring phenomena that approximate assignment to treatment and control groups.
	• Look for such naturally occurring phenomena when it is impossible or inefficient to try to manipulate variables and randomly assign cases.
When to use quasi-experiments	• When you need to use group rather than individual assignment.
	• When you cannot assign groups to comparison and experimental conditions, but you can assign treatments to preexisting groups.
	• When you can obtain data to improve the quality of the estimates by using matching techniques, such as propensity score methods.
When to use single-subject experiments	• When the research emphasis is on learning how to treat individual cases.
	• When the experimental treatments extend over enough time that the treatments can be started and stopped several times—without harm to the research participant, of course.
When to use regression discontinuity methods of assigning experimental participants	• When treating research participants equitably, by providing treatment to those most in need, is an important consideration, one that trumps random assignment.

CHAPTER 10

Searching and Sampling for Observations

Searching and sampling sites for observational research has much in common with other forms of sampling discussed in this volume.[1] Yet observational designs also involve unique challenges and a distinctive sampling logic when it comes to selecting the organizations, events, locations, and situations for observing people and the complex social processes that engage them. The unique challenges arise because the researcher must make a series of up-front decisions and then stay flexible as opportunities develop on the ground. Sampling observations is a complicated business, and this chapter provides some suggestions for choosing among several approaches. We advise you to read more on site and case selection, especially examples of successful observational studies, as you are developing the design and sampling plan for your study. Reading other studies that have confronted issues like your own can help you make sampling decisions before entering the field—and to revise them as you see adjustments that need to be made.

Instead of controlling, simulating, or otherwise engineering situations for study, as is done using other designs, observation requires that you find a naturally occurring phenomenon and search for chances to observe that natural experience.[2] Observational research in the social sciences is particularly distinct from experiments, especially randomized controlled trials (RCTs).[3] You search first for possible sites, and then for cases, and then you sample the occasions and situations that provide the possibility

---

[1] We use the term *sampling* generically to refer to all aspects of selecting cases, sites, people, and times for observation.

[2] Denzin (1971).

[3] Vogt, Gardner, Haeffele, and Baker (2011).

of observing the phenomena relevant to addressing your research question. You don't create the research situation as in an experiment, a survey, or an interview. Instead, you observe it unfolding. In the case of naturalistic observation, the researcher and the research processes are often covert. This means that you are more likely to observe an unvarnished occurrence of interest. You also may have to wait for the phenomenon of interest to occur naturally.[4] In the case of participant observation, you are more confident of witnessing what you want to witness, but the researcher's presence invariably alters the "naturalness" of the phenomenon even when the researcher is relatively covert. Observational designs, naturalistic and participant, overt and covert, require balancing practicality, potential interferences, and the likelihood that you will see what you need to see to answer research questions.[5]

Research questions serve as road maps for sampling observations, whether the decisions are made in advance or in the field. You decide what to observe considering what you know about the phenomenon of interest and the role that theory development or refinement plays in your research question. You begin by searching for general categories and potential resources. Then, from broad searching in these contexts, you make increasingly narrow sampling decisions about what to observe. This chapter provides an overview of how research questions shape both in-advance and in-the-field decisions about sampling. Research questions vary in terms of how much usable knowledge we have about something, and this factor influences our searching and sampling. Are we making initial observations, in a largely unexplored field, trying to figure out what we are witnessing in order to describe it? Or are we working with a theory that requires examining cases in real-life situations in order to elaborate or to test the theory? The issues involved in choosing when, where, what, and whom to observe share common features with other design options, and it is often worthwhile to consider how observational designs might be used in conjunction with other sampling strategies discussed in this volume.

We can offer no neat algorithm for sampling observations in light of research questions. Instead, we suggest three different lenses that you can use to help in sampling. We begin with an overview of three basic considerations for sampling observations, determining: (1) how appropriate or relevant a sample is; (2) how to access authentic opportunities to witness phenomena represented in our research questions; and (3) how to balance various practical and resource concerns. This discussion establishes a basis for considering sampling from the perspective of research questions more specifically. First, we look at the basic research questions (i.e., when, where, why, how, and whom) and how these influence sampling. Finally, we return to the role that theory plays and offer another perspective on how the five types of research questions used in Chapter 8 also guide sampling in observational research. The question types considered are descriptive, exploratory, explanatory, theory testing, and theory building.

---

[4] Consider the parallels between natural sciences and naturalistic observations. The television series *Planet Earth* had amazing footage of wildlife in natural habitat. One particularly stunning shot was of a shark leaping out of the water to catch a seal in its jaws. A patient videographer waited a lifetime for that footage! Social scientists who wish to observe what occurs naturally are often in the field for a long time. Chapter 4 includes several examples.

[5] See Chapter 4 for details about when research questions suggest observation is necessary.

OVERVIEW OF SEARCHING AND SAMPLING CONCERNS IN OBSERVATIONAL RESEARCH

Generally speaking, there are three overarching factors that guide searching and sampling decisions for observational research designs: (1) the appropriateness of the sample; (2) access to situations in the sample; (3) and practical, resource, and logistical concerns. First, appropriateness in observational research uses sampling logic determined by two factors: the *relevance* and *representativeness* of observation sites and particular occasions for your research questions. Observations are often made in the context of case studies and combined research designs, so sampling decisions may be nested or scaled, and choosing the unit(s) of analysis for your observation is a critical part of designing the study.[6] Representative occasions must first be relevant, but the two concepts overlap considerably and must be considered in tandem when searching and sampling. For example, research questions about the quality and access to health care in rural areas would require determining relevance by defining what "rural" means. You include among the potential cases or sites to be sampled only those that are relevantly defined as rural. A definition of rural may include demographic, historical, or other considerations. You may need to know how many hospitals and clinics are in the region, how many beds, doctors, how many people are served, or how many miles the average patient drives to get to a health facility, all before sampling representative sites from the "population" of relevant ones. After developing a definition of what *rural* means, and thereby defining the relevant population, you select cases and sites that best represent the concepts in your research question.

A second consideration is access to authentic observation occasions. Will the people even allow you to observe them? And even if they are welcoming, how likely are you to be able to witness what you want to observe when you select a particular case? Once you have access, you must also be confident that you are witnessing an authentic occasion of interest and not something staged for the researcher. How will you ensure that when you observe, you are seeing the same phenomenon that you would see if no researcher was present? Of course, there can be no way to know this, since you cannot observe what it would be like if you didn't observe. But still you can ask yourself: Are there things about my sample of sites and observations that skew what I am able to see? Three factors potentially bias the sample in ways that call authenticity into question. The first is a lack of breadth. The second is insufficient attention to changes over time and how these may bias the sample. Finally, a lack of depth or variations in the depth of data collection across the sample may be a source of distortion.[7] As an example, researchers observing time-on-task in elementary classrooms sampled numerous entire days over the course of a full academic year hoping to achieve a sample that was both deep and broad enough to capture authentic interactions and behavior and that also included significant variation. They sampled different "kinds" of school days, including Halloween and other atypical school days.[8] Only through this intensive and extensive

---

[6] Patton (2002); Ragin and Becker (1992).

[7] Patton (2002).

[8] Smith (2000).

sample of observations were they able to draw a complete and authentic picture of how much time schoolchildren actually spent on learning the official curriculum. In this case, as in many others in observational research, seeking representativeness through a broader random sample would not have been as effective.

Finally, there are practical, resource, and logistical considerations. Will you have the resources to observe when and where you would like? Is there enough time and money to make sufficient on-site observation practical? Or will inadequate resources limit the number of sites or the number of visits you can make? An equally important consideration is whether you can, in the allotted time, see enough of what you want and need to see to make it worthwhile. Resource constraints determine how much you will be able to witness. Is your sample extensive and representative enough to enable you to address the type of research questions you are asking? To draw on an example we cited in Chapter 4,[9] if you seek thick description of the life of bouncers, you need to consider how much time is needed and what kind of variation would help you answer your questions. If you want to be clearer about the bouncer life overall, you need to consider whether you should see bouncers in different clubs or different kinds of clubs with different clientele, balancing what you expect to see with the resources available. Your choices are strongly influenced by practical concerns, but you have to be able to justify choices to research audiences. Do you need to go "under cover" and work as a bouncer in clubs, or could you learn what you wanted to know by observing while quietly sitting in a corner with a drink pretending to be an ordinary customer?

Observational research is resource intensive, not only when you are on site observing, but also continuously in the care and feeding of your field notes and transcripts, and then during the coding, analyzing, and interpreting phases of the research. As you engage in these activities, it is important to document and justify the steps you took to observe the organizations, events, and situations in order to answer your questions. Convenience sampling that selects the most readily available opportunities is not acceptable because it has no rationale to support the coding, analysis, and reporting that conclude the research. Instead, you are guided by relevance and representativeness of your samples, by whether you can gain authentic access to them, and by the adequacy of your resources as you seek to answer your research question.

APPROPRIATENESS AND RELEVANCE OF THE SAMPLE

When you select among observational sites, cases, events, and times, your sampling is a deliberative process that requires tradeoffs and hard choices. Throughout this volume, we have referenced two strategies for sampling applicable to observational designs: purposive and probabilistic. Purposive sampling is focused on *relevance* in observational and other research designs. Probabilistic sampling is aimed at *representativeness*. It is tempting to simply map these two views of sampling developed for measurement-based designs onto observation, but this is not wholly appropriate to searching and sampling decisions in observational research. As discussed above, you first want your potential sites or cases to be *relevant* to the concerns that underlie your research questions.

---

[9] Calvey (2008).

Determining this is a matter of judgment (informed by evidence, of course), which is why purposive sampling is sometimes called judgment sampling. When your sites and cases are relevant, they could still vary in how much they are *representative* of the concepts identified in your research question. If your search for relevant sites and cases yields a large number of candidates, it may be appropriate to use probabilistic sampling to select sites for observation.[10] Or, and more typically, you could decide that the cases and sites you need in order to investigate your research question also have to be selected using your judgment rather than a statistical procedure.

When Do You Search and Sample for Relevance?

Relevance sampling might begin by searching the Internet or a database, using key words or criteria to develop a more specific idea about which observations will comprise a meaningful sample. In Chapter 11 on sampling for archival studies, we offer an overview of how searching determines sampling. It is much the same with observational research. Once you have found the "population" of relevant cases, you can then refine your search to a much smaller sample of resources you can actually use. The process is ongoing, and often requires refining the search terms several times, and it perhaps subtly reshapes your research question as you see different features and perspectives of your population of sites and cases.

The process ends, at least temporarily, when you can identify units that represent the relevant population and a subgroup of cases or examples that offer the possibility of answering your research question. In his classic 1971 essay on naturalistic inquiry, Denzin used home-based examples to illustrate how he sampled observations of family interactions. When studying mother–daughter interactions and sex role socialization, Denzin sampled spaces where these interactions were most likely to occur: bedrooms, kitchens, retail spaces, and even bathrooms.[11]

Relevance of the cases sampled may be fairly easy to determine in some situations. For example, one of us conducted a study of "postsecondary coaching" in high schools, where a designated professional was assigned specifically to help students plan for life after graduation and take the necessary steps to enact that plan. One relevance criterion was obvious: the searching process had to find high schools employing such designated coaches, a relatively rare incidence.[12] Then, there needed to be evidence that coaching was practiced long and deeply enough to observe its effects. Not just any high school with a well-established postsecondary coach would do; another component of the study was to document coaching effects on low-income and minority students. Thus, finding a relevant sample also meant locating specific schools attended by these students. The initial set was developed through searching; high schools were then sampled for representativeness, and a final sample selected for comparative case study.[13]

---

[10]This was the procedure used in the study of graduate students in counseling psychology discussed in Chapter 8: first judgment was used to identify relevant programs; then probabilistic sampling was used to pick among them.

[11]Denzin (1971).

[12]Difficulties in finding rare samples are discussed in Lee et al. (2001).

[13]Haeffele (2009).

When Do You Search and Sample for Representativeness?

If a case is relevant, then it is somewhat representative by virtue of being a member of a relevant set. Your job as researcher is to find the examples that represent your research question well or effectively—as "perfect examples," comparison examples, or even outliers and negative examples where you expect to see something different, so that the variation you are studying through your research questions can be witnessed. Patton offers 16 different sampling strategies for observational research, and his schema is not the only one available to the observational researcher.[14]

To understand the phenomenon you want to describe, explore, or begin to explain, you and the audiences of your scholarship both need reassurance that you have chosen an observational sample that is representative of its set: a population or a group of organizations, settings, occasions, or events to observe phenomena and variables of interest. While judgment is always involved, it is important for researchers to avoid picking only observation sites that fit their preconceptions. It is harder to avoid the influence of the unexamined assumptions that may be embedded in your research questions. It is much better to make your assumptions about the set of possible observation sites explicit and to inform your readers about those assumptions. Then you and your readers can determine whether the sites and cases you have selected represent the phenomena in a logical, credible way.

When selecting a representative subset of cases the decisions tend to be more difficult than when indentifying the initial pool or population of relevant potential cases. Random sampling and other statistically derived sampling procedures are designed to make these choices in an unbiased way. Observational researchers have the same obligation to seek unbiased samples, but their approaches will almost always be different. The subset that you select probably will not be chosen using random processes, although in certain cases it may be possible to do so. The key point is to be able to make a credible argument that you are not using a biased procedure or merely selecting cases because it is convenient.

Knowing that it is impossible to witness everything that might pertain to a research question, you strategically choose cases as representative of some special variables, concepts, or exceptional features. It is possible and often advisable to seek outliers for this purpose, and to see what contextual variation does to the sensitizing concepts, constructs, or ideas that shaped your research question. For example, you can locate sites by their reputation for exceptionality. You can create comparisons that highlight variables of interest or offer new insights. Or you can locate a few relevant cases that share a particular variable in order to witness variation in several contexts where that variable presents.

In the study of postsecondary coaching mentioned earlier, the role of coaching in high schools was studied in a combined design that included observation. To explore variables related to the coaching in context, two high schools were sampled from a relevant set by selecting schools based on their demographic and college-going profiles: for example, one school had an 80% poor and minority student populations with an 80% rate of college matriculation, a very high college-going rate in relation to its student demographics. The comparison case had only 20% poor and minority students, but

---

[14]Patton (2002).

also had 80% college attendance. By selecting cases with similar outcomes but an obvious difference (the relative percentage of poverty and minority students), observations yielded comparison data about the coaching process and outcomes in the two settings.

In observational studies, you often do not have the luxury of deciding in advance when to observe by using demographic or other profile data. Duneier's sociological study, *Sidewalk*, is an excellent example of this. He did not simply pick a "sidewalk" at random. Rather he intentionally chose to study the same neighborhood featured in Jane Jacobs's famous study conducted 40 years earlier.[15] One of his research questions concerned how the area had changed over time. Then Duneier went into the field and followed leads as they presented themselves.[16] We could call this a kind of snowball sampling that takes the form of following your opportunities. Snowball sampling is not uncommon once you have an entering wedge into a social context in which you are an outsider. Duneier became acquainted with one street vendor who was a key resource for introducing him to others in the street's economic and social system. The general point is that sampling criteria and opportunities will develop in the course of your study, and these may lead you in directions you did not initially intend to go. This kind of learning as you go is in the nature of, and one of the strengths of, observational research. If you didn't expect to be surprised from time to time and to learn how and what and whom to sample as you go, you probably would not have chosen an observational design in the first place.

ACCESSING OBSERVATION SITES

Sampling logic and key sampling ideas, often adapted from statistical models for qualitative research, must be coupled with some practical considerations. Chief among these is the likelihood you can access a site and the occasions and people that you want to observe. And even if the individuals with the power to grant you access approve, you will need to meet the standards of the research community regarding whether it is ethical for you to access the site and do the kinds of observations you want to do. A more thorough discussion of ethical matters follows in Part III of this volume, but research ethics influence sampling and access.

When you have identified a group of relevant cases, you are left with more practical sampling issues of access to the people and places that interest you. How likely are you to be able to find observational occasions where recruits are both willing and able? A persistent criticism of observational designs is the failure of some researchers to provide a rationale for their samples and how they developed case selection criteria, and then to explain their criteria in clear terms.

Decisions about observing in the field invariably include making choices about how "revealed" as a researcher you will be or how much you intend to participate in the social processes you observe. Choices range from being totally passive up to and including being a fully participating action researcher. As always in observational designs, you are less able to make up-front research decisions than you are with other designs, such as surveying. Rather than use the techniques of, for example, survey sampling, you

---

[15] Jacobs (1961).

[16] Duneier (2000).

document your decisions in a research or field journal; you keep memos that capture your thinking. This can be invaluable when you report your findings and offer others the opportunity to judge the decisions you have made and therefore the usefulness of your study. The question of how revealed you will be in the field is also an access issue: How does your covert/overt status in the field affect access and thus sampling decisions? Will you get more access if your presence is not known? Or will revealing your research intent open new doors to you? Decisions about how revealed to be in the field come early on, and they will shape your recruitment and contact strategies.

Witnessing Authentic Phenomena

How likely is it that you can observe something authentic and not staged for your benefit? The answer is closely related to decisions about how revealed to be. The more obvious it is that you are a researcher, the greater the potential that this can change the situation and the behaviors you are observing. This is a surprisingly complex matter, not just because of interpersonal dynamics, but also because it presents a set of ethical dilemmas, which we address in Chapter 16. As you select sites, you will have to get a feel for how likely you are to form relationships and how to handle yourself with others. This will be complicated and continuously developing, so it is a good idea to document insights that relate to the authenticity of your observations.[17]

Time is a factor, too. How much time do you need to be confident that you have witnessed something unstaged—or not overly influenced by your presence? The more time you spend, the more likely you are to witness genuine and useful phenomena. Kidder observed for 9 months in a fifth-grade class to get data for a thick description of the daily life of an exceptional teacher and her students in an economically depressed community.[18] The results of his many hours spent in that classroom yielded an unforgettable and richly textured portrayal. Your research question is an initial guide about how much time you will need to make it likely that you will witness authentic occasions and situations, but as with most things in observational research, your initial estimates are quite likely to be wrong—underestimates, most observational researchers would say.

DECISIONS INFLUENCED BY RESOURCES AND OTHER PRACTICAL CONSIDERATIONS

It is tempting to put time and money first when making decisions about projects, but in *research* projects resources should not be the only considerations; ideally, they are secondary to answering your research questions and developing usable knowledge. As stated above, increasing observational time helps build confidence that you are gaining access to unfeigned actions and that your accounts of them are faithful to reality. The

---

[17]For example, Venkatesh (2008), who studied a Chicago street gang, immediately identified himself as a (survey) researcher and quickly evolved into an ethnographer and a quasi-participating observer, while his key informant believed that Venkatesh's intent was to write a biography of his exploits as leader of the gang.

[18]Kidder (1990).

extensive time that high-quality observational research takes causes some researchers to shy away from this design. It is, in short, very resource intensive. Sampling the sites most relevant for answering your research questions may involve extensive travel. It is not uncommon for novice researchers to have to choose between the most relevant sites and cases and those that they can afford to study.

Some researchers are fortunate in being able to obtain support for the time, travel, and other costs of observational research. Doctoral candidates are not often in this group, yet their research questions may require extensive time in the field observing. Choosing closer rather than more distant sites may constitute a legitimate tradeoff. It may also mean studying just one case example with observation. Choices must be supported with appropriate justification and documentation and described in the section of the sampling procedures devoted to limitations. Another option is to choose a research question that someone is interested in funding. Many funders concentrate on specific topics and interests, and it is worth finding out which of these might coincide with your research interests. Recently, one of our institution's research centers was approached by a foundation that had learned of its scholarship in the field of school leadership. At the time of this writing, that foundation, whose philanthropic cause is early childhood education, is underwriting the cost of an international observational study by our research center on models of educational leadership that influence early learning.

Advanced graduate students may have access to support through fellowships, grants, and scholarships, both within and outside of their educational institutions. Again, this does not mean convenience sampling is acceptable. But it does mean that all researchers who are not independently wealthy have to balance multiple considerations in their choices of research design and case selection. An unknown, but probably large, number of novice researchers have been influenced by monetary considerations to abandon their first choice of an observational research topic in favor of a more fundable one, or even to give up on observational research and take up the analysis of existing databases rather than collect their own data.

FOUR BASIC SAMPLING DECISIONS

Another way to approach observational sampling issues is by answering four basic questions that are a natural part of any sampling plan. Using your research question, you need to decide, in brief, (1) when?, (2) where?, (3) what?, and (4) whom? We will consider them in this order, but these decisions are likely to be nearly simultaneous and impossible to separate in your thinking as you plan your sampling so that it best addresses your research question.

First, when will observation, a labor-intensive endeavor, be possible? The "when?" question becomes primary because coordination is required between the researcher and the people at the site. But you also must decide when to observe based on the likelihood that you can witness a sample of occasions, practices, and events of interest with the time and money available to you. You and the site must be available to see what matters most. Even though convenience sampling is inadequate as a reason for doing anything, you have to be realistic about what is possible, so your own availability and that of those you wish to observe can be balanced.

Second, where will you go? It may seem counterintuitive to make this the second question, and in fact, it is inseparable from the first. Once you have done the groundwork of searching and sampling, you will likely have to juggle sites and potential observation occasions within those sites. Again, resources will matter as you make the inevitable tradeoffs to get into the field. In our own work evaluating teacher professional development in Science Technology Engineering and Math (STEM), we focus on partnerships between schools and universities. To do this we usually decide when to go (Question 1) based on the nature of events we are likely to witness, often occasions where teachers, principals, and college faculty are gathered in partnership meetings. We must also decide which sites (Question 2) are likely to yield answers to our research questions about what makes STEM partnerships viable and sustainable in differing contexts. We have to make choices simultaneously about when and where, guided as always by over-riding research questions and purposes. When can we go and where will we see what we most want to see given our best hunches and given that we can't be everywhere at once, and that we might not always be welcomed at all times? Sometimes, even though a site nominally meets our sampling criteria, we recognize that what we can learn there is limited, and we move it down our list of priority cases.

Third, when you are in the field observing, what types of phenomena do you want to see, and how are these phenomena likely to manifest themselves? Can you both plan ahead and stay flexible in the field with the decisions you are making as you sample? You will have to sample from more opportunities than you can possibly follow up, so you have to think of how to use your time effectively as you choose when and what to witness. To continue with the STEM example, our interest is in the sustainability of partnerships that enable teachers to build supportive relationships with their university colleagues to benefit their students. How do you observe a partnership developing and maintaining itself? What are the occasions where this shared work is done? What do you most need to see to build an understanding of how partnerships form and mature so that usable knowledge results? How can we think about the partnerships over time and see a representative sampling of occasions that matter? These are not easy questions to answer, and fieldwork will continuously inform the answers. These questions are typical of the complexities involved. They illustrate that while observational researchers may sample only a few sites, or even only one, they usually collect hundreds (often thousands) of observations and sample from an even larger number of potential phenomena to observe.

Finally, you need to consider whom you want to observe. Population sampling is rarely the primary concern in observational research. But in any social science research, you must decide who is most interesting in order to answer your research question. To continue with our STEM partnerships example, we have had continuously to decide whom to visit. Ultimately, students are intended to be the main beneficiaries of the STEM partnerships, but we did not begin by observing students (although we did collect data about them from school records). In the early phases of the project, we observed gatherings of college deans, school district superintendents, and other policy makers. Next, we spent time with steering committees of leaders like principals, professors, and grant directors from universities. Now, after studying partnerships for several years, we are studying the fruits of the partnerships as we visit and observe teacher teams, teacher leaders, and the classrooms in which students are engaging with teachers.

SAMPLING AND THE FIVE TYPES OF RESEARCH QUESTIONS

One final way to think about sampling in observational designs is to return to the continuum of question types used in Chapters 4 and 8: (1) descriptive; (2) exploratory; (3) explanatory; (4) theory testing; (5) and theory building. First, there are research questions that require thick description of a phenomenon, and sampling decisions will seek to balance resource concerns with educated guesses about how much descriptive detail will be enough. You have first to understand what you are studying well enough to know what is relevant. This is a "what" type inquiry where we begin to "fix the phenomenon"[19] with "thick description" from the sites we sample.[20] Next are those exploratory research questions that imply elaboration on prior thick descriptions where questions are more specific and in which we explore variations we are coming to understand. This is another "what" type of inquiry, but one that is left open-ended so that new insights have room to emerge. Third, we come to "why" and "how" questions that seek to explain phenomena. Fourth are questions that ask us to test prior findings as a means of establishing an emerging theory. Finally, we conclude with research questions that seek to refine or build upon a theory and to create the possibility of using the research results to further our scholarship and to shape practice.

To illustrate sampling decisions for each of the five question types, we offer an extended example. Let us consider the theory or empirical generalization that "small class size increases student learning." This generalization is widely believed but not fully confirmed. It has received much attention and has shaped educational policy in numerous school districts and several states. The theory rose. Then it sank when it failed to pan out as a panacea for education's woes and when its huge cost clashed with a major economic downturn. The "hunchy" nature of the implied theory makes it interesting: we think we know this is true, but we really don't know; it just seems so obvious on the face of it. Even if it is true, we still want to know how and why it is, if our goal is usable knowledge. Thus the commonsense nature of the theory makes it a useful example, and you could do an easy search and find investigations of various subtheories and alternative explanations. The most likely answer to the question "Does small class size increase student learning?" is: "It depends" . . . followed by a string of qualifying variables in complex interrelationships. For example, the relation is stronger in the United States than in many other countries and in the United States it is stronger for economically disadvantaged students than for affluent ones.[21] Observational research may be especially helpful in the study of complicated and intricate human problems and relations such as this one.

Let's assume there are two broad theories about class size effects. The first theory is a quantity theory: small class size increases student learning because teachers have more time to pay attention to individual students and can do more of what they have been doing to move the class ahead. The second theory is a quality theory: small class size increases student learning by improving instruction as teachers adopt better methods to fit student needs that are not possible with larger groups. You could combine the

---

[19] Merton (1976).

[20] Geertz (1973).

[21] See Pong and Pallas (2001).

theories: more time afforded by smaller classes means more and better teaching and figuring out what works for students. However, there are many other explanations. For example, one study found that improved morale was a cause for increased learning in small classes and schools—happier teachers teach better and increase student learning.[22] We will use the second theory—the quality theory—to provide examples of observational research illustrating all five types of research questions and what each suggests for sampling.

Sampling for "Thick Description" in Response to "What?" Questions

We go into the field to describe when we are interested in establishing that a phenomenon exists or exploring the meanings that people ascribe to their actions and experiences. In observational designs, we may seek corroborating evidence of actions that back up words we have taken from interviews or to describe life as we witness it. When our questions are asking for descriptions, we will likely need multiple observations at the same site in order to describe thickly enough to understand the phenomenon of interest.

For example, a descriptive question about class size could be "What produces increased student learning in small classes?" You try to establish the phenomenon by answering this question by searching for factors at work in increasing student learning by increasing teachers' instruction. These may later contribute to testing or building a theory. Initially your work will involve a very small number of cases observed in depth.

How do you sample descriptive cases? Observation would be required for thick description of what happens in small classes, so you could sample relevant cases of increased student achievement in schools implementing the small class policy. If you relied on state test score databases to find districts and schools that had better results after implementing a small class policy, you could choose sites by random selection from that population. But you would be more likely to take a nonrandom sample but still locate places that had evidenced increases in learning. Some states adopted this policy in recent years. Those states would be promising if you wanted to sample probabilistically through random sampling. Or, you could purposively seek a school district that has pursued small class size as a policy and take its definition of "small" as your working definition. Data archives that provide evidence of increased student achievement would help you identify districts and then schools within them where learning increased.[23] You would not be able to observe all the small classes, so you could draw your sample classes from the same school as a way to witness the class size question in one micropolicy context, again using evidence of increased learning to find promising schools. You might study only one primary grade or even only one class and observe it in depth. If you know that a particular case is an instance of precisely what you are looking for, it makes sense to study a sample of one in depth. That approach is not anecdotal; it is targeted at answering a specific research question.

---

[22] Lee and Loeb (2000).

[23] Increasingly, as data archives give researchers the capability to select classes where achievement levels are identifiable within the same school and grade, sampling for educational research can become more refined.

Sampling to Explore Described Phenomena in Depth

Exploratory research questions are likely to be best answered by investigating a few settings with more numerous observations. Exploratory questions often develop from the study of a thick description; they follow the descriptive phase that established a phenomenon for study. Explorers either search broadly or look deeply into the phenomenon to discover what they can in response to what, when, where, why, and how questions. The differences between sampling for descriptive and exploratory approaches can be more a matter of degree than of kind. Descriptive studies, by definition, develop detailed descriptions to answer "what?" questions. Exploratory observations are more probing; they often seek to identify (and describe) key variables and uncover (and describe) connections among them.

If we were conducting an exploratory study of the effects of class size, we might seek a few sites for in-depth observation that we would expect to be particularly illuminating. Or, we might want to study more sites with shorter, more frequent, and structured observations, balancing depth with breadth. Once again we would seek increased learning in a purposive sample and likely seek sites in our sample districts or schools that offered the best chances to witness the effects of various class sizes as they were manifested in practice.

From our observations, we might conclude that small class size alone does not seem to change teachers' instructional practices in ways that account for differences in learning between small and large classes. But we might notice that other practices at the school, such as instructional coaching and differentiated instruction (where teaching methods differ for particular students' needs), seem to contribute to qualitative differences in instruction. If we do observe such practices, we have identified variables—instructional coaching and differentiated instruction—that raise interesting questions about their relationship to class size and student learning that we can't explain without further investigation.

Sampling for Explanatory Studies

Often, when you want to explain something, you will seek a few well-chosen comparative cases to examine possible causal connections and explanations. Ideally, these cases will be alike in many ways, except for important differences in key categorical variables you want to study.[24] Statistical research that seeks to explain causes and effects begins as observations of ordinary occurrences. Only when there is a theory for testing or elaboration can these categorical variables be converted into continuous variables that facilitate experimental designs. The development of continuous numerically coded variables makes possible the final stages of a research process that can begin with discovery and end with explanation.

We can think of descriptive, exploratory, and explanatory research questions as three steps in theory development in a roughly sequential relationship. Explanatory studies come closest to establishing a basis for theory, a theory that could be tested or fleshed out by observation. Explanations begin as observations that can later be tested

---

[24]Cronbach (1975) writes that statistical analysis of continuous variables relies on observation of categorical variables that make researchers aware of possible explanations and causal connections.

by designs that include experiments. Experimenters often owe the theories that they test to someone's prior observations. Without observation, no one would notice or begin to believe that some observable factor caused or at least helped explain something of significance.

To review the class size example, we now have some thick descriptions of what goes on in small classes, and some new and possibly important variables in a web of possible connections. We have explored and observed that instructional coaching and differentiating instruction seem to improve small class outcomes, but we don't know how they interact or what causes changes in student learning.

Our sampling concern for an explanatory study would be to locate sites with confirmatory evidence of improved student outcomes, and that have the three variables of interest (small class size, instructional coaching, and differentiated instruction) present or absent in various combinations. These sites will be representative of a relevant set we can identify that may begin to explain what's going on in small classes. We might want to find stellar examples of instructional coaching or differentiated instruction being used as specific strategies intended to ensure that class size reductions translate into improved learning.[25] Archival data can tell us which schools have the necessary student learning outcomes, and we can narrow the sample with other methods, such as interviews with people who can identify schools with our variables of interest. We are likely to seek a few cases where we can observe over time in order to refine our questions and our ideas about the relative influence and interactions of the three variables.

An explanatory study might culminate in a hypothesis; in our school example, this hypothesis could be that small class size works in combination with other specific instructional variables to foster increases in student learning. Instructional coaching and differentiated instruction might be hypothesized to be the intervening or mediating variables that explain the link between smaller classes and increases in student learning. A chief goal of theory-building work is finding and then testing possible mediating variables. A classic example is the link between arthritis and reduced numbers of men's heart attacks, which researchers first established through observation and studying patients' records. The link, or mediating variable, was aspirin, which men with arthritis took more often than those without arthritis; aspirin was the cause of the "benefits" of arthritis. If differentiated instruction is the variable that is behind the link between small classes and increased learning, one question might be, do we need small classes, or can we go directly to the cause (differentiated instruction), even in normal-sized classes? This question could then be tested in a subsequent study.

Sampling to Test an Emerging Theory

To sample cases for purposes of a theory-testing investigation that looks for causal connections, relevance is your guide. You will likely seek out specific cases to test the hypotheses implied by the theory. You might sample for maximum variation among cases in order to understand and characterize cross-cutting themes or patterns as they play out in different contexts.[26] You might sample for extreme cases—either stellar

---

[25] In this case, we would be applying a relevance criterion. For an overview of criteria that include the idea of stellar examples see Patton (2002) and Vogt et al. (2011).

[26] Lincoln and Guba (1985).

examples or cases with particular unique features in light of the theory.[27] You may select several relevant cases for comparison or to help you use "predictable contrasts."[28] As always, your rationale for sampling and the criteria you use to establish relevance must be well considered and documented.

In our class size example, our theory-testing study would seek to explain the phenomenon of rising student achievement as it related to small class size, instructional coaching, and differentiated instruction. After establishing a school sample with the desired student achievement parameters, we might sample for cases that (1) combine all three variables, (2) combine class size reduction with one other variable, and (3) employ class size reduction alone. Other combinations are possible, such as schools that employ the instructional variables but do not reduce class size. If resources permit these could be studied as well. A broad question might be "does small class size strategically combined with focused instructional interventions increase student learning?"

To test this question we would need a robust study that includes multiple sites in order to make a claim that we understand how small class size functions as a means of improving student learning results. Observation alone may be insufficient for testing the theory, but observation continues to be critical to understanding what actually happens in those classes. In this case, observation may be logically supplemented with an experiment that controls the variables. However, setting up major and hugely expensive experiments with real students in real schools is extremely difficult for an ordinary researcher. In our example, the sampling process we used is actually seeking "natural experiments," or naturally occurring comparison groups, that serve the same purpose as assigning schools or teachers or students to experimental groups but are more feasible in most circumstances.

Sampling to Establish a Theory

Theory building can be undertaken with in-depth exploration of a few cases. As in theory testing, relevance will be established through criteria that help you sample from possible sites. You will likely seek a sample that gives you cases that are exemplary in some way—often compared with some negative examples. Prior descriptive, exploratory, explanatory, and theory-testing studies provide the basis for your sampling criteria. The special nature of the examples buttresses your confidence in the theory you are building. Theory building is a distinct approach that is considered, in some circles, philosophically different than theory testing.[29] It is often focused on *how* variables produce their effects.

In our class size example, prior observations contributed important elements for an emerging theory. They identified additional key instructional variables which, when combined with class size reduction, seem to be important factors in improving student learning. Sampling of a few exemplary cases—positive and negative—can set the stage for additional observation and verification, leading to elaboration of the theory and its potential contribution to the scholarship of educational improvement.

---

[27] Vogt et al. (2011).

[28] Schwandt (2007).

[29] Schwandt (2007).

Scholars working in the qualitative research tradition, in which observational designs developed, are often less interested in testing a theory that is explanatory and predictive than it is in considering the rich milieu in which multiple factors play out in a particular context. A common manifestation of this occurs in research questions about culture. Those who study culture often believe that simple theories that are truthful in every context are basically impossible. Instead, theories of culture are built within the contexts in which culture is observed. A sample of a few observation sites is used. Can a theory ever be "built" this way? The answer is yes, given time—lots of time, multiple studies, many observations, repeating our research sequence many times. This process is the basis for "grounded theory," which most certainly does not emerge from a single observational study.[30]

CONCLUSION

Observational research designs face distinctive sampling challenges, often related to how opportunities present themselves in the field. This chapter has approached these challenges three different ways:

- By looking at issues of relevance and representativeness, access, and resources;
- By considering four basic sampling decisions: when, where, what, and whom; and
- By considering sampling in light of five types of research questions: descriptive, exploratory, explanatory, theory testing, and theory building.

Most sampling for observations is purposive; you seek cases that are relevant to your research question rather than sampling randomly from a known population. Depending on the nature of the research question, you may sample more or fewer sites, observe more or less often at a given site, and encounter more or fewer logistical hurdles. Determining the defensible criteria by which you select your samples is a critical component of your research design, and an important part of your study documentation.

The table on page 197 summarizes these and related points about selecting and sampling for observational research.

---

[30] Glaser and Strauss (1967).

SUGGESTIONS FOR FURTHER READING

Sampling naturalistic and participant observation situations, participants, and occasions is an important and complex topic. Because these two designs are frequently part of case studies or combined designs and have roots in ethnography, much has been written to help researchers justify their choices. Otherwise, findings that come from these designs are sometimes dismissed as unusable because they are not generalizable. You will find more resources coming from the qualitative tradition even though observational designs may generate both quantitative and qualitative evidence. Most observational research uses purposive sampling, but several resources offer other sampling approaches. The following readings are helpful for deciding when to sample and how to justify your choices.

A Few Basics

A few resources that provide practical advice and an overview include Patton's *Qualitative Research and Evaluation Methods* (2002), which gives a helpful overview of purposive sampling with 16 different frameworks and unique ways to consider units of analysis for choosing when, where, who, and what to observe. The book is highly accessible too, and makes a good case for information-rich cases and their value in research. Patton further includes purposeful (i.e., purposive) random sampling, an approach that builds confidence among audiences who believe in randomization. He even takes on the perennial sample size question. Other texts deal broadly with observational research as part of case studies or ethnographies. *The Art of Case Study Research* (Stake, 1995) and *Case Study Research: Designs and Methods* (Yin, 2009) are classics. A reissued ethnography classic with sampling advice is *Ethnography: Principles in Practice* (Hammersley & Atkinson, 2007).

Digging a Little Deeper

There are several ongoing controversies about observational sampling. Two such controversies come from the qualitative tradition as it develops its own logic and vocabulary that distinguish it from the quantitative tradition. The first controversy is finding words to capture the distinctive qualitative perspective and signify its differences from quantitative reasoning and methodology. We refer again to the seminal text *Naturalistic Inquiry* (Lincoln & Guba, 1982), which is one of the first sources where this controversy is discussed and a new expression developed: the idea of an observational phenomenon as "fitting" rather than sampled. For a more recent overview, we recommend "Rethinking Observation: From Method to Context" (Angrosino & Mays de Perez, 2000). The second controversy addresses the generalizability of findings when samples are small and not random. A helpful essay, "Increasing the Generalizability of Qualitative Research" (Schofield, 2007), offers a concise overview of this controversy and a novel approach to the problem. Current arguments in favor of different sampling approaches, including the idea that sampling does not matter, as well as ideas about the usefulness of observational designs for ethnographic and case study research, can be found in the most recent *Sage Handbook of Qualitative Research* (Denzin & Lincoln, 2011).

CHAPTER 10 SUMMARY TABLE

WHEN DETERMINING KEY SAMPLING ISSUES, CONSIDER:

- Relevance and representativeness as you sample to observe cases and situations that allow you to describe, explore, and explain phenomena.
- How access can be negotiated and authentic observations ensured.
- How to address logistical and resource issues.

WHEN MAKING FOUR BASIC SAMPLING DECISIONS, ASK:

- When to observe?
- Where to observe?
- What types of phenomena to observe?
- Whom to observe?

WHEN SAMPLING BASED ON YOUR RESEARCH QUESTIONS, DECIDE ON SAMPLING METHODS TO USE:

- When you are seeking to characterize a phenomenon that requires "thick description."
- When you seek to explore in depth to verify and/or elaborate a description, seeking variables and patterns in your observations and data.
- When you seek to explain connections among variables by witnessing them in all the complexity of real life, often asking for comparisons and causes.
- When you seek to test an emerging theory using naturally occurring comparative cases.
- When you seek to establish a theory through exemplary cases.

Interdisciplinary research - methods & methodology
- subject, objects, validity
- much ie has a component of critical reflection
- knowledge is partial, provisional, plural
- validity measures are based on internal / group standards, but must be open to ex. crit.

CHAPTER 11

Sampling from Archival Sources

Sampling is central to the process of archival research. As we saw in Chapter 7, it is also at the heart of most survey research. But the target of the sampling is different in most archival work. Survey researchers sample cases, potential respondents, from whom they collect data. Archival researchers sample data that has already been generated and/or assembled by others. There is little doubt that archival research is the most frequent type of research published in the major journals in sociology, political science, and economics. The same is true in many journals in applied fields such as social work and education. This means, in brief, that archival sampling is the most frequent kind of sampling in social research, but it is probably the least frequently discussed in research methods textbooks. Again, we researchers who write methodology textbooks often do not preach what we practice.

As we discuss in Chapters 8, 9, and 10, for interview, experimental, and observational researchers the emphasis is more on recruiting research participants than on sampling them. But, for most other social scientists, sampling is crucial, and it has increasingly become a matter of sampling from archives. Sampling has been transformed by the availability of huge archives. Until the 1960s the typical research project in the social sciences was comprised of a small number of cases and an even smaller number of variables. Often, a single researcher would make the observations and collect the data. Methods of quantitative analysis were designed with such "small-N" studies in mind. The chief analytic concern was to reduce the dangers of overgeneralizing from a small sample—from whence the focus on statistical inference and the rise of the ubiquitous p-value.

Today economists, political scientists, sociologists, and researchers in applied disciplines such as business, policy studies, education, and social work most often work with very large archived datasets. Concern with statistical significance has diminished (not disappeared) if for no other reason than that with very large sets it can be hard to find a relationship that is *not* statistically significant, that fails to meet the minimum threshold of $p < .05$. The availability and use of massive data archives fundamentally alters the nature of research. Having thousands of cases and dozens of variables transforms the nature of research questions. And the relevant statistical tools change too. In general, the emphasis has shifted from estimating the likelihood that a particular finding could have occurred by chance (null hypothesis testing) and toward assessing the adequacy of complex models. The sampling problem has been redirected. In small-N research it was (and is) recruiting a large enough number of cases. In large-N archival research, it is devising methods to navigate oceans of cases. Workshops for quantitative researchers focus on topics such as how to find one's way through "Modern Massive Data Sets (MMDS)."[1]

Depending on the kind of archival data you have, different sampling techniques can be appropriate. But the basic principles of sampling are always relevant. The discussion of types of survey sampling in Chapter 7 (probability, nonprobability, stratified, systematic, purposive, etc.) can be applied quite directly to sampling from archives. The criteria leading to decisions about when to use what kind of sampling are the same. To quickly review:

- Choosing the population from which you will sample determines the quality of your work as much as the methods of sampling you use.
- Probability samples are preferable whenever possible.
- Convenience sampling is almost always hard to justify.
- Purposive (or judgment) samples have an important role to play—especially if targeting specific cases is more important to the research question than is generalizing to a broader population.
- A representative, nonbiased, small sample is preferable to a large but biased sample.
- Among nonbiased samples, bigger samples are better.

These and similar valid generalizations apply to all varieties of sampling, whether you sample in order to survey or to select useful cases and variables from archives.

WHEN DO YOU SEARCH AND WHEN DO YOU SAMPLE?

In archival research you usually do both searching and sampling, and it can sometimes be difficult to distinguish between the two. You might have to search for an appropriate archive. If there is more than one potential archive, you have to investigate them to decide which one is most important for your work. Or, you might decide that you have to use more than one. Once you have settled on an archive, you often have to both search within it and sample from it. If you are using a newspaper archive, for example, you will usually sample particular years, or sections, or randomly sample among issues. After that process of sampling, you will then have to search for articles or passages dealing with your particular topic. If you are looking for Web pages or blogs your search may find few enough that you can study the entire population of Internet documents. More likely you will find many blogs and will have to sample among them. If you are

[1] Presentations at one workshop, held in 2008, can be found at *mmds.stanford.edu*. The CDC held a symposium on a similar theme, "Massive and Emerging Data in Public Health," in May 2011: *www.cdc.gov/sag*.

conducting a research synthesis, your population is often all the research reports on a topic. When that is the case, the search aims to find the population. And, within the research reports you have found, you will probably use judgment (or purposive) sampling to extract some kinds of data while not using others. In brief, searching and sampling are often intertwined in archival research.

When Do You Stop Collecting Data: When Do You Have Enough?

This is an important question in all kinds of research, but it is perhaps especially pressing in archival research, where the potential sources can be hugely extensive. When collecting quantitative data you can sometimes use criteria based on statistical power, much as experimental researchers do. But generally, statistical power is easy to achieve in huge data archives since one of the main determinants of power is the size of the sample. Hence, as always, judgment is required. When collecting qualitative data, whether from archives or in other ways, researchers often refer to reaching the saturation point as the moment when it is no longer useful to collect data. The term *saturation* originated in grounded theory,[2] but the concept is crucial in all considerations of sampling, including in archival research. A similar idea from economics is the point of diminishing returns, the point at which the yield in useful data does not justify the effort necessary to collect more of it. A systematic method in meta-analysis provides a criterion to stop looking for more studies to synthesize: If you would have to find an improbably large number of studies that contradict your initial conclusions, then it makes little sense to continue searching. In archival research, as in other types, you need a criterion for determining when you should stop collecting data. Of course, the criterion should be justifiable. "I got bored" or "I ran out of time" are perhaps common reasons, but they are inexcusable.

All forms of archival research involve sampling. We will use the same framework to discuss sampling that we used in Chapter 5 to discuss the main options in archival research designs: (1) reviews of research literature, (2) database archives, (3) organizational records, (4) textual studies of documents, and (5) new media, especially various Internet sources such as blogs.

SAMPLING RESEARCH LITERATURE
TO BUILD UPON AND SYNTHESIZE IT

The importance of using the literature review to orient your research is largely beyond dispute. However, the value of that review will depend significantly on the quality of the previous work on your research question and the quality of the ways you sample it. Reviewing a seriously flawed research literature may be useful for helping you avoid pitfalls, but this is not what most methodological writers have in mind when they enjoin you to take the literature review seriously.[3]

---

[2] See Bowen (2008) for a discussion of saturation in grounded theory.

[3] Pawson (2006) reminds us and provides a good example of how even methodologically weak studies can contain "nuggets of wisdom." An excellent overview of the process of searching and sampling is available in Card (2012), chapter 3.

The literature review, even a review of an excellent literature, will be of limited value if you use biased methods of finding and selecting the literature to review. Basic principles of sampling are the same in all forms of research. Your sample needs to be representative of the population or universe about which you want to generalize, and it needs to be large enough that you can be confident that you aren't basing any generalizations on a small number of unusual cases. But sampling in research reviews is not based on a known or even knowable population, particularly when that population includes unpublished sources. Hence, for research reviews, sampling is searching for members of the population. Whatever methods of sampling you use for reviewing the literature, your responsibility as a researcher is the same as in any research—to fully inform the reader what you have done and why you have done it.

Meta-analysts usually aim to search out and analyze the entire population of research reports. They don't want to do a sample, they aim for a census. They often recommend going to what might seem heroic lengths to have as complete a population as possible—one that includes "all" research reports, including unpublished ones. We put "all" in quotes because there are inevitably practical limits—most often perhaps, for the readers of this book, research reports in languages other than English. Even when researchers are largely successful at collecting the entire population of research reports, there remains a reporting problem. Just as we will see below with newspapers, what a research review summarizes is the available *documents* on a topic, *not the topic*.[4] If all the research on a topic contains a bias (for example, it omits an important ethnic group or an important variable), a meta-analyst might summarize the sources perfectly, but that summary may not lead to a valid conclusion about the topic. This problem is crucial to understanding *all* archival research, not only reviews of research literature. The summary can be no better than the documents (data) summarized. This fundamental point can sometimes get lost in the discussions of the methods used to find and review the documents.

When Do You Use Electronic Databases to Do Your Searching?

While you will usually supplement electronic searches with other methods—such as the "ancestry" method of checking the citations in articles you read—the answer is simple: *always*. There is no substitute for using electronically searchable databases. Note the plural. One database is virtually never sufficient. The degree of overlap between different sources is often considerable, but it is never complete. The specific databases you use will vary by field and by your research question. The three most likely to be important in the social and behavioral sciences are: SocioFile, PsychINFO, and Google Scholar.[5] But others—such as the Social Science Citation Index, Arts & Humanities Citation Index, Dissertation Abstracts, and ERIC—can usually provide additional crucial leads.

Note that there are three types of retrieval possible using these searching tools: (1) the original basic findings, (2) the "ancestor" citations listed in these basic findings, and

---

[4]For some kinds of writing, such as the history of a discipline, the documents may be the topic; see the section on documents on pp. 210–212.

[5]Google Scholar is the new kid on the block, and some researchers think it compares poorly to more traditional alternatives, but its coverage is broad, and you can't beat the price—free. See van Aalst (2010) for a review.

(3) the "descendent" citations that build upon the original set. First you find a set of research reports on your topic. Then you check the citations in those reports for further leads. Finally you search (in citation indices) for research reports that have cited the initial set. Many of the sources on your final list will be in your initial basic set of research reports, but the ancestry and descendent methods almost always lead to several interesting additions. So, when searching, don't settle for only one form of searching, but use the results of your initial search to guide you toward further sources.

Typically, when using these sources, the database allows you to search using titles, keywords, and abstracts. But it is getting increasingly likely that one will be able routinely to search in the full texts of the articles. One interesting study of full-text searching, compared with the more limited methods generally in use, found that the full-text searching identified *10 times* more articles.[6] The author also believed that the additional articles he found through full-text searching enabled him to uncover not only a greater number of articles, but relevant ideas and information that would have otherwise been neglected. This comparison was made comparing science databases—the Science Citation Index (traditional) and ScienceDirect (which allows full-text searches)—but the same advantages are likely in social research articles, when appropriate databases become available.

The saturation question—when is it OK to stop collecting data?—is often quite salient in research reviews. The investigators always have limitations when reviewing any extensive body of literature. When do you spend how much time pursuing which documents? What are the likely consequences of omitting unpublished research reports or those published in Japanese—or French or German? How serious a limitation is it if you do not pursue every research report, no matter how obscure? Saturation in research synthesis is usually thought of in terms of the "fail-safe N," which refers to the number of as yet undiscovered studies you would have to discover to have some possibility of their making any difference to your conclusions. In meta-analysis, this number can often be computed quite precisely. When you have made a thorough search and calculated your effect sizes and confidence intervals, you can then calculate how many more studies with contradictory results you would have to find to require you to change your conclusions. If the number is improbably large, you can be fairly confident that it is OK to stop looking. But the *number* of potential omitted studies may matter less than their characteristics. For example, if you don't have any studies in Spanish, Chinese, or Arabic (English's companions among the largest language groups), you ought to be very nervous about the external validity of your conclusions.

In Chapter 5, we suggest that even if the majority of studies on your topic aren't amenable to meta-analysis, you can still do "mini-meta-analyses" of those that are. This situation is actually quite common. There may be a relatively small number of research studies on a topic and some of them will probably be theoretical or single-case studies or interview studies. These may be important to your research, but they cannot be summed for a meta-analysis effect size. For the research that is appropriate for a meta-analysis, what is the minimum number of research studies you need to find if you are to conduct a worthwhile mini-meta analysis and synthesize the data that can be quantitatively summarized? The answer is just two, according to the authors of an excellent review of

---

[6] Kostoff (2010).

the sample size and analytic options in meta-analysis.[7] The authors recommend using meta-analytic techniques even with a sample size of two, not because such a small size is ideal, but because the alternatives are worse. Meta-analysis at least provides (usually in advance) transparent and replicable rules of decision making about which studies to include and how to analyze them—usually using confidence intervals rather than (or in addition to) *p*-values when the samples are very small.

When Is It OK to Be Selective Rather Than Comprehensive?

Again, the first point to remember is that you probably cannot be comprehensive and study the entire population of research reports on a subject. And, if you include unpublished reports in your definition of the population, you *cannot know* whether you have found the entire population. It is better, we think, to use reasonable criteria to make reasonable selections. Then admit there were limits on what you included. As Dirty Harry once said, a researcher's "gotta know his [or her] own limitations." It is best to know your and your study's limitations and to describe them fully. Here is a hypothetical example describing how you searched for and found your sources, and the limitations of your procedures. Despite the limitations, if your search and your description of it were this thorough, it would be hard to fault what you did.

> I searched for articles in refereed journals, books, and book chapters, published beginning in January 1980 through December 2011 in either English or Spanish (the languages I read). The following three databases were used: SocioFile, PsychINFO, and Google Scholar. The following search terms were used: . . . . The search produced 287 candidate research reports. I was able to access 242 (84%) of these. After reading abstracts and skimming full texts of those 242 reports, 118 (49%) were selected because they reported the results of primary research, and because they provided data on one or more of my study's variables. When two or more research reports in the list of 118 were written by the same author or authors, I conducted a search for research reports citing those authors. The *Social Science Citation Index* and *Google Scholar* were used for this second search. In this way another 23 research reports were identified. That brought the final number of research reports included in this review to 141.

What are the limitations here? First, reports are included only if they have been published in books or refereed journals. That leaves out dissertations, conference papers, and various other unpublished material. That is unfortunate, especially because there continues to be evidence of "publication bias" of various sorts. Research that is published may differ in systematic ways from research that is not. The most discussed example of potential bias has to do with statistical significance. There seems no doubt that articles with statistically significant outcomes (small *p* values) are somewhat more likely to be accepted for publication, even when nonsignificant results (such as no difference between treatments) can be equally important for policy or practice. The extent of publication biases can never be known for certain, and it probably differs from field to field. One option, the one taken by our hypothetical research reviewer, is to assume

---

[7]Valentine, Pigott, and Rothstein (2010).

that much (*not* all) of what is valuable in dissertations, conference papers, and other unpublished sources eventually gets published. If something has to be left out (and it does) because there is no practical alternative (and there isn't), excluding unpublished research reports is probably the least harmful choice.

Other limitations include the fact that research published before 1980 and after 2011 is excluded as is research in languages other than English and Spanish. Again, that is unfortunate. Indeed, there might well be hidden gems published in the 1930s or in Russian or Chinese. But, what are the practical alternatives—become a historian, search in languages you don't know, and hire translators? Researchers conducting meta-analyses are more likely than others to try to analyze a "complete" population. But even in meta-analysis, the complete population is a chimera—an imaginary monster you will never be able to capture.

Here is an example from an excellent meta-analysis of research on elementary and secondary school mathematics programs. In it Slavin and Smith do a meta-analysis of sample sizes in primary studies; they found striking relationships between sample size, research design, and results obtained. Here we focus on the criteria the authors used to find the studies they synthesized: "*All* published and unpublished sources were investigated exhaustively and systematically in an effort to locate *every* study that might meet the inclusion criteria."[8] But they did not study reports in languages other than English, nor did they investigate those published before 1970. In addition, the authors applied design-specific criteria: to be included the study had to use random assignment or matching, have pretest data, and last 12 or more weeks. So words like *all* and *every* have to be taken with a grain of salt. This is *not* a criticism as much as a reminder not to overstate one's case. One must have selection criteria, some of them are limitations, and all should be described fully—as they are in this article.

A final reason that selection criteria are so important is that the number of research studies and the number of meta-analyses summarizing them have increased dramatically in recent decades. The number of citations to meta-analyses in PsychINFO roughly tripled between the 1980s and the early 2000s; the increase in MEDLINE citations was even greater (from 497 in 1980–1989 to 9,622 in 2000–2005, an increase of nearly 40 times). The rate of research production in medicine as of 2010 was 75 clinical trials and 11 systematic reviews *per day*. As one group of authors asks, "How will we ever keep up?"[9] Keeping up is facilitated by electronic searching (see the relevant sections below), by uniform standards of reporting the results of primary research,[10] and by checklists and criteria for conducting and reporting meta-analytic research. The Cochrane Collaboration in medical research and the Campbell Collaboration in social research specify protocols for collecting data and analyzing them as well as reporting the results. Such standards mean that reviewers of the research literature will have a good idea of what will be available in research reports and where to find it. But keeping up remains a fast-moving target.

---

[8] Slavin and Smith (2009, p. 502; emphasis added).

[9] Viechtbauer (2008); Bastian, Glasziou, and Chalmers (2010).

[10] For example, see the uniform requirements in biomedical journals by the International Committee of Medical Journal Editors: *icmje.org*. For psychology and education, see Zientek and Thompson (2009).

DATABASE ARCHIVES

As with most forms of archival research, both searching and sampling are required when using database archives. First you choose the most appropriate database. Then you sample cases and variables within that database. While access to some databases is restricted, for many of them, access poses few problems for qualified researchers (and even for the general public). Indeed compilers of some important but underutilized data archives—such as the U.S. Census Bureau's American Community Survey—sometimes make considerable effort to facilitate their use by holding workshops and training sessions open to interested researchers.

Using archives and selecting from them is a form of sampling. Even when you use an established database, you virtually never use all the variables it contains, and you rarely use all the cases. For instance, say you have the following research questions: as compared to entering the labor market directly after high school graduation, are there earnings benefits to attending a community college and completing a degree or certificate, and if so, how big are they? To address your questions you would likely use one or more of the large databases available from the NCES.[11] These contain thousands of cases and hundreds of variables. But you would not use them all. First, based on your research question, you would select your variables. You would probably choose no more than two or three outcome variables, such as employment record and average annual salary. Your independent variable would be fairly simple and dichotomous: graduated from high school with no further education versus entered a community college and earned a degree or certificate within 3 years. You might also select a dozen or so covariates based on your knowledge of the topic gleaned from your research review. Again, depending on your target population you would not use all the cases. In the example of comparing community college degree earners to students who ended their educations with high school, you would not use as cases students who did not graduate from high school, nor would you use those who did graduate from high school and went directly to a 4-year college. After sampling the variables and cases of interest to you and putting them in a separate file, you would probably have retained thousands of cases and dozens of variables. But your working dataset would likely be quite small compared to the original database. You sample from the original database to address your research questions.

Longitudinal studies very often employ archived data and are retrospective. The alternative to archival retrospective studies is prospective studies in which researchers prepare to gather follow-up data at some point(s) in the future. Archival retrospective studies can be undertaken immediately. This advantage means that most longitudinal studies are in fact archival. Selecting good archival sources for longitudinal studies means selecting those with long runs of data. Good archives also collect data in consistent ways from year to year, which enables the researcher to adhere to the old adage, "if you want to measure change, don't change the measure." One such archive is the General Social Survey (GSS), which has been surveying adults for decades about their social and political beliefs, attitudes, and values. It has long been a favorite archive

---

[11] The National Center for Educational Statistics has been conducting longitudinal studies of high school graduating classes since the 1970s. See Lin and Vogt (1996) for an example using these.

of researchers in political science and sociology. Studies of long-term effects will also inevitably be studies of effects that are distant in time, and sometimes this is what researchers seek. For example, research questions that have been asked using the GSS archives include, "Did growing up in the 1960s leave a permanent mark on attitudes and values?"[12]

Sometimes researchers use longitudinal or trend data when their primary goal is to investigate what future outcomes are likely to be. A good example of this kind of research, using the National Assessment of Educational Progress (NAEP), asks the question, "How large an effect can we expect from school reforms?"[13] The NAEP has collected student achievement data from millions of pupils from elementary through secondary schools. There is no other dataset that comes close to its depth, breadth, and quality on the subject of student achievement. The authors of this study investigated what it might be reasonable to expect as outcomes of school reforms. "Reasonable" can be reasonably decided by asking "as compared to what?" If a reform improves or intends to improve an outcome measure by, say, 10%, is that a lot or a little? If, in studying the history of student achievement in thousands of schools with millions of students in nationally representative samples, researchers have never found a change of more than 5%, then an improvement of 10% is an ambitious goal or a remarkable achievement. If, on the other hand, changes of 20% have routinely occurred and can be documented with extensive archival data, then 10% could be embarrassingly small. Collecting evidence from archives that have extensive longitudinal data enables researchers to answer such questions.

Archives of social, political, and educational data are breathtaking in their number and depth. But they pale in comparison to the archives available to biomedical researchers. When seeking to collect data on issues of public health and epidemiology, researchers have concluded (judging by their behavior) that archives contain the best data for answering many questions. To give readers an idea of what is available, we illustrate with four database examples and the kinds of research that have been undertaken using them with special emphasis on social, behavioral, and policy research questions rather than strictly biomedical ones. Have inequalities in death rates between different social groups widened in recent years? Using the National Vital Statistics System, which records *all* deaths and their causes, researchers found that the gap had increased; this occurred because of declines in death rates for the upper socioeconomic groups and a lack of change (or even increases) in death rates for lower socioeconomic groups.[14] Racial disparities can also be studied collecting data from archives. For example, researchers using the Health Employer and Data Information Set documented that disparities are widespread in Medicare health plans as measured in over 400,000 observations of individuals' health outcomes.[15]

The Behavioral Risk Factor Surveillance System (BRFSS), a nationally representative telephone survey of health behaviors and medical problems, was used to study the

---

[12] Davis (2004).

[13] Konstantopoulos and Hedges (2008).

[14] Ahmedin, Ward, Anderson, Murray, and Thun (2008). The NVSS is administered by the National Center for Health Statistics.

[15] Trivedi et al. (2006). The same database was used to demonstrate that women were less likely to get good-quality care for diabetes and heart disease (Bird et al. 2007).

relation between income, health insurance, and the use of key medical services by nearly 200,000 respondents. Interestingly, having health insurance was a stronger predictor of the use of medical services than was income; *both* the rich and the poor people who did not have health insurance were less likely to have had a cholesterol check or to have undergone various kinds of cancer screening.[16] Whether such screening is always a good idea and whether it can lead to overdiagnosis and overtreatment are the questions raised by our final example. The debate has been especially intense concerning mammograms for breast cancer and prostate-specific antigen (PSA) tests for prostate cancer. The issues are very complicated, but the data are exceptionally rich. One study using the Surveillance, Epidemiology, and End Results (SEER) database examined the records of 123,000 men who had been diagnosed with prostate cancer and concluded that many of them had been overtreated. Others agree that the archival data collected from the SEER database are the best to use to resolve the question, but disagree strongly about the level of overtreatment.[17]

While the availability of such databases containing thousands and even hundreds of thousands of cases is unlikely to resolve any complicated and controversial issues, they at least make it possible to start from a foundation of solid evidence rather than hunch, speculation, and ideology. The researcher's task when aiming to facilitate evidence-based discussion of important issues is to search for and select among the best available archival sources and then to sample variables and cases within them. Finally, it is always important to remember that no database archive is without bias and flaws. Being a critical user, not merely a passive consumer, of database archives is as important as good methods for finding, selecting among, and sampling cases from these sources. When you use a database archival source you will have an opportunity, one might even say an ethical obligation, not only to address your research question, but also to contribute to the literature on the quality and use of that database[18] and to describe the limitations to your conclusions that stem from the imperfections in the database.

ORGANIZATIONAL RECORDS

When you decide to do research in organizational records, there are several typical steps in the process of searching, sampling, and selecting. First you have to choose the kinds of organizations that have features relevant to your research question. This amounts to identifying your population or the target group about which you want to generalize. Then it is necessary to specify the particular organizations among the population of organizations: you sample from that population. With large populations of organizations, your sampling methods may include some form of probability sampling, but more commonly, judgment or purposive sampling is used, much in the way that a researcher selects among potential interviewees. When you are studying a single organization as a case study, your next most important question is: a case of what? You should have an explicit or implicit population in mind when conducting this or any other kind of case study.

---

[16] Ross, Bradley, and Busch (2006).

[17] Shao et al. (2010). See also the editorial responses to the article in the same issue of the journal.

[18] Herrera and Kapur (2007) is a key source.

Next, of course, is the issue of gaining access to records, particularly when the organizations you plan to study are not public institutions. Some organizational records are public. You can consult many records without seeking anyone's consent. Even for private organizations, such as hospitals and corporations, many records are public. That is because private hospitals and schools are subject to strict state and sometimes federal reporting procedures. Corporations, even though privately owned, are public in the sense that they must provide financial data to stockholders and government agencies. When records are not routinely available to researchers, part of your searching and sampling process will be to establish good relations with those who can grant you access. Failing good relations, for some classes of public organizational records, researchers may resort to the Freedom of Information Act (FOIA). Originally passed in 1966, the FOIA has been successfully used by some researchers (and many journalists) to gain access to documents the U.S. government was not necessarily happy to release. In subsequent decades, many states (e.g., California, Illinois, Michigan, New York, and Texas) have passed more-or-less stringent state versions of the FOIA.

When you have identified your population and sampled from it, then the issue becomes sampling among the records and, within the records, sampling data contained in them. Unlike when you consult database archives, when you study organizational records the data are neither designed nor arranged for the use of an external researcher. And sometimes the "access" you are given will be too generous, and you will be overwhelmed by a data dump. In that case, sampling records and the data they contain will have to be preceded by a great deal of reviewing, sorting, and categorizing.

Finally, your approach to sampling organizations' records will be influenced by the importance of those records as a source for your data. Sometimes you study organizational records as your sole or main source of data. In other circumstances organizational records supplement what you have learned using other methods such as interviews or participant observation. When the latter is the case, your sampling strategies will often be shaped by questions that you generate in the course of your interviews and observations.

The number of options available to researchers is truly enormous. Organizational records may not always give researchers datasets with huge numbers of cases, but they can provide access to information about questions that is available in no other way. As with database archives, the best way to give readers a sense of the range of options in using organizational records is through illustration, mini case studies, one might call them. For example, two of the authors of this book conducted a study using nonpublic files of a state education agency. The agency had not been satisfied with the quality of the evaluations of its grant-sponsored programs, chiefly because it was not easy to use the information in those evaluations as an aid to policy making. The agency contracted with the researchers to review its past evaluations and make recommendations. The availability of these records enabled the authors to make policy recommendations and to further a research agenda focused on improving grant evaluations.[19]

A second example addressed interdisciplinary graduate-level research. It made use of the records of one of the National Science Foundation's (NSF) grant programs, specifically its Integrative Graduate Education and Research Traineeship program. The records

---

[19]This is briefly discussed in Vogt et al. (2011).

accessed were 129 successful grant proposals.[20] The proposals were not obtained from
the NSF. Rather the list of successful awards was obtained from the NSF; the authors
then contacted the principal investigators (PIs) who won the awards. The proposals and
other records were obtained from these PIs. The authors were able to gain insight into
the nature of interdisciplinary research in engineering and the sciences and compare it
with interdisciplinary work in the humanities and social sciences.

A third example used records of private commercial organizations to examine the
reliability of awards in blind-tasting competitions for U.S. wines.[21] The wine industry
in the United States is large and growing. Consumers use the results of competitions to
guide their buying choices. But the reliability of the judging from one competition to
the next is very low; indeed the distribution of gold medals almost perfectly mirrors a
random distribution. Tasting seems to be an inexact science.

Organizational records from medical institutions are often used to construct consumer ratings of hospitals, clinics, health centers, and other health organizations.[22]
And private medical records, such as diagnostic observations, have been analyzed using
intensive textual analysis methods (see the next section) to better understand not only
the content of the documents but their "life histories," how they were used.[23]

As a final example, one of the authors recently completed work as part of a team
doing a contract evaluation of a state government agency.[24] The contractor was the state
legislature, which had specific questions in mind for the evaluators. One component of
the work was to answer the research question, how does this state agency compare to
its counterparts in other (selected) states? The contract spelled out specific variables for
comparing across the state agencies, and also specified which states to use for the comparison. Some of the specified comparison variables included state population demographics, service population demographics, scope of agency authority and responsibilities, funding, staffing, regional delivery systems, and productivity indicators. Thus, the
population and sample had been identified, along with the variables of interest. What
ensued was a good example of the process we described above: finding the archived
organizational records, sampling from among them, sampling from the data within
them, and continuous review, sorting, and categorizing.

In sum, for researchers searching for and selecting from archival data, organizational records constitute a huge source of high-quality data. But they are not used as frequently in research reports as are publicly available database archival sources. There are
at least two possible reasons. First, the records and the data in them are more likely to be
textual than quantitative, which requires more time-consuming analyses. Second, much
more effort on the part of the researcher is usually required to gain access and to put
together data from organizational records, which are collected for purposes other than
research. But organizational records have much potential despite the fact that searching
for and sampling from them can be arduous.

---

[20] Borrego and Newswander (2010).

[21] Hodgson (2009).

[22] Bevan (2006).

[23] Prior (2008a, 2008b).

[24] Evergreen Solutions (2008).

TEXTUAL STUDIES OF DOCUMENTS

The first step in studies of archived texts is finding a set of documents useful for addressing your research question. You will have already, in the design stage of your research, determined whether your textual studies of documents will focus on the texts themselves, on the phenomena the texts represent, on the contexts in which the texts emerged, or some combination of the three (see the discussion in Chapter 5). Once you have identified the basic strategy, your search can range from the highly difficult and complicated to the fairly simple and straightforward. Often you will have more than one set of documents from which to choose. Once you have chosen among these, and have selected the source of your documents, then you need to select and sample the documents in that source. Your choice of searching and sampling strategies is very consequential for the quality of your research for the obvious reason that *all* sources are incomplete and *all* methods for collecting data from them are imperfect. Often the best approach is to combine sources of data. Much as an interview researcher does not talk with only one interviewee, or an observational researcher does not observe a site only once, triangulating the perspectives from multiple documentary sources is almost always advisable.

Your documents will often be published or otherwise publicly available. News media remain an important source. And choices among news media are usually complicated by the number and variety of options: newspapers, weekly or monthly magazines, websites sponsored by television networks, and so on. Multiple sources relieve the worries associated with having only one source, but increase the burdens of choice. Once you have made your decisions, based on a careful consideration of which sources are most appropriate for your research questions, then you sample within these sources.

Newspapers are perhaps the paradigm case because they have been studied the longest and continue to be widely used by researchers. Although newspapers may eventually be replaced as the news media evolve and become more electronic, they have always been among the most widely used documentary sources. Choice among the relevant newspapers is necessary for many reasons, most importantly because no newspaper can report on everything, and all newspapers have editorial policies. Editorial policies are roughly equivalent to sampling bias or publication bias. If you are studying particular events, such as civil disturbances, or crimes, or political rallies, and so on, you don't want to make the assumption that lack of coverage means the lack of an event. One strategy for compensating for gaps in any single newspaper is to use more than one. Another approach is to supplement newspapers with another kind of source, such as public records of the events you are interested in. The best strategy is virtually always to combine sources[25]—much as in multimethod research or interviewing multiple witnesses. As in literature reviews, in which the absence of research on a problem does not equal the absence of a problem, gaps in the documentary information do not necessarily equal gaps in the world.

Sometimes the question is less *what* the events were and more *how* the media reported them. Are you using newspapers or other texts to study the subjects on which they report or to study the nature of those texts? As an example of the latter, one study examined the accuracy of the reporting of medical news on the front pages of major

---

[25] See Maney and Oliver (2001) for an insightful example that illustrates the complexities involved in using multiple documentary sources.

newspapers and compared this reporting to the research as described in medical journals. In both instances, search engines (LexisNexis, MEDLINE, and Google Scholar) were used to find the relevant articles.[26] The conclusion was that newspapers had a tendency to overreport *preliminary* findings and to underreport multistudy summaries that confirmed preliminary conclusions. This tendency is probably due to newspapers' greater emphasis on newness than on accuracy. There can be a difference between newsworthy (in the sense of catching a reader's eye) and being worthy of sustained attention. This kind of bias seems inevitable in news media.

When Do You Use Computer-Assisted Methods for Searching and Sampling Texts?

Whenever you can. Once you have your working model of verbal texts, the things that shape them and the things to which they refer, then more specific searching, sampling, and analytical questions arise. Although words are definitely qualitative data, they may be searched, sampled, and analyzed either quantitatively or qualitatively, by software or by "brainware."

Sampling of texts as well as their analysis is increasingly performed using computer programs to search for and select data. As it gets easier to read documents directly into computer programs and as these programs become more advanced, this approach will probably become routine. Still, when one wants to test the accuracy of a computer program, the almost inevitable technique is to compare the program's selections and codings to "hand" coding.[27] In such comparisons of computer software to human "brainware" the computer programs fare well, especially with large bodies of textual materials, but there still seems no substitute for actually reading the texts if one wants to know what they say. The computer programs are almost always best at *finding* passages with relevant information. Yet, you still have to tell the software, in more or less detail, what to look for.[28] The words, phrases, and concepts for which the programs search are defined by the researcher, usually on the basis of familiarity with the texts.

When one uses computers to help search, sample, and analyze texts, this is usually called *content analysis*. And some commentators are fairly insistent about this label—that it *only* refers to machine-assisted analysis. If your analysis was based on traditional methods of reading and thinking about your texts, you might reasonably think of it as content analysis, but you could actually be criticized for calling your analysis of content "content analysis." Despite the fact that it is still hard to dispense with ordinary reading and (perhaps less ordinary) thinking, this traditional research method (reading and thinking) seems not to have an agreed-upon descriptive label. In brief, while computer programs are often still surprisingly rudimentary for *analyzing* texts, they are powerful aids for *searching* and *sampling* texts. The two approaches are complementary: the human tells the computer what to look for and the computer finds passages that the

---

[26] Lai and Lane (2009).

[27] For examples, see Simon and Xenos (2004), Laver, Benoit, and Garry (2003), Klebanov, Diermeier, and Beigman (2008), and Anderson-Connolly (2006).

[28] One of the most persuasive partial exceptions to this rule is Quantitative Narrative Analysis; see Franzosi (2010).

human is likely interested in reading. The human reads the passages and then redirects the computer to search for new words, passages, and themes.

Text mining or data mining is one of the most promising areas of computer-assisted searching and sampling and one that, it is not very risky to predict, will be increasingly employed in research using texts as a main source of data.[29] Particularly if you are searching in large amounts of text, there is no reasonable alternative. The texts to be searched and sampled could be quite traditional, such as print documents like newspapers and books. But even for traditional documents, the currently most effective methods for searching and sampling have become widespread only with the increasing availability of means to read text into computer files so that they can be searched and sampled using high-speed computing. We stress, once again, that text mining still is much more useful for searching and sampling than for understanding texts. Understanding texts still demands abilities that are not yet automated, such as critical reading and thinking.

Like most people, academics tend to be fascinated by themselves, so it comes as no surprise that many examples of text mining are concerned with the better understanding of academia. In one interesting example, the discipline of economics, as reflected in its published research over four decades, was compared to other disciplines, as reflected in their journals. The authors concluded that the fields of economics and sociology had distinct focal concerns.[30] Another study used data mining to investigate educational journals and books. Not only did it address the contents of the articles, but it used network analysis to examine how they were linked in the networks constitutive of the field of educational research.[31] The largest such study we know of is being conducted by the National Information Standards Organization, which is building a database to assess scholarly impact. Using 40-plus measures of scholarly impact, this project is collecting data from over 100,000 journals, newspapers, and magazines and from more than 2,000 institutions.[32] The three examples discussed in this paragraph are cases of text mining from traditional texts, "old" media. Text and data mining are even more prevalent and essential when studying so-called new media, which have proliferated greatly in recent years.[33] These are the topic of our next section.

NEW MEDIA, INCLUDING VARIOUS INTERNET SOURCES

When studying newer media—such as blogs, Web pages, and tweets—and the networks they make possible, one will almost inevitably sample. Any idea of a total sample or population of sources is likely to be wildly impractical, although a few exceptionally powerful computer networks can study millions of cases. Produced with hardware and software, the new media have to be investigated with it too. Data mining in the study of traditional texts is an extremely handy supplement; with documents available in the new

---

[29] Cohen and Hunter (2008) provide a brief and clear introduction in an open-access journal.

[30] Goldschmidt and Szmrecsanyi (2007).

[31] Carolan and Natriello (2005).

[32] The NISO website is very informative about text mining of academic sources; see *www.niso.org*.

[33] The mining of quantitative data has become widespread enough to have its own journals—for example *Statistical Analysis and Data Mining*, published by Wiley.

media, data mining is usually the only way to study one's subject. Because data mining documents on the Internet, such as Web pages, is so computer intensive, one ordinary computer may not be up to the task. "Web crawlers" that search Web pages using distributed networks of otherwise idle computers (such as university computer labs after closing time) are one solution that has been proposed and implemented.[34]

One striking recent example used Twitter to assess the mood of the nation and then used the mood thus assessed to predict stock market trends, specifically the Dow-Jones Industrial Average (DJIA).[35] The authors' procedures illustrate many of the searching and sampling methods that can be used to obtain data from the new media. To conduct the study the authors examined 9.8 *million* public tweets over a period of 10 months in 2010. They used two kinds of software—one that they created, the other publicly available—to assess the moods expressed in the tweets. First they had to cull spam and other nonpersonal messages as well as punctuation. Then they had to identify and select those messages that contained explicit statements about their authors' moods. Grouping together all the selected tweets published on the same days, they then used those daily data to make a time-series dataset that could be compared to the time series of daily DJIA closing values. They found that shifts in mood improved the ability to predict shifts in the DJIA 3 or 4 days later. Whether they could actually gather and analyze the data fast enough to *predict* (rather than "retrodict") is a different question, which is addressed in our companion volume on analysis. Here our focus is on sampling. The authors point out one important limitation of their sampling frame despite their gigantic sample: the U.S. stock market is influenced by individual and institutional decisions worldwide, but currently tweeters are mostly English speaking and live in the United States.[36] This is a nice illustration of the fact that a large sample is not necessarily drawn from the appropriate population nor is it inevitably without bias.

Almost as striking as the Twitter-tweet article and the searching and sampling techniques it used was how the authors chose to publish their results. The results appeared, instantaneously upon submission, in something called "archive," that is, *arXiv.com*. This is an online, fully automated e-publishing service run by Cornell University Libraries that is accessible by any reader. It publishes works in physics, mathematics, computer science, statistics, and other fields. By late 2010, this archive contained over 600,000 publications; it currently processes some 200 submissions per day. The use of this e-print archive is free of charge and illustrates what many prognosticators claim is the future of publishing. The online world and the new media not only provide multiple sources of data, they also give us many outlets for publishing analyses of them.

We conclude this section by returning to the Web forum example we introduced in Chapter 5. In contrast to the Twitter research just reviewed, which required a massive investment of computational time by a team of computer science experts, researchers with more modest resources could use this Web forum or others like it to conduct important research. Suppose your research question was "Among male and female

---

[34]Thelwall (2001). See also Thelwell (2011) for further discussions of the use of social networking sites for the study of human communication as well as graphic methods for depicting the results.

[35]Bollen, Mao, and Zeng (2010). The article is available freely online and provides an excellent overview of this kind of Internet text searching for scholarly purposes.

[36]A somewhat parallel study, with more of an international emphasis, which studied Wikipedia is Ratkiewicz, Menczer, Fortunato, Flammini, and Vespignani (2010).

participants ('posters'), are there differences in the frequency and types of advice asked for and offered?" You could use the statistical capabilities of the website to determine the overall ratio of male to female posters and their relative activity levels on different message boards. Then you could sample among the discussion threads and seek examples of advice being requested and offered. Avatars available in each post either overtly identify the poster's gender, or allow you to go to the user profiles to find that information. Since, in this case, you are interested in the texts themselves, the texts of the posts could be copied. Qualitative data analysis software could be used to search for words and themes associated with giving and getting advice. As we can see, even this relatively simple research question would require an explicit study design that lays out the sampling process and the potential sources of data, and the data collection itself would involve several sequential steps. However, this level of effort could be positively rewarded by the quantity, depth, and quality of the source material. We would be very surprised if there were not an enormous increase over the next few years in the mining and interpreting of such sources of rich archival data.

CONCLUSION

Sampling for archival research differs in several ways from sampling as practiced in the other research designs we have reviewed. First, people do not have to be recruited, persuaded, or paid to participate in the study—as is not uncommon in survey, interview, and experimental research. Archival researchers need not seek permission from observational sites, survey respondents, interviewees, and experimental participants. Instead, the archival researcher usually downloads data from a website. Second, much archival research is inconceivable without computer-assisted searching for cases, whether the object of the search is research studies, variables in databases, organizational records, documents, or websites. Third, and related to the first two points, is that the number of cases is usually vastly greater in archival research. The sampling problem is not one of encouraging a sufficient number of interviewees, respondents, or participants to join and persist in the study. Rather, it is devising an appropriate rationale for selecting among many thousands of cases and hundreds of variables.

Despite these differences, sampling is fundamentally similar in archival and other research designs. In all designs, the population from which you sample must be appropriate to the research question. And the sample must be representative if you are to use it to generalize from the sample to the population. A huge N of cases and variables drawn from an official government database does obviate the need to find a relevant population and draw a representative sample from it. The table on page 216 reviews and summarizes these and related points concerning sampling from archival sources.

SUGGESTIONS FOR FURTHER READING

Several of the sources cited in the Further Reading section for Chapter 5, especially the more general texts, are also relevant for this chapter on searching and sampling. Here we mention readings focused more exclusively on finding archival data and sampling from it once you've found it. Noel Card's (2012) *Applied Meta-Analysis for Social Science Research*, especially Chapter 3, is particularly good for searching for and sampling from research reports.

Since most searches will be done electronically on the Internet and World Wide Web, many sources that can help you with your searches will also be located there, but it can be hard to find them if you don't already know what they are and how to use the Net and the Web. While in the long run the best way to learn about online searching may be by searching online, in the short run most people need help to get started. The field of archival searching and sampling is characterized by some elementary and some highly advanced resources—and not much in between. Two good books with which you can begin are Shaw's *Mastering Online Research* (2007) and Hartman and Ackermann's *Searching and Researching on the Internet and World Wide Web* (5th edition, 2010). Thelwall's already cited article "Investigating Human Communication and Language from Traces Left on the Web" (2011) is both excellent and brief. Finally, remember that if you have access to a research library you should be able to find people working there who specialize in what is sometimes called data librarianship.

The knowledge needed for sampling from archives once you've found them tends to be both more localized and more highly technical. A short overview of database archives and their quirks is Herrera and Kapurs's excellent article "Improving Data Quality: Actors, Incentives, and Capabilities" (2007), which we've already cited. A book such as Feldman and Sanger's *The Text Mining Handbook* (2007) covers a lot of ground and is both advanced and helpful. But we think that the most useful guidance for sampling from archives will come from the archival sources themselves. This is most obvious in the case of private collections and organizational records, which are often completely inaccessible without specific permissions and local guidance. For general social science research it is usually most effective to start by going (online) to data repositories. (See Vartarian's *Secondary Data Analysis* [2010] for a good list of secondary data bases.) A very handy website with links to almost everything we've ever wanted to use is *www.secondarydataanalysis.com*. It is associated with Smith's handy *Using Secondary Data in Educational and Social Research* (2008).

Four widely used repositories are the Inter-university Consortium for Political and Social Research (ICPSR), Bureau of the Census, the National Center for Educational Statistics (NCES), and the CDC. Each of these is huge and can be a bit difficult to penetrate, but each is admirably well organized and has excellent and friendly staffs. When you have found the database you want to use then you can consult its associated technical literature for guidelines for how to sample from it. The knowledge you need does tend to be localized, however. Tricks of the trade that are great for the Human Relations Area Files won't do you much good while working with the Early Childhood Longitudinal Survey. Finding your way through more traditional archives, such as collections of institutional documents, tends to be even more dependent on the goodwill of the people working there. No matter how much some might wish it, in social research there's no avoiding social interaction.

CHAPTER 11 SUMMARY TABLE

USING ARCHIVAL SOURCES

When to search	• When you are seeking appropriate archival sources. • When you are looking within an archive for relevant data. • When you are trying to find the entire population of texts on a topic (as with a research synthesis or meta-analysis).
When to sample	• When you have selected an appropriate archive and need to sample cases from within it.

SAMPLING RESEARCH LITERATURE

When to use electronic databases to search	• Always, but also always use more than one, depending on your field of study and your research question.
When is it OK to stop collecting data?	• When you have made a thorough search and you calculate that you would have to find many more articles to make a difference in the conclusions you draw.

DATABASE ARCHIVES

When to sample from database archives (vs. using all records)	• Virtually always; selecting variables and cases that are relevant to your research question is the norm.

ORGANIZATIONAL RECORDS

When to sample from organizational records	• When your research question requires that you select from among records rather than study all records. • After a process of reviewing, sorting, and categorizing.

TEXTUAL STUDIES OF DOCUMENTS

When to sample from textual archives	• When your source archives are very large, such as newspaper archives. • When you are studying a particular phenomenon and need to sample from multiple text records/reports.
When to use computer-assisted text searching and sampling	• Whenever possible after you have your own working model of the texts and the language in them (so you can direct the software appropriately). • When you can compare the software selections to those produced without software.

NEW MEDIA, INCLUDING INTERNET SOURCES

When to use sampling within new media	• Most of the time, given the burgeoning amount of data online. • After a process of searching and narrowing the field of potential data sources.

CHAPTER 12

Sampling and Recruiting
for Combined Research Designs

If you have decided that your research question should be addressed through a combined research design, then you have already dissected your question into its component parts. Each of those parts indicates one or more research methods from which you will gather and analyze data within your combined design. In order to gather those data, you will need to decide how to select your "cases," through making important sampling decisions for each component of your study.

Depending on your design components, we recommend reading the relevant sampling chapters in this volume as well as consulting specific detailed texts and reviewing previous studies and their sampling methods. In this chapter, we illustrate our discussion with several prototypes of combined designs, the sampling issues they may raise, and how these issues might be addressed.

As with the rest of this volume, we will not begin with the traditional decision between quantitative versus qualitative methods. As we have discussed elsewhere, making this distinction a priori potentially sets up a false dichotomy that can lead you off track regarding your research design and execution. For example, conventional wisdom may say that large samples are used in quantitative studies, while small samples are used in qualitative studies. This, however, is not always true. When researchers want to pilot quantitative questions for a survey, they might very well select a small sample for that purpose. When researchers want to gather open-ended responses for eventual qualitative analysis, they might very well administer the questionnaire to large numbers of people. As with every phase of your project, your research question will determine the best way to design your project, select your samples, and gather your data. The quant–qual distinction becomes important in the measurement, coding, and analysis phases and is discussed in our companion volume.

One distinction is very important: samples fall into two categories—either probability or purposive samples.[1] Which you select for each component of your combined

---

[1] We do not use the dichotomous categories of probability/nonprobability as we did in the survey sampling chapter, because we do not recommend using some types of nonprobability sampling techniques, such as convenience sampling. Therefore, in this chapter, we have narrowed the latter category to purposive samples.

research design will be determined by the purpose of your research project. A fairly detailed discussion of probability and purposive sampling is presented in Chapter 7 on sampling in survey designs.[2]

In a combined research design, you will need to not only select sampling methods appropriate for each component of your design, but also to select them based on their compatibility, that is, their appropriateness for collecting combinable data. Analytic methods for combining data are reviewed in our companion volume.

Besides the probability/purposive sampling distinction, another general classification scheme for sampling designs is often useful. This scheme involves the relationship among the samples you will select for the different components of your design. The relationships can be classified as being one or more of four types: (1) identical samples, (2) parallel samples, (3) nested samples, and (4) multipopulation samples.[3] Identical samples are obviously the same, that is, using the same group for two or more parts of your study. Parallel samples are different, but are selected from the same population. In samples with a nested relationship, one sample is selected for one part of the study, and a subset of this sample is used in another part of the study. Multipopulation samples are drawn from two or more different populations. Examples of each sampling method are shown in Table 12.1 for different research questions regarding student learning.

In the following sections, we employ examples to illustrate different sampling options. The sampling classifications of probability/purposive, as well as the four sampling relationships described above, are used, as appropriate, to clarify some of the sampling decisions in the examples.[4]

TABLE 12.1. Relationships among Samples: Student Learning Research Examples

Sampling method	Research question	Example
Identical samples	What effect does a specific intervention have on student learning?	Administer a pretest and a posttest to the same group of students before and after the intervention.
Parallel samples	How do two interventions differ in their effects on student learning?	Randomly select two groups of students from a population; administer one intervention to one group and a different intervention to the other; compare the results.
Nested samples	What do students believe they learned and on what do they base this belief?	Survey a large group of students regarding their beliefs about the learning experience; interview a subset of the larger group to examine the basis for their beliefs.
Multipopulation samples	How do the effects of an intervention differ for urban and rural students?	Select one group of students from an urban population and one group from a rural population; administer the same intervention to both groups; compare results.

[2] For an excellent comparison between probability and purposive sampling techniques, see Teddlie and Yu (2007, Table 1, p. 84).

[3] Collins, Onwuegbuzie, and Jiao (2006). We have altered their terminology somewhat.

[4] A general summary of sample size recommendations is found in Onwuegbuzie and Collins (2007, Table 3). For discussions of when to focus on effect sizes and confidence intervals (rather than on hypothesis testing) when calculating sample size, see Parker and Berman (2003) and Kelley and Rausch (2006).

WHEN SHOULD YOU USE PROBABILITY SAMPLES IN YOUR COMBINED DESIGN STUDY?

As discussed in Chapter 7 on survey sampling, you choose to use probability samples when you want to maximize generalizability to the broader population; or, in other terms, to maximize the external validity of your study. Some combined research designs seek to do this, and should employ sample selection techniques similar to those used in simpler survey or archival designs. As with simple designs, you must follow standard protocols in order to recruit a large enough representative sample using a formal sampling frame.

One example of a study that would use probability sampling might be when your research question requires people in a certain type of organization to answer both forced-choice and open-ended survey questions. Your study has two parts: you want to know *how* people answer the forced-choice questions, and you want to know *why* they answered as they did through collecting responses to the open-ended questions. In this case, you could use cluster sampling (a form of probability sampling described in Chapter 7) to randomly select the organizations, then administer the survey to every employee in those organizations. You can conduct the two parts of your study simultaneously; both sets of questions can be administered at the same time to the same (identical) sample.[5]

In this study design, there is probably little concern about whether the two components (analysis of the forced-choice survey responses and analysis of the open-ended responses) will be compatible at the data integration stage, since they clearly were developed to be integrally related. You are using the same sampling method for both parts of your study, so you will not create unique sampling concerns with each part. Your probability sampling will allow you to make statistical inferences and generalize your survey results to the broader population.

Another type of design seeking generalizable findings might separately employ a probability sample and a purposive sample. You might want to survey a representative sample of a population, then later purposely select cases to observe from among the survey respondents that represent extremes or a range of variations within that sample. In this case, it would be important to assure that your initial sample is representative, not only so your findings can be generalizable, but also so that it will be likely to include the variations you seek to study in depth.[6]

There could be any number of situations in which your sampling choices create potential problems with representativeness and subsequent generalizability. For instance, similar to the first example, suppose you are conducting a study in which the first step is again a survey of employees in a particular type of organization, and a subsequent step is on-site observations of selected cases from among the responding organizations. Making sure you have a representative sample at the outset of your combined design study will be extremely important so that you do not compound an initial sampling error with your later sampling and data collection. Suppose that, instead of cluster sampling as we described in the first study, you instead asked for organizations to *vol-*

---

[5] An example of this study design is found in Parasnis, Samar, and Fischer (2005), a study of deaf college students' attitudes.

[6] An example of this type of sampling in a combined design is found in Lasserre-Cortez (2006).

unteer for your study. Right away, you have created a kind of convenience sample of willing participants, leading to automatic sampling bias and sampling error. As you later select the subsample to participate in the on-site observation phase, if you again ask for volunteers, you now compound the original bias by selecting the "most willing among the willing." How realistically will your findings represent the actual situations that exist among these types of organizations? In other words, how valid is this study? However, you often have no choice but to use volunteers among the volunteers, for, it must be remembered—both as a practical matter and in terms of the ethical conduct of research—that in a sense, *all* samples are samples of the willing, of volunteers, since all research participants, except those observed in public places, must give their informed consent.

As a rule of thumb, when you want to generalize, you need to use probability sampling of some type to set the stage for subsequent data collection, analysis, and interpretation, which may include additional types of sampling for different purposes.

WHEN SHOULD YOU USE PURPOSIVE SAMPLES IN YOUR COMBINED DESIGN STUDY?

Purposive samples should be used in your combined design study when you want to garner a variety of perspectives on an issue, or when your cases fit certain characteristics that are important to your study, such as being "typical," or being "outliers," or being part of a group receiving specific "treatment," or representing a range of variation along a continuum, or representing a particular combination of interesting characteristics. It's no surprise, given the term, that "purposive" samples are selected with a particular study purpose in mind! In the previous section on when to use probability sampling, we referenced some examples that combined probability sampling with purposive sampling, but we will discuss purposive sampling in more detail here.

In one study, researchers were investigating economic development opportunities in rural communities in India. In the first phase of their study, they employed a purposive sample to garner the viewpoints of a variety of professions. This sample was selected on the basis of providing maximum variation: trying to get as many perspectives as possible. The data from this phase were used to create a questionnaire that was later administered to a random sample of households in rural villages, using a stratified random sampling strategy.[7] The first phase provided a broad range of data upon which to base the questionnaire, since the purposive sample included so much deliberate variation. The findings from the questionnaire, since they were administered to a representative sample, could then be generalized to the larger rural population.

In another combined design study, only purposive sampling was used. In this case, researchers were exploring how persons infected with hepatitis C (HC) make decisions concerning alcohol consumption. This study began with semi-structured interviews with HC patients being treated at a university teaching hospital. Participants were purposively selected to ensure variability across three variables of interest: gender, race/ethnicity, and level of alcohol use. A second component of the study sampled archival data from electronic sources: posted narratives regarding the experience of HC-related

---

[7]Blattman, Jensen, and Roman (2003).

illness, and threaded HC discussions on forum websites. Narratives and discussion threads were purposively selected for their references to alcohol use. Of over 600 discussion threads, a systematic sample of every third thread was used in order to make the data analysis manageable and to attempt to limit the interrelatedness of the threads.[8]

In this example, the study was exploratory, attempting to identify new factors, not previously used, to determine how alcohol use influences decisions. As an exploratory study, the goal was not to generalize to a larger population, but rather to seek new variables that might be used for subsequent larger-scale studies.

Sometimes a mixed methods study is so large and comprehensive that it requires a sampling process that will provide both the necessary breadth and a manageable number of cases. For example, a very large study employed two-stage purposive sampling to create a study population for both interview and survey research. The researchers were seeking to conduct a national study of youth smoking cessation programs. Given the national scope of the study, they needed to establish a logical sampling frame that would provide insight into a variety of programs in diverse settings. Since most tobacco cessation programs operate at the county level, their first-stage sampling frame was all U.S. counties ($N = 3,142$). They eliminated counties with populations under 10,000 ($N = 689$), leaving nearly 2,500 counties for their study. They stratified the county sample by urbanization, socioeconomic status, youth smoking prevalence (based on national survey data), and tobacco control expenditures, resulting in 24 strata that could be used for later comparisons. The researchers then applied a snowball sampling strategy to identify actual smoking cessation programs for qualitative study. They initially identified "key informants" from government and not-for-profit records and websites, and then asked these informants for contact information regarding others involved in youth tobacco cessation programs. They continued this process until no new names appeared on their lists. Finally, they interviewed these informants (over 1,300) and identified 756 smoking cessation programs for survey administration and additional interviews.[9]

In case study research, sampling is almost always purposive. Cases are selected for their conceptual categorical characteristics related to the phenomenon of interest you want to study. In comparative case studies, the selected cases often represent divergent or contrasting characteristics. As we mentioned in Chapter 6, case study research is inherently iterative, with findings used to continuously refine both research questions and data collection. Thus, the initial cases selected for study may reveal that additional cases should be included, or may indicate that the original selection criteria need to be modified and different cases selected.

WHEN SHOULD YOU USE BOTH PROBABILITY AND PURPOSIVE SAMPLES IN YOUR STUDY?

The obvious answer to when to use both probability and purposive samples is when the intent of your project and your research question requires that you do. Some of the examples we have already presented used both types of samples. It certainly would not be unusual, as some of our preceding examples demonstrate, that in a combined design,

[8] Stoller et al. (2009).

[9] Curry et al. (2007).

one component would require a probability sample and another component would require a purposive sample.

Let's say your project involves market research with an overall intent of product improvement, and you are interested in finding out how people use a certain product and what might be done to improve this type of product in the future. You could use cluster sampling (very common in market research) to administer a simple forced-choice survey, but if you stop there, you would garner only limited information based on the ideas you had when you constructed the survey. What if you haven't thought of every potential answer? How will you know if people are using this product in new and creative ways? How will you know if there are new ideas out there to improve the product in ways that you haven't yet imagined? Your research question has at least two parts, and is more complex than a simple survey design can address. To conduct this more in-depth analysis, you decide on a combined design in which you first select and survey a cluster sample, then interview a subsample of the survey respondents (perhaps using a focus group format), then conduct observational research with another subsample of the interviewees. This is an example of a design in which you would include both probability and purposive sampling.

This would obviously be a sequential study (survey first, then interviews, then observations) using a "nested" sampling design, with each new sample being a subset of the preceding sample. Your initial survey would be administered to a probability sample, using systematic cluster sampling techniques to identify important groups within your population of interest. When you review your survey responses, you can identify respondents that used the product of interest in various ways, and select a subgroup to contact for follow-up interviews. This would be a purposive sample of participants selected because they represent a variety of perspectives on the product and its use. Finally, from among the interviewees, you could select another purposive subset, probably those representing particular important categories of interview responses, and arrange to observe them using the product.

In this example, the purpose of the research was not primarily to study the population, but rather to garner ideas for product improvement. Therefore, although probability sampling was used in the initial phase, generalizing the results to the broader population was only the first step of the process. The survey step would give you a good idea of what the population as a whole thought of the product and in what ways it was being used. But your study would be incomplete without addressing the primary objective— product improvement. Thus, the predominant phases of your combined design (those most closely addressing your project intent) were the qualitative components of interviewing and observing.

It is entirely possible to utilize both experimental methods using random assignment and purposive sampling methods in a combined design. For example, in a recent federal research grant proposal, the authors were interested in studying the effects of professional development training on science teachers' knowledge, classroom methods, and subsequent student achievement. One logical way to do this is to randomly assign teachers to receive the professional development training and compare their results to those of teachers who did not participate. (The comparison group would have the opportunity to participate at a later date.) Once the random assignment was made, the training would be delivered, and a subgroup of teachers purposively selected for further study. Both quantitative data (from tests and surveys) and qualitative data (from interviews and observations) would then be collected to determine how much teachers had learned, how they deployed this learning in their classrooms, and how much their students learned as a result. The same methods would be used to study nonparticipating (control group) teachers so that comparisons could be made between the groups.

The preceding example represents the most common type of multimethod sampling in experiments: combining purposive sampling of sites with random assignment to control and experimental groups within the sites.[10] In one interesting example of an experimental study of the effect of praise on children's motivation to learn, researchers conducted a series of six experiments.[11] The students were all in the fifth grade but were located in schools in different cities: a small town in the Midwest and large city in the Northeast. The schools and classrooms were purposively selected to maximize variation among different ethnic groups. This procedure is very important for increasing external validity in nonrandom samples.

Another kind of purposive sampling, less common but not rare, is on-site investigation of sites where an experimental approach was successful and other sites where it was not. The basic idea is to uncover and investigate in detail the causes for the different outcomes and to understand through observational and interview research the variability shown in the experiment.[12]

A third way of combining methods of sampling is the survey experiment. In this approach, random assignment is used to conduct an experiment among subgroups of the respondents in the survey's random sample. The beauty of this method of combined sampling is that it unites two very strong approaches to case selection and assignment—random sampling and random assignment. Sometimes, when one combines methods of design and sampling the purpose is to correct for weaknesses—as when surveys (representative but superficial) and interviews (deep but not representative) are combined. With the survey experiment, two powerful methods are linked.[13]

From these examples, we can see that multiple ways to combine probability and purposive sampling are possible; depending on your combined design, you may use them simultaneously or sequentially in a variety of configurations.[14]

CONCLUSIONS

There are numerous ways to blend the parts of your study, and each part requires choosing among specific sampling techniques. As always, the overall purpose of your study (e.g., exploration or generalizability) and your specific research questions will determine both your study design and your choices of sampling methods.

The two main categories of sampling useful for combined designs are probability sampling and purposive sampling. Probability samples are needed when you want to

---

[10] Shadish et al. (2002) have a good general discussion of this widespread practice.

[11] Mueller and Dweck (1998).

[12] Plewis and Mason (2005).

[13] For good discussions and examples, see Gaines et al. (2007) and Krysan et al. (2009).

[14] Collins et al. (2006) provide examples of at least eight designs that use some combination of two sampling techniques.

generalize your findings to the larger population; purposive samples are selected when specific characteristics of your cases are important to your study.

Depending on your design, your samples may be identical, parallel, nested, or multipopulation. The relationships among your samples should be carefully considered and should make sense in light of your research questions. Care must be taken to avoid compounding sampling errors when taking successive samples for different components of your combined study design.

As we repeat often in this volume, once you have decided *when* to use which type of sampling, figuring out how to create your sampling frames and recruit your participants will take additional research and contemplation. For "how to" guidance, we recommend consulting specialized sources on sampling techniques.[15]

The table on page 225 summarizes the guidance discussed in this chapter.

SUGGESTIONS FOR FURTHER READING

In addition to providing a good discussion about probability and purposive sampling, Teddlie and Yu's article "Mixed Methods Sampling: A Typology with Examples" (2007) provides ideas for creative ways to sample, including sequential, concurrent, and multilevel sampling. The authors provide a list of useful guidelines to consider when sampling in combined research designs. Plowright's book *Using Mixed Methods: Frameworks for an Integrated Methodology* (2011) devotes two sections to sampling in mixed methods studies, with additional reading recommendations also provided.

---

[15] Tashakkori and Teddlie (2003, Chap. 10) is a good place to start.

CHAPTER 12 SUMMARY TABLE

WHEN SHOULD YOU USE PROBABILITY SAMPLING IN YOUR COMBINED DESIGN?

- When you want to generalize your findings to a larger population.
- When you are able to recruit a large enough sample.
- When you can create a formal sampling frame.

WHEN SHOULD YOU USE PURPOSIVE SAMPLING IN YOUR COMBINED DESIGN?

- When you want to garner a variety of perspectives on an issue, or
- When your cases fit certain characteristics that are important to your study, such as:
  - Being "typical,"
  - Being "outliers,"
  - Being part of a group receiving specific "treatment,"
  - Representing a range of variation along a continuum, or
  - Representing a particular combination of interesting characteristics.

WHEN SHOULD YOU USE BOTH PROBABILITY AND PURPOSIVE SAMPLING IN YOUR COMBINED DESIGN?

- When one or more components of your design require probability sampling in order to make generalizations, and one or more components require in-depth study of specific cases of interest.
- If you do sequential sampling, when you can assure that the sampling process will not create or compound sampling error.

WHEN SHOULD YOU USE IDENTICAL, PARALLEL, NESTED, OR MULTIPOPULATION SAMPLES?

Identical samples	• When you need to hold the participants constant while testing the effects of a variable (such as an intervention or treatment).
Parallel samples	• When you can reasonably select two random samples from a larger population in order to administer different treatments to them and compare effects.
Nested samples	• When you seek more in-depth information from a subgroup of a larger sample.
Multipopulation samples	• When you need to hold the intervention or treatment constant in order to compare results across different populations.

PART III

Research Ethics
The Responsible Conduct of Research

INTRODUCTION TO PART III

The term *ethics* refers to good conduct toward others; it also refers to the branch of philosophy that studies good and bad conduct and the moral obligations or responsibilities we have toward others. It is important to emphasize the phrase "toward others" in the definition, because a purely self-interested act can be neither ethical nor moral, although it could be morally neutral. Taking good care of your health because you want to live a long and full life is a fine thing to do, but it only becomes a moral act if, for example, you are taking care of yourself because others are dependent on you. Or, helping another person could be a moral or ethical thing to do, but not if you were motivated only by the hope of a reward. Ethics is a complicated subject and one that is as old as recorded thought. We can only sketch a few main points here before turning to the narrower questions of applying ethical principles to research in the social and behavioral sciences.

Ethics is a matter of commitment to and behavior guided by certain values. Scientists can probably never be value free or value neutral. Instead, scholars in the social sciences tend to put the values of scientific research above other values, such as religious, political, and ideological values. What are the values of scientific research? Various lists have been proposed.[1] Some examples can illustrate the types of values that have been proposed. One value of scientific research is organized skepticism; this seems built into most notions of scientific research. Scientific skepticism entails the systematic questioning of knowledge claims. This questioning can come into conflict with any orthodoxy that stresses conformity to beliefs, whether political, social, or religious. Another value

---

[1] One of the best known is Merton's (1973); see also Shamoo and Resnik (2009).

researchers usually support is open access to data, ideas, and information. This value might easily conflict with others' values, such as a government's wish to maintain control over data and information in order to promote such values as social stability—or to guard national security. Finally, ethics almost always involves making decisions and choices about which principles should apply and what kind of conduct is ethical in particular situations. Unthinking or habitual actions are rarely, if ever, considered as ethical.

Why are we waiting until comparatively late in this book to begin the discussion of research ethics? Some writers on research methods think one should start with ethics. And they are correct that ethical considerations are relevant at all stages of your research from the initial formulation of the research question through design, sampling, and analysis. But ethical considerations tend to become most practically relevant *after* you have decided on your research question, picked a design strategy, and devised a sampling plan. Moralists can enjoin us to make research ethics guiding principles in our lives, but many of us won't quite get around to serious ethical deliberations until it is time to approach the institutional review board (IRB). The IRB wants to know what you are going to do and to whom and why. Before applying to the IRB for approval of your plan to conduct research on human subjects (IRBs continue to use the term "human subjects" although most social researchers prefer "participants") you've got to have a plan. For instance, if you are writing a doctoral dissertation, you usually need an approved dissertation proposal, which includes your design and sampling choices, as part of what you submit to the IRB. So we discuss research ethics after design and sampling because we see research ethics as a branch of *applied* philosophy, which is related to *actions* in specific areas of conduct—not as normative ethical philosophy, which focuses on what people should *believe* more than on what they should *do*. In short, it is more relevant and clearer how to apply ethical principles to actions when you have a plan of action that includes your design (what to do) and sampling choices (with whom it will be done).

We cannot tell you how to make ethical decisions, but we do discuss when, in the course of research, the need to make them is likely to occur. We review situations when ethical sensitivity is likely to be required and when the danger of a breach of ethical principles is great. Answers to the question "when to use which ethical safeguards" vary from discipline to discipline and, within disciplines, from design to design. If research ethics can be defined as good conduct toward others in the course of conducting research, the next obvious question is: which others? We will categorize our discussions of research ethics in two ways, first in terms of those toward whom researchers have ethical responsibilities. Second, we will examine how these responsibilities differ between types of research, especially types of research categorized by design as we have defined it in Part I of this volume. We display the framework for our discussion in Figure III.1.

Our general topic is researchers' ethical responsibilities toward others. The first row of Figure III.1 (row A) emphasizes that norms of research ethics may be either legal or moral or both. Sometimes researchers' responsibilities are the right thing to do (they are moral or ethical), but they are not necessarily enforced by legal rules and administrative regulations. Of course, in any society there tends to be a lot of overlap between moral and legal rules. However, except in a pure theocracy, the overlap is never complete, and the boundary between the moral and the legal fluctuates. For example, in the late 20th

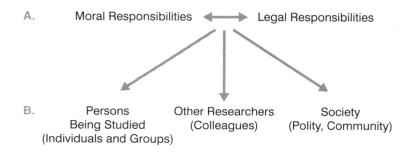

FIGURE III.1. Researchers' ethical responsibilities toward others.

century, principles of conduct toward research subjects that had been in earlier decades ensured only by professional norms became formal rules supported by various legal sanctions. The general trend in recent decades has been to convert what had been ethical principles (protecting subjects) into legal rules (safeguarding participants). While we discuss rules and regulations governing research, these vary from time to time, from nation to nation, and even from state to state in the United States. Consequently, we put more emphasis on the ethical principles on which rules and regulations are or should be based.

Our responsibilities as researchers can be divided into the three fairly distinct groups listed in the second row of the figure (B): persons being studied, other researchers, and the broader society or community. The most important of these, especially in the social and behavioral sciences is the first: the persons whom we study. While the ethical issues raised by studying people are clearly paramount in the social and humanistic disciplines, they are quite complex and they differ significantly with the designs researchers use. The issues involved in the ethical conduct of research can vary greatly depending on whether we are surveying respondents, interviewing informants, experimenting on participants, observing persons in social settings, reviewing the archival records of individuals and groups, or any combination of these. These issues will be examined in our next six chapters on survey, interview, experimental, observational, archival, and combined research designs.

In the remainder of this introduction to Part III, we review general issues in research ethics that cut across designs, but that differ in terms of those toward whom researchers have ethical responsibilities. Many of these issues refer to responsibilities toward the community of researchers and toward the broader society. But, again, pride of place in research ethics in the social sciences will always be given to the people we study. We begin there, and the ethical implications of studying people will be the central topic of the six chapters of Part III.

RESPONSIBILITIES TOWARD THE PERSONS BEING STUDIED

The theory and practice of research ethics in the social sciences bear the marks of their origins. Those origins were largely in medical abuse, and truly evil actions were taken in the name of "medical" research, most notoriously by Nazi physicians in the Second

World War. Reaction to those atrocities led to the Nuremburg trials of war criminals and to the Nuremburg Code of the late 1940s. The Code contains 10 regulations governing proper conduct of medical research, particularly clinical experiments. The 10 points, which have been applied very broadly, are:

1. Human subjects should give informed consent.
2. The research should have potential benefit.
3. Human experimentation should be based on the results of prior animal experimentation.
4. The research should avoid all unnecessary physical and mental suffering and injury.
5. No experiment should be conducted when there is reason to believe that it will result in death or injury, except perhaps when the experimental physicians also serve as their own subjects.
6. The risks should not be greater than the potential benefits.
7. Protections must be in place for subjects against even remote possibilities of harm.
8. Experiments should be conducted only by scientifically qualified persons.
9. The subjects should be free to end the experiment at any stage.
10. Researchers should stop the experiment if they discover that the research may be causing harm to the experimental subjects.[2]

Since the 1940s, there has been a sometimes gradual and sometimes rapid movement in the direction of increased rights for human subjects. Lest one believe that abuses only date from remote times and places, the infamous Tuskegee experiments serve as a reminder that evil can occur anywhere, in this case, in Alabama. These experiments allowed some 400 African American men with syphilis to go untreated in order to chart the course of the disease. This went on for decades (between 1932 and 1972), long after effective cures for the disease became available (in the late 1940s).[3] It wasn't only Nazis who allowed patients to suffer avoidable harm. Discovery of this abuse at least had the positive effect of leading to the National Research Act in the United States. This Act gave rise to IRBs, established in 1981. These boards must approve all research involving human subjects that is federally funded or takes place at an institution receiving federal funds. The rules enforced by IRBs are not very different from those stated in the Nuremberg Code, but they apply to any research using humans, whether medical or not, including surveys, interviews, experiments, observations, and archival investigations.

---

[2]The text has been reproduced or summarized many times since it was first published in the United States in *Trials of War Criminals before the Nuremberg Military Tribunals under Control Council Law No. 10*, Vol. 2, pp. 181–182. Washington, DC: U.S. Government Printing Office, 1949. The Code has been expanded upon but not fundamentally changed in subsequent documents such as the Belmont Report.

[3]Reverby (2009) provides one of the fullest accounts. Reverby was also central in exposing an even worse instance of researcher immorality; in Guatemala during the Second World War, U.S. researchers *intentionally infected* people with syphilis.

While the basic principles on which modern research ethics are based have remained quite consistent since the promulgation of the Nuremburg Code, the rules implementing those principles have evolved with changes in social and political contexts and with advances in research technology. At the time of this writing (Fall 2011) the U.S. Department of Health and Human Services is on the verge of issuing a major revision in the rules governing "Human Subjects Research Protections." The Department has been soliciting reactions to proposed changes which aim to enhance "protections for research subjects" while simultaneously "reducing burden, delay, and ambiguity for investigators."[4] Among the likely changes are fewer regulations governing interviews and surveys of adults conducted by social and behavioral researchers; this would be probably accomplished by making it easier for studies to qualify for exemption from review or for expedited review. On the other hand, stricter and more consistent regulations can be expected in the areas of maintaining information privacy and data security. This reflects the growth of research using huge databases; when using these databases, the risks are "not physical but informational." It remains to be seen whether the changes will lessen the criticisms of IRB rules reviewed in the next two paragraphs or will give rise to new ones.

It is hard to overemphasize the progress that the rigorous application of regulations protecting research participants represents. Still, some researchers have resented them. Many researchers working on topics that apparently pose little threat to anyone, such as anonymous surveys of adults, have felt annoyance at the delays that even "expedited" IRB reviews can entail. But problems with enforcement of ethics regulations go beyond irritation at minor delays. Institutional Review Boards have, in many cases, become bureaucracies, and bureaucracies have well-known tendencies to expand the numbers and details of rules seemingly for their own sake. This is especially likely to occur when key concepts—such as harm, benefit, risk, and informed consent—are difficult to define, differ according to context, and thus require extensive interpretation if they are to be applied to specific cases. One author has called the proliferation of rules and the actions they cover "ethics creep."[5] Others think of it as galloping bureaucratic inflation of rules. As Howard Becker put it, what was originally a set of safeguards to prevent physicians from abusing research subjects (they were not called "participants" until later) "has turned into a serious, ambitious bureaucracy with interests to protect, a mission to promote, and a self-righteous and self-protective ideology to explain why it's all necessary."[6] Researchers can differ about the label and about the extent of the problem, but there is little doubt that IRBs are exercising increasing control over a wider range of research practices. This control can seem particularly irksome to researchers gathering qualitative data, especially those using participant observation and open-ended informal interviewing. IRBs want researchers to specify in advance exactly what they intend to do, but much of qualitative research is built upon discovering next steps in the course of the research, not specifying a protocol in advance.

---

[4]The text of the proposed regulations and the rationale for them can be found in the U.S. Government *Federal Register, 76* (2011, pp. 44512–44531).

[5]Haggerty (2004). Haggerty examines in depth the Canadian system of enforcing research ethics. Becker (2004) and Bosk (2004) (cited below) are commentaries by U.S. researchers on his work. See also Schrag (2010).

[6]Becker (2004, p. 415).

Some researchers who gather qualitative data are concerned because IRBs usually have many representatives from medical and biological research. They should; that's where serious harm usually occurs. But biomedical researchers can easily believe that "ethnographic research, when compared to the standard of the randomized clinical trial, is so slipshod that it cannot have any benefit. Without a plausible benefit, it is hard for IRB members to justify any risk, however remote."[7] There is considerable debate about whether rules originally meant for medical research are appropriate in the social sciences.[8] Whatever one's assessment of the effects, there can be little doubt that the breadth and depth of IRB oversight have increased in terms of what counts as (1) research, (2) risk of harm, (3) informed consent, and (4) confidentiality and anonymity.

Here we make five general points about these issues. That is because specific IRB rules and regulations can vary in how they are implemented from one institution to the next, and laws and regulations are continually being revised at the federal level. Hence, we focus on general points that apply to researchers using any design when studying people. They indicate times when heightened sensitivity or caution may be needed.

First, IRBs do not monitor the actual *conduct* of research. They review and approve (or reject) *proposals*. Reviews of the conduct of research are most likely to arise when there has been a complaint concerning harm to humans. Then several questions arise. Was a research protocol submitted to the appropriate IRB? If so, did the IRB approve it? If so, did the researchers do what the approved proposal said they were going to do? If the answer to these three questions is yes, then the IRB and the sponsoring institution may be liable for any harm to participants. If the answer is no, then the burden of liability will rest much more heavily on the researcher.

Second, researchers often believe that otherwise good rules for protecting the people who are studied in research projects are also sometimes used as a pretext to avoid scrutiny. Administrators who fear evaluation will sometimes use "privacy" of clients or patients or students or prisoners to deny access to data—even when privacy can be fully guaranteed, for example, by the use of anonymous institutional records. Even researchers who strongly support protections for human research participants can be highly suspicious of administrators who "play the rights card" as a form of obstructionism that can get in the way of important research. There are few easy ways around such barriers, although the Freedom of Information Act (FOIA) can provide some leverage for investigators conducting archival research on federal documents, and many states have comparable open-access laws.

Third, it is very important to remember that you, as a researcher, have limited ability to protect the anonymity and confidentiality of the people you study. For example, you do not have the kinds of rights to safeguard your sources that a journalist does. Journalists are protected by constitutional provisions guarding freedom of the press, and those protections extend to journalists' sources. But there is no constitutional guarantee of freedom of research. Therefore your sources have no such rights either. If your notes are subpoenaed, you will probably have to give them up—or risk jail time. Incarceration for failing to inform on your informants is rare, but it does happen. Also, there is no social researcher analogue to doctor–patient or lawyer–client privilege to

---

[7]Bosk (2004, p. 419).

[8]For an argument and some evidence that worries about the medicalization of social research are mostly ill-founded alarmism, see Hedgecoe (2008).

safeguard, for example, interviewees' information—unless you happen to be a physician or an attorney and the research participants are patients or clients. In short, be careful not to promise a kind of confidentiality you cannot deliver.

The fourth general point about responsibilities toward the people we study is that they need to give their *informed* consent before they participate in the research. But good research practice for certain kinds of questions often requires that participants not be told which treatment they will receive, or what the purpose of the study is, because this knowledge might influence how they react to the intervention. Also, defining what it means to be truly "informed" is not simple. How well do research participants need to understand the information they are given?[9] Finding the fine line between informed consent and good research practice often challenges researchers. The American Evaluation Association has published a useful collection of articles on the subject of research ethics[10] and the *Standards for Educational and Psychological Testing*[11] is crucial in those fields. The best way to keep up with developments in this quickly changing area is to consult the websites of the major professional organizations in your field of specialization as well as checking with the IRB at your institution, which will often maintain a website describing any new regulations or new ways they are being interpreted.

Finally, our fifth point is that preparing IRB proposals can be very helpful in creating succinct, understandable descriptions of your research project, and can help you clarify and hone your research design. The project description you create for the IRB can be modified for use on participant informed consent forms, perhaps by condensing details, simplifying language for a lay audience, or laying out your research plan in clear and concise steps. While the process can sometimes seem bureaucratic and cumbersome, it can be approached as being important not only to protect your participants, but also to improving your research project. All researchers can benefit when serious and informed people systematically review and comment on their work; the IRB review can reasonably be thought of as an opportunity as well as a requirement.

RESPONSIBILITIES TOWARD OTHER RESEARCHERS

The community of scholars is built on a foundation of openness and trust. This means that it is vulnerable to abuse by the unscrupulous. This vulnerability is the price we pay for an open system. More regulation of the relations among researchers could probably curb some abuses, but that might not be worth the price paid in loss of creativity and loss of research freedom. Strict governmental controls over researchers' activities are usually associated with low research quality and despotic regimes. Most researchers would probably agree that an informal system of values and sanctions would be better—at least until they have a complaint; then they may feel that "there oughta be a law." Today, researchers' obligations toward other researchers and the community of

---

[9]Walker et al. (2008) discuss this issue; the research participants were unemployed workers signing up for a job training program.

[10]Fitzpatrick and Morris (1999).

[11]American Educational Research Association (1999). This volume is jointly sponsored by the American Educational Research Association, the American Psychological Association, and the National Council on Measurement in Education.

scholars are mostly maintained by an informal system of rewards and sanctions. This means that when ethical issues come up, they will usually have to be resolved by discussion and deliberation rather than by appeals to formal rules.

What do we mean by an informal system? Here is an example. One of the authors of this book was once an editor of a publication to which potential authors were invited to contribute. If they accepted the invitation, they committed to writing an *original* article for the publication. But one author who accepted the invitation sent us an article that he had also sent to another journal. At the last minute, as we were ready to go into production, he informed us that his contribution had just been published in the other journal. This meant that we could not publish it. The author's actions were a clear violation of long-standing rules of journals and professional organizations against multiple submissions of a research article. We could have reported this violation to the journals and to the relevant scholarly organizations. Instead, despite delays in publication, we worked with the author to correct the problem. We attempted no formal sanctions. But what about informal sanctions? Well, we would probably never work with that author again, and, if asked, we would be reluctant to recommend that others do so. That does not sound like much, perhaps, but in a relatively small community based on trust, it is not necessarily inconsequential.

We can briefly discuss researchers' obligations or responsibilities toward colleagues and the community of scholars under three headings: collegiality, honesty, and fairness. When ethical sensitivity is needed and when the possibility of the breach of norms occurs, it usually does so in one of these three categories.

Collegiality

When you work with colleagues, it is important to fulfill reasonable expectations that you pull your weight, meet deadlines, and so on. The example of the multiple submissions of the same research article just discussed was a violation of norms of collegiality as well as of the official policies of professional organizations and scholarly journals. Not only were the editors inconvenienced and their time wasted, but also the other contributors had to wait longer to see their contributions published. The violation was not grave, and it was probably due more to carelessness than to dishonesty, but careful accuracy is also a norm of responsible conduct, and one that is especially relevant in the scholarly community.

Good colleagues share their ideas, methods, and data. Most progress in our knowledge and understanding of important issues in social research has come as a result of the interaction of ideas, methods, and findings from many sources. Of course, some contributions are more important than others, but no one starts out by making major contributions and hardly anyone ever really does so totally on their own. We are all indebted to current and previous colleagues. We can only repay that debt by cooperating with other colleagues. As the old saying goes, it's not nice to kick down the ladder you used to climb to the top.

It is also important to share concerns about and to discuss ethical issues with colleagues. Such discussions usually lead to better decisions and they help to maintain the informal set of norms on which ethical behavior is based. Finally, if you are a faculty member and your colleagues are students, such as graduate assistants or undergraduate student workers, as a researcher you have an obligation to be their mentor, not just their boss. The students should be seen as future members of the community, not merely as employees. The mentoring should focus on research techniques, of course, but also on ethical values and practices, thus helping to prepare the next generation of ethical scholars.

Honesty

Honesty toward other researchers first involves presenting findings accurately. When researchers honestly present findings, they do not exaggerate their importance, nor do they hide the limitations of the research design and the conclusions, nor do they engage in questionable practices such as deleting inconvenient outliers. Equally important, researchers should not take more credit for the research than is their due. If others, such as graduate students, helped write a research report or did some of the data gathering or reviewed the literature, they should be acknowledged, and perhaps listed as coauthors. In addition to giving credit where it is due, it is important not to take credit where it is not due. It is fairly common for senior researchers to be asked to sign on as coauthors when they have made few contributions to the project leading to the publication. This can sometimes be acceptable, if, for example, the senior author has been brought in to review the data analysis for accuracy—but the limits of such contributions should be signaled in some way. Some journals even have systems for precisely specifying the portions of the research and the publication for which each author was responsible.

Of course, the greatest academic dishonesty of all is plagiarism. This is the use of the ideas, data, and/or words of another without acknowledging their originator. One common attempt at defense is ignorance. It is quite remarkable how often students do not know that to cobble together verbatim paragraphs from various sources is an unacceptable way to "write" a paper. One way to tell that sometimes students have been miseducated, and that they really do not know they are plagiarizing, is that not infrequently they carefully list in the bibliography all the sources from which they have plagiarized.

Sometimes plagiarism could happen unintentionally, but probably not nearly as often as inadvertent plagiarism is claimed as a defense. Well-known writers have tried to exonerate themselves by claiming that it was all an accident. And it could happen. In discussions with colleagues, we have often heard versions of a familiar nightmare scenario. When writing your lecture notes you use some of the best sources in the field and take extensive notes, including some verbatim passages. As you revise your notes from semester to semester, some fragments of the original verbatim texts remain. Having used these notes a few times, they have become "yours," and you don't quite remember that you didn't actually write some of those snappy phrases you are using. Then, you employ those phrases in a publication and someone remembers having read them before. You've been caught.

While there are simple tools you can use to avoid verbatim plagiarism (they are called quotation marks), the situation can get murkier when it comes to ideas. It actually is hard to know where one's ideas have come from—how much they are original to you and how much they are minor variations on a theme heard in another context. In any case, it is important to be scrupulous in giving credit, not just for self-protection, but also out of common decency. Think of it this way: how would you feel if you read a new and important book, one that was getting lots of credit in the press, and you realized that chunks of that book had been lifted from something you had written? "Violated" is a word that people have understandably used to express their outrage in such situations.

Fairness

When issues of fairness are raised in the academic community, they are probably most frequently linked to questions of fairness in peer review. Peer review is the foundation upon which the rewards system in academic life is built. Peer review determines who gets published, who obtains grants, and who receives promotion and tenure. While the peer review system has very important consequences for university researchers' professional lives, it is very difficult to determine its fairness in specific cases. Unlike plagiarism, multiple submissions, and data fudging, which can all be detected and demonstrated with reasonable certainty, violations of the norms of fairness in peer review are hard to prove. Peer review is based on professional judgment, not ultimately on matters of fact. When important consequences are tied to subjective processes, occasions for violations of the ethical norm of fairness can be frequent and consequential. There is little that you as a member of an academic community can do that is more important than to make your peer review work as rigorously honest and fair as you know how. Part of that fairness includes maintaining strict confidentiality.

RESPONSIBILITIES TOWARD THE BROADER SOCIETY/COMMUNITY

Two millennia ago, Hippocrates expressed the nub of the matter in three words: *Primum non nocere*,[12] or "First do no harm." This principle is usually applied to individuals, but it is equally relevant when thinking of researchers' responsibilities to the broader society. Researchers who engage in unethical practices hurt not only colleagues and research participants, but the broader society as well. As with all realms of ethical issues, sometimes enforcement of ethical norms is accomplished through informal means and sometimes through formal legal sanctions. While incentives to act responsibly toward one's colleagues are mainly a matter of reputation and moral suasion, responsibilities toward society can be enforced by more severe penalties, including jail time in some instances.

Moral Suasion

The work of most researchers in the social and behavioral sciences is subsidized by the broader society[13]. A few researchers are independently wealthy or have day jobs and pay their own way. Some others write books that may sell well enough that they can support their research with their royalties. But most of us receive grants and/or work in organizations supported in whole or in part by tax dollars and tax-exempt status. When such researchers (including the authors of this book) are inefficient, they are wasting public

---

[12] Why Hippocrates, a Greek physician, should always be quoted in Latin is a scholarly curiosity.

[13] We leave out of consideration here the separate category of researchers who work for private for-profit corporations doing product development, market research, and so on.

resources that could be used to do something useful. Slipshod work is a betrayal of the public trust. Pursuing this line of argument, one could also argue that it is important to work on socially significant topics, not just on interesting puzzles—while admitting that it is not always easy to know what will prove to be socially significant in the long run.

While the impact of unethical research practices tends to be less severe in the social than in the biomedical sciences, social research can have important consequences for the broader society. Research findings can sometimes influence social and political policy in major ways. For example, much educational policy in the 1960s and 1970s was directly influenced by the Coleman Report,[14] which at the time probably summarized the best available information. *A Nation at Risk*, based on dramatically less data than the Coleman Report, also had a major impact on education reform movements in the 1980s and 1990s.[15] After 2000, several states spent billions of dollars reducing class size on the basis, at least to some extent, of the findings of Project STAR conducted in Tennessee in the late 1990s.[16] We know the field of education research and policy best, and our examples often come from that area of social policy, but it is hardly the only area where social scientists can have a big influence. Economists have perhaps the most direct effects, with their reports influencing everything from stock prices to the consumer confidence index. While some of us might hope someday to see a President's Council of Sociological Advisors, the economists seem to have a corner on that market. Ironically, unlike most major organizations of social scientists in the United States, the American Economic Association does not have a formal code of ethics. The general point is that one's research can have consequences and an ethical researcher is alert to these.

Legal Penalties

Research misconduct as defined by the Office of Research Integrity is a legal—not a moral—infraction. Most legal infractions would be considered unethical by researchers in the social and behavioral sciences even if they were not illegal. In any case, if you take public dollars to conduct your research, especially federal dollars, then your results and your data are not yours alone. They belong to the public, and others can use the Freedom of Information Act to obtain them if you have not made them available.

The most common infraction that leads to legal action is fraud—usually data falsification. Fraud seems to be less common in the social and behavioral sciences than it is in the physical and biological fields. Or, more likely perhaps, fraud in the social and behavioral sciences is less often discovered, perhaps because less is at stake when a researcher cheats in order to make some social science point as opposed to when researchers conceal data that would eliminate the profits on a successful painkiller that has the pesky side effect of causing heart problems and stroke (consider the case of Celebrex), or when they falsify data on the effects of childhood vaccines on autism.

But fraud in our disciplines is hardly unknown. The case of Cyril Burt is perhaps the most famous. He falsified data (literally made it up) on pairs of identical twins (many of whom did not exist) so that he could "prove" that IQ was mainly heritable.

---

[14] Commonly known as the "Coleman Report" for its lead author, James Coleman, *Equality of Educational Opportunity* was published in 1966.

[15] Published in 1983 by the National Commission on Excellence in Education.

[16] See Finn and Achilles (1999).

He appeared to have been "on a mission," so sure he was right that inconveniences like inadequate data couldn't be allowed to get in the way. And he persuaded many people for a long time. His dishonesty went undiscovered for 20 years, and many researchers and policy makers were influenced by his intellectual swindle. Given that it took two decades to catch a high-profile researcher like Cyril Burt, it is probably the case that if researchers in the social and behavioral sciences are to behave honestly, they will have to be motivated more by moral principles than by the fear of getting caught. The chances of discovering dishonesty in social research seem fairly low. We have little to maintain our ethical standards apart from a scrupulous commitment to honesty.

Conflicts of interest are an area of ethical concern that straddles moral norms and legal sanctions. There are quite specific rules, for example, about how much stock you can legally own in a company that stands to benefit from your research. But conflicts of interest are potentially very broad and apply to many areas that are not covered by formal regulations. There are generally two types of conflict that are pertinent to social science research: first, potential conflicts between the interests of the researcher and the interests of his or her study participants; and second, competing interests between the goals of the researcher and the goals of others, such as funders or employers. For any funded study, your consent forms must include the funding source, and must indicate if the funding creates any conflicts of interest for the researchers. If you, the researcher, could benefit financially or otherwise from an individual's participation, a potential conflict of interest exists between your interests and those of your participants, and must be disclosed when seeking informed consent.

In an example of the first type, conflict of interest between researcher and participants may arise in situations such as those in which potential participants feel compelled to participate, either overtly or by inference, because they may fear reprisal or deprivation of benefits. This conflict overlaps with the general category of harm to research participants, and must be examined in each situation for either actual or potential coercion. In the second type, competing interests between the researcher's and funders' goals, a research study may be compromised by this conflict. For example, say a private foundation funder wants to underwrite a research study but has a definite motive in mind for finding certain predetermined results. The funder may then exert influence on the researcher to modify the study design, the analysis procedures, or the findings. In this case, the funder's motives are in conflict with the researcher's presumable motive of conducting a valid and reliable study.

Finally, when you know of or suspect fraud, or illegal conflict of interest, do you blow the whistle? Do you have an ethical obligation to the broader society to do so? The history of what has happened to whistle-blowers is not encouraging.[17] Still, if you are committed as a researcher to honest work for the benefit of the broader society that supports you, it might be hard to resist speaking out.

We have been able here to offer little more than a quick overview of the circumstances under which ethical issues might arise. In the next six chapters, our emphasis is on ethical issues involving the people who make our research possible by letting us study them. That discussion will be organized under three rubrics—principles that are salient for our fulfilling our responsibilities to the persons we study: consent, harm, and

---

[17] See Shamoo and Resnik (2009) for details on several cases.

TABLE III.1. Typical Research Ethics Issues by Specific Design Types

Chapter	Design type	Research ethics issues
13	Survey	• Anonymity of respondents and their responses. • Privacy and informed consent.
14	Interview	• Confidentiality of interviewees. • Protections from any harm that might come from probing sensitive issues. • Informed consent.
15	Experimental	• Limiting deceptive practices. • Curbing physical or psychological harm. • Informed consent. • Debriefing.
16	Observational research	• Maintaining the anonymity of individuals and organizations. • Informed consent. • Covert observation.
17	Archival research	• Varies by the type of data in the archive. • Privacy of data in records.
18	Combined designs	• Does the use of multiple methods of data collection and their possible interactions cause problems for the subjects or ethical issues for the researcher?

privacy. We discuss each of these as they relate to the various phases of your research project: design, sampling, data collection, and analysis and reporting.

Each of the six chapters in Part III looks in depth at ethical questions related to specific research designs. We again organize the discussion by design because ethical obligations to the people (individuals or groups) we study, and the problems that occur in trying to fulfill those obligations, tend to vary by design. Table III.1 provides an overview of the main issues addressed in each chapter.

CHAPTER 13

Ethics in Survey Research

It might seem that ethical concerns in survey research would be relatively minor, especially as compared with either participant observation or experiments, both of which entail considerably more direct contact and interaction with the people being studied. You certainly intervene in the ordinary course of people's lives less in survey research than in any major design category except archival research. Another feature of survey designs and sampling methods that makes them relatively uncomplicated in terms of ethical issues is that, as compared to interviews and observation research, surveys are highly structured and the work is mostly frontloaded. This means that many of the ethical choices you have to make are built into the design and are made before you come into contact with respondents. By comparison, the less structured methods used in interviews and observational research mean that unanticipated issues are more likely to arise, and you are more likely to have to make your ethical decisions on the fly and have less time for deliberation. Still, many ethical issues and problems are embedded in the design of survey research, and others can occur in the course of data gathering and analysis.

In a well-designed survey with a good sampling plan, it is a relatively straightforward matter to obtain informed consent and to avoid causing harm to respondents. The chief ethical problem in survey research is guarding the anonymity or confidentiality of the respondents and their responses or, in other terms, maintaining respondent privacy. People sometimes believe that the promised anonymity is sham, and sometimes they are right. The cartoon strip *Dilbert* expresses this well when, from time to time, Dilbert's boss says something like "I see that on your anonymous employee survey you said that you. . . ." It is true that sometimes surveyors promise anonymity or confidentiality but don't deliver. This is especially the case when there is an ulterior motive behind the research (such as snooping on employees). When that is the case, it probably is not even accurate to call the survey activity research. It is, instead, prying or spying.

Sometimes surveys aren't even real. One category of phony survey is the SUGS: selling (or soliciting or slandering) under the guise of surveying. Commercial, political, and religious marketers all use SUGS. You know the kinds of questions: "Would you be happy if for just pennies a day you could make your home more beautiful—and how do you feel about vinyl siding?" Blatant sales pitches are perhaps less disreputable than the so-called "push poll": "Doesn't it make you mad when politicians in Washington . . . , and would you be surprised to learn that Senator X from your state advocates . . . , and would you like to contribute to an organization that will put a stop to . . . ?" No respectable social researcher would be involved in this sort of fraud. It isn't even research, of course.[1] We do not mean to suggest that marketing research is illegitimate or that political research is inherently unethical. Companies have a legitimate interest in learning what kinds of products their customers want, and responsible politicians should know about their constituents' social and political values. Surveys are useful tools for pursuing this kind of knowledge. The ethical principles relevant to survey research are the same regardless of the researchers' goals—whether the research is conducted, for example, by companies for applied purposes, such as gauging customer satisfaction, or is undertaken by universities for more basic goals, such as describing demographic trends.

We suggested in the Introduction to Part III that one of the best ways to seek ethical guidance when employing particular research designs is to consult the websites of the relevant professional organizations. For survey research, a very good one is the code of professional ethics of the American Association for Public Opinion Research (AAPOR). This five-page document provides a good overview of the main issues likely to arise in the context of surveying.[2] The majority of the points in the document discuss researchers' ethical obligations to colleagues and to the broader society. This emphasis makes sense in survey research because surveys raise comparatively fewer ethical concerns about the well-being of respondents—as compared, for example, to experiments. The ethical principles in the AAPOR document that deal with survey respondents are the usual ones: (1) ensuring respondents' informed consent, (2) avoiding harm to respondents and (3) maintaining confidentiality and/or anonymity of respondents and their responses. We discuss each of these. Of the three, privacy is most important for survey research, since obtaining informed consent is usually comparatively routine and the possibility of harming individual respondents in survey research is fairly remote. Under each heading—consent, harm, and privacy—we discuss research activities in which ethical issues might emerge: (1) design, (2) sampling, (3) data collection, and (4) analysis and reporting.

CONSENT: INFORMED PARTICIPANTS WILLINGLY JOINING THE RESEARCH PROJECT

Design

Obtaining consent is a straightforward matter in most survey research designs. Potential respondents not wishing to participate in a survey can throw a paper questionnaire in the waste basket, hang up the phone, or shut the door in the face of the surveyor. Freely given consent can become an issue, however, especially when surveyors have some real

[1] While phony research is probably most common in surveys, it can be found everywhere. An egregious example is one of the scandals associated with Merck's Vioxx; one supposed clinical trial was actually disguised marketing designed to encourage physicians to prescribe the drug. See Hill, Ross, Egilman, and Krumholz (2008).

[2] Available at *www.aapor.org.*

or perceived authority over respondents, such as employers over employees, teachers over students, social workers over clients, or physicians over patients. In those circumstances, potential respondents may wrongly believe they must respond or that failure to respond will put them at some kind of disadvantage. Even worse, researchers may feel that their employees, students, or clients are obliged to participate in the survey. The ethical principle for researchers is simple: it is unethical for survey researchers to use their authority to imply that potential respondents are under an obligation to respond to survey questions. Confusion can arise among potential respondents because some surveys and survey-like questionnaires *are* mandatory. The U.S. Census is the most obvious example, and many other government surveys involve mandatory reporting by individuals and institutions. While these reports may be used extensively by researchers conducting archival or secondary analysis studies, they are not themselves research and do not fall under the category of research ethics.

Ethical actions by governments are a separate topic and one we address only occasionally. But one example deserves mention because it illustrates several potential ethical problems with survey research. Early in 2011, various news media reported that the U.S. Army compels soldiers to take a "spiritual fitness test." The mandatory test was instituted because some researchers believed that soldiers who are spiritually fit can handle battle-related stress better than those who are not. The "test," in the form of a survey, asks questions quite similar to those on opinion surveys, which are designed to make generalizations about populations and subgroups. In opinion surveys, these questions (about prayer, religious beliefs, and so on) raise few ethical issues because they are voluntary and anonymous. But the Army's questions are compulsory and are done for the purpose of diagnosing individuals' "problems," not for generalizing about groups. A soldier who scores poorly on the test is informed of the "deficiency"; he or she is offered a computerized training session to help "improve spiritual fitness." Not surprisingly, some soldiers have objected on various Constitutional grounds (separation of church and state, privacy, and others). A suit in federal court is probable. The general point is that it is not usually the questions themselves that are ethical or unethical, but who is asked, whether they can refuse to answer, and what use is made of the answers.

Informed consent requires that the researcher make clear the purposes of the research so that respondents know the kind of research in which they are participating. Fully disclosing the nature of the research and its purposes includes informing participants of any conflicts of interest (real or perceived) the researcher might have. For example, if the researcher runs a consulting firm and sells survey results for profit, this constitutes a conflict of interest. In survey research, such conflicts tend either to be rare or obvious (as in the case of market research) and tend to be a relatively small problem, but it is one to which the conscientious researcher will attend. Conflict of interest is one of several areas of research ethics that is regulated by legal and institutional rules as well as by moral and ethical principles.

Sampling

Forms of sampling that involve recruiting from and making contacts within networks can raise ethical issues about consent. For example, snowball sampling can exert pressure. Sales people know this well: "Your neighbor three houses down just agreed to consider a home security system. Wouldn't you like to keep your family safe like Mr.

Jones has?" And quota sampling, of the sort done in shopping malls or outside of polling places, where the researchers buttonhole potential respondents, can also make consent feel somewhat less than freely given. But these pressures are relatively minor. Other forms of persuading respondents to participate in the survey, such as being polite and flashing a winning smile, aren't neutral but hardly seem to constitute undue or unethical influence on adult respondents.

Data Collection

Respondents may agree to participate in your survey because they did not fully understand how you intended to ask them questions. Perhaps they did not realize that you would not welcome their desire to skip some questions or to reply with something other than your predetermined categories of answers. You might want respondents to pick one option from a list while some of them want to pick all that apply. Or, they may have agreed to answer questions about a general topic but they do not want to answer some particular questions. As a researcher, you will want to design your survey for flexibility, both to make informed consent as meaningful as possible and to avoid alienating respondents with rigid rules about how they must answer questions.

Analysis and Reporting

The researcher's main ethical obligation to respondents (as it is to colleagues and to the general public) is fair and accurate methods of analysis and reporting. Respondents' consent implies a belief on their part that you will honor your ethical obligation to present what they say honestly and accurately and not distort what they say to serve some other purpose.

HARM: PREVENTING INJURY TO RESPONDENTS

Design

Harm to respondents is rarely a major issue in survey research. It is not completely fanciful to imagine survey questions that could cause harm merely by being asked, but any such harmful questions, particularly when a respondent is under no obligation to answer them, are quite rare. Of course, some respondents may be upset by the content of questions. When one of us was on a team conducting a pencil-and-paper survey in group settings about tolerance of nonconformity, one respondent threw down his pencil and marched out of the room, announcing in a loud voice, "This survey isn't about tolerance. It's about homos!" And he slammed the door on the way out. While the survey did include some questions about attitudes toward homosexuals, the survey also referred to members of many other social, political, and religious groups. The reaction of the door slammer was the most extreme negative reaction, but it wasn't the only one. Quite a few respondents seemed to be made uncomfortable by the content of the survey, so much so that the researchers eventually decided to follow up subsequent surveys by asking for volunteers to participate in focus group discussions about their reactions to the questions on the survey. We learned that many respondents, about one out of five or six, found merely *thinking about* social, political, and religious diversity to be an unpleasant experience. We did not believe that asking respondents to think about controversial issues constituted inflicting harm, particularly since those taking the survey were adults. However, our experience did lead us to stress even more strongly on subsequent surveys that there were no right or wrong answers and that respondents were free to skip any questions they did not want to answer. And we would recommend being very emphatic about respondents' right to skip questions, especially when surveys deal with controversial issues, as they often do. Our experience did make us more reluctant to use our survey with populations that might be considered more vulnerable than our young adults. (As a note, we had never thought that these survey questions were appropriate for minors.)

Sampling

Sampling in surveys always involves sampling from a known or implied population. Selecting that population should be done with considerations of possible harm to the potential respondents. While we think that occasionally colleagues go overboard by worrying about any possible harm to any potential respondent, no matter how remote the likelihood of such harm, researchers do have to be sensitive, particularly when asking questions about issues regarding which respondents are likely to have strong feelings. It is possible to imagine, for instance, that an elderly "Tea Party" member, when asked questions about increasing taxes, could have a heart attack. The best one can do, unless one is willing to abandon all research on controversial topics, is to let potential respondents know about the general topic in advance of the survey and to assure them that they are free to skip a question or stop at any time. Finally, if your research question is such that your target population includes children, to avoid any potential distress that your questions might cause, you should probably consider other means of data gathering, such as interviews and observations. It is much easier to explain and reassure young research participants in interviews than in surveys.

Data Collection

When collecting data in surveys, especially in face-to-face data collection, it is easy to get frustrated when respondents want to skip or do not understand questions. Your responsibility is to be encouragingly neutral (if that's not an oxymoron). While you want to avoid unanswered questions and the missing data problems they cause, it is certainly inappropriate to be aggressive and insist upon an answer when a respondent is hesitant to give one.

Analysis and Reporting

Since surveys are routinely analyzed and reported using aggregate data analysis and reporting, potential harm to individual respondents is, in most circumstances, moot. Any serious harm to respondents is likely to come from breaches of privacy and confidentiality—not from the mere act of answering questions. Violations of the ethical norm of privacy are discussed in the next section.

However, aggregating data in analysis and reporting can cause harm. We think the possibility of harm, not only to groups but to individuals, is potentially great when the reporting can contribute to stereotyping. Poor reasoning and reporting that fosters stereotyping is remarkably common. For instance, several 2010 news reports of survey data stated that senior citizens were opposed to health care reform because they worried that money would be taken away from Medicare to provide funds for the uninsured. The typical headline was "Seniors Oppose Health Care Reform." What is wrong with this kind of reporting? Even if the statement were true of some large percentage of senior citizens, there were still millions about whom it was not true. Those millions of individual senior citizens who support health care reform were stereotyped. Such reporting stereotypes not only groups but also—indirectly—individuals. It is unethical because it can foster discriminatory behavior among the lay public. Such reporting also isn't accurate or intelligent, but that's not our concern here.

The first question one should ask when encountering a statement such as "seniors oppose reform" should be: All, most, or some? The second question is: Is this true after controlling for variables such as education, income, and gender? A responsible researcher, we believe, will answer these questions before they are asked and will not succumb to journalistic headlining when reporting research results. One example of harmful stereotyping is the way gender differences in students' math test scores are reported. (Tests are essentially surveys of knowledge.) One often hears that boys are better at problems requiring spatial reasoning, while girls are better at problems requiring calculations. Anyone who has thought about this statement knows that it cannot possibly refer to all boys and all girls. Rather, it means that boys got a higher *average* score on spatial reasoning problems and girls got a higher *average* score on problems involving extensive calculation. A thinking person knows that these averages include a huge range of individual differences. But far too many people (including teachers and parents) don't think this way. They stereotype, with unfortunate consequences for students—such as a thoughtless teacher assuming an individual girl is bad at spatial reasoning. Of course, in this case, it is the teacher's reasoning, not the student's, that should be called into question.

Ethical reporting (as well as intelligent reporting) requires that researchers report distributions, ranges of scores, variations within averages, and margins of error, as well as mean differences. Ethical reporting discusses limitations fully. Things always go wrong with all forms of research. Survey research, especially when the surveys are of difficult-to-reach populations, is plagued with uncertainty. Good research practice includes making sure that your questions are valid and that your recording of the answers is reliable; these research practices are essential to good ethical practice.[3] In sum, accurate reporting is important. We believe it is unethical to report survey results in such a way that they can lead incautious readers to jump to harmful conclusions.

Even when it is accurate and does not stereotype, reporting of survey research results can lead to consequences of questionable ethicality. Suppose your survey shows that the people living in a particular Afghan village are strong supporters of the Taliban. Even when the report is nuanced and explains what "strong" means (a high percentage and/or a high level of intensity) and discusses whether there is a minority and how big it is, the data report could have serious consequences. Will the military use this

---

[3] See Asher (2010) for an entertaining and informative discussion.

information to impose restrictions on this village—or to bomb it? Is that an ethical use of your data? Should you have conducted the study in the first place? Your answers will depend on whether you think the war against the Taliban in Afghanistan is just and on whether you think social scientists ought to be doing militarily relevant research. While we are sure that researchers shouldn't falsify their data and that they should not report their results in ways that could lead to stereotyping, there is room for a great deal of legitimate disagreement on many issues concerning the topics on which it is ethical to conduct research.

PRIVACY: ENSURING RESPONDENTS' ANONYMITY AND/OR CONFIDENTIALITY

Privacy is generally discussed under the rubrics of confidentiality and anonymity. These are usually the chief concerns in survey research, and they are tied to consent and harm. Most people consent to surveys because they are assured of the anonymity of their responses, and any harm that comes to respondents is most likely to be the result of violating those assurances about privacy. Which is preferable, anonymity or confidentiality? The distinction between them is when researchers don't know the identity of the respondents (anonymity) versus when they know but promise not to tell (confidentiality). Anonymity is generally preferable because it is a stronger safeguard. But it may be harder to ensure anonymity than one might imagine, and depending on your research design and sampling plan, it may not be possible.

Design

The main design issues that affect privacy of respondents are related to the mode of survey administration. For example, if you survey respondents face to face, which is the method still preferred by many survey organizations, anonymity is automatically compromised. Telephone surveys, even those using random-digit dialing, often involve knowing the name of the person who pays for the phone. Of course, the same is true of e-mail surveying. One common solution is to use an e-mail list as your sampling frame. When potential respondents are contacted by e-mail, those willing to be surveyed are then directed to go to a website where anonymity can be "guaranteed." We put guaranteed in quotation marks because no information has ever been totally secure from snoopers. And, as the 2010 and 2011 revelations and public distribution of secret government documents by WikiLeaks attests, that is as true of modern, electronic modes of communication as other kinds. It may be easy to purloin a few letters, but this can be a minor matter compared to the data dumps that made the news in 2010–2011. Using "snail mail" may actually be the safest for privacy (despite what your credit card company says), even if it is slow and expensive. If potential respondents to a mail survey do not consent to be surveyed, they throw away their mail. If they do consent, they mail back the survey in an envelope that includes no identifying information. However, if your research question leads you to want the ability to recontact respondents, for example to interview them, then there is a conflict—one that is hard to resolve—between wanting the option of recontacting respondents and wanting to maintain their anonymity. For this reason, many social science survey research studies rely on assurances of confidentiality in lieu of being able to guarantee anonymity.

Sampling

Any form of snowball sampling involves getting names or contact information from some respondents regarding other potential respondents. Anonymity is therefore compromised. Snowball sampling is usually conducted when the researcher plans to use face-to-face surveying, so anonymity is impossible in any case. Still, respondents further along the reference chain are likely to wonder, "How did you get my name?" The provider of the contact in a snowball sample need not be an individual. It is quite common to use an organization, such as a professional group or a union, to get a list of contacts to recruit for a survey, but potential respondent concerns about privacy can keep success rates remarkably low.[4] Concerns are similar with more advanced forms of snowball sampling, such as respondent-driven sampling (RDS). As discussed in Chapter 7, the basic idea is to give respondents coupons they can give to others who might be interested in participating. The coupons have value, particularly in the kinds of communities often studied with RDS. For example, at least one investigator found that the RDS coupons were used to bolster the dominance hierarchy in a community of injection drug users.[5]

Data Collection

Privacy in data collection is closely related to the mode of survey administration. As discussed above, privacy is easier to ensure when the survey is self-administered by respondents rather than conducted face to face. For sensitive questions one can increase privacy, even in face-to-face surveys, by using the randomized-response technique or RRT. This method was invented in the 1960s and has been successfully used in many contexts to improve the accuracy of and response rate for answers to sensitive questions. An RRT survey contains two redundant versions of the sensitive question—for example: (1) I have done X—True or False or (2) I have not done X—True or False. The instructions might read: "If you were born in the first half of the year (January through June) answer question (1); if you were born in the second half of the year (July through December) answer question (2)." That is the randomization technique.[6] The researcher gets the answer but does not know which question was answered. The respondents' privacy is maintained, but since the probability of answering the two questions is known, the researcher can calculate the percentage of respondents who have done X. Since RRT is a well-established method, it has been extensively studied. It preserves the anonymity of respondents' answers to questions and has been found to be more accurate than other methods.[7] And, as an added bonus for being ethically attuned to the sensibilities of your respondents, the method also often yields higher response rates than does asking about

---

[4]See Wells et al. (2003) for a detailed description of the difficulties researchers can encounter.

[5]Scott (2008).

[6]This example is actually from a variant recommended by Tan et al. (2009).

[7]Lara, Strickler, Olavarrieta, and Ellertson (2004) and Lensveldt-Mulders, Hox, van der Heijden, and Mass (2005).

sensitive questions directly. Whenever it is possible to use, we think RRT is the ethical choice when surveying respondents on highly sensitive questions.

Finally, what do you do when you learn, in the course of survey data collection, that a respondent is harming others, perhaps even other respondents? You've promised confidentiality but you learn that a respondent is engaged in child abuse or illegal pollution. Should you tell the authorities, "blow the whistle?" The law isn't clear; it varies by illegal activity, and it can vary from state to state. But it is clear that a survey isn't a confessional, or a consultation with a lawyer, or a session with a therapist, so the same protections do not apply. If your notes or your data files are subpoenaed, you'll have to give them up or pay the legal penalty. But what if there is no subpoena? Do you still blow the whistle? This kind of question is more likely to arise in interview and observational research, but it is not wholly absent in survey research. We have more questions than answers when it comes to such problems. Making ethical choices often involves deciding which value is more important to you in a particular instance.

Analysis and Reporting

Even when you don't know the identity of a particular respondent, it is possible that you or someone else could figure it out—if you report data in such a way that individual respondents' answers can be studied. When you collect bits of data, especially demographic information—such as age, occupation, education level, residence, marital status, and the like—it can be relatively easy to identify a respondent. Your goal might simply be to control for background data, but such data can be turned into identifiers. Think about it: how many 42-year-old female lawyers living in Fort Wayne can there be?

We have argued that it is good practice to make your data available to other researchers, and that there is something close to an ethical obligation to do so. But there can be a conflict between making data available and the privacy of respondents. When researchers report their findings in survey research, they almost invariably do so using aggregate statistics, which means that there is no way that individual respondents or their answers to questions could be identified. But data summaries are of limited use to other researchers. If other researchers want to reanalyze your data, they need the actual data files, not merely summary tables.[8] There are ways around this apparent conflict between wanting to make your data available to the community of researchers and protecting the privacy of your respondents. You can take your lead from procedures used by some of the leading survey archives.

Many people analyzing survey research data in fact use survey archives rather than collecting their own data. While it would theoretically be possible for researchers to identify individual respondents, most of the larger national datasets use two safeguards to protect the privacy of respondents. The National Center for Educational Statistics (NCES) is typical in what it does to prevent users from determining the identity of individual cases. First is a legal safeguard: it is illegal and the penalties for breaking the law can be quite harsh. For example, trying to determine the identity of teachers or professors or students answering a questionnaire is illegal. Violations are a class

---

[8]An exception is the correlation and/or the covariance matrix; these are summary statistics, but they can be used by other researchers doing meta-analysis and structural equation modeling.

E felony punishable by up to 5 years in jail and a fine of as much as $250,000.[9] So, what is private information and what are the rules?[10] In addition to protecting specific information, such as names, social security numbers, and so on, the rules also protect against the use of other information that, alone or in combination, can be linked to and lead with reasonable certainty to the identity of a specific case. The second safeguard, used by the NCES and most other federal agencies, is so-called data perturbation. This involves making small random changes in the data that do not affect averages and other aggregate statistics, but do make it difficult, in fact nearly impossible, to identify individual cases even were one tempted to do so.

The moral of the story for individual researchers is that, if you are making your database available to a broader community of researchers, you should probably do some data perturbation of your own. This is not a simple task, but programs exist for doing it, and it is unethical to share your data without having done so. What good is your promise to keep data private if you then just give them to others without sufficient safeguards?

One final note about privacy when using survey archives: analyzing the data from one database archive is often no problem; the data are well disguised to prevent breaches. But merging more than one database with another can be very difficult and usually requires special permissions that are difficult to obtain. Say, for example, you wanted to relate scores on a statewide high school mathematics achievement test with high school grades, and these two sets of data are separate. To merge them, you would need to get permission to use students' identifiers, such as social security numbers or state ID numbers. Using these identifiers could require getting permission from two separate state agencies, each of which would consult with its lawyers. And when in doubt, we have found, lawyers have a distressing tendency to "just say no." This is not a fanciful example. On one occasion, when we were conducting research funded by a state (research in which that state presumably had an interest), we found it impossible to obtain the needed permissions from the relevant state agencies.

CONCLUSION

Apart from archival research, which requires little if any interaction with persons, survey research is the least intrusive of the major research designs. Interviews, experiments, and observational research all raise more—and more ethically demanding—challenges for researchers. Nonetheless, as we have seen in this chapter, and as is summarized in the following table, survey research is not without potential for producing ethically problematic consequences. The consequences may be milder in degree but are not fundamentally different in kind from the ethically dubious practices that can occur with other research designs. The main issues in survey research, as with other types, are research participants' voluntary consent, protection from harm, and privacy. The table on page 252 summarizes ethical issues in survey research.

---

[9]See the National Center for Educational Statistics statement at *nces.ed.gov/statprog*. Ironically, perhaps, that's the same jail time and fine as for pirating a DVD, which suggests either that privacy is undervalued or DVDs are overvalued.

[10]The best source is the Institute of Education Sciences' technical brief NCES 2011-601, available at *nces. ed.gov/pubs2011*.

SUGGESTIONS FOR FURTHER READING

Most textbooks and handbooks on survey research have modest sections devoted to ethical issues and most general books on research ethics contain modest sections on survey research. The books focusing mainly on survey research often deal with ethical issues such as how to maintain anonymity while still being able to recontact respondents for follow-up questions. For these kinds of issues the sources cited in Chapters 1 and 7 are relevant.

Israel and Hay's *Research Ethics for Social Scientists* (2006) succinctly reviews the basic philosophical approaches to research ethics, including survey and interview research. The book's international focus is particularly welcome because it documents the great diversity that exists in national systems for regulating social science research. Denmark, for example, determined that while biomedical research needs regulation by ethics committees, no such committees are needed for social science research.

Because surveys are usually used to collect quantitative data, several chapters in Panter and Sterba's *Handbook of Ethics in Quantitative Methodology* (2011) are relevant. Most of the chapters are focused either on analysis and measurement issues or on researchers' responsibilities to their professional colleagues, but it is a remarkably thorough volume for treating those issues and goes well beyond the normal summaries of IRB rules that are typical of many works on research ethics.

As always in discussions of research ethics, the emphasis is on biomedical research, even when focusing on methods not usually thought of as biomedical, such as survey research. One good example is a superb study sponsored by the National Research Council called *Cells and Surveys: Should Biological Measures Be Included in Social Science Research?* (2001).

Many of the ethical issues related to analysis and reporting touched on in this chapter are covered in greater depth in the fairly technical volume by Bethlehem, *Applied Survey Methods: A Statistical Perspective* (2009); this is a more generally interesting book than its title might suggest, containing, for example, good sections on Internet surveying and suggestions for guarding the privacy of data.

On the question of ethical issues that can arise when surveying vulnerable populations, an edited volume by Kroll and colleagues, *Toward Best Practices for Surveying People with Disabilities* (2006), contains many insightful chapters.

CHAPTER 13 SUMMARY TABLE

CONSENT

Design	• Be certain not to imply that participation is compulsory. • Informed consent requires explaining to respondents both the purposes of the research and any conflicts of interest you might have.
Sampling	• Snowball sampling or any other forms of network sampling, such as RDS, may pressure potential respondents to participate.
Data collection	• Make sure respondents know that they may skip questions and are not compelled to answer in the preferred format.
Analysis and reporting	• Respondents' consent ethically implies that you, the researcher, will analyze and report what they say fairly and accurately.

HARM

Design	• Respondents can be distressed when survey questions ask them to think about topics that make them uncomfortable, such as controversial issues.
Sampling	• Even in surveying, one of the least intrusive of the major research designs, one must exercise extra caution when studying vulnerable populations.
Data collection	• Harm is a fairly remote possibility when collecting data with surveys, but it is somewhat more likely in face-to-face surveys.
Analysis and reporting	• Beware of publishing or otherwise disseminating data that could cause respondents harm—information that others could use to treat them in ways to which they object. • Avoid stereotyping respondents, and by implication, the populations from which they were drawn.

PRIVACY

Design	• Anonymity will be difficult or impossible with some designs, many of which include identifiers (e.g., for recontacting those who did not respond to the first contact).
Sampling	• Snowball sampling and its descendents, such as RDS, mean that researchers will know the identities of respondents.
Data collection	• Face-to-face data collection opens dangers of privacy breaches, but methods such as RRT can mitigate these. • When in your research you learn of respondents' illegal activities, are you legally and/or ethically obliged to report these activities—or to keep them in confidence?
Analysis and reporting	• Making your data files available to other researchers may enable them to discover the identities of your respondents. Use methods of disguising data, such as "perturbation."

CHAPTER 14

Ethics in Interview Research

We have talked in other chapters about the similarities and differences between survey and interview research. The overriding similarity is that the two designs are based on the same assumption: that one can learn important things by asking people questions and analyzing their answers. The differences are mainly in the kinds of questions asked and the methods for coding and recording the answers. It's often a matter of breadth (surveys) versus depth (interviews). But the basic structure of the intellectual activity of surveying and interviewing is similar—and so are the kinds of ethical issues that pertain to the two kinds of research, which is why, in this chapter on interviews, we use the same outline we employed in Chapter 13 for discussing the ethics of surveying. First, we consider the problems of obtaining informed consent from potential interviewees. Second, we examine issues of potential harm that could come to them in the process of being interviewed. Third, we address challenges that can arise when trying to maintain interviewees' privacy. Under each of these three headings (consent, harm, and privacy) we discuss, in turn, potential ethical consequences of different approaches to overall interview design, recruiting interviewees, gathering data from them, and analyzing and reporting the results.

Although the basic structures of interviewing and surveying are parallel, interviews typically demand much more of research participants. The interview usually takes more of their time, demands more attention, asks for more in-depth reflection, may address difficult topics, and requires them to exert more effort to construct their answers. An interview usually intrudes more into participants' lives than does a typical survey. To take an extreme example, when we think of the police interrogating or "sweating" a suspect, we don't imagine them providing a survey for the suspect to fill out; rather, they conduct an interview. With the greater intensity of the typical interview comes a greater salience of ethical issues.

As with surveys, the possibility of direct harm to interviewees from the process of being asked questions and answering them is comparatively small. The potential for harm to interviewees is greatest when privacy is breached. Considering the very nature of the act of interviewing, anonymity is all but impossible, and that makes the burden of confidentiality greater. At a minimum, the answers given by specific interviewees will be known by at least one person (the researcher), and these answers tend to be much more deeply revealing of personal details than are typical survey answers. Any dangers can be subtle and hard to predict, which increases the responsibility of researchers who are attempting to obtain the highest level of informed consent possible.

CONSENT: INFORMED PARTICIPANTS WILLINGLY AGREEING TO BE INTERVIEWED

Design

The basic design you use to gather interview data varies with the nature of your research question. Interviewing takes many forms and has many different research purposes, and the nature of informed consent will vary accordingly. One distinction is between interviews that seek internal/subjective responses and those that ask interviewees for more external/objective information (see Chapter 2 for more discussion). If you are seeking objective information from knowledgeable informants, it will usually be easier to provide full disclosure about your research goals in the informed consent form. Sometimes it is even helpful to include in the consent form a list of the questions you hope to ask. Whether it is a matter of gathering oral history narratives from people who have witnessed events, or asking interviewees to explain how their organization works, or seeking a description of the politics of decision making in different scientific disciplines and laboratories,[1] providing potential interviewees with a full description of what you seek is relatively easy in informational interviewing.

On the other hand, if you want to explore personal meanings and feelings with your interviewees, and to discuss sensitive subjects with them (such as how they deal with making life-and-death medical decisions),[2] you probably do not yourself know in full detail the questions you will ask. New questions will often emerge from the answers interviewees give to your initial broad exploratory questions. In this kind of interview, the consent form will necessarily be more vague about the content of the questions you plan to ask and sometimes even about the purposes of the research. Exploratory research about personal meanings is, for obvious reasons, more difficult to specify in advance than confirmatory research that gathers factual information. Of course, the consent form can be very specific about the rules and state that "your participation is voluntary; you need not answer any particular questions; you can stop the interview at any time; your identity and your replies will be held in the strictest confidence," and so on. All this is important, but it is IRB boilerplate language. Informing potential interviewees about the purposes of the research can be more challenging—sometimes, as we have found in our own research, because the interviewees are not all that interested.

In the course of the research, the specific application of IRB confidentiality rules can be more complicated than one might suspect. When do you promise confidentiality? The easy answer is: always. This is a good thing to do, and you are obliged by the IRB to do it, but you should be aware you can only make a *personal* promise. Unlike journalists, researchers are not protected by the First Amendment. They have no right to keep their sources confidential if they are requested by the police to reveal them. If

---

[1] Knorr-Cetina (1999).

[2] Bosk (2008).

your field notes or tapes are subpoenaed, it is illegal for you to destroy them. The First Amendment provides for freedom of the press, but contains no provisions for freedom of research. Nor are you covered by doctor–patient privilege, unless you are a medical or psychological doctor. Attorney–client privilege is also a well-established protection. But a sociologist or an anthropologist or an educational researcher has no such safeguards. So be cautious when promising that you won't tell, because you might be legally or morally obligated to do so. You are not a priest in a confessional; there are no statutes or legal precedents that allow you to keep secrets, and you should make this clear to potential interviewees.

Sampling and Recruiting

Social researchers often interview members of vulnerable populations, and this raises particular concerns about informed consent. Children or others (such as the mentally impaired) who may not truly understand what is being asked for when consent is requested raise special problems. This is one of those areas where legal and administrative regulation is extensive. As always, you need to check the current regulations, starting with your IRB.[3] These regulations do change. Using a book published last year, and written 2 years before that, is not good practice when you are dealing with laws and rules that evolve and that may be unstable as different interpretations of ethical principles are instituted by various national and local authorities.

One thing doesn't change: you don't ever want to imply that agreeing to be interviewed is anything other than completely voluntary. As with surveys, so also with interviews: many people have experienced interview-like situations that are not a matter of choice—with employers, police officers, tax officials, and others—so you need to make it clear that you, as a researcher, are not in the kind of position that can compel response. And you might *seem* to be in a position to compel compliance if you are, for example, a professor studying your students or a social worker studying your clients.[4] In the oral description, *before* giving the consent form to the potential interviewee, you could say, "Your participation is voluntary, of course," or words to that effect. It probably sounds even stronger to say "I am asking you if you want to volunteer." There's a subtle difference between those two ways of putting it, but it is a difference that some of our anecdotal evidence suggests can be an important one. If you are worried that you might be unduly pressuring possible interviewees, try to use phrasing that makes it easy for them to bow out.

One potential barrier to participation in interviews is the consent form itself. Meant to protect research participants, it can drive them away. "I'm happy to talk to you, but I won't sign anything," is the way one interviewee put it to one of us. Obviously, signed consent forms make the names of interviewees known to the IRB, are placed in the data-files, and can constitute a threat to privacy. There are methods IRBs can use to approve nonwritten or verbal consent (federal policies allow this), but some IRBs are apparently unaware of or unwilling to adopt such policies, and some may not be too happy when you try to explain the rules to them.

---

[3]For a detailed recent survey, see Shamoo and Resnik (2009, Chapter 13). The relevant federal regulations are the Code of Federal Regulations, Title 45, Part 46; available at *www.hhs.gov/ohrp/humansubjects*.

[4]For a good review of some of the issues involved, see Shaw (2003).

Data Collection

Because IRB informed consent assurances offer *you*, the researcher, little or no protection, you should decide how far you are willing to go to protect confidentiality, and then you need to inform your interviewees accordingly. Otherwise, they won't be giving you fully informed consent. The protection that informed consent forms offer your informants is potentially dependent upon your willingness to make a personal sacrifice if need be—for example by defying a subpoena asking for your notes or tapes. That is why it is usually ill advised to respond affirmatively to the statement: "If I tell you something about X, will you promise not to tell?" The safe answer is: "I'm sorry. I can't do that. Depending on what you tell me, I might be legally or morally compelled to report it. So, don't tell me."

Another question that comes up surprisingly frequently is: when does the interview begin and end? What parts of your interactions with interviewees are covered by rules of informed consent? As you chat with them and get acquainted while explaining the purposes of the research and answering questions about it, you may learn important things that never get mentioned in the interview itself. In addition to discussions before the consent form is signed, it often happens that interactions continue after the interview. One interesting article describes the various experiences of 10 interview researchers, including the different ways interviewees conveyed information after the interview was technically over, and how the researchers handled this.[5] Seeing this diversity in the data collection process makes it clear that you can't have rules for everything in advance. That is why it is important to have not only IRB rules, but also ethical principles, to guide you in your actions and decision making.

The question of what parts of the interview may be used comes up most frequently, or most obviously (and the procedures are well-honed), in journalistic interviews. Practices developed in journalism can be instructive. When the journalist Bob Woodward interviewed members of the Bush White House and then the Obama White House about their decision making and the conduct of the wars in Iraq and Afghanistan, many people talked to him with remarkable frankness. These were public officials recounting public events. But they did not always want attributed to them the information they seemed happy to divulge to Woodward. Many interviews were conducted "on background," which meant that the information could be used but not attributed to a particular source. Other information was, in the course of the interview, declared "off the record." This meant "it could be not used unless the information was obtained elsewhere."[6] While much in these procedures is particular to journalism and its jargon, the ideas are applicable in many kinds of interviews. What parts of the interview can you *not* use? When someone agrees to be interviewed and signs the consent form, their consent can still be "turned off" temporarily. Turning the audio recorder on and off is one technique. But can you turn off your memory? In any case, when an interviewee asks you, "You're not going to use that, are you?" your answer has to be "Not if you don't want me to."

Your consent form and your explanation of it should make it clear that consent can be withdrawn or put on hold. This will be important both for ethical reasons and for recruiting reluctant interviewees. Explaining all this without making potential interviewees impatient or uneasy is no simple matter. It is more a matter of art than of method.

---

[5] Warren et al. (2003).

[6] Woodward (2008, 2010, p. xiv).

Analysis and Reporting

When giving their consent, many potential interviewees worry about their privacy, which means they worry about how you are going to report what you have learned from them. Methods for concealing identities in interview research are similar to those used in survey research, but interview data, especially quotations, are harder to mask than checkmarks on a Likert scale.[7] It is simple to de-identify survey data quickly. Enter the data into a spreadsheet and destroy the original forms. But even after the tapes are destroyed, interview transcripts contain much potentially identifying information. While it is standard practice to destroy recordings after they have been transcribed, it highlights a potential conflict of values—between privacy and accurate reporting. Recordings contain data that are difficult to transcribe, such as pauses, tones of voice, and emotional states. These can be very important in data analysis and interpretation.

Be sure to let respondents know what you plan to do with the data you collect from them and others, how you will keep tapes and transcripts locked up, and how they will not contain labels that can be used to link the records with their names. And make sure they know that if your results are published, the results are public. What interviewees say will be summarized and/or quoted. There is no useful equivalent of summary statistics for reporting interview data. Of course, the analysis will summarize by discussing themes and patterns in the responses, but most readers want to see these generalities illustrated with quotations from individual interviewees. Such quotations are crucial to good reporting—but can be an entering wedge for a snoop.

HARM: PREVENTING INJURY TO INTERVIEWEES DURING THE INTERVIEW

Design

The chances of actually harming someone in the conduct of interview research are fairly remote, but when your research question requires probing sensitive subjects in an interview, there is the possibility that this can lead to psychological distress on the part of interviewees. A good informed consent discussion and consent form will alert potential interviewees to this possibility so that they can decide whether or not to volunteer.

Another consideration occurs when your design employs focus groups, especially when the discussion deals with controversial topics. Focus group sessions can range in tone from working group seminars to brainstorming sessions to shouting matches. If you anticipate the latter, it is important to warn interviewees that sometimes focus groups can get raucous and contentious, and that they might find this to be stressful. They may also experience unaccustomed peer pressure from other participants in the group.

Sampling and Recruiting

The possibility of harm depends greatly on the vulnerability of interviewees. When should you take special steps to "empower" informants? A big concern among many interview researchers is inequalities in the power of researchers and informants. As one influential scholar put it in a widely read book on research interviewing, "the interviewee-interviewer

---

[7]Israel and Hay (2006) provide a good overview of ways to conceal identities in Chapter 6.

relationship is marked by a striking asymmetry of power."[8] Interviewers are in control; they ask the questions. They shape the answers in many ways, for example, by communicating through a pause that they expect a longer, more detailed answer—or that they are looking for a shorter one by seizing the first opportunity to move on to the next question. The issue of empowerment is particularly important when informants are vulnerable in one way or another (children, patients, prisoners, the homeless, the unemployed, etc.). In these cases, it might be especially hard for interviewers to avoid shaping the responses of informants. When there is a great inequality in power, interview researchers have advocated taking various steps toward the empowerment of the informants.

Of course, informants are not invariably in a subordinate position or totally without resources. In the first place, *they* have the information you seek. You cannot proceed with your study without their cooperation. The role of researcher is sometimes that of a supplicant anxiously requesting participation. The researcher's dependence may not always be clear to informants, but it is likely to be very real, especially for researchers relatively early in their careers. We don't imagine that many researchers actually say, as part of their informed consent routine: "Please help me finish my project or I won't be able to write my dissertation [obtain a grant, get tenure]," but such thoughts must be in the backs of their minds from time to time.

The rules of informed consent are a natural resource that informants can use to protect themselves from dominance by the researcher. They have the information without which researchers can do nothing. The shield of informed consent and protections of the rights of participants are most important in interviews where in-depth and highly personal information is collected. Anonymity is all but impossible in the actual interview situation. Even in the write-up, results cannot easily be pooled into anonymous statistical averages.

Finally, we wish to stress that many research questions do not lead the researcher to interview vulnerable informants. For example, we were part of a team that interviewed state higher education leaders and other state officials. These interviewees considered their time to be a precious resource. We agreed and were grateful for access to it. We traveled to their states, to their offices. We asked the questions, but *they* invariably shaped the interviews. This kind of interviewing is more common than the methodological literature sometimes suggests. Informants are not invariably members of vulnerable populations. In fields such as administration, business, political science, and the ethnography of science, informants are often people of high rank, successful in their fields, who have no need to be empowered. Blanket statements about empowerment should be qualified by reference to the specific informants and their situation. We need to remain sensitive to the problem of "groups oppressed by research,"[9] and to make sure not to contribute further to any such oppression. But in a list of history's oppressors, researchers rank pretty low—at least as compared to religious fanatics, racists, criminals, fascists, communists, and tyrannical rulers of all types.

Data Collection

Again, as with survey research, direct harm is unusual in the process of data collection during interviews. Still, interviews do often involve extensive probing and pressing

---

[8] Mishler (1986, p. 117).
[9] Kelly (2006, p. 37).

interviewees with follow-up questions to encourage them to clarify what they say or to pursue a topic in more depth.[10] Also, discussions can get quite heated in focus group interviews, and some interviewees may find this stressful, whereas in the one-on-one interview the researcher usually adopts a more passive or neutral role, even while probing. Probing and focus groups on controversial topics should probably be avoided with members of vulnerable populations.

Analysis and Reporting

When you have a dual role as a researcher and as a practitioner, occasions for harm to interviewees are possible in data analysis, reporting, and use. For example, if you are a social worker doing research that involves your clients, the clients could be put at a disadvantage. *Future* clients might benefit from what you have learned as a researcher, but your current clients, the interviewees, might not—especially if the same data analysis is or can be used for two purposes: evaluating clients for research purposes and assessing them for eligibility for access to services. Practitioners who are also researchers have to be careful not to disadvantage research participants who are also recipients of services. This can be a worry in several fields, such as medicine, education, and social work.

One step to avoid harm in data analysis and reporting is to have your interviewees review your summary (notes, transcript, etc.) of the interview before you use it in your research. This is often called *member checking*, and, when practicable, it is often wise. Some researchers advocate clearing only matters of fact (not notes and transcripts) obtained from an informant before using them. Asking for clearance or even permission can be important in some circumstances, particularly when issues of confidentially are paramount. Some researchers have gone further and even given informants veto power over their *interpretations*. In most circumstances, that is going too far. Empowering your informants should not require self-abnegation and abandoning your responsibility as a researcher to provide the best interpretations you can. A researcher is not a ghost-writer.

PRIVACY: ENSURING INTERVIEWEES' CONFIDENTIALITY

Design

By design, anonymity, while common in surveys, is very rare in interviews. Anonymity and confidentiality vary by mode of interviewing. When one thinks of an interview, the typical picture that comes to mind is a face-to-face conversation. But other forms of interviewing exist, with different possibilities for maintaining interviewees' privacy. And it seems inevitable that other forms will increasingly supplement, though not replace, the expensive and time-consuming method of the face-to-face interview. The telephone was the first new technology to supplement or replace the face-to-face interview—with the "ear-to-ear" mode. Video-chatting and e-mail interviewing have also become options. Conference calls are sometimes used for virtual focus group interviews. As we discussed in Chapters 2 and 8, there are circumstances where telephone

---

[10]See Dick (2006) for a direct comparison (using the same subjects and covering the same topics) of interview and survey methods of data collection, especially follow-up questions.

and other nondirect methods are preferred by interviewees. In one study, adolescents discussing sensitive topics (risky sexual behaviors) preferred and were more forthcoming in e-mail communications. The authors recommend the approach, even though it made their IRB very nervous and reluctant to approve the design.[11]

Is an e-mail interview or a discussion in a chat room or a conference call really an "interview"? One could stipulate a definition that would exclude anything but the traditional face-to-face interview, but these other forms of communication will surely persist and probably expand as part of the researcher's toolkit. These other forms have already made substantial inroads into businesses, schools, and homes. We assume that they will become more frequently used in research. What does that mean for privacy? One of the drawbacks of new modes of interviewing is the ease with which privacy can be breached. Because something said or written or depicted in an electronic communication can be posted on the Internet and become available worldwide in a matter of seconds, potential threats to privacy are much greater than with a face-to-face interview, even one that has been audio- or videotaped.

Sampling and Recruiting

Some form of snowball sampling is very common in recruiting people to be interviewed. This kind of sampling can range from following up on a casual recommendation in an interview to the more rigorous methods used in respondent driven sampling. Whatever the method, people are identified. You couldn't approach them to try to recruit them and get their consent otherwise. Interviewing people encountered haphazardly is rare and even more rarely is it part of a good research plan. So, you know something of the people you approach that makes you think they might be good candidates for your research, and the people who recommended them know that they made the recommendation. Word gets around that you are buttonholing people to get them to participate in your study. The content of interviewees' responses to your questions is usually easier to keep confidential than the fact that they have been interviewed—or been asked to be interviewed. Some people might be displeased that other people have been interviewed—such as employers, who don't want to see an "investigation" proceed with the help of their employees. So be alert to the potential harm that can come to interviewees simply from participating (or being asked to participate) in your study, quite apart from what they say in the interview.

When you sample and recruit from vulnerable populations, you will often have to obtain the consent of those who are responsible for the vulnerable individuals' welfare. For example, if your research question involves interviewing children, you will need permission from parents or guardians. Can you maintain the child's privacy? What if a parent or school official wants to know, claims she or he needs to know, or has a right to know? Again, unless you can assert that you are, for example, a psychologist acting in a counseling capacity, you may have limited legal grounds on which to deny their request. Does a child or a student have a right to privacy—privacy from a parent or a teacher? Clearly the rights of children and students are limited in some circumstances, while in other cases children might have more protections than adults. This is another of those contested areas in which changes in rules may be frequent and where it is important for

---

[11]See Hessler et al. (2003).

you to seek the most up-to-date information available. Usually the best places to start are with your IRB and by consulting the relevant federal guidelines.[12]

Data Collection

The site for the interview is important for maintaining privacy. The main consideration in selecting a site is the comfort of the interviewees, that is, where they feel that their privacy is best assured.[13] This means offering alternatives with the full understanding that since interviewees will choose different places, this adds another contextual variable to the interpretation of your data. If some interviewees want to meet in your office, others in a cafeteria, and still others in their homes, comparing interviews in these very different contexts will increase your analytical burden. But interviewee choice and comfort should usually trump your desire to hold constant such variables as the interview site.

Finding appropriate sites that are sufficiently private can be more complicated in focus group interviews. Privacy in focus groups is obviously a function of how many people you have in the room. You, the researcher, will hold everything said in strict confidence. But you will not be the only person in the room. To protect the privacy of each individual discussant, you need to stress how important it is for all discussants to protect that privacy, but interviewees are not bound by IRB rules. For interviewees to discuss their experiences with friends is their choice when they have participated in individual interviews. Gossiping about focus groups is probably an even greater temptation. In focus groups, you have to try to protect the privacy of interviewees when you don't really control it.

Interviewer researchers must make some record of the interview. Ultimately this data record almost always becomes a written document, either as notes or a transcript. The kind of written document it becomes depends on how interviewees respond to your requests to record what they say. The privacy of a verbal, conversational interaction in an interview changes in character when it is recorded. Unless it is recorded, it is, like a musical performance, gone forever, except in memory. It is becoming less frequent for interviewees to object to voice recording. Yet, you will probably still find some interviewees who will give permission to take notes, but not to record electronically. Some interviewees will be made uncomfortable by any note-taking process, perhaps especially if it is done on a computer. And some will even object to notes in any form. Then you need to take field notes as soon after the interview as possible. The nature of the data collection is the interviewees' choice—unless you have determined that your research question can only be properly addressed with verbatim transcripts and that interviewees who will not consent to audio recording cannot be included in your research.

Sometimes when you have permission to take notes, you could decide against doing so. You might not want to break eye contact in a particularly intense interview, so you don't take anything more than the briefest notes, which you supplement from memory as soon after the interview as possible. The potential gain in rapport has to be balanced against the possible loss in accuracy of your notes. Accuracy is important when considering privacy. An interviewee's right to privacy arguably includes the right to an accurate portrayal of what he or she says.

---

[12] See footnote 3 in this chapter.

[13] See Herzog (2005) for a sensitive account.

Privacy in data collection is influenced by the methods you use for recording the data, for turning what the interviewees say into a written document. The history of privacy in interviewing has evolved along with recording techniques.[14] Knowing shorthand was once a useful skill for an interviewer. Sometimes stenographers were hired and took notes from behind screens to maintain interviewee privacy. Stenographers were replaced by tape recorders the size of small suitcases; these tended to intrude on the rapport between researcher and interviewee, but had the advantage, perhaps, of being very visible, hard to ignore, and a reminder that one was speaking "for the record." Now, digital recorders that are small enough to conceal easily are no longer just for spies, but are a routine technology used in recording interviews. This opens the possibility for abuse. We know of a small number of cases of researchers who have effectively said, "OK, no recording, but is it OK if I take notes?" having already turned on a recorder concealed in a briefcase. Being stealthy is easier than it once was. You don't even have to transcribe the recordings yourself to keep your secret, given the increasing quality of transcription software. When microrecorders and even cell phones can be used for stealth recording, the ethical integrity of the researcher is even more important. Abuse of the trust between researchers and the persons they study seems particularly sleazy in a face-to-face interview. And, it is not only unethical, of course, but could lead to fairly serious sanctions.

Analysis and Reporting

Publishing your results has more perils for participants' privacy in interview research than in survey research. Sharing your data with other researchers, such as by archiving it, presents similar dangers. However, in some cases, you may have no choice. If you receive financial support from the U.S. federal government or from a UK granting agency, the data may have to be made available; they belong not only to you. This means that you need to take steps to share the data and the results in ways that reduce the possibility that someone could uncover the identities of the interviewees. This can be harder than it might seem. Things can be complicated when some of your interviewees want to be identified—for example, to go on record as stating their position.[15] Identifying some but not others can be a delicate task.

Another kind of possible compromise to interviewees' identities occurs if you are doing your research in a place or an organization and you want to describe its features. You want, in other words, to discuss the social context of your interviewees. For example, say you are studying doctoral students in the sociology department of a private university in a small town in the Midwest. Say you interviewed 20 doctoral students. How hard would it be to figure out the identity of the department? Of course, you could use pseudonyms or no names at all for the interviewees, but by combining information about the university and the department with data about the individuals' backgrounds—age, gender, ethnicity, and so on—it could be relatively easy for someone to figure out who was saying what. You might have to disguise identities of organizations or individuals to the point that this weakened your analysis. If you were studying gender and race relations among graduate students by studying one graduate department and you didn't

---

[14] See Lee (2004) for a fascinating discussion.

[15] See Guenther (2009) for this and other issues related to "naming names."

want to give the genders and races of the individual interviewees, this could be a serious limitation to your analysis or the comprehensibility of your findings.

To preserve the interviewees' privacy, you are going to have to omit some information, such as features of and location of the site or demographic information about the interviewees. You will change some information by providing pseudonyms. More awkwardly, especially if you are a researcher who values accuracy and detests falsification, you might sometimes have to provide pseudo-data—data that would mislead someone trying to uncover the identity of particular interviewees. Which data do you omit, which do you fudge? Answering that question can involve making a difficult judgment that requires weighing the analytic and privacy advantages of different options. As is so often the case in research ethics, it's not enough to "talk the talk" or even to "walk the walk." What you need to do is "think the thought." In other words, you need to engage in serious deliberation about tradeoffs as you decide how to conduct your research. The general rule (all else being equal) is to delete or alter the identifying information, the omission of which would have the fewest analytic consequences. The general rule is clear, but applying it to specific research data is often complicated.

CONCLUSION

In the summary table on pages 264–265, you will notice that in addition to new points about consent, recruiting, and privacy in interview research, many of the themes seen in the chapter on ethics in survey research recur here. That repetition is intentional. It is required by the similar structures of the two designs for collecting data—asking people questions, and recording and studying their answers. While interviews and surveys are not usually activities with great potential for doing harm—except when private information becomes public in ways that are unsafe or unpleasant for the interviewees—many ethical issues confront the conscientious researcher.

SUGGESTIONS FOR FURTHER READING

If you want to read deeply and broadly about research ethics, you have little choice but to read works on biomedical ethics. Often, the most interesting sources dealing with biomedical ethics are written by social researchers, so they partake of the two worldviews. As with surveying, many of the most extensive discussions of ethical issues relevant to interviewing are focused on ethics in medical settings. Bosk's book *What Would You Do?: Juggling Bioethics and Ethnography* (2008) is probably the best of these. Bosk is a sociologist with a long career of interviewing people—patients, physicians, and even professional ethicists—in hospitals and clinics so as to construct an ethnography of ethics. He is particularly attuned to the ambiguities in his roles as both an observing and largely passive researcher and consultant participating in medical decision making. Bosk's is the main source we would recommend beyond the works already cited in this chapter and in the earlier chapters on interviewing.

CHAPTER 14 SUMMARY TABLE

CONSENT

Design	• Be certain not to imply that participation is compulsory. • It is usually more difficult to describe the research in enough detail that interviewees can give their informed consent when the research question explores interviewees' feelings and meanings (as compared to seeking external information). • Informed consent requires explaining to respondents both the purposes of the research and any conflicts of interest you might have. • Promises of confidentiality are ultimately *personal* promises made by the researcher. Communications between interviewee and researcher are not guaranteed by such protections as attorney–client privilege and interviewees should be told this as part of informed consent.
Sampling	• Snowball sampling or any other forms of network sampling, such as RDS, may pressure potential respondents to participate. • When sampling from vulnerable populations, investigate the latest rules and regulations that pertain, starting with your IRB. • For some populations, nonwritten consent may be necessary or more appropriate.
Data collection	• Make sure respondents know that they may skip questions and are not compelled to answer in the preferred format. • In the course of the interview, consent can be turned on and off. Inform potential interviewees that signing the consent form does not oblige them to answer all questions or to let you use anything you learn in the interview.
Analysis and reporting	• Respondents' consent ethically implies that you, the researcher, will analyze and report what they say fairly and accurately. • Interviewees should be told, as part of informed consent, how you plan to report what you have learned (e.g., if you plan to use extensive quotations).

HARM

Design	• Interviewees can be distressed when questioned about sensitive topics or controversial issues. • The stress of participating in an interview can sometimes be greater in a focus group than in an individual interview.
Sampling	• Researchers must exercise extra caution when studying vulnerable populations, and additional IRB rules apply to them.

Data collection	• Harm is a fairly remote possibility when collecting data with interviews; it is somewhat more likely when collecting data on sensitive topics and sometimes also in focus group interviews.
Analysis and reporting	• Beware of publishing or otherwise disseminating data that could cause interviewees harm—information that others could use to treat them in ways to which they object. • When you have a dual role of researcher and practitioner, be sure not to disadvantage research participants who are also clients, students, and so forth. • Consider member checking to increase the accuracy of your reporting of interviewee data. • Avoid stereotyping respondents, and by implication, the populations from which they were drawn.

PRIVACY

Design	• Anonymity will be difficult or impossible in most interviews. • Alternatives to face-to-face interviews can raise more privacy concerns because of the ease with which these can sometimes be broadly distributed.
Sampling	• Snowball sampling and its descendents, such as RDS, mean that researchers will know the identities of respondents. • The privacy of interviewees includes the fact that they have been interviewed, not only the content of what was said in the interview. • Vulnerable populations may have both greater and lesser protections of their privacy. Rules are extensive and they can change frequently.
Data collection	• The site for the interview is important for privacy and should usually be decided by interviewee choice. • Face-to-face data collection opens dangers of privacy breaches, which is one of the attractions of alternatives such as e-mail. • When in your research you learn of respondents' illegal activities are you legally and/or ethically obliged to report these—or to keep them in confidence? • The development of recording technologies that are easy to conceal increases the importance of the ethical integrity of the researcher in maintaining interviewees' privacy.
Analysis and reporting	• Making your data available to other researchers may enable them to discover the identities of your respondents. • To preserve the privacy of interviewees the researcher will usually have to omit some background information and use methods of concealment such as pseudonyms.

CHAPTER 15

Ethics in Experimental Research

Discussions of ethics in experimental research often refer to the so-called medical model. When Goffman introduced the term,[1] he was referring to a model of treatment, not of research. He specifically meant hospitalization or institutionalization of the mentally ill, which he believed had much in common with the "tinkering trades," such as clock repair in the 19th century: you drop off the clock in the shop and pick it up when it is fixed. More recently, the term medical model has expanded to include a concept of research, specifically biomedical experimental research as applied to fields other than medicine. The term is also used to mean ethical decision-making in IRBs that is thought to be inappropriate to the special needs of nonexperimental social science research. Are we too influenced by the medical model in discussions of research ethics in the social sciences? And what exactly is wrong with that model? While it is frequently claimed that the medical model has too much influence in ethics reviews of social science research proposals, there is not a lot of data one way or another.[2]

One form of the medical model arises from the origins of modern research ethics, which emerged largely from reactions to abuses in medical research. Ethical standards were formulated to prevent such abuses, which had usually occurred in experiments. And because medical research is associated with experimentation, we do have a medical model of research. The experiment, specifically the randomized controlled (or clinical) trial—the RCT—is widely considered to be the norm or the ideal model by biomedical researchers, and most experimentalists in the social sciences agree. Hence the medical model in research ethics means the RCT and the ethical issues that occur when implementing this design.

In discussions of protecting the people we study, experimental design always takes a prominent place, and for good reason. By definition, experiments involve intervention and manipulation of subjects. Opportunities for direct harm are greater when you assign

---

[1] Goffman (1961).

[2] Two sides of the issue are nicely captured in empirical studies of how IRBs (or their equivalents in Canada and England) work, one claiming that IRBs are unnecessarily bureaucratic and stifle innovation—Haggerty (2004)—and one claiming that these fears are largely groundless—Hedgecoe (2008). These are important works because they provide evidence in a field where strong opinions usually overwhelm weak evidence.

treatments than when you ask questions in surveys and interviews, or observe people in natural settings, or review their records. This means that the balance of ethical concerns tends to be different in experimental research. Research participants' informed consent, possible harm to them during the conduct of the research, and their privacy after the research is concluded are important in all forms of research. But in survey, interview, observational, and archival research, the most important of these is usually privacy, because any harm that can come to participants is most likely to have a breach of privacy as its source. Informed consent involves explaining this. By contrast, violations of privacy are fairly rare in experimental research, in part no doubt because the emphasis in reporting is on comparing average outcomes in the treatment and control groups. Dangers to participants are likely to be a consequence of receiving (or not receiving) the experimental treatment. Informed consent in experimental studies means explaining such dangers to potential participants.[3]

Before we begin our discussion of consent, harm, and privacy in experimental research, we need to address a preliminary question: *When is an experiment not research?* When might an investigation be better described as an innovative and deliberate effort to improve practice? We started our discussion of experimental design in Chapter 3 by noting that experimentation is a traditional way of learning what works, one that is as old as human inquiry. Today, many practitioners continue that tradition when they "experiment" with various approaches to carrying out their responsibilities. They try out new things, keep careful records, and analyze the data in those records to decide what to try next. Sometimes they write up the results of that experimentation for publication. Physicians' and psychologists' case studies are a good example. A slightly different approach occurs when conscientious practitioners systematically review their records to find areas in need of improvement and, on the basis of their reviews, conduct more experiments. Among the people we know who have engaged in this type of experimentation are social workers, psychologists, university professors, high school teachers, physicians, educational administrators, and department managers. They experiment, intending to use what they learn in their own practice.

The federal definition of *research* is systematic investigation aimed at producing generalizable knowledge. If the knowledge produced is for your own use, it is not technically research. Does it become research if you decide that others might be interested? If that is so, can you be taken to task for not having run your research protocol by an IRB? Does action research, undertaken to learn how to improve a specific program or practice, with no concern about its relevance to outsiders, qualify as research that needs regulation by IRBs and the federal agencies they represent? We are convinced that the distinctions are often unclear at best between the rigorous and systematic self-study done by conscientious practitioners on the one hand and the kind of activity that requires official regulation on the other. By "requires official regulation" we mean subject to IRB review. When your research does not officially qualify, and is not subject to legal regulation, then, as an ethical practitioner-researcher, you should apply moral and ethical principles in the absence of legal ones.

---

[3] As always, researchers do well when making ethical choices to consult the codes of ethics of the relevant professional organizations. For experiments in the social and behavioral sciences the most influential one is that of the American Psychological Association (APA). The principles stated in the code of the American Educational Research Association (AERA) are closely parallel, but place more emphasis on experiments with minors.

We often mention in this volume that ethical research must necessarily also be high-quality research. Using research participants' time and subjecting them to risk is unwarranted if the research has no possible benefit. And it can have no benefit if it is conducted so poorly that nothing can be learned from it. All else being equal, ethical research will also be research that uses the highest-quality design, sampling, and analytic standards. It is easy to think of examples of unethically *low* quality—such as carelessness in data collection or inappropriate techniques in analysis. But opinions about what constitutes high quality are more subject to dispute. Some researchers believe that the superiority of randomized experiments is so indubitable that using another design violates one's ethical obligations to participants and the populations from which they are drawn. Others, comprising a smaller yet vociferous group, believe that any experimental research on humans (or other animals) is fraught with ethical problems.[4] Neither position is likely to be invariably correct. Both err by overstating their case. Where we agree is in the belief that when researchers try to make better methodological decisions, they also improve their likelihood of better ethical research conduct.

Be that as it may, avoiding doing harm to experimental participants is a crucial ethical responsibility. It is difficult to discuss the full range of potential harms that could occur in experiments because experiments are conducted on such a broad range of topics. On the other hand, since it is relatively easy to screen out projects that participants should never be asked to join, most difficult ethical decision making occurs at the stage of obtaining consent to do the research—first from the IRB, then from the participants. Consent is a relatively simple matter in surveys, interviews, and archival research. But, in experimental research (as in observational research), fully describing the project to potential participants so that they can give their informed consent can be quite demanding.

CONSENT: INFORMED PARTICIPANTS WILLINGLY JOINING THE RESEARCH PROJECT

Design

Providing potential participants sufficient information to freely decide whether they wish to join the research project can require striking a delicate balance between too much information and not enough. Standard consent-form boilerplates vary in length, but the clear trend has been for them to grow over the years, despite little evidence that this improves the decisions participants make.[5] The more complicated your research design, the more work is involved in explaining it to potential participants so that their consent can be fully informed. Ensuring that the consent is truly voluntary can be particularly difficult when the population is composed of minors or others (e.g., people with Alzheimer's or psychiatric patients) who might have trouble understanding what the experiment involves for them.[6]

---

[4] Many of the arguments are reviewed in Mark and Lenz-Watson (2011).

[5] Stunkel et al. (2010).

[6] Stiles, Epstein, Pogthress, and Edens (2011) stress the importance of the voluntariness of the consent as well as that the researchers have to disclose the risks and assess whether the potential subjects understood them.

Another complicated issue arises when deception is part of your design. This is often thought to be necessary in some types of social research. For example, if you are studying the influence of beliefs on behavior, what subjects believe about the purposes of your research is likely to influence their behavior. If you reveal the purposes of your research in advance, it will be difficult to assess reactions to the treatment. And some types of experiments are quite impossible without deception or surprise. Goffman and Garfinkel's "breaching experiments" are a stark example.[7] The idea is to violate a norm to see how strongly people react to that; the reaction is a way to gauge the strength of the norm. Milgram conducted this type of experiment in the early 1970s on the New York City subway. He had his graduate students approach riders and politely ask them to give up their seats. The strength of the norm was indicated by the fact that everyone, including the student researchers, was made quite uncomfortable by the activity.[8] Of course, this kind of approach to social research would make no sense if you announced what you were doing in advance and passed out consent forms.

Another kind of deception can occur when researchers have a conflict of interest. Informed consent requires that researchers be explicit about the purposes and the methods of the research so that respondents know the kind of research in which they are being asked to participate. In experimental research, as in all other designs, a relevant disclosure to the potential participants one is trying to recruit is information concerning any conflicts of interest researchers may have. Conflicts of interest arise when researchers' interests (financial, personal, political, etc.) could interfere with their actual or perceived ability to responsibly conduct the research for which they are attempting to recruit participants.

Typically in experimental research, the most important duty is fully describing any risks of participation in the study. The risks may be compared with the benefits—especially when there are few potential benefits *to the participants* or to the population from which they have been drawn. Very often, any benefits to participants in social research will be minimal at best. The decision often involves weighing risks *to participants* against benefits *to other people*. That kind of comparison is morally dubious, especially when the risks to participants are concrete while the benefits are high sounding and vague: the growth of scientific knowledge, the advancement of society, or the development of knowledge of possible value in the future.

Both risks and benefits each have two dimensions: probability and size.[9] Each needs to be addressed individually. Then they need to be considered together. Let's start with the risk of harm to participants in the research. If we can rate the probability of harm and the size or severity of harm on scales of large, medium, or small, we can produce a 3×3 matrix (Table 15.1), which will include nine possible combinations of probability and severity of harm for any research project. Obviously the greatest risk is represented by Cell A, a large probability of a large harm. The least problematic is Cell I, a small probability of a small harm. The cells from A to I are not a rank order scale. Even a small probability of harm, if the harm is grave, as in Cell C, could be unacceptable—if, for example, "only" 2 out of 1,000 participants die.

Possible harms are almost always discussed in the context of potential benefits. An increased risk of death might be acceptable—if the benefit were great enough. For

[7]Goffman (1985); Garfinkel (1966).

[8]These experiments are described in Blass (2004).

[9]This discussion is based on Shamoo and Resnik (2009, pp. 247–248).

TABLE 15.1. Probabilities and Sizes of Research Harms			
	Size of harm		
Probability of harm	Large	Medium	Small
Large	A: large-large	B: large-medium	C: large-small
Medium	D: medium-large	E: medium-medium	F: medium-small
Small	G: small-large	H: small-medium	I: small-small

example, if the research participants were terminally ill patients who knowingly volunteered, and if the benefit were a cure for a deadly disease, and if the cure might come in time to help them, then the risk–benefit ratio might be acceptable. Of course, such a hypothetical example of extreme risk and enormous benefit is hard to imagine in most social and behavioral research.

When we think of the benefits of the research, we can construct the same kind of matrix—a 3 × 3 grid showing nine possible combinations of probability and size of the benefits (Table 15.2). This yields a similar grid except that the values of the cells are reversed. Cell A, a large likelihood of a big benefit, is the most desirable. Cell I, a small chance of a small benefit, is least acceptable, although it is probably the most common in social and behavioral research.

Combining the two matrices gives the researcher 81 choices: 9 × 9 = 81. Furthermore, there are at least three possible recipients of any benefits: (1) research participants, (2) scientific knowledge, and (3) society at large. That brings the total to 243 (81 × 3 = 243). This seems like a ridiculously large number, but IRBs routinely attempt to weigh these numerous factors when making decisions. Finally, these matrices and the decisions based on them assume that we actually know, or can accurately estimate, the probabilities and severity of harms and the probabilities and sizes of benefits. Most often, however, these are unknown. One reason we conduct experiments is to find out what these unknown values are. A fundamental fact in the ethical conduct of research is that neither researchers nor IRBs can *fully* inform potential experimental subjects for the simple reason that no one really has all the necessary information.

Another cost is the cost of *not doing* the research—this cost could be borne by society, science, by people in the future, and even by participants in the experiment. This is a point initially made by Rosnow and Rosenthal in their influential discussions

TABLE 15.2. Probabilities and Sizes of Benefits from Research			
Probability of benefit	Size of benefit		
	Large	Medium	Small
Large	A: large-large	B: large-medium	C: large-small
Medium	D: medium-large	E: medium-medium	F: medium-small
Small	G: small-large	H: small-medium	I: small-small

of ethical decision making. Rather than use the categorical levels of risk, benefit, and probability that we have, they employ continuous conceptions of them, not unlike supply and demand curves. When you are uncertain how to handle the various risks and benefits in your research, using Rosnow and Rosenthal's graphic "decision diagonals" can be a very helpful way to organize your thinking.[10]

Sampling and Assigning

Although in statistical theory, experimental participants are first selected from a population by random sampling and then randomly assigned to control and experimental groups, in reality the procedure is usually first to *recruit* a pool of possible participants and then obtain their consent to be randomly assigned to treatment and comparison groups. Random assignment needs to be explained, and researchers have often found this frustratingly difficult. Sometimes problems with explanation arise because the treatments and the assigning mechanisms are complicated to the point that most participants do not find them easy to understand.[11] Resistance to randomization is naturally greatest when the experimental treatment is considered an advantage. Then assignment to the control group can be thought of as denial of treatment, especially when potential participants overestimate the benefits they might receive by being in the experimental group.[12] And they often overestimate; why else would they sign up? When expectations might be too high, informed consent means that you need to dampen participants' enthusiasm—without driving them away. It is sometimes helpful to call random assignment a lottery. Because a lottery seems a less offensive concept to many people than random assignment, it can reduce their resistance, and a lottery is an accurate description of what actually happens. Another form of randomization, especially common in quasi-experiments, is group randomization. Then consent needs to be obtained from the groups or organizations. And a type of secondary consent may also be required—the consent of the individuals within the groups, such as teachers in schools or clients in clinics.

Explaining what happens to participants who are *not* assigned to the experimental (or treatment) group also includes explaining what the experiment envisions for them: no treatment, an alternative treatment, or a placebo. The last case is controversial because it can involve deception: the placebo is believed to be a real treatment but is not. An approach that can eliminate the need for deception is one form or another of blinding: subjects do not know whether they have received the real treatment or an intentionally ineffective treatment (and in a double-blind experiment, neither do the researchers). Placebos are rare in social research, although placebo-like reactions to unintentionally ineffective treatments may sometimes be among the more important social and psychological effects of participating in an experimental trial.

When it is difficult to recruit participants willing to be randomly assigned to treatment or nontreatment groups and when allocating resources fairly would suggest that people most in need of the new treatment should get it first (assuming the treatment is beneficial), you should consider using *regression discontinuity* (RD) methods of

---

[10] See Rosnow and Rosenthal (2011) for a good general account.

[11] Walker et al. (2008).

[12] The psychology of overestimating benefits in drug trials is discussed in Jansen et al. (2011).

assigning participants to experimental and control conditions.[13] As described in Chapter 9 of this volume, the RD design sacrifices little in statistical power or in the precision of the estimates of effect sizes. And it does so using a method that has much to recommend it in terms of research ethics, specifically the equitable distribution of resources. The only drawback is that RD puts more technical demands on the researcher than does comparing the means of randomly assigned groups.

Data Collection

Describing the treatment is not enough to ensure informed consent. You need also to explain the procedures to be used for collecting data about outcomes and how intrusive or uncomfortable or time-consuming they might be. The range of possible methods for data collection is vast: a test of knowledge, physical measurements, completing an attitude scale, producing written artifacts, monitoring subsequent behaviors, and so on. When the method of data collection is likely to be unfamiliar, such as using special equipment to measure reaction times, fuller explanations are necessary. When there will be a debriefing session after the experiment, it needs to be described as well, especially if the debriefing session will be long or complex, as is common in experiments involving deception. Finally, if there is to be a *stopping rule*, this requires careful explanation. When there is a stopping rule, interim data are collected and analyzed. If the analysis indicates that the probability of benefit is very low (or that the treatment is causing harm), the experiment can be discontinued. Stopping rules are rare in social research but increasingly common in biomedical research. This may be a case where the medical model has something to teach us. Even in social and behavioral research, it seems an unethical waste of participants' time and society's resources to slog along to the end if there are no likely benefits and nothing more can be learned. There may be no great harm to participants, but if you can envision no possible benefit to anyone (except what you've already learned: that the treatment didn't work out) it is usually better to discontinue the project.

Analysis and Reporting

The main ethical obligation to participants in analysis and reporting is the use of fair and appropriate methods. Participants' consent is implicitly contingent on your unbiased and accurate description of the experiment and analysis of its results. When you have a real or perceived conflict of interest that might taint the analysis and reporting, describing that conflict as part of the consent procedures is also advisable.

HARM: PREVENTING INJURY TO EXPERIMENTAL PARTICIPANTS

Design

While privacy is the biggest concern in surveys and interviews, which have comparatively low risk of inflicting injury, causing harm in the course of the research is the central concern in experiments. But how much harm has the conduct of experiments in the social

---

[13]The best general source is Shadish et al. (2002, Chap. 7).

sciences actually caused? The record is perhaps less alarming than is sometimes implied. When writers want to discuss examples of dangerous social science experiments, they usually refer to studies that are 40 or 50 years old—most often to some of the work of Stanley Milgram in the 1960s and Philip Zimbardo in the early 1970s. This is not the place to describe these studies, which have been summarized and debated repeatedly. Suffice it to say that Milgram studied people's willingness to follow orders even when they thought that by doing so they were inflicting serious harm on others; and a central part of Milgram's design required deceiving subjects.[14] Zimbardo's experiments required no deception. Subjects were placed in a simulated prison where they played the roles of guards and prisoners. The guards quickly became sadistic, the prisoners rioted, and the experiment had to be stopped abruptly.[15] (Compare the stopping rule discussed above.)

What lessons can we draw from these two iconic examples? First, the actual harm to research participants was comparatively minor. An unspecified number of the participants were upset when they found out what they were capable of doing. In some cases, this self-knowledge was quite distressing for them. Also, in the guard-versus-prisoner experiment, there was a possibility that the role playing could have gotten out of hand and have led to genuine physical harm. Still, the injuries participants received in these and other social research experiments were comparatively minor—compared to the outrages in biomedical research during the same era and subsequently. If the harm was relatively slight, why have these studies been so controversial? In part, the controversy occurred because the authors studied controversial topics. The ease with which apparently ordinary individuals could be turned into authoritarian sadists made some people angry at the researchers. It made others despair of the human condition.

The second lesson is that ethics reforms beginning in the 1970s, as institutionalized in IRBs, appear to have been quite successful in reducing research that involves as much risk of harm and as much deception as these studies did. There have been few if any comparable scandals about social science experiments conducted in the 1980s and 1990s. It is almost inconceivable that Milgram or Zimbardo could get their designs approved by an IRB today. Is this a loss to science? It is hard to say. We know that it is possible to study Milgram and Zimbardo's general topic—conformity to roles and norms we'd like to think people would be better at resisting—with only minor risk of harm, although probably not very easily without deception. The topic continues to interest researchers. The question of whether newer studies have led to as much knowledge about human behavior cannot be settled here, but it is clear that they have set off fewer ethical alarm bells.[16] Today, even quite minimal risk of harm in social research experiments is seldom approved by IRBs. Deception about the purposes of the experiment is more often approved, but the deception has to be slight and researchers often have to make a rigorous argument to get even a slight and short-lived deception approved.

Sampling, Recruiting, and Assigning

Identifying a vulnerable population from which to sample and recruit is a choice with important ethical implications. Of course, you may wish to study a particular population

---

[14] A good source putting the experiments in context is Blass (2004).

[15] Zimbardo's work is widely available. His review with two of his graduate students is the most complete succinct account (Haney, Banks, and Zimbardo, 1973).

[16] A good example, discussed briefly in Chapter 3, is Willer et al. (2009).

precisely because it is vulnerable and you hope that your research will help by, for example, devising better methods of intervention to curb school bullying or increasing awareness of social and psychological problems. The definition of what constitutes a vulnerable population can change, and has done so in surprisingly complex ways. Not too long ago, women were routinely so labeled and were "protected" from potentially dangerous research. But the inclusion movement of the 1990s changed some of the designated categories. Groups that were once excluded so as to protect them now wanted to be included.[17] There are many reasons to broaden inclusion, but among the most important is that you can't very well generalize about gender, age, and ethnic groups unless you include them in the study. It would be not only scientifically inappropriate, but also ethically inappropriate to do so.

One important vulnerable population is composed of people who are economically needy since it is easier to recruit them by offering to pay them to participate. Paying research subjects has a long history and it has usually been controversial. Are you exploiting needy people? Or is payment for research more like a part-time job, an opportunity to pick up some extra cash? Are you simply paying people for their time, or are you pressuring them to subject themselves to risk? To answer these questions, research projects have to be addressed on a case-by-case basis, but when the risk is minimal, providing incentives to participate seems unobjectionable, and it is often justified because it would otherwise be too difficult to recruit a sufficient number of participants.

How many participants do you need? Analytically speaking, the larger the number of participants, the better the accuracy of treatment effect estimates. Cost prohibits unnecessarily large groups of participants, and so do ethical considerations. One wants to keep the number exposed to potentially dangerous treatments to a minimum. Looking at it the other way around, the number in the comparison group denied access to a potentially beneficial treatment should also be kept to the lowest number consonant with the needs of the research for valid and precise estimates of treatment effects. When seeking to determine the number of participants exposed to potentially dangerous (or denied potentially beneficial) treatments to the minimum number needed to conduct a valid study, you will usually have to conduct a statistical power analysis. A power analysis gives an *estimate* of the number of cases needed to detect a significant effect. It must be stressed that a statistical power calculation is an estimate based on data that are themselves usually estimated. But power analyses provide the best guidelines we have. Both scientific and ethical considerations oblige researchers to conduct them whenever they are feasible.

When assigning potential participants to the treatment and comparison groups it is important to remember that those assigned to the comparison groups may consider this a source of harm. Harm can be thought of not only as likely to arise from the treatment but also from the denial of treatment. These harms of denial are sometimes less likely to be perceived as grave when the comparison group receives the standard treatment— as opposed to a placebo or no treatment. And receiving the standard treatment is quite common in social research. For example, when a new learning method is introduced in schools as part of a field experiment, the comparison group schools are neither closed down nor do they undertake phony placebo methods of instruction. Still, participants who receive the standard rather than the experimental treatment are likely to believe

---

[17] Epstein (2007) provides a thorough and thoughtful account.

they have been denied something potentially beneficial. And if there were no grounds for that belief, why would you, as an ethical researcher, be conducting the experiment?

In sum, when planning for sampling and recruiting, the line between protecting and excluding potential participants is often unclear. And when assigning recruited participants to experimental treatments, the line between exploiting and denying can also be blurred. A good decision probably will not often be made on the basis of unchanging ethical principles. What counts as a good decision will likely vary with the political climate and with the beliefs and wishes of the potential participants.

Data Collection

Participants can drop out or refuse to provide data at any time. People can agree in general to participate, but not want to continue when they see what is actually involved. When participants want to drop out, of course you aren't pleased, and it's OK to try to dissuade them, but an effort to dissuade that is more than a polite request violates a fundamental ethical principle. Conversely, participants may want to continue with the experimental treatment, intervention, program, or procedure when you think it is time to invoke a stopping rule. When the data collected and your interim analysis of those data indicate that it is a waste of resources to continue, but the participants disagree, are you ethically obliged to persist? Probably not, but if you are going to conduct an interim data analysis that could lead to termination of an experiment, participants should be apprised of this before they consent to join the study.

Debriefing can be seen as a form of data collection. Debriefing after an experiment is not merely a human subjects issue that helps repair any harm from a deceptive experiment; it is also crucial for understanding how participants behaved under treatment and for discovering further hypotheses to test.

Analysis and Reporting

When the topics are important (and one hopes that no one is doing research on unimportant topics), accuracy is at a premium. There are four main ways that accuracy can be put at risk: *falsification, conflicts of interest, exaggeration including stereotyping,* and *poor methods*. It hardly seems necessary to make an argument against falsification. Yet the frequency of falsification scandals—again, biomedical research leads the way—makes one wonder how many people believe that they can, or actually do, get away with falsifying evidence. From Cyril Burt's fabrication of data about the heritability of IQ in the mid-20th century to Andrew Wakefield's claims about the origins of autism, whose fraudulence was discovered in the early 21st century, the urge to make a point, to make the data match preconceptions, has led people to take remarkable risks with their careers and, more important, with other people's lives. Because we doubt that cheats like Burt or Wakefield would be open to ethical suasion, it's hard for us to know what to do except to plead: Please don't do it. Have some self-respect. Show some common decency.

Many scandals stem directly or indirectly from conflicts of interest. The most obvious conflicts occur when researchers who are testing the quality of a product or procedure are paid for their work by those who have a proprietary interest in the outcome. The pharmaceutical industry has often been caught at this, as have their hirelings. An interesting wrinkle on the researcher-for-hire phenomenon is ghostwriting: the company writes up its own research report and pays a "respectable" researcher to sign it and publish it as its author. Conflicts of interest occur in social research too. Project evaluation researchers, who sometimes use quasi-experiments and even RCTs, are a good case in point. These researchers often evaluate projects that pay their fees. This awkward relationship is sometimes mandated by funding agencies that require grant projects to set aside a portion of their budget to hire evaluators. An ethically less dubious approach is for the funding agency to hire the evaluators directly. Details aside, the ethical mandate is clear: when publishing the results of their work as research, evaluators should reveal the sources of their funding and related conflicts of interest, such as ties with the organizations they studied. When you are simply an employee, many practices that are fully acceptable would be inappropriate should you try to pass off your work as independent research, at least without a full disclosure.

Some conflicts of interest can be more subtle. We would all like our experiments to turn out "right," for our hypotheses to be confirmed, and for our findings to be interesting. If our papers are discussed and frequently cited, that can lead to promotions and other career benefits—in addition to a sense of personal well-being. All this can encourage exaggerations that occasionally border on—or cross the border into—stereotyping of the participants and the populations from which they were drawn. In the discussion sections of otherwise sober papers, authors can become remarkably exuberant, and journals apparently allow this, perhaps because the editors believe that the audience of researchers can easily dismiss excessive enthusiasm. Before you allow yourself to get carried away, it is good to remember that less technically savvy readers usually read only the discussion sections and the press releases.

Exaggeration can also be subtle. Let's return once more to the iconic examples of Milgram and Zimbardo. They were fairly cautious about not claiming too much for their research, and they did not maintain that no participants were able to resist the urge to succumb to authoritarian impulses. But they certainly didn't linger over their outliers. Almost immediately, press reports left out nearly all qualifications to the alarming generalizations about what people are capable of doing. The authors probably could not have stopped the exaggeration of their results had they tried. Still, the exaggerations came close to stereotyping not just this or that group, but human beings as a whole. Surely the participants who did *not* just follow orders, who did *not* become sadistic, are as interesting as those who did. But at the time Milgram and Zimbardo conducted their research, reporting standards did not encourage nuance. And it still seems true today that there is usually less reward to the researcher whose results are complicated, nuanced, and discussed in terms of likely margins of error.

We discuss good quality data analysis and reporting in our companion book on "when to use what analysis methods." Here, it suffices to say that poor reporting techniques, such as dichotomizing continuous data,[18] the use of extreme-groups designs,[19] or reporting p values without effect size estimates and confidence intervals,[20] not only fail to meet minimum professional standards. They are unethical as well. Not conducting high-quality analyses of the data you collect wastes participants' time. Poor standards

[18] Cohen (1983).
[19] Preacher et al. (2005).
[20] Cumming (2008).

in data reporting mean that the experiment not only puts participants at some risk, but does so while squandering possible benefits.

PRIVACY: ENSURING PARTICIPANTS' ANONYMITY AND/OR CONFIDENTIALITY

Design

Anonymity of experimental participants is difficult to maintain, so the default safeguard in most experiments is confidentiality. When your research question leads you to want the ability to recontact respondents, for example to interview them or to see if treatment effects were long-lasting, you will need to maintain contact information. This is a (perhaps necessary) threat to privacy.

Sampling and Recruiting

Any form of snowball sampling involves getting the names or contact information from some respondents about other possible respondents. This kind of recruiting is very frequent when trying to find participants for experiments.

When you use organizational or group randomization, it is much more difficult to maintain the privacy of the organizations than when you use individual randomization.

Data Collection

In most experiments, data collection is done face to face or in other ways in which the experimenter can hardly avoid knowing the participants' identities. In double-blind studies, the experimenters do not know the participants' group—treatment or comparison. When sensitive information is being gathered, one can separate those who recruit participants from those who collect the data and from those who analyze the data. This is good practice in terms of preventing bias and also provides additional privacy safeguards for participants.

Analysis and Reporting

We have stated several times in this book that it is good professional practice to make your data available to other researchers. However, this carries some risk to the privacy of research participants' confidential information, but probably less with experimental data than most other types. Experimenters often collect little data on the kinds of covariates that could be used to identify research participants. That is because good randomization techniques reduce the probability that covariates will have effects. When covariate data are collected (demographic information is the most common kind), this is mostly used as a check on the success of the randomization and to eliminate the possibility that other variables have intervened. This means that sharing the database is less of a threat in experimental than in other forms of research where covariates are at the heart of the analysis. Very often what other researchers, especially those conducting a meta-analysis, want their experimental colleagues to share is simply the variance–covariance matrix; this contains no identifying information.

CONCLUSION

Analyzing risk of harm is particularly important in experimental research designs. Experiments in the social and behavioral sciences may not pose the same risks of potential physical harms inherent in biomedical experiments; however, our matrices delineating the likelihood and size of potential harms indicate that a thorough analysis for any social experiment is imperative. As we stated in the introduction to the chapter, experiments involve intervention and manipulation of people. Any time that you recruit participants for treatment and nontreatment groups, they must receive the best possible explanation of the experimental process for truly informed consent. You must take special care to protect them during the actual experiment, including building in mechanisms to allow participants to withdraw or even to stop the study if necessary. And, while privacy issues may be less prominent than in other research designs, they must still be addressed using standard methods to protect data confidentiality. Key considerations for experimental ethics are reviewed in the table on pages 279–280.

SUGGESTIONS FOR FURTHER READING

Research ethics in experimental designs are, if anything, more dominated by medical examples than are other research designs. This may not be as unfortunate as some believe. At least it seems to us no great stretch to get ideas from examples involving the studies of human subjects in fields other than our own. A happy exception to the rule of the medical model in how we evaluate the ethics of research is Rosnow and Rosenthal's lively little book *People Studying People: Artifacts and Ethics in Behavioral Research* (1997).

Less lively, but very comprehensive, is Shamoo and Resnik's volume *Responsible Conduct of Research* (2nd edition, 2009). It is probably the best one-volume overview of ethical principles and regulations. It focuses mostly on experimental research. Most of the examples are not social or behavioral, but some are. And Shamoo and Resnik's book illustrates the generality of principles of ethical conduct across fields of research better than any other work with which we are familiar.

An extremely impressive piece of scholarship that stretched our thinking considerably is Epstein's *Inclusion: The Politics of Difference in Medical Research* (2007). Epstein is a sociologist who has written a piece of contemporary history about the changes in attitudes and policies (especially at the National Institutes of Health) concerning which sociopolitical groups should be included as participants in medical experiments. Epstein's empirical work on the history of methodological and political debates surrounding the issues of categorizing research participants provides the most nuanced general understanding of the issues that we have read.

CHAPTER 15 SUMMARY TABLE

CONSENT

Design	• Be certain not to imply that participation is compulsory. • Informed consent requires explaining to respondents the purposes of the research, the processes of the experiment, and any conflicts of interest you might have.
Sampling	• Explain the random assignment procedure you will use. Consider using regression discontinuity (RD) as an assignment method. • For group randomization, you may need two kinds of consent: group or organization, and individual. • Explain the treatment and nontreatment conditions, including use of placebos and/or application of standard treatments if appropriate.
Data collection	• Describe procedures for data collection. • Explain any debriefing process that may occur. • Make sure respondents know that they may drop out. • If you include a stopping rule, explain when this may be used.
Analysis and reporting	• Respondents' consent ethically implies that you, the researcher, will analyze and report what they say fairly and accurately.

HARM

Design	• Use of deception requires strong justification. • Size and likelihood of harm must be fully analyzed in the design phase.
Sampling	• Consider special protections and rules for vulnerable populations. • Determine whether offering compensation creates undue pressure to participate. • Conduct a power analysis to determine how many participants are needed to detect treatment effects. • When the treatment is perceived to be beneficial, consider whether assignment to the nontreatment group might be considered by participants to be a form of harm.
Data collection	• Assure that participants know they can drop out of the study. • Consider creating stopping rules based on preliminary data. • Debriefing participants may be a means of identifying and repairing harms such as stress and anxiety.

Analysis and reporting	• Participants in experiments may be easier to identify compared to survey participants, so employ standard confidentiality protections.
	• Reject unethical analysis and reporting practices, including data falsification and conflicts of interest that may affect reporting.
	• Avoid stereotyping respondents, and by implication, the populations from which they were drawn.

PRIVACY

Design	• Anonymity will be difficult or impossible with some designs, many of which include identifiers (e.g., for recontacting those who did not respond to the first contact).
Sampling	• Snowball sampling or similar referral processes mean that researchers will know the identities of respondents.
Data collection	• Face-to-face data collection creates dangers of privacy breaches.
	• To protect privacy consider separating those who recruit participants from those who collect and those who analyze the data.
Analysis and reporting	• Making your data available to other researchers may enable them to discover the identities of your respondents, but individual differences are rarely of interest in experiments, where the main focus analytically is group averages.

CHAPTER 16

Ethics in Observational Research

This chapter treats the ethical concerns inherent in observational research designs. As with any design in this volume, observational research has its particular set of ethical issues. Understanding ethical issues specific to observational research can help us make the decisions and take the actions necessary to fulfill the moral and legal obligations we have as researchers. These obligations include maintaining the anonymity of the individuals and organizations that we observe, acquiring informed consent, and safeguarding the study's ethical dimensions even when observing covertly.

Observational research has distinctive qualities that give rise to unique ethical concerns. First, observational research is quite unlike experimental research. The fact that experimental research is the basis of traditional ethical standards makes observational research an outsider, or at least an outlier, in some circles. This creates special challenges, because the assumptions of experimental designs are very different from those that underlie observational research. A second source of difference for observational designs is that relationships are more likely to develop between researchers and the people they study. Relationships can develop between the observer and the observed in both covert and overt observations. If people get to know and trust you, you can feel personal obligations acutely (and you should). Finally, you are unlikely to anticipate all the ethical dilemmas that will arise in the field, which places a particular responsibility on you, as the researcher, to be clear about the potential benefits and harms that may result from your decisions and actions. Clarity is needed about multiple obligations: to persons and groups, to the research community and your colleagues, and to society at large.[1] As an observational researcher, you have an ethical responsibility to think carefully before applying for IRB approval. And after entering the field you need to respectfully consider how you will witness unfolding social phenomena that will help you answer your research question.

As with our discussion of the ethical implications of other designs in this volume, consent, harm, and privacy are the main foci of this chapter. We can think about these

---

[1] See the Introduction to Part III for a more general overview of ethical obligations.

as phases in the research process, each with its particular ethical issues. First, you seek approval from institutional review and develop a plan for getting participants' informed consent in the field.[2] To seek informed consent, you take into consideration and explain potential harms that might arise in the conduct of research, balanced against possible benefits to the individuals and organizations, other researchers, and the broader society. Second are the risks of harm that arise from the actual conduct of the research. No research is ever risk-free, so the potential usefulness of answering a worthwhile research question must always be weighed and reweighed in the field as questions of potential harm to reputation, sense of trust, and other tangible and intangible harms arise. Finally, privacy can never be fully ensured, but it is particularly imperative in observational research to conceal identifiers of observation sites and occasions as well as the identities of individuals. Because your data consist of detailed descriptions and quotations from the field, maintaining privacy is especially challenging. Privacy must be reconsidered throughout the research process, through data collection, coding, analysis, and reporting. Privacy matters also extend to maintaining data securely, whether the data are material or virtual. This is an area of increased scrutiny as new electronic media raise unprecedented privacy concerns.

SEEKING AND ACQUIRING INFORMED CONSENT TO OBSERVE

Design

You choose observational designs because you see a need to witness the phenomena that sparked the formulation of your research question. Informed consent in observational research means that the participants know the purpose of your research and make informed choices about whether they will run the risks involved in joining the study. How you acquire consent differs with the observational design. Your first decision is to select either a naturalistic or participant observer design. The next question is informed consent.

If you have selected a naturalistic design, you are usually covertly watching natural social events as they unfold. In practice, your fieldwork may not be completely covert. Concealment and revelation are ongoing negotiations in participant observation, making design decisions all the more important.[3] You will not seek a signed consent waiver prior to most covert observation, but to be able to use your observations, you may be required to obtain consent after the fact. A covert, naturalistic design choice does not absolve you of ethical responsibilities. On the contrary, covert observation puts a greater burden on you to protect your participants from harm as they have no clear-cut refusal option. Most such covert, naturalistic observations are undertaken in public places where the people being observed have no reasonable expectation of privacy. When you seek permission to use as research data your observations of public phenomena, you need to ensure that unwitting participants understand, after the fact, that their consent is voluntary.

---

[2] We chose the term *participant(s)* for the individuals and groups you will observe. If you are in the field as a participant observer yourself, this can be confusing. We will use the terms *participant observer, naturalistic observer,* or *researcher* for those who seek to answer research questions.

[3] Lugosi (2006).

If you use a participant observational design, then you may or may not need to get informed consent, depending on the situation. This too is tricky, depending on how engaged you will be with the participants you observe and how private the observation situation. The more participatory you are, the more like an interview or a focus group the observation becomes. The more private the situation, the more likely people are to be unguarded, placing a greater burden on you to elicit informed consent. If you have consent for an interview or focus group, then observation of group events in the same setting is probably implied. You must be prepared as you plan the study to weigh design decisions carefully, judge how engaged you need to be to answer your research question, prepare to articulate your safeguards clearly for a skeptical IRB, and think ahead about what ethical dilemmas may arise in the field as you sample and develop relationships with participants. It is an open question whether ailing, uneducated, or marginalized persons can give informed consent under any circumstances, so you have to be careful about how you communicate with different audiences and in different settings.[4] Making adequate preparations about ethical choices is your responsibility, not only to those you observe, but to the community of scholars and to society.

Examples can be illustrative. We begin with naturalistic observation. One famous example is the study *Nickle and Dimed: On (Not) Getting by in America*.[5] To gather her data, Ehrenreich designed the study so that she worked covertly in a series of low-wage jobs to explore the lived realities of maids, waitresses, and others. Erhenreich had to balance her need to be covert with her concerns for the workers who become her colleagues and friends, confided in her, and provided her with the connections she needed to complete the book. Ehrenreich lived where her participants lived, washed clothing in local laundromats, and used public transportation as her participants did, deciding that this was the only way to really understand how people in the minimum-wage economy survived. It is unlikely that Ehrenreich could have so richly described this lifestyle if she had revealed herself to be a comfortably situated professional writer with broad access to resources.

The social science research literature includes exceptional examples of research that yielded surprising and useful results that could never have been gleaned in any other way than covert participant observation. Sociology and social psychology have been built on such classic works.[6] A more recent example is Drury and Stott's study of political action.[7] They participated in demonstrations, took sides, battled with police, and maintained—convincingly—that they could not have learned much had they *not* participated and taken sides.

In Calvey's study of Manchester bouncers, another covert participant observation,[8] trying to obtain consent would have stopped the research cold. He and others have argued that IRBs have gone too far in protecting participants, who don't see themselves to be nearly as vulnerable as academics perceive them. As the researcher, you must ask

---

[4]Institutional review includes special protections for vulnerable populations that we have discussed in other chapters in Part III of this volume. Consult your IRB or one of the many resources available in this subject. This chapter assumes that the researcher is studying adults who are capable of and free to consent.

[5]Ehrenreich (2001).

[6]The best known is probably Goffman (1961), discussed briefly in Chapter 4.

[7]Drury and Stott (2001).

[8]Calvey (2008).

yourself, "How close to the action do I need to be in order to get the necessary thick description and answer my research question?" And, of course, the design plan may change in the field as discoveries are made and followed up. Then, you must determine when you need to let the participants know what you have been doing and get their consent to proceed. Say that you begin your study as a covert researcher and then go back to seek consent to proceed overtly. If consent is denied, then some data from your covert, naturalistic observations may not be eligible to be used in your final analysis and report. Or you may face a daunting set of tasks, as Duneier did in his study of street vendors, when he retrospectively sought consent from people whose words had been captured by a hidden tape recorder.[9] This is why you need to make some prior assessments of whom and what you wish to observe, realizing that these may have to be adjusted in the field.

When you choose an overt participant observation design, where you are known to the other participants as a researcher, you will almost certainly need to seek up-front informed consent. When and how to do this is not always a straightforward decision because observational research is seldom a stand-alone design; it is usually combined with interview and/or archival research. Participant observational designs vary along a continuum of engagement with other participants, and this level of engagement is a design decision. Participant observation in combined designs may mean that consent is obtained as part of another method incorporated in the same study.[10] For example, if you have obtained participants' informed consent for interviews, this may cover subsequent observations. However, if you foresee that observation will likely follow the interview phase, it is better to obtain consent for both phases in advance. Your research may occur in reverse order; you may begin by merely observing a general meeting or other public or quasi-public event without revealing your identity as a researcher. As you become more engaged, conversations may occur spontaneously. Then you must make in-the-field decisions about whether or not a conversation at a public event or meeting has risen to the level of an interview or other data-gathering opportunity that requires the informed consent of participants. If it does, this may be awkward; you may have to interrupt the natural flow of social interaction to have someone sign a form. On the other hand, if you don't do this, you may be unable ethically to use the data from that conversation.

Common practices used in obtaining informed consent in observational research designs include offering some clear benefit to the participants and/or providing them the chance to review your work in some form. Your design decisions include thinking through what potential participant benefits might be. In an example from the field of bioethics, the researcher was invited to consult in medical decision making as well as observing it.[11] This allowed potential participants to consider the benefits of the study before giving consent. However, in this case, participants often expected more from the researcher than he felt comfortable trying to give. Another kind of benefit can be giving your participants first access to your findings. You not only learn about people for the purposes of your research, you try to provide them some interesting insights about themselves. You may offer to present your findings to the organization, or you may provide a cleaned-up transcript or synthesis for the participants to review for their corrections. In what is often referred to as member checking, participants review a synthesis

---

[9] Duneier (1999).

[10] See Chapter 18 for more discussion of informed consent in combined designs.

[11] Bosk (2008).

or report of some or all of your inferences and your theorizing about what you witnessed; they check the accuracy of descriptions and quotations and perhaps the fidelity of your theory. While the researcher is not obligated to accept the participants' views, the member check is useful for improving confidence in the data, analysis, and report. This approach allows you to elaborate your findings and correct any misconceptions. To be ethical, you must follow through with any agreements or promises you make as to how you will use participant input. Be careful what you promise; researchers have had their work vetoed and their studies gutted by participants who were promised too much. It is important to protect participants' autonomy, but yours has value as well. In any case, offering to share results and giving the opportunity for member checks are ways to increase the likelihood of getting consent, of generating valid and usable knowledge, and of protecting participants' rights.

The design phase is crucial to getting the ethics of the study right. If you know your purpose and can share it with others, you can seek IRB approval for your study and be prepared for the unanticipated. Decisions you make up front about how engaged and how directive or intrusive you intend to be can protect you and your participants. That being said, there are occasions where research becomes impossible if consent is an absolute. Some of the best sociological research of the 20th century came about from covert observations wherein the potential for harm and loss of privacy was balanced against the compelling nature of the research questions.[12] But not much research of this sort gets approved in the 21st century.

Sampling

Moving from designing to sampling, observational researchers address ethical concerns about when informed consent is necessary. The researcher has to balance the relevance and representativeness of the sample with the potential harm, including breaches of privacy. The real-life character of observational research means these decisions are sometimes made in the field as we sample. You are always making choices that are sampling decisions. What meetings do I attend? Who will I talk to? Do I watch this or that? In each situation you decide, do I observe passively or participate actively? How public the setting is will contribute to these decisions.

If you are a covert observer who has sampled public events for observation, then informed consent cannot be acquired up front in the usual ways. Of course, IRB approval is required in advance. Consent may need to be sought later if, for example, describing what you have observed could identify or harm the people you have studied. If you are sampling more private settings and/or you are revealed as a researcher, then the answer to the question "Do I need informed consent from the participants?" is "maybe."[13] In general, the more private the situations you sample, the more ethically imperative it is to identify yourself as a researcher and seek consent.

---

[12] Wells (2004).

[13] Calvey and others have asked the question "Consent for what?" and it is surprisingly difficult to make prior stipulation of everything that might happen as you observe. This and other related concerns leave "informed consent" seeming like little more than a legal fig leaf for the university and the research enterprise generally. It is no substitute for respect and empathy for the human condition and a neutral stance toward your findings.

Some of our own fieldwork has taken us to public and quasi-public meetings and training sessions in a variety of organizational settings. Conversations develop, particularly as we visit the same settings repeatedly and get to know people. We are overt as researchers and evaluators, but we seek to make others comfortable with us so that we can learn about the phenomena of interest, in our case, school-university-community partnerships.[14] We often get into conversations that turn into quasi-interviews. Generally, we get informed consent in advance, because in this research we are not sampling the kinds of settings where wildly unexpected things happen. Still, we sometimes find ourselves in the position of judging whether or not to ask someone with whom we are conversing to sign a form giving us consent to use what they are saying in our research. One loose criterion we use to guide our decisions is asking and answering the question: How directive are we being in this conversation relative to our research and/or interview questions? If we are shaping the conversation more than just listening to the voices of others, it is a good idea to make this clear and ask for consent.

We try to avoid most of these contingencies by distinguishing interviews and focus groups from observations as a priori design and sampling decisions. Once a conversation begins to seem like an unanticipated interview, we have three options. One option is to postpone the interview so that we can be more engaged and directive at a later time. This works best in situations where the researcher role will be acknowledged and accepted. The second option is to let the conversation proceed but do little to direct it. We then develop a sampling strategy to follow up later with more directed interviews, possibly with additional participants, on the same topics that came up in conversation. It is here that the concept of data saturation arises. When we have sampled conversations in the observational field, we may follow up by having more conversations that seem to corroborate or negate what we heard in prior conversations. Sampling will involve engaging an adequate number of participants or engaging them a sufficient number of times, although there is no definitive way to decide how much is enough.[15] The third option is to allow the conversation to proceed and seek informed consent later.

An instructive example that explores sampling issues and consent comes from a study referenced previously, Duneier's *Sidewalk*.[16] This 5-year study of street vendors on Sixth Avenue in New York's Greenwich Village began as casual observations by Duneier as a private individual who walked by the vendors daily and became intrigued by a book vendor named Hakim. Duneier decided to study the street vendors, building on a 1960s sociological study about life on the same New York sidewalks.[17] Duneier had to be flexible as his sample developed on the streets, and he had to respond both proactively and retrospectively to the issue of informed consent.

Hakim was his main contact and through Hakim, Duneier sampled from a network of participants in mostly public situations. Because the street is public, Duneier decided that informed consent was not needed until he sampled for private interviews in coffee shops, homes, and other settings. After 2 years of relying on field notes, Duneier began using a tape recorder concealed under a milk carton, again reasoning that the sidewalk

---

[14]Baker (2011).

[15]Patton (2002).

[16]Duneier (1999).

[17]Jacobs (1961).

is public, so no consent was needed. Duneier's nearly continuous presence made his interactions natural and less intrusive than if he had sampled from organizational contexts or private and semiprivate spaces. Later, Duneier retrospectively got as many of the taped participants to give informed consent as possible to allow him to use their words. In another sampling decision, Duneier allowed the members of his network to tape interviews and on-the-sidewalk conversations; he could not elicit informed consent himself, but used the reporting phase to address the privacy concerns that arose from this sampling approach. Finally, Duneier asked Hakim and a few key participants for member checks.

To summarize, the more you participate, the more you know people well, and the more you expect to direct what you observe and what you hear, the more likely you are to need informed consent—and, often, the more awkward it is to ask for it. Asking for consent that requires a signature is a great conversation stopper, so prior planning is an essential ingredient of sampling.

Data Collection

For participant observation, your consent process should describe how you plan to collect and record your observational data. For example, there are special populations who must be given particular consideration when they are observed, particularly if images or audio files will be part of the data collection. Field notes are sometimes considered a better approach than videotaping or audio recording. Consent may be more freely given when the data collection and recording is in writing. Electronic audio and video recordings raise privacy concerns for participants and IRBs alike. With written notes, it is easier to conceal identities, since there are no electronic files with individual voices or images that might be released. Privacy is protected when field notes are taken with your own shorthand and then elaborated later as part of the research record.[18] Arguably, the authentic voices of your participants may matter more than ease of consent, so determining how your data are to be collected and recorded involves decisions that must be carefully weighed. Whatever your methods of gathering data, you will also develop your own identifiers and pseudonyms to use in your data files, and these must be carefully protected. When concealing data identifiers, you should consider encrypting your files. This is easier to do than many researchers realize.

Analysis and Reporting

Many decisions about analysis and reporting are made in the design phase, so you will have a good idea of how you plan to handle the data and will have shared this plan with the appropriate audiences. Potential audiences for your analysis plans are other researchers, the IRB, and the participants, whose informed consent should include some overview of analysis and reporting. It is a good idea to review your files and make sure that you have consent from everyone with whom you had an engaged, relatively private, and directed conversation. This is especially true if you are quoting or using electronic files or images of those persons in your reports. This is mere clerical work if you have been careful in gathering and retaining informed consent, but having done it

---

[18] Mack, Woodsong, MacQueen, Guest, and Namey (2005).

will reassure you that you can use report findings respectfully with the confidence that informed consent provides.

Through informed consent, participants are agreeing to how you intend to share findings: as a presentation, report, article, book, or through any kind of electronic media. It is important to understand that research is designed to produce generalizable knowledge to be shared with others. Participants need to understand that they will be described and perhaps quoted. If a participant tells you something off the record, that request must be respected and the data should not end up in the final reports. If you wish to make use of something obtained off the record, go back to sampling and find other sources and/or research designs to fill in the gaps.

AVOIDING AND MINIMIZING HARM TO PARTICIPANTS WHILE CONDUCTING THE STUDY

Design

Designers of observational studies must anticipate potential harm and follow the advice offered earlier: use your purposes and research questions to guide you to design an ethical study that puts no one at unnecessary risk. Because the main risk in an observational design is a breach of privacy, you need to be particularly aware of this risk. A key element is including an opt-out provision that is clear to the participants and that you take seriously. When observing naturally occurring social phenomena, it may not seem like your study can cause much harm. Rather than causing harm, it is more likely you will observe harmful events and situations, and you may not often have an opportunity to help. But harm is a broad concept. One could argue that harm includes the kind of intangible injuries that can occur when researchers are not respectful of diverse opinions and differing perspectives, special vulnerabilities and personal sensitivities, and the potential for loss of privacy and reputation.

When observing those whose views differ from your own or who have perspectives that you do not fully understand or appreciate, you are ethically obligated to observe with a compassionate eye for what you can learn.[19] There isn't much point in undertaking social research otherwise. For example, Duneier's study of sidewalk vendors required deep sensitivity about experiences unlike his own that shaped the lives and identities of his participants.[20] Without that sensitivity—if he had predetermined notions preventing him from appreciating others' perspectives—he could never have so richly described the lives of these people and provided such deep insights into life on the sidewalk. Nor could he have developed ethical responses to the dilemmas that developed in the field, some of which have been provided as examples in this chapter.

Vulnerable populations are a key concern of IRBs, and some of these populations are clearly identified. However, you may have to recognize other kinds of vulnerability. Once in the field, your observations may cause you to notice particular vulnerabilities of individuals and organizations. In the conduct of most observational research, potential

---

[19]To be an ethical and insightful researcher, you need not be sympathetic to the beliefs and goals of the people and organizations you observe. Ezekiel's (1995) study of neo-Nazis and skinheads is a case in point.

[20]Duneier (1999).

harms tend to be intangible. It is possible to cause participants distress if the setting is one in which personal sensitivities, traumas, or difficult subjects come up. You are obligated to refrain from any exploitation of these vulnerabilities, although you will likely report them in some way in your findings. In such cases, it may also be prudent to anticipate legal obligations ahead of time, especially if you should learn something that must be reported to authorities.

Finally, tangible and intangible losses must be considered and prevented by determining what is really necessary to achieve your purposes and answer your research question from the design phase forward. Tangible losses include things like bodily harm or financial loss. For example, organizational observation may reveal behaviors that could result in someone's loss of a job. Intangible losses may include betrayed trust, anxiety, depression, embarrassment, or other personal pain caused by the observation. Many of these harms can be traced to breaches of privacy. In all cases, respect for others and the sincere desire to learn from observing them must guide your design.

Sampling

For observational designs, you will likely find sites, activities, behaviors, and events to sample wherein you can learn by seeing phenomena in all their complexity. When the researcher has questions that cannot be answered without observing, decisions about where to go and whom and what to observe must minimize vulnerability while still locating relevant cases. Because the most common harms result from loss of privacy, many of the informed consent safeguards discussed above pertain to sampling as well. Participation and directiveness by the researcher and the relatively public or private nature of the situation are all factors that alter the calculus of harm.

To return to an example we have used before, Calvey observed nightclub bouncers covertly by working as one of them at different "doors" around urban Manchester.[21] He maintained a covert identity as a bouncer and was accepted as a member of that community. Here, Calvey's privacy and identity had to be protected, but those bouncers needed protection as well. So, in his design and sampling decisions, Calvey had to consider carefully where to go and who to talk to; otherwise, he would not have had a relevant sample. He had to sample situations where the violence of the bouncer culture could be witnessed in both public and private interactions. Obviously, he was unable to seek informed consent. It was conceivable that those he knew in the field could come to harm in the violence-ridden world of bouncers if his identity became known, so he continued to protect his identity even after the study was completed. He took pains to sample so that the small world of Manchester nightclubs did not put his participants at risk of greater harm by making it easy to identify the clubs and individuals. Fortunately, most social science research projects do not entail such serious perils.

Data Collection

Observational research always requires adjustments in the field. No one who does this kind of research fails to be surprised by some of the things she or he encounters. Here again, your research question should be your primary guide. You are looking for specific

---

[21] Calvey (2008).

kinds of things, not fishing. The lens of your research question helps you focus appropriately, as you may see and hear things that are interesting or even sensational but are not really relevant to your research purposes. If you do learn something that could harm someone during data collection or if you see that you are causing harm, you have several options: (1) you can address the problem at the site; (2) you can withdraw from the site; or (3) you can stop the study.[22] The first option implies that you have means to adjust your work and that you have guidelines regarding recourse if something or someone else is causing harm. The second option involves more sampling. The third involves redesigning the study to prevent the harm.

Secure your research materials in the field as agreed in your consent process. Such measures are necessary to prevent harm, just as they are necessary to protect your consent arrangements. Again, use of shorthand and keeping identifiers secure protects privacy in the field. Covert observation will likely increase security, but will require you to commit your observations to field notes or a field journal as soon as you leave the field. Ensuring that your memory is fresh is as important as accurate note taking when you are overtly participating and observing. Care of field notes in terms of accuracy and potential bias when the field notes are elaborated in memos, journals, and early drafts of your findings are ethical concerns as much as they are concerns about research quality. Computer files should be password protected and perhaps encrypted.

Analysis and Reporting

Harm to participants can occur after the study is done. Thick description reveals variation and complexity at the observation site. No persons or organizations are perfect, yet you must protect reputations and be sensitive to different perspectives represented in the findings as well as guarding participants' identities. Your analysis must probe for deeper meanings and not settle for an uncomplicated view of the phenomenon under study. You must represent the full dataset accurately in order to offer a fully realized view of the observational situation and the people in it. Your reporting must be unbiased, not sensationalized, and should consider the likely uses of your research reports, anticipating potential harm.

When a potential harm is recognized, the researcher has to weigh the harm and tell the story without sentiment or embellishment.[23] There is nothing like genuine empathy for your participants and appreciation for the complex nature of lived reality to counter harm. This is ultimately why we do thick description in the first place, to offer a sensitive and nuanced report based on a strong design, effective sampling, and careful data collection and analysis. Observational designs alone often do not provide enough detail for a full story that illuminates the phenomenon of interest. One way to prevent harm in reporting is to use triangulated data sources, like interviews or archival analysis, to amplify and elaborate observations for a more accurate portrayal of your findings.

Member checking and taking care to ensure the privacy and security of your research materials continue to be relevant in the analysis and reporting phase. Reading

---

[22] The exception is harm that rises to the level of legal sanction. Learning that children are being abused is an example of harm that must be reported to authorities. *Suspecting* that they may be abused puts you in a more ethically and legally ambiguous position.

[23] Patton (2002).

reports of many observational studies can be instructive, particularly when the authors have done their jobs well and explained their decisions as choices and not as academic abstractions. It is only by carefully considering the findings and plumbing them for meaning and implications that we can be sure that ethics have been given due diligence. When you have observed disreputable practices or uncovered failed organizations, you should still probably leave the writing of exposés to journalists. Almost by definition, exposés violate participants' privacy, which is the topic of the next section.

ENSURING PARTICIPANT PRIVACY

Design

You should be thinking about participants' privacy as you design your project. Consider carefully your role as an observational researcher. Do not ask more of your participants than you need. Observational designs create personal connections, and this places responsibility on you, from the design stages forward, to ensure that your research questions guide you to respect participants' privacy and safeguard confidentiality. Assurances of confidentiality are your personal promises to the participants that you will do your best to maintain their privacy even if this makes your work more difficult or might alter your study.

Returning often to your research questions and design prevents fishing expeditions that may compromise privacy. Used correctly, design decisions set the tone for the research and provide guidance as you sample, collect and analyze data, and report findings with privacy in mind.

Sampling

Privacy concerns appear when you first search for sites that fit your criteria and then sample among situations and individuals that provide opportunities to witness phenomena of interest. Anticipating the need to conceal where you have been and who you observed, your first obligation is to sample effectively. Poor sampling can make privacy hard to protect. For example, convenience sampling compromises privacy, as when researchers study their own or nearby organizations. It is very difficult to conceal participants' identities in these cases. Often, following leads in the field can become a form of snowball sampling, in which a participant in one observational setting refers you to other settings and participants. Obviously, when referrals are involved, people in the referral network know each others' identities, creating the need for enhanced privacy protections. Sampling also raises special privacy concerns when outlying, negative, or highly unique cases are sought, as these might be more easily identified than "typical" cases.

Data Collection

The principal approach to maintaining privacy during data collection is prevention. Avoid overreaching and choose data collection techniques that are less rather than more invasive, depending on your purposes. Field notes and other textual data are the least invasive approach, and they have been the mainstay of observational research for many decades. But field notes do not have the power to capture and share exact behaviors and utterances after you leave the field. Videos, audio recordings, and still photographs provide the opportunity to virtually "revisit" the observational setting in some detail. However, these methods require a heightened attention to maintaining privacy. Should you decide you need to use any of these techniques, you must be very clear when seeking IRB approval about how the images you collect will be used, maintained, and eventually archived or destroyed.

During the observation process, you may witness illegal activity, and even participate in it to avoid compromising the study and your identity and safety. You have to make decisions about how you will respond in the field and later, remembering that as a researcher you have no special legal privileges that protect you or your sources. Trust between the observer and the participants can also be compromised, leaving you with nothing to collect, analyze, and report.[24]

Data is also a privacy concern after it is collected. You have to decide how you will use, store, and dispose of your data. Storage in actual and virtual files requires safeguarding them from unauthorized use. You will provide assurances to your IRB and participants that material data are under lock and key and that electronic media are pass-code protected and/or encrypted and available only to researchers. Participants' identities may even be concealed from other research team members if privacy is likely to be compromised. Whenever possible, use coded identifiers as a precaution, but remember that protecting the key to the codes is also required. Not many of us have to worry that our data could be used by assassins as Wood did in her study of the civil war in El Salvador,[25] but the precautions she took can serve as a model of ethically appropriate behavior in collecting and managing data.

Analysis and Reporting

In observational research, data collection and the first steps in analysis are often simultaneous.[26] Throughout data collection and analysis, the ethical obligations to secure materials and obscure identities are the same. Analysis adds an additional ethical feature, however. If you gathered data, you are obliged to consider analyzing it. Otherwise, you have put participants' privacy at needless risk and are perhaps biasing your results in the process.

As with all ethical questions, it is your obligation to know why you made each choice and to share your reasoning with audiences and participants. During data analysis, if you have used electronic files and/or still photography, you have the advantage of reviewing your observations for accuracy and testing your emerging ideas, themes, clusters, and the other patterns in the data. The same permanent, often electronic, files that allow for accurate analysis can make for more exciting reporting, but also involve the need to employ greater privacy protections.

---

[24]Spano (2006) describes how he had to compromise his role as a neutral observer and become a participant in order to maintain rapport with the police officers he observed.

[25]Wood (2006).

[26]Texts in the qualitative research tradition offer cogent explanations for this overlap, sometimes called "constant comparative method" after Strauss and Corbin (1990).

While privacy in reporting may seem an after-the-fact issue, where pseudonyms are used and other obvious precautions taken, the foundations for these approaches to ensuring confidentiality are laid at the beginning, in the design phase. When seeking informed consent, you promised confidentiality and explained privacy risks and your safeguards for each. When protecting your participants from harm, you were focused and employed no more probing or risk taking than necessary. Now, you decide what to report and how to report it, given the needs of audiences and the privacy rights of participants. What can be reported to whom? Do all audiences of your findings require the same level of detail? How can the raw data be used to support the claims you make in your reports without compromising privacy? Will you need to change some identifiers or personal characteristics of participants to protect privacy? These are guiding questions to consider both as you design your project and as you prepare to share your results.

CONCLUSION

Naturalistic and participant observation designs are arguably among the most ethically challenging for researchers. Because these studies cannot be fully planned in advance there will always be considerable uncertainty about the ethical implications of actions you take during the research. Responses to ethical quandaries are likely to be less certain than in other forms of research. As a result, you must take your ethical responsibilities to protect privacy and prevent harm seriously, perhaps even more seriously than medical researchers and others who perform experiments in which the nature of the potential harm to participants tends to be clearer. Seriousness and ethical sensibilities are particularly required when you are highly engaged in the observational setting, either covertly or overtly. Being serious and sensitive means that you will return to your research purpose and think carefully about the ethical issues and questions that may arise in all phases of your study. By sharing your ethical deliberations and decisions about how to design, sample, collect data, and analyze and report findings, you help build the capacity of all observational researchers to behave ethically. A summary of ethical considerations discussed in this chapter is provided in the table on pages 295–296.

SUGGESTIONS FOR FURTHER READING

Reading widely in this area is recommended because the ethical dilemmas are complex and difficult to anticipate in naturalistic and participant observational designs. Our recommendations for reading on the ethical dimensions of observational designs share common features with earlier supplemental reading recommendations on the use of these designs and on observational sampling. Most of this scholarship comes from the qualitative tradition and has its roots in ethnography and case study research, and that is the source of our recommendations. Ethical discussions are ordinarily treated as part of a larger text and may appear embedded in chapters on these designs. Finally, we recommend a discipline-focused search as the ethics of nursing or social work research may differ from those of education, criminal justice, or other fields that apply social science research.

Dedicated Texts

We recommend three texts focused exclusively on the ethics of fieldwork. The first, *Ethics in Qualitative Research* (Mauthner, Birch, Jessop, & Miller, 2002) includes a chapter with the intriguing title, " 'Doing Rapport' and the Ethics of 'Faking Friendship' " and comes from a feminist perspective. This and other essays in the book address dilemmas of caring face-to-face work wherein relationships are forged, trust established, and personal feelings and reputations are on the line. The second text, *Fieldwork Participation and Practice: Ethics and Dilemmas in Qualitative Research*, frames observational ethics as "intentions, motivations, and ways of cognitively structuring the ethically sensitive situation" at least as much as "conforming to or violating a code (de Laine, 2000, p. 3). We add to this short list a classic, *The Politics and Ethics of Fieldwork*, which has informed much of the ethics of fieldwork since (Punch, 1986), and its update, "The Politics and Ethics of Qualitative Research" (Punch, 1994).

Essays on Ethics

Many texts in the qualitative tradition treat ethics as part of a survey of the observational designs, and handbooks often contain essays on this significant topic. We recommend two classic essays focused on ethics, "Educational Research and Outsider-Insider Relations" (Elliot, 1988) and "Doing Ethics: The Bearing of Ethical Theories on Fieldwork" (May, 1980). For an overview of issues in covert research see "Covert, Adversarial and Collaborative Research" (Lee, 1993). For the latest word, read relevant essays in recent editions of *The Sage Handbook of Qualitative Research*. Since the first edition in 1994, these have been updated with new articles and essays on topics relevant to naturalistic and participant observational designs, and no two of the four editions of this work are the same (Denzin & Lincoln, 1994, 2000, 2005, 2011).

CHAPTER 16 SUMMARY TABLE

CONSENT

Design	• Your observational design will be naturalistic or participatory; covert or overt; more passive or active; and more or less directive. Be aware of the effects of these choices on your ability to offer the promise of confidentiality. • Plan ahead for what you expect to happen, but remain flexible. • Be prepared to share your research purposes and benefits to an organization or setting. If appropriate, plan member checks.
Sampling	• Advance decisions about searching and sampling observations prevent harm and loss of privacy. • Identify only relevant and/or representative situations; once a setting is identified, be prepared to continue sampling, but also continue to select only relevant/representative situations. • Get advanced consent wherever possible, and seek it later as needed when sampling.
Data collection	• Plan how to record your observations and share these choices as you get consent for specific approaches. • Field notes protect privacy better than audio/video recordings, so it is easier to get consent.
Analysis and reporting	• Participants' consent ethically implies that you, the researcher, will analyze and report what they say fairly and accurately. • Interviewees should be told, as part of informed consent, how you plan to report what you have learned (e.g., if you plan to use images or extensive quotations).

HARM

Design	• Your design is a plan to minimize harm to yourself and others. • Consider a range of harms from the physical to the psychological. • You choose observational designs to understand others. Remember to respect diverse views, experiences, and vulnerabilities.
Sampling	• Consider risks such as privacy and reputational harm when searching and sampling. • Consider the relevance and representativeness of the sample balanced against risk. • Researchers must exercise extra caution when studying vulnerable populations, not only because additional IRB rules apply.
Data collection	• Harm is most likely in covert observations that are highly participatory. Be aware of your own vulnerability and that of others. • Take care to protect field notes and other artifacts.

Analysis and reporting	• Analysis must probe for deeper meanings and not settle for an uncomplicated view of the phenomenon under study. • Reporting must be unbiased and unsensational, considering likely uses of the reports and anticipating harms. • Member checks and care to ensure the privacy and security of your research materials continue to be relevant in this phase.

PRIVACY

Design	• In observational research, it is unlikely that you will promise anonymity unless you are covert in public. Otherwise, confidentiality is your personal promise.
Sampling	• Anticipate the need to conceal where you have been and who you observed, and sample strategically. Poor sampling can make privacy harder to protect.
Data collection	• Avoid overreaching and choose data collection techniques that are less rather than more invasive, depending on your purposes. • When in the field you learn of respondents' illegal activities, are you legally and/or ethically obliged to report these—or to keep them in confidence? • Secure privacy by protecting identifiers and characteristics of participants as individuals, groups, or organizations. • Decide how you will record, use, store, and dispose of your data, whether it is text, audio files, or images.
Analysis and reporting	• Concealing identity in all your materials can prevent confidentiality breaches. • Decide what to report and how to report it, given the needs of audiences and the privacy rights of participants. Once your data are available to other researchers, they may discover the identities of your participants. • To preserve the privacy of participants the researcher will usually have to omit some background information and use methods of concealment such as pseudonyms.

Ethical Issues in Archival Research

Ethical concerns might seem fairly minor in archival research. And indeed, archival research does tend to be less likely to be directly harmful to research participants than, for example, experiments and covert observational research. Earlier chapters in Part III of this volume, on research ethics, have focused on research participants: getting their *consent*; avoiding *harm* to them in the course of the research; and preserving their *privacy* when the research is done. Very often in archival research, there are no human subjects—at least not actively participating ones, so the outline we used in previous chapters is less relevant. To discuss the important ethical issues that can arise in archival research we return to the five-part organization used in Chapters 5 and 11 on archival design and sampling: (1) reviews of the research literature; (2) database archives; (3) organizational records; (4) studies of documents; and (5) new media, especially Internet sources such as blogs and social networking sites. Ethical problems have emerged in each of these areas.

The range of archival research is wide. Reviews of the research literature and studies using database archives together comprise a clear majority of the pages published in the major scholarly journals in most fields. Much, in fact nearly all, natural experimental research is done with archival data, including some pioneering work using difference-in-difference designs to study social policy.[1] Studies of stock market behaviors and the vast array of statistics and indices generated by economists are based on archival data, and an archival component is very often an element in observational studies of organizations and many other combined designs. While some of the data used in archival research are private and require permission to use, most are public and available to any qualified researcher, or indeed anyone. Given that vast sources of data are available largely without restriction or IRB regulation, the popularity of archival research is understandable.

---

[1] Card and Krueger (2000); Dunning (2008).

ETHICAL PRACTICE IN REVIEWS OF THE RESEARCH LITERATURE

When reviewing the research literature, few ethical issues are salient. Beyond the researchers' clear professional obligations to be honest, not to cook the data, to avoid biases and the like, ethical concerns seem unlikely to occur in reviews of the literature, whether meta-analyses or more traditional reviews. Not surprisingly, there are few published sources examining the ethical conduct of research reviews.[2] Those who do discuss the ethical conduct of research syntheses emphasize issues of accuracy and fairness in reporting and analysis; these are issues that are important in any research project. The ethical imperative to be accurate and unbiased might be greater in a research synthesis than for a single study. Because more attention is sometimes paid to research syntheses than to individual studies, more can be at stake. An obvious example is best-evidence syntheses that practitioners use to decide how to conduct their work.

Literature reviews find and analyze documents. Not only are the cases documents and not people, they are usually public documents. The documents are the research subjects, even when they describe people; thus, issues of consent, harm, and privacy do not arise. They have already been taken care of in the primary research—or they should have been. You might be faced with an ethical dilemma about whether to use a particular research report if the data in it were collected using unethical methods. The data might be good, but the methods of obtaining them might have been unethical in your judgment. The problem of whether to use public data obtained by methods you consider ethically suspect is less likely to occur in literature reviews than other forms of archival research, but it can occur.

Permission can be an issue in research reviews. Research synthesizers are often encouraged to find unpublished research. One reason is that doing so provides a hedge against various kinds of publication bias.[3] When you use unpublished research, you are obliged to get permission from the authors before you attempt to synthesize preliminary findings that the authors have let you see as a courtesy. You will often hear a paper on your topic at a scholarly conference. Very often these papers are not distributed and are not available. If a summary is distributed, it may contain the words "not to be quoted without permission," or a similar injunction. Even if such summary documents are not copyrighted, it is unethical—although probably not illegal—to use them without permission.[4]

It is possible for harm to come to some people as a result of a research review. Documents and their authors have reputations. A research article might be considered "an insightful account," or "a ground-breaking study." Your research review, if it contains a critique of a highly regarded article, could damage the article's reputation, its author, and the reputation of the journal in which it was published. But public documents do not have rights. While authors are persons, and one can harm their reputations by demonstrating that their research is faulty, this is not normally considered an ethical matter

---

[2] We know of only one devoted to the topic: Cooper and Dent (2011).

[3] Emerson, Warme, and Wolf (2010) provide strong experimental evidence that such biases do indeed exist.

[4] Our impression is that the frequency of "not to be quoted" papers has declined in the last decade or so, perhaps because attitudes have changed, leading many scholars to "publish" their unpublished work on Web pages.

as long as one is honest in one's critiques or the critique is not motivated by a conflict of interest. Criticizing the work of others does place an ethical burden on you not to be careless or mean spirited in your critiques, as these can be harmful. Perhaps the most common critique in research reviews is to label a study too flawed to be included in the review. Excluding a study inappropriately or criticizing one too harshly breaks few rules (and libel is hard to prove), but an ethically minded researcher would make serious efforts to avoid unnecessarily harming the reputations of other researchers.

Having systematically reviewed all or most of the research literature on a subject, you are in an ideal position to spot plagiarism or other abuses, such as publication of the same materials in more than one place, which amounts to an author's self-plagiarizing. Sometimes you suspect plagiarism, but you aren't sure. In those cases, you can use one of the available online programs to run a check.[5] While you certainly do not want to use tainted data in your research synthesis, you also face a less certain ethical issue: whether and when you should become a whistle-blower when you discover plagiarized or other faulty sources. Part of your ethical obligations as a research synthesizer, one could argue, is to help preserve the integrity of the data—in this case the corpus of research reports. Something similar could be argued for researchers using database archives, which is the topic of our next section.

ETHICAL PRACTICES IN EMPLOYING DATABASE ARCHIVES

Issues similar to reviewing the research literature pertain when you use public databases. It is important to be honest and admit the limitations of the databases,[6] but issues of harm and privacy are moot in nearly all instances. It is usually impossible for researchers, or those who use their findings, to identify any individuals. Hence, the anonymity of research participants is assured—almost. We add that qualifier because the history of secret documents is also the story of how the information in them has been uncovered. With increasingly sophisticated data mining technologies and a not inconsiderable number of people willing to leak information, there can be no absolute guarantees. But in an uncertain world, the safety of data in large public databases is probably greater than the security of data collected using most other designs.

When using large well-established databases, consent mostly has to do with getting permission from the custodian of the database. The people whose data are in the records are often anonymous and usually do not need to be consulted—although there are some cases where this has been contested, especially in medical research. To get permission to use these databases, you have to establish your bona fides as a legitimate researcher. As with the data collected in survey research (see Chapter 13), it is theoretically possible, using covariates, to identify individuals. This is not much of an issue with the large well-established data archives, where rigorous efforts to de-identify records are the norm, but many small data archives exist in researchers' private collections. While the responsibility to maintain privacy is initially that of the owner or custodian of the archived data,

---

[5] One free program is the document cop (*www.doccop.com*). See Lundberg and Shafer's online discussion, "Detecting and Preventing Plagiarism," published in *MedPage Today*, January 31, 2011. As journal editors, they routinely use programs to detect plagiarism.

[6] See Herrera and Kapur (2007) for a sobering review.

after you gain access to it, you also have an obligation—especially if the safeguards used in the initial archiving were inadequate.

The obligation to protect the data in databases cuts both ways. Before you follow the sometimes required and often recommended practice of making your data available to other researchers, it is important for you to take precautions to maintain the privacy of the people and organizations you have studied. Because it is increasingly recommended and sometimes even mandatory that you make your data available in order to publish results based on it, the importance of this ethical consideration for individual researchers is likely to grow, even for individual researchers whose shared data are composed of nothing more than de-identified rows and columns in a spreadsheet.

ETHICAL OBLIGATIONS WHEN USING INSTITUTIONAL RECORDS

Researchers using records are rarely interested in specific cases and the identities of particular individuals, but when one wants to link records from different sources, individual identifiers are needed. Even in these cases, it is relatively easy to make records anonymous. Alarmism about every possible kind of harm that anyone could imagine can be used to deny access to important research evidence. It is difficult to maintain the accountability of institutions if their records cannot be examined. The feeling of many researchers is that privacy regulations are sometimes used as a screen for incompetence, to avoid evaluation.

Your confidentiality agreements often have to cover the institutions themselves as well as the individuals in them. Typically, a researcher will use pseudonyms for institutions. While pseudonyms often work well to disguise the identity of individuals, it is more difficult to achieve anonymity in the case of institutions. Readers familiar with the field the researcher is examining often have little difficulty guessing the identity of the organizations or institutions discussed. This is especially the case because social science researchers naturally want to put the institutions into social contexts, and there are good reasons for doing so. But each contextual variable (organizational size, location, date of founding, etc.) makes it easier to identify the organization or institution being studied. Using pseudonyms then may amount to little more than what one author refers to as "thin veiling." A transparent pseudonym probably protects the researcher from "accountability while leaving respondents quite vulnerable to identification."[7]

When researchers plan to use organizational records to study children or medical patients—whether paper documents or electronic media—issues of confidentiality and anonymity are often more important. For educational records, the Family Educational Rights and Privacy Act (FERPA) of 1974 provides broad protections for students attending institutions receiving U.S. Department of Education funding. Similar protections are in place for medical records, most importantly through the Health Insurance Portability and Accountability Act (HIPAA) of 1996. In both cases, individuals' access to their own records is ensured while the privacy of their data is protected. When using documents covered by these laws, be sure also to remember that many states have regulations that build on and expand the scope of these federal regulations.

---

[7] Guenther (2009).

On the other hand, when you want to study public organizations and their documents, you have some legal recourse should you be refused access. Even private organizations—if they accept considerable amounts of public funding, have tax-exempt status, and/or are subject to state and federal regulation—sometimes have to open their records to you even when they do not wish to do so. As discussed in Chapter 11, federal and state freedom of information acts can be used to pry loose documents from unwilling hands. But the fact that some institutions may be legally obliged to give you access does not mean that you can ethically trample their sensitive information when there is no good research reason to do so. Journalists may do this. A story is a story, after all. But ethical researchers might wish to maintain higher standards even when not legally compelled to do so.

Documents, even public documents, can be used to injure. Investigative reporters have often used information in public records (births, marriages, divorces, purchases, and the like) that proved embarrassing or unpleasant for the recipient of journalistic attention. Researchers could possibly inflict similar harms, perhaps especially researchers writing biographies. And remember that researchers do not have the constitutional protections of journalists. It is very rare to successfully sue a journalist for libel. A researcher might not have the same kinds of successful outcomes in the courts that journalists usually experience.

As is typical in discussions of ethics and morality, values are often in conflict. In studies of organizations, accountability and freedom of information on the one side may clash with privacy on the other, particularly for those organizations that are private or that have some of the same rights as do "persons," such as corporations.

ETHICAL ISSUES USING DOCUMENTS, INCLUDING PUBLIC DOCUMENTS

Permission to use documents (including the institutional records discussed in the previous section) has been the subject of some dispute. For example the use of documents can be controversial when deciding whether de-identifying the records suffices to protect privacy and eliminates the need for informed consent. In the course of their practice, professionals (physicians, educators, psychologists, social workers, etc.) almost always maintain records as paper and/or electronic documents. The data in these documents may constitute important research evidence for improving practice, but questions can arise when these data are used for research. In general, an effort to improve professional practice does not, as such, require IRB approval, because it is not "research," in the sense of being intended to produce generalizable, published reports. Endeavors to improve practice may be based on research, such as best-evidence syntheses. Of course, responsible practitioners keep records. Then the data from these records can be used in research. Such data from records (as long as it has been de-identified) also seldom requires IRB approval or requires only an expedited review that focuses on the safeguards for de-identifying the records.

We know of one case in which a school official intended to "finesse" the IRB, although, as we will see, he may have gone to greater lengths than necessary. He introduced a new program for the children in a school, which was backed by considerable research suggesting that it would be beneficial. He did this in his capacity as an educational administrator, not as a researcher. But he intended all along to do research on the program and its implementation for his doctoral dissertation. He believed that, had he identified the project as "research" from the outset, he would have had to go through a lengthy IRB approval process and would have had to get consent forms from *every* parent, which is almost never possible. He saw himself as doing something like "data laundering." But, he *probably* could have introduced the program and studied it for his dissertation without the ruse. He *probably* could have had his project reviewed under the provisions of "expedited review," which is appropriate when the data are collected for purposes other than research. "Purposes other than research" include taking steps to improve the quality of professional practice. We emphasize the word *probably* because the question of whether a program is exempt from federal human subjects regulations, or whether it is eligible for expedited review, has been interpreted differently by researchers, various IRBs, and the federal Office for Human Research Protections (OHRP).[8] In any case, this researcher intervened in the school in his capacity as a school administrator. That intervention generated records containing data. He later wrote his dissertation using only the data in those records. His proposal had been approved as an instance of secondary analysis of existing data.

When it comes to archival documents in the traditional sense—old manuscripts not available electronically (if such still exist)[9]—the temptation to falsify seems to be great. There have been several famous cases of forgery, and their discovery, dating back at least to the Renaissance.[10] The chicanery continues. Several news reports in the media in 2010 and 2011 tell of an amateur historian, doing research in the National Archives, who falsified a date (changed April 14, 1864, to 1865) so as to claim that a document he found in the archives was probably the last document Lincoln signed. The historian, Thomas Lowry, wanted to be famous. By increasing the document's historical significance, he first gained fame, and then when he was caught, shame. Actually what he did was illegal, not only unethical, but the statute of limitations had passed by the time his falsification was discovered, so he was not prosecuted. Access to archival data of the type we have been discussing is often quite restricted, sometimes for fear of damage to the documents and sometimes because of concerns about privacy. The smaller and more private the archive (such as family records of interest to a biographer), the more restrictions there might be. Establishing good relations with the guardians of such archives can be more important for you as a researcher—and for the owners of the documents who want to protect sensitive family materials—than any legal rules and regulations.

Finally, what do you do about documents that are now public but were obtained by ethically dubious, and possibly illegal, means—such as WikiLeaks documents about the Afghan war or Swiss banks? Now that they are public, are they fair game or do they still carry the taint of their origins? And are their origins really tainted? Reasonable people could, and do, disagree.

---

[8] See Miller and Emanuel (2008) for an interesting discussion of the important case of quality-improvement research in emergency rooms and whether patient consent and IRB approval was needed.

[9] When the Dead Sea Scrolls become available online from Google, as happened in 2010, can anything long remain inaccessible?

[10] Perhaps the most notorious case is the Donation of Constantine in which the ninth-century emperor supposedly ceded control of the Roman Empire to the Catholic Church. Lorenza Valla, in 1440, proved it to be a forgery.

ETHICAL ISSUES WHEN USING BLOGS
AND OTHER SOURCES PUBLISHED ONLINE

Because blogs are public, and anyone can read these online diaries, there would seem to be little in the way of ethical concerns in using them. How can a researcher invade the privacy of individuals who publish their thoughts in the most public of all media? One limitation is copyright laws. In most nations, when a blog appears on the Internet, it is automatically protected by copyright. Copyright does not mean that materials are unavailable to the researcher as long as quotations are put within quotation marks and quoted passages do not exceed quite generous limits. When you are using these or other textual sources, you need to be familiar with the "fair use" provisions of the copyright laws in your nation and in the nations from which the documents come.

On the other hand, some researchers feel that it is wrong to use blogs in ways that the authors never intended, even if this is not technically illegal.[11] These concerns are even more reasonable for media such as chat rooms, which researchers could enter covertly using deceptive practices. On the other hand, when a chat room is open to anyone who wishes to join, and when the identity of the chatters is unknown or kept in confidence by the researcher, it is hard to see what an unethical breach of privacy might be.

The situation is even murkier when it comes to social networking sites such as Facebook or Twitter. Individuals post their information to share with friends. But what about friends of friends—or "fans" of friends of friends? For researchers studying modern culture or networking, such sources are crucial, and data mining techniques are rapidly developing. But how much do privacy protections apply in these circumstances? This question has been a subject of lively debate and litigation. The boundary between what is private and therefore protected and what is public and thus fair game will not be easy to draw. As we discuss further in Chapter 18, we recommend that, if your design includes research via the Internet, you consult the most up-to-date guidance. The Association of Internet Researchers has produced a free guide (in 2002—the most recent available version at the time of this writing) that provides helpful details regarding practical ethics considerations in internet research.[12]

WHEN MIGHT THE HONEST, CORRECT REPORTING
OF ARCHIVAL RESEARCH CAUSE HARM?

Our question here is: when are there some things we are better off not knowing? One example reported in various media in 2010 concerned a study of mortality rates of women during childbirth published in the British medical journal the *Lancet*. The study indicated that the number of women dying in childbirth had dropped by about one-third in the last three decades. It is still staggeringly high—over 300,000 per year—but there has been some improvement in recent decades. The ethical issue arose when the editor of the journal, Richard Horton, said he was pressured by advocates of women's health

---

[11]See Hookway (2008) for a discussion. For a different view, see Thelwall (2011).

[12]Available at the Association of Internet Researchers website: *aoir.org/reports/ethics.pdf*.

to delay the publication of the study until after crucial United Nations meetings about funding public health. The advocates thought that the release of the findings could lead to a reduction in public health funding. The question this example raises is: When do you as a researcher have an ethical obligation to worry about how your findings might be used? Should you delay publication of results if doing so could promote an outcome to which you were committed?

An older example comes from the work of Christopher Jencks, who wrote a book in 1972 called *Inequality: A Reassessment of the Effects of Family and Schooling.* Jencks concluded that schools were only marginally effective as engines of social change and were not very powerful institutions for promoting social mobility and economic equality. Jencks was criticized by people who did not really challenge his conclusions. Rather, critics feared that his findings, even if true, could play into the hands of conservatives who would use them to attack the school system and to justify cutbacks in funding to impoverished schools. Should Jencks have withheld the publication of his findings or perhaps not have studied the question in the first place?

Is it true that what you don't know can't hurt you—or, will the truth set you free? As researchers who have conducted numerous program evaluations, we have come to believe (a skeptic might say we have a vested interest in believing) that having accurate information about institutional effectiveness is better than basing policy on hunches and hopes or a political agenda. Consider the first example: if we can identify the causes of the decline in maternal mortality, might we not have a better chance of learning how to reduce it still further? In the second example, of course it is disappointing to learn that improving schools will not help reduce economic inequality very much. But isn't it better to base arguments for improving schools on reality rather than wishes? Aren't we better off, in efforts to promote social mobility, to identify effective policies and programs rather than to persist with approaches that at best produce limited improvements? Our rhetorical questions make our answers clear.

CONCLUSION

In all of these cases, it seems best to conclude with questions rather than with moralistic pronouncements. It is more common than not for values to be in conflict and for reasonable people to disagree about which values should take priority over others. Usually federal regulations as implemented by local IRBs are clear and uncontroversial enough, but many ethical issues arise that do not necessarily fall under the purview of regulatory agencies. In archival research, the three most common gray areas are: when to blow the whistle on flawed or deceptive data documents or files; when to use ostensibly good data from a tainted source; and when to withhold an accurate and honest report because some interested parties think that the knowledge contained therein could do more harm than good. The table on page 306 summarizes the ethics guidance discussed in this chapter.

SUGGESTIONS FOR FURTHER READING

Books on research ethics for archival data tend to focus on privacy, especially digital privacy and the Internet. This makes sense because most data, including traditional historical documents, are accessed on the Internet. Discussions of digital data security range from advanced computer algorithms to conspiracy theories and ways to avoid Big Brother's scrutiny.

A good, brief overall guide to the topic of ethically conducting research on the Internet is McKee and Porter's *The Ethics of Internet Research* (2009).

Serious techniques for ensuring privacy and anonymity of archived data can often be quite, well . . . technical. An excellent example discussing the relative merits of various methods mentioned in this chapter (plus some others not mentioned) is *Privacy-Preserving Data Mining* (2008), edited by Aggarwal and Yu.

More general discussions based in large part on legal and social theory are available in two very thought-provoking books by Daniel Solove: *The Digital Person: Technology and Privacy in the Information Age* (2006) and *Understanding Privacy* (2010). Another excellent book along these lines, one that is somewhat more philosophical than the first two, is Helen Nissenbaum's *Privacy in Context: Technology, Policy, and the Integrity of Social Life* (2009).

Another useful area for ethical insights pertinent to researchers is the profession of journalism, which tends to combine archival and interview methods. Foreman's *The Ethical Journalist: Making Responsible Decisions in the Pursuit of News* (2010) is a good all-purpose textbook. Smith's *Ethics in Journalism* (2008) discusses many instances both in the United States and elsewhere when journalists were confronted with ethical dilemmas and how they resolved them—or failed to do so.

CHAPTER 17 SUMMARY TABLE

CONSENT

Design	• Consent is an issue in research reviews only when your design calls for synthesizing unpublished, preliminary research. • If your design calls for using private databases, consent from the data's owner is required. • In the study of public institutions consent to use records may not be needed, but it is always required for private records. • Using public documents requires no consent, but it will be required if your design leads you to study private documents in private collections. • When your design requires using online documents and data, defining what is public and fair game versus what is private and requires consent is not simple. Your decisions about what to use will as often be determined by your sensibilities as by clear rules.
Sampling	• It may be that some research reports or portions of a data archive or some institutional records or documents (whether paper or online) are not available for sampling without consent. You are obliged, as you search archived data, to adhere to the consent agreements you made about what may and may not be sampled.
Data collection	• Data collection in archival research is limited to those documents, records, and other data stipulated in the consent agreements. There are few limits for public materials, except those imposed by honesty, fairness, and accuracy.
Analysis and reporting	• As you analyze and report your data, you may encounter data that are technically covered by your consent agreements, but to which you suspect that keepers of the archival data might not have consented to give you access had they known what you would find. Should this happen you may be confronted with an ethical dilemma.

HARM AND PRIVACY[a]

Design	• Harms through breaches of privacy are most likely in research designs that examine private or proprietary data. Institutional records and private document collections are most susceptible to this source of harm.
Analysis and reporting	• Sampling, data collection, and analysis in archival research can rarely cause harm in themselves except as they are steps on the way to reporting research findings. • Reporting private data, or public data that some people would prefer to keep private, is the main potential source of harm through invading privacy.

[a]Because the harms that can occur as a result of archival research arise from breaches of privacy, harm and privacy are discussed together in the table.

Ethical Considerations
in Combined Research Designs

In the preceding chapters of Part III, we have discussed ethical issues specific to research designs that use surveys, interviews, experiments, observations, and archival data. Two of these research methods, surveys and archival techniques, involve relatively low risk to research participants. Interviews, observations, and experiments can involve considerably more risk, depending on the specifics of the research design, sampling techniques, data collection, analysis, and reporting methods. When you use a combination of these methods in your research design, you can potentially compound the ways that risk can be incurred and you must plan accordingly.

If your research questions have led you to a combined design, you already know that things are going to be more complicated than they would be with a single-method research study. In this chapter, we consider issues of consent, harm, and privacy as they relate to combined research designs. While we cannot tell you how to make definitive ethical decisions and employ particular safeguards for each and every situation that may arise, we provide suggestions for how and why such decisions can be made for combined designs. As you analyze your study design and its component parts, we recommend that you consult the relevant preceding chapters for more detail regarding specific ethical concerns for each part of your study. We also highly recommend that when you have complex research designs, you discuss them with interested colleagues or, if you are in the early stages of your research career, consult one or more experienced mentors to guide you through the ethical considerations raised by your study.

CONSENT

Design

Because combined designs utilize multiple research methods, they have the potential to compound consent considerations. These include adequately describing your research plan; fully assessing potential conflicts of interest in all components of your design; and planning to maintain confidentiality or anonymity across all aspects of your data collection, analysis, and reporting. All of these considerations have the potential to add up or to multiply as a result of interactions among the various components of your combined research design. All must be included in the information provided to potential participants to obtain consent.

Adequately Describing Your Research Plan

In all likelihood, your design is complex in structure because of the compound nature of your research question. When you have several methods in play (concurrently or consecutively), your research project may be difficult to describe as you balance the use of understandable language with enough detail to adequately assure participant understanding. You don't want to overwhelm your consent forms with pages of methodology explanation because that will be confusing to potential participants, may obscure the most important information, and may even scare them off from a virtually harmless project. On the other hand, you don't want to oversimplify, possibly understating or omitting important details of what participants will actually be asked to do. An adequate description of your research would include a general overview of the project and its purpose, key steps (such as an observation phase followed by an interview phase), explanations of which parts involve the potential participants and what data will be collected in each part, and anticipated analyses and uses of the data.

If applicable, preparing IRB descriptions and protocols can be a good process to help you create succinct and understandable accounts of your project. If you create your basic project description first, this can be modified for use on the consent forms, possibly by substituting lay terms for technical terms, slightly condensing descriptions, and so on. Since your consent forms must accompany your IRB application, creating these simultaneously can be an efficient and effective process, especially for complex combined research designs. It is helpful to remember that while the IRB process is intended to protect research participants, it also provides the researcher with opportunities to hone and improve the research design. Most IRBs want to work with you to promote good, ethical research, and can be a valuable resource in this respect.

Adequately Assessing Conflicts of Interest in Various Elements of Your Design

For any funded study, whether you plan to employ single or multiple methods, your consent form must disclose the funding source. For a combined design, it is possible for one portion of the work (say a survey or experiment) to be underwritten by one funding source, and other portions (for example, qualitative work that supplements quantitative findings) to be funded by another source. If you, as the investigator, stand to benefit financially or otherwise from participants' involvement in any component of your research design, there may be conflicts with your participants' interests and these must also be disclosed.[1] If you are using a combined design, it is quite possible that you have assembled a team of researchers to conduct parts of the study based on their relevant expertise, and thus you must assess each team member's potential conflicts of interest

---

[1] Financial benefit is not always easy to define. One criterion is contained in the old saw: "It's OK to make a living doing research, but not to make a profit."

relative to each component of your study and include any such conflicts as information for potential participants to consider when giving informed consent.

Sampling

As with all studies, when conducting a combined research design, you must use extra cautions when studying vulnerable populations. Special legal protections are in place for these groups and can limit how you sample, the topics you can study, and the methods you can employ to do so. For these types of studies, special IRB consent provisions apply, and individual IRB rules may differ from institution to institution.

Data Collection

In a combined design, it is entirely possible that for some aspects of your study, confidentiality will be reasonably easy to maintain throughout the data collection process. For example, administering a paper survey without identifiers generally safeguards participants' identities. If you follow up with interviews based on your survey findings, and you recruit a new group of participants for the interview phase, you can also take steps to protect the confidentiality of the interviewees. However, if you want to interview from the same group that took the survey in the first phase, you must have a way to contact the surveyed individuals, meaning that you must have identifying information included in the survey. The more important it is to keep track of participants through various phases of your investigation, the more difficult (and more important) it is to be able to protect individual identification. Any such risks that may arise during data collection should be explained in the consent form.

Obtaining informed consent can be particularly tricky for participants in research conducted via the Internet. At the time of this writing, research ethicists are struggling with the challenges that electronic media pose for social science research. While an in-depth analysis of this issue is beyond the scope of this volume, we recommend that, if your design includes collection of responses via the Internet, you consult the most up-to-date guidance on how to include appropriate consent procedures. The Association of Internet Researchers offers a free guide (created in 2002) that provides helpful details regarding practical ethics considerations that can be applied in both simple and combined study designs.[2]

Analysis and Reporting

As you consider your study design, you will need to determine how the analysis and reporting process will create the potential for identifying information to emerge. For example, if your design involves qualitative descriptions of "outlier" cases based on a combination of archival data analysis, interviews, and observations, it may be possible that a given case is so unique that it can be clearly identified and thus compromise participant confidentiality. In such studies, it would be important to make this risk clear to participants, and to include provisions in the consent form regarding subsequent communication with participants to review the findings and obtain specific permission to release the data.

---

[2] Available at the Association of Internet Researchers website: *aoir.org/reports/ethics.pdf*.

Complete anonymity for subjects is very difficult, if not impossible, to assure in most combined design studies. After all, a combined design, by its very nature, employs multiple methods to study a phenomenon, each of which may require you to be able to track participants through the course of the study. An exception would be a design in which you analyze publicly available data archives (without individual identifiers) to isolate potentially important variables, and then use that information to create and conduct an anonymous survey from a random sample in a population. As an example, one of us used General Social Survey (GSS) questions, administered to a sample of the national population, to design an anonymous survey to circulate to local teachers.[3] But in most combined designs, especially those involving experiments, interviews, and observations, you will know your participants' identities and thus cannot assure anonymity when obtaining informed consent.

HARM

Design

In a combined design, you need to review all components of your study for situations that could cause stress to participants or other potential harm. For example, if you are studying a sensitive or controversial topic such as addictive behavior, sexual behavior, or criminal activity, it is possible that participants risk legal repercussions or social stigmatization if identified. Even if their confidentiality is well protected, they could experience mental or emotional stress from particular interview questions. This type of risk can be greater in focus group interview situations. On-site observations can create the same type of stress or risk of reprisals for participants. Experimental procedures and conditions need special scrutiny to determine potential harm to participants. Studies of organizations such as businesses, schools, or community groups often employ combined research designs. These require detailed review regarding potential harm to workers, students, or members through the possibility of real or perceived coercion to participate; threats to safety, employment status, or reputation; and mental or emotional stress.

Sampling

When conducting a combined research design, you must use extra cautions while studying vulnerable populations, and you must follow specific legal and IRB guidelines when doing so. If your combined design study takes you to areas and/or people that are geographically and/or culturally removed from your own locale and experience, then you need to consider cultural context and local definitions of harm when designing your investigation. Different countries, and often the various cultures within those countries, have different written and unwritten rules about what constitutes appropriate practice when searching and sampling from archives, recruiting interviewees, recruiting for social experiments, and/or selecting sites for observations. For example, adequately sampling particular ethnic subpopulations may present difficulties, such as occurred when Pew and Gallup conducted independent surveys of Muslim Americans in 2007 and 2008. The two surveys utilized national probability samples but encountered difficulty reaching large enough samples for their telephone surveys because of the languages in which

---

[3] Vogt and McKenna (1998).

the surveys were conducted, and because one survey used only landline phone contacts. As it happens, many recent immigrants rely solely on cell phones, which left many out of the potential interview sample.[4] This may have led to potential harm through overgeneralizing from a biased sample and subsequent stereotyping based on the conclusions.

Data Collection

The potential for harm to participants is fairly remote for data collection in studies that involve surveys or archival research, or some combination of the two. The potential for harm to participants is somewhat more likely for interviews (especially if they probe sensitive or controversial topics), focus group interviews, and observations. And finally, experiments pose the most risk of harm to participants, and thus merit the most scrupulous analysis of those potential risks. In a combined design, you will likely employ two or more of these methods, and thus you should assess potential harm during data collection for each of your design components as well as any consequences that may arise from participation in multiple phases of your study.

Analysis and Reporting

In all the preceding chapters of Part III, we have noted specific types of harm that can arise from the way you handle the data you collect. Depending on the components of your combined design, you can determine which of these apply to your study. For designs that use interviews or observations (or a combination of these), you will want to consider using member checking to increase the accuracy of your findings and reports.

As in any study, avoid the potential for harm caused by group stereotyping, taking findings out of context, or reporting data in ways that make participants potentially identifiable. Referring again to the Pew and Gallup surveys of Muslim Americans mentioned earlier, the two surveys produced significantly different findings regarding racial demographics, educational attainment, and employment. Any of these findings, if reported without acknowledging the study limitations, could lead to stereotyping of this American subpopulation. To the credit of the survey organizations, those limitations were reported and the differences between the two sets of results were formally described, explained, and published. While this example refers to two separate survey studies, the same kinds of issues can potentially arise within separate components of your combined study.

PRIVACY

Violations of participant privacy can be considered a particular form of harm. When individuals consent to participate in your study, they have a reasonable expectation that their privacy will be protected as described in the informed consent agreement. For most studies, you will obtain this consent in advance, giving participants the particulars of your investigation and their part in it. However, some study designs raise unique issues regarding privacy. For example, covert observation of uninformed subjects creates

[4]For a more complete discussion of why findings differed between methods, see *pewresearch.org/pubs/1144/muslim-americans-pew-research-survey-gallup*.

particular ethical concerns. It may be important to you that the people you observe are unaware that you are doing so, but is it fair to them? We discuss this issue in more detail in Chapter 16, but here we will say that including covert observation in your combined design can pose serious privacy concerns.[5] It would be better to avoid these issues by modifying your design to include nonparticipant (but not covert) observations.

As noted earlier in this chapter, if you combine archival research or survey research with other methods such as observation, interviews, or experiments, you automatically eliminate the possibility of anonymity for your research subjects. In these types of studies, your focus will be on maintaining privacy by establishing confidentiality safeguards throughout your design components. You should review all components of your design to determine if each poses particular privacy risks.

Sampling

Studies of vulnerable populations require attention to special protections. These include privacy protections, and you must consider all relevant federal, state, local, and institutional rules that apply.[6] If your design employs recruitment techniques such as snowball sampling or respondent-driven sampling (RDS), identities of respondents are necessarily known to the researcher and to other participants. You must determine if this knowledge poses privacy threats to your participants, and decide if these are manageable and warranted based on the relative benefits of your study.

In studies that utilize sampling procedures and recruitment via the Internet, keep in mind that e-mail and most personal computers are not secure. IP (Internet Protocol) addresses can be tracked to specific computers, if not to specific individuals. Data transmitted via the Internet can potentially be viewed by others not associated with your project. Another consideration is that, for Internet survey research, it is usually important that respondents submit data only once. This means that as the researcher, you may want to incorporate an identifier such as an e-mail address. Doing so means that confidentiality could potentially be compromised. One option is to recruit potential respondents using e-mail lists, but then refer them to a third-party survey site (many are commercially available) where they may participate in the survey.

Finally, if your study includes identifying sites for observation, the process of site selection can raise privacy issues. Do participants at these sites know how and why they have been selected? What data were considered in making the selection, and does the use of these data pose privacy threats? Documenting the process and criteria for site selection and making these clear to participants will highlight any privacy considerations that may arise.

Data Collection

In any design that includes face-to-face data collection, the potential for privacy breaches exists. Interviews, observations, and experiments all include personal encounters between and among researchers and participants. Even if you, the researcher, diligently

[5] For an example and a detailed discussion of this topic, see Calvey (2008).

[6] The most up-to-date source for federal regulations at the time of this writing is the Code of Federal Regulations, Title 45, Part 46; available at *www.hhs.gov/ohrp/humansubjects*.

maintain the privacy of participants as promised, it is completely possible that participants themselves will divulge information, not just about themselves, but also about other participants. In fact, participants may actually want to be identified by name.[7] If your research deals with sensitive subjects, you may consider ways to shield participant data from other participants, for example by forgoing focus group interviews in favor of individual interviews.[8]

With many combined designs, it is important to match data elements across various stages of the investigation. This always involves assigning some type of identifier to the data. For example, pretest results usually must be matched to posttest results. Demographic data may need to be matched to experimental results so that relevant variables can be taken into account during data analysis. Longitudinal studies always need a way of tracking participant data over time. Any time your data collection requires you to assign identifiers, you must devise specific plans to protect participant privacy. We discuss possibilities for such protections in the next section.

Analysis and Reporting

Data analysis often includes matching data elements across study components. To protect participant privacy, your plan might include destroying the identifiers after data analysis, although this will compromise the ability for subsequent study by you or others. Another possibility is to employ data perturbation methods that don't compromise your key variables and findings, but that limit the potential for participant identification. When the risk is high, as it tends to be when using multiple and combined sources of data, you should probably consider data encryption, which makes it difficult for unauthorized persons to access your data. Many commercial and some freeware programs are available.[9] For qualitative study components, you could employ pseudonyms as a method of identity concealment. However, these are often not very effective unless you disguise other data as well.

In combined designs, analyzing data for one component of your study could potentially affect how data is analyzed and reported for another. It is possible for these types of interactions to compromise participant privacy. For example, you may have created identifiers to link participant data across parts of your study. As you analyze the various parts, it may be possible to refine your findings to the point where you have categorized respondents into discrete groups based on particular study variables. If these groups are sufficiently unique, even if you destroy the individual identifiers, it may still be possible to identify the individuals in each group. As we said in an earlier chapter, "How many 42-year-old female lawyers living in Ft. Wayne can there be?" If this level of detail is not necessary to answer your research question, you may consider forgoing the extended analysis in favor of more general findings.

When reporting results, determine if your key findings can be reported in aggregate form. Doing so can reduce the risk of individual identification. However, if your study group is small, or if your study requires reporting of qualitative findings such

---

[7] For an example and a discussion of this issue, see Guenther (2009).

[8] For a good discussion of specific issues related to participant privacy in focus group research, see Smith (2005).

[9] Popular database programs such as SQL and MS Access contain encryption options.

as descriptions or quotations, you must take care that participants are aware of your intentions up front, and that they give specific permission for use of their data in your reports. As we mentioned earlier, member checking can allow you both to check for accuracy and to obtain such specific permissions.

CONCLUSION

When you settle on a combined design to answer your research question, you create the potential for new variations on the ethical concerns of consent, harm, and privacy pertinent to research on humans in the social and behavioral sciences. Single research methods carry their own types of risks to research participants, so combining these methods can often compound the potential for risk. As a researcher, it is your obligation to study each part of your design, assess the risks inherent in each part, and also to look for interactions among methods that may create additional opportunities for introducing risk to your participants.

In combined research designs, especially if they incorporate qualitative methods such as interviewing and observations, your ethics vigilance does not end with informed consent. For each method you employ, ethical considerations must be analyzed for each stage: design, sampling, data collection, and analysis and reporting. The more complex your design, the more complex your ethical issues may be. While there are no one-size-fits-all prescriptions for how to assess and manage the risks in social science research, the risks can be identified and managed with appropriate attention and care. For specific situations relevant to your study, we recommend that you become thoroughly familiar with laws, rules, and institutional requirements, as well as standards of ethical research conduct. (Many pertinent references have been provided in the chapters of Part III.) Also be sure to consult experienced colleagues and mentors and study ways that ethical issues were handled in other studies similar to your own.

The table on pages 315–316 summarizes the ethical guidance provided in this chapter.

SUGGESTIONS FOR FURTHER READING

Although written for qualitative researchers, Guillemin and Gillam's article "Ethics, Reflexivity, and Ethically Important Moments in Research" (2004) discusses concepts that can be useful for combined designs, distinguishing between "procedural ethics" (meeting legal and institutional requirements) and "ethics in practice" (dealing with situations that arise during the course of research activity). Kimmel's book *Ethics and Values in Applied Social Research* (1988) provides detailed information regarding ethical problems that can arise in social research, from case selection through reporting results. The author uses case study examples that illustrate ethical considerations in combined research designs. The book also provides suggestions for additional reading.

CHAPTER 18 SUMMARY TABLE

CONSENT

Design	• Combined designs have the potential to compound consent considerations.
	• Use of multiple methods can make it difficult to describe the research in enough detail to adequately assure participant understanding.
	• Different parts of the research may raise separate potential conflicts of interest, all of which should be described when obtaining consent.
	• The capacity to maintain confidentiality may differ across components of the combined research design, and should be explained to potential participants when obtaining consent.
	• Combined designs rarely can promise anonymity, since they often involve interviewing, experiments, and/or observation.
Sampling	• When sampling for different parts of a combined design study, researchers must consider whether each sampling method exerts pressure to participate, involves vulnerable populations, or requires nonwritten consent.
	• When sampling for a combined study conducted via the Internet, it may be difficult to assure that potential subjects comprehend consent information or that they are of legal age to consent (18 or over).
Data collection	• Inform potential interviewees that signing the consent form does not oblige them to answer all survey and/or interview questions nor does it oblige them to let you use or attribute anything you learn from them in the study.
Analysis and reporting	• Participants have the ethical right to assume, when consenting, that the researcher will analyze and report responses, experimental results, and/or observations fairly and accurately.
	• Participants should be told, as part of informed consent, how data from each component of your combined design will be analyzed and reported.

HARM

Design	• All components of combined designs should be reviewed for situations that may cause stress or other potential harm (e.g., peer pressure in focus groups, interview questions on sensitive or controversial issues, experimental procedures or conditions, observational settings).
	• Organizational studies often use combined designs and need special scrutiny regarding potential harm to workers or members through potential coercion, safety, and other concerns.
Sampling	• As with all study designs, researchers must exercise extra caution when studying vulnerable populations to whom additional IRB rules apply.

Sampling *(cont.)*	• Cultural context and local definitions of harm should be considered in combined designs that involve recruiting interviewees and/or performing on-site observations, particularly in areas geographically and culturally different from the researcher's own locale.
Data collection	• Harm is fairly unusual for data collection in surveys and archival study components; somewhat more likely for interviews (especially for sensitive or controversial topics), focus groups, and observations; and potentially most likely for experiments. • For combined studies, harm during data collection should be assessed for individual components as well as interrelated components.
Analysis and reporting	• As with any study design, avoid harmful effects of analysis and reporting, such as group stereotyping, taking findings out of context, or reporting data in ways that make subjects potentially identifiable. • For designs that use interviews and/or observations, consider using member checking to increase accuracy of data reporting.

PRIVACY

Design	• Combined designs that utilize covert observation require special diligence about privacy issues. • Combining surveys and interviews/observations automatically eliminates the possibility of anonymity. • You should review all components of your combined design to determine if each affords different privacy considerations.
Sampling	• With snowball sampling and RDS researchers know the identities of respondents. • Vulnerable populations have need of special privacy protections. • In studies that utilize sampling procedures and recruitment via the Internet, keep in mind that e-mail and most personal computers are not secure. • In designs that use observation, site selection may raise privacy issues.
Data collection	• Face-to-face data collection (as in interviews and observations) may raise the potential for privacy breaches. • If data collection involves assigning identifiers to responses (as in interviews and surveys) and other records (as in archives and observations), consider how these will be protected.
Analysis and reporting	• Consider whether data analysis and reporting for one design component could affect how data is analyzed and reported for another, and whether these interactions could cause harm to research subjects. • Making your data available to other researchers may enable them to discover the identities of your respondents and/or research sites. Options such as data perturbation reduce this risk. • To preserve the privacy of research subjects, the researcher will usually use methods of concealment such as pseudonyms.

Conclusion
Culmination of Design, Sampling, and Ethics in Valid Data Coding

Our goal in this book is to provide a reasonably complete and helpfully arranged set of guidelines for readers preparing to undertake a research project. We begin with the initial selection of the design, move to methods for obtaining cases to study with that design, and conclude with considerations for carrying out the research plan in an ethically responsible way. At that point, the researcher is nearly ready to begin collecting data. But there is one more crucial step, one that should be informed by the first three. That step is deciding on an approach to data coding. Data coding rounds out what we think of as a full "design package" that prepares you for data analysis. Thus we conclude this volume with a chapter on data coding. Data analysis, and its related issues of coding and measurement, is an intricate topic and it demands a volume of its own, which will soon be available as a companion book.[1]

We describe a sequence of choices in research methodology that begins, as a first step, with selecting a research design, which is the procedure or strategy you will use to collect data. Our broad design categories are (1) surveys, (2) interviews, (3) experiments, (4) observations, both participant and naturalistic, (5) archival research, and (6) combined designs. The choice of design, we argue and try to illustrate, is most effective when the decision is shaped mainly by the demands of your research question. After you choose your design strategy, the next step is to identify a target population that is appropriate for your research question and compatible with the design you have chosen to investigate it. From that target population, you then need to find and select cases—be they people, organizations, regions, programs, or documents.[2] Cases have to be found and/or sampled and/or recruited. In experiments, they also have to be assigned to treatment and control groups. The target population and the methods used to obtain cases to

---

[1] Tentatively titled *When to Use What Methods of Analysis.*

[2] We use cases because it is the most generic term (except perhaps units of analysis). Terms more typically used vary by design, for example, respondent, interviewee, participant, informant, and so on.

study will be determined by the design used. That is why we organize our subject matter by design when discussing searching for, recruiting, selecting, sampling, and assigning cases. We also organize by design when discussing research ethics. Ethical issues become concrete at the intersection of design strategy and case selection. While there are many overriding principles of research ethics that apply in nearly all cases, their application in practice varies greatly depending on who or what is studied and how they are studied, which is why we also organize the ethics chapters by design types.

The structure of our presentation shifts as we take up data coding. Methods of coding are related to procedures for measurement and analysis, and they cut across designs. Researchers using each of the major designs apply a variety of coding and analysis schemes to their data. Hence, organizing by design, which was effective for discussing case selection and research ethics, would involve too much repetition and thus be clumsy for a discussion of coding.

The purpose of data coding is to prepare data so that they reliably and validly express key concepts in your research questions; this, in turn, enables you to analyze the data in reliable and valid ways. Coding forms a transition point in the flow of a research project. Coding refers back to the concepts implied in your research question, and it also refers forward to your analysis plan. How you decide to code your data is based on the character of the concepts in your research question. The most widely used generic labels for the conceptual issues and problems involved in coding and measurement are the *validity* and *reliability* of the codes (validity is also important in design and analysis). Researchers whose work does not involve numerical data sometimes use alternative terms for these concepts, such as *trustworthiness* to indicate validity and *dependability* for reliability. We use *reliability* and *validity* only because they are currently somewhat more generic or, at least, more widely used.[3]

Labels aside, coding decisions significantly shape the analysis options open to you. Because coding is a point of transition between design and analysis, it is also a transition point between "when" questions and "what" questions. We move from our focus in this book on *when* to use which kind of method (design or sampling or ethics safeguard) when collecting your data, to the focus in our companion volume: *what* techniques to use when you have this kind of data (coded in a particular way) to analyze. In short, readers will note an increasing frequency of "what" questions and a decline in the number of "when" questions—a transition that will intensify as we move to the volume on analysis.

We have been referring to the subject of this concluding chapter as *coding*. However, in the quantitative tradition in research, it is often called *measurement*. Measurement, in this tradition, is usually defined as assigning numbers to differences in variables, and that is an apt definition. Applying the term *measurement* to qualitative data would often seem peculiar. Much so-called measurement for qualitative data involves making categorical distinctions for which there is no particular need to assign numbers: categories such as male/female, Protestant/Catholic, assertive/passive, guilty/innocent, yes/no, and so on. But one must code these distinctions, whether verbally or numerically. For that reason, we use *coding* as the generic label. *Measurement*, or assigning *numbers* to coded observations, is a subcategory of the more general process of coding.

---

[3]Many researchers collecting qualitative data use the terms *reliability* and *validity*, but few researchers dealing with quantitative data use the terms *trustworthiness* and *dependability*.

It is often not possible to separate coding and measurement, particularly when concepts are coded numerically. Furthermore, coding and measurement are naturally linked via a continuum of data handling that ends in analysis. Hence, the discussion will sometimes drift, when discussing coding, into measurement and analysis—and vice versa. This kind of drift is better than imposing rigid distinctions that exist only in textbooks, not in the practice of research.

A *reliable* and *valid* research procedure consistently and accurately codes a meaningful *concept*. The three key terms are *reliable, valid*, and *concept*. Concepts are more difficult to define than validity; validity is more difficult to define than reliability; reliability is more difficult to establish than methods of coding. In this introduction, we begin with the easier and move to the more difficult topics. This is pedagogically effective; it is useful for *learning* the subject: first coding, then reliability, then validity, then concepts. But this is usually not a good order for *applying* what is learned to planning effective research. One should, most methodologists would say, start with the concept, then move to a valid way to define and investigate the concept. Only then does one take up coding and measuring and testing those codes for reliability.

WHEN TO USE QUALITIES OR QUANTITIES, NAMES OR NUMBERS, CATEGORIES OR CONTINUA?

And now, finally, we come to the issue with which many researchers like to begin. Should the research be quantitative or qualitative? We have postponed the decision between quantitative and qualitative methods until comparatively late in the decision process because of the way we understand the differences between them. We see qualitative research as the right choice when the investigators' research questions are best answered by collecting and analyzing qualitative data. Similarly, the question of whether to use quantitative research is answered positively when the research questions can be effectively addressed by collecting and analyzing quantitative data. This understanding of the difference between the two can be thought of as the *soft* version, but there is also a *hard* version.[4] Adherents of the hard version see qualitative and quantitative *not* as mere practical differences between approaches to collecting and analyzing data to answer research questions. Rather, quantitative and qualitative research are seen as worldviews or paradigms that are seldom tolerant of one another because they are believed to be fundamentally incompatible. Rather than soft, pragmatic questions—for example, can we better answer our questions with qualitative interview data or quantitative survey data?—the hard, worldview approach is more likely to debate the merits of scientism and positivism versus postmodernism and phenomenology. We think the hard version is mostly an unfortunate digression. We know that many friends and colleagues disagree, so we will conclude simply by pointing to the most important practical or pragmatic consideration leading to our position. Progress in knowledge is often the result of applying new approaches to problems or combining methods of investigation previously kept distinct. The hard or worldview understanding of qualitative and quantitative research

---

[4] Our understanding of the soft versus hard definitions of qualitative and quantitative research owes much to a discussion with Burke Johnson who, while he influenced our thinking, might not completely agree with our conclusions.

stops that progress dead in its tracks by making it less likely that researchers will consider alternative approaches.

For us, the most fruitful approach to answering the question of when the research should be qualitative and when quantitative depends on how the researcher's concepts are defined as variables. That, in turn, has to do with both the purposes of the researcher and with the substantive nature of the variables. Some concepts and the way to handle evidence for them seem to fit cleanly in one type or the other; there appears little doubt about whether to use words or numbers to code the evidence. But even non-numerical categories sometimes admit of degrees.

For example, is a person a Catholic or not? If we wanted to study Catholics, how would we make the categorical decisions about whether individuals were Catholic? What are the attributes of a Catholic and, of those attributes, which ones matter most? Are there necessary and/or sufficient conditions? To construct a workable indicator or operational definition, you could just ask people, "Are you a Catholic?" Your operational definition would be that those who say yes are Catholic and those who say no are not. But doing this runs the risk of using unstable, unreliable definitions. One person might say, "Yes, I'm a Catholic; even though I no longer attend church, I identify with Catholicism because my parents were Catholic and raised me to hold certain values that I still hold." Another interviewee might have the same background, but answer the question, "No, although I was raised Catholic and still hold many Catholic values, I no longer attend church." So how do you define the concept you want to study? Do you use as indicators specific practices and beliefs, such as attending church every Sunday or believing in the infallibility of the Pope? If there are several indicators, can you turn them into a scale of "Catholicness," with some people ranking as highly Catholic and others only slightly Catholic?

Other variables seem clearly quantitative; they are continuous, not categorical. Age, income, and height are three examples. You could replace these with names or categories, but to do so would be to lose data, even to discard it. Old/young, rich/poor, tall/short are crude categories that break up continua. But, for some purposes, categorical approaches to continuous data make sense. For example, take the variable of age and the purposes of the researcher. If the issue was legal eligibility, a political scientist might be interested in whether respondents were old enough to vote, a social work researcher in whether informants were old enough to qualify for Medicare. In these cases, differences between informants in their 20s and in their 50s, important for many other research questions, might be irrelevant for these issues of legal eligibility.

Even height, which would seem unambiguously numerical, can sometimes, depending on *substance*, be better treated as a categorical variable. A classic example comes from genetics, specifically Mendel's peas. Mendel studied several characteristics of peas, such as their color, shape, and height. The peas were either tall or short. If you cross-pollinate tall plants and short plants, you do not get medium plants. Rather, you get some plants that are tall and some that are short, in predictable proportions. In this case, what might be thought of as substantively or naturally continuous is, upon closer examination, naturally categorical.

After you've made your decisions about the substantive and conceptual nature of your variables, as shaped by research questions and purposes, *then* you can know how to code and measure them, which in turn shapes your choices of analytic techniques. Concepts should shape coding, which is a substantive issue worthy of serious attention. It should not be treated as a mere preference for numbers or words.

WHAT METHODS TO USE TO CODE CONCEPTS
WITH RELIABILITY AND VALIDITY

What methods should one use to code concepts in ways that are reliable and valid? Reliability and validity are related but distinct. They are terms for different aspects of the process of investigating concepts. Reliability refers to the consistency of coding or measurement. Validity refers to the appropriateness and accuracy of coding or measurement. Reliability and validity are linked in one fundamental way: an unreliable measure cannot be valid. However, reliability alone does not guarantee validity.[5]

Reliable coding and measurements *may be* invalid. If you were to measure blood pressure with an oral thermometer, doing so could be quite reliable (consistent) but it would be invalid. If two investigators used oral thermometers to measure the same individuals' temperatures, they would likely get similar or identical readings. Or, if readings for several individuals were taken at 2:00 P.M. and again 3:00 P.M. they would tend to be highly correlated. But despite all their reliability, these would be invalid measurements of blood pressure.

Unreliable coding and measurements *must be* invalid. To illustrate how an unreliable measurement must be invalid, consider the following: Say you used a blood pressure cuff (an appropriate, valid instrument) to measure a patient's pressure at 10-minute intervals and the readings were 30 over 300, 180 over 20, and 6 over 3. These measures are so inconsistent (unreliable) that they cannot be a valid (true, accurate, or appropriate) measure of anything. In sum, reliability is a necessary condition for validity, but it is not sufficient. Other than this important link, the two concepts are quite distinct. Because reliability is the simpler of the two, we begin our discussion with it.

WHAT METHODS TO USE TO IMPROVE RELIABILITY

Reliability refers to the consistency or dependability of coding and measurement. This can mean consistency in the measurement instruments or in the persons doing the measuring and coding—or some combination of the two. If two of your research assistants code the same videotape, do they do so in the same way? If you judge a performance on Tuesday, will you use the same criteria on Thursday? If you have five survey questions, all intended to measure facets of the same variable, do your respondents interpret the questions and answer them in the same way?

Consistency in research is relatively easy to determine, especially when numerical coding is used. Then consistency can be measured quite precisely with reliability coefficients, which are usually correlation coefficients. Consistency can be more difficult to ascertain when verbal coding is used, as it often is, for example, in observational work. Two participant observers of the same social situation could get together and compare observations, but this is quite rare. Indeed, it could be argued that two different participant observers would, by definition, not be observing the same situation. And when more than one observational study of the same setting is undertaken, this often involves

---

[5]While validity is also important in design and analysis (where it means "appropriate"), we focus here on coding and measurement.

one researcher challenging the reliability and validity of the data coding of another.[6] Reliability of verbal coding is more testable when the data are made up of texts. Texts (interview transcripts, newspaper articles, and so on) do not vary depending upon who is looking at them. The interpretations of texts may vary, of course, but not the basic data.

Consistency in making subjective judgments can be taught and learned. Whether it is Olympic judges rating diving contests or pathologists grading cancer tumors or social psychologists identifying helping behaviors, it is possible for researchers to learn to improve their intersubjective agreement, which is one definition of objectivity. This kind of consistency is usually called interrater reliability. It is one of three main types of reliability. The other two are test–retest reliability and internal consistency reliability. The labels of these types of reliability clearly indicate the kind of consistency they address. Because the three are distinct, researchers should test for all the types of reliability relevant to their studies. All three types of reliability (and subtypes of each) are measured by coefficients that range from 0.0, when there is no consistency, to 1.0 when the consistency is perfect. For most research purposes, test–retest reliability and interrater reliability need to be quite high: .80 or .90 would be a good rule of thumb.

Internal consistency reliability is used for multiple indicators of the same concept. For example, one six-item measure of neighborhoods' commercial decline had a reliability of .91.[7] That means that when one item indicated decline the others had a very strong tendency to do so as well. And, when one item indicated lack of decline, the other items also pointed in that direction. Reliability based on internal consistency is usually measured by Cronbach's alpha (the related technique of factor analysis is also used for the same purpose). Like other reliability coefficients, Cronbach's alpha ranges between 0.0 and 1.0. Usually, .70 is used as a *minimum* threshold for satisfactory reliability of a multi-item scale. Any such cutoff is somewhat arbitrary, but this one is very widely used.

Scales with levels of reliability lower than .70 can severely underestimate, and perhaps miss altogether, true relations between variables. Reliability is necessary for accuracy in measurement. Unreliability equals error. And when reliability coefficients are in the .50s or .60s (or lower), underestimates of the size of a relationship can be grave. For example, if two variables are *perfectly* correlated in actuality, but they are measured with reliabilities of .55 and .60, then mathematically the highest possible measured correlation between them is .574. So, a correlation that would be 1.0 if the variables were measured without error can be no higher than .57 with mediocre reliability. This underestimation is called attenuation.

These technical considerations derived from the study of quantitative data should not disguise the fact that reliability, however named, is crucial in all forms of research. It is equally important for researchers who envision collecting qualitative data and coming to qualitative conclusions. Forms of dependability or consistency of observation and coding in qualitative research include (1) repeated observations, such as member checking, (2) observations by more than one researcher, and (3) the consistency of a set of observations of the same phenomenon. Without some consistency in observations—

[6] For a very instructive example, see the conflicting ethnographic studies of what caused the high number of deaths in a heat wave in Chicago in Duneier (2006) and Klinenberg (2006).
[7] Browning, Wallace, Feinberg, and Cagney (2006).

regardless of whether those observations are coded with names or numbers—it would be hard to claim that you know anything at all.[8] And you surely could not replicate research findings if observations and measurements had no consistency whatsoever. Human communication rests on consistency in identifying and labeling phenomena. Researcher communication is the same. If researchers lived in private worlds and did not use the same words for the same things, they could make no credible knowledge claims.

WHAT METHODS TO USE TO ENHANCE VALIDITY

Questions of validity apply to all stages of a research project, from design through sampling, coding and measurement, and analysis. Discussions of research methods often refer to four major categories of validity. To put the discussion of validity in coding and measurement in context, here is a brief review of the four categories:

- *Internal validity* refers to the relevance of the design and the evidence gathered with it to answering the questions of interest to the researchers. Are the type of design and the ways it is implemented likely to yield the best evidence for addressing the subject of your research? This kind of validity is addressed mostly in Part I of this book.

- *External validity* has to do with the generalizability of the findings to cases other than those you have studied, from samples to generalizations about populations. Unless one has studied the entire population of interest, this kind of validity will be important. And even when one has studied the whole population, future populations are usually of interest. External validity is the main criterion for judging the quality of the selection of populations and samples as discussed in the chapters of Part II.

- *Evidence-inference validity* has to do with the appropriateness of the analysis methods used to interpret the data collected. This is discussed in our companion volume on analysis. In the experimental tradition, this is known as "statistical-conclusion validity," but that label is too narrow to describe a general issue relevant for all researchers.[9]

- *Construct validity* is the heart of validity as it pertains to data coding; it is our focus in this concluding chapter. Construct validity means that the definitions of the constructs or concepts are true and appropriate. The codes, indicators, and measures researchers use to study the constructs have to be accurate and appropriate as well. Other types of validity in coding and measurement are often

---

[8] See Denzin and Lincoln (2005) for work stressing the importance of *distinguishing* between qualitative and quantitative approaches to reliability and validity—rather than taking a unitary approach as we have here. Most of the best work stressing the structural and conceptual similarities of reliability/validity in numerical and verbal data has been done by political scientists. Important examples include Adcock and Collier (2001); Brewer and Hunter (2006); and Goertz (2006).

[9] The originators of this classification were Campbell and Stanley (1963). See Shadish et al. (2002) for the fullest elaboration of the original classification of types of validity.

thought of as subcategories of construct validity, and that is how we deal with them here.

Some of the most interesting classic discussions of research methods have centered on which of these types of validity is most important and why. Cook and Campbell thought that internal validity was the most fundamental. Cronbach countered that external validity is equally or more important. Many recent writers have claimed that construct validity is the most important and further that, properly understood, it includes the others. Discussions of validity have been extensive and vigorous. A proliferation of confusing subtypes and attempts at synthesizing them does not yield unambiguous guidelines for the practical researcher. But the extensiveness of the discussion, as annoyingly abstruse as it sometimes can be, is perhaps an indication of the importance of the topic.[10]

It is clear that all four categories of validity are crucial. All four are necessary to a good research project, and no one of them is sufficient. A failure to attain validity in any one aspect of a project can undermine the entire project. It is a good idea, whether you are a beginner or a seasoned veteran, to use a validity checklist to help you make sure you have not omitted anything.[11]

Again, in this chapter, we focus on construct validity. This can be roughly defined as the extent to which the data you are gathering and coding is pertinent to your research question. In other words, are you studying what you intend to study? How closely are your survey questions geared to the information you want from informants? Do your definitions and measurements of your outcome variable make sense in terms of your research questions? These are validity questions, they can be difficult to answer, and there is almost never a definitive answer. Indeed, it is usually easier to get agreement that a design or sample or method of coding is *invalid* than that it is valid. Much of the reason for this is that, unlike estimates of reliability, assessments of validity are more dependent on judgment than on statistics.

There are statistical measures of validity. But these are less certain than measures of reliability. Consistency (reliability) is inherently simpler than appropriateness (validity). When judging reliability one uses similar measures of the same thing; the coefficient is a correlation between, for example, identical uses of the same measure on the same sample (test–retest reliability) or on multiple raters' assessments of the same phenomenon (interrater reliability). Validity, by contrast, may be assessed by correlating *different* measures of *different* phenomenon.

For example, are grades in a training course for future employees a valid predictor of supervisors' ratings of the job performance of those employees (predictive validity)? To continue with the example of job performance, if you have three assessments of the same thing (performance) you would expect them to be closely related if performance

---

[10] Cook and Campbell (1979); Cronbach (1975); Messick (1993). For brief general discussions, see Thorndike (2005), Vogt (2007), and the works cited therein. For a good example of the extensive debates common in the field, see *Educational Researcher* (2007, Vol. 36, No. 8, pp. 437–486), where several well-known scholars addressed the issues. Adcock and Collier (2001) provide an excellent review of the proliferation of types as well as a persuasive attempt to bridge the gap that divides the study of quantitative and qualitative data.

[11] Shadish et al. (2002) is the *locus classicus*; their lists are especially relevant to experimental research. Creswell (2003) helps fill the gap for other forms of research.

were a valid concept. You could have more confidence in your evaluation of the employees' performance if the assessments were closely related than if they were not. Say the measures are supervisors' ratings, customer satisfaction surveys, and monthly sales. When measures of the same concept (job performance) differ, that could be because one or more of the measures is inadequate, but it could also be because the concept is flawed. Treating job performance (the concept) as a single, unitary construct might be erroneous. The reason for the lack of agreement among the measures may be that the three assessments (supervisor ratings, customer satisfaction, and sales) are assessing different things and not different aspects of the same thing. That is a frequent question in matters of validity: *are these different things or are they different aspects of the same thing?* Coding is not only a technical matter. It is also determined by the clarity of the researchers' understanding of the concepts being coded.

WHAT TO USE TO CODE CONCEPTS VALIDLY

As always, you begin with your research question. In one way or another, the question is composed of concepts. A concept is a general or abstract idea of something. To discuss the abstract concepts of poverty, prejudice, democracy, intelligence, religiosity, and so on, one needs to define these abstractions. Abstract concepts such as prejudice or intelligence cannot usually be studied directly. Further specification is required. You supply those specifications of a complex or abstract concept by using simpler or more concrete terms. These terms are often components of the more general concept. For example, two definitional components of democracy are civil liberties and free elections. Such components are often characterized as necessary and/or sufficient conditions. Civil liberties and free elections are necessary conditions. A nation (or other polity) that is missing either of these does not qualify as a democracy. A list of all the necessary conditions usually suffices to define whether a case counts as an instance of a concept, such as whether a nation qualifies as a democracy.

Next the researcher has to specify how the necessary components are defined. At this point you get closer to the level of operational definitions, and here a key coding decision intrudes: when do you code the component or concept categorically, or in terms of ranks, or continuously? Does the nation guarantee civil liberties—*yes or no*? Does it do so *more or less* than other ostensible democracies? Can you construct a *continuous rating scale* and assign a number to the level or degree of civil liberties in the nation?

Very often, you have to discuss the components of components. The process of specification continues, sometimes through several levels of specification, until you finally arrive at definitions that are concrete enough to enable you to gather objective evidence about them. For example, civil liberties may be necessary if a nation is to be judged a democracy, but how does one define civil liberties? Does the necessary and sufficient definition of civil liberties include freedom of the press, of speech, of assembly, of religion? And how do you define each of these? For example, does *any* government restriction mean that there is *no* freedom of the press?

Your coding decisions will be shaped by your concept. What does it mean to say that citizens of a polity have civil liberties? Are civil liberties a unitary construct that is, in a very real sense, either present or absent? Is the idea of just a little bit of civil liberty a sham? If a nation has serious protections for freedom of the press but freedom of

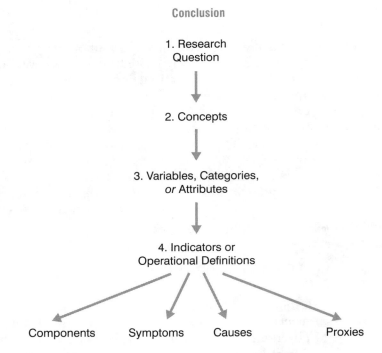

FIGURE 1. Valid coding of concepts.

assembly is hedged about with restrictions, would it qualify as having civil liberty? Can a nation with an official religion, even if the nation has freedom of the press, qualify as having civil liberties and therefore properly be considered a democracy—or not?

These kinds of complex decisions about your concepts are not rare. They are—or should be—routine. We have sketched the typical process of making your concepts researchable in Figure 1.

Your research question leads you to your concepts (Lines 1 and 2 in the figure). Say your question is: Are democratic nations more or less likely to go to war with one another than nondemocratic nations? For that question you would need to specify your concepts: democratic, nondemocratic, and war. Or your research question might be: what is the comparative influence on children's academic achievement of their socioeconomic status (SES), their academic aptitude, and the quality of the school they attend? Then influence, SES, aptitude, school quality, and achievement would be the concepts you would need to specify. Or, one final example: Are unemployed workers more likely to find work after participating in an occupational training program? Here, you would need to describe what you meant by unemployed, find work, participating, and training program. After you have defined these concepts, they can become your variables (Line 3).

A variable is a component of a phenomenon studied by a researcher. A variable can change, can vary, can be expressed as more than one value, or can be described by various values or categories. If it cannot change or be described in different categories it is not a variable, but rather a constant. Variables may be continuous or categorical. In the latter case, we often refer to them as categories or *attributes*.[12]

---

[12]*Attribute* is the term preferred by researchers using qualitative comparative analysis, and it works well for many categorical concepts. See Rihoux and Ragin (2009).

Few researchers in the social and behavioral sciences work with concepts that are easy to define, code, and measure. Therefore, to make them manageable, we have to use *indicators* or *operational definitions* of our concepts (Line 4 in Figure 1). There can be subtle distinctions between the two terms but it is also common to use them more or less interchangeably. An indicator is an easily identified and coded phenomenon that can be used to study a more abstract concept. Operational definitions describe how researchers will observe, code, and record a phenomenon. They describe the actions (operations) used to categorize or measure a variable. When you operationalize one of your variables you decide how you will recognize, categorize, and record it. Indicators and operational definitions all have the same function: to make variables or attributes concrete enough to be coded.

The concrete ways we code our data usually imply something substantive about what we are studying. How might the indicators or operational definitions be substantively related to the concept? As indicated in the bottom row of Figure 1, there are four ways. They could be components, symptoms, causes, or mere proxies.

- An indicator can be a *component*, part of the definition of the concept, as when many theorists see free elections as a definitional component of democracy, possibly along with other components. So, while you might well use free elections as an indicator of democracy, they are also a component. Such components can also be conditions of a concept. They may be sufficient conditions, necessary conditions, or a group of necessary conditions which are, together, sufficient.

- An indicator can be a *symptom* caused by the concept. This approach is the basis of the modern practice of structural equation modeling, but it is much older than that. For example, in a 19th-century sociological classic, Durkheim used changes in laws to trace changes in moral values.[13] He did this because laws—written codes—were easy to study. He did not think that laws were part of the definition (a component) of moral values. Rather, the two tended almost always to evolve together because, Durkheim believed, a society's moral values shaped its laws, at least in the long run. A society's laws were a symptom (indicator) of its moral values. This assertion was an important substantive assertion, not just a measurement convenience.

- An indicator can be a *cause* of the concept. For example, a standard definition of prejudice is: an irrational negative belief about someone or something in the face of evidence to the contrary. One indicator of prejudice is irrationality. That is because irrationality is a component of prejudice, *and* because irrationality causes prejudice.

- Finally, an indicator can be a mere *proxy*. Sometimes you cannot directly study the concept you are interested in, perhaps because it is too general or abstract. For example, the overall quality of medical services in a nation is a complex, multicomponent concept. But researchers interested in comparing medical services across nations have sometimes used a fairly simple proxy—infant mortality rate is probably the most common one.

---

[13] Durkheim (1893).

To sum up, let's look in a bit more detail at two examples. Intelligence testing is a familiar example, because the early history of measurement research was pioneered by psychology and educational testing, especially focused on the concept of intelligence. Intelligence cannot be studied directly. Rather, one studies its presumed *components* such as spatial reasoning and verbal ability. *Indicators* of these, such as scores on solving puzzles and on vocabulary tests, are often used as the operational definitions of the components. But there is much controversy in the study of intelligence. No one thinks that puzzle solving *is* intelligence; it is a mere indicator. But what about spatial reasoning? Is it an indicator, a higher-level indicator, perhaps, of the more general concept of intelligence? Or is spatial reasoning (like verbal ability) one of several components of intelligence? And in recent decades, a new dimension has been added to these classic debates: the concept of multiple intelligences as elaborated by Howard Gardner. He originally proposed seven intelligences and more recently added an eighth. They are spatial, linguistic, logical-mathematical, kinesthetic, musical, interpersonal, intrapersonal, and naturalist. Critics have claimed that, while this is a reasonable list of abilities, all abilities are not forms of intelligence. The debate goes on. While it might seem mostly about words, it is really about concepts and how we understand them, which has important practical implications (in education most obviously) as well as implications for the practice of research, especially coding and measuring our variables.

As in the field of intelligence and its components, in the study of democracy and its components, one's understanding of the concept leads directly to coding and measurement decisions. Intelligence is usually defined as a continuous variable. Democracy is usually defined as a categorical variable or an attribute. In studies of intelligence, the concept is defined in such a way that the indicators and components of intelligence, such as verbal ability, are never considered as simply present or absent. Intelligence *could be* defined categorically, but this is rare except in casual speech. Democracy *could be* defined by a score on a continuum, and some researchers actually do this, but it is more common to think of it as either present or absent. And almost all the indicators or components of democracy are defined categorically. For example, a nation either has free elections or it does not. Researchers often argue about how to define free elections, but they are seeking definitions that allow them to make categorical distinctions. In brief, *valid coding and measurement depend on the concepts*. That is or should be the rule, not the exception. When exceptions are made to that rule, the quality of the research never benefits.

What does it mean in practice to say that coding and measurement should depend on our understanding of concepts? Most importantly, it means that we should not twist concepts to make them fit the exigencies of data handling. Rather, we should construct our coding and measurement schemes to reflect our concepts.

Reliability is a tricky problem. Validity is very difficult. And conceptual analysis is extremely challenging. Because techniques of reliability are easier to discuss, we sometimes let them swamp attention to concepts. Techniques should be the handmaiden of concepts, not a distraction from thinking about them. There seems to be a tendency in research to brush past difficult concepts with a nod and a few quick sentences so that we can quickly move to the less problematic, but also less important, parts of the project, such as technical measurement issues or the practicalities of making observations. Among quantitative researchers, extreme operationalism is one strategy for replacing the difficult with the simple, but mostly by ducking the key issue. The most famous example is the phrase "IQ is what IQ tests measure," which means that you don't need to think about the concept because you've got an indicator. Among qualitative researchers one way to avoid difficult conceptual issues is simply to say "the researcher is the instrument," which means that you don't have to think about what's going on, but can just assume that it all somehow is taken care of inside the researcher's head. But if we believe that concepts refer to phenomena in the world, such as democracy or intelligence, we need to do better than that. We are arguing, in other words, for a realist understanding of concepts. They are not merely convenient labels. If that is all concepts were, there would not be much point in studying them.

Although data coding can be discussed generically as we have done in the above pages, many of the issues you are likely to encounter differ among specific designs. Table 1 briefly sketches some of those differences. You can see that many of these questions have been raised and discussed in the design chapters, illustrating once again how coding grows naturally out of design choices. To repeat, coding not only refers forward to analysis. It relates back to your project's roots in design.

By contrast, and to orient this discussion of data coding toward future steps in your research project, we offer Table 2. It lists what we think a researcher should *always* do in the area of coding and measurement. It sums up many of the points we have made in the above paragraphs. Such a list, offering generic advice, is possible because many problems of coding and measurement cut across all research traditions and designs.

TABLE 1. Typical Coding and Measurement Questions by Specific Design Types

Design type	Coding/measurement questions
Survey	What procedures do you use so that your questions capture your concepts? How do you know whether your respondents understand your questions? What do you do to determine whether your scales are reliable?
Interview	When do you use a comparatively structured or unstructured set of interview questions? When should you use multiple coders to code responses (and intercoder reliability) and/or software to generate your data codes?
Experimental	How do you code and measure treatments (categorically or continuously) and outcomes—behaviors, self-reports, or objective measures?
Observational research	When do you go into the field with theories in mind and when do you approach the site with as few preconceptions as possible? How do you structure your field notes? When do you use multiple coders (and intercoder reliability) and/or software to generate your data codes?
Archival research	When the data are precoded, do you recode existing codes?
Combined designs	When do you use multiple methods of coding and measurement, and when can the possible interactions of different coding methods cause conceptual or analysis problems?

TABLE 2. What Procedures Should You Always Use to Achieve the Reliable and Valid Coding and Measurement of Concepts and Indicators?

- Specify how your concepts are defined and how their components are related.
- Make coding and measurement dependent upon conceptual analysis rather than defining your concepts by what is convenient to study.
- Explain how your indicators relate to the general concepts (components, symptoms, cause, or necessary/sufficient conditions?).
- Decide how to code (names, ranks, numbers) *after* your conceptual work, not before.
- Justify your coding/measurement choices (for example, why have you categorized a continuous variable?).
- Explain the validity of your observations, codes, and/or measurements and specify the steps you have taken to handle threats to validity.
- Use a checklist to ensure you have not forgotten any important threat to validity.
- Explicitly discuss the reliability of observations, codes, and/or measurements.
- Consider all types of reliability relevant to your study (e.g., both test–retest and internal consistency).

CODING DECISIONS SHAPE ANALYTIC OPTIONS

Your coding choices will limit the range of the types of analytic techniques that are available to you. While all analytic methods can be used with all designs, not all analytic methods are possible once your data have been coded. The distinction between quantitative and qualitative methods was not of great moment in the design chapters, but it will be in most discussions of analysis. That is because analytic methods are tied to the methods of coding that have been used. The ties do not always bind permanently. Data can be recoded to make them align with a particular analytic method you wish to use. Initial data coding and recoding are not absolutely determinative even at the analysis stage, because some kinds of data—textual, categorical, and ranked—can be studied with either quantitative or qualitative techniques.

It remains true, however, that types of data, and the way you code them, do importantly limit the range of appropriate techniques. In some respects the general procedures from initial coding through analysis are quite parallel when working with qualitative and quantitative data. This is illustrated in Figure 2. We see that both start out with initial coding. More fine-grained, advanced, or higher-order work is needed on the coded data to get it ready for analysis. Whether one calls this "measurement," as is common in research on quantitative data, or "axial coding," to borrow a phrase from grounded theory, the procedure is first, with initial coding, to get data ready for collection, sorting, and recording and then to prepare the data thus collected for further analysis.

We have been talking as though there were only two ways data are coded: verbally and numerically. A third type is visual data, which includes examples such as maps, satellite images, videotapes, and X-rays. In part because these tend not to be used as extensively in most social sciences as verbal and numerical data (geography is an exception), and in part because visual data are often converted into verbal and/or numerical data, coverage of visual data in this book is not as extensive as it is for words and numbers. Visual data mostly enter the discussion in the analysis stages with the graphic

Quantitative data

Initial coding → Measurement → Analysis

Qualitative data

Initial coding → Higher-order coding → Analysis

FIGURE 2. From initial coding through analysis.

representation of verbal and numerical data such as concept maps, causal diagrams, and various graphing techniques. Numerous methods of visual analysis, very prominent in network analysis, for example, will also be important in our later discussions of analysis methods.

That said, verbal and numerical codes and methods of analysis are still the master categories. Some differences among them are obvious. When your research questions require you to deal with many cases, the shorthand of a numerical summary is very handy; words can be clumsy. By contrast, when studying single cases and small groups, numerical coding can be silly. Even when your data are numerical, if your group is small, often only simple counts are appropriate. A parent with two daughters and one son is not likely to say "fully 67% of my children are female." But one of us served on a dissertation committee in which the following sentence appeared in an early draft: "Of the 14 interviewees, 28.6% thought that the treatment was unfair, while 57.1% believed it was fair and 14.3% had no opinion." It could have been more reasonable to say: four thought it was unfair, eight thought it was fair, and two had no opinion. Or would it be better simply to say "Most thought it was fair"? Judgment is always involved in these decisions.

Direct observations can be recorded as words or numbers, and the two are often merged. You can count events that you have identified and coded verbally: "In a typical hour on the playground, 42% of the interactions among boys involved physical aggression." This statement refers to qualitative judgments that you have observed, qualitatively categorized, then counted and numerically analyzed. Sandelowski and colleagues called this practice "quantitizing,"[14] by which they mean converting qualitative data into quantitative—usually words into numbers. It is a common practice and one that is often necessary in mixed or multimethod research. Transformations of data of one type into another can make it possible to merge data into one dataset that can be analyzed. Quantitizing data or its opposite, "qualitizing" data, raises more complicated issues than might at first seem likely. First there is the question: what are data? They often do not start out as, and are not inherently, qualitative or qualitative. We obtain data by coding our observations (visual or aural) into symbols (numbers, words, or other symbols), which we can then analyze. We often go back and forth between qualitative and quantitative. For example, to count the number of times something happens, we usually begin by qualitatively categorizing cases. If something is in the category, we count it; if it is not we don't. After we count instances of a phenomenon, and analyze the resulting data, we then often conclude by making a qualitative judgment—for example, that the data are meaningful, important, or significant.

---

[14]Sandelowski, Voils, and Knafl (2009).

While quantitizing and qualitizing are both common, one type of qualitizing is almost always a bad idea. In a now-classic little article on the "cost of dichotomization," Jacob Cohen explained why this frequent practice constitutes unjustifiable "data mutilation."[15] Before the widespread availability of computer data analysis, when calculations were done by hand, dichotomizing (or otherwise categorizing) continuous data was often the researcher's only practical alternative. But "this practice of our grandparents" (they are now, a generation later, our great-grandparents) should never be followed. It amounts to throwing away the majority of your data. Cohen focused on dichotomizing prior to analysis, but it is also a relevant topic when planning data coding. When it makes sense to code your data categorically or qualitatively, by all means do it. But, if you code your data categorically, you can never go back. You can always categorize continuous data, but you can't usually "continuize" categorically coded data. If you have naturally continuous data—income, age, numbers of students in schools, populations of towns, and so forth—*never* categorize it at the initial coding and data collection stage. You may want to do so at the analysis stage, and that can be part of a reasonable analysis strategy, but it is *always* a potentially grave mistake when collecting data and assigning initial codes.

This is an unusually strong note on which to conclude. The tone is much less conciliatory than most of our recommendations have been. We hasten to add that the strength of that recommendation has nothing to do with a preference for quantitative or qualitative data as such. Reasoning about evidence, whether for purposes of explanation, prediction, understanding, causality, or generalization, uses the same conceptual tools whether the data are names, ranks, numbers, or pictures. Whatever their form, data are mute on these issues. The data do not speak for themselves. You have to speak for the data regardless of the symbols used to collect and record the data. But the way you handle the data can either limit what you can say or open up possibilities.

We have not been shy about stating, sometimes quite forcefully, what we believe researchers ought to do, the order in which they ought to do it, and why we think so. Our checklists and the summary tables with which we end each chapter and in which we give a roll call of when to use what are, however, guidelines and recommendations—not rules. It is a big step from these rosters of suggestions to rules of method. Indeed, we think that looking for rules is usually the wrong way to go about planning research. Rather than the one best thing to do, we think of a suite of more or less advisable things to do. Our guidelines and recommendations are meant to enhance and encourage choices because, we think, to borrow a phrase from a different context, a choice is a terrible thing to waste. Even the order in which we structure the choices—from design, through identifying cases to study, to research ethics and finally data coding—is more a matter of advice than advocacy.

Whatever our specific recommendations, the general attitude of mind that motivates them is methodological pluralism. One consequence of this pluralism is that it increases the range of choices. That range is broad and is increased exponentially when one is looking to combine multiple methods. And pluralism itself is pluralistic—there is a plurality of different types of pluralism.[16] We know that researchers, perhaps especially beginning researchers, are often eager to get to work. We would never discourage

---

[15] Cohen (1983).

[16] Reiss (2009).

enthusiasm, and we know that methodological pluralism can seem like putting off the time when you can get down to work. But in research, getting to work means thinking long and hard about options in design, case selection, and ethical behavior. The fact that we advocate using multiple methods (see especially Chapters 6, 12, and 18), despite the exacerbation of the choice problem that doing so entails, is an indicator of how seriously we mean it. Any increase in the already large set of choices is a cost, but also an opportunity. That is the most important lesson this book tries to convey. Little matters as much as exercising your intellect when selecting research methods. Choices based on habit, whim, or authority will be good ones only if you are lucky. We think that methodological choices are more likely to be effective if they are based on systematic deliberation. We have tried to give researchers suggestions and guidelines for the sometimes daunting task of selecting their research methods.

SUGGESTIONS FOR FURTHER READING

The same sources relevant to this concluding section can also be consulted for our earlier discussions of the relations of theory, research questions, and designs in the Introduction to Part I. Both sections deal with the conceptual (almost epistemological) parts of research design. The standard model or paradigm is still often referred to as the *hypothetico-deductive* model. In this model, you begin with a theory; from the theory you deduce a testable hypothesis; then you test it using the techniques of null hypothesis significance testing (NHST). The best account we know of this approach is Aneshensel's *Theory-Based Data Analysis for the Social Sciences* (2002). A different approach, one that we think has a chance of becoming the new dominant paradigm, uses *multiple* working hypotheses to conduct *multiple model inference*. The models are compared and ranked according to the strength of the evidence for each—not rejected or "failed to rejected" one at a time. The most accessible introduction to this information-theoretic approach is *Model Based Inference in the Life Sciences* (2008) by David Anderson. The big problem with NHST, Anderson argues, is that when using it you test a hypothesis you don't care about; NHST, he says, is "only of historical interest at this stage," except perhaps in small RCTs.

Discussions of validity are, if anything, too available. Because of the proliferation of often abstruse discussions, Adcock and Collier's article "Measurement Validity: A Shared Standard for Qualitative and Quantitative Research" (2001) is especially welcome. It provides an excellent review of the pullulation of types of (and dozens of labels for) validity and makes a strong case that it is possible to bridge the gap between the ways validity is understood when studying qualitative versus quantitative data. Shadish, Cook, and Campbell's classic *Experimental and Quasi-Experimental Designs for Generalized Causal Inference* (2002) is valuable in many ways, not the least of which is their lists of threats to validity, which are especially relevant to experimental research. Creswell's *Research Design: Qualitative, Quantitative, and Mixed Methods Approaches* (2003) expands on their lists to include forms of research besides experimental and quasi-experimental designs.

Some of the best work wrestling with the conceptual issues of the relation of research on qualitative and quantitative data has been done in political science. King, Keohane, and Verba's *Designing Social Inquiry: Scientific Inference in Qualitative Research* (1994) started an important and enormously influential discussion; their volume stressed the similarity of the two styles of research, but at the cost, their critics claim, of subsuming qualitative *under* quantitative. Ten years later the debate continued in Brady and Collier's edited collection *Rethinking Social Inquiry: Diverse Tools, Shared Standards* (2004). Reading the two books together is exceptionally thought provoking.

Finally, Goertz, in *Social Science Concepts: A User's Guide* (2006), shows that it is not only theoretically possible, but practically possible, to think about concepts in ways that transcend the qual–quant divide—and it is refreshing to do so. His work was very important to our thinking about the relations among concepts, variables, and indicators.

Glossary

We have aimed for simple, generic, and nonpartisan definitions in this glossary, but it is probably impossible to avoid offending someone. That is because no aspect of research methodology is uncontroversial; this includes the "proper" use of terms. Among researchers, as well as other social groups, the politics of identity formation can be broad and deep and may sometimes extend even to remarkably strong feelings about which words to use and whether they should be capitalized or hyphenated. We try to pay attention to such nuances, but ultimately we define terms in this glossary in ways that will be most useful to readers of this book, that is, we define them as we use them in the volume.

Our glossary is a targeted reference resource, not a general-purpose methodological dictionary.[1] Rather, as in the rest of the book, we concentrate on aspects of the definitions that are relevant to selecting research designs and methods. We do not repeat the full discussion of every term used in the text, because to do so would merely rearrange the entire book into alphabetized chunks. The focus is on key terms that readers will encounter in more than one place in this book. If a term occurs only once, either it is defined where it is used or, in our judgment, it is too elementary for the typical reader to need a definition. For discussions of terms fuller than those provided in the glossary, readers should refer to the pages identified in the index and to other sources. Finally, terms used in definitions that are themselves defined in the glossary are indicated by italics.

Action research Investigations designed to learn how to accomplish a social goal. Program *evaluation research*, especially when conducted in collaboration with research participants, is a common form of action research.

Anonymity A guarantee of research participants' privacy. Anonymity means that participants cannot be identified because their identities are unknown. Anonymity is a stronger privacy safeguard than *confidentiality*.

Archival populations Documents or other records from which a researcher samples. One example would be the research reports selected for use in a *meta-analysis*. Another would be a database archive from which a researcher selects cases and variables.

---

[1] For that, see Vogt and Johnson (2011).

Archival research   Studies conducted by researchers who study data that they do not generate themselves—data that exist prior to the beginning of the investigation. Archival research data may be collected from numerical records, verbal documents, or visual artifacts, including those found on websites. When data are collected from database archives, the research is often called *secondary data analysis*.

Between-subjects design   A study in which comparisons are made between groups of subjects, such as members of the control and experimental groups in an experiment. Also called between-participants study, especially when the participants are persons. (Compare *within-subjects design*.)

Bias   Error in collecting or analyzing data that systematically over- or underestimates what the researcher is interested in studying. (Compare *random error*.) A biased method of sampling for a survey would be to survey only your friends; in an experiment, a biased procedure would be having participants volunteer to be in either the treatment or the comparison group. (See *selection bias*.) The most common way to eliminate bias is to use methods of randomization, such as *random sampling* or *random assignment*.

Blinding   A procedure used to reduce *bias* by keeping participants, researchers, and/or data analysts ignorant of (blind to) a treatment. Double blinding occurs when both participants and researchers do not know which treatment is administered. Triple blinding includes data analysts in the circle of ignorance. Blinding is rare in nonexperimental research.

Blocks   Groups to which experimental participants are assigned; they are similar to, and have the same purpose as, strata in sampling for survey research. (See *stratified sampling*.) A "blocking" variable is one the researcher wishes to control. The participants are placed into groups determined by scores on the blocking variable. Participants with similar scores are assigned *at random* to blocks. Each block is then given a different experimental treatment. In an experiment with one control and two treatment groups, three blocks are needed. With only one treatment and one control, the blocks become *matched pairs*. Blocking is important when the sample size is small. The smaller the sample, the less likely it is that *random assignment* will equalize the control and experimental groups.

Case   A generic term for something a researcher studies. Cases can be persons, institutions, events, or any other phenomena examined by a researcher. Data about cases are recorded in rows (which are also called "records") in spreadsheets and statistical packages; *variables* are recorded in columns. (See *case study, participant, subject, unit of analysis*.)

Case study   Intensive examination of one phenomenon or a small number of instances of a phenomenon. The goal in a case study is deep understanding of a small number of cases rather than broad knowledge of data about variables drawn from many cases. Depending on the research question, a case study may be descriptive, exploratory, or explanatory, and will usually employ a combination of methods, including observation, interviews, and *archival research*.

Causal process or mechanism A link that explains a causal relation among phenomena or a clarification of how a cause operates. For example, if smaller classes caused increases in student learning, a causal process would explain how they did so—perhaps by giving teachers more time to work with individual students, allowing for different methods of instruction, improving teacher morale, making the classroom more welcoming to students, or some combination of these. The process or processes at work could differ at different instructional levels—from the elementary grades through graduate school. Causal processes can be uncovered in a wide variety of ways, from experimentation to naturalistic observation.

Cause A phenomenon that leads to a change in another phenomenon. Some researchers see the study of causation as their central purpose; others believe that this has no legitimate place in social research. We find the assumption of causation to be indispensable both in research and in day-to-day lived experience. But neither causation in general nor any particular cause can be proven. Proof belongs only to the abstract and purely conceptual worlds of mathematics and formal logic. In studying the empirical social world, we make do with approximations of proofs; these usually take the form of evidence for the degree of likelihood of causal relations between phenomena.

Cluster sampling A type of sampling used when it is impossible or impractical to sample a population directly, often because there is no good list (or *sampling frame*) of the population's individual members. For example, there is no usable list of all college students in the United States, but a list of all colleges is easy to obtain. Colleges can be treated as clusters of students. First one would sample colleges (clusters) and then, within colleges, students. Cluster sampling is also called multistage or multilevel sampling, and it is very widely used. (Compare *group randomization*.)

Cohort study A cohort is a segment of a population, members of which have some characteristic in common, often age. For example, all U.S. citizens born in 1990 are a cohort. A cohort study investigates the same group (cohort) over time, but not necessarily the same individual members of the cohort. (Compare *panel study* and *cross-sectional study*.)

Combined research designs Any use of more than one research design to study the same phenomena. The concept of combined design usually, but not necessarily, includes combining methods of coding and analysis. (Compare *mixed methods research* and *multimethod research*.)

Comparative case study research Systematically investigating in depth a small number of instances of a phenomenon in order to draw conclusions about the phenomenon. The two basic approaches are (1) to study cases that are different in many ways but have one thing in common and (2) to study cases that are similar in many ways but differ in one important respect.

Confidence intervals Margins of error for an estimate. Confidence intervals define the range of values with a known probability (called confidence "level") of including the true population value. The wider the confidence interval, the higher the confidence level will be; the narrower the interval, the lower the confidence level. The tradeoff is between precision (narrowness) and certainty (level). Decisions about the tradeoff between interval width (margins of error) and confidence levels (degrees of certainty) are usually made using the 95% and 99% levels, but this is merely traditional. Different levels may be used if, for example, you wanted a more precise estimate (narrower interval or margins of error) and were willing to accept a lower confidence level (e.g., 80 or 90%) in order to get it. The upper and lower values of a confidence interval are called "confidence limits."

Confidentiality A means of protecting the privacy of research participants by concealing their identities and shielding links to the data pertaining to them. This protection is less strong than *anonymity*, where the researcher does not know participants' identities and cannot link their data to them. When the information is confidential, the researcher knows but promises not to reveal private information. This promise may be legally limited. Unlike journalists and their sources, most researchers and the people they interview or the institutions they study are not protected by constitutional guarantees.

Confirmatory research Investigations aimed at answering questions concerning the relevance or applicability of a generalization, usually a *theory*. The research aims to confirm or disconfirm a specific generalization. (Compare *exploratory research* and *descriptive research*.)

Conflicts of interest Ethical and legal problems that arise when the interests of researchers are at odds with the possibility of objective, unbiased research and/or with the interests or rights of research participants. The first type of conflict of interest is often defined legally, especially with federally funded research. Rules may be quite specific about, for example, how much stock you can legally own in a company that stands to benefit from your research. But conflicts of interest are much broader than those covered by formal regulations. While some social researchers may own stock in the companies they study or may develop products (assessment tools, for example) that are investigated in evaluation research, this is comparatively rare in the social and behavioral sciences. In social research, the most common conflicts of interest are probably those between the interests of researchers and those of the research participants. Covert observations, experimental deception, and violations of privacy might sometimes be useful for the researcher's purposes, but they are rarely in the best interests of the people or institutions being investigated. Conflict of interest rules also apply to what researchers must disclose on *informed consent* forms.

Consent See *informed consent, harm,* and *privacy.* The relative importance of these three key ethical concerns tends to vary from one design and project to another.

Content analysis Usually, the conversion of verbal texts into quantitative data, through methods such as determining the frequency of words or phrases or characterizing relationships among words and phrases in texts. It can be performed by hand or by using computer programs. (Traditional methods of analyzing the content of texts by reading and thinking about them is also sometimes called "content analysis," but some purists who strongly object to the use of that term label it "non-computerized analysis.")

Convenience sample A method of selecting phenomena (places, events, persons, documents, and so on) to study based solely on what is easy for the researcher rather than on the relevance or representativeness of the sample. Feasibility is always a consideration in sampling, but feasibility is not merely convenience. (Compare *judgment sample* and *purposive sampling*.)

Counterbalancing A method for dealing with the effects of order on the delivery of experimental treatments. When the order in which participants receive experimental treatments could affect their reactions to those treatments, counterbalancing means presenting treatments in random orders to ensure that you can distinguish between order effects and treatment effects.

Covariate A variable other than the independent variable that is correlated with ("covaries" with) the dependent variable, but that is not the focus of the research. When attempting to make causal inferences, researchers try to control for covariates and thus eliminate them as possible explanations. In experiments, this control is accomplished mainly by *random assignment*.

Covert research A study conducted without the knowledge of the persons or institutions being studied. *Naturalistic observational* research is almost by definition covert. *Participant observation* may be covert, as when a researcher is hired by an institution and pretends to be an ordinary employee, but has taken the job only in order to study the institution. Because of the legal and ethical implications of covert observation, this type of research is comparatively rarer than it was before *IRB* regulations.

Crossed design A type of *within-subjects design* used in assigning cases or participants to experimental conditions. In the crossed design, the subjects experience each experimental condition, and scores are compared before and after each treatment. In choosing a crossed design, the researcher determines that there is a research advantage in using a small sample and repeated measures. (The main alternative is the *between-subjects* or nested design, in which the participants are divided into groups, with each group experiencing only one experimental treatment and results are compared across the groups.)

Cross-sectional study An investigation of a "slice," or cross-section, of a population at a single point in time rather than over time. (Compare *cohort study* and *panel study*.)

Data mining Tunneling through large databases in order to find interesting or important relationships or patterns among variables. Data miners often use statistical techniques, such as principal components analysis, to find patterns in the data. Because of the joint emergence of powerful computer programs and huge databases, data mining research has become increasingly important, particularly in policy research.

Descriptive research   Investigations aimed at answering research questions that focus on describing phenomena thoroughly and in depth rather than investigating causal relationships or testing theories. (Compare *exploratory research* and *confirmatory research*.)

Design   The term is used to denote either the general method of data collection (such as surveys, interviews, experiments, etc.) or an overall plan for conducting a research project that includes methods of data collection, sampling, ethics, data coding/measurement, and strategies for analyzing and interpreting data. In this book, we have used the term both ways.

Effect size   Any of several measures of the magnitude of the effect of one variable on another. Effect size measures are usually reported in standard deviation units; this enables researchers to compare them across studies and populations.

Epistemology   The study of the origins of knowledge and the justifications of knowledge claims. Research methodology can be thought of as a type of applied epistemology. The strength of the ties between epistemological and methodological principles is a matter of some dispute. Opinions range from those who believe that epistemological beliefs *determine* methodological choices to those who find epistemological discussion mostly incidental to their research.

Ethical research   Ethics is a branch of applied philosophy, which is related to conduct in specific areas. Ethical research is only indirectly a matter of normative ethical philosophy, which focuses on what people should believe more than on what they should do. Research ethics can be defined as good conduct toward others in the course of conducting research. The relevant others are research participants, colleagues, and the broader society. We focus mainly on research participants, and we categorize the relevant areas of conduct toward them as ensuring participants' informed *consent*, avoiding *harm* to them, and preserving their *privacy*.

Evaluation research   Also known as program evaluation research (and in some circles as assessment), evaluation research involves investigations of the implementation, effectiveness, and impact of social programs or clinical interventions. Evaluation researchers also often gauge the effectiveness of products (both physical and psychometric) and personnel, including personnel training programs in companies and other organizations. Most designs and sampling methods discussed in this book have been used as tools for evaluation research.

Event-history analysis (EHA)   A form of survey research in which respondents are asked to recall biographical data concerning their past experiences. (A subtype of EHA used in medical research is called "survival analysis.") EHA combines some of the advantages of longitudinal methods such as *panel studies* with the ease of *cross-sectional surveys* in which data can be collected at one point in time.

Experimenter effect   Any *bias* in how participants respond to experimental treatments caused not solely by the treatments, but also by the experimenters who administer them. The effects can be due to the characteristics of the experimenters (e.g., gender, ethnicity) or to the experimenters' expectations.

Explanatory research Studies aimed at understanding or clarifying phenomena rather than predicting them. It is often easier to identify a pattern or predict an outcome (such as higher rates of graduation among females) than it is to understand it. An explanatory research question and project would attempt to elucidate the reasons behind the pattern or outcome. (Compare *causal process*.)

Exploratory research A type of study conducted in order to try to discover relationships, find patterns, or generate ideas rather than to test theories. (Compare *confirmatory research*.)

Field experiment An experiment conducted in a natural setting (the "field") rather than in a laboratory, which is an unnaturally pure setting. The researcher forgoes control over the research setting in hopes that the gains in *external validity* that may come from experimenting in the real world will offset the loss of control that comes from moving out of the laboratory.

Focus group interviews Often referred to as "focus groups," these interviews are conducted with around 8 to 12 individuals who have a common interest or trait which they discuss under the guidance of a researcher. The method is thought to be more effective for examining some kinds of topics, perhaps especially those related to small-group interactions. Survey researchers often use focus groups to learn how they might improve their survey questions.

Freedom of Information Act (FOIA) Passed in 1966, the FOIA provides procedures that individuals, including researchers, can use to obtain government information. It has been successfully used by some researchers (and many journalists) to gain access to documents and data that government agencies would otherwise not have released. Several state governments (e.g., California, Illinois, Michigan, New York, and Texas) have passed parallel state versions of the FOIA.

Full-text searching When you search for articles to read for your review of the research literature, most electronic databases allow you to search titles, abstracts, and lists of keywords. With full-text searching, as its name implies, the researcher can search entire research reports, not merely summaries and titles. It is probable that full-text searching will become the standard method as soon as sources such as PsychINFO and SocioFile make it available.

Grounded theory A method for inductively constructing theories based (mainly) on interview data. The term *grounded theory* is often used loosely to mean any theory based on analysis of qualitative data. It is also used more precisely to refer to the set of methods outlined by Glaser and Strauss in their 1967 book *The Discovery of Grounded Theory*, involving a process of coding, categorizing, and conceptualizing. This work and others built upon its ideas have been very influential in research methodology dealing with qualitative data.

Group randomization Random assignment to control and experimental groups done at the group rather than the individual level; groups are assigned rather than individuals. This is commonly done in *quasi-experiments* and in *evaluation research*. In most forms of *field research* it is easier to find groups than to identify unassociated individuals. Because most common analytic techniques are based on the assumption that individual randomizing has been conducted, serious analytic adjustments have to be made when group randomization is used.

Harm In the context of research ethics, harm refers to injury (physical, psychological, financial, reputational, etc.) to participants in the research. Harm may occur through breaches of *privacy* in the reporting of results as well as in the actual conduct of the research. It is important to remember that participants' definitions of harm may vary locally and culturally. Key considerations in weighing the danger of doing harm in the conduct of research are how likely the injury is to occur and how serious it is likely to be. The potential harms might range from likely but minor to unlikely but grave.

History effect An event, not under the researcher's control, that occurs during the course of a study which can influence the research outcomes. History effects make it difficult, and often impossible, to interpret the effects of an independent variable. The longer the life of the study, the more likely it is that history effects will occur.

Informant A person who provides a researcher (often an anthropologist) with key information about a culture or a social group. The term is also used to describe participants in interview research. Informants may also be those participants who lead researchers to other participants, such as in *snowball sampling*.

Informed consent In the context of research ethics, informed consent refers to the willing joining of the research project by participants who have full knowledge of the risks and rewards of the project. The concept of informed consent is simple. Implementation can be more complicated. Problems with ensuring informed consent include the fact that the research design may require that the participants not be told before the study begins which treatment they will receive or that they be unaware of the purpose of the study. (See *blinding*.) Also, determining how much knowledge research participants need in order to be fully informed can be far from simple and open to different interpretations.

Institutional review board (IRB) A committee to review research proposals that must be in place at any institution in the United States that receives federal funds—which is nearly all colleges and universities. The IRB's purpose is to protect human research participants from possible harms that could result from the research. Research must be approved by an IRB before it is conducted. IRBs are much less involved in monitoring research projects to ensure that they conform to the procedures stipulated in the approved proposal than they are in prior review.

Interaction effect A joint or combined effect of two (or more) variables on a third. The combined effect is different from the simple sum of the two variables. With an interaction the total is more than (or different from) the sum of the parts. For example, if tutoring alone improved students' scores on a test by 10% and if extra studying alone improved scores by 10%, but extra studying and tutoring *together* improved scores by 30%, the bonus would be due do an interaction effect. Investigators often undertake *combined research designs* hoping for such an interaction effect on the knowledge they obtain. Interaction effects are not always positive, of course; an obvious example is dangerous drug interactions.

Interviewer effects   Influences on the way persons being interviewed answer questions that are caused by the characteristics of the interviewers (e.g., age, gender, ethnicity). These effects can be important in face-to-face survey research as well as in interviews. When more than one interviewer is involved in a study, interviewer effects can become critical threats to *reliability* unless care is taken to assure consistency in interview techniques and presentation. (Compare *experimenter effects*, which have been studied more often than interviewer effects.)

Interview protocol   A list of questions and instructions for how to ask them that interviewers use to guide their work. The questions and the instructions can range from very general to highly specific.

IRB   Abbreviation for *institutional review board*.

Judgment sample   Also called a *purposive sample*, a judgment sample uses the researcher's knowledge and reasoning to select participants for interviews, observations, surveys, or experiments. In surveys and experiments, judgment sampling is often used as a substitute for formal statistical methods of sampling. In interviews and observations, judgment sampling is often more effective than random statistical methods. (Note: a judgment sample is not a *convenience sample*!)

Latin squares   Like *counterbalancing*, the Latin squares method is used to eliminate the effects of the order of the treatments in an experiment by randomly assigning the order of treatments. It is an extension of the randomized blocks design. (See *blocks*.) It is used to allocate treatments to participants—or, looking at it the other way around, it is a way to assign participants to treatments; the two are equivalent.

Matched pairs design   This method is used when an experimenter believes that participants have characteristics that may affect their reaction to a treatment. Participants are matched on those characteristics, often on the basis of scores on a pretest. After the pairs are determined, one member of each pair is assigned at random to the experimental group; the other is assigned to the control group. Groups receiving the same treatments are called *blocks*.

Member checking   In observational or interview research, submitting your data and/ or conclusions to participants ("members") so that they can check to make sure you have not misrepresented them. Member checking is more commonly done with data, such as interview transcripts, than with interpretations and conclusions. Most interview and observational researchers agree that member checking is a good idea, but opinions differ about how extensive it should be—whether it should extend to conclusions and interpretations, for example.

Meta-analysis A type of *research synthesis* in which the research is summarized and analyzed using *quantitative* techniques, especially standardized *effect size* measures. Meta-analysts often attempt to review the total population of studies on a topic, rather than to sample from the population.

Mini-meta-analysis A meta-analysis conducted on a subset of research reports, specifically those that contain the data necessary to do a meta-analysis. It is frequently the case that many of the research reports on your topic are not appropriate for a meta-analysis, but you can still conduct a mini-meta-analysis on those that are appropriate. Often the results of this mini-meta-analysis can be incorporated into a research synthesis that combines studies presenting quantitative and qualitative data.

Mixed methods research Also called "mixed research." Combining methods typically used with quantitative and with qualitative data. A common example is combining, in one study, quantitative coding and analysis of responses to survey questions on a topic with qualitative coding and analysis of responses to interview questions on the same topic—often asked of the same participants.

Model An abstract representation of a real phenomenon. The model is meant to depict the phenomenon and to simulate it—graphically, statistically, or verbally. Usually, the purpose of building a model is to test it. The hope is that what one learns by testing a model is to some extent applicable to reality, often as an explanatory tool. A well-known quotation about models by George Box is "All models are wrong, but some are useful."

Multimethod research Also called "combined research" in this book. Research that unites in one project different designs, sampling techniques, and/or methods of coding and analysis. As with *mixed methods research*, the goal is to improve understanding by combining the strengths of various methods. The main difference is that mixed methods research focuses on crossing the quant–qual divide. Multimethod researchers might also do this, but are equally interested in combining all methods, whether or not they are thought of as quantitative or qualitative. For example, combining quantitative data gathered from surveys and from experiments or combining qualitative data from interviews and from document analysis would be *multi*method research, but not *mixed* methods research.

Natural experiment A study of a phenomenon that has occurred naturally, without a researcher's intervention, but that approximates assignment to treatment and comparison groups. Natural experiments are particularly important when practical or ethical limits render impossible unnatural experiments (those that take place in an artificially pure laboratory). For example, if the topic is the effects of attending school versus not attending, researchers cannot randomly assign some students to the attend-school group (treatment) and others to the stay-home group (comparison). But the typical cycle of the school year provides an approximation of a *repeated-measures* experiment. Students attend school from September through May and then stop from July through August and then begin again. This allows for assessing the effects of the treatment (attending school) versus the comparison (not attending in the summer).

Naturalistic observation   A method of study that stresses investigating individual and social life in its natural settings, without intervention by a researcher. The goal is to study life as it occurs naturally, when it is not being studied. This kind of investigation is necessarily covert research. Because of ethical considerations and *IRB* regulations, it is rare today to be able to conduct this kind of research except in public settings where people have no reasonable expectation of privacy—and some interventionist IRBs make even this difficult.

Nested sample/nested variable   The phrases are used in several contexts. In nested sampling, used in combined designs, a sample is selected for one part of the study, and a subset of this sample is used in another part of the study. A nested variable is one located inside another, as cities are nested in counties and counties in states. Such variables are often examined in multilevel models. In experimental research, nested is the opposite of a *crossed design*.

Nonresponse bias   The term is most often used in survey research to describe the type of bias that occurs when respondents do not answer questions. It is also a problem in other forms of research (interviews and experiments), in which participants may not respond to all questions. Nonresponse leads to bias when those not answering are not a representative subgroup of the sample. They are probably not representative, and the researcher usually cannot determine whether they are representative or not.

Objective data   The idea of objective data is highly contested, so finding a definition on which all can agree is difficult, or perhaps impossible. The basic distinction is parallel to that between fact and opinion, with facts being objective and opinions being *subjective data*. Objective data are "objects" that exist independently of anyone's desires or beliefs. Some researchers deny that such objects exist. We have used the term *objective* in this book to indicate data that can be confirmed externally, that do not depend on reports of research participants. A person's broken finger is an objective fact; impartial observers can agree that it is broken. The degree of pain the person with the broken finger feels is subjective. The pain is undoubtedly real, but there is nothing for external observers to observe; they can only ask, "How much does it hurt?"

Operationalization of a variable   Also called "operational definition" of a variable. A description of the ways researchers will identify, observe, code, and measure a variable. Disagreement among researchers can sometimes be traced to the fact that they have operationalized variables differently. An otherwise good research study can be undermined by poor operationalization of variables.

Opportunity sampling   Taking advantage of opportunities in the course of your research to identify research participants to sample. Opportunity sampling is not *convenience sampling*. Convenience sampling is doing what's easy; opportunity sampling is being alert and flexible enough to recognize a chance to improve on your initial sampling plan.

Order effects   Experimental outcomes that occur when there is more than one treatment and the order of the treatments influences the outcomes. Similarly, in survey research, the order in which questions are asked can influence how respondents answer them. In both cases, the solution is random assignment—of the order of treatments or of the order in which the questions are asked. See *counterbalancing* and *survey experiment*.

Outlier   Loosely, any participant or case that is very unusual. A nation with a radically high rate of suicide might be called an outlier. In quantitative research, an outlier is often defined as a value or score that is three or more standard deviations above or below the mean. Whether outliers are defined quantitatively or qualitatively, they raise problems for researchers—and sometimes provide the best opportunities for interesting work.

Panel study   Survey research in which a group of people (called a *panel*) is surveyed two or more times. Sometimes called a true longitudinal study/survey.

Parallel samples   A term used to describe different samples that are selected from the same population. Often used in combined designs. (Compare *cohort study*.)

Participant   A generic term for something a researcher studies, best applied to people and their groups or organizations. It is used most widely in experiments and other designs (such as program evaluations) that entail the active involvement of the persons or institutions or programs being studied. "Participant" implies willing, informed, and active involvement in the research. For types of research in which willing involvement is not applicable—as when the objects of study are events or texts or historical trends or demographic patterns—*case* may be a more useful term. And "subject" is still widely used by federal agencies that regulate research.

Participant observation   A type of research in which the investigator participates in the group or organization being studied. Today, the researcher usually informs the group that he or she is an observer as well as a participant. Covert or "under cover" participant observation was once fairly common, but has been all but "IRBed" out of existence in social research, although not in investigative journalism.

Population   The group the researcher wants to describe or make generalizations about. Also called "target population." After selecting the population, the researcher samples from it and uses the data from the sample to describe the population or make generalizations about it. The sampling may be formal and statistically guided, as in *random sampling* in a survey, or shaped more by the researcher's judgment, as in selecting cases for a comparative case study.

Positivism   A philosophical position, much discussed in research methodology (especially by those who denounce the position), that the path to true knowledge lies in positive verification, usually through applying the scientific method. The term is mostly used vaguely except by historians describing groups such as followers of Comte in the early 19th century or members of the Vienna Circle in the early 20th. Few people today call themselves "positivists," but many people are so labeled by others. This name-calling mostly involves accusations of "scientism," defined as an excessive faith in the value of science.

Pragmatism   In research methodology, pragmatism is a philosophical position that judges knowledge claims by how useful they are to the community of researchers and users of knowledge. Pragmatism leads to a standard for judging research methods: the more a research method fosters growth in usable knowledge, the better the method. A poor method would constrict the growth of usable knowledge.

Privacy   A key component of research ethics that involves ensuring that participants' identities will be kept anonymous and/or confidential and that the data about them will be handled and saved in ways that prevent access by unauthorized persons. Most harm to participants that comes about as a result of research studies in the social sciences is due to violations of privacy.

Probability sampling   A method of selecting cases (individuals, cities, events, etc.) in which each case has a known probability of being selected for inclusion in the study. Because the probabilities are known, techniques of inferential statistics can be used to generalize from samples to populations. At some stage in probability sampling, random sampling must be used. In nonprobability sampling, as the name indicates, the probability of inclusion is not known. When the sample probabilities are not known, using inferential statistics to generalize about populations is technically inappropriate, although quite common.

Program evaluation   Using research methods to determine the implementation processes and effects of a project, policy, or program. It is usually based on a program theory of how a policy or intervention should create an effect, and it often employs a *combined research design*. (See *evaluation research*.)

Propensity score matching (PSM)   A form of *matched pairs* most often used when random assignment of the pairs has not been possible, as in a *quasi-experiment*. PSM combines scores on multiple variables into an overall propensity score. That score is then used to match the participants in the quasi-experiment. PSM is a powerful technique for quasi-experiments, but it requires a large number of cases/participants, is computationally complex, and in some cases does not approximate experimental results.

Protocol   A plan for conducting an investigation; the term is most commonly used for descriptions of how to administer experimental treatments. When a distinction is made between a *design* and a protocol, the design refers to the overall plan and the protocol refers to the detailed procedures.

Purposive sample   Also called a *judgment sample*, a purposive sample is one in which researchers choose participants deliberately (with a purpose in mind), usually in order to make the sample more representative. Purposive sampling is typically done when random statistical methods would be difficult or impossible. The term *purposive* is most often used to describe selecting among populations of potential experimental participants. The term *judgment sampling* is more often used in interviews and observational research. (Note: a purposive sample is not a *convenience sample*!)

Qualitative methods   Methods of coding and analyzing used for qualitative data including textual, oral, and graphic/visual data—or quantitative data that can be categorized and thus recoded as qualitative. All designs (surveys, interviews, experiments, observations, and archival) have been used to gather qualitative data. But kinds of analysis tend to be more restricted by types of data. In other words, it is usually easier to combine designs than methods of analysis. See *quantitative methods* and *mixed methods research*.

Quantitative methods   Methods of coding and analyzing used for quantitative data— or for qualitative data that has been quantified. All designs have been used to gather quantitative data including those (such as interviews and observations) that are typically thought of as qualitative designs. (See *qualitative methods* and *mixed methods research*.)

Quasi-experiment   A research study that resembles an experiment "to some degree" (quasi). Quasi-experiments are often an attractive alternative to true experiments, especially in real-world, rather than laboratory-world, contexts. (See *field experiment*.) Quasi-experiments may be used when the researchers are unable to assign individuals to control and experimental groups, but they can select groups at random to receive different treatments—or when they can assign treatments at random to groups of recruits or volunteers. Quasi-experiments are very common in studies of social, medical, and educational interventions when the units of analysis are agencies, clinics, and schools rather than individual clients, patients, or students.

Quota sampling   A combination of a *stratified* and a *convenience* sample, but the researcher's convenience is limited by the quotas. The quotas typically involve demographic characteristics. A quota sampling protocol might read: "Sample 50 adults at the mall this afternoon; at least 20 of them should be male and none should be accompanied by children." Like all non-*probability samples*, quota samples are of limited use for generalizing to populations.

Random assignment   Allocating experimental research participants to treatment and comparison groups using a mechanism that ensures that the assignment is done purely by chance. The purpose of random assignment is to eliminate differences between the groups, except differences due to chance. The larger the number of participants, the better random assignment works to equalize treatment and comparison groups.

Random error   Random variation; that is, variation in values or scores that is due entirely to chance factors. The opposite of random error is systematic error or *bias*. Bias occurs when factors other than chance influence the distribution of scores on a variable. Random error cannot be eliminated, but because it is randomly distributed, it can be estimated. (See *sampling error*.)

Random sampling or selection   The term *random sampling* is more often used to refer to surveys and *random selection* to experiments, but the underlying principle is the same: choosing participants, respondents, or cases so that each is determined entirely by chance, by a random process, such as flipping a fair coin. Random does not mean haphazard, whimsical, casual, or careless. Indeed, the process of random sampling requires careful planning and can be quite arduous. The cost may be high, but the reward is considerable—ability to draw legitimate statistical inferences about populations from sample data.

Randomized controlled trial (RCT)   An experimental approach applied to the study of effectiveness of a treatment, especially one not conducted in a laboratory. (See *field experiment*.) As with all experiments, two main characteristics of RCTs are (1) random assignment of cases to experimental and control groups and (2) researcher control over the implementation of the independent variable. The RCT is often referred to as the "gold standard" for assessing the effectiveness of social and educational interventions.

RCT   An abbreviation for randomized controlled trial or randomized clinical trial or randomized controlled clinical trial.

Regression discontinuity (RD)   A method of assigning participants to control and experimental conditions that uses a cutoff score, not random assignment. It is most often used when considerations of fairness (or political pressures) make it hard to use random assignment; rather, those most in need of the treatment are assigned to it. This *assumes* that the treatment is beneficial. Of course, if we *knew* that the treatment was beneficial, there would be little need to conduct an experiment. The method has been most often used in the evaluation of educational programs. It has been less widely used than it might otherwise have been, in part because it is computationally complex.

Reliability   The consistency or stability of an observation, measurement, or test from one instance to the next. This consistency is an indicator of a lack of error in the observations, measurements, or tests. Reliability is important because without it you can learn nothing at all; if your observations are completely erroneous, they are completely useless. The three main types of reliability are interrater reliability, test–retest reliability, and internal-consistency reliability. Their labels are clear indications of how they are used. They are all measured with types of correlation coefficient. We briefly describe each in turn:

- **Interrater reliability** is agreement or consistency among raters. Having multiple raters often improves the quality of the rating or scoring, but only if the raters are largely in agreement. Ratings often involve assigning numbers to qualitative assessments; the agreement among the scores of Olympic judges is a well-known example.
- **Test–retest reliability**, as its name implies, involves measuring the consistency among scores on two or more versions of tests administered to the same person(s).
- **Internal-consistency reliability** refers to the degree to which multiple items on a scale are measuring the same thing; if they are, they will be highly correlated. This is the kind of reliability most often reported in articles in social research, usually using the Cronbach's alpha statistic.

Repeated-measures design   A research design in which participants/cases are measured two or more times on a dependent *variable*. This is usually discussed as a type of experimental design, but it used much more broadly, as when an effect of a variable is gauged by measuring it before and after an event or a policy change. Also called *within-subjects design*.

Research   The systematic investigation of a topic. As readers of this book are aware, research can be conducted in many different ways. The federal government's definition of research, which is important for determining whether a project needs *IRB* approval, is systematic investigation aimed at producing generalizable knowledge, that is, knowledge not solely for private use but for public consumption. This means that if you are generating knowledge solely for your own use, for example if you are studying your own professional practice hoping to learn how to improve it, that study is not research requiring IRB approval. However, if you publish the results of your research, or plan to, then it does require IRB review. The line between the two is often unclear.

Research synthesis   A rigorous and detailed review of the research literature on a topic. The synthesis may be quantitative, in which case it is a *meta-analysis*, but it need not be. Indeed, many important research syntheses are not meta-analyses, strictly speaking, because they do not synthesize only quantitatively.

Respondent   A research participant who answers questions on a survey.

Sampling error   The differences between the sample and the population from which the population was drawn. When the sample is used to make inferences about the population, these differences will lead to errors in the estimates. Using *probability sampling* reduces error, and it allows you to estimate the error's size and its likelihood. The bigger the probability sample, the smaller the likely error. With nonprobability samples, you haven't a clue about the magnitude of the probable error; you might think you do, but you don't.

Sampling frame   A list or other record of all the cases (people, cities, institutions, etc.) in the population you plan to study. The sampling frame is almost never a perfect list of the members of the population, but it is the population that is accessible to you. This discrepancy between the frame and the population has to be added to *sampling error* as another limitation to the accuracy of your generalizations about the population.

Saturation point   The point in the course of one's research where it makes little sense to continue to collect data because it is unlikely that there is more that can be learned by doing so. The term originated in *grounded theory*, but it is used more broadly, especially in research on qualitative data. Similar concepts exist in research collecting quantitative data, such as the "fail-safe N" used in meta-analysis. (Compare *stopping rule*.)

Secondary data analysis   A type of *archival* research conducted on data, such as census files, that have been collected by others, often in database archives. More generally, secondary data and sources are those that are not original to the researcher. For example, if you observed and recorded events yourself, your research data would be primary; if your data are composed of the news accounts you read to learn about the events, your data would be secondary.

Selection bias   A bias that arises when the researcher cannot apply random techniques in sample selection or in assigning cases to control and experimental groups. It is often called "self-selection bias" because one of the most frequent sources of selection bias in social research is that we almost always rely on volunteers who self-select into the pool of participants—and, a greater concern, into the treatment groups.

Sensitizing concept   An idea that guides observation by making the researcher more alert (sensitive) to seeing certain phenomena. Sensitizing concepts can be thought of as proto-theories; they tend to be adjusted over the course of a research project as more observations are made. (See *theory, model*.)

Single-case experiments   *Within-subjects designs* applied to one case at a time, often in a clinical or therapeutic setting. Also known as single-subject experiments. Treatments are applied, stopped, and applied again. The experimenter assigns treatments to cases, not cases to treatment conditions. Repeated measures of the outcome variable are made following each change in the treatment. Theoretical understanding of variables thus studied tends to be built up inductively.

Snowball sampling   Finding study participants by asking initial contacts or informants for further contacts. It is used both by survey researchers to find comparatively large pools of respondents and by interview researchers to identify smaller numbers of informants. It is an especially helpful technique to use when populations are rare or difficult to access. The key assumption of snowball sampling is that members of your target population know one another. Following leads in observational field research is a form of snowball sampling in which a participant in one setting refers you to other settings and participants.

Statistical inference   Making inferences about a population by using probability theory and data about a sample. The usual summary of statistical inference is a *p* value. The *p* stands for probability, specifically the probability that a result (such as a correlation between two variables) is due to chance alone. More specifically still, the *p* value answers the question: How likely is it that a correlation of this size or bigger in a sample of this size could have been obtained by chance if there were no correlation in the population? Because statistical inferences are probability inferences, they should be made only when using *probability samples*. Of course, many important inferences are not statistical; making inferences by reasoning about evidence is a time-honored activity much older than the *p* value.

Statistical power   The ability to use a sample to detect a relationship in a population. The power of a statistical test is its ability to detect something that is there. Much like the magnification power of a microscope, the greater the power of a statistical test the smaller the things it can detect. You can increase statistical power by increasing your sample size.

Statistically significant   Said of a value or score that is larger or smaller than would be expected by chance alone. The fact that a finding is "unlikely to be due to chance" does not necessarily imply that it is "significant" in the sense of being important or relevant or noteworthy. Calculations of statistical significance result in *p* values. (See *statistical inference*.) A *p* value is uninterpretable unless it refers to scores calculated on a probability sample or to scores of groups that have been formed by random assignment. However, many uninterpretable *p* values are in fact calculated. A statistical program will often do this by default. The program doesn't know any better; you should.

Stopping rule   A decision, made before a research project begins, about when to terminate a study—if interim data analyses indicate that it may be harmful to participants and/or that the probability of benefit is very low. The ethical conduct of research would seem to require one to stop a research project not only when it is harmful to participants but also when there are few likely benefits to the participants or to society or to the advance of knowledge. Stopping rules are used increasingly in biomedical research, where interim analysis of data is common, but they remain comparatively rare in social research.

Stratified sampling   A method of sampling that begins by dividing the population into groups; the groups, called strata, are often based on demographic characteristics such as ethnicity, gender, or age. The researcher samples not from the population as a whole, but from the strata. Stratified samples are helpful when groups of interest to the researcher differ greatly in size and simply sampling from the population as a whole might not yield enough cases in each group. For example, if you wanted to compare the opinions of male and female nurses, simply sampling 1,000 members from the population of nurses might not give you a big enough sample of male nurses to make statistically significant comparisons. If you stratified the population by gender and randomly selected 500 female and 500 male nurses, you would have representative samples of each group, which you could use to make your comparisons. The samples would be representative of the strata, but together they would not be representative of the population. If you generalized from your pooled samples to the population, males would be overrepresented.

Subject A generic term for something a researcher studies; also called a *case*. Because "subject" carries connotations of subjugation and unwilling participation, *participant* is the preferred term whenever it is applicable. Note, however, that the official term in federal regulations, including those governing *IRBs*, is "human subjects."

Subjective data Information that can only, or most effectively, be obtained from the "subjects" of the research. Such data often pertain to individuals' values, beliefs, feelings, or opinions. Subjective data cannot be confirmed by outside observation. They depend on reports of research participants. For example, if external observers noted that a person had oatmeal every morning for breakfast, they could infer that she must like its taste. But if they wanted to know, they would have to ask her; perhaps she finds it bland and uninteresting, but eats it daily on the recommendation of her cardiologist. (Compare *objective data*.)

Survey experiment An experiment conducted using subsamples of survey respondents as participants. A typical procedure is to randomly select groups of survey respondents to reply to different forms of questions. The goal is often to improve the quality of survey questions, but more substantive goals may also be pursued. One of the attractive features of a survey experiment is that it can combine the advantages of random sampling and random assignment—an advantageous combination that is very rare.

Systematic error Bias, that is, error which is consistent (or systematic), not random or unpredictable. For example, if you used *systematic sampling* of the listings in a city telephone directory to indentify people to survey over the phone, and you used the results of your survey to generalize about the population of the city, your conclusions would be biased; they would contain systematic error. That is because your sample systematically would exclude people who had no phone, who had unlisted numbers, and who had only cell phones. By extension, it would also overrepresent people listed in the directory.

Systematic sampling Also known as "list sampling," systematic sampling involves selecting cases at regular intervals from a list. The typical procedure is to decide on your sample size and divide it into the list size. The answer is the size of the interval. For example, if you wanted a sample of 100 and the list contained 1,000, you would select every 10th person on this list. You would start at a randomly chosen place on the list between 1 and 10. *Systematic error* can be avoided only if the list contains no biases, such as excluding parts of the population or listing them in an order that could influence the results. As with any *sampling frame*, a list sample can be no better than the list from which it was drawn. It is always possible to draw a random sample from the list you have used to draw a systematic sample, but the practical difficulties of random sampling are often greater than those of list sampling.

Target population The group about which a researcher aims to draw conclusions. This is often called simply "the population"; "target" is used merely for clarification or emphasis.

Text mining A subset of *data mining* that focuses on verbal texts. Most data mining has been conducted by searching in quantitative datasets. The algorithms for searching for patterns seem better developed for quantitative datasets, but given that methods to read text into computer files so that they can be searched and sampled using high-speed computing are now routinely available, the future of text mining seems assured. It is probably most commonly used currently to mine texts available electronically, such as Web pages and social networking sites.

Theoretical research Investigations intended to create theories, not (initially) to test them. Theories are often the product of systematic research, typically research reviewing existing research. The theorist's premise is that sometimes we can get new knowledge merely by thinking hard about data that are already available. The process of theory creation is elusive. From theorists' descriptions we can say that it seems to involve a lot of reflection followed by leaps of insight followed by more reflection—"thinking until your head hurts and then thinking some more," in Heisenberg's phrase. Ultimately, the value of theoretical research depends on whether one's insights are useful to others in the field. While theoretical research might not be very common as the main goal of most social researchers, it is typically part of the early process of constructing a research question and crafting a research design to investigate the question.

Theory A statement that concisely summarizes relationships of phenomena or variables and/or explains how and why something occurs. Theories can be described in equations and graphically as well as in words. Many researchers believe that a research question should be based on a theory and that an appropriate theory is most likely to be found in a review of the research literature. Others argue that a theory should be the outcome of the research, not its starting point and that a better goal for research is to construct a theory inductively. (See *model.*)

Thick description Portraying a phenomenon, such as a behavior, in detailed context, because without the context, it cannot be fully understood. The term is used mostly in the context of observational and ethnographic research. Popularized by the anthropologist Clifford Geertz, it is now used broadly in other social science disciplines to mean a very detailed description of a phenomenon and its context.

Thought experiment A simulated experiment in which the simulation is conducted by imagining and reasoning about the likely outcomes of an experiment that we are unable to conduct, but one for which we can conceive of a range of likely outcomes had we been able to conduct it. Thought experiments have been most important in the physical sciences, but they can be an important step in social research as well, at least for refining research questions: "So if we were to set up an experiment, what do we think the likely outcomes might be, and how would we interpret them?"

Triangulation The use of several research methods or kinds of data to examine the same phenomenon. The term is borrowed from trigonometry, where triangulation is a way to calculate the distance to a point by viewing it from two other points that are a known distance apart. The term is mostly used in the context of *mixed methods research* and *multimethod research.*

Trustworthiness   The conceptual equivalent of *validity* applied to research on qualitative data. Multiple observations and triangulating with other sources of evidence add to the trustworthiness of an observation or conclusion.

Units of analysis   The entities—persons or things—a researcher studies. The units of analysis are determined by the research question. If you were studying academic achievement, your unit of analysis might be individual students or classrooms or schools. If the study required informed consent of the entities being studied, they would usually be called *participants*. If you were gathering data from archived educational records, the units might be called *cases*, which are recorded on the rows or "records" of a statistical package. The units of analysis might not always be the units of data collection or observation. For instance, if you were studying the academic achievement of different teachers' classrooms, you might collect data about individual students in the classrooms and pool the data to obtain classroom averages.

Validity   Few terms are as difficult to define as validity, in part because it has been defined, used, and categorized in many (literally dozens of) different ways. The conclusion to this book contains an extended discussion that we will not repeat here. Perhaps it suffices to say here that the basic questions researchers ask themselves when thinking about validity are: Are we truly studying what we intend to study, are the methods we use appropriate for the problem, and are the conclusions we draw accurate? Probably the two most common subtypes of validity are: (1) external validity, which refers to the degree to which the results drawn from the sample can be accurately generalized beyond the participants taking part in the study to the population at large and (2) internal validity, which refers to drawing correct conclusions about the sample, especially regarding causal effects. Extensive debates in research methodology have occurred concerning which of these two types of validity is more important and in what contexts.

Variables   The term is used loosely to mean any phenomena studied by a researcher. More specifically, variables are characteristics or attributes of the phenomena being studied that can vary; that can have different values, levels, or categories. The opposite of a variable is a constant, which by definition does not vary. The three most important categories of variables are (1) the independent variable, also known as the predictor variable, which loosely speaking is the *cause* in a study, (2) the dependent variable, also called the outcome or response variable, which loosely speaking is the effect in a study, and (3) a set of other types of variables that further specify the links between the independent and dependent variables; these are variously called intervening, mediating, moderating, and modifying variables.

Vulnerable populations   Groups of people who are particularly likely to be harmed by an experiment and/or who are in special need of help to understand the purposes of research before giving their informed consent, and/or who are especially vulnerable to breaches of their privacy. These could include children, the mentally retarded, and victims of crime. Vulnerable populations are a key concern of *IRBs*, and federal regulations define some of these populations precisely. However, the regulations probably do not cover all the kinds of vulnerability that researchers could encounter in their studies.

Within-subjects design A before-and-after study, also called a repeated-measures design. You measure, treat, and measure again. When the subjects are persons, it is called a "within-*participants*" design. This design is usually compared with the *between-subjects* approach. The standard model in *RCTs* is between-subjects. That means that there are control and experimental groups, and they contain different participants. By contrast, in the within-subjects model, each participant serves as his or her own control. When using a within-subjects design you have the highest certainty that there are no differences between participants receiving and not receiving treatment, because they are the same people. The simplest within-subjects design is a plain before-and-after study. You measure the participants before the experimental treatment and after. Of course, whenever in an experiment you use a pretest and a posttest of the dependent variable you are collecting data within-subjects, but in the between-subjects approach you are looking at two groups of subjects—those receiving treatment and those in the control group who do not receive treatment. In the within-subjects design, you collect data only on the treatment group; it is the only group you have.

References

Abdi, H., Edelman, B. Valentin, D., & Dowling, W. J. (2009). *Experimental design and analysis for psychology.* Oxford, UK: Oxford University Press.

Abern, M. R., Dude, A. M., & Coogan, C. L. (2010). Marital status independently predicts testis cancer survival—an analysis of the SEER database. *Urologic Oncology, 28.* Retrieved from *www.urologiconcology.org/article/ S1078-1439(10)00061-X/abstract.*

Adams, J. (2004). The imagination and social life. *Qualitative Sociology, 27*(3), 277–297.

Adcock, R., & Collier, D. (2001). Measurement validity: A shared standard for qualitative and quantitative research. *American Political Science Review, 95,* 529–546.

Ahmedin, J., Ward, E., Anderson, R., Murray, T., & Thun, M. (2008). Widening of socioeconomic inequalities in U.S. death rates, 1993–2001. *PLoS ONE, 3*(5), e2181.

Allison, P. D. (1984). *Event history analysis.* Thousand Oaks, CA: Sage.

Aloe, A. M., & Becker, B. J. (2011). Advances in combining regression results in meta-analysis. In M. Williams & W. P. Vogt (Eds.), *Handbook on innovations in social research methodology* (pp. 331–352). London: Sage.

Alvarez, R. M., Sherman, R. P., & VanBeselaere, C. (2003). Subject acquisition for web-based surveys. *Political Analysis, 11*(1), 23–43.

American Educational Research Association. (1999). *Standards for educational and psychological testing* (2nd ed.). Washington, DC: Author.

Anderson, D. (2008). *Model based inference in the life sciences.* New York: Springer.

Anderson-Connolly, R. (2006). On the state of the economic in sociology: A content analysis. *American Sociologist, 37*(4), 5–28.

Aneschensel, C. S. (2002). *Theory-based data analysis for the social sciences.* Thousand Oaks, CA: Sage.

Angrosino, M. V., & Mays de Perez, K. A. (2000). Rethinking observation: From method to context. In N. K. Denzin & Y. S. Lincoln (Eds.), *Handbook of qualitative research* (2nd ed., pp. 673–702). Thousand Oaks, CA: Sage.

Asher, J. (2010). Collecting data in challenging settings. *Chance, 23*(2), 6–13.

Atkinson, R. (2001). The life story interview. In J. F. Gubrium & J. A. Holstein (Eds.), *Handbook of interview research* (pp. 121–140). Thousand Oaks, CA: Sage.

Baker, P. J. (2011). Three configurations of school/ university partnerships: An exploratory study. *Planning & Changing, 42*(1/2), 41–62.

Baker, S. G., & Kramer, B. S. (2008). Randomized trials for the real world: Making as few and as reasonable assumptions as possible. *Statistical Methods in Medical Research, 17,* 243–252.

Bastian, H., Glasziou, P., & Chalmers, I. (2010). Seventy-five trials and eleven systematic reviews a day: How will we ever keep up? *PLoS Medicine, 7*(9), 1–6.

Becker, H. (2004). Comment on Kevin Haggerty. *Qualitative Sociology, 27,* 415–416.

Belli, R. F., Shay, W. L., & Stafford, F. P. (2001). Event history calendars and question list surveys:

A direct comparison of interviewing methods. *Public Opinion Quarterly, 65,* 45–74.

Bennett, A., Barth, A., & Rutherford, K. (2003). Do we preach what we practice?: A survey of methods in political science journals and curricula. *PS: Political Science and Politics, 36,* 373–378.

Berk, R. A. (2004). *Regression analysis: A constructive critique.* Thousand Oaks, CA: Sage.

Bernard, H. R. (2000). *Social research methods: Qualitative and quantitative approaches.* Thousand Oaks, CA: Sage.

Bevan, G. (2006). Setting targets for health care performance: Lessons from a case study of the English NHS. *National Institute Economic Review, 197,* 67–79.

Bhattacharya, H. (2008) New critical collaborative ethnography. In S. Hesse-Biber & P. Leavy (Eds.), *Handbook of emergent methods* (pp. 303–322). New York: Guilford Press.

Bifulco, R. (2002). Addressing self-selection bias in quasi-experimental evaluations of whole-school reform. *Evaluation Review, 26*(5), 545–572.

Bird, C. E., Freemont, A. M., Bierman, A. S., Wickstrom, S., Shah, M., & Rector, T. (2007). Does quality of care for cardiovascular disease and diabetes differ by gender for enrollees in managed care plans? *Women's Health Issues, 17*(3), 131–138

Blass, T. (2004). *The man who shocked the world: The life and legacy of Stanley Milgram.* New York: Basic Books.

Blattman, C., Jenson, R., & Roman, R. (2003). Assessing the need and potential of community networking for development in rural India. *Information Society, 19,* 349–364.

Bloom, H. S., Richburg-Hayes, L., & Black, A. R. (2007). Using covariates to improve precision for studies that randomize schools to evaluate educational interventions. *Educational Evaluation and Policy Studies, 29*(1), 30–59.

Bloor, M. (2005). Population estimation without censuses or surveys: A discussion of mark-recapture methods. *Sociology, 39,* 121–138.

Blumenthal, M. M. (2005). Toward an open-source methodology: What we can learn from the blogosphere. *Public Opinion Quarterly, 69,* 655–669.

Bok, S. (1999). *Lying* (2nd ed.). New York: Vintage.

Bollen, J., Mao, H., & Zeng, X. (2010). Twitter mood predicts the stock market. Available at *arXiv: 1010.3003v1.*

Bollett, A. J. (1992). Politics and pelegra: The epidemic of pellagra in the U.S. *Yale Journal of Biology and Medicine, 65,* 211–221.

Boote, D. N., & Beile, P. (2005). Scholars before researchers: On the centrality of the dissertation literature review in research preparation. *Educational Researcher, 34*(6), 3–15.

Borrego, M., & Newswander, L. K. (2010). Definitions of interdisciplinary research: Toward graduate-level interdisciplinary learning outcomes. *Review of Higher Education, 34,* 61–84.

Bosk, C. L. (2004). The ethnographer and the IRB: Comment on Kevin Haggerty, "Ethics Creep . . ." *Qualitative Sociology, 27,* 417–420.

Bosk, C. L. (2008). *What would you do?: Juggling bioethics and ethnography.* Chicago: University of Chicago Press.

Bowen, G. A. (2008). Naturalistic inquiry and the saturation concept: A research note. *Qualitative Research, 8*(1), 137–152.

Bowen, W. G., Chingos, M. W., & McPherson, M. S. (2009). *Crossing the finish line: Completing college at America's public universities.* Princeton, NJ: Princeton University Press.

Bracht, G. H., & Glass, G. V. (1968). The external validity of experiments. *American Educational Research Journal, 5,* 437–474.

Brady, H. E., & Collier, D. (Eds.). (2004). *Rethinking social inquiry: Diverse tools, shared standards.* New York: Rowman & Littlefield.

Brewer, J., & Hunter, A. (2006). *Foundations of multimethod research: Synthesizing styles.* Thousand Oaks, CA: Sage.

Browning, C. R., Wallace, D., Feinberg, S. L., and Cagney, K. A. (2006). Neighborhood social processes, physical conditions, and disaster-related mortality. *American Sociological Review, 71,* 661–678.

Bruner, J. (1990). *Acts of meaning.* Cambridge, MA: Harvard University Press.

Bryk, A. S., Sebring, P. B., Allensworth, E., Luppescu, S., & Easton, J. Q. (2010). *Organizing schools for improvement: Lessons from Chicago.* Chicago: University of Chicago Press.

Bryk, A. S., Sebring, P. B., Kerbow, D., Rollow, S., & Easton, J. Q. (1998). *Charting Chicago school reform: Democratic localism as a lever for change.* Boulder, CO: Westview Press.

Calvey, D. (2008). The art and politics of covert research: Doing "situated ethics" in the field. *Sociology, 42*(5), 905–918.

Campbell, D., & Stanley, J. (1963). *Experimental and quasi-experimental designs for research.* Chicago: Rand McNally.

Card, D., & Krueger, A. B. (2000). Minimum wages and employment: A case study of the fast-food industry in New Jersey and Pennsylvania. *American Economic Review, 90*(5), 1397–1420.

Card, N. A. (2012). *Applied meta-analysis for social science research.* New York: Guilford Press.

Carolan, B. V., & Natriello, G. (2005). Data-mining journals and books: Using the science of networks to uncover the structure of the educational research community. *Educational Researcher, 34*(4), 25–33.

Charmaz, K. (1991). *Good days, bad days: The self in chronic illness and time.* New Brunswick, NJ: Rutgers University Press.

Charmaz, K. (2006). *Constructing grounded theory: A practical guide thorough qualitative analysis.* Los Angeles: Sage.

Charmaz, K. (2008). Grounded theory as an emergent method. In S. Hesse-Biber & P. Leavy (Eds.), *Handbook of emergent methods* (pp. 155–172). New York: Guilford Press.

Chatterji, M. (2007). Grades of evidence: Variability in quality of findings in effectiveness studies of complex field interventions. *American Journal of Evaluation, 28*(3), 239–255.

Christian, L. M., Dillman, D. A., & Smyth, J. D. (2007). Helping respondents get it right the first time: The influence of words, symbols, and graphics in web surveys. *Public Opinion Quarterly, 71*, 113–125.

Classen, R. L. (2007). Ideology and evaluation in an experimental setting: Comparing the proximity and directional models. *Political Research Quarterly, 60*, 263–273.

Clifford, J. (1983). On ethnographic reality. *Representations, 1*(2), 116–146.

Code of Federal Regulations, Title 45 (2009). Available at *www.hhs.gov/ohrp/humansubjects*.

Cohen, J. (1983). The cost of dichotomization. *Applied Psychological Measurement, 7*, 249–253.

Cohen, J. (1992). A power primer. *Psychological Bulletin, 112*, 155–159.

Cohen, K. B., & Hunter, L. (2008). Getting started in text mining. *PLoS Computational Biolog, 4*(1), e20.

Collins, K. M. T., Onwuegbuzie, A. J., & Jiao, Q. G. (2006). Prevalence of mixed-methods sampling designs in social science research. *Evaluation and Research in Education, 19*(2), 83–101.

Cook, T. D., & Campbell, D. T. (1979). *Quasi-experimentation: Design and analysis issues for field settings.* Boston: Houghton Mifflin.

Cooper, H. (2010). *Research synthesis and meta-analysis* (4th ed.). Thousand Oaks, CA: Sage.

Cooper, H., & Dent, A. (2011). Ethical issues in the conduct and reporting of meta-analysis. In A. T. Panter & S. K. Sterba (Eds.), *Handbook of ethics in quantitative methodology* (pp. 417–443). New York: Routledge.

Couper, M. P., & Hansen, S. E. (2001). Computer-assisted interviewing. In J. F. Gubrium & J. A. Holstein (Eds.), *Handbook of interview research* (pp. 557–576). Thousand Oaks, CA: Sage.

Corbin, J., & Strauss, A. (2008). *Basics of qualitative research: Techniques and procedures for developing grounded theory* (3rd ed.). Thousand Oaks, CA: Sage.

Corden, A., & Hirst, M. (2008). Implementing a mixed methods approach to explore the financial implications of death of a life partner. *Journal of Mixed Methods Research, 2*(3), 208–220.

Creswell, J. W. (2003). *Research design: Qualitative, quantitative, and mixed methods approaches* (2nd ed.). Thousand Oaks, CA: Sage.

Creswell, J. R., & Clark, V. L. P. (2010). *Designing and conducting mixed methods research* (2nd ed.). Thousand Oaks, CA: Sage.

Cronbach, L. J. (1975, February). Beyond the two disciplines of scientific psychology. *American Psychologist, 30*(2), 116–127.

Crouch, M., & McKenzie, H. (2006). The logic of small samples in interview-based qualitative research. *Social Science Information, 45*(4), 483–499.

Culyba, R. J., Heimer, C. A., & Petty, J. C. (2004). The ethnographic turn: Fact, fashion, or fiction? *Qualitative Sociology, 27*(4), 365–389.

Cumming, G. (2008). Replication and *p* intervals: *p* values predict the future only vaguely, but confidence intervals do much better. *Perspectives on Psychological Science, 3*(4), 286–300.

Curry, S. J., Emery, S., Sporer, A. H., Mermelstein, R., Flay, B. R., Berbaum, M., et al. (2007). A national survey of tobacco cessation programs for youths. *American Journal of Public Health, 97*(1), 171–177.

Curtin, R., Presser, S., & Singer, E. (2005). Changes in telephone survey nonresponse over the past quarter century. *Public Opinion Quarterly, 69*, 87–98.

Dai, Q., Borenstein, A. R., Wu, Y., Jackson, J. C., & Larson, E. B. (2006). Fruit and vegetable juices and Alzheimer's disease: The kame project. *American Journal of Medicine, 119*(9), 751–759.

Dattalo, P. (2010). *Strategies to approximate random sampling and assignment.* New York: Oxford University Press.

Davis, J. A. (2004). Did growing up in the 1960s leave a permanent mark on attitudes and values? *Public Opinion Quarterly, 68,* 161–183.

de Laine, M. (2000). *Fieldwork, participation, and practice: Ethics and dilemmas in qualitative research.* London: Sage.

Denzin, N. K. (1971). The logic of naturalistic inquiry. *Social Forces, 50,* 166–182.

Denzin, N. K. (1978). *The research act: A theoretical introduction to sociological methods.* New York: McGraw-Hill.

Denzin, N. K. (2009). The elephant in the living room: Or extending the conversation about the politics of evidence. *Qualitative Research, 9*(2), 139–160.

Denzin, N. K., & Lincoln, Y. S. (2005). *Handbook of qualitative research* (3rd ed.). Thousand Oaks, CA: Sage.

Denzin, N. K. & Lincoln, Y. S. (2011). *Handbook of qualitative research* (4th ed.). Thousand Oaks, CA: Sage.

Department of Health and Human Services. (2011). Human subjects research protections: Enhancing protections for research subjects and reducing burden, delay and ambiguity for investigators. *Federal Register, 76,* 44512–44531.

Dick, H. P. (2006). What to do with "I Don't Know:" Elicitation in ethnographic and survey interviews. *Qualitative Sociology, 29,* 87–102.

Dillman, D. A., Smith, J. D., & Christian, L. M. (2009). *Internet, mail, and mixed-mode surveys: The tailored design method.* New York: Wiley.

Druckman, J. N., Green, D. P., Kuklinski, J. H., & Lupia, A. (2006). The growth and development of experimental research in political science. *American Political Science Review, 100,* 627–633.

Drury, J., & Stott, C. (2001). Bias as a research strategy in participant observation: The case of intergroup conflict. *Field Methods, 13*(1), 47–67.

Duneier, M. (1999). *Sidewalk.* New York: Farrar, Straus & Giroux.

Duneier, M. (2006). Ethnography, the ecological fallacy, and the 1995 Chicago heat wave. *American Sociological Review, 71,* 679–688.

Dunning, T. (2008). Improving causal inference: Strengths and limitations of natural experiments. *Political Research Quarterly, 61,* 282–293.

Durkheim, E. (1893). *De la division du travail social.* Paris: Alcan.

Duster, T. (2006). Comparative perspectives and competing explanations: Taking on the newly configured reductionist challenge to sociology. *American Sociological Review, 71,* 1–15.

Ehrenreich, B. (2001). *Nickel and dimed: On (not) getting by in America.* New York: Henry Holt.

Elliot, J. (1988). Educational research and outsider-insider relations. *Qualitative Studies in Education, 1*(2), 155–166.

Emerson, G., Warme, W. J., & Wolf, F. M. (2010). Testing for the presence of positive-outcome bias in peer review: A randomized controlled trial. *Archives of Internal Medicine, 170,* 1934–1939.

Emerson, R. M., Fretz, R. I., & Shaw, L. L. (1995). *Writing ethnographic fieldnotes.* Chicago: University of Chicago Press.

Epstein, S. (2007). *Inclusion: The politics of difference in medical research.* Chicago: University of Chicago Press.

Erikson, K. T. (1976). *Everything in its path: Destruction of community in the Buffalo Creek flood.* New York: Simon & Schuster.

Ezekiel, R. S. (1995). *The racist mind: Portraits of American neo-Nazis and Klansmen.* New York: Penguin.

Farmer, T., Robinson, K., Elliot, S. J., & Eyles, J. (2006). Developing and implementing a triangulation protocol for qualitative health research. *Qualitative Health Research, 16,* 377–394.

Farquharson, K. (2005). A different kind of snowball: Identifying key policymakers. *International Journal of Social Research Methodology, 4,* 345–353.

Fielding, N. (2004). Getting the most from archived qualitative data: Epistemological, practical, and professional obstacles. *International Journal of Social Research Methodology, 7,* 97–104.

Finn, J. D., & Achilles, C. M. (1999). Tennessee's class size study: Findings, implications, misconceptions. *Educational Evaluation and Policy Analysis, 21,* 97–109.

Fisher, R. (1939). *The design of experiments.* London: Macmillan.

Fitzpatrick, J. L., & Morris, M. (Eds.). (1999). *Current and emerging ethical challenges in evaluation.* San Francisco: Jossey-Bass.

Fontana, A. (2001). Postmodern trends in interviewing. In J. F. Gubrium & J. A. Holstein (Eds.), *Handbook of interview research* (pp. 161–175). Thousand Oaks, CA: Sage.

Fowler, F. J. (2008). *Survey research methods* (4th ed.). Thousand Oaks, CA: Sage.

Franzosi, R. (2010). *Quantitative narrative analysis*. Thousand Oaks, CA: Sage.

Freese, J. (2007). Replication standards for quantitative social science. *Sociological Methods and Research, 36*, 153–172.

Gaines, B. J., Kuklinski, J. H., & Quirk, P. J. (2007). The logic of the survey experiment reexamined. *Political Analysis, 15*, 1–20.

Gans, H. J. (1999). Participant observation in the era of "ethnography." *Journal of Contemporary Ethnography, 28*(5), 540–547.

Gao, S., & Fraser, M. W. (2010). *Propensity score analysis*. Thousand Oaks, CA: Sage.

Garfinkel, H. (1966). *Studies in ethnomethodology*. New York: Polity Press.

Gattone, C. F. (2006). *The social scientist as public intellectual*. Lanham, MD: Rowman & Littlefield.

Gawande, A. (2004, December 6). The bell curve: What happens when patients find out how good their doctors really are? *New Yorker*, pp. 82–91.

Geertz, C. (1973). Thick description: Toward an interpretive theory of culture. In *The interpretation of cultures: Selected essays* (pp. 3–30). New York: Basic Books.

Gendlin, E. T. (1981). *Focusing* (2nd ed.). New York: Bantam.

George, A. L., & Bennett, A. (2005). *Case studies and theory development in the social sciences*. Cambridge, MA: MIT Press.

Glaser, B. G., & Strauss, A. L. (1967). *The discovery of grounded theory: Strategies for qualitative research*. Chicago: Aldine.

Glenn, N. D. (2003). Distinguishing age, period, and cohort effects. In J. Mortimer and M. Shannahan (Eds.), *Handbook of the life course* (pp. 465–476). New York: Kluwer Academic.

Goertz, G. (2006). *Social science concepts: A user's guide*. Princeton, NJ: Princeton University Press.

Goffman, E. (1959). *The presentation of self in everyday life*. New York: Anchor.

Goffman, E. (1961). *Asylums: Essays on the social situation of mental patients and other inmates*. New York: Anchor Books.

Goffman, E. (1985). *Behavior in public places*. New York: Free Press.

Goldschmidt, N., & Szmrecsanyi, B. (2007). What do economists talk about?: A linguistic analysis of published writing in economic journals. *American Journal of Economics and Sociology, 66*, 335–378.

Gonzalez, R. (2009). *Data analysis for experimental design*. New York: Guilford Press.

Goodman, L. A. (1961). Snowball sampling. *Annals of Mathematical Statistics, 32*, 148–170.

Gorski, P. S. (2004). The poverty of deductivism: A constructive realist model of sociological explanation. *Sociological Methodology, 34*, 1–33.

Gosling, S. D. & Johnson, J. A. (Eds.). (2010). *Advanced methods for conducting online behavioral research*. Washington, DC: APA Press.

Grambsch, P. (2008). Regression to the mean, murder rates, and shall-issue laws. *The American Statistician, 62*, 289–295.

Greene, J. C. (2007). *Mixed methods in social inquiry*. San Francisco: Jossey-Bass.

Greene, J. C., Caracelli, V. J, & Graham, W. F. (1989). Toward a conceptual framework for mixed-method evaluation designs. *Educational Evaluation and Policy Analysis, 11*(3), 255–274.

Groves, R. M. (2006). Nonresponse rates and nonresponse bias in household surveys. *Public Opinion Quarterly, 70*, 646–675.

Groves, R. M., Fowler, F. J., Jr., Couper, M. P., Lepkowski, J. M., Singer, E., & Tourangeau, R. (2009) *Survey methodology* (2nd ed.). New York: Wiley.

Guba, E. G., & Lincoln, Y. S. (1982). *Naturalistic inquiry*. Beverly Hills, CA: Sage.

Gubrium, J. F., & Holstein, J. A. (Eds.). (2001). *Handbook of interview research*. Thousand Oaks, CA: Sage.

Guenther, K. M. (2009). The politics of names: Rethinking the methodological and ethical significance of naming people, organizations, and places. *Qualitative Research, 9*(4), 411–421.

Guillemin, M., & Gillam, L. (2004). Ethics, reflexivity, and ethically important moments in research. *Qualitative Inquiry, 10*(2), 261–280.

Gunter, B. (2008). Media violence: Is there a case for causality? *American Behavioral Scientist, 51*(8), 1061–1122.

Haarh, M. T., & Hrogjartsson, A. (2006). Who is blinded in randomized clinical trials?: A study of 200 trials and a survey of authors. *Clinical Trials, 3*, 360–365.

Haeffele, L. (2009, June). *Understanding the role of post-secondary coaches in high schools: A social capital analysis*. Paper presented at the annual meeting of the Student Financial Aid Research Network (SFARN), Indianapolis, IN.

Haeffele, L., Baker, P. J., & Pacha, J. (2007) *The Illinois best practice school study: 2003–2006. Research and Policy Report 1-2007.* Normal, IL: Center for the Study of Education Policy, Illinois State University.

Haggerty, K. D. (2004). Ethics creep: Governing social science research in the name of ethics. *Qualitative Sociology, 27,* 391–414.

Hammersley, M., & Atkinson, P. (2007). *Ethnography: Principles and practices* (2nd ed.). New York: Routledge.

Haney, C., Banks, C., & Zimbardo, P. (1973). A study of prisoners and guards in a simulated prison. *Naval Research Reviews, 9,* 1–17.

Harrison, G. W., List, J. A., & Towe, C. (2007). Naturally occurring preferences and exogenous laboratory experiments: A case study of risk aversion. *Econometrica, 75,* 433–458.

Hatt, B. (2007, March). Street smarts vs. book smarts: The figured world of smartness in lives of marginalized urban youth. *Urban Review, 39*(2), 145–166.

Hedgecoe, A. (2008). Research ethics review and the sociological research relationship. *Sociology, 45*(5), 873–885.

Hedges, L. V. (2007). Correcting a significance test for clustering. *Journal of Educational and Behavioral Statistics, 32,* 151–179.

Hedges, L. V., & Hedberg, E. C. (2007). Intraclass correlation values for planning group-randomized trials in education. *Educational Evaluation and Policy Analysis, 29,* 60–87.

Hembroff, L. A., Rusz, D., Rafferty, A., McGee, H., & Erlich, N. (2005). The cost-effectiveness of alternative advance mailings in a telephone survey. *Public Opinion Quarterly, 69,* 232–245.

Henrich, J., Boyd, R., Bowles, S., Camerer, C., Fehr, E., Gintis, H., et al. (2001). In search of *homo economicus*: Behavioral experiments in 15 small-scale societies. *American Economic Review, 91,* 73–79.

Hermanowicz, J. C. (2002). The great interview: 25 strategies for studying people in bed. *Qualitative Sociology, 25*(4), 479–499.

Herrera, Y. M., & Kapur, D. (2007). Improving data quality: Actors, incentives, and capabilities. *Political Analysis, 15,* 365–386.

Herzog, H. (2005). On home turf: Interview location and its social meaning. *Qualitative Sociology, 28*(1), 25–39.

Hessler, R. M., Downing, J., Beltz, C., Pelliccio, A., Powell, M, & Vale, W. (2003). Qualitative research on adolescents' risk using e-mail: A methodological assessment. *Qualitative Sociology, 26*(1), 111–124.

Highhouse, S. (2009). Designing experiments that generalize. *Organizational Research Methods, 12,* 554–566.

Hill, K. P., Ross, J. S., Egilman, D. S., & Krumholz, H. M. (2008). The ADVANTAGE seeding trial: A review of the internal documents. *Annals of Internal Medicine, 149,* 251–258.

Hobbs, D., & Wright, R. (2006). *The Sage handbook of fieldwork.* London: Sage.

Hodel, R., Hines, E. R., Ambrose, A., Mushrush, C., Pruden, S., Vogt, P., et al. (2006). *Recession, retrenchment and recovery: State higher education funding and student financial aid.* Study funded by the Lumina Foundation in collaboration with the Center for the Study of Education Policy at Illinois State University, the National Association of State Student Grant Aid Programs, and the State Higher Education Executive Officers. Available at *www.ecs.org* Document Number: 7257 or at *centereducationpolicy.illinoisstate.edu/initiatives/stateprofiles.*

Hodgson, R. T. (2009). An analysis of the concordance among 13 U.S. wine competitions. *Journal of Wine Economics, 4,* 1–9.

Holt, D. T. (2007). The official statistics Olympic challenge: Wider, deeper, quicker, better, cheaper. *The American Statistician, 61*(1), 1–8.

Honaker, J., Joseph, A., King, G., Scheve, K., & Singh, N. (1999). *Amelia: A program for missing data.* Cambridge, MA: Harvard University, Department of Government. Available at *http:// gking.harvard.edu/amelia.*

Hookway, N. (2008). Entering the blogosphere: Some strategies of using blogs in social research. *Qualitative Research, 8*(1), 91–113.

Horton, N. J., & Kleinman, K. P. (2007). Much ado about nothing: A comparison of missing data methods and software to fit incomplete data regression models. *The American Statistician, 61,* 79–90.

Humphreys, L. (1970). *Tearoom trade: A study of homosexual encounters in public places.* London: Duckworth.

Hutchinson, S. R., & Lovell, C. D. (2004). A review of methodological characteristics of research published in key journals in higher education. *Research in Higher Education, 45,* 383–403.

Hyde, V., Jank, W., & Shmeuli, G. (2006). Investigating concurrency in online auctions through visualization. *The American Statistician, 60*(3), 241–250.

Iacono, J., Brown, A., & Holtham, C. (2009). Research methods—A case example of participant observation. *Electronic Journal of Business Research Methods, 7*(1), 39–46. Available online at *www.ejbrm.com*.

Israel, M., & Hay, I. (2006). *Research ethics for social scientists.* Thousand Oaks, CA: Sage.

Jacobs, J. (1961). *The death and life of great American cities.* New York: Random House.

Jaeger, R. (1984). *Sampling in education and the social sciences.* New York: Longmans.

Jansen, L. A., Appelbaum, P. S., Kelin, W. M. P., Weinstein, N. D., Cook, W., Fogel, J. S., et al. (2011). Unrealistic optimism in early-phase oncology trials. *IRB: Ethics & Human Research, 33*(1), 1–8.

Jick, T. D. (1979). Mixing qualitative and quantitative methods: Triangulation in action. *Administrative Science Quarterly, 24*(4), 602–611.

Johnson, J. M. (2001) In-depth interviewing. In J.F. Gubrium & J.A. Holstein (Eds.), *Handbook of interview research* (pp. 103–120). Thousand Oaks, CA: Sage.

Johnson, R. B., & Onwuegbuzie, A. J. (2004). Mixed methods research: A research paradigm whose time has come. *Educational Researcher, 33*(7), 14–26.

Juster, F. T., Ono, H., & Stafford, F. P. (2003). An assessment of alternative measures of time use. *Sociological Methodology, 33*, 19–54.

Kadushin, C., Hecht, S., Sasson, T., & Saxe, L. (2008). Triangulation and mixed methods designs: Practicing what we preach in the evaluation of an Israel experience education program. *Field Methods, 20*(1), 46–65.

Kalkhoff, W., & Thye, S. R. (2006). Expectation states theory and research. *Sociological Methods and Research, 35*, 219–249.

Kaplowitz, M. D., Hadlock, T. D., and Levine, R. (2004). A comparison of web and mail survey response rates. *Public Opinion Quarterly, 68*, 94–101.

Kelley, K., & Rausch, J. R. (2006). Sample size planning for the standardized mean difference: Accuracy in parameter estimation via narrow confidence intervals. *Psychological Methods, 11*, 363–385.

Kelly, G. J. (2006). Epistemology and educational research. In J. L. Green, G. Camilli, & P. B. Elmore (Eds.), *Handbook of complementary methods in educational research* (pp. 33–56). Mahwah, NJ: Erlbaum.

Kennedy, C. H. (2005). *Single-case designs for educational research.* Boston: Allyn & Bacon.

Kidder, T. (1990). *Among schoolchildren.* New York: Perennial.

Kimmel, A. J. (1988). *Ethics and values in applied social research.* Newbury Park, CA: Sage.

King, G., Keohane, R. O., & Verba, S. (1994). *Designing social inquiry: Scientific inference in qualitative research.* Princeton, NJ: Princeton University Press.

King, G., & Zeng, L. (2007). When can history be our guide? The pitfalls of counterfactual inference. *International Studies Quarterly, 51*, 183–210.

Kirk, D. S. (2009). A natural experiment on residential change and recidivism: Lessons from Hurricane Katrina, *American Sociological Review, 74*(3), 484–505.

Klebanov, B. B., Diermeier, D., & Beigman, E. (2008). Lexical cohesion analysis of political speech. *Political Analysis, 16*, 447–463.

Klinenberg, E. (2006). Blaming the victims: Hearsay, labeling, and the hazards of quick-hit disaster ethnography. *American Sociological Review, 71*, 689–698.

Knorr-Cetina, K. (1999). *Epistemic cultures: How the sciences make knowledge.* Cambridge, MA: Harvard University Press.

Kohl, H. R. (1993). *From archetype to zeitgeist: Powerful ideas for powerful thinking.* Boston: Little, Brown.

Kong, T. S., Mahoney, D., & Plummer, K. (2001). Queering the interview. In J. F. Gubrium & J. A. Holstein (Eds.), *Handbook of interview research* (pp. 29–258). Thousand Oaks, CA: Sage.

Konstantopoulos, S., & Hedges, L. V. (2008). How large an effect can we expect from school reforms? *Teachers College Record, 110*(8), 1611–1638.

Kostoff, R. N. (2010). Expanded information retrieval using full-text searching, *Journal of Information Science, 36*(1), 104–113.

Kraemer, H. C., & Thiemann, S. (1987). *How many subjects? Statistical power analysis in research.* Newbury Park, CA: Sage.

Krueger, R. A., & Casey, M. A. (2009). *Focus groups: A practical guide for applied research* (4th ed.). Los Angeles: Sage.

Krysan, M., Couper, M. P., Farley, R., & Forman, T. (2009). Does race in matter in neighborhood preferences?: Results from a video experiment. *American Journal of Sociology, 115*(2), 527–559.

Kurasaki, K. S. (2000). Intercoder reliability for validating conclusions drawn from open-ended interview data. *Field Methods, 12*(3), 179–196.

Lai, W., & Lane, T. (2009). Characteristics of medical research news reported on front pages of newspapers. *PLoS Medicine, 4*(7), 1–7.

Lamont, M. (1992). *Money, morals, and manners: The culture of the French and American upper-middle class.* Chicago: University of Chicago Press.

Lamont, M. (2009). *How professors think: Inside the curious world of academic judgment.* Cambridge, MA: Harvard University Press.

Landry, P. F., & Shen, M. (2005). Reaching migrants in survey research: The use of Global Positioning System to reduce coverage bias in China. *Political Analysis, 13*(1), 1–22.

Lara, D., Strickler, J., Olavarrieta, C. D., & Ellertson, C. (2004). Measuring induced abortion in Mexico: A comparison of four methodologies. *Sociological Methods and Research, 32*(4), 529–558.

Larzelere, R. E., Kuhn, B. R., & Johnson, B. (2004). The intervention selection bias: An underrecognized confound in intervention research. *Psychological Bulletin, 130*(2), 289–303.

Lasserre-Cortez, S. (2006). *A mixed methods examination of professional development through whole faculty study groups.* Unpublished doctoral dissertation, Louisiana State University, Baton Rouge.

Leahey, E. (2007). Not by productivity alone: How visibility and specialization contribute to academic earnings. *American Sociological Review, 72*(4), 533–561.

Lee, R. M. (1993). *Doing research on sensitive topics.* London: Sage.

Lee, R. M. (2004). Recording technologies and the interview in sociology, 1920–2000. *Sociology, 38*(5), 869–889.

Lee, V. E., & Loeb, S. (2000). School size in Chicago elementary schools: Effects on teachers' attitudes and students' achievement. *American Educational Research Journal, 37*(1), 3–31.

Lee, V. E., Ready, D. D., & Johnson, D. J. (2001). The difficulty of identifying rare samples to study: The case of schools divided into schools within schools. *Educational Evaluation and Policy Analysis, 23*(4), 365–379.

Lensveldt-Mulders, G. J. L. M., Hox, J. J., van der Heijden, P. G. M., & Mass, C. J. M. (2005). Meta-analysis of randomized response research: Thirty-five years of validation. *Sociological Methods and Research, 33*(3), 319–348.

Levine, A. G. (1982). *Love Canal: Science, politics, and people.* New York: D. C. Heath.

Lewin, K. (1946). Action research and minority problems. *Journal of Social Issues, 2*, 34–46.

Light, R. J., & Pillemer, D. B. (1984). *Summing up: The science of reviewing research.* Cambridge, MA: Harvard University Press.

Lin, Y., & Vogt, W. P. (1996). Occupational outcomes for students earning two-year college degrees: Income, status, and equity. *Journal of Higher Education, 67*(4), pp. 446–475.

Lincoln, Y. S., & Guba, E. G. (1985). *Naturalistic inquiry.* Beverly Hills, CA: Sage.

Lipsey, M. W., & Wilson, D. B. (2001). *Practical meta-analysis.* Thousand Oaks, CA: Sage.

Lynn, P. (2003). Developing quality standards for cross-national survey research: Five approaches. *International Journal of Social Research Methodology, 6*(4), 323–336.

Lugosi, P. (2006). Between overt and covert research: Concealment and disclosure in an ethnographic study of commercial hospitality. *Qualitative Inquiry, 12*(3), 541–561.

Mack, N., Woodsong, C., MacQueen, K. M., Guest, G., & Namey, E. (2005). *Qualitative research methods: A data collector's field guide.* Research Triangle Park, NC: Family Health International. Available at *www.fhi.org/NR/rdonlyres/ezacxnbfb52irvkhkxxvf2z7vt5aglkcxlwxb3zobgbab3renayoc373plnmdyhga6buu5gvkcpmgl/frontmatter1.pdf.*

Mandell, M. B. (2008). Having one's cake and eating it too: Combining true experiments with regression discontinuity designs. *Evaluation Review, 32*(5), 415–434.

Maney, G. M., & Oliver, P. E. (2001). Finding collective events: Sources, searches, timing. *Sociological Methods and Research, 30*(2), 131–168.

Mark, M. M. (2008). Emergence in and from quasi-experimental design and analysis. In S. Hesse-Biber & P. Leavy (Eds.), *Handbook of emergent methods* (pp. 87–108). New York: Guilford Press.

Mark, M. M., & Lenz-Watson, A. L. (2011). Ethics and the conduct of randomized experiments and quasi-experiments in field settings. In A. T. Panter & S. K. Sterba (Eds.), *Handbook of ethics in quantitative methodology* (pp. 185–209). New York: Routledge.

Mathison, S. (1988). Why triangulate? *Educational Researcher, 17*, 13–17.

Mauthner, M., Birch, J., Jessop, J., & Miller, J. (2002). *Ethics in qualitative research*. London: Sage.

May, M. (2007). Use of mixed methods in a study of residence and contact disputes between divorced and separated parents. *International Journal of Social Research Methodology, 10*(4), 295–306.

May, W. F. (1980). Doing ethics: The bearing of ethical theories on fieldwork. *Social Problems, 27*(3), 358–370.

McDonald, S. (2005). Studying actions in context: A qualitative shadowing method for organizational research. *Qualitative Research, 5*(4), 455–473.

McKenna, B., & Vogt, W. P. (1995, March). *Suicide and the Gulf War: A test of Durkheim's theory of egoistic suicide*. Paper presented at the annual meeting of the Eastern Sociological Society, Philadelphia, PA.

McKnight, C., Des Jarlais, D., Bramson, H., Tower, L., Abdul-Quader, A. S., Nemeth, C., et al. (2006). Respondent-driven sampling in a study of drug users in New York City: Notes from the field. *Journal of Urban Health, 83*, i54–i59.

McKnight, P. E., McKnight, K. M., Sidani, S., & Figueredo, A. J. (2007). *Missing data: A gentle introduction*. New York: Guilford Press.

Menchik, D. A., & Tian, X. (2008). Putting social context into text: The semiotics of e-mail interaction. *American Journal of Sociology, 114*(2), 332–370.

Merton, R. K. (1973). *The sociology of science*. Chicago: University of Chicago Press.

Merton, R. K. (1976). *Sociological ambivalence and other essays*. New York: Free Press.

Merton, R. K. (1985). *On the shoulders of giants: A Shandean postscript*. New York: Harcourt Brace Jovanovich.

Merton, R. K. (1987). Three fragments from a sociologist's notebook: Establishing the phenomenon, specified ignorance, and strategic research materials. *Annual Review of Sociology, 13*, 1–28.

Merton, R. K., Fiske, M., & Kendall, P. L. (1990). *The focused interview*. New York: Free Press. [Original work published 1956]

Messick, S. (1993). *Foundations of validity: Meaning and consequence in psychological assessment*. Princeton, NJ: Educational Testing Service.

Miller, F. G., & Emanuel, E. J. (2008). Quality-improvement research and informed consent. *New England Journal of Medicine, 358*, 765–767.

Mishler, E. G. (1986). *Research interviewing: Context and narrative*. Cambridge, MA: Harvard University Press.

Moffitt, R. A. (2004). The role of randomized field trials in social science research. *American Behavioral Scientist, 47*, 506–540.

Moffitt, R. A. (2005). Remarks on the analysis of causal relationships in population research. *Demography, 42*, 91–108.

Moore, M. R. (2008). Gendered power relations among women: A study of household decision making in black, lesbian stepfamilies. *American Sociological Review, 73*(2), 335–356.

Moran, T. P. (2006a). Statistical inference and patterns of inequality in the global north. *Social Forces, 84*, 1799–1818.

Moran, T. P. (2006b). Statistical inference for measures of inequality with a cross-national bootstrap application. *Sociological Methods and Research, 34*, 296–333.

Morgan, D. L. (2001). Focus group interviewing. In J. F. Gubrium & J. A. Holstein (Eds.), *Handbook of interview research* (pp. 141–160). Thousand Oaks, CA: Sage.

Morgan, D., Fellows, C., & Guevara, H. (2008). Emergent approaches to focus group research. In S. Hesse-Biber & P. Leavy (Eds.), *Handbook of emergent methods* (pp. 189–206). New York: Guilford Press.

Moss, M. (2009). Archival research in organizations in a digital age. In D. Buchanan & A. Bryman (Eds.), *Handbook of organizational research methods* (pp. 395–408). Thousand Oaks, CA: Sage.

Mosteller, F., Nave, B., & Miech, E. J. (2004). Why we need a structured abstract in education research. *Educational Researcher, 33*, 29–34.

Mosteller, F., & Wallace, D. (1964). *Influence and disputed authorship: The Federalist*. New York: Addison-Wesley.

Mueller, C. M., & Dweck, C. S. (1998). Praise for intelligence can undermine children's motivation and performance. *Journal of Personality and Social Psychology, 75*, 33–52.

Munday, J. (2006). Identity in focus: The use of focus groups to study the construction of collective identity. *Sociology, 40*, 89–105.

Murray, D. M., & Blitstein, J. L. (2003). Methods to reduce the impact of intraclass correlation in group-randomized trials. *Evaluation Review, 27*, 79–103.

Myers, J. L., Well, A. D., & Lorch, R. F. (2010). *Research design and statistical analysis* (3rd ed.). New York: Routledge.

Nagel, E. (1961). *The structure of science: Problems in the logic of scientific explanation.* London: Routledge Kegan & Paul.

Newman, F. M., Smith, B., Allensworth, E., & Bryk, A. S. (2001). Instructional program coherence: What it is and why it should guide school improvement policy. *Educational Evaluation and Policy Analysis, 23*(4), 297–321.

NICHD Early Child Care Research Network. (2002). Early child care and children's development prior to school entry. *American Educational Research Journal, 39*(1), 133–164.

Onwuegbuzie, A. J., & Collins, K. M. T. (2007). A typology of mixed methods sampling designs in social science research. *Qualitative Report, 12*(2), 281–316.

Onwuegbuzie, A. J., Leach, N. J., & Collins, K. M. T. (2011). Innovative qualitative data collection techniques for conducting literature reviews/ research syntheses. In M. Williams & W. P. Vogt (Eds.), *The SAGE handbook of innovation in social research methods* (pp. 182–204). London: Sage.

Owens, R. G. (1982, Spring). Methodological rigor in naturalistic inquiry: Some issues and answers. *Educational Administration Quarterly, 18*(2), 1–21.

Palmer, C. R. (2002). Ethics, data-dependent designs, and the strategy of clinical trials: Time to start learning as we go? *Statistical Methods in Medical Research, 11*, 381–402.

Panter, A. T., & Sterba, S. K. (Eds.). (2011). *Handbook of ethics in quantitative methodology.* New York: Routledge.

Parasnis, I., Samar, V. J., & Fischer, S. D. (2005). Deaf college students' attitudes toward racial/ ethnic diversity, campus climate, and role models. *American Annals of the Deaf, 150*(1), 47–58.

Parker, R. A., & Berman, N. G. (2003). Sample size: More than calculations. *The American Statistician, 57*(3), 166–170.

Parry, O., & Mauthner, N. S. (2004). Whose data are they anyway?: Practical, legal and ethical issues in archiving qualitative research data. *Sociology, 38*, 139–152.

Patel, P., Roberts, B., Guy, S., Lee-Jones, L., & Conteh, L. (2009). Tracking official developmental assistance for reproductive health in conflict-affected countries. *PLoS Medicine, 6*(6), 1–12.

Patton, M. Q. (2002). *Qualitative research and evaluation methods* (3rd ed.). Thousand Oaks, CA: Sage.

Pawson, R. (2006). Digging for nuggets: How "bad" research can yield "good" evidence. *International Journal of Social Research Methodology, 9*, 127–142.

Pew Research Center. (2007). *Muslims in America: Middle class and mostly mainstream.* Available at *http://pewresearch.org/assets/pdf/muslim-americans.pdf.*

Piaget, J. (1955). *The child's construction of reality.* London: Routledge.

Platt, J. (2001). History of the interview. In J. F. Gubrium & J. A. Holstein (Eds.), *Handbook of interview research* (pp. 33–54). Thousand Oaks, CA: Sage.

Plewis, I., & Mason, P. (2005). What works and why: Combining quantitative and qualitative approaches in large-scale evaluations. *International Journal of Social Research Methodology, 8*, 185–194.

Plowright, D. (2011). *Using mixed methods: Frameworks for an integrated methodology.* London: Sage.

Pong, S., & Pallas, A. (2001). Class size and eighth-grade math achievement in the U.S. and abroad. *Educational Evaluation and Policy Analysis, 23*, 251–273.

Preacher, K. J., MacCallum, R. C., Rucker, D., & Nicewander, W. A. (2005). Use of extreme groups approach: A critical reexamination and new recommendations. *Psychological Methods, 10*, 178–192.

Presser, S., Couper, M. P., Lessler, J. T., Martin, E., Martin, J., Rothgeb, J. M., et al. (2004). *Methods for testing and evaluating survey questions.* New York: Wiley.

Prior, L. (2008a). Repositioning documents in social research. *Sociology, 42*(5), 821–836.

Prior, L. (2008b). Researching documents: Emergent methods. In S. Hesse-Biber & P. Leavy (Eds.), *Handbook of emergent methods* (pp. 111–126). New York: Guilford Press.

Punch, M. (1986). *The politics and ethics of fieldwork.* Newbury Park, CA: Sage.

Punch, M. (1994). The politics and ethics of qualitative research. In N. K. Denzin & Y. S. Lincoln (Eds.), *Handbook of qualitative research* (pp. 83–97). Thousand Oaks, CA: Sage.

Ragin, C. C. (2008). *Redesigning social inquiry:*

Fuzzy sets and beyond. Chicago: University of Chicago Press.

Ragin, C. C., & Becker, H. S. (1992). *What is a case? Exploring the foundations of social inquiry.* Cambridge, UK: Cambridge University Press.

Rashotte, L. S., Webster, M., & Whitmeyer, J. M. (2005). Pretesting experimental instructions. *Sociological Methodology, 35,* 163–187.

Ratkiewicz, J., Menczer, F., Fortunato, S., Flammini, A., & Vespignani, A. (2010). Characterizing and modeling the dynamics of online popularity. *Physical Review Letters, 105.* Retrieved from *http://prl.aps.org/pdf/PRL/v105/i15/e158701.*

Raudenbush, S. W. (2004). What are value-added models estimating and what does this imply for statistical practice? *Journal of Educational and Behavioral Statistics, 29,* 121–129.

Raudenbush, S. W., Martinez, A., & Spybrook J. (2007). Strategies for improving precision in group-randomized experiments. *Educational Evaluation and Policy Analysis, 29*(1), 5–29.

Read, J. G., & Oselin, S. (2008). Gender and the education-employment paradox in ethnic and religious contexts: The case of Arab Americans. *American Sociological Review, 73*(2), 296–313.

Reiss, J. (2009). Causation in the social sciences: Evidence, inference, and purpose. *Philosophy of the Social Sciences, 39,* 20–40.

Rennie, D. L., & Fergus, K. D. (2006). Embodied categorizing in the grounded theory method. *Theory and Psychology, 16*(4), 483–503.

Reverby, S. M. (2009). *Examining Tuskegee: The infamous syphilis study and its legacy.* Chapel Hill: University of North Carolina Press.

Rihoux, B., & Ragin, C. C. (2009). *Configurational comparative methods: QCA and related techniques.* Thousand Oaks, CA: Sage.

Robinson, G., McNulty, J. E., & Krasno, J. S. (2009). Observing the counterfactual?: The search for political experiments in nature. *Political Analysis, 10,* 341–357.

Rosnow, R. L., & Rosenthal, R. (2011). Ethical principles in data analysis: An overview. In A.T. Panter & S. K. Sterba (Eds.), *Handbook of ethics in quantitative methodology* (pp. 37–58). New York: Routledge.

Ross, J. S., Bradley, E. H., & Besch, S. H. (2006). Use of health care services by lower-income and higher income uninsured adults. *Journal of the American Medical Association, 295,* 2027–2036.

Rubin, D. B. (2006). *Matched sampling for causal effects.* Cambridge, UK: Cambridge University Press.

Rubin, D. B., & Little, R. (2002). *Statistical analysis with missing data* (2nd ed.). New York: Wiley.

Rudner, L. M., & Peyton, J. (2006). Consider propensity scores to compare treatments. *Practical Assessment, Research and Evaluation 11*(9), 1–9. Available at *http:/pareonline.net.*

Rutter, M. (2007). Proceeding from observed correlation to causal inference: The use of natural experiments. *Perspectives on Psychological Science, 2,* 377–395.

Ryan, T. P. (2007). *Modern experimental design.* Hoboken, NJ: Wiley.

Salant, P., & Dillman, D. (1994). *How to conduct your own survey.* New York: Wiley.

Salganik, M. J., & Heckathorn, D. D. (2004). Sampling and estimation in hidden populations using respondent-driven sampling. *Sociological Methodology, 34,* 193–239.

Sandelowski, M., Voils, C. I., & Knafl, G. (2009). On quantitizing. *Journal of Mixed Methods Research, 3*(3), 208–222.

Sanders, D., Clarke, H. D., Stewart, M. C., & Whitley, P. (2007). Does mode matter for modeling political choice?: Evidence from the 2005 British Election Study. *Political Analysis, 15,* 257–285.

Schlosser, L. Z., Knox, S., Moskovitz, A. R., & Hill, C. E. (2003). A qualitative examination of graduate advising relationships: The advisee perspective. *Journal of Counseling Psychology, 50*(2), 178–188.

Schneiderhan, E., & Khan, S. (2008). Reasons and inclusion: The foundation of deliberation. *Sociological Theory, 26*(1), 1–24.

Schochet, P. Z. (2010). The late pretest problem in randomized control trials of education interventions. *Journal of Educational and Behavioral Statistics, 35*(4), 379–406.

Schofield, J. W. (2007). Increasing the generalizability of qualitative research. In M. Hammersley (Ed.), *Qualitative inquiry in education: The continuing debate* (pp. 181–203). Thousand Oaks, CA: Sage.

Schrag, Z. M. (2010). *Ethical imperialism: IRBs and the Social Sciences, 1965–2009.* Baltimore, MD: Johns Hopkins University Press.

Schumann, H., & Presser, S. (1981). *Questions and answers in attitude surveys: Experiments in question form, wording, and context.* New York: Academic Press.

Schwalbe, M. L., & Wolkomir, M. (2001)

Interviewing men. In J. F. Gubrium & J. A. Holstein (Eds.), *Handbook of interview research* (pp. 203–220). Thousand Oaks, CA: Sage.

Schwandt, T. A. (2007). *Dictionary of qualitative inquiry* (3rd ed.). Thousand Oaks, CA: Sage.

Scott, G. (2008). "They got their program, and I got mine": A cautionary tale concerning the ethical implications of using respondent-driven sampling to study injection drug users. *International Journal of Drug Policy, 19*, 42–51.

Senese, P. D., & Vasquez, J. A. (2003). A unified explanation of territorial conflict. *International Studies Quarterly, 47*, 275–298.

Shadish, W. R., Cook, T. D., & Campbell, D. (2002). *Experimental and quasi-experimental designs for generalized causal inference.* New York: Houghton Mifflin.

Shamoo, A. E., & Resnik, D. B. (2009). *Responsible conduct of research* (2nd ed.). New York: Oxford University Press.

Shao, Y., Albertsen, P. C., Roberts, C. B., Lin, Y., Mehta, A. R., Stein, M. N., et al. (2010). Risk profiles and treatment patterns among men diagnosed as having prostate cancer and a PSA level below 4.0. *Archives of Internal Medicine, 170*, 1256–1261.

Shaw, I. F. (2003). Ethics in qualitative research and evaluation. *Journal of Social Work, 3*(1), 9–28.

Sigaud, L. (2008). A collective ethnographer: Fieldwork experience in the Brazilian Northeast. *Social Science Information, 47*(1), 71–97.

Singer, E. (2004). Confidentiality, risk perception, and survey participation. *Chance, 17*, 30–34.

Singer, J., & Willett, J. (2003). *Applied longitudinal data analysis.* New York: Oxford University Press.

Slavin, R., & Smith D. (2009). The relationship between sample sizes and effect sizes in systematic reviews in education. *Educational Evaluation and Policy Analysis, 31*, 500–506.

Smith, B. (2000). Quantity matters: Annual instruction time in an urban school system. *Educational Administration Quarterly, 36*(5), 652–682.

Smith, M. (2005). Ethics in focus groups: A few concerns. *Qualitative Health Research, 5*(4), 478–486.

Snow, J. (1855). *On the mode of communication of cholera.* London: Churchill.

Spano, R. (2006). Observer behavior as a potential source of reactivity: Describing and quantifying observer effects in a large-scale observational study of police. *Sociological Methods and Research, 34*, 521–553.

Spradley, J. P. (1979). *The ethnographic interview.* Fort Worth, TX: Harcourt Brace.

Spradley, J. P. (1980). *Participant observation.* Fort Worth, TX: Harcourt Brace.

Stake, R. E. (1995). *The art of case study research.* Thousand Oaks, CA: Sage.

Stephan, W. G., & Vogt, W. P. (Eds.). (2004). *Education programs for improving intergroup relations: Theory, research, and practice.* New York: Teachers College Press.

Stephens, N. (2007). Collecting data from elites and ultra elites: Telephone and face-to-face interviews with macroeconomists. *Qualitative Research, 7*(2), 203–216.

Stewart, R. (2006). *The places in between.* Orlando, FL: Harcourt.

Stiles, P., Epstein, M., Poythress, N., & Edens, J. (2011). Formal assessment of voluntariness using a three-part consent process. *Psychiatric Services, 62*, 87–89.

Stoller, E. P., Webster, N. J., Blixen, C. E., McCormick, R. A., Perzynski, A. T., Kanuch, S. W., et al. (2009). Lay management of chronic disease: A qualitative study of living with Hepatitis C infection. *American Journal of Health Behavior, 33*(4), 376–390.

Strauss, A. (1987). *Qualitative analysis for social scientists.* Cambridge, UK: Cambridge University Press.

Strauss, A., & Corbin, J. (1990). *Basics of qualitative research: Grounded theory procedures and techniques.* Newbury Park, CA: Sage.

Strug, L. J., Rohde, C. A., & Corey, P. N. (2007). An introduction to evidential sample size calculations. *The American Statistician, 61*, 207–212.

St. Sauver, J. L. (2006). Protective association between nonsteroidal anti-inflammatory drug use and measures of benign prostatic hyperplasia. *American Journal of Epidemiology, 164*, 760–768.

Stuart, E. A., & Rubin, D. B. (2008). Best practices in quasi-experimental designs: Matching methods for causal inference. In J. W. Osborne (Ed.), *Best practices in quantitative methods* (pp. 155–176). Thousand Oaks, CA: Sage.

Stunkel, L., Benson, M., McLellen, L., Sinaii, N., Bedarida, G., Ezekiel, E., et al. (2010). Comprehension and informed consent: Assessing the effect of a short consent form. *IRB: Ethics and Human Research, 32*, 1–9.

Sudman, S. (1976). *Applied sampling.* New York: Academic Press.

Tan, M. T., Tian, G.-L., & Tang, M.-L. (2009). Sample surveys with sensitive questions: A non-randomized response approach. *The American Statistician, 63*(1), 9–16.

Tanur, J. M. (Ed.). (1992). *Questions about questions: Inquiries into the cognitive bases of surveys.* New York: Russell Sage Foundation.

Tashakkori, A., & Teddlie, C. (Eds.). (2003). *Handbook of mixed methods in social and behavioral research.* Thousand Oaks, CA: Sage.

Teddlie, C., & Tashakkori, A. (2009). *Foundations of mixed methods research: Integrating quantitative and qualitative approaches in the social and behavioral sciences.* Thousand Oaks, CA: Sage.

Teddlie, C., & Yu, F. (2007). Mixed methods sampling: A typology with examples. *Journal of Mixed Methods Research, 1*(1), 77–100.

Tedesco, J. C. (2007). Examining Internet interactivity effects on young adult political information efficacy. *American Behavioral Scientist, 50*(9), 1183–1194.

Thelwall, M. (2001). A web crawler design for data mining. *Journal of Information Science, 27,* 319–325.

Thelwall, M. (2011). Investigating human communication and language from traces left on the web. In M. Williams & W. P. Vogt (Eds.), *The SAGE handbook of innovation in social research methods* (pp. 163–177). London: Sage.

Tingley, D. (2006). Neurological imaging as evidence in political science: A review, critique, and guiding assessment. *Social Science Information, 45,* 5–32.

Torrieri, N. K. (2007). America is changing and so is the census: The American Community Survey. *The American Statistician, 61*(1), 16–21.

Trivedi, A. N., Zaslavsky, A. M., Schneider, E. C., & Ayanient, J. Z. (2006). Relationship between quality of care and racial disparities in Medicare health plans. *Journal of the American Medical Association, 296,* 1998–2004.

Trzeniewski, K. H. (Ed.). (2010). *Secondary data analysis: An introduction for psychologists.* Washington, DC: American Psychological Association.

Udry, C. (2003). Fieldwork, economic theory, and research on institutions in developing countries. *American Economic Review, 93,* 107–111.

Valentine, J. C., Pigott, T. D., & Rothstein, H. R. (2010). How many studies do you need? A primer on statistical power for meta-analysis. *Journal of Educational and Behavioral Statistics, 35,* 215–247.

Van Aalst, J. (2010). Using Google Scholar to estimate the impact of journal articles in education. *Educational Researcher, 39,* 387–400.

Van Maanen, J. (1988). *Tales of the field.* Chicago: University of Chicago Press.

van Staa, T.-P., Leufkens, H. G., Zhang, B., & Smeeth, L. (2009). A comparison of cost effectiveness using data from randomized trials or actual clinical practice: Selective Cox-2 inhibitors as an example," *PLoS Medicine, 6*(12), 1–10.

Vartarian, T. P. (2010). *Secondary data analysis.* Oxford, UK: Oxford University Press.

Venkatesh, S. (2008). *Gang leader for a day.* New York: Penguin.

Viechtbauer. W. (2008). Analysis of moderator effects in meta-analysis. In J. W. Osborne (Ed.), *Best practices in quantitative methods* (pp 471–487). Thousand Oaks, CA: Sage.

Vogt, W. P. (1997). *Tolerance and education: Learning to live with diversity and difference.* Thousand Oaks, CA: Sage.

Vogt, W. P. (2002, April). *What are the grounds for choosing research methods? And do multimethod options exacerbate the choice problem?* Paper presented at the annual meeting of the American Educational Research Association, New Orleans, LA.

Vogt, W. P. (2007). *Quantitative research methods for professionals.* Boston: Allyn & Bacon.

Vogt, W. P. (2008, August 27). The dictatorship of the problem: Choosing research methods. *Methodological Innovations Online, 3*(1). Available at *http://erdt.plymouth.ac.uk/mionline/public_html/viewarticle.php?id=72.*

Vogt, W. P., Gardner, D., Haeffele, L., & Baker, P. (2011). Innovations in program evaluation: Comparative case studies as an alternative to RCTs. In M. Williams & W. P. Vogt (Eds.), *The SAGE handbook of innovation in social research methods* (pp. 289–320). London: Sage.

Vogt, W. P., & Johnson, R. B. (2011). *Dictionary of statistics and methodology: A nontechnical guide for the social sciences* (4th ed.). Thousand Oaks, CA: Sage.

Vogt W. P., & McKenna B. J. (1998, April). *Teachers' tolerance: Their attitudes toward political, social, and moral diversity.* Paper presented at the annual meeting of the American Educational Research Association, San Diego, CA.

Walker, R., Hoggart, L., & Hamilton, G. (2008). Random assignment and informed consent: A case study of multiple perspectives. *American Journal of Evaluation, 29*(2), 156–174.

Warren, C. B., Barnes-Brus, T., Burgess, H. Wiebold-Lippisch, L., Hackney, J., Harkness, G., Kennedy, V., et al. (2003). After the interview. *Qualitative Sociology, 26*, 93–110.

Wasserman, J. A., Clair, J. M., & Wilson, K. L. (2009). Problematics of grounded theory: Innovations for developing an increasingly rigorous qualitative method. *Qualitative Research, 9*(3), 355–381.

Webb, E. J., Campbell, D. T., Schwartz, R. D., & Sechrest, L. (2000). *Unobtrusive methods: Nonreactive research in the social sciences.* Thousand Oaks, CA: Sage. [Original work published 1966]

Webster, M., & Sell, J. (Eds.). (2007). *Laboratory experiments in the social sciences.* New York: Elsevier.

Weinreb, A. (2006). The limitations of stranger-interviewers in rural Kenya. *American Sociological Review, 71*(6), 1014–1039.

Weisberg, H., Krosnick, J., & Bowen, B. (1996). *An introduction to survey research, polling, and data analysis* (3rd ed.). Thousand Oaks, CA: Sage.

Wejnert, C., & Heckathorn, D. D. (2008). Web-based network sampling: Efficiency and efficacy of respondent-driven sampling for online research. *Sociological Methods and Research, 37*, 105–134.

Wells, H. M. (2004). Is there a place for covert research methods in criminology? *Graduate Journal for Science Education, 1*(1), 1–19.

Wells, Y., Petralia, W., DeVaus, D., & Kendig, H. (2003). Recruitment for a panel study of Australian retirees. *Research on Aging, 25*, 36–64.

Weston, C., Gandell, T., Beauchamp, J., McAlpine, L., Wiseman, C., & Beauchamp, C. (2001). Analyzing interview data: The development and evolution of a coding system. *Qualitative Sociology, 24*(3), 381–400.

Wibeck, V., Dahlgren, M. A., & Oberg, G. (2007). Learning in focus groups: An analytical dimension for enhancing focus group research. *Qualitative Research, 7*(2), 249–267.

Willer, R., Kuwubara, K., & Macy, M. W. (2009). The false enforcement of unpopular norms. *American Journal of Sociology, 115*(2), 451–490.

Williams, M., & Vogt, W. P. (Eds.). (2011). *The SAGE handbook of innovation in social research methods.* London: Sage.

Willis, G. B. (2005). *Cognitive interviewing: A tool for improving questionnaire design.* Thousand Oaks, CA: Sage.

Winchatz, M. R. (2006). Fieldworker or foreigner? Ethnographic interviewing in nonnative languages. *Field Methods, 18*(1), 83–96.

Wood, E. J. (2006). The ethical challenges of field research in conflict zones. *Qualitative Sociology, 29*, 373–386.

Woodward, B. (2008). *The war within: A secret White House history, 2006–2008.* New York: Simon & Schuster.

Woodward, B. (2010). *Obama's wars.* New York: Simon & Schuster.

Yang, Y., & Land, K. C. (2006). A mixed models approach to the age-period-cohort analysis of repeated cross-section surveys, with an application to data on trends in verbal test scores. *Sociological Methodology, 36*(1), 75–97.

Yang, Y., & Land, K. C. (2008). Age-period-cohort analysis of repeated cross-section surveys: Fixed or random effects? *Sociological Methods Research, 36*(3), 297–326.

Yin, R. K. (2009). *Case study research: Design and methods.* (4th ed.). Thousand Oaks, CA: Sage.

Zientek, L. R., & Thompson, B. (2009). Matrix summaries improve research reports: Secondary analyses using published literature. *Educational Researcher, 38*, 343–352.

Zoppi, K., & Epstein, R. (2001). Interviewing in medical settings. In J. F. Gubrium & J. A. Holstein (Eds.), *Handbook of interview research* (pp. 355–384). Thousand Oaks, CA: Sage.

Index

An *f* following a page number indicates a figure; a *t* following a page number indicates a table.
Page numbers in bold refer to entries in the Glossary.

Action research, 44, 81, 267, **335**
Administration, 19–23, 20*t*, 27, 42–43
Age effects, 24–25
AMELIA software program, 132
American Association for Public Opinion Research (AAPOR), 242
Analysis. *see* Data analysis
ANCOVA, 59, 163
Anonymity, **335**
    combined research designs and, 309–310
    ethics and, 232–233
    experimental design and, 277–278, 280
    interviews and, 255, 258, 259–263, 265
    surveys and, 247–250, 252
Archival populations, **335**
Archival research, **336**. *see also* Literature review
    covariates and, 175–176
    data coding and, 329*t*
    database archives, 93–95
    ethics and, 239*t*, 297–306
    new media, 99–100
    organizational records, 95–96
    overview, 3*t*, 86–88, 100–102, 317–318
    research questions and, 4
    resources for data, 87
    sampling and, 6, 118, 119*t*, 198–216
    textual studies of documents, 96–98, 97*f*

theory and, 12
types of, 89–93
types of data available for, 88
when to use, 14*t*, 88–89, 89–93
Attributes, 81, 326, 326*f*. *see also* Variables
Authenticity, 187, 197

Behavioral Risk Factor Surveillance System (BRFSS), 17, 206–207
Between-subjects design, 57, 58*f*, 65, **336**
Bias, **336**
    combined designs, 220
    identifying and recruiting people for interviews and, 142
    interviews and, 44–45
    literature review and, 201
    nonresponse bias, 131
    random assignment and, 163–164
    simple versus multipart research questions, 104
    surveys and, 17, 21
Biomedical research, 206, 266
Blinding, 57, 65, **336**
Blocks, 59, 165, 175, **336**

Case study, 33, 84, 110, 112, 113, 115–117, 207–208, 221, **336**
Cases, **336**. *see also* Participants; Respondents; Sampling
    adding to an experiment, 166–167
    interview sampling and, 147–154

observational designs and, 184–186
    overview, 5–6, 115–117
    random assignment and, 51
    relevance and, 184
    selecting, 116
Categorical independent variables, 60–61
Causal homogeneity, 116–117
Causal mechanisms, **337**
    archival designs and, 94
    experimental design and, 54–56, 55*t*, 65
    indicators and, 327–328
    interviews and, 37–38, 47
    observational designs and, 73
    sampling and, 116–117
Cause, 73, 176, 193, 327, 330, **337**
Centers for Disease Control (CDC), 17
Change over time, 23–25, 81, 82
Clinical interviews, 32. *see also* Interviews
Cluster sampling, 126, 140, 219–220, **337**. *see also* Sampling
Coding. *see also* Data analysis; Measurement
    analytic options and, 330–333, 331*f*
    concepts and, 325–329, 326*f*, 329*t*, 330*t*
    interviews and, 33–34
    overview, 2, 2*f*, 317, 318–319
    quantitative and qualitative measurements and, 319–320
    reliability and, 321, 321–323

Cohort effects, 24–25
Cohort study, 23–24, 29, **337**
Collection of data. *see* Data collection
Combined designs, **337**
  data coding and, 329*t*
  ethics and, 239*t*, 307–316
  experimental design and, 66
  logistical considerations in, 110–111, 111*t*
  overview, 3*t*, 6–7, 103, 112–113, 317–318
  research questions and, 4
  sampling and, 6, 118, 217–225
  simple versus multipart research questions, 104–106, 105*t*
  types and qualities of, 106–110
  when to use, 14*t*, 106, 107*t*, 113
Comparative case study research, 146, **337**
Comprehensive criteria, 203–204
Computer-assisted methods, 211–212, 216
Concept
  coding validly, 325–329, 326*f*, 329*t*, 330*t*
  data coding and, 319, 319–320, 321
  reliability and validity and, 321
Conference calls, 259–260
Confidence intervals, 135, 166, 202–203, 276, **337–338**
Confidentiality, **338**
  archival designs and, 300
  ethics and, 232–233
  experimental design and, 277–278
  interviews and, 253–255, 256, 259–263, 264
  surveys and, 247–250, 252
Confirmatory research, 38, 254, **338**. *see also* Explanatory research
Conflicts of interest, 238, 275–276, 308–309, **338**
Consent, **338**. *see also* Informed consent
  archival designs and, 306
  combined designs, 307–310, 315
  experimental design and, 267, 268–272, 270*t*, 279
  interviews and, 254–257, 264
  observational designs and, 295
  surveys and, 242–244, 252
Consistency, 321–323
Construct validity, 323–325. *see also* Validity
Content analysis, 211–212, **338–339**

Context
  observational designs and, 68–69, 69*f*, 71–72
  textual studies of documents and, 97–98, 97*f*
Continuous independent variables, 60–61, 66
Convenience sampling, **339**. *see also* Sampling
  archival designs and, 199
  identifying and recruiting people for interviews and, 141
  overview, 140
  quota samples and, 127–128
  surveys and, 126–127
Counterbalancing, 162, **339**
Covariates, 175–176, **339**
Covert research, 74–75, 294, **339**
Covert/participant research, 74*f*, 75–76. *see also* observational designs
Crossed design, 58–59, 58*f*, 65, 165, **339**
Cross-sectional design, 24–25, 30, **339**

Data analysis. *see also* Coding
  archival designs and, 298–299, 306
  combined designs, 309–310, 311, 313–314, 315, 316
  data coding and, 330–333, 331*f*
  experimental design and, 272, 275–277, 277–278, 279, 280
  interviews and, 257, 259, 262–263, 264, 265
  observational designs and, 287–288, 290–291, 292–293, 295, 296
  overview, 2, 2*f*, 18, 317
  surveys and, 244, 245–247, 249–250, 252
Data coding. *see* Coding
Data collection
  combined designs, 309, 311, 312–313, 315, 316
  ethics in archival research and, 306
  experimental design and, 272, 275, 277, 279, 280
  interviews and, 256, 258–259, 261–262, 264, 265
  observational designs and, 287, 289–290, 291–292, 295, 296
  surveys and, 244, 245, 248–249, 252
Data mining, 212–213, 299, 303, **339**, 353–354

Database archives. *see also* Archival research
  archival designs and, 201–203, 297
  overview, 93–95, 100, 102
  sampling and, 201–203, 205–207, 216
  when to use, 95
Decision making, 147–154, 187–188, 197
Depth, 68–69, 69*f*
Descriptive research, 38, 47, 69, **340**. *see also* Exploratory research
  identifying and recruiting people for interviews and, 143, 144
  observational designs and, 181, 190, 191
Design, **340**
  overview, 2, 2*f*, 3, 3*t*
  research questions and, 4–5, 9–10
  theory and, 10–12, 10*f*, 12*f*
Detail, 68–69, 69*f*
Developing a theory. *see* Theory development
Documents in research. *see* Archival research; Literature review; Textual analysis

Effect size, 166, 173, 276, **340**
Electronic databases, 201–203, 216. *see also* Database archives
E-mail interviews, 42–43, 47, 152, 259–260. *see also* Interviews
E-mail surveying, 21–22, 132–133. *see also* Surveys
Epistemology, vii–ix, **340**
Ethical research, 268, 308, 314, **340**
Ethics
  archival designs and, 239*t*, 297–306
  combined designs, 239*t*, 307–316
  experimental design and, 239*t*, 266–280
  interviews and, 239*t*, 253–265
  observational designs and, 78–79, 239*t*, 281–296
  overview, 2, 2*f*, 3*t*, 6, 227–229, 229*f*
  responsibilities to other researchers, 229*f*, 233–236
  responsibilities to society/communities, 229*f*, 236–239
  responsibilities to the persons being studied, 229–233, 229*f*
  surveys and, 239*t*, 241–252

Ethnography, 40, 94
Evaluation research, 41, 74*f*, 81, **340**. *see also* Program evaluation
Event-history analysis (EHA), 25, 30, **340**
Evidence-inference validity, 323. *see also* Validity
Exaggeration including stereotyping, 275, 276
Experimental design
  advantages and disadvantages of, 54–56, 55*t*
  basic types of, 56–63, 57*f*, 58*f*, 60*f*, 65–66
  combined designs, 222–223
  compared to observational designs, 180–181
  covariates and, 175–176
  data coding and, 329*t*
  ethics and, 239*t*, 266–280
  gold-standard thinking and, 49–50
  identifying and recruiting people for interviews and, 141
  observational designs and, 80
  overview, 3*t*, 4–5, 48–49, 63–66, 267, 317–318
  randomized control trials (RCTs) and, 50, 159–175, 171*f*
  research questions and, 4
  sampling and, 6, 117–118, 119*t*, 159–179
  surveys and, 21
  theory and, 11
  when to use, 14*t*, 50–63, 55*t*, 57*f*, 58*f*, 60*f*, 65–66
Experimental group size, 164–166
Experimenter effects, 162, **340–341**
Explanatory research, 147, **341**
  identifying and recruiting people for interviews and, 143, 145, 157
  interviews and, 38, 47
  observational designs and, 69, 181, 190, 192–193
Exploratory research, 157, 181, 190, 191, **341**. *see also* Descriptive research
External data, 143–144, 157
External validity. *see also* Generalizability; Validity
  experimental design and, 53–54, 55–56
  overview, 323
  random sampling and, 122–123
  sampling and, 116

Face-to-face administration of a survey. *see also* Surveys
  ethics and, 248, 265
  overview, 27
  when to use, 19–23, 20*t*, 29
Face-to-face administration of an interview, 42–43, 47, 152. *see also* Interviews
Field experiment, 274, **341**
  combined designs, 110–111
  experimental design and, 60, 65, 169–170
  when to use, 179
Field observation, 189. *see also* observational designs
Focus groups interviews, 41–42, 47, 153–154, 158, **341**. *see also* Interviews
Forensic interviews, 32. *see also* Interviews
Formal interviews, 43, 47. *see also* Interviews
Freedom of Information Act (FOIA), 208, 232, **341**
Full-text searching, 202, **341**

Generalizability. *see also* External validity
  experimental design and, 163
  nonprobability sampling and, 130–131
  random sampling and, 122–123
  sampling and, 116, 121
  size of survey samples and, 133–138, 136*f*, 137*f*
Gold-standard thinking, 48–50. *see also* Experimental design
Grounded theory approach, 38–39, 200, **341**
Group administration of surveys, 22. *see also* Surveys
Group interviewing, 41–42, 47, 153–154, 158. *see also* Interviews
Group randomizing, 162–163, 178, **342**. *see also* Randomized control trials (RCTs)
Group size, 164–166

Harm, 230–232, **342**
  archival designs and, 306
  combined designs, 310–311, 315–316
  experimental design and, 267, 268–271, 270*t*, 272–277, 279–280
  interviews and, 253–254, 257–259, 264–265

observational designs and, 288–291, 295–296
  surveys and, 244–247, 252
History effect, 52, 55*t*, **342**

Identical samples method, 218, 218*t*, 225. *see also* Sampling
Incentives, 151–152, 160–161
Individual randomizing, 162–163, 178. *see also* Randomized control trials (RCTs)
Informal interview questions, 40, 43, 47. *see also* Interviews; Questions
Informants, 34–35, **342**. *see also* Cases; Participants
Informed consent, **342**. *see also* Consent
  ethics and, 233
  experimental design and, 268–272, 270*t*
  interviews and, 254–257, 255, 256, 258, 264
  observational designs and, 282–288, 288
  surveys and, 242–244, 252
Institutional records. *see* Organizational records
Institutional review board (IRB), **342**. *see also* Ethics
  archival designs and, 297, 301–302
  combined designs, 308
  experimental design and, 267, 270
  interviews and, 254–255, 256, 260
  observational designs and, 281, 283–284, 285, 288–289
  overview, 228
  responsibilities to the persons being studied, 230–232
Interaction effect, **342–343**
Interactive design methods, 109–110, 113. *see also* Combined designs
Internal consistency reliability, 322. *see also* Reliability
Internal data, 143–144, 157
Internal validity, 53–54, 55–56, 161–162, 323. *see also* Validity
Internet sources
  archival designs and, 99–100, 297, 303
  combined designs, 309
  sampling and, 212–214, 216
Internet surveying, 21–22. *see also* Surveys

Internet-based interviews, 42–43, 152. *see also* Interviews

Interrater reliability, 322. *see also* Reliability

Interview protocol, 35, 40, 45, **343**

Interviewee. *see* Cases; Participants

Interviewer effects, 21, **343**. *see also* Bias

Interviewers, 43–45. *see also* Role of the researcher

Interviews
    compared to surveys, 33–36
    data coding and, 329*t*
    ethics and, 239*t*, 253–265
    focused group interviews, 41–42
    identifying and recruiting people for, 141–158
    interview text and, 43–45
    modes of conducting, 42–43
    observational designs and, 80, 83
    overview, 3*t*, 31–32, 45–47, 317–318
    questions and, 37–40
    research questions and, 4, 143–147
    sampling and, 117, 119*t*
    selecting and recruiting for, 6
    structure in, 39–40
    types, approaches and procedures, 36–45, 47
    when to use, 14*t*, 31–36, 47

Intraclass correlation (ICC), 176

Introductory review, 90. *see also* Archival research

IRB, **343**. *see also* Institutional review board (IRB)

Iterative design methods, 109–110, 113. *see also* Combined designs

Job interviews, 32. *see also* Interviews

Journalistic interviews, 31–32. *see also* Interviews

Judgment sampling, **343**. *see also* Sampling
    archival designs and, 199
    identifying and recruiting people for interviews and, 141
    overview, 140
    surveys and, 128–129

Laboratory environment, 59

Laboratory experiment, 60, 65, 169–170, 179

Latin squares, 165–166, **343**

Legal considerations, 237–238

Life history interviews, 39. *see also* Interviews

Likert scale, 26–27, 30

Literature review. *see also* Archival research; Meta-analysis
    ethics in archival research and, 297, 298–299
    overview, 86–87, 89–93, 100
    sampling and, 200–204, 216
    theory and, 12, 12*f*

Longitudinal data, 110–111, 205–206. *see also* Archival research

Mail surveys, 21–22. *see also* Surveys

Manipulation checks, 60

Matched-pairs design, 59, 167–168, **343**

Meaning, 35, 72

Measurement, 2, 2*f*, 318–319, 321–323. *see also* Coding

Media, 210–211. *see also* New media

Medical model, 266

Member checking, 259, 284–285, 311, **343–344**

Meta-analysis, **344**. *see also* Archival research
    database archives and, 202–203
    literature review and, 201
    overview, 89–93, 102
    saturation and, 200
    selection criteria and, 204
    textual studies of documents and, 97
    when to use, 91–92

Methodological rigor, 32. *see also* Interviews

Mini-meta-analysis, 92, 202, **344**

Missing data, 131–132

Mixed method research, 7, 164–165, **344**. *see also* Combined designs

Model, 266, 334, **344**

"Modern Massive Data Sets" (MMDS), 199

Moral suasion, 236–237

Multilevel sampling, 126, 163. *see also* Sampling

Multimethod research, 7, **344**. *see also* Combined designs

Multipart research questions, 104–106, 105*t*. *see also* Research questions

Multiple data sources, 111*t*

Multiple methods, 111*t*

Multiple researchers, 110–111, 111*t*, 113

Multipopulation samples method, 218, 218*t*, 225. *see also* Sampling

Multistage sampling, 126. *see also* Sampling

Natural experiments, **344–345**
    compared to observational designs, 180–181
    covariates and, 175–176
    experimental design and, 62, 66
    overview, 170–172, 171*t*
    when to use, 179

Naturalistic observational designs. *see also* observational designs
    overview, 67–68, 73–76, 74*f*, 85, 317–318
    research questions and, 4
    sampling and, 6
    when to use, 14*t*, 76–79

Naturalistic observations, 281–296, **345**

Naturalistic/covert research, 74–75, 74*f*. *see also* observational designs

Naturalistic/overt research, 74*f*, 75. *see also* observational designs

Nested design, 58–59, 58*f*, 65, 165

Nested samples method, 218, 218*t*, 225, **345**. *see also* Sampling

New media
    archival designs and, 99–100, 297, 303
    interviews and, 259–260
    overview, 100, 102
    sampling and, 212–214, 216

Nonprobability sampling, 122, 126–131, 140. *see also* Sampling

Nonresponse bias, 131, **345**

Note taking
    interviews and, 32, 261–262
    observational designs and, 287, 292

Objective data, 16, 39, **345**

Observation sites, 186–187

Observational designs. *see also* Naturalistic observations; Participant observational designs
    data coding and, 329*t*
    decision making and, 187–188
    distinguishing between naturalistic and participant observational designs, 73–76, 74*f*
    ethics and, 239*t*, 281–296
    overview, 3*t*, 67–69, 69*f*, 81–85, 317–318
    research questions and, 4, 190–195
    sampling and, 6, 118, 119*t*, 180–197
    when to use, 69–73, 76–81, 85

Office for Human Research Protections (OHRP), 302

Online sources. *see* Internet sources
Open-ended questions, 37–39, 219.
    see also Questions
Operational definitions, 327–328
Operationalization of a variable,
    345
Opportunity sampling, 39, 142,
    346. *see also* Sampling
Oral history archives, 94. *see also*
    Archival research
Oral history interviews, 39. *see also*
    Interviews
Order effects, 162, **346**
Organizational records. *see also*
    Archival research
    ethics in archival research and,
        297, 300–301
    overview, 95–96, 100, 102
    sampling and, 207–209, 216
Outcomes, 54–56, 55t, 65
Outlier, 109, 281, 309, **346**
Overt/participant research, 74f, 76.
    see also observational designs

Panel study, 23, 29, **346**
Parallel samples method, 218, 218t,
    225, **346**. *see also* Sampling
Participant observational designs,
    346. *see also* observational
    designs
    ethics in observational research
        and, 281–296
    overview, 67–68, 73–76, 74f, 85,
        317–318
    research questions and, 4
    sampling and, 6
    when to use, 14t, 79–81
Participants, **346**. *see also* Cases;
    Participant observational
    designs; Respondents;
    Sampling
    adding to an experiment,
        166–167
    ethics and, 229–233, 229f
    experimental design and,
        159–179
    interviews and, 33–34, 141–158,
        147–154, 157, 253–254,
        257–258
    observational designs and, 76–81
    overview, 5–6
    random assignment and, 51
    surveys and, 15–17, 33–34,
        35–36
Period effects, 24–25
Permission, 298
Per-respondent cost, 21
Phenomena, 97–98, 97f, 187, 189
Photography archives, 94
Plagiarism, 235–236

Political processes, 69–70, 206
Poor methods, 275, 276–277
Population, 127, **346**. *see also*
    Target population
Positive-outcomes bias, 104. *see*
    also Bias
Positivism, viii, 319, **347**
Pragmatism, ix, 105–106, **347**
Predictions, 94
Pretest sensitization, 59, 65
Pretests, 59, 65, 167–168, 178–179
Privacy, **347**
    archival designs and, 306
    combined designs, 311–314, 316
    experimental design and, 267,
        277–278, 280
    interviews and, 253–254, 255,
        259–263, 261–262, 265
    observational designs and,
        291–293, 296
    surveys and, 247–250, 252
Probability sampling, **347**. *see also*
    Sampling
    archival designs and, 199
    combined designs, 217–218,
        219–220, 221–223, 225
    observational designs and,
        183–184
    overview, 122–126, 140
    purposive sampling and,
        221–223
Program evaluation, 23, 49, 52,
    62, 81, 335, **347**. *see also*
    Evaluation research
Propensity score matching (PSM),
    173–174, **347**
Protocol, 40, **347**
Proxy, 327–328
Publishing research results. *see*
    Reporting research results
Purposive sampling, **348**. *see also*
    Judgment sampling; Sampling
    archival designs and, 199
    combined designs, 217–218, 219,
        220–223, 225
    identifying and recruiting people
        for interviews and, 141–142
    overview, 140
    probability sampling and,
        221–223
    surveys and, 128–129
Push polls, 242
P-value, 122, 123, 198

Qualidata archive, 94
Qualitative methods, **348**
    archival designs and, 94, 200
    data coding and, 330–333, 331f
    experimental design and, 48
    interview sampling and, 153

overview, 4
    when to use, 319–320
Quantitative methods, **348**
    data coding and, 330–333, 331f
    experimental design and, 48
    overview, 4
    when to use, 319–320
Quant–qual debate, viii, 319–320
Quant/qual debate/distinction, 4, 7,
    48, 112, 117, 217, 319–320
Quasi-experiments, **348**
    covariates and, 175–176
    experimental design and, 61, 66,
        167–168
    overview, 170, 171t, 172–174
    when to use, 179
Questions. *see also* Research
    questions
    interviews and, 37–40, 47
    sampling and, 117–119, 118t,
        119t
    structure in, 39–40
    surveys and, 16–17, 25–27, 30
Quota sampling, 127–128, 140,
    348

Random assignment, **348**
    combined designs, 222–223
    ethics in experimental research
        and, 271–272
    experimental design and, 51, 55t,
        65, 163–164, 165
    quasi-experiments and, 61
Random error, **349**
Random sampling, 122–123, 140,
    349. *see also* Sampling
Randomized block design,
    164–166
Randomized control trials (RCTs),
    349
    alternatives to, 170–175, 171t
    compared to observational
        designs, 180–181
    covariates and, 175–176
    ethics and, 266–280
    experimental design and,
        159–175, 171f, 178–179
    gold-standard thinking and,
        49–50
    overview, 49, 65
    research questions and, 54–56,
        55t
    when to use, 50, 51–53
Randomized field trials (RFTs),
    169–170. *see also* Field
    experiment
Randomized-response technique
    (RRT), 248–249
RCT, **349**. *see also* Randomized
    control trials (RCTs)

Recruitment. *see also* Sampling
  experimental design and, 160–
    161, 177, 178–179, 271–272,
    273–275, 277
  interviews and, 147–154, 157–
    158, 255, 257–258, 260–261
  overview, 5–6
Regression, 59
Regression discontinuity (RD)
    designs, **349**
  ethics in experimental research
    and, 271–272
  overview, 170, 171*t*, 174–175
  when to use, 179
Relevance, 182, 183–186, 197
Reliability, **349–350**
  data coding and, 318, 319, 321
  methods to use to improve,
    321–323
  overview, 328–329, 330*t*
Repeated-measures designs,
    164–165, **350**
Replacement, 123–124
Replication, 56, 65
Reporting research results
  archival designs and, 303–304,
    306
  combined designs, 309–310, 311,
    313–314, 315, 316
  ethics and, 245–247
  experimental design and,
    168–169, 179, 272, 275–277,
    277–278, 279, 280
  interviews and, 257, 259,
    262–263, 264, 265
  observational designs and,
    287–288, 290–291, 292–293,
    295, 296
  surveys and, 244, 249–250,
    252
Representativeness of a sample.
    see also Sampling
  archival designs and, 199
  experimental design and,
    160–161
  identifying and recruiting people
    for interviews and, 141
  observational designs and, 182,
    183–186, 197
  size of survey samples and,
    133–138, 136*f*, 137*f*
Research, 1–2, 307–308, **350**
Research ethics. *see* Ethics
Research interviews. *see* Interviews
Research questions. *see also*
    Questions
  change over time and, 23–25
  combined designs, 218*t*
  focus of, 54–56, 55*t*

interview sampling strategies
    and, 143–147, 157
interviews and, 37–40, 47
observational designs and, 69,
    181, 190–195
observational sampling and,
    188–189, 197
overview, 4–5, 9–10
randomized control trials (RCTs)
    and, 52–53
sampling and, 117–119, 118*t*,
    119*t*, 190–195
simple versus multipart research
    questions, 104–106, 105*t*
surveys and, 22–23
theory and, 10–12, 10*f*, 12*f*
Research synthesis, 89–93, 91–92,
    102, **350**. *see also* Archival
    research
Respondent-driven sampling
  combined designs, 312
  interview sampling and, 153
  overview, 140
  surveys and, 129–130, 248
Respondents, 33–34, 35–36,
    242–244, **350**. *see also* Cases;
    Participants
Response rate, 18–19, 131–133
Retrodiction, 94
Retrospective studies, 205–206
Rigor, 32
Role of the researcher, 43–45, 47,
    257–258

Sample design, 23–25, 29–30
Sample size
  archival designs and, 199
  experimental design and, 164,
    178
  interview sampling and, 149
  surveys and, 133–138, 136*f*, 137*f*
Sampling
  archival designs and, 198–216,
    306
  combined designs, 217–225, 309,
    310–311, 312, 315–316
  compared to searching, 199–200
  decision making and, 188–189
  ethics and, 245
  experimental design and,
    159–179, 271–272, 273–275,
    277, 279, 280
  identifying and recruiting people
    for interviews, 141–158
  interviews and, 33–34, 255,
    257–258, 260–261, 264, 265
  literature review and, 200–204
  nonprobability sampling,
    126–131

observational designs and,
    80–81, 82, 180–197, 285–287,
    289, 291, 295, 296
  overview, 2, 2*f*, 3*t*, 5–6, 27,
    115–119, 118*t*, 119*t*, 121,
    138–140
  probability sampling and,
    122–126
  random assignment and, 51
  research questions and, 143–147,
    190–195
  response rate and, 18–19,
    131–133
  size of survey samples and,
    133–138, 136*f*, 137*f*
  surveys and, 121–140, 241–242,
    243–244, 248, 252
Sampling error, 137, 137*f*, 220, **350**
Sampling frame, 124–125, **350–351**
Saturation point, 200, 202, **351**
Scientific disciplines, 48
Screening, 148
Searching, compared to sampling,
    199–200
Secondary data analysis, 86, **351**.
    see also Archival designs
Secondary sources, 14*t*, 86, 118. *see
    also* Archival research
Seeking information, 39
Selection, 5–6. *see also* Sampling
Selection bias, 53, 117, 169, **351**
Selection criteria, 203–204
Self-administration of a survey, 17,
    19–23, 20*t*, 27, 29. *see also*
    Surveys
Semantic differential scaling (SDS),
    26, 30
Semistructured interview questions,
    39–40, 83. *see also* Interviews;
    Questions
Sensitizing concepts, 70–71, 82,
    351
Simple random sampling, 122–123,
    124, 140. *see also* Sampling
Simple research questions, 104–
    106, 105*t*. *see also* Research
    questions
Single-case study research, **351**
  overview, 171*t*, 174
  sampling and, 115–117
  when to use, 179
Snowball sampling, **351**
  ethics in interview research and,
    260, 265
  ethics in survey research and, 248
  interview sampling and,
    152–153, 158
  overview, 140
  surveys and, 129–130

Social desirability bias, 17. *see also* Bias
Social interviewing, 41–42, 47. *see also* Interviews
Social processes, 69–70, 206
Sociology, 97–98, 97*f*
Solomon four-group design, 59, 60*f*
Split-plot designs, 164–165
Statistical analysis, 73
Statistical archives, 93–95
Statistical inference, 123, 134, 198, 351–352
Statistical power, 134–135, 166, 178, 352
Statistical techniques, 131–132
Statistically significant, 104, 105*t*, 124, 133–134, 166, 198, 203, 352
Stopping rule, 272, 352
Stratified random sampling, 125–126, 140. *see also* Sampling
Stratified sampling, 352
Structured interview questions, 39–40. *see also* Interviews; Questions
Subjective data, 16, 353
Subjects, 51, 229–233, 229*f*, 353. *see also* Participants
SUGS (selling under the guise of surveying), 241–242
Surveillance, Epidemiology, and End Results (SEER) database, 207
Survey experiments, 21, 353. *see also* Experimental design; Surveys
Surveys
 administration of, 19–23, 20*t*, 29
 compared to interviews, 33–36
 data coding and, 329*t*
 ethics and, 239*t*, 241–252
 nonprobability sampling, 126–131
 observational designs and, 80
 overview, 3*t*, 15, 27–30, 317–318
 probability sampling and, 122–126
 question formats used in, 25–27, 30
 research questions and, 4
 response rate and, 18–19, 131–133
 sampling and, 6, 23–25, 29–30, 117, 119*t*, 121–140, 198

 size of survey samples and, 133–138, 136*f*, 137*f*
 when to use, 14*t*, 15–19, 29
Synthesis of studies, 200–204. *see also* Archival research
Systematic error, 353. *see also* Bias
Systematic review, 90, 102. *see also* Archival research
Systematic sampling, 124, 140, 353. *see also* Sampling

Target population, 141, 150–151, 159–160, 178, 205, 245, 317, 353. *see also* Population
Targeted questions, 37–38, 47. *see also* Questions
Telephone administration of an interview, 42–43, 47, 152, 259–260. *see also* Interviews
Telephone administration of a survey. *see also* Surveys
 Behavioral Risk Factor Surveillance System (BRFSS) and, 17, 206–207
 overview, 27
 when to use, 19–23, 20*t*, 29
Testing a theory. *see* Theory-testing model
Text mining, 212–213, 299, 303, 353–354
Texts, textual studies of documents and, 97–98, 97*f*
Textual analysis. *see also* Archival research
 ethics in archival research and, 297, 301–302
 overview, 96–98, 97*f*, 100
 sampling and, 210–212, 216
 when to use, 98
Theoretical research, 93, 354
Theory, 10–12, 10*f*, 12*f*, 354
Theory development
 archival designs and, 92–93
 identifying and recruiting people for interviews and, 143, 146, 157
 observational designs and, 69, 181, 190, 194–195
Theory-testing model
 archival designs and, 92–93
 identifying and recruiting people for interviews and, 143, 145–146, 157
 interviews and, 38

 observational designs and, 69, 181, 190, 193–194
 research questions and, 10–12, 10*f*, 12*f*
Therapeutic interviews, 32. *see also* Interviews
Thick description, 71–72, 190, 191, 354
Thought experiment, 45, 354
Treatment fidelity, 60, 66
Triangulated methods
 combined designs, 111, 111*t*, 113
 observational designs and, 69, 72, 83
Triangulation, 83, 111, 354
Trustworthiness, 33–34, 318, 355

Units of analysis, 61, 115*n*, 196, 317*n*, 355
Unstructured interview questions, 39–40, 83. *see also* Interviews; Questions

Validity, 355
 data coding and, 318, 319, 321
 experimental design and, 53–54, 55–56, 55*t*, 161–162
 methods to use to enhance, 323–325
 overview, 328–329, 330*t*
 random sampling and, 122–123
 sampling and, 116
Variables, 355
 experimental design and, 51–52, 60–61, 65, 66, 161–162, 178
 nonprobability sampling and, 130–131
 observational designs and, 70–71, 73, 77–78, 81
 overview, 326, 326*f*
 quantitative and qualitative measurements and, 319–320
Variation, 68–69, 69*f*
Video chatting, 259–260
Volunteering for studies, 219–220
Vulnerable populations, 288–289, 355–356. *see also* Harm

Websites, 21–22, 99–100, 212–214, 216
Whistle-blowing, 238, 249
Within-subjects design, 57, 57*f*, 65, 356

About the Authors

W. Paul Vogt, PhD, is Emeritus Professor of Research Methods and Evaluation at Illinois State University, where he has won both teaching and research awards. Before coming to Illinois State as an administrator and faculty member, he held similar posts at the University at Albany, State University of New York. He has also been a visiting researcher at l'École des Hautes Études en Sciences Sociales in Paris (1980) and at the University of London Institute of Education (1986). Dr. Vogt's areas of specialization include research design and data analysis, with particular emphasis on combining qualitative, quantitative, and graphic approaches. He has also served as principal program evaluator for many funded projects and continues to be active in this field. His publications include *Dictionary of Statistics and Methodology* (4th edition), *Quantitative Research Methods for Professionals*, *Education Programs for Improving Intergroup Relations* (coedited with Walter G. Stephan), and *The SAGE Handbook of Innovation in Social Research Methods* (coedited with Malcolm Williams). He is also editor of three four-volume sets in the series Sage Benchmarks in Social Research Methods: *Selecting Research Methods*, *Data Collection*, and *SAGE Quantitative Research Methods*. He blogs about research methods at *vogtsresearchmethods.blogspot.com.*

Dianne C. Gardner, PhD, is Associate Professor of Educational Administration at Illinois State University. Prior to joining the faculty at Illinois State, she began her career at Alverno College in Wisconsin, a pioneering organization in higher education assessment and evaluation, and also as a speech diagnostician in several Wisconsin school districts. She worked as a consultant on program evaluation and assessment of student learning at the University of Wisconsin–Madison in the College of Agricultural and Life Sciences and the Departments of Zoology and Educational Leadership and Policy Analysis. Dr. Gardner's research interests include assessment, organizational development, program evaluation, P20 systems, and qualitative research methodology. She currently serves as a program evaluator for state- and federally funded education programs.

Lynne M. Haeffele, PhD, is Senior Research Associate in the Center for the Study of Education Policy at Illinois State University, where she provides research, evaluation, policy analysis, and management expertise for projects in teacher preparation, teacher professional development, higher education policy, and STEM education. Prior to joining Illinois State, she served as Chief Deputy Superintendent for the Illinois State Board of Education. She also won state and national awards as a high school science teacher and has taught teacher preparation courses. Dr. Haeffele's research interests include combining research designs, applying research findings to policy and practice, program evaluation, and the topical areas of college readiness, organizational performance, and school–university partnerships. She currently serves as a consultant and program evaluator for several state- and federally funded education programs.